THE COLLECTED COURSES OF
THE ACADEMY OF EUROPEAN LAW

Volume XXX/1

Justifying Contract in Europe

Political Philosophies of European Contract Law

THE COLLECTED COURSES OF THE ACADEMY OF EUROPEAN LAW

Edited by: Professor Neha Jain, Professor Claire Kilpatrick, Professor Sarah Nouwen, and Professor Joanne Scott

Assistant Editor: Joyce Davies

The Academy of European Law is housed at the European University Institute in Florence, Italy. The Academy holds annual advanced-level summer courses focusing on topical, cutting-edge issues in Human Rights Law and The Law of the European Union. The courses are taught by highly qualified scholars and practitioners in a highly interactive environment. General courses involve the examination of the field as a whole through a particular thematic, conceptual, or philosophical lens or look at a theme in the context of the overall body of law. Specialized courses bring together a number of speakers exploring a specific theme in depth. Together, they are published as monographs and edited volumes in the Collected Courses of the Academy of European Law series. The Collected Courses series has been published by Oxford University Press since 2000. The series contains publications on both foundational and pressing issues in human rights law and the law of the European Union.

OTHER TITLES IN THE SERIES INCLUDE:

Contemporary Challenges to EU Legality
Edited by Claire Kilpatrick and Joanne Scott

Reframing Human Rights in a Turbulent Era
Gráinne de Búrca

New Legal Approaches to Studying the Court of Justice
Revisiting Law in Context
Edited by Claire Kilpatrick and Joanne Scott

EU Law Beyond EU Borders
The Extraterritorial Reach of EU Law
Edited by Marise Cremona and Joanne Scott

Freedom of Religion, Secularism, and Human Rights
Edited by Nehal Bhuta

EU Administrative Law
Third Edition
Paul Craig

What's Left of the Law of Integration?
Decay and Resistance in European Union Law
Julio Baquero Cruz

EU Legal Acts
Challenges and Transformations
Edited by Marise Cremona and Claire Kilpatrick

Constitutionalization of European Private Law
Edited by Hans W. Micklitz

Justifying Contract in Europe

Political Philosophies of European Contract Law

MARTIJN W. HESSELINK

OXFORD
UNIVERSITY PRESS

OXFORD
UNIVERSITY PRESS

Great Clarendon Street, Oxford, OX2 6DP,
United Kingdom

Oxford University Press is a department of the University of Oxford.
It furthers the University's objective of excellence in research, scholarship,
and education by publishing worldwide. Oxford is a registered trade mark of
Oxford University Press in the UK and in certain other countries

First Edition published in 2021

Impression: 2

Published in the United States of America by Oxford University Press
198 Madison Avenue, New York, NY 10016, United States of America

British Library Cataloguing in Publication Data
Data available

Library of Congress Control Number: 2020952421

ISBN 978-0-19-284365-4 (hbk.)
ISBN 978-0-19-284368-5 (pbk.)

DOI: 10.1093/oso/9780192843654.001.0001

Printed and bound by
CPI Group (UK) Ltd, Croydon, CR0 4YY

Preface

The project

No theory starts from nowhere. And sometimes theoretical enquiries are rooted in very concrete experiences. So too, the idea for this book was triggered by my personal experiences in the past two decades with the academic and political debates on European contract law.

These experiences started in the Study Group on a European Civil Code where we drafted and discussed texts that later ended up in the Draft Common Frame of Reference. It was followed by my membership of the European Commission's Expert Group that prepared a draft for the Commission's proposal for a Common European Sales Law. In both the Study Group and the Expert Group the membership consisted chiefly of academics, specialising, in particular, in (comparative) positive private law. Yet, the questions we were discussing were clearly not positive at all but normative: they were concerned with what European contract law *should* become. Moreover, they were also explicitly political. The political dimension became quite concrete when the European Commission invited us to discuss our drafts with (selected) stakeholder representatives, i.e. Brussels-based lobbyists for small businesses, banks, notaries, consumers, and others. Even more tangibly political was my experience in writing reports on European (consumer) contract law for the European Parliament and presenting and discussing these in Brussels at public hearings of the Parliament's Legal Affairs Committee.

However, the experience that most directly inspired this project was in a group of academics who together wrote a manifesto on social justice in European contract law, in response to the European Commission's action plan, where we denounced the Commission's attempt at the time to obscure the political nature of contract law making while at the same time setting a blatantly 'neoliberal' agenda for its contents. Our manifesto was generally well received. However, it also raised questions. The most fundamental one was: what do you mean by social justice and what does it have to do with contract law? Besides, it was quite obvious that our own text was political too, not merely because it came from the left, but also because it constituted a delicate compromise between several quite divergent views.

Through these experiences, I became increasingly interested in whether something more articulate, more grounded in theory, could be said about the normative political questions on European contract law. I decided to explore this question by setting up a course that I ended up teaching for a decade in different European universities.[1] The name of the course varied but its format was always essentially the same. It submitted six fundamental political questions of European contract law to six leading

[1] Université Panthéon-Sorbonne (Paris I) (2010), Católica Global School of Law (Lisbon) (2011–2018), Sciences Po (Paris) (2016–2018), University of Amsterdam (2010–2019), University of Catania (2019), the Academy of European Law (2019), and the European University Institute (2020).

contemporary political theories. The result was a developing matrix of the political philosophy of European contract law. Initially, I used Kymlicka's introduction to political philosophy as the core reading for the course.[2] But when my research project got more advanced I switched to versions of the present manuscript, culminating, in 2019, in the General Course for the Academy of European Law at the European University Institute (EUI) in Florence.

A genuine attempt to do equal justice to the various political theories and their authors is what accounts for the considerable amount of time that has gone into this project, far more than I had anticipated. In many cases, what started out as sceptical curiosity, and in some cases even a degree of hostility ('reading the enemy'), led me—via better understanding—to a greater appreciation of the worldviews at hand, without necessarily always becoming convinced by them. This made the fact of reasonable pluralism (Rawls' phrase) almost palpable. My hope is that the book conveys some of this sensation to the readers as well.

The European Civil Code movement was inspired by strong European private law idealism that today seems to belong to the past. Yet, this book is not driven by nostalgia for the 'grand project' of the European civil code.[3] As I will explain in more detail in the introduction, the main focus of this book is not on the recent history of European contract law but on its future. Still, what this project has in common with that 'grand project' is a shared interest in the basic structure of European private law as part of the basic structure of the European Union. This led me to ask what might be referred to as 'grand questions', to adopt a normative focus on European contract law as it should be, and to refrain from taking the positive European contract law 'acquis' for granted as the starting point for the critical analysis. The fundamental political questions of European contract law that are central to this book are more general and abstract because they aim to contribute to a better understanding of the normative foundations and possible futures of European contract law.

Acknowledgements

During the decade that I worked on this project, many people have contributed to it in various ways. I am very grateful for their interest and generosity.

As mentioned, this book took shape in parallel with a course I taught in universities across Europe. I would like to thank the colleagues who invited me to teach a class in the Master's programmes and summer schools directed by them: Pierre Legrand at Paris I, Joseph Weiler, Miguel Maduro, and Luís Barreto Xavier at Catòlica, Christoph

[2] W. Kymlicka, *Contemporary Political Philosophy: An Introduction* (2nd ed., 2002).

[3] Having said that, arguably a European civil code, provided that it is done in the right way (i.e. through a thoroughly inclusive and deliberative democratic process and expressing a strongly materialised conception of private autonomy) is our best hope today for re-coding capital, taking back democratic control, and ensuring equality. For a superb diagnosis of the key role played by general private law (property, contract, and company law) in creating capital, see K. Pistor, *The Code of Capital: How the Law Creates Wealth and Inequality* (2019).

Jamin and Horatia Muir Watt at Sciences Po, Antonio Las Casas at Catania, and Claire Kilpatrick and Joanne Scott at the Academy of European Law. In addition, I would like to express my special gratitude to the many students in my classes throughout these years for the animated discussions we had and for the excellent questions they asked and the pertinent observations they offered. I hope that the spirit of our lively debates is also reflected in the style of this book.

Some of the draft chapters underwent particularly intense scrutiny, at the Centre for the Study of European Contract Law's annual summer schools on private law theory (2016–2019), not only from the junior researchers, but also, and especially, from my co-teachers Aditi Bagchi, Hanoch Dagan, and Lyn Tjon Soei Len. I thank them for the exciting exchanges, which usually continued over dinner. These have been among my best experiences in academia.

At the University of Amsterdam, a group of colleagues set up a reading group where we discussed several draft chapters before I left for the EUI. I would like to thank Marija Bartl, Nik de Boer, Laura Burgers, Christina Eckes, Aukje van Hoek, Mirthe Jiwa, and Candida Leone for all their comments.

Finally, I am very grateful to all those who contributed to turning my manuscript into a book. Agata Poznańska did an excellent job as a research assistant in implementing the publisher's citation style. Brianne Bellio, as a project editor, and Viki Kapur, as a production editor, at Oxford University Press, skilfully guided the book through the various production stages. Throughout the entire writing, editing, and production process, Joyce Davies, the assistant editor of the Academy of European Law Collected Courses series, ensured, kindly but firmly, steady progress at each turn and solved the numerous practical questions that came up along the way.

Fiesole, autumn 2020

Table of Contents

Detailed Table of Contents

List of Abbreviations

General

AFSJ	area of freedom, security and justice, a grouping of home affairs and justice policies designed to ensure security, rights, and free movement within the EU
B2B	business to business
B2C	business to consumer
BEUC	Bureau Européen des Unions de Consommateurs, the European Consumer Organisation
CESL	Common European Sales Law (proposed and withdrawn)
CFR	Common Frame of Reference (European Commission proposal)
CFREU	Charter of Fundamental Rights of the European Union
CISG	United Nations Convention on Contracts for the International Sale of Goods (Vienna, 1980) (the 'Vienna Sales Convention')
CJEU	Court of Justice of the European Union
CLS	critical legal studies movement
CRD	Consumer Rights Directive, adopted in 2011
DCFR	Draft Common Frame of Reference
ECC	European civil code (idea)
ECHR	European Convention on Human Rights
GDP	gross domestic product
GNI	gross national income
GVCs	global value chains
HDI	Human Development Index
IMCO	Internal Market and Consumer Protection committee of the European Parliament
JURI	Legal Affairs committee of the European Parliament
P2P	peer-to-peer
PECL	Principles of European Contract Law
Rome I	Regulation (EC) 593/2008 of 17 June 2008 on the law applicable to contractual obligations
SEA	Single European Act 1986
SE	*Societas Europea*, the European company
SIN	Standard Information Notice (European Commission)
SMEs	small and medium-sized enterprises
TEU	Treaty on European Union
TFEU	Treaty on the Functioning of the European Union
UNIDROIT	International Institute for the Unification of Private Law

Journals

AJCL	*American Journal of Comparative Law*
Am. Sociol. Rev.	*American Sociological Review*
Colum. L. Rev.	*Columbia Law Review*
CMLR	*Common Market Law Review*
ELJ	*European Law Journal*
ERCL	*European Review of Contract Law*
ERPL	*European Review of Private Law*
Geo. Wash. L. Rev.	*George Washington Law Review*
Harv. L. Rev.	*Harvard Law Review*
Hastings L.J.	*Hastings Law Journal*
ICLQ	*International and Comparative Law Quarterly*
JCMS	*Journal of Common Market Studies*
J. Legal Stud.	*Journal of Legal Studies*
Law Contemp. Probl.	*Law and Contemporary Problems*
MLR	*Modern Law Review*
OJLS	*Oxford Journal of Legal Studies*
U. Chi. L. Rev.	*University of Chicago Law Review*
Va. L. Rev.	*Virginia Law Review*
Yale L.J.	*Yale Law Journal*
YEL	*Yearbook of European Law*
ZIP	*Zeitschrift für Wirtschaftsrecht*

1
Introduction

1. Rethinking European Contract Law

A. Contract's Reasons in the European Union

The aim of this book is to rethink the normative foundations of European contract law. In particular, it asks what, if anything, the political institutions of the EU ought to do about contracts. More concretely, it addresses some of the most fundamental political questions of European contract law from the different perspectives of leading contemporary political theories. The result is a critical discussion of political philosophies of European contract law, or, put differently, of contract's reasons in Europe. Not only does this contribute to a better understanding of European contract law and its reasons, but by deepening and widening our views on what European contract law ought to look like it also opens up democratic space for the consideration of concrete alternative futures for contract law in the EU, and for finding better justifications for those parts of the EU contract law *acquis* we want to retain. In this way, the book aims to move the academic and political debates on European contract law beyond *acquis* positivism, market reductionism, normative intuitionism, private law essentialism, and methodological nationalism.

B. Beyond *Acquis* Positivism

After the defeat of the Common European Sales Law proposal in 2014, most participants in the European civil code debate, which had dominated the scene during this century's first decade and a half, abandoned the Europe-wide foundational discussion on the future of European private law and moved on to different subjects. Many of them turned their attention to the EU private law *acquis*. They did so in various ways: commenting on consumer protection directives and the interpretations of these by the Court of Justice; dissecting private law elements from economic-sector-specific regulation and trying to make regulatory sense of them; testing certain premises or consequences of the *acquis* empirically; or critiquing the existing EU private law and proposals for new European legislation as being intrinsically 'neoliberal'. Others returned to their respective national debates on how to domesticate the steady flow of private law legislation coming from Brussels.

There is nothing wrong per se with this more positivistic, and perhaps even more realistic turn taken by recent European private law scholarship. Perhaps it is even a natural reaction to the demise of a project with distinctly utopian traits (or dystopian, depending on one's point of view). However, the current strong focus by European

Justifying Contract in Europe: Political Philosophies of European Contract Law. First Edition. Martijn W. Hesselink, Oxford University Press. © Martijn W. Hesselink 2021. DOI: 10.1093/oso/9780192843654.003.0001

private law scholarship, in both its doctrinal and critical versions, on the private law as it is proposed, enacted, and interpreted by the EU institutions, risks leaving us with a significant gap. If European private law scholarship is going to limit itself from now on to neo-positivism, neo-empiricism, and neo-Foucauldian critique (however justified) that fails to tell us what a better EU private law might look like, then we risk losing sight of potential alternative futures for private law in Europe.

Therefore, we need to re-open, in a better way, the fundamental normative debate about what European private law could and should look like: to imagine how it could be different, and to explore whether some of the alternatives would perhaps be better, and more justified. Moreover, even for the EU private law that we want to retain—perhaps a lot—there must be better reasons than the single-minded justification offered by the European Commission in recent decades, i.e. that EU private law must be instrumental to economic growth ('justice for growth'), which seems to have been determined by the European Commission's understanding of a functioning internal market (Article 114 TFEU) exclusively as a growing market, where consumers confidently shop across borders. The failure of the 'grand project' does not mean that we must now also avoid the grand questions.[1] We should not throw the baby out with the bathwater. We should avoid sliding from healthy realism into 'utopophobia' (Estlund).[2] Indeed, today more than ever we need a rich variety of convincing and attractive alternative accounts of private law across borders as it could be and perhaps ought to be, and, in some cases, of alternative and more convincing justifications for EU private law as it is.[3] In summary, what we urgently need in Europe today is normative private law scholarship.

Many legal scholars shy away from normative theory. They consider it too speculative or too abstract to be of any practical use to, for example, European private law makers. However, uncertainty about the answer does not diminish the importance of a question. Demands for social and interpersonal justice will not go away. And as to abstraction, normative questions can be just as concrete as positive ones. There is no correlation between the is/ought-distinction, on the one hand, and different levels of abstraction, on the other. Just as empirical legal studies can improve on our intuitions regarding facts, so too can normative legal scholarship assist in articulating and elucidating our normative intuitions, thus opening up the possibility for insights that may both broaden and deepen political and doctrinal debates on law. We should resist naturalistic reductions of legal scholarship to science as measurement. Society needs normative accounts of law, and so does democracy. This does not mean, of course, that normative political theory of private law, in its turn, should be detached from the reality of actually existing European contract law. On the contrary, this book will consistently address, contextualize, and critically discuss salient political choices made by both EU and domestic contract law makers.

[1] Cf Micklitz, 'Failure or Ideological Preconceptions? Thoughts on Two Grand Projects: The European Constitution and the European Civil Code', in K. Tuori and S. Sankari (eds), *The Many Constitutions of Europe* (2010) 109–142.

[2] I.e. the unreasonable fear of utopianism. See Estlund, 'Utopophobia', 42 *Philosophy and Public Affairs* (2014) 113, at 116.

[3] This also applies for the boundaries of the EU, and hence the scope of EU law, which are both contingent.

C. Beyond Market Reductionism

Most of the contract law *acquis communautaire* (i.e. the existing EU contract law) is justified by the European legislature exclusively in market terms. In particular, the official purpose of the various EU directives in the field of contract law is to contribute to the proper functioning of the internal market by approximating certain aspects of the contract laws of the EU Member States (Article 114 TFEU). In addition, within these harmonization measures 'a high-level of consumer protection', as required by Article 169 TFEU, is often considered instrumental to the market-building aim as well: consumer protection boosts consumer confidence, which, in turn, will lead to more cross-border shopping. Moreover, the European legislature's understanding of a functioning market in recent decades has been an extraordinarily reductive one: a properly functioning market is a growing market. Thus, according to the official justifications, EU contract law making has been directly—and almost exclusively—at the service of economic growth within the EU.

Remarkably, much of the critique of internal market instrumentalism is equally economically reductionist in its focus. This is true, in particular, for those who understand much of European private law—and indeed of the EU in general—as being essentially 'neoliberal'. Much of this critique is rooted in classical Marxian materialism. In its most radical forms, it regards normative political theories, and their reference to justice, as mere ideology, proposed either as a result of naivety or even bad faith. In more moderate versions, the focus is on socio-economic reform, based on (sometimes radically) different 'political economy' conceptions of the market and the role of private law therein, without giving up, however, the understanding, shared with the Commission, of private law as a mere socio-economic institution.

In contrast, this book aims to move the debate beyond both types of market reductionism. Even though contract law is undoubtedly a very important economic institution, its societal role, and hence its political justification, cannot be reduced, without loss, to its economic function. Even in a society with much more economic growth or significantly less economic inequality, respectively, there would still be good reason to discuss the normative foundations of contract law. First, because we need a reason or standard for deciding whether the prevailing levels of growth and inequality are acceptable, and, secondly, because we should at least consider whether reasons and concerns other than socio-economic ones (think of interpersonal justice and human rights) should override or supplement socio-economic considerations, in at least some cases and perhaps in many.

D. Beyond Normative Intuitionism

The focus in this study is on leading contemporary political theories and their implications for fundamental questions of European contract law. The expectation is that a critical discussion and comparison of these accounts can enrich the political and academic debates on European contract law by broadening and deepening the debate. In particular, it can be shown that positions that have been taken in these debates can be traced back to more fundamental disagreements of principle, and, vice versa, that each of the leading contemporary political theories has something to say on some of the most fundamental political questions of European contract law. In other words, the consideration and critical comparison of contemporary political philosophies of European contract law will not only open our eyes to potential alternative futures for contract law in Europe, but it will also help us in understanding and articulating what exactly is wrong with certain existing European contract law rules or a reform proposal made by a politician or scholar that we are inclined to reject intuitively, without too much reflection upon the reasons for our misgivings.

It should be emphasized, however, that the focus here on political theories does not mean to suggest that intuitions have no legitimate place in the political debate on (European) contract law and its foundations, nor even that normative theories of contract law should play an important role in the political debate. In particular, this book does not take any position, at least not as a starting point,[4] on the epistemic status of normative contract theory. In other words, it does not assume that the questions central to this work are ones about the truth of political and contract theories, or that political theorists and contract law theorists know a particular method for arriving at that truth. Moral realism and cognitivism are not the only points of view from which an attempt to move the debate on (European) contract law in a more normative direction can be considered meaningful. Nor does the focus in this work on reasons and justification imply a commitment to any strong form of rationalism. The only starting point in this regard is that often citizens and law makers are, or might be, moved by reasons. Therefore, views on contract law cannot be reduced, without significant loss in understanding, to the mere 'preferences' that economic agents sometimes are said to find themselves with and strategically to act upon. Nor does it seem plausible, whatever one's view on the role of agony and other emotions in politics, that law making and political debate is and should never be informed by arguments. All that this book assumes as a starting point is some human agency in the contract law making process, i.e. some capacity and inclination in human beings to be convinced, and to change their minds, when confronted with reasons offered by others.

E. Beyond Private Law Essentialism

At the core of most leading contract law theories lies a claim concerning contract law's essential nature or value (e.g. autonomy, solidarity, or efficiency). Thus, we find strong agreement on contract law having an essence, but equally strong disagreement as to what exactly contract law's essence might be. Note that essentialist claims are extraordinarily strong claims: they hold that in the absence of the element considered essential, contract law would no longer be contract law. By definition, divergent essentialist claims, proclaiming a certain value as contract's core or ultimate value, are mutually exclusive. From the point of view of each essentialist theory, whatever characteristic the other theories are proposing as essential cannot but be merely accidental. The claim of essentialism is a metaphysical claim. In a pluralist society it is not self-evident,

[4] The question will be considered explicitly in Chapters 3 and 9.

to say the least, that metaphysics can provide convincing reasons for the justification of generally applicable rules. Moreover, essentialist claims are uncompromising. They imply that if we do not take whatever is contract law's asserted essential value as its foundational and organizing principle then we are denaturing contract law. 'Whatever you are proposing, it is not contract law properly understood', is how such claims tend to go. Uncompromising views seem fundamentally at odds with democratic polities where it rarely is the case—especially over time—that the winner of the debate or the vote takes all. Therefore, contract law essentialism seems difficult to match with the practical reality (if not the essence) of democratic government. Moving beyond contract law essentialism—i.e. to de-essentialize contract law and its theory—obviously does not mean that essentialist contract law theories, their claims, and their proposals will be disregarded altogether. In particular, proposals deriving from essentialist theories should not be barred from becoming part of a democratic compromise, at least not for that reason. What they will lose—i.e. what will be disregarded—is merely their exclamation mark, as it were.[5]

In contrast to essentialist and other monist views of contract law, which are reductionist, the aim of this book is to show complexity. The idea is that we will better understand the normative foundations of (European) contract law, and will be better placed to debate its future, if we critically discuss and compare very different—often radically opposed—normative theories. This does not mean, however, that this book aims at completeness (whatever that would mean). Rather, it aims to show different views of the cathedral, to reflect upon these differences, and to address the question of what the existence of such very different perspectives should entail for (European) contract law. On the other hand, therefore, the aim here is also to go beyond mere perspectivism or an academic 'style exercise'.[6] Thus, arguments coming from different political theories will not merely be juxtaposed, but will be critically discussed, compared, and their merits will be assessed in concluding normative observations, which will thus not be made 'from nowhere' (see later, in Section 3).

F. Beyond Methodological Nationalism

With today's widespread disaffection towards the EU, also seen among legal scholars, it has become almost counter-current to consider and propose new ideas for Europe. However, that is exactly what the present book aims to do for private law: to open up the political debate by presenting and critically discussing concrete alternative futures, based on different contemporary normative political theories, which go beyond the Commission's market reductionism.[7] This does not mean that the book is per se

[5] In this regard, there exists a parallel between essentialist and constitutionalist claims, both aiming to trump other claims—in the words of Kennedy—by adding an exclamation mark (D. Kennedy, *A Critique of Adjudication: Fin de Siècle* (1997), at 331).

[6] Obviously, there is nothing against style exercises, especially if they are done as brilliantly, as in R. Queneau, *Exercices de style* (1947). Specifically in the field of political theory, see also S. Lukes, *The Curious Enlightenment of Professor Caritat: A Novel of Ideas* (1995), which I will come back to in Chapter 2.

[7] The Commission's view is crucial, from a political point of view, since it has the exclusive right of initiative for new EU legislation. See Art. 17 TEU.

biased towards 'more Europe'. All it does is to move beyond methodological nationalism, i.e. the assumption that political views and values differ chiefly between nations, not (or to a lesser extent) between groups transcending national boundaries. This book adopts a transnational point of view from which to rethink the Europeanization of contract law. And the fundamental normative questions on European contract law that the book discusses from this transnational perspective include, notably, the very question of whether contract law should be national, European, global, sub-national, or a combination of these.

2. The Political Philosophy of European Contract Law

A. Fundamental Political Questions

We cannot know in advance which existing rules, doctrines, or aspects of European contract law citizens may want to contest or which new ones they may want to propose. Yet, a number of questions with regard to contract law in Europe that seem politically salient can still be formulated. Some of the most central ones, it is submitted, include the following: (1) Does contract law need to have a democratic basis? (2) Should contract law be national, European, or global? (3) Should contracts have legally binding force and, if so, what should this entail in terms of remedies? (4) Should contract law protect weaker parties? (5) Should the freedom of contract be limited for reasons of public policy or public morality? (6) Should contract law be partly optional? Each of these questions and their political relevance will be fully introduced at the beginning of the respective chapters. Therefore, I will not further elaborate on them here.

These will be the six questions central to this inquiry. I am fully conscious that this brings an element of 'framing', as political analysts call it, to the organization of the book. It could be objected that by selecting these six particular questions as fundamental questions of European contract law, and by discussing these, from the perspective of political theory, as questions concerning what we could call the basic structure of European contract law, certain aspects of contract law in Europe are placed in the foreground—which inevitably suggests that other questions are less politically salient. My answer is that I am aware of this and that the reader should be as well. However, there exists no real alternative.[8] There is no fully neutral and uncontroversial way of presenting the political stakes in European contract law. In particular, an approach taking the contract law *acquis* as a starting point, even for a critical analysis, would not have been any more neutral. On the contrary, it would have risked naturalizing the status quo, obscuring its contingency, and reifying 'the changeable decisions of a political lawgiver'.[9] All I can offer is what, I suggest, are good reasons for this selection. In view of (1) the existing political and academic debates on European contract

[8] On how we shape the world, bringing order to it by drawing distinctions, which are never neutral, and on how these distinctions both reflect and reinforce existing power relationships and produce new ones, see M. Foucault, *The Order of Things: An Archaeology of the Human Sciences* ([first published 1966] 1994).

[9] J. Habermas, *Between Facts and Norms: Contributions to a Discourse Theory of Law and Democracy* (1996), 'Postscript', at 447. On law's contingency, see Venzke, 'What If? Counterfactual (Hi)Stories of International Law', 8 *Asian Journal of International Law* (2018) 403.

law and the arguments exchanged therein; (2) the general concerns and focal points of the contemporary political philosophies that will be discussed; and (3) the idea that the basic structure of contract law, as part of the basic structure of society (to use a Rawlsian phrase), should be under particularly strict scrutiny when it comes to thinking and rethinking private law, these six questions seemed to me to be the most fundamental—indeed 'constitutional'—ones.[10]

B. Leading Contemporary Political Theories

Similarly, in advance of actual proposals and contestations we do not know which reasons will eventually be invoked by citizens and by the law making institutions. We do not know this for existing systems, doctrines, rules, or remedies of contract law and still less so for ones that could be proposed or considered in the future. The main public justifications and contestations of European contract law that have already been put forward in the political and academic debates must of course be discussed. Beyond these, we will have to resort to normative theories. Therefore, central to this book will be a critical discussion of the responses to our six political questions that can be derived from leading contemporary political theories, in particular the following six theories: utilitarianism (notably, welfarism and the normative law and economics based on it); liberal-egalitarianism (the political theory closest to social-democracy); libertarianism (or neoliberalism); communitarianism (or neo-Romanticism); civic republicanism; and discourse theory.

Here too there is a clear risk of framing. One might ask, for example, whether feminism is not a leading contemporary political theory. While there is no doubt that some of the most prominent contemporary political philosophers are feminists it is not clear that feminism is best understood as a single political philosophy.[11] Many of these theorists self-identify at least as much as liberal-egalitarians (focusing on rights), discourse-theorists (rethinking the public sphere), or communitarian (advocating identity politics) as they are outspoken feminists. Therefore, the political ideas and critique on subjects such as domination (patriarchy), intersectionality, commodification, and the boundary between public and private spheres—that are highly relevant to (European) contract law, as we will see—will be discussed here not from a singular feminist normative point of view, but rather from the perspectives of the various feminist strands in normative political and legal theory.[12] Others will miss Marxism, which undeniably remains a prominent political theory. However, Marxists, classical

[10] In Hesselink, 'The Politics of a European Civil Code', 10 *European Law Journal* (*ELJ*) (2004) 675, I formulated as many as 50 political questions on European contract law that, I argued, should be answered by the democratic legislator before the more technical drafting by experts could legitimately commence. However, clearly, not all political questions, whatever their importance, were also fundamental ones. Here, the focus is on the latter.

[11] Perhaps only a past middle-age white male law professor would classify feminism in this way. Similarly, my selection of fundamental political questions of European contract law might also be biased by male privilege, backgrounding issues that would matter more from one singular feminist perspective.

[12] In addition to different normative approaches, many (perhaps most) prominent contemporary feminist contributions engage in critical theory. For varieties of feminist legal theory, see the contributions to R. West and C. G. Bowman (eds), *Research Handbook on Feminist Jurisprudence* (2019), Part I.

and contemporary, would fundamentally reject the normative focus on justice, rights, and reasons adopted in this book.[13] Therefore, the first Marxist response to the questions central to this book would be that these are fundamentally the wrong kind of questions to ask about (European) contract law. This was a reason for not structurally discussing Marxism in this book. Still, as in the case of feminism, at several specific points throughout the book pertinent Marxist arguments will be addressed (e.g. with regard to exploitation, adaptive preferences, and hegemony).

3. Starting Point

A. A Radically Democratic Hunch

This book submits six fundamental political questions of European contract law to six contemporary political theories. The expectation is that these theories will have something valuable to say that can contribute not only to a better understanding of European contract law and its normative foundations, but also to bringing about a better and more just European contract law. In other words, this book understands the political theories as potentially effective ideas, with a vocation to have an impact on the future of European contract law. This starting point has a number of implications.

First, it constitutes a certain *a priori* for the analysis and the discussion. The *a priori* is only a weak one. It is not an assumption or a presumption—nothing more than a hunch. But in spite of its weakness it is radical. It is what Habermas referred to as a 'radically democratic hunch'.[14] If we understand normative theories of contract law as meant, at least in part, to have an impact on the future of (European) contract law then they must be understood as theories proposing ideas that can be effective in a democratic society. Not only has the EU enshrined the democratic principle in Article 10 TEU, as a matter of positive constitutional EU law, but also it does not make any normative sense—and this is the radically democratic hunch—to explore what contract law ought to look like in an undemocratic society. Whether this radically democratic *a priori* necessarily leads to the conclusion that contract law itself must also have a democratic basis (or that instead a society can still be democratic if its contract law has no democratic basis) and, in particular, what exactly this would entail—i.e. what we mean by a democratic society and a democratic contract law—is a separate question on which this inquiry adopts no *a priori* view. On the contrary, this is one of the fundamental political questions of European contract law that I will address in this

[13] On the classical Marxian view, both private law and justice are nothing more than ideology—part of the superstructure meant to legitimate, through false consciousness, the existing economic structure of society (the base). See K. Marx, *A Contribution to the Critique of Political Economy* (1859), Preface, at 8–9. Marx famously rejected the notions of rights and distributive justice as 'obsolete verbal rubbish'. See Marx, 'Critique of the Gotha Programme' [first published 1875], in D. McLellan, *Karl Marx: Selected Writings* (2nd ed., 2000) 610, at 615. And from the Marxian perspective, all contracts are exploitative, simply because they reproduce economically determined power relationships. Specifically with regard to labour contracts, see K. Marx, *Capital: An Abridged Edition* (D. McLellan (ed.)) (1995), at 323. See also the young Marx's poignant characterization of commercial contracts as 'mutual plundering'. Marx, 'On James Mill' [1844], in D. McLellan, *Karl Marx: Selected Writings* (2nd ed., 2000) 124, at 130.

[14] Habermas (n. 9) xiii.

book—indeed the very first one (in Chapter 3). However, whatever the answer to this question (and the other questions posed in this book) may be, in a democracy it will have to be argued for. In other words, unlike authoritarian regimes, which can resort to violence, in a democracy arguments and debate will have to play a role in making political ideas become effective.

This brings us to a second implication. In a democracy, it is unthinkable that generally applicable laws will be based on one single underlying value or principle. In other words, the radically democratic hunch implies a pluralistic hunch. Like the democratic hunch the pluralist hunch is only a weak one. And it entails another weak *a priori*, i.e. the starting point that Rawls refers to as 'the fact of reasonable pluralism'.[15] This is the fact that reasonable disagreement concerning worldviews is to be expected as a permanent condition of modern constitutional democracies.[16] Therefore, the pluralism of political views on (European) contract law will be centre-stage in this book. As Tony Judt wrote, 'fox-like, Europe knows many things'.[17] Similarly, as we will see, European contract law and its theory also know many things.[18]

This leads to a third implication. As stated earlier, most contributions to contract theory try to capture the essence of contract law. They try to understand why we have contract law and to determine its true normative or conceptual foundation. Although such truth and truth-like claims will play a central role in the analysis, the focus here will be different. The central question will be what a democratic society should make of these various truth or truth-like claims concerning what ought to be the normative foundation of its contract law. In other words, the normative questions, and the answers to these, as proposed by (or deriving from) political theories, will remain normative but they will not be understood here as ideal theories only. They will be discussed as questions and answers for a society that understands itself as fundamentally committed to democracy (whatever that may mean) and that, therefore, finds itself in what Waldron refers to as the 'circumstances of politics'.[19] As Waldron points out, reasonable disagreement exists not only concerning worldviews and ultimate values but also with regard to conceptions of justice that are meant as a response to the fact of reasonable pluralism (such as Rawls' theory). Therefore, justice claims are also within the circumstances of democratic politics. For the purposes of our inquiry this means that we will discuss them on an equal footing with other political arguments, i.e. as responses to the same fundamental political questions and therefore as located on the same plane (while, of course, duly addressing their normative claim to priority).

This, in turn, leads to a fourth implication. The answers to fundamental political questions of contract law given by a pluralist society committed to democracy will

[15] J. Rawls, *Political Liberalism* ([first published 1993] 2005), at 36.

[16] J. Rawls, *Justice as Fairness: A Restatement* (2001), at 33–34: 'the diversity of religious, philosophical, and moral doctrines found in modern democratic societies is not a mere historical condition that may soon pass away; it is a permanent feature of the public culture of democracy'.

[17] T. Judt, *Postwar: A History of Europe Since 1945* (2005), at 7. The reference is to the line from the Greek poet Archilochus, i.e. 'the fox knows many things, but the hedgehog knows one big thing', famously used as a metaphor for the difference between pluralists and monists by I. Berlin, *The Hedgehog and the Fox; An Essay on Tolstoy's View of History* ([first published 1953] 2009).

[18] For an earlier account of a European contract law for foxes, see Hesselink, 'Five Political Ideas of European Contract Law', 7 *European Review of Contract Law* (*ERCL*) (2011) 295.

[19] J. Waldron, *Law and Disagreement* (1999), at 102.

always have to be compromises, at least to some degree. They will be the result of give and take, and of balancing values and principles. This leads to another weak premise, i.e. the notion that European contract law will and should be a compromise between very different views and ideas of contract law in Europe. However, compromises cannot be made out of uncompromising views. Therefore, in a democracy (as opposed to an authoritarian regime) the propensity for compromise of a theory is important to its potential as an effective political idea. So, while this book does not take as a starting point that the answers to the fundamental political questions of European contract law must be justifiable by public reasons (the question whether it should will, of course, be discussed), it does assume that the more partisan the arguments are, the less likely it is that they will have a strong impact on any compromise guided by reasons (as opposed to different types of political power). This is why the uncompromising or fundamentalist nature of certain political views will be considered as an important element in our critical discussion.

There is a fifth and final implication. To some, the present inquiry may come across as a typical elite project, detached from the real concerns of the people. While much of the criticism of the roles of various elites in politics is entirely legitimate, claims setting up 'the elite' against 'the people', in the singular, are different. They are populist. If we understand populists as those who claim to speak on behalf of the real people, understood as a monolithic homogeneous unit, then populism is fundamentally anti-democratic because it is anti-pluralist.[20] It denies the pluralism of views in society that is the premise of any democratic politics. Instead, it claims that, in our case, the entire (European) contract law debate is illegitimate, because it disregards the concerns of the real people, whom the populist politician or theorist claims to be somehow uniquely well placed to capture, voice, and represent.[21] Conversely, in the current political climate in Europe (and beyond) where populism continues to be a major political factor, a book that aims to show the width and depth of the pluralism of ideas that exist, in our case, with regard to contract law and its Europeanization, and to critically engage with various arguments, can contribute to resisting the populist fallacy of a singular 'the people' with uniform concerns, aspirations, values, and principles.[22] Thus, one motivation for writing this book is the belief that showing a pluralism of legitimate reasons is the best response we have against populist claims, based on fantasies of a homogeneous people.[23]

In summary, following from the starting point of understanding normative political theories as potentially effective ideas, aspiring to making an impact on, in our case, the future of European contract law, this book takes the radically democratic hunch, the

[20] J.-W. Müller, *What Is Populism?* (2017).

[21] Cf. N. Urbinati, *Me the People: How Populism Transforms Democracy* (2019).

[22] This includes the populist reduction of contemporary politics to a battle between right and left populism, as proposed by C. Mouffe, *For a Left Populism* (2018).

[23] At the risk of stating the obvious, I underline here the fundamental difference between proponents of essentialist and monistic contract law theories, on the one hand, and populists, on the other: when monist theorists argue that one single value or principle should be the foundational value or principle of politics, or, in our case, of (European) contract law, then they are not claiming to speak on behalf of singular people. They do not deny the plurality of values existing in society; they only try to convince everyone else that one single value or principle is supreme.

fact of reasonable pluralism, the circumstances of politics, the need for compromise, and the rejection of populism as weak premises for its analysis.[24]

B. Critique and Justification

Normative arguments, in particular justificatory and contestatory discourses, will be centre-stage in this book. Their strength will be tested, not only on their own terms (immanent critique), but also on the basis of pertinent arguments deriving from other political theories (external critique), and in terms of the weak premise adopted in this book, i.e. that the political theories under discussion, and the arguments derived from them, will be understood as aspiring effective ideas for a democratic society. This critical stance differs from the more radical, foundational critique coming from critical legal studies, much of which is fundamentally sceptical with regard to normative theory and the power of reasons. In contrast, this book regards a commitment to the unforced force of the better argument as central to meaningful critique.

At the end of each chapter and in a final chapter, I will formulate some concluding observations. These will be partly analytical, pointing to similarities and differences between the various political theories in their responses to the question at hand. However, they will also be normative, trying to distinguish between stronger and weaker answers to the question under discussion. Thus, although each of the conclusions will be reached in discussion with the political theories central this book, the main aim is not to determine an overlapping consensus or some common core. It is the strength of the reasons that counts, not the number of political theories supporting them. At the same time, it is clear that the analysis will not yield a grand theory of European contract law, not only because a critical discussion of six contemporary political theories remains narrow as an informational basis for such a theory, or that arguments other than political ones may also have to inform normative contract theory (which, however, seems doubtful), but also because the reasonable pluralism of worldviews suggest the unlikelihood of finding compelling normative reasons in support of a fully fledged blueprint for an ideal, fully justified European contract law.

4. Objectives and Outline

A. Main Aim

As previously stated, the main aim of this book is to rethink the normative foundations of European contract law. For this purpose, I will engage in critical discussions of contemporary political theories concerning the answers they give to fundamental political questions of European contract.[25] In doing so, I aim to contribute to an

[24] In other words, in the eyes of anyone who rejects the radically democratic hunch, the fact of reasonable pluralism, the circumstances of politics, the need for compromise, or embraces populism, the present analysis starts on the wrong foot.

[25] For an earlier attempt, see Hesselink (n. 18).

understanding of the ways in which European private law is political that goes deeper, and is more nuanced, than existing one-dimensional accounts limited to, for example, a left-right continuum,[26] varieties of welfarism,[27] diachronic narratives featuring one dominant paradigm at a time,[28] or space-time analyses in terms of national political traditions or 'legal consciousnesses'.[29] The focus will be explicitly normative, i.e. on European contract law as it ought to be. The answers derived from the various political theories will frequently be counterfactual. Therefore, they can serve as principled grounds for critique and as normative bases for reform proposals.[30] At the same time, this book can also be understood as a critical introduction to the political philosophy of European contract law: a new field of study at the crossroads of European law, contract law, and political philosophy.

B. Pluralism

Any contemporary normative theory of contract law in Europe that aims to become an effective political idea will have to take into account, one way or another, a number of pluralities that are part of the reality of contract today. These include the pluralities of contract types, of contract law systems, of roles of contract law, of values attributed to contract law, and indeed of contract theories. As a theme running through all the chapters, this book will therefore explore what the presence of this multitude of contract pluralities should mean for the normative theory of European contract law. One important dimension of pluralism, including political and value pluralism, is that the same question may be understood differently from different perspectives. So too, the various political theories under discussion here, as we will see, frequently understand our fundamental political questions of (European) contract law quite divergently. Each of these theories highlights different aspects of the same question, understanding it as raising different sub-questions, as it were.

C. Outline

The remainder of the book is organized as follows.

[26] See Kennedy, 'The Political Stakes in "Merely Technical" Issues of Contract Law', 10 *European Review of Private Law* (*ERPL*) (2002) 7. For the EU, see Hesselink (n. 10); B. van Zelst, *The Politics of European Sales Law* (2008); C. Mak, *Fundamental Rights in European Contract Law: A Comparison of the Impact of Fundamental Rights on Contractual Relationships in Germany, The Netherlands, Italy and England* (2008).

[27] Wilhelmsson, 'Varieties of Welfarism in European Contract Law', 10 *ELJ* (2004) 712.

[28] Habermas (n. 9) ch. 9.1; Kennedy, 'Three Globalizations of Law and Legal Thought: 1850–2000', in D. Trubek and A. Santos (eds), *The New Law and Economic Development: A Critical Appraisal* (2006) 19.

[29] See e.g. H.-W. Micklitz, *The Politics of Justice in European Private Law: Social Justice, Access Justice, Societal Justice* (2018), Part I.

[30] In a sense, this book may be regarded also as a case study in political philosophy, where political theories are applied to—and tested for—the case of European contract law and its making. While it is mainly directed at those interested in European private law and its theory, some of the arguments may be relevant (*mutatis mutandis*) for other subjects of private law or European law as well, and some insights obtained for this specific case may also feed back into wider political philosophical debates.

Chapter 2 provides context. It briefly presents the states of play in the two debates which this book aims to bring together, i.e. European contract law and political philosophy, and is intended for those readers who are not familiar with these debates. The first section offers an introduction to the Europeanization of contract law. Its main purpose is to set the scene, as it were, without unduly framing the argument. Thus, it introduces the main milestones, players, acts, and controversies. The objective is to provide the reader with a general but concrete sense of what we are talking about when we speak of 'European contract law'. This may be helpful, in particular, for European readers familiar mainly with their own national contract laws, and perhaps especially for readers from outside the EU. Experts on the subject may decide to skip this section. The second section, similarly, provides a brief introduction into normative political philosophy. It sketches the main traits of some of the leading contemporary political theories, with a special focus on aspects relevant for (European) contract law. Like the first section, it does not take any strong positions. It is meant, in particular, for lawyers with no background in political philosophy, and thus philosophers will probably prefer to move on directly to the next section. Finally, a third section further sets the scene by briefly presenting the various pluralities with which any contemporary theory of contract law is confronted, i.e. the variety of contract types that parties may conclude, the different systems of contract law existing in the Member States of the EU, and the various roles that contract law plays in our lives. The section concludes by briefly introducing the main stances one may adopt, as a law maker or as a theorist, towards these pluralities, i.e. monism, pluralism (constrained or unconstrained), and neutralism.

The core of the book follows: six chapters dedicated each to a fundamental political question of European contract law.

Chapter 3 concerns the relationship between contract law and democracy. The central question is whether contract law, in order to be legitimate, must have a democratic basis, and what this would entail. This leads to a normative institutional comparison between legislators, courts, legal academics, and economic-sectoral experts as the protagonists in contract law making. In addition, beyond the matter of institutional choice, the question of democratic legitimacy may lead to the question whether there are any limits as to the kind of reasons ('public reasons') that can justify the law, in our case European contract law.[31]

Chapter 4 addresses the Europeanization of contract law, a subject already introduced briefly in Chapter 2. This time, however, the discussion is from a normative perspective: can the Europeanization of contract law be justified? Or are there perhaps more convincing reasons why contract law should remain national or become global?

Chapter 5 is dedicated entirely to what may be regarded as the most fundamental political question of contract law (and is usually considered the core question of contract theory), i.e. what justifies the legally binding force of contract law? What business do public institutions have in recognizing and enforcing private agreements? Could a society decide not to enforce contracts and still be sufficiently just? And if indeed

[31] Much of what will be discussed in Chapters 3 and 4 applies equally to fields of private law other than contract law.

a society ought to publicly recognize and enforce contracts, then which remedies should it make available (minimally or maximally)?

Chapter 6 discusses whether contract law can and should differentiate between different types of contracting parties with regard to their relational or social weakness: should contract law protect certain weaker parties? And if so, who should count as worthy of protection and what kinds of protection should they be granted? Given that consumer protection has been central to EU contract law, this question goes to the core of the justifiability of the European contract law *acquis*.

Chapter 7 asks whether a society committed in principle to the legal recognition and enforcement of contracts is nevertheless free to—or even *required* to—withhold recognition and enforceability from certain contracts, by declaring them 'null' or 'void' under contract law doctrines such as 'good morals' or 'public policy', because of their unacceptable content, purpose, or consequences. This is the classical question of freedom of contract, which can be rephrased, to a large extent, in contemporary terms of 'commodification' and, for the EU, as the question of the moral limits to the internal market.

Chapter 8 focuses on a distinctive characteristic of an important portion of contemporary rules of contract law that sets them apart not only from public law but also from other branches of private law (e.g. property and family law), i.e. that these rules can be set aside freely by the contracting parties. Contrary to national civil codes, however, positive EU contract law does not include many instances of non-mandatory rules. This raises the question of what exactly justifies the existence of such optional rules: should public institutions be providing elaborate sets of contract law rules if private parties can set them aside as they please, and, if so, what kind of considerations should determine the content of such rules? Similar questions can be asked with respect to other instances of optional contract law, such as choice of law in cross-border contracts.

Finally, Chapter 9 presents the main conclusions of this inquiry and also offers a few wider concluding observations.

Formulated in this way, the key questions addressed in this book may seem rather abstract. However, as the chapters will show with a host of contemporary examples, they are of central relevance to the very concrete practice of European contract law making today. The examples will include leading court cases from the Court of Justice and from national courts, salient provisions in EU directives and national civil codes, and many other actions and actors involved in the EU and national contract law making processes in Europe. In this sense, the book can also be read as a critical reconstruction of the making of European contract law during more than two decades of political and academic debates. Still, the discussion will not limit itself only to existing (positive) contract law. Rather the focus will be on both the *acquis* and its reasonably conceivable alternatives. The account will therefore also be counterfactual on two levels. First, the answers to the normative questions discussed here include possible alternatives that may not even have been discussed in the European-contract-law-making institutions (and are, in this sense, 'unheard of'). Secondly, the questions will not derive from—or follow the structure of—the *acquis* (including the failed *acquis*, i.e. legislative proposals that were withdrawn); instead, they will be abstract in order to leave enough space for the normative and critical dimensions of the analysis.

A final comment on scope. It follows from the commitment of this book to consider European contract law beyond *acquis* positivism that the discussion here refuses to entrench the EU's geographical boundaries, and consequently, the geographical scope of EU law. After years of enlargement, in 2020 for the first time a Member State left the EU. Yet, not only will it take many years to fully assess the impact of Brexit on EU private law, but also re-accession of the UK, or a (by then former) part of it, for example Scotland, still remains fundamentally possible, and in any case entirely thinkable. Therefore, the geographical scope of the normative considerations in this book has not suddenly become limited to the 27 current Member States. Similarly, even though enlargement is not a specific theme in this book, no aspiring new Member State (whether Turkey or another) is in principle excluded from its scope. This is expressed in the title and the subtitle of the book, which do not refer to the 'European Union' but to 'Europe' and 'European', respectively.

2
Context

This chapter sets out the context in which the fundamental political questions of European contract law will be raised. It situates the normative discussion and sets the scene for it. In particular, it briefly introduces some of the milestones in the process of Europeanization of contract law, the core characteristics of the contemporary political theories central to our discussion, and the various pluralities that are part of contract's reality.

1. European Contract Law

The Europeanization of contract law is a political process (or project) that has been taking place for more than three decades now. For a long time it moved at an ever increasing pace; today, it is developing more steadily. It has involved a variety of different actors and actions. The main landmarks and its principal players will be introduced briefly in this section. The objective is to provide a general first impression and short history of the field in which the political questions under discussion in this book are situated, i.e. what is usually referred to as 'European contract law'. Each of these acts and actors will be seen again in the following chapters, where they will be discussed critically. The objective here is merely to set the scene.

A. The *Acquis Communautaire*

Since 1985, the European legislator has enacted a host of legislative measures in the area of contract law. In the first two decades, the most important directives in the field of contract law—some of which have already been revised in the meantime—included On Doorstep Selling (1985), Commercial Agents (1986), Consumer Credit (1987), Travel Packages (1990), Unfair Terms (1993), Time Shares (1994), Distance Selling (1997), Consumer Sales and Guarantees (1999), and Late Payment (2000).[1] Most of

[1] Directive 85/577/EEC to protect the consumer in respect of contracts negotiated away from business premises, OJ 1985 L 372; Directive 86/653/EEC on the coordination of the laws of the Member States relating to self-employed commercial agents, OJ 1986 L 382; Directive 2008/48/EC on credit agreements for consumers, OJ 2008 L 133; Directive 90/314/EEC on package travel, package holidays and package tours, OJ 1990 L 158; Directive 93/13/EEC on unfair terms in consumer contracts, OJ 1993 L 95; Directive 2008/122/EC on the protection of consumers in respect of certain aspects of timeshare, long-term holiday product, resale and exchange contracts, OJ 2009 L 33; Directive 97/7/EC on the protection of consumers in respect of distance contracts, OJ 1997 L 144; Directive 1999/44/EC on certain aspects of the sale of consumer goods and associated guarantees, OJ 1999 L 171; Directive 2000/35/EC on combating late payment in commercial transactions, OJ 2000 L 200.

Justifying Contract in Europe: Political Philosophies of European Contract Law. First Edition. Martijn W. Hesselink, Oxford University Press. © Martijn W. Hesselink 2021. DOI: 10.1093/oso/9780192843654.003.0002

these directives concerned only consumer contracts (i.e. business to consumer, B2C). A few others, such as the ones on commercial agency and on late payment, by contrast, were concerned exclusively with commercial contracts (i.e. business to business, B2B).

Although these various directives lay down certain very detailed rights and obligations for the contracting parties, they are not directly applicable to the contracts they aim to regulate. As directives, they do not address the contracting parties, only the Member States, who must transpose them into their national legal systems.[2] Therefore, strictly speaking these directives do not create any EU *private* law: they have no direct horizontal effects and, therefore, on their own, do not create any contractual rights and obligations. Having said that, the Court of Justice has held consistently that a private party can rely on a directive whenever a Member State has failed to transpose it in a timely and adequate manner: the national courts, then, must interpret the existing national law, as far as possible,[3] in conformity with that directive ('harmonious interpretation').[4] By contrast to directives, regulations are directly applicable in the Member States. However, in the area of contract law their number has been rather limited. The most prominent examples presently include the Regulation on Air Passenger Rights in the Case of Denied Boarding, Cancellation and Long Delay (2004) and the 'Rome I' Regulation on the Law Applicable to Contractual Obligations (2008).[5] In addition to these sources of secondary EU law, an example of primary EU law of contracts also exists, even though most people would not intuitively regard it as such: pursuant to the second paragraph of Article 101 TFEU, on competition law, any agreements that are prohibited by that provision are automatically void. Thus, from the perspective of contract law, Article 101 TFEU is one of the possible sources of invalidity of contracts, in this case cartel agreements.

One of the most striking features of the existing EU contract law is its fragmented nature. The *acquis communautaire* in the area of contract law contains no general rules, applicable to all kinds of contracts concluded by any type of party, on, say, the formation, validity, interpretation, performance, and breach of contracts—what is usually referred to as 'general contract law'. Instead, it merely stipulates limited sets of rather specific rules that only apply to certain specific types of contracts (e.g. timesharing or consumer credit agreements) or problems (e.g. late payment or unfair terms), concluded by specific parties (e.g. consumers, air passengers, or self-employed commercial agents). As a result, the outlook of EU contract law is markedly different from that of the contract laws that all Member States had previously been familiar with in the jurisdictions in the civil law tradition on the Continent and the common law systems of the UK and Ireland. The explanation for this contrast lies in the limited competence of the EU legislator: any act of EU legislation requires a specific legal basis

[2] See Art. 288 TFEU.

[3] The usual limit is *contra legem* interpretation.

[4] See e.g. Case C-106/89, *Marleasing v. La Comercial Internacional de Alimentación* (EU:C:1990:395); Case C-240/98 to Case C-244/98, *Océano Grupo Editorial SA v. Rocio Murciano Quintero (and Others)* (EU:C:2000:346); Case C-555/07, *Seda Kücükdeveci v. Swedex GmbH & Co. KG* [2010] ECR I-00365 (EU:C:2010:21), at para. 56.

[5] Regulation (EC) 261/2004 establishing common rules on compensation and assistance to passengers in the event of denied boarding and of cancellation or long delay of flights, OJ 2004 L 46; Regulation (EC) 593/2008 on the law applicable to contractual obligations, OJ 2008 L 177 (hereinafter 'Rome I').

justifying the particular legislative measure.[6] The founding treaties, as they currently stand, do not provide any general legal basis for a European private law or contract law. Therefore, 'the approximation of laws', including in the area of contract law, necessarily has to be what the European Commission calls 'sector specific'—providing targeted solutions to existing problems. For contract law, this basis has been found primarily (although not exclusively) in problems relating to the construction and proper functioning of the internal market (now Article 114 TFEU). In its *Tobacco* ruling, the Court underlined that a measure adopted on this basis 'must genuinely have as its object the improvement of the conditions for the establishment and functioning of the internal market', which means that 'mere disparities between national rules',[7] in our case of contract law, are not sufficient to justify harmonization on the basis of Article 114 TFEU.

B. The Action Plan

In a 1989 resolution, the European Parliament requested that 'a start be made on the necessary preparatory work on drawing up a common European Code of Private Law'.[8] This political appeal sparked a lively academic debate on the desirability and feasibility of a European civil code.[9] There were forceful pleas from both advocates and opponents to the idea.[10] In 2001, the European Commission picked up on this debate and published a communication on European contract law in which it asked the stakeholders, such as political institutions, legal practitioners, consumer and business associations, and academics, whether the existing state of European contract law led to any problems for the functioning of the Internal Market.[11] This was followed, in 2003, by another communication entitled—quite programmatically—'Action Plan', in which the Commission identified a number of existing problem areas and suggested a 'mix of non-regulatory and regulatory measures' in order to solve those problems.[12] The Commission also announced that it intended to elaborate, with the assistance of academic researchers, a 'Common Frame of Reference' (CFR). It explained that such a CFR should 'provide for best solutions in terms of common terminology and rules'. In the next follow-up communication, entitled 'The Way Forward',[13] the Commission further elaborated these plans. In particular, it provided a 'possible structure of the

[6] Art 5 TEU (principle of conferral).

[7] Case C-376/98, *Federal Republic of Germany v. European Parliament and Council of the European Union* ('*Tobacco Advertising*') (EU:C:2000:544), at para. 84.

[8] European Parliament resolution of 26 May 1989, OJ 1989 C 158, at 400. See also the European Parliament resolution of 6 May 1994, OJ 1994 C 205, at 518.

[9] See e.g. A. S. Hartkamp *et al.* (eds), *Towards a European Civil Code* (1994).

[10] Contrast Lando, 'Why Codify the European Law of Contract?', 3 *European Review of Private Law* (*ERPL*) (1997) 525, with Legrand, 'Against a European Civil Code', 60 *Modern Law Review* (*MLR*) (1997) 44.

[11] Commission Communication, 'On European Contract Law' (COM(2001) 398 final).

[12] Commission Communication, 'A More Coherent European Contract Law: An Action Plan' (COM(2003) 68 final).

[13] Commission Communication, 'European Contract Law and the Revision of the *Acquis*: The Way Forward' (COM(2004) 651 final).

CFR',[14] which happened to be almost identical to that of the Principles of European Contract Law that had been published by a group of academics a few years earlier.[15]

C. The Consumer Rights Directive

In these three communications, the Commission's focus had been, quite generally, on 'European contract law', without any distinction between B2B and B2C contracts. This changed, however, in the aftermath of the referendums on the European Constitution in the Netherlands and France. As Diana Wallis MEP pointed out in 2006:

> it is hardly the time to be seen to be moving towards anything that remotely resembles a European Civil Code; if the voters of Europe did not want a constitution it is hardly the moment to force a civil code, even just a contract code on them. The political moment, the political context is not right; however, as with the constitution, the practical arguments in favour of greater harmonisation will remain.[16]

The Commission decided to narrow down the focus of the project. The result, following a green paper on the review of the consumer *acquis*,[17] was a proposal for a 'Directive on Consumer Rights', published in 2008.[18] The CRD-proposal was eventually adopted only in part. The full harmonization of sales remedies and of unfair terms law (including black and grey lists), that would no longer have permitted the Member States to provide consumers with any greater protection, was rejected by the Council. As a result, a Consumer Rights Directive, with a much narrower substantive scope than originally proposed, was eventually adopted in 2011.[19]

D. The Draft Common Frame of Reference

Meanwhile, in 2009 an international network of researchers had published a Draft Common Frame of Reference (DCFR),[20] consisting of principles, definitions, and model rules plus a commentary. The DCFR covered most subjects of patrimonial law, including contract law (both general and specific), tort law, property law, and the law of trusts. The Commission's Proposal for a Consumer Rights Directive had not referred explicitly to the DCFR, nor did its content seem to have been much inspired by it.[21]

[14] Ibid. Annex I.

[15] H. Beale and O. Lando (eds), *Principles of European Contract Law, Parts I and II, Prepared by the Commission on European Contract Law* (2000).

[16] Wallis, 'European Contract Law—The Way Forward: Political Context, Parliament's Preoccupations and Process', 1 *ERA Forum Special Issue on European Contract Law—Developing the Principles for a 'Common Frame of Reference' for European Contract Law* (2006) 8.

[17] Commission Green Paper, 'On the Review of the Consumer *Acquis*' (COM(2006) 744 final).

[18] Commission Proposal for a Directive On Consumer Rights of 8 October 2008 (COM(2008) 614 final).

[19] Directive 2011/83/EU on consumer rights, OJ 2011 L 304 (hereinafter 'Consumer Rights Directive').

[20] C. von Bar *et al.* (eds), *Principles, Definitions and Model Rules of European Private Law: Draft Common Frame of Reference (DCFR), Outline Edition* and *Full Edition* (2009).

[21] Cf. Hesselink, 'The Consumer Rights Directive and the CFR: Two Worlds Apart?', 5 *ERCL* (2009) 290.

This raised some doubts as to the political future of the CFR and the optional instrument. However, in 2010, in response to questions from the European Parliament at her confirmation hearing, Viviane Reding, the incoming Vice-President of the European Commission and Commissioner for Justice, Fundamental Rights and Citizenship, stated as a core ambition for her mandate, 'the move from the first building blocks of European contract law (common frame of reference, standard terms and conditions, consumer rights) to a European Civil Code'.[22] Thus, with the Lisbon Treaty securely ratified in all the Member States, the idea of a European civil code was suddenly back on the political agenda. In that same year, the European Commission launched a new consultation on 'Policy Options for Progress Towards a European Contract Law for Consumers and Businesses'.[23] At the same time, the Commission set up an 'expert group' entrusted with the task of turning the academic DCFR into a draft for a Commission proposal for an instrument on European contract law.[24] In 2011, the Commission presented the outcome of the expert group's work as a 'feasibility study'.[25] After a short informal consultation concerning that text, in the autumn of 2011 the Commission published a proposal for a regulation on a Common European Sales Law.[26]

E. The Failure of the Common European Sales Law Proposal

The proposed Regulation intended to introduce a self-standing set of contract law rules, as a second national regime, into the laws of the Member States, which could be opted into by parties (both B2C and B2SME) to cross-border sales and related service contracts. The proposal did not meet with a warm welcome. A number of national Parliaments took the unusual step of issuing 'reasoned opinions' holding that the proposal violated the subsidiarity principle (the so-called 'yellow card procedure').[27] The European consumer organization BEUC rejected the proposal because it expected that the result of the regulation would be effectively to deprive consumers of the protection existing under their national (consumer) contract laws, which are warranted by Article 6 Rome I.[28] An influential group of German academics, in contrast, criticized the proposal for the opposite reason of unduly restricting party

[22] Notice to Members, Hearing with Viviane Reding, Commissioner-designate for Justice, Fundamental Rights and Citizenship, 7 January 2010 (CM\800797EN.doc; PE431.139v02-00).

[23] Commission Green Paper, 'On Policy Options for Progress Towards a European Contract Law for Consumers and Businesses' (COM(2010) 348 final).

[24] See Commission Decision 2010/233/EU of 26 April 2010 setting up the Expert Group on a Common Frame of Reference in the area of European contract law, OJ 2010 L 105/109.

[25] Commission Expert Group on European Contract Law, *Feasibility Study for a Future Instrument in European Contract Law*, 3 May 2011.

[26] Commission Proposal for a Regulation on a Common European Sales Law (COM(2011) 635 final).

[27] The reasoned opinions came from the British House of Commons, the Belgian Senate, the Austrian Parliament, and the German Bundestag and Bundesrat. For details, see http://www.ipex.eu/IPEXL-WEB/dossier/document/SEC20111165.do#dossier-COD20110284 (last visited 15 June 2020).

[28] 'Common European Sales Law: the Commission's Proposal For a Regulation (COM(2011) 635 final), BEUC's Preliminary Position 21 March 2012'; 'BEUC and Ecommerce Europe joint call to reject CESL', joint letter sent to all Members of the European Parliament on 20 February 2014.

autonomy, and generally for its poor quality.[29] Others, taking the Commission's political choices as given, made various textual proposals for improvement.[30] In 2014, the Common European Sales Law (CESL) proposal was discussed in a plenary debate in the European Parliament, followed by a vote where it was adopted, at first reading, by a large majority.[31] The Council had not yet voted on the proposal. However, when the new European Commission came in, six Member States sent a letter to the new Commissioner for Justice, arguing that the proposed regulation on a CESL 'cannot be a suitable solution' and 'worse, it may reduce confidence in the single market.'[32] The following month, the incoming Juncker Commission decided to withdraw the proposal.

F. The Digital Single Market

The withdrawal of the CESL proposal was accompanied by the announcement of a 'modified proposal in order to fully unleash the potential of e-commerce in the Digital Single Market'.[33] A year later, in 2015, the Commission published proposals for two new directives, one on contracts for the supply of digital content and the other on contracts for the online and other distance sales of goods.[34] The latter proposal, on goods, was replaced in 2017 by a modified proposal essentially extending its scope to include offline sales, after both the European Parliament and the Council, during the discussion on the original proposal, had warned about the risk of legal fragmentation, stressing the need for coherent rules for distance and face-to-face sales. This led the Commission to the conclusion that the time was ripe for the full harmonization of consumer sales law, 'covering all sales channels, in order to create a level playing field for all businesses selling goods to consumers'.[35] Both directives were adopted days before the election of the new European Parliament in 2019.[36]

[29] Eidenmüller *et al.*, 'The Proposal for a Regulation on a Common European Sales Law: Deficits of the Most Recent Textual Layer of European Contract Law', 16 *Edinburgh Law Review* (2012) 301.

[30] Statement of the European Law Institute on the Proposal for a Regulation on a Common European Sales Law (COM(2011) 635 final).

[31] European Parliament Legislative Resolution of 26 February 2014 on the Proposal for a Regulation of the European Parliament and of the Council on a Common European Sales Law (COM(2011)0635—C7-0329/2011—2011/0284(COD)) (P7_TA-PROV(2014)0159). There were 416 votes for, 159 against, and 65 abstentions. Cf. also 'Optional European Sales Law Receives Strong Backing by the European Parliament' (European Commission MEMO/14/137, Strasbourg, 26 February 2014).

[32] Letter of 18 November 2014 from the Ministers of Justice of Austria, Finland, France, Germany, the Netherlands, and the UK to Vera Jourová, the Commissioner for Justice, Consumers and Gender Equality (unpublished, on file with the author).

[33] Commission Communication to the European Parliament, the Council, the European Economic and Social Committee and the Committee of the Regions, 'Commission Work Programme 2015, A New Start' (COM(2014) 910 final), Annex 2, at 12, proposal no. 60: 'Modified proposal in order to fully unleash the potential of e-commerce in the Digital Single Market'.

[34] Proposal for a Directive on Certain Aspects Concerning Contracts for the Supply of Digital Content (COM(2015) 634 final); Proposal for a Directive on Certain Aspects Concerning Contracts for the Online and Other Distance Sales of Goods Brussels (COM(2015) 635 final).

[35] See Amended Proposal for a Directive on Certain Aspects Concerning Contracts for the Online and Other Distance Sales of Goods, 31 October 2017 (COM(2017) 637 final), especially 'Explanatory Memorandum', at 2–3, and proposed preliminary Recital (7).

[36] Directive 2019/770 on certain aspects concerning contracts for the supply of digital content and digital services, OJ 2019 L 136; Directive 2019/771 on certain aspects concerning contracts for the sale of goods,

G. Regulatory Silos

While most politicians and academics were concerned with the ECC-DCFR-CESL project, important developments were taking place elsewhere, much more quietly and away from the spotlight. Micklitz was the first to call attention to what he refers to as 'European regulatory private law', i.e. the private law elements present in the regulation of a broad variety of markets, in particular the new markets resulting from privatization, for example telecommunications, postal services, electricity, gas, transport, health care, education, and from the opening up of already existing national markets, such as the market for financial services, in particular. These sectors function as relatively closed entities (as 'regulatory silos'), each with its own set of rules and standards (being a mix of private law, public law, and private regulation), transnational community of experts, and dispute resolution mechanisms.[37] Each of these silos has a higher degree of normative coherence—at least in the eyes of the relevant professional community—than the European contract law of which only a small section of each silo is also a part.

H. The Court of Justice

Moreover, in recent years the activism of another key player, i.e. the Court of Justice, has caught the attention of many observers, not only legal scholars but also political scientists, the former often supportive, the latter usually more critical. Whatever the legitimacy of the Court's activism,[38] there is little doubt as to its reality. Interestingly, some of the Court's most controversial rulings have been in private law cases. And specifically in the field of contract law, the Court's preliminary rulings often also have gone far beyond the narrow determination of the meaning of a directive in the light of its objectives. In particular, with regard to the Unfair Terms Directive, in a series of bold judgments the Court has taken decisions that are unlikely to have been on the horizon of any of the original law makers.[39] In doing so, the Court has become one of the main drivers of the further Europeanization of contract law and a key protagonist in shaping and transforming EU contract law. This role became all the more visible once the European legislator's project for European contract codification, which had previously retained so much of the academic and political attention, had run aground and, consequently, the European legislator had opted for a much more modest agenda.

amending Regulation (EU) 2017/2394 and Directive 2009/22/EC, and repealing Directive 1999/44/EC, OJ 2019 L 136.

[37] Micklitz and Svetiev, 'The Transformation(s) of Private Law', in H-W. Micklitz, Y. Svetiev, and G. Comparato (eds), *European Regulatory Private Law—The Paradigms Tested*, EUI Working Papers, LAW 2014/04 69, at 78.

[38] This question will be addressed in Chapter 3.

[39] Landmark rulings include Case C-244/98 *Océano Grupo Editorial SA v. Rocio Murciano Quintero (and Others)* (EU:C:2000:346) and Case C-415/11, *Mohamed Aziz v. Caixa déstalvis de Catalunya, Tarragona i Manresa (Catalunyacaixa)* [2013] (EU:C:2013:164).

I. A New Deal for Consumers

In 2018, the European Commission announced a 'New Deal for Consumers'. The proposal was a direct response to 'Dieselgate'. It was much more modest in scale than the original 'New Deal', i.e. the series of radical reform programmes that the American President Roosevelt launched in the 1930s to overcome the Great Depression. The main shift brought about by the European Commission proposal was a marked change in language, from 'justice for growth' towards 'delivering a fairer single market' and 'strengthening consumer rights'.[40] So, more a new tone than a new deal, it would seem. As far as contract law is concerned,[41] a directive was proposed and rapidly adopted, in 2019. This directive brought a further consolidation and piecemeal extension of the scope of already existing remedies, most notably the introduction of certain contract law remedies against unfair commercial practices.[42]

J. Brexit

The referendum vote in the UK in favour of Brexit in 2016 was followed by speculation about its possible implications, both direct and more remote, also in the field of European contract law. For example, a so-called 'hard Brexit', where the UK left the EU without any agreement on the future relationship, would also mean an abrupt exit by the UK from EU contract law, not only in terms of applicable rules but also of institutions, most notably the jurisdiction of the Court of Justice. In various 'softer' versions of Brexit, the EU contract law *acquis*, both present and future, including its interpretation by the Court of Justice, would remain relevant to varying degrees depending on the agreement reached. When the UK formally left the EU in 2020 the future relationship between the two was still under negotiation, and it seems likely that it will take several years to fully to take shape, if there is ever going to be a stable end state. However, in any of the scenarios under consideration, there is likely to be a shift, more or less gradual, in the political relevance of the civil/common law divide, both for the general European private law debate and for specific instances of EU contract law making. With Ireland as the only remaining common law jurisdiction within the EU (and Malta as a mixed system), it is foreseeable that in coming years, little by little, EU contract law will become more civilianized, while the common law is likely to be increasingly regarded as largely external to EU law, indeed as mainly relevant for external (contractual) relationships.

40 Commission Press Release of 11 April 2018, 'A New Deal for Consumers: Commission Strengthens EU Consumer Rights and Enforcement' (IP/18/3041).

41 For civil procedure, notably collective redress, the proposals were more innovative.

42 Directive (EU) 2019/2161 on the better enforcement and modernisation of Union consumer protection rules, OJ 2019 L 328, Art. 3 (amendments to Directive 2005/29/EC concerning unfair business-to-consumer commercial practices in the internal market, OJ 2005 L 149).

2. Political Philosophy

A. Introduction

Political philosophy asks fundamental questions concerning politics, government, and political institutions. Normative political philosophy is concerned, in particular, with the question of what makes a just society. This question of social justice connects political philosophy to moral philosophy. While moral philosophy concentrates mainly on the responsibilities, individual and collective, that we have towards each other, normative political philosophy is concerned primarily with the role that public institutions ought to play in making a society become more just. Clearly, within different theories different institutions play quite different roles. From the perspective of political philosophy, the central question under examination in the present book is what role, if any, European contract law, as an institution, has to play in making our society become or remain a (fully or sufficiently) just society. Conversely, from the perspective of European contract law the central question is what arguments and reasons contemporary political philosophy has to offer that could deepen and widen the political debate on the present and future state of European contract law.

Although each individual political theory is unique, it will sometimes be convenient, for reasons of exposition, to lump some of them together under common labels. In fact, their authors themselves often do this. Rawls, Dworkin, Raz, and Nussbaum, for example, all explicitly present their own respective theories as 'liberal'. And in many contexts this is indeed very useful, for example when we contrast them with utilitarian or communitarian theories. It also helps to prevent philosophical argument from becoming too personalistic and scholastic: it is not the authority of the philosophers that counts, but their arguments. On the other hand, however, by definition a focus on certain common features is always reductive to some degree and never neutral: when we place certain common features in the foreground, other divergent features will inevitably move to the background, which may give the impression that these differences are somehow less important. These are well known characteristics and problems of taxonomy.[43] However, as long as we are conscious of this particular political dimension of taxonomy there is no reason to be very anxious about it. In any case, we cannot avoid the problem (no taxonomy is not an option). Therefore, throughout this book I will refer to utilitarianism, liberal-egalitarianism (or liberalism), libertarianism (or neoliberalism), communitarianism (or neo-romanticism), civic republicanism, and discourse theory as some of the leading contemporary political philosophies. However, within each chapter I will frequently discuss the ideas of certain specific philosophers in more detail, in which cases I will sometimes use adjectives such as 'Razian liberal' or 'Razian' *tout court*.

The present section will provide a first, very general introduction to the main strands in contemporary political philosophy and their relevance to European contract law. The aim is to set the scene for the following chapters, where fundamental normative questions of European contract law will be discussed from the perspectives

[43] See M. Foucault, *The Order of Things: An Archaeology of the Human Sciences* ([first published 1966] 1994).

of each of these political philosophies and their respective cognate contract law theories. What we are looking for, then, are (potentially) 'effective moral ideas'.[44] This approach differs fundamentally from other recent political accounts and theories of (European) contract law.[45]

My objective is to present each of these theories in their best light and their strongest interpretation (the principle of charity),[46] i.e. not as strawmen, but rather as ideal types or models. This charitable interpretation does not exclude, of course, a brief introduction to some of the main objections that have been directed against each of these theories. However, the critical examination of the theories and of their implications for (European) contract law will be reserved for the core discussion of fundamental normative questions in the following chapters.

As a final introductory remark, it is perhaps good to mention at the outset that, as we will see, the theories differ not only with regard to their normative starting points (ultimate values and core principles), but also in respect of their factual bases, i.e. the social, economic, psychological, and historical realities they presume, emphasize, or claim applicability or particular relevance for.

B. Utilitarianism

1. The Principle of Utility

According to utilitarians, the ultimate aim of the law should be to maximize the total amount of utility in society. In the words of Jeremy Bentham, '[t]he general object which all laws have, or ought to have, in common, is to augment the total happiness of the community'.[47] Utilitarianism is a comprehensive theory of value which extends to both individual and political morality,[48] and beyond.[49] This comprehensive nature of the theory is generally considered to be one of its strongest features. However, for our purposes this is less relevant since our concern here is not with individual choice ('may I breach my contract?') but only with collective or public choice ('how should the government respond to breaches of contract?'). We will therefore concentrate here on social utility and its maximization.

Utility has been defined in different ways by different utilitarians. For the classical utilitarians, the concept referred to the hedonistic idea of 'pain and pleasure'.[50] In more recent times, however, 'welfare' and 'preference satisfaction' have become the more

[44] L. Murphy and T. Nagel, *The Myth of Ownership: Taxes and Justice* (2002), at 188.

[45] On this, see Chapter 1.

[46] Cf. Davidson, 'On the Very Idea of a Conceptual Scheme', 47 *Proceedings and Addresses of the American Philosophical Association* (1973–1974) 5, at 19: 'charity is not an option, but a condition of having a workable theory'.

[47] Bentham, *An Introduction to the Principles of Morals and Legislation* [first published 1789], ch. 1, in J. S. Mill and J. Bentham (eds), *Utilitarianism and Other Essays* (2004) 97, at 97.

[48] Think of Bentham's famous slogan: 'it is the greatest happiness of the greatest number that is the measure of right and wrong'. See the Preface to J. Bentham, *A Fragment on Government* (1776).

[49] See, critical, e.g. A. Sen, *The Idea of Justice* (2009) 239: 'The utilitarian tradition, which works towards beating every valuable thing down to some kind of an allegedly homogeneous magnitude of "utility"'.

[50] J. Bentham, *An Introduction to the Principles of Morals and Legislation* (n. 47) 65; Mill, 'Utilitarianism', in J. S. Mill and J. Bentham, *Utilitarianism and Other Essays* (2004) 272.

recurrent standards. Although these notions are certainly not identical, what they do have in common, and what distinguishes them from other normative standards, is that they refer to factual states of affairs, and thus are subject, in principle, to empirical measurement. In addition, utilitarianism is a consequentialist theory.[51] It is fundamentally forward-looking,[52] justifying policies and laws entirely in terms of their overall net positive consequences, without any regard to their origin.[53] What matters is whether a policy, a law, or the recognition of a right will make society better off—not whether it is somehow right in view of past decisions and actions. Whatever happened in the past is by now water under the bridge.[54] Moreover, utilitarianism not only focuses exclusively on social utility, it also requires its maximization. Therefore, it is not sufficient for the government to show that a given policy increases social welfare (e.g. beyond a certain minimum): the choice for the particular policy is fully justified only if it produces more social welfare than any of the available alternatives.

Originally, in the eighteenth and nineteenth centuries, utilitarianism was quite a progressive and radical political movement and, for that reason, also controversial.[55] It attacked feudal privileges, and its reform agenda generally tended towards more egalitarian outcomes, such as universal suffrage. John Stuart Mill, for example, was a famous advocate of women's rights.[56] However, today's utilitarians often tend to defend the status quo: they had an effective programme for contesting the privileges of a small elite, but have less to offer for small and unpopular minorities seeking to assert their rights against a large majority opinion.[57]

2. Criticism

Philosophers, especially in the deontological tradition since Kant, have raised important objections against utilitarianism. Rawls wrote his theory of justice explicitly as an alternative to utilitarianism. Today, several familiar pertinent objections against utilitarianism exist.[58] Most of these also apply directly to leading 'economic' theories of contract law.

[51] The term consequentialism was introduced (critically) by Anscombe, 'Modern Moral Philosophy' 33 *Philosophy* (1958) 1, at 12: 'It is a necessary feature of consequentialism that it is a shallow philosophy.'

[52] For the distinction between 'backward-looking and forward-looking normative argument', see B. William, *Ethics and the Limits of Philosophy* (1985), at 8.

[53] Whereas all utilitarian and welfarist theories are consequentialist theories, not all consequentialist theories are utilitarian or welfarist. An exclusive focus of consequences does not necessarily imply that only one type of consequences (happiness or preference satisfaction) should count: distributional consequences or violations of fundamental rights and freedoms too are potential consequences of institutional arrangements or rule and policy choices, just as much as welfare consequences. Humean conventionalism, for example, takes a broad range of consequences into account.

[54] Utilitarianism has this prospective nature in common with philosophical pragmatism and its corollary, functionalism.

[55] See E. Hobsbawm, *The Age of Revolution 1789–1848* ([first published 1962] 2007), at 287 ff.

[56] J. S. Mill, *The Subjection of Women* (1869).

[57] See W. Kymlicka, *Contemporary Political Philosophy: An Introduction* (2nd ed., 2002), at 46.

[58] See e.g. J. Rawls, *A Theory of Justice* (1971), at § 5–6; M. C. Nussbaum, *Frontiers of Justice: Disability, Nationality, Species Membership* (2006), at 72 ff; J. Raz, *The Morality of Freedom* (1986), at 267 ff; R. Dworkin, *Law's Empire* (1986), at 288 ff; A. Sen, *Development as Freedom* (1999), at 58 ff; Kymlicka (n. 57) ch. 2; Driver, 'The History of Utilitarianism', in E. N. Zalta (ed.), *Stanford Encyclopedia of Philosophy*, available at https://plato.stanford.edu/entries/utilitarianism-history/ (last visited 18 June 2020).

The most fundamental question raised with regard to utilitarian theories is: why utility? Is a society that maximizes happiness and minimizes pain a better society for that reason alone? Happiness as the ultimate value was famously attacked by Nozick. He introduced the idea of an experience machine that people could be hooked onto and which would make them feel happy for the rest of their lives.[59] Perhaps some people would be curious to try this once, but is a society where everyone is connected to such an 'experience machine' for their entire lives (if this were actually possible) the best society that could be imagined? Is there any value in such a state of affairs and should the government maximize the availability and the use made of such machines? In response, utilitarians have substituted their purely hedonistic notion of utility with the concept of preference satisfaction or even with the satisfaction of informed and rational preferences (i.e. those which are in the agent's own best interest), thus moving away from a purely factual (and measurable) notion of utility. However, preferences, and even informed and rational preferences, may also be problematic, because these in fact may be so-called 'adaptive' preferences, i.e. desires that are adapted to whatever happens to be available.[60] The 'preferences' that people have depend to a large extent on the options they can realistically choose from.[61] Indeed, as Marxists have long pointed out, the preferences that people happen to have for certain institutions may be shaped to an important extent by the very economic and political institutions one is trying to justify on utilitarian grounds.

In addition to this fundamental question, there is also the more practical problem of how to measure utility. Can happiness and utility be expressed in a number? And, although they may all bring me happiness, are very different things such as the first day of Spring, an Ajax victory, grilled swordfish, catching a train just before it departs, and reading John Stuart Mill, actually commensurable? Even if we do not require utility to be measured in cardinal numbers but accept that our preferences are to be determined in ordinal numbers, can I really decide a meaningful order among such very different things and reduce their complex meaning for me to the relative amount of satisfaction they give me? Utilitarians may answer that, if pressed, we can order our preferences in utility functions. However, even if this is true, Raz points out that this would still change the nature of the exercise: the result would amount to nothing more than our utility function *when pressed* to choose among what in our own estimation are really incommensurable values.[62]

Even if we accept the reduction of value and meaning to one single notion of welfare and express our individual 'preferences' by establishing a relative order among seemingly incommensurable sources of welfare expressed in the shape of a utility function, then there still remains the problem of interpersonal comparison. Utility functions are expressed in ordinal not cardinal numbers. They express a hierarchy of (expected)

[59] R. Nozick, *Anarchy, State and Utopia* ([first published 1974] 2006), at 42 ff. See earlier Berlin's idea of a happiness machine or pill (Berlin, 'John Stuart Mill and the Ends of Life', in I. Berlin (H. Hardy ed.), *Liberty* (2002) 218, at 222).

[60] Elster, 'Sour Grapes—Utilitarianism and the Genesis of Wants', in A. Sen and B. Williams, *Utilitarianism and Beyond* (1982) 219; J. Elster, *Sour Grapes: Studies in The Subversion of Rationality* ([first published 1983] 2016), at 110 ff and passim.

[61] Nussbaum (n. 58) 73; Sen (n. 58) 62.

[62] Raz (n. 58) 348.

preference satisfaction in relative terms, which says nothing of the intensity of the satisfaction in absolute terms. This makes comparison and aggregation among different individuals very problematic. If strawberry ice cream ranks at the bottom of my list and at the top of yours this seems to suggest that you like strawberry ice cream better than I do. But is this really true? Perhaps strawberry ice cream still makes me happier than it could ever make you feel. Indeed, the only thing we really know is that you like nothing better than strawberry ice cream. This problem is insurmountable, for the simple reason that one cannot arrive at interpersonal comparison or aggregation without moving from the subjective to the objective. Indeed, all solutions to this problem that have been proposed substitute the essentially subjective notions of happiness, welfare, or preference satisfaction, with a more objective notion, such as 'willingness to pay', expressed in money.[63]

There is a more fundamental difficulty with the aggregation into a single amount of social utility: it neglects, as Rawls famously put it, the 'separateness of persons'.[64] In the utilitarian calculus human beings are reduced to mere carriers of utility.[65] The kind of interpersonal trade-offs that utilitarian social morality requires fails to treat individuals, in Kant's expression, as aims in themselves and reduces them to mere means for the aims of others.[66] In practical political terms, this means, for example, that minorities are in structural danger of being sacrificed to the preferences of the majority. More generally, existing rights—famously derided by Bentham as 'nonsense upon stilts'[67]—and other entitlements of individuals can be sacrificed to the greater good of maximizing utility. But does it really not matter, turning specifically to questions of private law, that I was the owner of the property or that you actually agreed to perform the contract?[68]

Another distinguishing feature of utilitarianism, that has also attracted major criticism, is that it takes no direct interest in the way the total amount of happiness, preference satisfaction, or wealth in a society is divided among its members. What matters is the sum total of utility or welfare, not its distribution. Utilitarians are interested in the size of the cake, not its division. A society with more total happiness in it is better off, for that reason alone, than a society with a slightly lower total amount of happiness but much more equally distributed. Even if one regards, as most people will, increasing happiness and reducing suffering (without wasting resources) as important policy aims for any government it does not necessarily follow that maximizing social welfare should be the only aim. Why should not some trade offs be accepted between social welfare and other concerns, such as a fairer distribution of the overall welfare? Why is a society with 100 units of happiness which are all in the hands of one single person, while all others live in total misery (i.e. have zero happiness), a better one than

[63] On the concept of 'willingness to pay', see later, in Section 2.B.4.

[64] Rawls (n. 58) 27–29; see also Raz (n. 58) 271 ff.

[65] See B. Williams, *'Moral Luck': Philosophical Paper 1973–1980* (1981), at 4: 'As a Utilitarian agent, I am just the representative of the satisfaction system who happens to be near certain causal levers at a certain time.'

[66] Categorical imperative (second formulation). See I. Kant, *Grundlegung zur Metaphysik der Sitten* ([first published 1785] 1974), at 61.

[67] J. Bentham, *Anarchical Fallacies; Being an Examination of the Declaration of Rights Issued During the French Revolution* (1792), republished in J. Bowring (ed.), *The Works of Jeremy Bentham*, Vol. II (1843).

[68] We will come back to this question in Chapter 5.

a society with only 90 units but distributed much more equally?[69] Is it really only the size of the pie that matters or also its division? In Dickens's novel *Hard Times*, Sissy recounts how Mr M'Choakumchild had explained Prosperity to her, and asked her whether a nation where there were fifty millions of money was a prosperous nation, and whether she was in a thriving state. According to Sissy: 'I thought I couldn't know whether it was a prosperous nation or not, and whether I was in a thriving state or not, unless I knew who had got the money, and whether any of it was mine.'

A final methodological problem with utilitarianism is that it suffers from the same reductionism that naturalism generally suffers from. If science is reduced to measurement then in many fields, but certainly in moral and political philosophy, important parts of the picture risk being removed from our investigative and argumentative horizon.[70] Utilitarian moral and political reasoning claims to be based on firmer ground than other moral and political theories. However, in fact, as Taylor makes clear, these claims to a firmer foundation are illusory:

> What is really going on is that some forms of ethical reasoning are being privileged over others because in our civilisation they come less into dispute or look easier to defend. This has all the rationality of the drunk in the well-known story who was looking for his latch key late one night under a street lamp. A passer-by, trying to be helpful, asked him where he had dropped it. "Over there" answered the drunk, pointing to a dark corner. "Then why are you looking for it here?" "Because there's so much more light here", replied the drunk.[71]

Therefore, Taylor concludes, the utilitarian reduction is arbitrary. Similarly, there is more that matters to a human life than can be expressed in mere preferences. We cannot reduce men and women to the economists' *homo economicus*—in the words of Dworkin, to 'a human being whose interests are exhausted by his preference curves'.[72] Similarly, the focus of welfarists on outcomes obscures the importance of human agency, for it ranks states of affairs (outcomes) independently of their sources.[73] Are our choices conditioned entirely by the preferences with which we find ourselves, or are human beings also moved by reasons?[74] In other words, not only the methodologic but also the anthropological assumptions of utilitarianisms are reductionist.[75]

3. Varieties of Utilitarianism

Partly in response to these criticisms, utilitarians have modified their theories over time. As a result, today many different versions of utilitarianism exist. An important distinction—and highly relevant to legal questions—is the distinction between fact

[69] R. Dworkin, 'Is Wealth a Value?', 9 *Journal of Legal Studies* (*J. Legal Stud.*) (1980) 191.

[70] S. Shapin, *The Scientific Revolution* (1996), at 162; J. Habermas, *Between Naturalism and Religion* (2008), at 2, who refers to 'uncritical faith in science' as 'hard forms of naturalism'.

[71] C. Taylor, 'The Diversity of Goods', in A. Sen and B. Williams, *Utilitarianism and Beyond* (1982) 129, at 139.

[72] R. Dworkin, *Justice for Hedgehogs* (2011), at 18.

[73] Sen, 'Utilitarianism and Welfarism', 76 *Journal of Philosophy* (1979) 463.

[74] O. O'Neill, *Bounds of Justice* (2000), ch. 2.

[75] See generally, A. Supiot, *Homo Juridicus; Essai sur la fonction anthropologique du droit* (2005).

utilitarianism, which requires a welfare enhancing outcome in every single case, and rule utilitarianism, which accepts trade-offs between different cases if the net result of the rule's or policy's application is positive. Another relevant distinction is the one between direct utilitarianism and indirect utilitarianism. Supporters of the latter approach point out that what matters, from a utilitarian perspective, is the outcome not the rationale of a given policy. Therefore, if a non-directly-utilitarian policy is welfare-enhancing it must be supported. So, for example, if the protection of individual rights makes people better off in their own estimation, then this is a good thing even if these rights are officially protected (e.g. by the constitution), not with a view to increasing social welfare, but with a view to treating people as ends in themselves. Similarly, if it can be established as an empirical matter that people care about equality, then for that reason (and to the extent of this 'taste' they happen to have for equality) egalitarian policies may have to be pursued by the government.[76] Finally, we can distinguish between total and average utilitarianism. If we focus exclusively on total utility a society can be made better off by the mere addition of another life even if this reduces the average happiness in society. In order to avoid this 'repugnant conclusion',[77] concentrating on average utility has been proposed. However, this leads to new problems because under that standard it might be advisable to kill all the unhappy people (or only the ones who would not be missed too much by others). Not all these different rescue strategies are mutually compatible. Nor do all different versions of 'utilitarianism' seem best described by the label of utilitarianism. For example, is a theory that only counts 'reasonable' preferences still a utilitarian theory?

4. Welfarism and Cost Benefit Analysis

One of the most influential contemporary heirs to utilitarianism is the economic analysis of law, a branch of scholarship concerned with the economic determinants and consequences of law. In principle, the economic analysis of the law amounts to nothing more specific than a form of consequentialism applied to law. However, much of the law and economics scholarship, including prominent contributions to contract theory and the European contract law debate, is based, explicitly or implicitly, on a welfarist notion of some sort. In line with Becker's claim that the economic approach can provide 'a unified framework for understanding *all* human behaviour', and with its basic assumption that individuals are maximizers of their own utility or welfare,[78] these scholars are interested in the 'economic efficiency' of legal rules and institutions. They regard a social state of affairs as efficient if no alternative state would make at least

[76] On a 'taste for fairness', see L. Kaplow and S. Shavell, *Fairness Versus Welfare* (2002), at 21. Note that, on this view, if no one cares about justice, rights, or fairness, a society has no reason to pursue any justice- or fairness-oriented policies, or to protect human rights.

[77] D. Parfitt, *Reasons and Persons* (1984), ch. 17.

[78] See G. S. Becker, *The Economic Approach to Human Behavior* (1976), at 5 and 14 (emphasis in original). Other economists have been quite dismissive of this kind of project. See F. A. Hayek, *Law, Legislation and Liberty: A New Statement of the Liberal Principles of Justice and Political Economy*, Vol. III *The Political Order of a Free People* ([first published 1979] 2003), at 201–202 (footnote 35): 'The childish attempts to provide a basis for "just" action by measuring the relative utilities or satisfactions of different persons simply cannot be taken seriously.... But most economists begin to see that the whole of the so-called "welfare economics", which pretends to base its argument on inter-personal comparisons of ascertainable utilities, lacks all scientific foundation. The idea of basing coercive actions by government on such fantasies is clearly an absurdity.'

one person better off (in their own estimation) without making anyone else worse off (Pareto efficiency) or, alternatively, if the winners gain so much that they could compensate the losers and still be better off (Kaldor-Hicks efficiency, cost-benefit analysis). When scholars in law and economics advocate a certain rule, economic system (as in the 'Washington consensus'),[79] or legal system (as in the 'legal origins' thesis that was followed by the World Bank),[80] because of its economic efficiency, such normative law and economics usually relies on some kind of utilitarian normative assumption. Often these assumptions are implicit but explicit defences of normative law and economics in utilitarian terms also exist. A radical example is the book *Fairness Versus Welfare* by Kaplow and Shavell, who argue that all policies should be based exclusively on welfare considerations. The (tautological) reason they give is that if other considerations were to play a role, notably considerations of justice and fairness, policies would risk being adopted that make no one better off or even make everyone worse off.[81]

In cost benefit analysis, welfare is sometimes reduced to wealth. A society, then, is considered a better one to the extent that it is wealthier. The assumption is that a wealthier society is a happier one or one where there is more welfare. And this assumption is based on the idea that something is in the hands of those who value it most when it is held by the highest bidder. In other words, on this view, an individual's 'willingness to pay' expresses her preferences (and not, for example, her initial wealth). This idea provides the basis, for example, for comparing the welfare in different countries in terms of their gross domestic product (GDP) or gross national income (GNI). The great advantage of this approach is that in this way human welfare becomes relatively easy to measure and can be expressed in very precise numbers. However, this reduction also removes from the picture a number of factors (the presence of violence, discrimination, poverty, etc.) that are very important for the welfare of most people.[82] This conception, reducing welfare to wealth, was adopted by prominent scholars in law and economics, in particular by Posner in the 1970s,[83] but has been rejected by others who uphold a more inclusive notion of welfare.[84]

As stated earlier, some form of utilitarianism is often invoked (or implicitly assumed) as the basis for cost benefit analysis and normative law and economics. However, this is not uncontroversial, even among legal economists. Kornhauser, for example, acknowledges that the difficulties in interpersonal comparison and

[79] Cf. critical, J. Stiglitz, *Globalization and Its Discontent* (2002), at 53 ff and passim.

[80] See La Porta, Lopez-de-Silanes, and Shleifer, 'The Economic Consequences of Legal Origins', 46 *Journal of Economic Literature* (2008) 285; the World Bank's *Doing Business* reports available at www.doingbusiness.org (last visited 18 June 2020).

[81] Kaplow and Shavell (n. 76).

[82] Others, in particular Sen, have proposed a much broader concept of human welfare. See Sen (n. 58); United Nations Development Programme, *Human Development Report 2016*. His capabilities approach evaluates the welfare of individuals in terms of the options they have for life fulfilment. This approach became the basis for the Human Development Index (HDI).

[83] See R. Posner, *Economic Analysis of Law* (1st ed., 1973), at 357. However, Posner soon distinguished the wealth maximization that he advocated from utilitarianism, which he defined more narrowly. See Posner, 'Utilitarianism, Economics, and Legal Theory', 8 *J. Legal Stud.* (1979) 103. Critical of wealth maximization, Dworkin, 'Is Wealth a Value?' (n. 69). See also E.-J. Mestmäcker, *Legal Theory Without Law: Posner v. Hayek on Economic Analysis of Law* (2007), at 13: 'Wealth maximisation is no substitute for the purpose of law in general.'

[84] See e.g. M. D. Adler, *Well-Being and Fair Distribution: Beyond Cost-Benefit Analysis* (2012).

aggregation of welfare are insurmountable.[85] Moreover, to the extent that normative law and economics is attracted to utilitarianism, that attraction is not necessarily mutual. Many utilitarians will reject cost benefit analysis (and certainly the precept of wealth maximization) as unacceptably reductive. This will have to be kept in mind in the following chapters, when I will be presenting existing law and economics scholarship in the area of European contract law as a form of utilitarianism. Although the familiar arguments against utilitarianism usually apply also against the 'economic' arguments that are put forward in the European private law debate, and against the understanding of contract law on which it is based, there is a further argument against this scholarship—i.e. excessive reductionism—that does not apply equally to the more sophisticated and inclusive versions of utilitarianism. In other words, although utilitarianism provides the most promising (and therefore most often invoked) basis for a normative economic theory of law, normative claims made by legal economists are not necessarily always the most convincing claims made in the name of utilitarianism.

Economic analysis, positive and normative, has been applied extensively to contract law. While the theories of 'efficient breach' and of 'default rules' are probably among the most famous ones, economic analysis has in fact been applied to every conceivable doctrine and question of contract law, especially in the US where economic analysis became the dominant paradigm in contract law theory (and also became quite influential in judicial practice). In the relevant literature, the focus has been heavily on American contract law but many of the law and economics theories have also been influential in Europe, including in civil law jurisdictions—perhaps most extensively in Germany, as we will see in the following chapters.

C. Liberal-Egalitarianism

1. Liberal Equality and Social-democracy

Liberal-egalitarianism is usually regarded as the school of thought that provided a philosophical justification for the welfare state.[86] It includes the work of such influential philosophers as Rawls, Dworkin, and Nussbaum. Liberal egalitarians have in common—in contrast to libertarians—that they define freedom as something more than mere non-intervention by the state (negative liberty).[87] State action—in particular, through just institutions—may also be liberty-enhancing. Indeed, they argue, appropriate institutions are indispensable for creating and maintaining the conditions for equal freedom. I will follow the practice in philosophical discourse of referring to these philosophers as 'liberal-egalitarians' or even as 'liberals' *tout court*. This use of terminology may come as a surprise—and may even seem confusing—to some

[85] See L. A. Kornhauser, 'On Justifying Cost-Benefit Analysis', 29 *J. Legal Stud.* (2000) 1037.

[86] Kymlicka (n. 57) 88.

[87] See e.g. H. L. A. Hart, 'Utility and Rights', 79 *Columbia Law Review* (*Colum. L. Rev.*) (1979) 828, at 835–836 (against Nozick): 'But it is of course an ancient insight that for a meaningful life not only the protection of freedom from deliberate restriction but opportunities and resources for its exercise are needed. Except for a few privileged and lucky persons, the ability to shape life for oneself and lead a meaningful life is something to be constructed by positive marshalling of social and economic resources. It is not something automatically guaranteed by a structure of negative rights.'

Europeans, since in countries like France, Germany, and indeed my own home countries, the term 'liberalism', both in general political discourse and in political theory is often still associated with the right-wing tradition, discussed later, in Section 2.D, that I will refer to as 'libertarianism' (or 'neoliberalism'). Liberals (in the sense of liberal-egalitarians) on the European continent, situating themselves on the left of the political spectrum, have usually referred to themselves as 'social democrats'.[88] The reason why, nevertheless, I follow the American terminology in a book on European contract law is that in the political-philosophical literature, which is dominated today by the English language, this has become the current practice. The philosophers whose views I will be discussing refer to themselves as 'liberals' or 'liberal-egalitarians', and not usually as 'social democrats'.[89]

2. Liberal Perfectionism

Throughout the book, I will draw a further distinction within liberal-egalitarianism: between liberal perfectionism, on the one hand, and political liberalism, on the other. Following Rawls, this has become a familiar—but contested[90]—distinction in political philosophical discourse. At the core of classical liberalism were the values of personal autonomy (Kant) and individuality (Mill). The central ideal was that of a free person who shapes her own life through her own choices and in accordance with her own conception of what is valuable in life, i.e. of what amounts to a good life. Modern heirs to that liberal ideal of the autonomous person—i.e. to this idea of human perfection—are usually called (and refer to themselves as) liberal perfectionists. A prominent contemporary liberal perfectionist is Raz. According to Raz, an autonomous life is a more valuable life than the life of someone who 'drifts through life unawares', without ever exercising her capacity to choose.[91] The ideal is 'self-authorship': 'the autonomous person is a (part) author of his own life'.[92] In his view, this is an objective moral truth, i.e. independent of what the person whose life it is thinks about the value of autonomy. That makes the theory a perfectionist theory.[93] For Raz, the value of autonomy is closely connected to value pluralism.[94] According to Raz, the task of the state with regard autonomy is not limited to refraining from intervention (negative liberty). Real autonomy depends on the availability of a sufficiently diverse range of

[88] Cf. J. Habermas, *Between Facts and Norms: Contributions to a Discourse Theory of Law and Democracy* (1996), at 58 (with reference to Rawls): '"liberal" according to Anglo-American usage and "social-democratic" from a European viewpoint'. Cf. also R. Bellamy, *Political Constitutionalism: A Republican Defence of the Constitutionality of Democracy* (2007), at 96 (with regard to Dworkin): 'largely social-democratic understanding'.

[89] Apparently, the change of meaning of the term 'liberalism' in the US was a deliberate step taken by the Roosevelt administration that regarded 'social-democracy' as unattractive because it sounded too much like 'socialism'. Cf. *Wikipedia*, 'Liberalism in the United States', available at https://en.wikipedia.org/wiki/Liberalism_in_the_United_States and 'Modern Liberalism in the United States', available at https://en.wikipedia.org/wiki/Modern_liberalism_in_the_United_States (last visited 18 June 2020). Generally, on the different uses of the term 'liberalism', see Gaus and Courtland, 'Liberalism', in E. N. Zalta (ed.), *Stanford Encyclopedia of Philosophy*, available at https://plato.stanford.edu/entries/liberalism/ (last visited 18 June 2020).

[90] See later, in Section 2.C.3.

[91] Raz (n. 58) 371 and 382.

[92] Ibid. 369.

[93] Ibid. 265.

[94] Ibid. 367.

valuable options, which, in turn, each depend on the presence of social forms for those different possible courses of life. Therefore, the state has the task of making autonomous choices possible by ensuring the presence of a sufficiently wide range of different valuable options (positive liberty). Raz's liberalism has been explicitly relied on with regard to contract theory, especially, albeit in quite divergent ways, by Kimel and Dagan.[95]

3. Political Liberalism

Although many people value autonomy, in pluralist societies like our own we cannot take for granted that everyone will subscribe to the ideal of the autonomous person. Therefore, self-authorship as a response to value pluralism will not convince those who attribute foundational importance to culture and tradition, as communitarians do,[96] or those who believe that they should live in accordance with the commands of their God, as expressed in a sacred text.[97] They will never adhere to liberal principles as principles deriving from their ideal of a person living a good life. At best, they may accept certain liberal principles as a guide for living together as citizens in mutual respect of each other's personal values. In other words, in a pluralist society liberal perfectionism, rather than being a solution to the problem of value pluralism has become a part of the problem, just like any other form of moral perfectionism.[98] As a response to what Rawls calls 'the fact of reasonable pluralism', philosophers like Larmore, Rawls, and Nussbaum have proposed a merely political liberalism that addresses us solely in our political role as citizens, not in our capacity as full ethical persons.[99] Nussbaum's and Rawls' politically liberal theories have been applied to European contract law by Tjon Soei Len and Klijnsma respectively,[100] while Bagchi has adopted the Rawlsian frame more widely with regard to private law questions.[101]

However, political liberalism has also met with severe criticism. First, it is argued, political liberalism is bound to create difficulties within one person, whenever that person does not happen to adhere also privately to liberal principles. Rawls relies on a rather sharp distinction between the public and the private, i.e. our roles as citizens and all our other roles. However, as Kymlicka points out, there are likely to be spillover effects.[102] Secondly, Rawls's political liberalism has been accused of being unrealistic at the political level. Non-liberals (such as communitarians and libertarians), comprehensive liberals (like Dworkin), and others sympathetic to Rawls's project (like

[95] D. Kimel, *From Promise to Contract: Towards a Liberal Theory of Contract* (2005); Dagan, 'Pluralism and Perfectionism in Private Law', 112 *Colum. L. Rev.* (2012) 1409.

[96] See later, in Section 2.E.

[97] Cf. M. C. Nussbaum, 'Perfectionist Liberalism and Political Liberalism', 39 *Philosophy and Public Affairs* (2011) 11.

[98] C. Larmore, *The Morals of Modernity* (1996), at 131.

[99] See further later, in 2.C.3.

[100] L. K. L. Tjon Soei Len, *Minimum Contract Justice: A Capabilities Perspective on Sweatshops and Consumer Contracts* (2017); Klijnsma, 'Contract Law as Fairness' 28 *Ratio Juris* (2015) 68. See also Kordana and Tabachnick, 'Rawls and Contract Law', 73 *George Washington Law Review* (*Geo. Wash. L. Rev.*) (2005) 598; Scheffler, 'Distributive Justice, the Basic Structure and the Place of Private Law', *Oxford Journal of Legal Studies* (*OJLS*) (2015) 1.

[101] See e.g. Bagchi, 'Distributive Injustice and Private Law', 60 *Hastings Law Journal* (*Hastings L.J.*) (2008) 105.

[102] See Kymlicka (n. 57) 236.

Habermas), all argue that the idea of political liberalism will not work in practice. An overlapping consensus on political principles—that very different worldviews and ultimate values would reach consensus on, and that the supporters of each of these divergent worldviews would be able to insert, for the right reasons, as a module into their respective comprehensive doctrines—would either be too thin to provide a workable basis for a constitutional democracy or would have to exclude too many religions and worldviews that today enjoy vast support and are not usually regarded as being wholly unreasonable.[103] Therefore, many observers conclude, justice as fairness in reality remains a comprehensive liberal theory, that competes, at the same political level, with, Christian, nationalist, libertarian, socialist, and other proposals for political principles.

4. Comprehensive Liberalism

Finally, a third category may be distinguished (at least in theory), between perfectionist and political liberalism, i.e. comprehensive liberalism. These are liberal theories that are not based on a conception of the moral person as a self-creating person, or the good life as an autonomous life, or autonomy as the ultimate value. However, at the same time they do not address us merely in our capacity as citizens. One of the most prominent proponents of such a comprehensive liberalism is Dworkin. Dworkin rejects perfectionism on the moral ground that the state should remain neutral towards different conceptions of the good life (or, as he puts it, of 'how to live well')[104] and on the practical ground of the 'endorsement constraint', i.e. that one cannot derive value from something unless one personally (internally) attributes value to it; therefore the state's attempt to impose its values upon its citizens will not work and may even be counter-productive. The rejection of perfectionism logically includes the rejection of liberal perfectionism. However, as has been pointed out,[105] Dworkin's comprehensive liberalism seems almost indistinguishable from liberal perfectionism. If the state must be neutral because people's lives go better when they make their own value choices then in fact the state is neutral in the name of the value of personal autonomy and is therefore not a neutral state after all.[106] Sen may also be regarded as a comprehensive liberal. His idea of justice is not based on any particular conception of the person, but it is also not meant to be merely political.[107] On the other hand, however, Sen has been a strong advocate of the right for individuals to exit from traditions and for each person to establish their own hierarchy among their senses of belonging.[108] The best explanation for that right seems to be the ideal of the autonomous person. Therefore, although non-perfectionist comprehensive doctrines can easily be imagined,[109] conversely, it is not entirely clear exactly what a comprehensive

[103] See Dworkin (n. 72) 66–67: 'Rawls's constructivist project, at least as he sometimes conceived it, is impossible.... What set of views about the character of free and equal persons could generate either of the two principles of justice and yet be adopted at a Tea Party convention.'

[104] Ibid. 13.

[105] Nussbaum (n. 97) 5.

[106] Especially in his later work, Dworkin's liberalism seems to shift more towards a conception of the good life.

[107] Sen (n. 49).

[108] A. Sen, *Identity and Violence: The Illusion of Destiny* (2006).

[109] Indeed they have always existed. Think of determinism.

non-perfectionist liberalism would look like. Obviously, that question does not have to be resolved here. And in any case, there is no doubt that both Dworkin and Sen are prominent liberal egalitarians. The same applies for Shiffrin, who, as we will see, has focused much of her work specifically on contract law.[110] For the purposes of this book most of the time the terms of 'liberal perfectionism', 'comprehensive liberalism', and 'ethical liberalism'[111] can be used interchangeably; the important distinction within liberal egalitarianism, at least for our purposes, seems to be between these, on the one hand, and political liberalism on the other.

D. Libertarianism

1. Libertarianism, Neoliberalism, Ordoliberalism

Libertarians understand liberty as the absence of interference by others, including especially the government (freedom as non-interference, or 'negative' liberty).[112] In particular, what libertarians like Hayek, Nozick, and Friedman have in common is that they advocate free markets as inherently just (and not merely efficient),[113] oppose egalitarian redistributive policies as fundamentally unjust, and regard society as a mere aggregate of individuals.[114] Indeed, contrary to the republican freedom of the ancients, libertarian freedom is fundamentally individualistic. In the words of Fried, 'liberty is individuality made normative'.[115] Libertarians are usually committed to the idea of a sharp private/public law divide,[116] strong and unrestricted property rights, and unfettered freedom of contract.[117] However, although the views of these thinkers

[110] E.g. Shiffrin, 'Paternalism, Unconscionability Doctrine, and Accommodation', 29 *Philosophy and Public Affairs* (2000), 205.

[111] R. Forst, *Contexts of Justice: Political Philosophy Beyond Liberalism and Communitarianism* (2002), at 56.

[112] C. Fried, *Modern Liberty and the Limits of Government* (2007), at 60: 'Liberty is an absence. It is an absence of restraints purposely placed on me by others and especially by government'. Cf. the (critical) expression by R. Dworkin, *Taking Rights Seriously* (1977), at 267: 'liberty as license'.

[113] Cf. Kymlicka (n. 57) 102: 'not everyone who favours the free market is libertarian, for they do not all share the libertarian view that the free market is *inherently* just' (emphasis in original). This rationale is distinct, in particular, from a defence of deregulatory policies on consequentialist grounds, as being efficient, i.e. welfare enhancing.

[114] Nozick (n. 59), at 32–33: 'Why not hold that some persons have to bear some costs that benefit other persons more, for the sake of the overall social good? But there is no *social entity* with a good that undergoes some sacrifice for its own good. There are only individual people. Using one of these people for the benefit of others, uses him and benefits the others. Nothing more. What happens is that something is done to him for the sake of others. Talk of overall social good covers this up. (Intentionally?)' (emphasis in original). Cf. P. Pettit, *Republicanism: A Theory of Freedom and Government* (1997), at 9: 'Self-described libertarians tend to think of the people as an aggregate of atomized individuals.'

[115] Fried (n. 112) 22. See also, ibid. 19: 'Individuals come first. Whoever says otherwise is trading in metaphors.' Constant, the 'first apostle of modern liberty' (ibid. 16), defined liberty as 'the triumph of individuality'. See B. Constant, *Mélanges de littérature et de politique* (1829), at vi: 'par liberté, j'entends le triomphe de l'individualité, tant sur l'autorité qui voudrait gouverner par le despotisme, que sur les masses qui réclament le droit d'asservir la minorité à la majorité'.

[116] Critical L. Raiser, *Die Zukunft des Privatrechts* (1971), at 18: 'Heute, nach mehr als 70 Jahren einer ungemein bewegten politischen Geschichte läßt sich die Vorstellung von der Eigenständigkeit des Privatrechts im Sinne eines gegenüber dem öffentlichen Recht abgedichteten Systems von liberalen Rechtsprincipien nicht mehr aufrechterhalten.'

[117] As we will see in Chapter 5, at the heart of one strand of libertarian contract theories (so called 'transfer' theories) there is also a property-like entitlement conception of contractual rights.

are quite similar in these respects, and for this reason they are often taken together under the label of libertarians, there are also considerable differences between them, as we will see.[118]

Libertarianism often is referred to also as neoliberalism and I will do the same here.[119] However, there is some risk of confusion. First, because neoliberalism is 'neo' only with reference to classical nineteenth-century liberalism, especially its laissez-faire aspect. Therefore, neoliberalism should not be confused with the (social-democratic) liberal-egalitarianism we saw earlier, which many philosophers refer to as 'liberal'. Secondly, in political and general discourse today 'neoliberal' is frequently used in a much wider and more imprecise sense.[120] Thus, for example, the EU's internal market instrumentalism or impact assessments, which are best explained by (utilitarian) efficiency considerations,[121] are sometimes referred to and criticized as being 'neoliberal', in spite of the fact that the libertarian case for free markets is non-(indeed anti-) instrumental.[122] In popular discourse 'neoliberalism' sometimes becomes a label for almost any evil of our time.[123] In Europe, even the term 'liberal' is sometimes used (critically) in this very wide (but strictly pejorative) sense.

2. Self-ownership

Nozick wrote his book *Anarchy, State, and Utopia* as an attack on liberal-egalitarianism, in particular Rawls's *A Theory of Justice*, which had been published a few years earlier.[124] In Rawls's theory there are no pre-institutional individual entitlements: individuals are morally entitled only to what is legitimately theirs under institutions that are just according to the principles of justice, notably the difference principle. In contrast, the idea of pre-legal and pre-institutional, and indeed pre-societal, entitlements,

[118] See Vallentyne, 'Libertarianism', in E. N. Zalta (ed.), *Stanford Encyclopedia of Philosophy*, available at https://plato.stanford.edu/entries/libertarianism/ (last visited 19 June 2020); Kymlicka (n. 57) ch. 4.

[119] See e.g. M. Foucault, *Naissance de la biopolitique: cours au Collège de France 1978–1979* (2004), at 80 ff.

[120] W. Streeck, *Gekaufte Zeit: Die vertagte Krise des demokratischen Kapitalismus* (2013), does not define neoliberalism but seems to identify it (at 54 ff) with the liberalization of markets. Harvey offers the following definition: 'Neoliberalism is in the first instance a theory of political economic practices that proposes that human well-being can best be advanced by liberating individual entrepreneurial freedoms and skills within an institutional framework characterized by strong private property rights, free markets, and free trade. The role of the state is to create and preserve an institutional framework appropriate to such practices.' D. Harvey, *A Brief History of Neoliberalism* ([first published 2005] 2007), 2. This consequentialist focus on well-being excludes many leading libertarians from this definition of neoliberalism, most notably Hayek.

[121] Market efficiency is essentially a collectivist objective while neoliberalism (libertarianism) is individualist at heart. See C. Taylor, *Modern Social Imaginaries* (2004), at 78–79, pointing out that the Smithian notion of an invisible hand, on which 'neoliberal boosters of the market' rely in our day: 'is not an order of collective action, for the market is the negation of collective action'.

[122] See e.g. Müller-Armack, *Wirtschaftslenkung und Marktwirtschaft* (1947), at 113: 'Die Marktwirtschaft ist ein formales und neutrales Organisationsmittel'.

[123] The label 'neoliberalism' is sometimes used somewhat more precisely to indicate a package of economic measures (austerity, market liberalization, privatization, etc.) that was originally referred to, in the 1990s and early 2000s, mostly by opponents, as the 'Washington Consensus'. See e.g. J. E. Stiglitz, *Globalization and Its Discontent* (2002), at 74: 'the Washington Consensus policies are sometimes referred to as "neo-liberal", based on "market fundamentalism", a resuscitation of the laissez-faire policies that were popular in some circles in the nineteenth century'. Obviously, there is a difference between a political theory and a package of economic measures. At best, an attempt could be made to justify such economic measures in neoliberal (in the sense of libertarian) terms, i.e. with reference to a specific conception of the person and the state.

[124] Nozick (n. 59).

is central to Nozick's theory.[125] The opening sentence of the book states: 'Individuals have rights, and there are things no person or group may do to them (without violating their rights).'[126] In Nozick's view, property is an absolute, pre-positive right. This places him squarely in the natural law tradition—i.e. whatever the positive law says, I am morally entitled to whatever I own since I obtained it from the rightful owner who, in turn, also got it from the previous rightful owner, and so on. Rightful acquisition thus fully legitimizes my unrestricted ownership. Nozick also applies the same idea of entitlement to the fruits of physical strength, natural talents, and whatever other characteristics individuals happen to have. He refers to this as 'self-ownership'. According to Nozick, the state has no right to take from me what is naturally mine. Therefore, re-distribution by the state amounts to a form of theft. For Nozick, a just distribution is simply whatever distribution results from people's free exchange: 'each person receives his marginal contribution to the world'.[127] In this way, Nozick's theory provides a normative basis for unrestricted capitalism.

The idea of legitimacy of ownership by acquisition in free exchange logically leads back to the first owner and raises the question of initial acquisition. Assuming that at the time of the original occupation of a piece of land scarcity already existed, there needs to be a ground justifying that one person, who wanted the property, got it and not the others, who also wanted it. The idea of first come, first served, depends on a contingency which seems morally arbitrary. The answer that joint property owned by all will not lead to a productive use of the property (the 'tragedy of the commons')[128] and that therefore the initial ownership must be given to the person who can make the most productive use of it (the first capitalist) and hire the others to work for her, clearly is a utilitarian argument that is not available to a libertarian trying to demonstrate individual entitlement. It is not clear that Nozick has solved or could solve the problem of initial acquisition.[129] Given that it is the moral rightfulness of this initial acquisition that is supposed to provide the justification for the entire theory of entitlement, this is a major problem with Nozick's version of libertarianism.[130]

3. Spontaneous Order

Hayek wrote his most famous book, *The Road to Serfdom*, during the Second World War.[131] In this book, he argued forcefully in favour of a spontaneous order and against governmental planning. In particular, he warned against the idea of social justice. Social justice is a mirage, he argued, because a society, if it exists at all, cannot be just or unjust, for justice is a virtue of individuals alone. Social justice is also a dangerous

[125] Nozick (ibid.) explicitly rejects Rawls' theory of justice as a 'manna-from-heaven model' (ibid. 199). He writes: 'things come into being already held' (ibid. 219).

[126] Ibid. ix.

[127] Ibid. 302.

[128] The concept was introduced by G. Hardin, 'The Tragedy of the Commons', 162 *Science* (1968) 1243, with reference to an example given by W. F. Lloyd, *Two Lectures on the Checks to Population* (1833), at 30–32.

[129] Cf. Fried (n. 112) 148: 'Property hurts liberty by limiting the liberty of some as it establishes the liberty of others.'

[130] 'Left-libertarianism' holds that unappropriated natural resources belong to everyone in some egalitarian manner. See Vallentyne (n. 118).

[131] F. A. Hayek, *The Road to Serfdom* ([first published 1944] 2005). The first edition was published also in an abridged form, during World War II, in the *Reader's Digest*.

notion, in his view, because distributive decisions taken by the government in its name (even when made in the utmost good faith) will inevitably lead to ever further planning and ultimately to totalitarianism.[132] Nobody can know what needs, aspirations, preferences, etc. everybody has: Hayek calls this our incurable ignorance. In particular, any central government by definition lacks complete knowledge. The only way to solve this problem of our incurable ignorance is by leaving distribution to the casual outcome of the market mechanism: a spontaneous order instead of a planned society. While Nozick's philosophy is rarely invoked in European contract law discourse, the ideas of Hayek have been explicitly endorsed by several scholars in the European private law debate.[133]

4. Ordoliberalism

A version of neoliberalism that has had considerable influence among German theorists and policy makers (e.g. in the way Germany responded to the Euro-crisis) is called ordoliberalism. This is a school of thought, founded in the 1930s,[134] by scholars belonging to the Freiburg school of economics. It is named after the journal 'Ordo', where several of their main contributions were published, including Böhm's very influential article '*Privatrechtsgesellschaft und Marktwirtschaft*' (private law society and market economy).[135] The core idea of ordoliberalism is that the state should create and maintain a legal order or framework, within which free markets and undistorted competition can thrive. That order should be constituted by strong public institutions, ideally protected by an 'economic constitution'; all other, private dealings should be left to the 'private law society'. Although the state should refrain from any concrete interference with the economy through economic policies, the emphasis on strong public institutions significantly differentiates ordoliberalism from laissez-faire libertarianism.[136] Ordoliberalism is also more socially oriented than most other (e.g. Chicago school and Hayekian) versions of libertarianism. The founders of ordoliberalism did not reject the idea of social justice (unlike Hayek), nor progressive taxes and minimum wages (under certain conditions). Indeed, the idea of a 'social market economy', today enshrined in Article 3(3) TEU, was originally an ordoliberal

[132] Contrast K. Polanyi, *The Great Transformation: The Political and Economic Origins of Our Time* ([first published 1944] 2001), an equally famous book of the same year arguing the exact opposite, i.e. that 19th century market liberalism (the utopia of free, unregulated markets) was at the root of fascism. For a contemporary reappraisal, see C. Joerges and J. Falke (eds), *Karl Polanyi, Globalisation and the Potential of Law in Transnational Markets* (2011).

[133] See e.g. Smits, 'European Private Law: A Plea For a Spontaneous Legal Order', in D. M. Curtin *et al.*, *European Integration and Law* (2006) 85; Grundmann, 'Information, Party Autonomy and Economic Agents in European Contract Law', 39 *Common Market Law Review* (*CMLR*) (2002) 269.

[134] It is sometimes suggested that the roots of ordoliberalism in the 1930s were connected to Nazism (e.g. Somma, 'Private Law as Biopolitics: Ordoliberalism, Social Market Economy, and the Public Dimension of Contract', 76 *Law and Contemporary Problems* (*Law Contemp. Probl.*) (2013) 105, at 114), but the opposite is true. Several of the founders risked their lives speaking out against the Nazis. And at the University of Freiburg they led the opposition against rector Heidegger. Cf. Joerges, 'What Is Left of the European Economic Constitution? A Melancholic Eulogy', 30 *European Law Review* (2005) 461, at footnote 15.

[135] Böhm, 'Privatrechtsgesellschaft und Marktwirtschaft', 17 *ORDO: Jahrbuch für die Ordnung von Wirtschaft und Gesellschaft* (1966) 75.

[136] Cf. Joerges (n. 134) 466. Generally, on the distinct ordoliberal version of 'neoliberal governmentality', see Foucault (n. 119) 77–190.

concept.[137] Ordoliberal ideas were promoted and implemented, both in Germany and in the EU, by Christian democrats (CDU). They have been held responsible, in part, for the economic success of Germany after World War II (*Wirtschaftswunder*).[138] The most prominent ordoliberal politician was Ludwig Erhard, at first Secretary for the Economy and later Chancellor, who was responsible for the enactment of the *Gesetz gegen Wettbewerbsbeschränkungen* which established a competition authority, the *Bundeskartellamt* (Federal Cartel Office), in 1958.

Many German theorists, both supporters *and* opponents of ordoliberalism, consider the ordoliberal reading of the EU's founding treaties—as an 'economic constitution'—as the orthodox reading, even though this reading has been much less influential (if not entirely absent) in most other founding EU Member States.[139] Given that in the ordoliberal view of freedom of contract is a key element in the economic constitution it is not surprising that German theorists, both supportive and critical of ordoliberalism, have also read European contract law in an ordoliberal fashion.[140] Thus, on this reading, contract law is part of the depoliticized institutional framework—in this respect not different from the European Central Bank—that assures the proper functioning of a market with free competition.

Although Hayek did not regard himself as an ordoliberal,[141] contemporary scholars with ordoliberal sympathies often combine these with Hayekian ideas.[142] As Joerges explains, this entails a shift in emphasis from private to public distortions of competition.[143]

5. Chicago School

Friedman was one of the leading exponents of the Chicago School of Economics. He consistently refers to his philosophy, not as libertarian, but as 'liberal', re-vindicating the term.[144] Friedman considers himself to be 'in the same philosophical tradition' as Hayek.[145] He argues for free markets, free enterprise, and laissez-faire for direct, but also for indirect, instrumental reasons. First, free enterprise is good per se, as an aspect of freedom. Secondly, he argues, economic freedom is a precondition for political

[137] Müller-Armack (n. 122) 65: 'soziale Marktwirtschaft'.

[138] J.-W. Müller, *Contesting Democracy: Political Ideas in Twentieth-Century Europe* (2011), at 153.

[139] See Chapter 4, with further references.

[140] Grundmann, 'The Structure of European Contract Law', 4 *ERPL* (2001) 505, at 515: 'the thinking of the ordoliberal school which is still the theoretical basis of the business regulation concept in the Community'; Somma, 'Social Justice and the Market in European Contract Law', 2 *ERPL* (2006) 181, at 189: 'It is rather trite to say that the guiding principles of modern EU economics are based on the ordoliberal perspective'. Cf. B. Lurger, *Grundfragen der Vereinheitlichung des Vertragsrechts in der Europäischen Union* (2002) 396.

[141] However, Hayek considered the ordoliberals to be his allies fighting for the same cause, i.e. the battle against socialism. With regard to the ordoliberal expression of 'social market economy', he wrote: 'I regret this usage though by means of it some of my friends in Germany have apparently succeeded in making palatable to wider circles the sort of social order for which I am pleading.' (Hayek (n. 78), Vol. II *The Mirage of Social Justice* ([first published 1976] 2003), at 180, footnote 26).

[142] E.g. Mestmäcker (n. 83).

[143] Joerges (n. 134) 30.

[144] M. Friedman, *Capitalism and Freedom* (2002), at 5–6: 'The rightful and proper label is liberalism.... Partly because of my reluctance to surrender the term to proponents of measures that would destroy liberty, partly because I cannot find a better alternative, I shall resolve these difficulties by using the word liberalism in its original sense—as the doctrines pertaining to a free man.'

[145] Ibid. xii.

freedom,[146] although not a sufficient condition.[147] He rejects most of contemporary state policies, including in particular redistributive ones, albeit not all (he endorses direct aid to the poor).

E. Communitarianism

1. General

Also communitarianism is nothing like a single theory or cohesive school of thought.[148] Still, what such different philosophers as Sandel, Taylor, and Walzer have in common is an emphasis on community, traditions, and the local, as opposed to the individual, rational, and universal.[149] Modern communitarianism, in the first place, has been a response to liberal-egalitarianism. Communitarians reject what they regard as liberalism's exacerbated individualism or 'atomism'. They point out that people are born into groups (families, religious communities, nations) and grow up developing a sense of belonging to those groups and their respective ways of life. They underline that the individual is not unencumbered but always already situated, and that individual choices and preference are deeply embedded and rooted in social and cultural practices and traditions. They emphasize that identity is not a matter of autonomous choice, at least not entirely, but also heteronomous, at least in part. Communitarians reject the liberal ideal of the neutral state. Instead, they claim that the state should be a vehicle for the promotion of the 'common good'. This common good is frequently, but by no means necessarily, understood in a religious sense.[150] Communitarianism is not only a perfectionist theory; it also supports paternalism, where this is needed in order to prevent people from making the wrong choices.

Thus, communitarianism is rather a substantive approach to politics. Where for utilitarians politics should be guided by the aggregate preferences of all concerned, the liberals distinguish between the right (individual rights and social justice) and the good (personal values and preferences) stipulating the priority of the former over the latter, and where civic republicans and Habermasians, as we will see, adopt a rather procedural approach, communitarians argue that politics should be guided by the

[146] Similar, Müller-Armack (n. 122) 70: 'Zusammenhang von Wirtschaftslenkung und geistiger und politischer Unfreiheit'.

[147] Friedman (n. 144) 10. Nor is political freedom a necessary condition for economic and civil freedom (ibid. ix).

[148] Cf. Taylor, 'Cross-Purposes: the Liberal-Communitarian Debate', in N. Rosenblum (ed.), *Liberalism and Moral Life* (1989) 159, at 163: 'portmanteau term'.

[149] Leading communitarian texts include: M. J. Sandel, *Liberalism and the Limits of Justice*, ([first published 1982] 2nd ed., 1998); M. Walzer, *Spheres of Justice: A Defense of Pluralism and Equality* (1983); A. MacIntyre, *After Virtue*, (3rd ed., 2007); C. Taylor, *Sources of the Self; The Making of Modern Identity* (1989).

[150] For a catholic reading, see e.g. *Catechism of the Catholic Church*, at no. 1897–1927, especially no. 1921: 'Authority is exercised legitimately if it is committed to the common good of society', and no. 1924: 'The common good comprises "the sum total of social conditions which allow people, either as groups or as individuals, to reach their fulfillment more fully and more easily"—reference to Pastoral constitution on the church in the modern world, *Gaudium et Spes*' (Second Vatican Council, 1965). See also, J. Finnis, *Natural Law and Natural Rights* (1980), at 154–160. Cf. J. Rawls, *Political Liberalism* ([first published 1993] 2005), at footnote 511: 'Deriving from Aristotle and St. Thomas, the idea of the common good is essential to much of Catholic moral and political thought.'

community's values and traditions. In practical terms, for the purpose of this book, this also means that communitarianism more often than any of the other theories offers concrete and sometimes quite outspoken answers to our political questions of European contract law. This distinctive characteristic is often expressed by indicating that communitarianism is based on a 'thick' conception of the good,[151] in especially stark contrast to liberalism where, for example, Rawls's key concept of 'primary goods' is deliberately based on a comparatively 'thin' conception of the good.

Contemporary communitarian philosophers often explicitly build upon Hegel's critique of classical (especially Kantian) liberalism,[152] or are heirs to the nineteenth century's romantic tradition of Herder.[153] It is difficult to locate communitarianism on a simple political spectrum from left to right: there are elements both of conservative reaction and progressive reform in most communitarian writings;[154] sometimes they are backward-looking and nostalgic, while on other occasions they may be forward-looking and optimistic.[155]

The typical method adopted in communitarian reasoning is the hermeneutical one of trying to understand 'our' traditions and 'our' culture, where we came from, and what this entails for our future.

2. The Liberal-communitarian Debate

As said previously, according to communitarians politics is about the definition of the common good. In the words of Sandel:

> The communitarian critics, unlike modern liberals, make the case for a politics of the common good. Recalling the arguments of Hegel against Kant, they question the liberal claim for the priority of the right over the good, and the picture of the freely choosing individual it embodies. Following Aristotle, they argue that we cannot justify political arrangements without reference to common purposes and ends, and that we cannot conceive of ourselves without reference to our role as citizens, as participants in a common life.[156]

Or, as Taylor puts it, in the liberal view, 'the common good is constituted out of individual goods, without remainder'.[157] Liberal-egalitarians responded to the communitarian criticisms. This led to the liberal-communitarian debate that dominated political philosophy in the 1980s. The liberal critique of communitarianism is that traditions often oppress or exclude individuals, especially when they belong to minorities or other vulnerable groups.[158] As Kymlicka put it, 'the problem of the exclusion

[151] See M. Walzer, *Thick and Thin; Moral Argument at Home and Abroad* (1994).

[152] E.g. C. Taylor, *Hegel and Modern Society* (1979).

[153] Cf. C. Larmore, *Patterns of Moral Complexity* (1987), ch. 5.

[154] R. Dworkin, *A Matter of Principle* (1985), ch. 8, especially at 198, refers to communitarians as 'conservatives', but this seems reductive. Walzer, for example, is an outspoken social-democrat.

[155] Kymlicka (n. 57) 273.

[156] Sandel, 'Morality and the Liberal Ideal', in M. J. Sandel, *Public Philosophy* (2006) 152.

[157] Taylor, 'Cross-Purposes: The Liberal-Communitarian Debate', in D. Matravers and J. Pike (eds.), *Debates in Contemporary Political Philosophy* (2003), 166.

[158] See e.g. M. C. Nussbaum, *Sex and Social Justice* (1999).

of historically marginalized groups seems endemic to the communitarian project'.[159] On the liberal view, adherence to tradition and identity is ultimately a matter of individual choice: every person should be free to decide on the hierarchy among her own allegiances and is entitled to have options to exit an oppressing tradition.[160] Or, put descriptively, the idea of society as an ethical community in any thick sense (i.e. a community of substantive values) misdescribes the kind of societies we live in today, which are structurally pluralist.[161] This point was eventually conceded by Walzer. If the liberal account is incorrect as a description, i.e. if we do not really live in an individualist or atomist society, then the problems and dangers that communitarians warn about do not exist. If, in contrast, the liberal account is descriptively correct, then this means that respect for our community and its tradition would mean respect for individualism and atomism.[162]

3. Nationalism

One instance of communitarianism with particular relevance for the European private law debate has been nationalism. Nationalists are communitarians whose preferred community is the nation. If nationalism is the political principle according to which the political and the national unit should be congruent,[163] then we can refer as 'private law nationalists' to those who believe that private law should be located at the political level of the nation state.[164]

4. Communitarian Private Law

Contemporary communitarian political theorists do not explicitly address contract law. However, there are a number theories of private law that fit particularly well with communitarian political philosophy, in some cases because they are connected to the predecessors of today's communitarianism, such as Hegelianism and romanticism.

A good example is neopandectism, the contemporary heir to the Historical School that was a reaction against the law of reason. Savigny understood the law as an expression of the *Volksgeist*, a concept akin to the thinking of Herder and Hegel. The Historical School was part of the Romantic rejection of products of the Enlightenment, most notably the French Revolution. Savigny, one of the main leaders of the Historical School, fiercely rejected the idea, proposed for example by Thibaut, of a civil code after the model of the French Civil Code. In a similar vein, neopandectists such as Zimmermann, explicitly invoking Savigny,[165] argued that it was too early for a

[159] Kymlicka (n. 57) 259.

[160] See also Habermas (n. 88) 324: 'actors are not simply *at the mercy* of their lifeworld' (emphasis in original).

[161] See Sen (n. 49) 247: 'Proposals to see a person merely as a member of one social group tend to be based on an inadequate understanding of the breadth and complexity of any society in the world.'

[162] M. Walzer, 'The Communitarian Critique of Liberalism', in D. Miller (ed.), *Thinking Politically: Essays in Political Theory* (2007) 96, at 107.

[163] For this definition, see E. Gellner, *Nations and Nationalism* (2nd ed., 2006), at 1. Similar, E. J. Hobsbawm, *Nations and Nationalism: Programme, Myth, Reality* (1990), at 9. I will come back extensively to nationalism, with further references, in Chapter 4.

[164] Cf. G. Comparato, *Nationalism and Private Law in Europe* (2014).

[165] Zimmermann, 'Roman Law and the Harmonization of Private Law in Europe' in A.S. Hartkamp *et al* (eds), *Towards a European Civil Code* (4th ed., 2010) 27.

European civil code. Others, while rejecting Savigny's mysticism, nevertheless emphasize the historical development of the law's authority.[166]

Similarly, the understanding of law as an expression of legal culture and, consequently, of legal differences as cultural differences,[167] although sometimes argued for on postmodernist grounds as incommensurable discourses,[168] often appeals to culture and tradition in a more communitarian sense.[169] Thus, the idea that when confronted with questions of law, even when engaging in legal comparison, we are always deeply influenced by our own respective legal traditions[170] is very similar to Sandel's idea that as 'encumbered selves' we are all already situated.[171] A third example is the—contested—understanding of the common law as essentially customary law, i.e. as emanating from a society's understanding over time of right and wrong, or decent business conduct, transformed into law by judges.[172] A final example is the idea (or metaphor) of legal families, especially in its original, uncritical version.[173]

F. Civic Republicanism

1. Neo-republicanism

Contemporary republicans aim to revive certain classical republican ideals that were found in (or are attributed to) the classical Greek city-states, the Roman republic,[174] the renaissance Italian city-states,[175] and the American revolution.[176] These ideals include active citizenship, public deliberation (moving from a 'vote-centric' to a more 'talk-centric' democracy,[177] 'a republic of reasons'[178]), a commitment to freedom as it was understood prior to liberalism,[179] and virtuous politicians. Core republican

[166] N. Jansen, *The Making of Legal Authority; Non-Legislative Codifications in Historical and Comparative Perspective* (2010).

[167] See e.g. Collins, 'European Private Law and Cultural Identity of States', *ERPL* (1995) 353; P. Legrand, *Fragments on Law-As-Culture* (1999); Sefton-Green, 'Cultural Diversity and the Idea of a European Civil Code', in M. W. Hesselink (ed.), *The Politics of a European Civil Code* (2006) 71.

[168] Legrand (n. 167); P. Legrand, *Que sais-je? Le droit comparé* (1999).

[169] Cf. (sceptical) R. Unger, *What Should Legal Analysis Become?* (1996), at 127 (critical): 'The idea of law as the expression of a unique form of life drastically exaggerates the unity and continuity, and understates the made-up character, of the cultures manifest in law.'

[170] Legrand, 'European Legal Systems Are Not Converging', 45 *International and Comparative Law Quarterly (ICLQ)* (1996) 52.

[171] Sandel (n. 149).

[172] See Hayek (n. 78) Vol. I *Rules and Order* ([first published 1973] 2003), at 78. This view is rejected as naive, for example, by H. Collins, *Regulating Contracts* (1999), at 82; B. Z. Tamanaha, *On the Rule of Law: History, Politics, Theory* (2004), at 70; and Posner, 'Law and Economics in Common-Law, Civil-Law, and Developing Nations', 17 *Ratio Iuris* (2004) 66, at 77.

[173] See e.g. R. David, *Les grands systèmes de droit contemporain* (1969); K. Zweigert and H. Kötz, *Introduction to Comparative Law* (3rd ed., 1998). For a critical assessment, see M. Siems, *Comparative Law* (2nd ed., 2018), ch. 4.

[174] In the accounts of Sallust, Livy, and Tacitus.

[175] See in particular N. Machiavelli's *Discorsi* (1531). Cf. Q. Skinner, *Machiavelli: A Very Short Introduction* (2000), ch. 3.

[176] See especially A. Hamilton, J. Madison, and J. Jay, *The Federalist Papers* (1787). Cf G. S. Wood, *The Radicalism of the American Revolution*, Part II (1991).

[177] Kymlicka (n. 57) 290.

[178] C. R. Sunstein, *The Partial Constitution* (1993), ch. 1.

[179] See especially Pettit (n. 114); Q. Skinner, *Liberty Before Liberalism* (1998).

ideas include popular sovereignty and self-rule, which motivated the Dutch, English, American, and French revolutions against external or internal domination, and the rule of law, i.e. 'the empire of laws and not of men'.[180]

One strand in neo-republicanism regards active political participation as a core aspect of a good life. The perfectionist ideal of what we may call ethical republicanism (also referred to as civic humanism) is that of a citizen of the Athenian city-state or of the Roman republic (think of Cicero), who finds fulfilment, as 'a political animal',[181] in his active engagement in the well-being of the *polis*, the state being 'prior by nature to the individual'.[182] In the words of Arendt, the political in the sense of the *polis* is:

> a space where freedom as virtuosity can appear. This is the realm where freedom is a worldly reality, tangible in words which can be heard, in deeds which can be seen, and in events which are talked about, remembered, and turned into stories before they are finally incorporated into the great storybook of human history.[183]

The most direct implication for private law of the realization of this ideal of the political life would be negative in that the public realm would be much more important and extensive, as a consequence of which, it seems, the scope of application for private law, and for private contracts, would be much reduced. On the other hand, however, the idea of the civil code as the *constitution civile*, which tells citizens how to behave vis-à-vis each other, resonates with notions of virtuous citizenship, which suggests that private law could perhaps serve as a 'seedbed of civic virtue'.[184]

Some perfectionist versions of republicanism tend towards communitarianism. They understand the polity as an ethical community whose common good should be furthered collectively through political action. Think, for example, of Rousseau's core concept of a unitary 'volonté générale',[185] which 'always tends towards the public good'.[186] However, as Habermas points out, the notions of the 'general will' and the

[180] J. Harrington (J. G. A. Pocock, ed.) *The Commonwealth of Oceana and a System of Politics* ([first published 1656] 1992), at 8, explicitly following Aristotle and Livy. The expression was famously cited by J. Adams, *Novanglus Essays* (1775), Essay 7, as 'a government of laws, and not of men', followed by the Constitution of Massachusetts 1780, Art XXX, and by the US Supreme Court in *Marbury v. Madison*, 5 U.S. 1 Cranch 137 (1803). On the structural tension between these two republican aspirations (the government of the people by the people and the government of the people by laws, self-rule, and law-rule), and their circular relationship, see Michelman, 'Law's Republic', 97 *Yale Law Journal* (*Yale L.J.*) (1988) 1493.

[181] Aristotle, *Politics*, 1253a: 'man is by nature a political animal'.

[182] Ibid.

[183] H. Arendt, *Between Past and Future* (2006), at 153. On the public and the private realms and on freedom being located exclusively in the former, see also H. Arendt, *The Human Condition* ([first published 1958] 2nd ed., 1998), ch. II, especially at 31. Critical, e.g. Unger (n. 169) 169: 'Its appeal would rest upon a one-sided and indefensible picture of human dispositions. In practice, a minority of talkers and self-promoters would find expanded opportunities for preferment while the majority would shrink from this oligarchy of busy-bodies.'

[184] Cf. M. A. Glendon, *Rights Talk: The Impoverishment of Political Discourse* (1991), at 14, who uses this term with reference to families, religious communities, and other social groups in civil society.

[185] See also *Déclaration des droits de l'homme et du citoyen de 1789*, Art. 6: 'La Loi est l'expression de la volonté générale. Tous les Citoyens ont droit de concourir personnellement, ou par leurs Représentants, à sa formation.' A core text of the French revolution, today it still counts as positive law in France with constitutional status (see Conseil Constitutionnel, Décision no. 73-51 DC 27 December 1973).

[186] J.-J. Rousseau, *Le contrat social* (1762), Book II, ch. 3, at 371. The general will thus seems to consist of 'the transcendent incarnation of the citizens' common interest that exists in abstraction from what

'common good' are problematic in pluralist societies: 'All the radical varieties of Rousseauianism labor under this moral overburdening of the virtuous citizen. The assumption of republican virtues is realistic only for a polity with a normative consensus that has been secured in advance through tradition and ethos.'[187] Under classical republicanism the common good was best taken care of by an elite, which excluded large sections of society from politics, i.e. slaves, women, and those without property.[188] Most contemporary republicans reject this legacy of 'excluding from the political community all those whose voices would—by reason of supposed defect of understanding, foreignness of outlook, subservience of position, or corruption of interest—threaten disruption of a community's normative unity'.[189] Still, certain republican understandings and proposals—for example with regard to the EU—remain based on the idea of politics as the pursuit of the common good, less ethical-communitarian perhaps and certainly not elitist, but nevertheless unitary.[190]

Modern republicanism in its more influential contemporary version, as developed in particular by Pettit and Skinner, is neither perfectionist nor communitarian. The core of this 'civic republicanism', as it is usually referred to, is the political value of freedom as non-domination. This notion also goes back to the understanding, rooted in history (especially the Roman republic, the English civil war, and the American revolution) that as a person you can only be free if you live as a citizen in a republic or commonwealth where you do not risk the arbitrary interference in your life by others, which would be the case notably if you were the subject of a monarch.[191] However, it is not perfectionist in that it does not imply a commitment to an active political life or any other conception of a good life. Obviously, civic republicans do not subscribe to one single theory, with no disagreements. For example, with regard to judicial review of constitutionality, there are both republican defences and attacks, and in both cases in the name of roughly the same shared principles of political liberty, democracy, and deliberation.[192]

2. Non-domination

The core political value of contemporary civic republicanism is freedom as non-domination. A person is unfree to the extent that she is dominated by the arbitrary

any of them actually wants', C. Bertram, 'Jean Jacques Rousseau', in E. N. Zalta, *Stanford Encyclopedia of Philosophy*, available at https://plato.stanford.edu/entries/rousseau/ (last visited 22 June 2020).

187 Habermas (n. 88) Appendix I (Popular Sovereignty as Procedure), at 473.

188 Cf. Wood (n. 176) 145 ('enlightened paternalism'). Less critical, H. Arendt, *On Revolution* ([first published 1963] 2006), at 271.

189 Michelman (n. 180) 1495.

190 See e.g. Scharpf, 'Legitimacy in the Multilevel European Polity', 1 *European Political Science Review* (2009) 173, at 176: 'governments are under a "republican" (and output-oriented) obligation to use the powers of government for the common good of the polity.'

191 The idea of the President becoming a monarch was central to Representative Schiff's closing statement in the Trump impeachment trial.

192 See, *pro*, Michelman (n. 180); Sunstein, 'Beyond the Republican Revival', 97 *Yale L.J.* (1988) 1539, and *contra*, Bellamy (n. 88), and, specifically with regard to rights, Bellamy, 'Rights, Republicanism and Democracy', in A. Niederberger and P. Schink (eds), *Republican Democracy: Liberty, Law and Politics* (2013), ch. 10. See further Chapter 3.

choices of another person. Thus, the opposite of a free person is a slave.[193] As Pettit underlines, this understanding of liberty differs from both negative liberty and positive liberty, as they were famously distinguished by Berlin.[194] Negative liberty, celebrated as we saw by libertarians, demands non-interference, especially from the state.[195] What matters is the absence of actual interference. This means that from the perspective of negative liberty someone who is at the mercy of someone else who has the prerogative or capacity to interfere but refrains from—or fails in—doing so (e.g. a benign tyrant, a distracted slave-holder) is, to that extent, free. On the other hand, someone who lives under legitimate laws (the outcome of an inclusive and deliberative democratic process) that, however, interfere with her capacity to do as she pleases, is considered, to that extent and for that reason, unfree from the perspective of negative liberty. In contrast, from the point of view of republican liberty the possibility of arbitrary interference (by the tyrant or slave-holder) makes the person unfree, while legitimate laws do not lead to domination and therefore do not reduce one's freedom. In a similar way, from a republican perspective positive liberty, i.e. freedom as self-realization, the core value of liberal perfectionism, may be both too much (when it leads to domination of others, e.g. economic domination) and insufficient (when it depends on the whim of a dictator).

This also has direct implications for private law. Think of property rights or the freedom of contract. From a civic republican point of view, consider the position of a person living in a dictatorship that adopts a laissez-faire economic policy (think of Pinochet's 'economic miracle'). Even if the state does not at present interfere with her property or contract (e.g. because opponents are still left alone), she nevertheless enjoys no—or only severely impaired—freedom of contract or property rights. The state apparatus may at any time decide to interfere (quite brutally) with her freedom, perhaps by accusing her of being a subversive communist agitator and confiscating her personal property, while leaving large landowning families untouched. Indeed, there is no reason to think that contract law, as an institution, should somehow be excluded from the non-domination test. On the contrary, Pettit's explicit highly critical discussion of the freedom of contract (as we will see in Chapter 7) leaves no doubt as to whether contract law too must meet the republican standard of not being conducive to, or even merely allowing for, domination. As Sunstein puts it, republican theories are not hostile to private rights or private autonomy; however, 'on the republican point of view, the existence of realms of private autonomy must be justified in public terms'.[196]

[193] This conception of freedom goes back to Roman law. See the *Digest*, section 'De Statu Hominum', especially D.1.5.3 (*Gaius libro primo institutionum*): 'Summa itaque de iure personarum divisio haec est, quod omnes homines aut liberi sunt aut servi.' Cf. Skinner (n. 179) 41: 'The essence of what it means to be a slave, and hence to lack personal liberty, is thus to be *in potestate*, within the power of someone else.'

[194] See Pettit (n. 114) 21. For the distinction, see Berlin (n. 59) 166 ff. Berlin's distinction builds upon Constant's distinction between the liberty of the ancients and the liberty of the moderns. See B. Constant, *De la liberté des anciens comparée à celle des modernes* ([first published 1874] 2010).

[195] Cf. T. Hobbes, *Leviathan* ([first published 1651] 1985), ch. XXI (Of the Liberty of Subjects): 'Liberty, or freedom, signifieth (properly) the absence of opposition; (by opposition, I mean external impediments of motion); ... a Free-man, is he, that in those things, which by his strength and wit he is able to do, is not hindered to do what he has a will to.'

[196] Sunstein (n. 192) 1551.

There is a line of criticism, going back to Hobbes,[197] according to which republicans confuse personal liberty with political liberty. However, according to civic republicans there is no confusion at all. They mean it: 'their thesis—to put it as bluntly as possible—is that it is only possible to be free in a free state'.[198] And they are not taken aback by 'Hobbes's incapacity (or perhaps refusal) to see any connection between public and private liberty'—a connection that lies at the heart of the republican argument.[199]

According to a different kind of criticism, republicanism, as a political theory of freedom, not a theory of justice, answers the question of when we are free, but fails to tell us what we owe to each other.[200] Thus, a society whose basic institutions ensure us freedom as non-domination is not necessarily also a just society. However, as Forst has argued, the theory could be transformed into (or read as including) a theory of justice, by adopting as its core principle that no one should be dominated by—i.e. subject to—norms or institutions that are not reasonably justifiable to her.[201]

3. Deliberation

While the notion of political freedom as non-domination was a neo-Roman rediscovery,[202] the belief in political deliberation is a distinctly American contribution to republican thought.[203] In contrast to other approaches to politics (libertarian, liberal, and, especially, utilitarian) it does not regard political views and positions as individual preferences exogenous to the political process, but as opinions that are revisable in response to information and—especially—reasons offered by others in a process of public deliberation. Some republicans regard public deliberation as a collective attempt to get closer to the truth about the common good; others are less perfectionist and more relativist and pluralist about conceptions of the good, and regard public deliberation as a way of determining constraints to legitimate political action. Similarly, with regard to the civic virtues that citizens cultivate through deliberation, some republicans emphasize the benefits of virtuous (i.e. public spirited and incorruptible) citizens and politicians for the quality of the political process and outcomes, while others claim that virtuous citizens are also better persons leading more fulfilling

[197] See Hobbes (n. 195) ch. XXI:

> The Libertie, whereof there is so frequent, and honourable mention, in the Histories, and Philosophy of the Antient Greeks, and Romans, and in the writings, and discourse of those that from them have received all their learning in the Politiques, is not the Libertie of Particular men; but the Libertie of the Common-wealth ... There is written on the Turrets of the city of Luca in great characters at this day, the word LIBERTAS; yet no man can thence inferre, that a particular man has more Libertie, or Immunitie from the service of the Commonwealth there, than in Constantinople. Whether a Common-wealth be Monarchicall, or Popular, the Freedome is still the same.

[198] Skinner (n. 179) 61.

[199] Ibid. 77.

[200] Forst, 'A Kantian Republican Conception of Justice as Nondomination', in Niederberger and Schink (eds) (n. 192) 154. See also Fricker, 'Epistemic Justice as a Condition of Political Freedom?', 190 *Synthese* (2013) 1317, who argues that non-domination is best understood as a thoroughly generic liberal ideal of freedom that depends upon epistemic justice as one of its essential conditions, because non-domination requires contestation and contestation requires epistemic justice, i.e. being taken seriously as a giver and receiver of knowledge.

[201] Forst (n. 200).

[202] Skinner (n. 179).

[203] Sunstein (n. 192) 1548.

lives.[204] Finally, the commitment to deliberation is closely connected to a concern for political equality. Equality is understood here in the substantive sense of having equal opportunities to contribute to the deliberation, by offering reasons and information from one's own point of view (i.e. as one is actually situated), and thus influence its outcomes. In particular, the negative impact (sometimes devastating) of economic inequality on political equality has consistently been a prominent republican concern.[205]

G. Discourse Theory

Habermas is widely regarded as Europe's most influential contemporary philosopher. The range of his philosophical work, spanning from social theory to epistemology, philosophy of language, moral theory, political theory, and legal theory, is breath-taking, while his critical interventions in societal and political debates have been manifold. Building on his work, and partly criticizing it, today there also exists a wide range of contributions to the discourse theory of law and politics from other philosophers.

1. Communicative action

The first generation of thinkers in the Frankfurt School had been rather pessimistic about the fate of modernity, i.e. the project of the Enlightenment. In their critical diagnoses, the autonomy of the self-reflective person was being replaced gradually by a purely instrumental rationality which was leading to technocracy, consumerism, and ultimately the eclipse of reason.[206] In contrast, Habermas developed an interdisciplinary theory of society that, although equally critical of instrumental reason, was more optimistic about society's capacity to respond. Central to his theory was his postulate that societies are characterized not only by strategic action, led by instrumental reason, but also by communicative action, guided by a distinct type of rationality, i.e. communicative reason, that cannot be reduced to instrumental reason. When different people try to coordinate their actions, a person acts strategically, based on instrumental reason, if she regards the others merely as an obstacle in the way between her and her chosen ends. However, a person engages in communicative action when she tries to coordinate her actions with others, and resolve any conflicts between them consensually. Habermas also goes to great lengths in critically demonstrating how modern societies increasingly are integrated through the mediums of money and bureaucratic power that are 'colonizing' our 'life world'[207]—a process in which law plays an important instrumental role.[208] However, he argues, the pessimistic view is

[204] In its original meaning, a person occupied entirely with his private affairs, to the neglect of his public role, was called an 'idiot' (ἰδιώτης). Cf. R. Bellamy, *Citizenship: A Very Short Introduction* (2008), at 97.

[205] Montesquieu, *De l'esprit des lois* (1748), Book V, ch. III–VI: 'L'amour de la république, dans une démocratie, est celui de la démocratie; l'amour de la démocratie est celui de l'égalité.'

[206] See especially, M. Horkheimer and T. W. Adorno, *Dialectic of Enlightenment* ([first published 1944] 1997); M. Horkheimer, *Eclipse of Reason* (1947); H. Marcuse, *One-Dimensional Man* (1964).

[207] A striking example of colonization is the ongoing push towards running universities as businesses, where financial incentives are accepted as normal, and where success in competitions for 'research grants' has become the holy grail.

[208] Habermas, *The Theory of Communicative Action* (1981), Vol II, VIII.2.C, at 356 ff.

reductionist[209] because societies always also integrate through 'communicative action', i.e. by trying to convince each other with the force of the better argument. The foundation for this postulate Habermas finds in the formal pragmatic philosophy of language ('the linguistic turn'). From this he derives the insight that when people communicate with each other, in their utterances they always make certain validity claims (usually implicitly), whether this be with regard to their own sincerity or the truth or rightness of what they are saying. It is here, i.e. in 'communicative action' where people try to convince each other, that we find a type of reason that is intersubjective[210] and cannot be reduced to instrumental reason. And it is here also that hope resides that a society will be able to defend itself against the instrumental reason that is driven by economic and bureaucratic power, and to reclaim those parts of our lifeworld that have already been colonized.[211]

2. The Discourse Principle

In Habermasian terminology, the concept of 'discourse' does not refer to just any kind of speech or narrative,[212] but has the specific meaning of offering reasons with a view to convincing others, in cases where disagreement has arisen.[213] The disagreement may relate to a theoretical question, concerning the truth of a proposition, but also—and most relevant here—to a practical question, concerning the rightness of norms for action. For the purposes of the latter, Habermas developed the discourse principle 'D' of argumentation, according to which 'only those norms can claim validity that could meet with the acceptance of all concerned in practical discourse'.[214]

On the basis of the discourse principle, Habermas developed his 'discourse ethics', which is a discourse theory of morality.[215] For the justification specifically of moral norms, the discourse principle takes the form of the universalization principle 'U': 'A norm is valid when the foreseeable consequences and side effects of its general observance for the interest and value-orientations of each individual could be jointly accepted by all concerned without coercion.'[216] The universalization principle is Habermas's post-metaphysical version of Kant's categorical imperative, moving from a subjectivistic and hence individualistic conception of practical reason, situated

[209] With this criticism, Habermas breaks not only with the critical theory of the Frankfurt School's first generation, but obviously also with classical Marxism, especially its deterministic rejection of reason as bourgeois ideology.

[210] By contrast, Kant's conception of reason resides ultimately in the self-conscious individual, a metaphysical conception of reason that it is Habermas's explicit aim to overcome.

[211] By reserving an important place for individual and collective agency, Habermas's theory of society goes directly against Luhman's systems theory of society which is based entirely on functional differentiation. For the controversy, see J. Habermas and N. Luhmann, *Theorie der Gesellschaft oder Sozialtechnologie: Theorie-Diskussion* (1971).

[212] Contrast e.g. M. Foucault, *L'ordre du discours* (1971).

[213] Habermas (n. 208) Vol. I, at 19–23.

[214] J. Habermas, *Erläuterungen zur Diskursethik* (1991), 12; Habermas (n. 88) 107; J. Habermas, *The Inclusion of the Other* (1998), at 41.

[215] The term discourse 'ethics' in the title of the book, although in line with prevalent terminology at the time, is confusing today since it ignores the distinction between ethics and morality that the book itself aims to draw. See J. Habermas, *Justification and Application* (1993), at 2.

[216] Habermas, *The Inclusion of the Other* (n. 214) 42.

ultimately in the critical self, to an intersubjective one, to be found in a procedure for dialogue and argumentation among all affected persons.[217]

Like the categorical imperative, the principle requires universal acceptability. This leads to a sharp distinction between moral, ethical, and pragmatic discourses.[218] While moral discourses refer to the universal duties that all human beings have towards each other, ethical discourses refer to values, traditions, and identities with a view to determining what to do in order to live a meaningful and authentic life. Pragmatic discourses, then, are concerned with the best means for achieving given (individual or societal) ends. It is important to point out that Habermas's procedural conception of morality is cognitivistic, not decisionistic, i.e. it offers a procedure for determining moral truths (or, rather: truth-like validity), with regard to which we can learn by including everyone's point of view, but which explicitly and fundamentally always remains open to a better argument.

3. The Democratic Principle

Law's claim to validity does not derive directly from morality, as natural lawyers believe. Positive laws do not claim universal application, but only for a specific time and place ('the changeable decisions of a political lawgiver').[219] Moreover, considerations other than morality, such as ethical and pragmatic considerations, also inform law making.[220] Therefore, the universalization principle cannot be applied directly in order to determine law's legitimacy, i.e. its claim to validity. On the other hand, the reduction by legal positivists of the law's validity claim to its mere pedigree (determined through Kelsen's 'basic norm' or Hart's 'rule of recognition') is also rejected by Habermas, as 'blind decisionism'.[221] It may explain compliance with the law as strategic action but not as communicative action. Therefore, the discourse principle must be adapted in order to do full justice to law's 'facticity and validity'.[222] Thus, Habermas's concept of legitimacy, unlike that of Weber or Luhmann, is not purely factual but also normative. It asks not merely which laws people actually follow, but also which ones they have reason to follow. And with reference to those reasons, he steers a middle ground between natural lawyers, who see it as the lawgiver's task to implement moral principles, and legal positivists, who accept laws as long as they have the right pedigree. Habermas postulates that in our contemporary societies legitimacy cannot but be democratic. It is important to underline, however, that in a discourse theory's understanding, democracy is not primarily a matter of voting but of deliberation and reason-giving. This leads to the democratic principle, which states that 'only those statutes may claim legitimacy that can meet with the assent (*Zustimmung*)

[217] J. Habermas, *Erläuterungen zur Diskursethik* (1991), at 12. Cf. Forst, 'Diskursethik', in H. Brunkhorst, R. Kreide, and C. Lafont (eds), *Habermas Handbuch* (2009), IV.3, at 306.

[218] Habermas, 'Diskursethik: Notizen zu einem Begründungsprogramm', in *Jürgen Habermas Philosophische Texte*, Vol. 3, at 108: 'der Universalisierungsgrundsatz funktioniert wie ein Messer, das einen Schnitt legt zwischen „das Gute" und „das Gerechte", zwischen evaluative und streng normative Aussagen.'

[219] Habermas (n. 88) 'Postscript', 447.

[220] Ibid. 151–152.

[221] Ibid. 'Postscript', 453.

[222] This would be a literalistic (and inadequate) translation of *Faktizität und Geltung*, the original German title of *Between Facts and Norms*.

of all citizens in a discursive process of legislation that in turn has been legally constituted'.[223] Thus, Habermas's theory of law is at heart a democratic theory.

4. The Co-originality of Private and Public Autonomy

Another core idea in Habermas's political theory is the 'co-originality of private and public autonomy'.[224] With this expression, Habermas means to convey that private and public autonomy mutually pre-suppose each other. In practical terms, the room for individual self-determination must be granted and determined (guaranteed by human rights and other subjective rights) through a process of collective self-determination (popular sovereignty), while at the same time collective self-determination depends on citizens having sufficient private autonomy (e.g. some property rights, freedom of contract, etc.). Thus, democracy and *Rechtsstaat* are not in tension, as is often thought, but in a (virtuous) circular connection, mutually re-enforcing each other. In other words, with the co-originality thesis Habermas's proceduralist understanding of law's legitimacy transcends the opposition between the liberal and the republican accounts.[225]

The co-originality thesis has direct implications for our understanding of private law. First, it directly rejects private law separatism (the claim to the 'autonomy of private law').[226] Private law making cannot be understood merely as the implementation of moral principles, as certain contemporary Kantians suggest.[227] Private law is not merely a matter of the right, which—as also in Habermas's understanding (see earlier)—has priority over the good, but legitimately may be informed also by other considerations, for example pragmatic ones. Secondly, it means that private law's legitimacy depends fundamentally on its democratic credentials.[228] For, as Habermas explicitly underlines, it is also true for private law that its addressees must be able to understand themselves as its authors.

5. The Procedural Paradigm of Private Law

In contrast to most other contemporary philosophers (but in line e.g. with Locke, Kant, and Hegel), Habermas explicitly engages in private law theory.[229] His reading is diachronic, in terms of successive paradigms.[230] The 'liberal' paradigm, which was

[223] Habermas (n. 88) 110.

[224] See ibid. 127, 314, and 409.

[225] According to Möllers, 'Demokratie und Recht', in H. Brunkhorst, R. Kreide, and C. Lafont (eds), *Habermas Handbuch* (2009), III.13, at 259, it transcends the opposition between liberalism and communitarianism. However, Habermas explicitly contrasts the 'liberal' view with the 'republican' view (see especially n. 88, at 3.1.4) (and attacks them both). Having said that, Habermas's understanding of republicanism is more communitarian than civic, taking Rousseau as the paradigmatic republican, contrasting him with Locke, who serves as the paradigmatic liberal.

[226] For this claim, see especially E. Weinrib, *The Idea of Private Law* (1995), ch. 8. See further Chapter 5.

[227] See e.g. A. Ripstein, *Force and Freedom* (2009).

[228] See Habermas (n. 88) 409. Similar, Unger (n. 169) 6.

[229] Habermas (n. 88) section 9.1.

[230] For a similarly historical account, see Kennedy, 'Three Globalizations of Law and Legal Thought: 1850–2000', in D. Trubek and A. Santos (eds), *The New Law and Economic Development: A Critical Appraisal* (2006) 19. In contrast, C.U. Schmid, *Die Instrumentalisierung des Privatrechts durch die Europäische Union: Privatrecht und Privatrechtskonzeptionen in der Entwicklung der Europäischen Integrationsverfassung* (2010), at 15–67 and 68–92, rejects Habermas's idea of consecutive paradigms and regards three paradigms as coexisting today, as a mix.

based on formal equality, can no longer be upheld today in the light of the existence of massive inequalities (an implicit rejection of contemporary libertarian theories).[231] However, the 'social-welfare' paradigm, which was a direct response to these inequalities, must also be rejected because it merely compensates for their effects, making individuals become clients of the welfare state which paternalistically *reduces* their private autonomy,[232] while sharing the same premises, i.e. 'the *productivist* image of a capitalist industrial society'.[233] Therefore, Habermas proposes as a new third paradigm of private law, a purely procedural understanding, according to which persons in a society mutually grant each other private rights, and where the legitimacy of these rights depends entirely on the degree to which each person is able to regard herself not only as an addressee but also as an author of private law.[234]

6. The Right to Justification

As mentioned earlier, the discourse principle is a principle of argumentation at the most general level, which needs to be operationalized with regard to different types of questions. Habermas has done this, in particular, with regard to pragmatic, ethical, and moral questions which require discourses in terms of purpose, the good, and the right, respectively.[235] Forst builds upon this differentiation, by distinguishing four 'contexts of justice',[236] i.e. ethical, legal, political, and moral. These are normative contexts where a person is addressed in different capacities, and each with its own type of appropriate justificatory reasons.[237] And a society can be considered just to the extent that it does justice to persons in all these dimensions and unites these contexts in the appropriate manner.[238] Indeed, Forst argues, every person has a right to justification of norms and actions affecting her.[239] This is the right to demand justification by reasons that are both general and reciprocal, which entails a moral veto right against unjustified actions or norms.[240] Generality means that no one's point of view should be excluded, while reciprocity signifies that no one may claim a privilege, be it in terms of content or of reasons (e.g. by projecting one's own 'higher truths' onto others). The right to justification is the most basic moral right that each person has. This marks an important difference between Forst's right to justification and Habermas's discourse principle. While Habermas, as we saw, grounds the discourse principle in the presuppositions of communicative action, Forst gives the right to justification a moral grounding. This is necessary, he argues, 'for otherwise moral persons might indeed

[231] Habermas (n. 88) 407.
[232] This critique was already present in Habermas (n. 208) Vol. II, especially at 346–351.
[233] Habermas (n. 88) 407 (emphasis in original).
[234] Ibid. 408.
[235] Habermas, 'On the Pragmatic, the Ethical, and the Moral Employments of Practical Reason', in J. Habermas, *Justification and Application* (1993), at 1. See also Habermas (n. 88) 109.
[236] Forst (n. 111).
[237] And each with its own specific type of autonomy, i.e. ethical, legal, political and moral autonomy, respectively. See ibid. Forst fully elaborates this, and adds social autonomy, in R. Forst, *The Right to Justification: Elements of a Constructivist Theory of Justice* (2013), ch. 5. On this, see further Chapter 5.
[238] Forst (n. 111) 5.
[239] Forst, *The Right to Justification* (n. 237).
[240] Ibid. 6.

know *how* they should justify their actions but not *that* they are obliged to do so in a moral context'.[241]

3. Contract Law Pluralities

A. Introduction

Before we move on to our six fundamental political questions, a third element to set the scene should be added. The normative questions cannot be asked entirely in the abstract. They must be empirically situated in reality, at least to some degree. In particular, it seems, any normative theory of (European) contract law will have to take into account the several pluralities that are part of the reality of contract in Europe today. These include: the rich variety of contract types concluded regularly by contracting parties; the different systems of contract law existing in the 27 Member States of the EU; the multitude of roles that contract law plays in our lives; and the many values that contract law is said to embody according to different contract theories. This section briefly introduces each of these pluralities. The existence of these multiple contract types, systems, roles, and theories must be kept in mind, as part of a reality check for possible answers, and in order to avoid unduly reductionist views of the reality of contracting when considering our normative political questions of European contract law in the following chapters.

B. Types of Contracts

1. Taxonomy

There exists a great diversity of contract types that could be considered, in principle, and be covered by a theory of (European) contract law. Moreover, there is a variety of different ways to distinguish between different types of contracts (including the idea that contract should not be regarded as a separate category at all).[242] This is explained by the fact that there are many different rationales for distinguishing between contract types and also different perspectives from which such distinctions can be made, for example the legal point of view of one's own legal system, or the empirical point of view of the most frequently concluded contract types, or the point of view of a normative contract theory. None of these rationales or points of view can be said to be neutral or autonomous. For example, the choices made by contracting parties will depend on the contract types recognized and regulated by their own legal system, which, in turn, may be interpreted and critiqued from the point of view of a normative theory, for example one that regards it as the government's task to contribute to human flourishing by making a sufficiently wide and diverse range of attractive ready-made types of contract available.[243] In other words, there is no such thing as a neutral contract

[241] Ibid. 57. See also ibid. 77. For an exploration of the main implications of the right to justification for contract law and its theory, see Hesselink, 'The Right to Justification of Contract', 33 *Ratio Juris* (2020) 196.
[242] See G. Gilmore, *The Death of Contract* (1974).
[243] This is the core argument made by H. Dagan and M. Heller, *The Choice Theory of Contracts* (2017).

taxonomy. Although the various distinctions that can be found often overlap, in part, they also differ significantly in other respects.

2. Nominate and Innominate Contracts

In civil law jurisdictions, there is the familiar distinction between nominate and innominate contracts, which refers, respectively, to those contracts that are specifically regulated, usually in the civil code, and those that are not. The nominate contracts in most classical codes go back to the contract types (or, rather, sources of obligation) in Roman law, prior to the acceptance of the binding force of a mere agreement (a *nudum pactum* in Latin—hence, *pacta sunt servanda*), which became the basis for the development of a general law of contract. Modern codes have added specific sets of rules regulating more modern contract types as well, such as, in some countries, franchising,[244] medical treatment,[245] or, as an example deriving from EU law, timesharing.[246] In most civil codes (and also in the DCFR), the number of provisions on specific contracts far exceeds those on contracts in general.

3. Onerous and Gratuitous Contracts

Another familiar distinction is the one between contracts for value (or onerous contracts) and gratuitous contracts. Some legal systems, notably those belonging to the common law tradition, where 'consideration' is a requirement for enforceability, even limit the definition of a contract entirely to the former, thus excluding gifts from the definition of contract and from contract law's substantive scope of application. In other legal systems (i.e. ones where agreement rather than consideration is traditionally regarded as the founding principle), however, the contract of donation is simply considered one among many other enforceable contracts (usually subject to certain formal requirements). Thus, in the civil law tradition civil codes usually dedicate a specific section to this specific type of contract.

Obviously, removing gratuitous contracts from the scope of contract law and contract theory has the immediate effect of making contract law, and the principles that should justify it, look much more commercial than if gifts, gratuitous loans (commodate), agency without remuneration (mandate), and marriage are included as well.

As a recent development, it should be noted that in the digital economy, the counterperformance in a contract for value may not necessarily have to be a price in money but may well consist in sharing one's personal data.[247]

[244] Usually prescribing extensive precontractual information duties on the franchisor. See e.g. the Spanish *Ley de ordenación del comercio minorista* of 1996 and the Belgian *Loi relative à l'information précontractuelle dans le cadre d'accords de partenariat commercial* of 2005.

[245] See e.g. Dutch Civil Code, Book 7, Title 7, Section 5.

[246] Directive 2008/122/EC on the protection of consumers in respect of certain aspects of timeshare, long-term holiday product, resale and exchange contracts, OJ 2009 L 33.

[247] Directive (EU) 2019/770 (n. 36), Art. 3, and Recital (24): 'Digital content or digital services are often supplied also where the consumer does not pay a price but provides personal data to the trader.' See also Directive (EU) 2019/2161 (n. 42), Recital (31): 'contracts for digital services under which the consumer provides personal data to the trader without paying a price'.

4. Relational and Discrete Contracts

A further distinction, that became quite prominent in contract theory the 1990s, is the one between relational and discrete contracts. According to the relational contract theory, the spot sales contract that is often taken as paradigmatic in contract law doctrine and theory actually only represents a rather limited segment of contract practice; most contracts, relational contract theorists claim, are relational and therefore should be governed by different principles, such as contractual solidarity and cooperation.[248] The notion of 'lifetime contracts' takes this debate one step further. It is based on the idea that certain contracts that are crucial for people's lives and that we tend to depend upon throughout our entire lifetime (medical insurance, utilities, work), albeit not necessarily constantly with the same counter-party, should have a special status and be much more intensely regulated, especially with a view to the protection of those persons who are most vulnerable.[249] The 'gig' economy further complicates the picture because self-employed individuals such as artists, ICT experts, and journalists may hop happily from one gig to another, but they are often much more vulnerable than regular employees because they depend on a continuous succession of new short-term and single-project contracts. This was brought home quite dramatically when the COVID-19 crisis broke out.

5. Business-to-Business and Business-to-Consumer Contracts

EU contract law discourse often distinguishes between business-to-business (B2B) and business-to-consumer (B2C) contracts. This distinction is closely related to the categories of commercial law, consumer law, and civil law. These distinctions express the idea that ordinary contract law rules are not (entirely) appropriate for consumer contracts, because consumers need (additional) protection, while, conversely, they should also be modified for commercial contracts since commercial parties require legal certainty more than contractual fairness. Each of these claims has been contested. Much of the discussion has concentrated on the question of whether small and medium-sized enterprises (SMEs), especially sole traders, should be entitled to a similar protection as consumers, for example with regard to unfair contract terms. This would, of course, tend to undermine the rationale for this categorical distinction. With the arrival of the sharing—or, as the European Commission prefers to call it, the collaborative[250]—economy, the category of peer-to-peer (P2P) contracts has raised the further question of how these should be treated, especially whether in some cases a non-professional party should be protected against another non-professional (consumer to consumer, C2C). Some contract theories try to bypass these complexities by postulating that commercial contracts should be regarded as the core of contracting.

[248] See e.g. Macneil, 'Contract Adjustment of Long-Term Economic Relations Under Classical, Neo-Classical and Relational Contract Law', 72 *Northwestern University Law Review* (1978) 854. Others, e.g. Eisenberg, 'Relational Contracts', in J. Beatson and D. Friedmann (eds), *Good Faith and Fault in Contract Law* (1995), have pointed out that contract law has already undergone a transformation (doctrines of good faith, frustration or change of circumstances, contextual interpretation, etc.) as a result of which the new features that a relational contract law would bring are in fact already present in modern general contract law.

[249] U. Reifner and L. Nogler (eds), *Life Time Contracts: Social Long-Term Contracts in Labour, Tenancy and Consumer Credit* (2014).

[250] Commission Communication 'A European Agenda for the Collaborative Economy' (COM(2016) 356 final).

However, as Dagan and Heller rightly point out, 'calling business contracts the core does not make it so'.[251]

6. Domestic and Cross-border Contracts

A final familiar distinction is the one between purely domestic contracts and contracts between parties based in different jurisdictions. Under traditional private international law rules and theories, it has been the task of conflict rules to domesticate such cross-border contracts by indicating one national legal system as the applicable law, while usually allowing the parties themselves to overrule the default conflict rule through their own choice of law.[252] However, that latter principle always has been subject to certain limitations on the free choice of law and to exceptions for overriding rules (*lois de police*).[253]

In addition to conflict rules, moreover, there also exist international instruments containing regimes of substantive contract law rules for cross-border contracts. The United Nations Convention on Contracts for the International Sale of Goods (CISG) is a prominent example at the global level;[254] the optional CESL would have been another at the European plane.[255]

7. Normalization

Clearly, none of these distinctions is neutral. Each of them highlights aspects that are regarded as salient from a specific normative perspective. Placing these aspects, rather than others, in the foreground tends to have a normalization effect and, thus, to contribute to the framing of the normative debate. Indeed, most monist contract law theories, and all the essentialist ones, depend on restrictive definitions of contract as a result of which parts of the law that do not match with their ultimate value or principle are conveniently classified as something else than contract. Such limitative definitions are not necessarily made in bad faith. They may also express the normative position that nothing else than what could be explained in terms of contract law's single underlying principle (e.g. corrective justice or the promise principle) should properly count as contract law. The best we can do, in this regard, is to be conscious of the reifying effects, and the potential normative implications, of the contract law taxonomy we use.[256]

The approach chosen in this book is to adopt a very broad and open notion of contract and to address the main political questions explicitly. However, taking a very general, inclusive starting point, as in this study, can help to secure avoidance of the problem only very partially. Indeed, the very idea of quite general, fundamental questions of contract law could be associated (mistakenly but understandably) with

[251] Dagan and Heller (n. 243) 57: 'Calling business contracts the core does not make it so. We do not get closer to a general theory of contract by excluding the vast bulk of contracting that occurs in the spheres of family, home, consumer transactions, and employment.'

[252] See, respectively, Art. 4 and Art. 3 of Rome I (n. 5).

[253] See, respectively ibid., Arts 5–8 and Art. 9.

[254] United Nations Convention on Contracts for the International Sale of Goods (Vienna, 1980).

[255] Commission Proposal for a Regulation on a Common European Sales Law (COM(2011) 635 final).

[256] E.g. Schwartz and Scott, 'Contract Theory and the Limits of Contract Law', 113 *Yale L.J.* (2003) 541, limit their theory explicitly to contracts between 'firms'.

classical general contract law, where the parties are assumed to have equal freedom and power. Yet, the opposite approach, in which no general notion of contract is assumed, is not necessarily to be preferred, as it will be readily associated with the death of contract thesis, which may or may not be convincing,[257] but in any case, it is hardly more neutral. Nor is a view 'from nowhere' available, either generally or specifically with regard to contract law and justice. Moreover, the inclusive, pluralist definition of contract is certainly not compatible *only* with classical laissez-faire contract law. On the contrary, think of the fair price principle—in some respects the opposite of laissez faire—that has also been proposed in contemporary theory,[258] as a principle of general contract law. Thus, parts of what will be addressed here as 'contract law' may also be discussed in—or even be central to—theories of 'private law', 'the law of obligations', 'consumer law', 'market regulation', 'the common law', 'labour law', 'EU law', or 'transnational law'. It is submitted that the perspective on contract adopted here, understood in a very inclusive and pluralist sense (without any definition, more as a field), is the best available starting point for a discussion of normative contract theory for a society characterized by pluralism.[259]

C. Systems of Contract Law

1. National Systems

In Europe, there exist as many contract law systems as Member States. Or even more, since in some countries there is more than one system of contract law—notably Scots law and the law of England and Wales in the UK. Each of these systems has its own national legal sources, its national legal practice, system of adjudication, and scholarship.

2. Legal Families

Comparative lawyers have customarily grouped national legal systems into 'legal families'.[260] Thus, some legal systems are categorized as belonging to the civil law tradition, others to the common law. The civil law of contract goes back to Roman law (the Corpus Iuris Civilis, in particular the Digest) which became the basis of the *ius commune*, before each civil law jurisdiction adopted its own civil code.[261] The common law of contract goes back to medieval forms of action, developed over time through precedents, and was later supplemented by statutes but was never codified.[262]

257 The question will be addressed in Chapter 5.

258 Gordley, 'The Just Price: The Aristotelian Tradition and John Rawls', 11 *ERCL* (2015) 197.

259 Another possible charge is that of a disciplinary imperialism, aiming to extend the power of contract law, contract lawyers, and contract theorists. On the related risks of the contractualization of society (hand in hand with the privatization of public services), see later, in Section 3.D.6.

260 See e.g. R. David, M. Goré, and C. Jauffret-Spinosi, *Les grands systèmes de droit contemporain* (12th ed., 2016); Zweigert and Kötz (n. 173). For a different approach, see P. G. Monateri (ed.), *Comparative Contract Law* (2017).

261 R. Zimmermann, *The Law of Obligations: Roman Foundations of the Civilian Tradition* (1996).

262 A. W. B. Simpson, *A History of the Common Law of Contract: The Rise of the Action of Assumpsit* (1975). In the 1960s, the English and Scots Law Commissions jointly drafted a contract code, but it was never enacted. See H. McGregor, *Contract Code Drawn Up on Behalf of the English Law Commission* (1993).

However, more recent comparative law work has thoroughly deconstructed the notion of legal families, each with a mother (or core) system and offspring (or satellites). Today, it is more frequently regarded as an essentially hegemonistic—if not neo-imperialistic—political project.[263] As a result, contemporary comparative work is usually based on the more neutral idea of country reports.[264]

3. The Subversive Effect of Comparative Law

Inevitably, the mere existence of so many different contract law systems in neighbouring countries, especially when they are quite similar socio-economically and culturally, has a certain subversive effect.[265] Legal comparison makes one's own national positive law appear more contingent. This also seems to suggest that the idea of a universal contract law theory, meant to apply for all contract law systems, such as most essentialist theories claim to do, is in fact implausible. At the very least, comparative contract law will show that not all existing contract law systems fit equally well with a given theory, which raises the question of which is wrong: one legal system, another legal system, or the theory, or none of these?[266] And to the extent contract theories claim merely to be interpretative or reconstructive of the law of one single jurisdiction (typically the author's own), then, it seems, the subversive effect of comparison may affect confidence in contract theory as well, especially its epistemological soundness: if contract theories differ from country to country, then what kind of theoretical knowledge and understanding are we really talking about? On the other hand, however, the relative ease with which in recent decades contract law experts succeeded in drafting an International Convention on the Sale of Goods, and principles of European contract law and of international commercial contracts, grounded (sometimes rather loosely) in legal comparison, seems to suggest the existence of universal contract law principles. Indeed, some theorists have set out to uncover the common normative foundations of Western contract law, formulating essentially a new natural law of contract.[267] Again, there is nothing neutral about the choice between a subversive or a common core approach, foregrounding, respectively, differences and similarities in legal comparison. That choice is already political.

4. How Many Systems of Contract Law Are There in the EU?

EU law adds another level of complexity. As we saw, in recent decades contract law in the EU has undergone a rapid Europeanization. This has raised the question of whether EU contract law constitutes a new system of its own, or whether it should

[263] Cf. Hesselink, 'Civil Law', in M. T. Gibbons (ed.), *The Encyclopedia of Political Thought* (2014) 522, with further references.

[264] See especially the various volumes published by the ongoing project, launched in 1993 in Trento, on the 'Common Core of European Private Law'.

[265] Fletcher, 'Comparative Law as a Subversive Discipline', 46 *American Journal of Comparative Law (AJCL)* (1998) 683; Muir-Watt, 'La fonction subversive du droit comparé', *Revue Internationale de Droit Comparé* (2000) 503.

[266] To use a Rawlsian term, it will be difficult to find a reflective equilibrium between a contract theory, on the one hand, and understandings of contract law informed by various different contract law systems, on the other.

[267] See, in particular, J. Gordley, *Foundations of Private Law: Property, Tort, Contract, Unjust Enrichment* (2006).

be regarded exclusively as being part of the respective contract laws of the Member States, or indeed whether all these national contract laws together should now be regarded as being part of one big multi-level European system of contract law. Moreover, it is not self-evident whether this question of 'how many systems?' is a purely analytical question or a normative one.[268] Thus, the arrival of EU contract law may have added a new level to the already existing plurality of contract law systems. Whether this is and should be the case is the question central to Chapter 4. For now, it suffices to note that EU law is a reality that a contemporary contract law theory can no longer ignore. However, in this regard, it should be noted that there appears to exist a remarkable mismatch between most leading normative contract law theories and the reality of EU contract law. On the one hand, most of the characteristics of contract law that one would expect under traditional contract law theories are absent in EU contract law, while, on the other hand, under those theories the most salient characteristics of the existing EU contract law remain unaccounted for.[269]

D. Roles of Contract Law

In our society today, the law of contract plays a number of well-known characteristic roles: contract law is coercive, it is distributive, it ensures entitlements, it provides a standard for interpersonal conduct, it facilitates transactions, and we often depend on it. These are not necessary or inevitable characteristics or essential elements of any contract law system. Nor are they contract law's only roles; others may be relevant as well, depending on the context. Rather, these are some of the main general roles of contract law as we know it here and now, i.e. in Europe in the early twenty-first century. They will have to be addressed, it seems, by any theory that is meant to explain, justify, or criticize our current contract law systems, including European contract law.[270] The brief account here is meant as introductory and descriptive. It presents the main roles contract law happens to have, quite apart from whether it is good or bad, or right or wrong, for (European) contract law to have those roles. These normative questions will come up in the discussion in the following chapters.

1. Coercion

Contract law is coercive. It forces people to do what they do not or no longer want to do.[271] A party who fails to comply with her contractual obligation can be ordered, by

[268] See Hesselink, 'How Many Systems of Private Law are There in Europe? On Plural Legal Sources, Multiple Identities and the Unity of Law', in L. Niglia (ed.), *Pluralism and European Private Law* (2013) 199.

[269] See Hesselink, 'Contract Theory and EU Contract Law', in C. W. Twigg-Flesner (ed.), *Research Handbook on EU Consumer and Contract Law* (2016) 508.

[270] There are overlaps among some of these roles. The degree of overlap depends on the way in which each of them is defined. This, in turn, is determined, in part, by the perspective from which the matter is addressed. The contemporary political theories, that were introduced in the previous section and will be discussed throughout this book, offer such perspectives. For now, it will suffice to note that, despite certain overlaps, it still makes sense, from the perspective of at least some normative contract theories, to distinguish between these particular roles.

[271] Hale, 'Coercion and Distribution in a Supposedly Non-Coercive State', 38 *Political Science Quarterly* (1923) 470.

a court, specifically to comply with the obligation, or to pay damages equivalent to the value of the performance to the plaintiff. In case the defendant fails to comply with a court order to perform her primary contractual obligation to perform the contract, or her secondary obligation to pay damages, public officials will assist the plaintiff to seize the assets of the defendant with a view to satisfying her claim from the proceeds. Thus, the legally binding force of a contract is warranted by the state, which claims the monopoly for the legitimate exercise of force.[272] There exists, therefore, an important difference in this regard between the voluntary performance of a contract, on the one hand, and the exercise of contract remedies, on the other. Voluntary compliance with an agreement, in principle, is something that directly affects the parties alone. In contrast, the legally binding force of contract involves others (third parties) as well.[273] In particular, it involves the exercise of state power, which entails the involvement of state officials.

2. Distribution

Contract law is distributive in that it contributes to determining how much each of us has in terms of wealth, opportunities, the social bases of self-respect, or other.[274] It may perhaps seem that only a contract law that protects certain groups of weaker parties is distributive. However, the law maker's choice not to protect weaker parties, individually or as a group, through contract law is equally distributive. Any rule choice concerning contract law is likely to make certain groups in society better off than others.[275] There is no default—no distributively neutral baseline.[276]

3. Entitlement

Contractual rights and their protection are not just a good idea. A contractual claim is not meant merely to provide a judge in a contract dispute with a good argument that could be defeated by other, better arguments. Contract law—and more broadly, private law—determines what belongs to whom: not necessarily what should belong to whom, but what actually is mine and what is yours ('mine and thine'). Contract law secures entitlements in that it creates and protects claims and defences of persons vis-à-vis other persons. The absence of secure entitlements (i.e. the presence of legal uncertainty) may lead to instability and ultimately a 'condition of war of everyone against everyone'.[277]

The entitlement-creating aspect of contract law overlaps, in part, with the distributive nature of contract law, while the entitlement-protecting aspect is closely related to the coercive nature of contract law, which were both discussed earlier. Still, it makes sense to mention the relationship between contract law and entitlement as a separate

[272] M. Weber (G. Roth and C. Wittich, eds), *Economy and Society* ([first published 1921] 1978).

[273] Shiffrin (n. 110).

[274] Cf. the title of J. Bentham's *Constitutional Code* (1843), Chapter III: 'Civil or Distributive Law', and the opening sentence of J. Bentham, *Principles of the Civil Code* (1843): 'Every thing which the legislator is called upon to distribute among the members of the community, may be reduced to two classes: 1st, Rights. 2d, Obligations.'

[275] Kronman, 'Contract Law and Distributive Justice', 89 *Yale L.J.* (1980) 472.

[276] Murphy, 'The Practice of Promise and Contract' in G. Klass, G. Letsas, and P. Saprai (eds), *Philosophical Foundations of Contract Law* (2014), ch. 9.

[277] Hobbes (n. 195) ch. XIV.

characteristic as well (also in the context of critique), because even the absence of a fair distribution or of effective enforcement does not necessarily preclude the presence of entitlements. The fact that someone is extremely wealthy does not mean that she is not (and ought not to be) the owner of a certain specific thing. Nor does it preclude her generally from having valid contractual claims against other persons in society, even if these others are very poor. As to coercion, contractual rights may (and usually do) exist well before (and even in the total absence of) their enforcement. Thus, they can be placed, as receivables, on a business's balance sheet, their value may be subject to taxation, and the spontaneous performance by the promisor does not amount to an undue payment.

4. Standard

Private law provides a public standard for interpersonal conduct. Private law rules tell citizens how they should behave vis-à-vis each other and what kinds of conduct they may expect from each other in their private dealings. These rules, therefore, can be regarded as the parameters of permissible conduct in the market-place,[278] as rules of just conduct,[279] or even as the civil constitution.[280]

5. Facilitation

Contract law assists business persons and others in making credible commitments.[281] Thus, contract law facilitates transactions. Even if it is true that in healthy business relationships business solutions to disputes are preferred over legal solutions, and contracts are invoked only when the relationship is already breaking down, as a last resort,[282] then still much of the strategic action by business partners takes place in the shadow of the law, i.e. with an awareness in both parties that the contractual stipulations could be enforced. Moreover, many contracts are not relational at all. It is therefore likely that without the legally binding force of contract there would be fewer transactions. And it seems even plausible that without the legal enforceability of contracts an economy of the kind that we are familiar with could not function properly.[283] If contract law facilitates transactions, the question arises of what contracts should be facilitated by contract law. Should courts simply enforce any contract presented to them or should there be limits?

6. Dependence

As a practical matter, the impact of contract law on our lives is difficult to avoid (unlike e.g. the rules of tennis) because, especially since privatization, for many important aspects of our lives many of us depend, at least in part, on contracts—think of nutrition, utilities (including access to the internet), work, housing, health, education,

278 P. S. Atiyah, *Essays on Contract* (1986), at 53.
279 Hayek (n. 78) 123.
280 Carbonnier, 'Le code civil', in P. Nora (ed.), *Les lieux de mémoire*, Vol II (1986) 293, at 309.
281 R. Cooter and T. Ulen, *Law and Economics* (6th ed., 2012), at 286.
282 Macaulay, 'Non-Contractual Relations in Business: A Preliminary Study', 28 *American Sociological Review* (*Am. Sociol. Rev.*) (1963) 1.
283 A. Smith, *An Inquiry Into the Nature and Causes of the Wealth of Nations* (1776), at 910.

financial affairs, transport, communication, being a couple, leisure.[284] Again, our general dependence on contracts is contingent. It could be (and has been) different in other times and places.[285] Moreover, the specific dependence on—and generally the impact on our lives of—specific types of contracts may vary a great deal among individuals and social groups. However, this does not make it any less true that the dependence of many people on certain types of contracts, in some cases throughout their entire lives ('life time contracts'),[286] constitutes another respect in which the contract law we have profoundly affects our lives. Dependence on the contract, for parties in certain contractual relationships, may partly overlap with distributive implications, especially in terms of vulnerability and precarity, but cannot be reduced to it.

7. Multi-tasking

There exist obvious tensions among the various tasks and roles contract law has in our society and in each of our lives today. This image of a multi-tasking contemporary contract law inevitably raises normative questions concerning whether one of these roles should perhaps enjoy primacy, or whether maybe all these functions (if they are commensurable) can be reduced to one essential function or role of contract law. And if not, then the question will arise how a multi-functional contract law can, and should, remain functional in case the various roles of contract law pull in different directions. A modern theory of contract law, it seems, should try to respond to this fact of multiple contract law roles.

E. Contract Theories

There exists a broad variety of quite diverse contract theories. Most of the best-known contract theories are normative, at least in part. Normative (or prescriptive) contract law theories focus on contract law as it should be, in contrast to positive or descriptive theories that address contract law as it is and that try to understand or explain its existence and operation, for example in terms of its role in society.[287] Most normative theories are ideal theories. They provide accounts of what contract law should ideally look like, available to be used as an external standard for evaluating positive contract law (i.e. the contract law existing in a given society) or as a blueprint for contract law reform. Or, indeed, they aim to be recognized as already partly reflected in the legal materials once these are properly reconstructed; this latter role is particularly relevant for legal systems, such as common law jurisdictions, where legislative reform of contract law seems unlikely for the near future.[288] In particular, many normative

[284] Cf. Hesselink, 'Who Has a Stake in European Contract Law?', 3 *ERCL* (2005) 295.

[285] Cf. Dagan and Heller (n. 243) 43: 'in a world of profound interpersonal interdependence—that is, in our actual world—the ability legitimately to enlist other individuals to [their] goals is crucial, even if not analytically indispensable'.

[286] Reifner and Nogler (eds) (n. 249).

[287] An overview and critical discussion of such theories (and more) can be found in S. Grundmann, H.-W. Micklitz, and M. Renner, *Privatrechtstheorie* (2015).

[288] Cf. Unger (n. 169) 37: 'The ideal conceptions representing law as an imperfect approximation to an intelligible and defensible plan are thought to be partly already there in the law.'

contract theories are explicitly a part, an aspect, or an application of more general political theories, or can be traced back to one of these. Utilitarian, liberal, libertarian, communitarian, republican, and discourse theories of contract law, for instance, explain and justify contractual obligation on the basis of their more general values and worldviews, as we will see in Chapter 5 and throughout this book.

Thus, we are confronted with a diverse collection of normative contract theories, all well-articulated, but each with its own starting point, based on a conception of what is valuable in human life, an understanding of the human condition, or an ideal of the person. Indeed, the battles between contract theories, although fortunately entirely peaceful, sometimes remind us, to some extent, of religious wars.[289] Moreover, contract law rules can become applicable to anyone coming within their scope of application. This would not pose any problem if the world was organized as in Lukes' philosophical satire, *The Curious Enlightenment of Professor Caritat*,[290] where all the utilitarians live in Utilitaria, the communitarians in Communitaria, the libertarians in Libertaria, and—who knows—the liberal perfectionists in Daganistan. For such a world, a collection of appropriate monist contract law theories would be the perfect solution. However, in the real world, where we live in pluralist societies, the fact that the rules of contract law become applicable to anyone within its territorial scope means that this is likely also to include persons (perhaps many) who reject the ultimate value or ideal on which some of these theories are based. Given that contract law has an important impact on people's lives, in various ways, as we just saw, what, if anything, does this entail for the justification of contract law, both positive law and proposals for its reform? This question is perhaps particularly pressing for the basic structure of contract law, which seems determined, for an important part, by a legal community's answers to the kind of fundamental questions central to this book.

F. Monism versus Pluralism

When submitting six different political questions of European contract law to six different political theories with a view to improving and deepening our understanding of the political philosophy of European contract law, one might start out with quite different kinds of expectations. First, one might expect (or seek) to find one single theory to have the best answer (or the single right one) to all these questions. Alternatively,

[289] The French wars of religion are Rawls' core reference for pluralist societies' need for political liberalism. See e.g. Rawls (n. 150) xxiii–xxiv:

> During the wars of religion people were not in doubt about the nature of the highest good, or the basis of moral obligation in divine law. These things they thought they knew with the certainty of faith, as here their moral theology gave them complete guidance. The problem was rather: How is society even possible between those of different faiths? ... Thus, the historical origin of political liberalism (and of liberalism more generally) is the Reformation and its aftermath, with the long controversies over religious toleration in the sixteenth and seventeenth centuries.

Obviously, neither contract law nor contract theory had any part in those wars.

[290] S. Lukes, *The Curious Enlightenment of Professor Caritat: A Novel of Ideas* (2nd ed., 2009).

however, one may anticipate discovering some truth or merit in more than one of the theories and expect (or seek) a combination of these elements as the best outcome of the European contract law making process. Thus, the fact of the plurality of different normative political theories raises the question of whether European contract law should (or does) have a monist or pluralist normative basis.

The answer to this question could be regarded as a matter of different personalities and personal characters. This is what Berlin famously suggested in his essay *The Hedgehog and the Fox*.[291] Some writers and thinkers—the hedgehogs—see the world in terms of one big idea or principle (Plato, Proust), while others—the foxes—pursue many different ideas and values that could not necessarily be reduced to one (Aristotle, Montaigne).[292] However, this is certainly not the only possible way to address the matter. Indeed, the debate in political theory on monism versus pluralism[293]—and the related debate on political perfectionism versus political neutrality—has several other important dimensions. In other words, quite different types of arguments have been proposed in favour of and against positions taken in the pluralism debate. In particular, there exist epistemological, moral, and pragmatic arguments for and against political pluralism. Epistemological arguments focus on the possibility of knowing the truth about the objective value of certain ways of life or conceptions of the good (cognitivism versus non-cognitivism), for example because they exist out there, whether or not anyone happens to adhere to them (realism versus anti-realism). Moral arguments make claims concerning the equal rights (to equal concern and respect, or to justification) of people (individuals or groups) with different conceptions of the good. Pragmatic arguments relate to the possibility of a stable consensus on valuable ways of life and worldviews, which may not be within reach, while our society nevertheless seems to need at least some laws—both a constitution and ordinary laws, including perhaps a law of contract—here and now.

In the various debates on pluralisms—ethical, moral, political, constitutional, legal pluralism—three main positions can be distinguished: monism, constrained pluralism, and radical pluralism. Thus, with regard (European) contract law, first, there are those who argue that contract law is ultimately or essentially based on one single value or principle (monists). In their view, others who attribute a different ultimate or founding value to contract law, or a plurality of these, are wrong. On the other hand, there are those who believe that contract law is based on a composite of several values and principles, which are not necessarily commensurable, and among which there exists no hierarchy. As an example, think of the DCFR, which, according to its

291 I. Berlin, *The Hedgehog and the Fox: An Essay on Tolstoy's View of History* ([first published 1953] 2009). Almost equally famously, Dworkin took up the challenge and wrote the book *Justice for Hedgehogs* (2011), the summary of all his theories, presented, in authentically hedgehog vein as a coherent, seamless system of integrity and single right answers. For an earlier assimilation of Berlin's hedgehog/fox distinction to the monism versus pluralism debate in normative European contract law theory, see Hesselink, 'Five Political Ideas of European Contract Law', 7 *ERCL* (2011) 295.

292 The central question in the essay was what was Tolstoy: a hedgehog or a fox? Berlin's answer: a fox who aspired all his life to being a hedgehog.

293 The same applies for the debate on legal pluralism.

drafters, was based on the 'underlying principles' of freedom, security, justice, and efficiency.[294] Finally, there are those who argue that contract law is based on a composite or compound of values, which, however, is subject to—and constrained by—a conception of justice that is autonomous with regard to the various values. The pertinent understanding of justice may be more procedural or more substantive (principle of neutrality, principles of justice, discourse principle, the right to justification, public reason).

These are three main groups of positions with regard to the plurality of values, and in response to the presence of a variety of normative conceptions of (European) contract law: monism, unconstrained pluralism, and constrained pluralism. As a practical matter, monists will usually aim to find and implement the best or the right theory of (European) contract law as a matter of philosophical speculation and/or reconstruction of the legal materials; unconstrained pluralists will tend to argue for pure majoritarianism; and constrained pluralists will typically argue for a form of constitutional democracy. The question of the relationship between contract law and democracy will be central to Chapter 3.

The debate between monists, constrained pluralists, and unconstrained pluralists is closely connected to the debate on political perfectionism and political neutrality. Political perfectionists believe in objective values and in objectively more valuable ways of life. They argue that given the objective truth of their own worldview, there is nothing against the implementation of their conception of the good by the government, for example through (European) contract law. Others, however, are sceptical with regard to the objective truth of values and the notion that one way of life is inherently more worthy than others, and they doubt (on epistemological, moral, or pragmatic grounds) the possibility for political institutions legitimately to determine these true values and their implications. They therefore claim that the state should remain neutral with regard to different conceptions of the good.

Concerning political neutrality, further distinctions can be drawn. First, there is the difference between neutrality of consequences, neutrality of aims, and neutrality of justifications. A precept of neutrality of consequences means that the state should not do anything that favours one way of life over another. That is a very demanding principle (if full compliance is at all possible). Neutrality of aims means that legislation must not be motivated by or in terms of partisan agendas (neutral legislative intent). Neutrality of justifications means that, whatever the legislative intent or the consequences of specific legislation, the state ensures (especially through its main institutions) that society is organized in a way that can be justified with reasons that no one can reasonably reject (public reasons). Moreover, views also differ with regard to the scope of political neutrality, asking where the government is required to remain neutral with regard to different conceptions of the good: only when it comes to constitutional essentials; in all constitutional matters; or with regard to the entire basic structure of society, all core institutions, all core rights, or even all legislation?

[294] DCFR, at 47. The main relevance of the catalogue lies in Art I.–1:102 (1) DCFR, pursuant to which the rules of the DCFR 'are to be interpreted and developed ... in accordance with their objectives and the principles underlying them'.

Even though the question of pluralism is more central to some political theories than others, each of them has a view on the remaining ground for its competitors, so to speak,[295] as we will see throughout this book. Clearly, from the point of view of monist theories, policies and laws informed by a plurality or compound of values and principles, as proposed by pluralist theories, are just instances of partial compliance, with the only specificity that in this case the less than full compliance is principled.

[295] Cf. J. Raz, *Ethics in the Public Domain* (1994), at 79: 'every (comprehensive) moral theory must address the question: How are those who disbelieve it to be judged and treated?'

3
Democratic Basis

1. Introduction

A. Contract Scholarship's Dirty Little Secret

Should (European) contract law have a democratic basis? This apparently straightforward question gives rise to a series of further questions: What do we mean by a democratic basis? Is this an all-or-nothing question or rather a matter of degree? What would be the alternatives to a democratic contract law? And so on. In considering the possible answers that are offered by—or can be derived from—leading contemporary political theories, hopefully we will obtain a clearer grasp of what we mean when we say that our contract law is democratic or, as the case may be, undemocratic, and why that matters.

We explore these questions against the backdrop of what Unger referred to as the dirty little secret of contemporary jurisprudence, i.e. its discomfort with democracy.[1] If anywhere, the discomfort is probably strongest in private law. Private law theorists produce blueprints for complete systems of contract law, while doctrinal private law scholars offer comprehensive drafts for reform. Among these scholars, there exists widespread scepticism, if not outright anxiety, about the idea of their proposals ending up in the hands of democratic legislatures. Private law exceptionalism has a long pedigree, partly perhaps because modern private law preceded modern democracy.

Discomfort with democratic contract law should not be confused, of course, with adherence to a different conception of democratic law making than the one Unger (or others) would subscribe to. In particular, democratic law making should not be identified (certainly not as a premise to our inquiry) with legislation.[2] Therefore, more concretely this chapter also explores whether any existing discomfort with democratic contract law making—whichever institution(s) that would involve—is justified from the perspective of leading contemporary political theories. Nor are all theorist and doctrinal scholars sceptical about a democratic private law. Indeed, the assumption of many seems to be that private law is law and, therefore, simply has to be democratic. Still, this private law anti-exceptionalist stance not only often remains implicit, but also its implications have not always been thought through fully and consistently for private law. Put differently, much of private law theory has not fully internalized its

[1] R. Unger, *What Should Legal Analysis Become?* (1996), at 72. Endorsed by J. Waldron, *Law and Disagreement* (1999), at 8. Similar, R. Forst, *Justification and Critique: Towards a Critical Theory of Politics* (2014), at 4: 'All too often political philosophy continues to live in a pre-democratic era. It accords priority to teleological values which are supposed to ground a just or good social order, where those who are subjected to this order do not feature in it as authors.'

[2] But see Waldron (n. 1) 9, remarking that contemporary philosophers of law are 'intoxicated with courts'.

Justifying Contract in Europe: Political Philosophies of European Contract Law. First Edition. Martijn W. Hesselink, Oxford University Press. © Martijn W. Hesselink 2021. DOI: 10.1093/oso/9780192843654.003.0003

democratic commitments. Therefore, another task of this chapter will be to tease out different democratic views of contract law.

B. Judges, Legislators, Professors, and Regulatory Silos

As a starting point for our normative inquiry, we can take the historical-comparative observation that in various times and places different actors have been the main protagonists in contract law making. These have included, in particular, courts, legislators, legal academics, and, most recently, (other) technical experts. The original common law of contract was entirely judge-made. It is alive and well today, but on important subjects, such as frustration of contract, unfair contract terms, the rights of third parties, and consumer rights it has also been complemented, and replaced in part, by various statutes.[3] In civil law jurisdictions, the law of contract law is contained chiefly in the civil codes, most of which were enacted by legislatures, which does not necessarily mean that they have always been democratic.[4] Moreover, in many civil law jurisdictions courts rather than the legislature are the main protagonists in contract law making. In several countries, legal academics have been heavily involved, as legal experts, in the drafting of contract law codifications and reforms that in some cases were merely rubber-stamped by the legislator. More recently, sectoral technical experts in finance, energy, transport, and food have played a key role, within what have been referred to as 'regulatory silos',[5] in setting regulatory standards, usually a mix of private and public, with a varying regulatory impact on contractual relationships, especially in newly privatized sectors of the economy. Thus, updating Van Caeneghem's famous typology, we can refer to the main contemporary actors in contract law making as judges, legislators, professors, and regulatory silos.[6] Our normative question, then, is which of them—or which combination of them—ideally ought to be our contract law makers today?

C. Legitimacy

Sometimes the addressees of contract law rules may want to challenge these rules because of the way they came about, either rejecting the authority of the contract law maker or objecting to the procedure the law maker adopted. In other words, they may want to question the legitimacy of the contract law applicable to them. This raises the question of whether the different possible contract law makers are equally legitimate.

[3] See the Law Reform (Frustrated Contracts) Act 1943, Unfair Contract Terms Act 1977, Contracts (Rights of Third Parties) Act 1999, and Consumer Rights Act 2015, respectively.

[4] Think only of the several civil codes that were adopted in Europe before universal suffrage or under authoritarian regimes.

[5] See Micklitz and Svetiev, 'The Transformation(s) of Private Law', in H.-W. Micklitz, Y. Svetiev, and G. Comparato (eds), *European Regulatory Private Law—The Paradigms Tested*, EUI Working papers, LAW 2014/04, 69, at 78.

[6] Cf. R. C. Van Caeneghem, *Judges, Legislators and Professors: Chapters in European Legal History* (1987).

The answer depends on what we mean by legitimacy.[7] Moreover, while some political theorists understand legitimacy and justice as two independent concepts, others, as we will see, regard legitimacy as dependent on justice. In either case, several more specific questions arise concerning the legitimacy of (European) contract law making. Is the involvement of one specific contract law maker required to the exclusion of all others, or would some kind of combination (a joint effort) be optimal? Is the horizontal division of labour between different contract law making institutions chiefly a question of comparing existing alternatives in terms of their likely good and bad consequences, or also a question of justice? Are the existing divergencies between countries in this regard an entirely normal and valuable consequence of cultural diversity or does the legitimacy of private law making depend on more universal principles? Or, indeed, is it perhaps entirely irrelevant which law maker implements a blueprint for contract law reform as long as it is a text of high quality in terms, for example, of justice, autonomy, efficiency, or tradition? Is it perhaps a mistake to think that contract law needs any democratic legitimation at all—a confusion of private with public autonomy, given that contract law will always become applicable to a person only as a result of her own choice to conclude a contract ('self-legislation')? As we will see in this chapter, some political theories are more concerned about some of these specific questions than about others.

D. What Democracy?

If, indeed, a democratic basis for (European) contract law is required from a justice or a legitimacy point of view, then the next question is what this entails. In other words, what would amount to a sufficiently or fully democratic contract law? Would a majority vote in parliament suffice? Or is much more required, for example inclusive deliberation and active participation from citizens in civil society? Or, negatively, is it the absence of distortional influence from certain players who lack a clear democratic mandate (e.g. self-empowering bureaucrats or economically powerful corporations) that matters most?

Think of the recent example of the contract law reform in France in 2016,[8] which was adopted by presidential decree.[9] Was it fully legitimated by the fact that the President of the Republic was elected directly by French citizens and that the government

[7] Legitimacy refers to the basis for the validity (*Geltung*) of norms or authority. For a social scientist, it refers to what makes norm compliance (empirically) more likely. See e.g. M. Weber, *Economy and Society*, Vol. I ([first published 1921] 1978), at § 6; Scharpf, 'Legitimacy in the Multilevel European Polity', 1 *European Political Science Review* (2009) 173, at 173. For a moral theorist it refers to the reasons why the relevant social norm, legal rule, court ruling, etc. *should* guide human action. See e.g. J. Habermas, *Between Facts and Norms: Contributions to a Discourse Theory of Law and Democracy* (1996), at 135; Waldron, 'The Core of the Case Against Judicial Review', 115 *Yale L.J.* (2006) 1346. Here we will be concerned mainly with the latter (i.e. normative) concept of legitimacy.

[8] Ordonnance n°2016-131 du 10 février 2016 portant réforme du droit des contrats, du régime général et de la preuve des obligations.

[9] See Art. 38(1) French Constitution. However, see also Art. 34 in conjunction with Art. 24(1), which seem to suggest that at least the fundamental principles of contract law must be determined by an act of parliament.

adopting the decree[10] responds to the elected parliament,[11] or because the requirement for presidential decrees to be ratified subsequently by parliament[12] sufficiently ensured democratic control? Or, on the contrary, was it deeply undemocratic, as the Senate held unanimously,[13] on the grounds that the reform of the law of contract was too important[14] and too political[15] to be withheld from Parliament, and that in practice the likelihood of meaningful *ex post* democratic control and amendment of a reform already entered into force, would be minimal?[16]

As another example, was the way in which the European Commission organized the process towards a 'Common Frame of Reference', which was meant to provide the basis for a legal instrument on European contract law, far too technocratic and therefore wholly lacking legitimacy, as claimed by the Social Justice Group among others?[17] Or, was it, on the contrary, one of the most inclusive consultations in European legislative history, as the Commission kept emphasizing relentlessly?[18] And consider the withdrawal by the (unelected) European Commission of the Common European Sales Law proposal (CESL),[19] encouraged by an unpublished letter from six (out of 28) Member States to the Commission,[20] even after it had been adopted in first reading by the European Parliament by a vast majority and after an intense political debate[21]—was this a troublingly undemocratic move?

More generally with regard to the EU context, does stakeholder involvement—a recurrent practice in EU contract law making—make contract law making become more democratic (because various interests are considered) or less democratic (because the lobbyists of economically powerful stakeholders will always be the most effective)? And if 80 per cent of European legislation passes through 'trialogue', i.e. negotiations between the Commission, Parliament, and Council that take place behind closed

[10] See Art. 38(2) French Constitution.

[11] See Art. 20(3) and Art. 49 French Constitution.

[12] Art. 38(2) French Constitution.

[13] Rapport n°288 (2013–2014) de M. Thani Mohamed Soilihi, fait au nom de la commission des lois.

[14] See ibid. 19: 'Le code civil est l'un des textes fondateurs du droit français ... L'importance de l'enjeu semble exiger que le Parlement s'en saisisse, afin qu'un débat public puisse avoir lieu.'

[15] Ibid. 21: 'La réforme du droit des obligations pose des questions politiques majeures, qu'il revient au seul Parlement de trancher'.

[16] Ibid. 16 and 22–23. The Senate appealed to the Constitutional Council which, however, sided with the government, holding that the delegation measure was sufficiently precise in its scope and objectives. See Conseil Constitutionnel, decision n° 2015-710 DC of 12 February 2015, at para. 5.

[17] See Study Group on Social Justice in European Private Law, 'Social Justice in European Contract Law: A Manifesto', 10 *ELJ* (2004) 653, at 658.

[18] See EU Justice Commissioner and Vice-President of the European Commission V. Reding, 'The Next Steps Towards a European Contract Law for Businesses and Consumers', Keynote Speech at the Conference Towards a European Contract Law, Leuven, 3 June 2011, at 9–10.

[19] See Commission Communication to the European Parliament, the Council, the European Economic and Social Committee and the Committee of the Regions, 'Commission Work Programme 2015, A New Start' (COM(2014) 910 final), Annex 2: List of Withdrawals or Modifications of Pending Proposals, at 12, proposal no. 60.

[20] Letter of 18 November 2014 from the Ministers of Justice of Austria, Finland, France, Germany, the Netherlands and the United Kingdom to Vera Jourová, the Commissioner for Justice, Consumers and Gender Equality.

[21] European Parliament legislative resolution of 26 February 2014 on the Proposal for a Regulation of the European Parliament and of the Council on a Common European Sales Law (COM(2011)0635—C7-0329/2011—2011/0284(COD)) (P7_TA-PROV(2014)0159). There were 416 votes in favour, 159 against, and 65 abstentions.

doors, can the EU's 'ordinary legislative procedure' (where the European Parliament is co-legislator), through which most EU contract law is adopted today, still count as truly democratic?[22]

As a final example, think of the claim, made by some theorists (and endorsed also by non-theorists), in common law jurisdictions, that judge-made law is legitimate, not in spite of being undemocratic, but because it is democratic. This is based on the idea that the common law has some unique democratic characteristics, especially in terms of agenda setting, resolving problems, and providing remedies exactly there where they truly matter,[23] thus empowering the people much more directly than would be the case through abstract legislation.[24] That claim is distinct from the idea that the application by courts of abstract rules to concrete cases will inevitably imply a degree of law making, especially in the case of open-ended standards such as good faith and fair dealing.[25]

These examples, and others that we will see, illustrate that the answer to our question of whether contract law should have a democratic basis depends not only on political principles but also on what we mean by a democratic basis, both in general and specifically with regard to private law, i.e. the law that deals with horizontal relationships.

E. Voting and Deliberation

A further question is whether democratic basis and legitimacy are only a matter of institutions or also a matter of procedure and perhaps even of content. Once we have sorted out which institution is the more legitimate (European) contract law maker (or which combination of several institutions), does that settle and exhaust the questions of a democratic basis and of legitimacy? Perhaps legitimate democratic law making requires much more. Maybe the political debate is not truly democratic unless it has a certain deliberative quality, for example when the participants aim to convince each other with better arguments. That would turn our attention to the quality of the debate and of the arguments. It raises the question of whether the basis of European contract law can be truly democratic if a parliamentary vote was grounded in arguments that should not have a place in democracy, for example because these arguments fail to treat all citizens as equals. Conversely, if the quality of the debate and arguments is so important, perhaps other institutions that display a high quality of argumentation, such as courts in their rulings, could also boast some democratic credentials—maybe even better credentials than certain legislatures? What is at stake here is the difference between vote-centred and talk-centred conceptions of democracy.

[22] Cf. Cooper, 'Where European Democracy Goes to Die: EU Leaders Are Fast-Tracking Legislation. Critics Say Lawmaking Is Pushed Out of Public View', *Politico*, 7 December 2016, available at www.politico.eu/article/where-european-democracy-goes-to-die-european-parliament/ (last visited 2 July 2020).

[23] On situation-sense, see K. N. Llewellyn, *The Common Law Tradition: Deciding Appeals* (1960), at 121 ff.

[24] See e.g. J. C. P. Goldberg and B. C. Zipursky, *Recognizing Wrongs* (2020), at 127–128, who assimilate the right to civil recourse to the right to vote, understanding both as political rights ensured in a liberal democracy.

[25] See Hesselink, 'The Concept of Good Faith', in A. S. Hartkamp *et al.* (eds), *Towards a European Civil Code* (4th ed., 2011) 619.

F. Power Struggle

As a matter of realism, i.e. beyond ideal theory, the answers to the normative questions of the need for a democratic basis for (European) contract law depends, at least in part, on the available or conceivable alternatives, none of which will be perfect.[26] Therefore, the question can also be rephrased in terms of institutional comparison: when it comes to contract law making, what is the appropriate division of labour between the different political institutions (and other public and private actors)?

As a further matter of realism, the horizontal division of labour with regard to the making of private law is not merely a question of detached institutional comparison: it has also been a battleground in the struggle for power between judges, legislators, and professors, and, we could add today, technical experts, with different victors in different times and places.[27] In other words, any outcome of the power struggle—any resulting division of labour—is going to produce winners and losers.

G. Constitutionalization

There is the further question, within each jurisdiction, of the proper vertical division of labour, in particular whether private law making should be subject to some form of judicial review, for example by a constitutional court. In addition to this institutional dimension, the constitutionalization of (European) private law has the obvious substantive dimension of whether democratic decisions should be constrained, through judicial review, by constitutional rights and values. The German experience has been paradigmatic in this regard. After World War II, the Federal Constitutional Court (*Bundesverfassungsgericht* or *BVerG*), started reviewing the 1900 *BGB* (the German civil code) in the light of the new post-War constitution. Or, to be more precise, it demanded from the civil courts a re-interpretation of that code, in particular of its open-textured 'general clauses' on good morals and good faith in the light of the value system enshrined in the constitution and in the rights protected by it ('indirect horizontal effect'). In principle, the impact of the constitution might extend to any field of private law and any provision of the civil code, thus effectively transforming private law into applied constitutional law.[28] It meant the end of the (perceived) autonomy of private law as a self-contained value system. In practice, this meant that the *Bundesgerichtshof*, the supreme ordinary court in civil and criminal matters, became subject, in its interpretation of the *BGB*, to review from the *BVerfG* in terms of the constitution, in particular fundamental rights. In other words, in terms of the question that concerns us here, the constitutional court became the ultimate authority—the supreme law maker in more realist terms—on all private law matters where constitutional values might be at stake, which, as already stated, in principle could include any subject of private law.

[26] N. K. Komesar, *Imperfect Alternatives: Choosing Institutions in Law, Economics, and Public Policy* (1994).

[27] Van Caeneghem (n. 6).

[28] The idea is well expressed by the notion of the 'total constitution', introduced by Kumm, 'Who Is Afraid of the Total Constitution? Constitutional Rights and Principles and the Constitutionalization of Private Law', 7 *German Law Journal* (2006) 341.

At the EU level, with regard to the horizontal effects of constitutional rights and values, the situation has not yet reached this stage. However, expectations are that the Charter of Fundamental Rights of the European Union may have a similar impact upon EU private law, especially on the interpretation and review of secondary EU law, i.e. directives and regulations (indirect horizontal effect). Moreover, within the scope of application of EU law (e.g. directives), constitutional principles may also have direct horizontal effect.[29] Several leading EU law cases come to mind, which were in fact contract cases.[30] In some of these cases, such as *Mangold*, the ruling of the Court of Justice was quite controversial. The question of whether private law making should take place at the national or the European level (or the regional or the global one), i.e. the vertical division of labour within the EU with regard to contract law making, will be the subject of Chapter 4. However, the activist law making by the Court raises the specific question—even if the Europeanization of private law is generally accepted—of whether it is legitimate for a European *court* to set aside (either formally or substantively, via the duty to interpret national law in a manner consistent with European law) statutes that were adopted by the (national) democratically elected legislator. This question concerns what have been referred to as 'diagonal conflicts' between different law making institutions within the EU.[31] Several observers believe that the Court of Justice wholly lacked political legitimacy in these landmark cases. Others, however, see specific democratic potential, deliberative or experimental, in the constitutionalization of (European) private law.[32]

H. The Core Question

Quite a broad variety of conceptions (or models) of democracy exists.[33] Even limiting ourselves to those proposed by the six contemporary political theories central to this book, it will be impossible, as a practical matter, to discuss critically all the various aspects introduced here of our core question, i.e. whether contract law should be

[29] See generally on the constitutionalization of European contract law, the contributions to S. Grundmann (ed.), *Constitutional Values and European Contract Law* (2008) and to H. Collins (ed.), *European Contract Law and the Charter of Fundamental Rights* (2017).

[30] E.g. Case C-106/89, *Marleasing SA v. La Comercial Internacional de Alimentacion SA* (EU:C:1990:395); Case C-91/92, *Paola Faccini Dori v Recreb Srl* (EU:C:1994:292); Case C-240/98 to Case C-244/98, *Océano Grupo Editorial SA v. Rocio Murciano Quintero (and Others)* (EU:C:2000:346); Case C-397/01, *Bernhard Pfeiffer and Others v. Deutsches Rotes Kreuz, Kreisverband Waldshut eV* (EU:C:2004:584); Case C-144/04, *Werner Mangold v. Rüdiger Helm* (EU:C:2005:709); and Case C-555/07, *Seda Kücükdeveci v. Swedex GmbH & Co. KG* (EU:C:2010:21).

[31] See Joerges, '"Deliberative Political Processes" Revisited: What Have We Learnt About the Legitimacy of Supranational Decision-Making', 44 *Journal of Common Market Studies (JCMS)* (2006) 779, at 794. By definition, diagonal conflicts between the European Court and national legislatures in cases such as *Mangold* have both a vertical and a horizontal dimension. Since the critique of the Court's dealing with such cases is usually presented mainly as a critique of the EU and, crucially, the main proposed solutions tend to be in the direction of renationalization, these diagonal conflicts will be discussed more fully in Chapter 4.

[32] Gerstenberg, 'Constitutional Reasoning in Private Law: the Role of the CJEU in Adjudicating Unfair Terms in Consumer Contracts', 21 *ELJ* (2015) 599; Mak, 'First or Second Best? Judicial Law-Making in European Private Law', *Centre for the Study of European Contract Law Working Paper Series No. 2016-12*, available at SSRN: https://ssrn.com/abstract=2847586 (last visited 2 July 2020).

[33] For a general, historical overview, see D. Held, *Models of Democracy* (3rd ed., 2006).

democratic, from the perspectives of all the political theories under consideration in this book. Nor is this necessary. For if we let each theory speak for itself, as it were, we will find that each of them will emphasize some aspects, but not others, as the normative core of our question.

The main focus here will be on (European) contract law. However, most of the arguments in this chapter (and the next) will be pertinent more widely to the relationship between private law and democracy.

2. Libertarian

A. The Priority of Liberty

Libertarians and neoliberals have not always been the most valiant guardians of democracy. Their strong focus on property rights and economic freedoms seems to have made certain libertarians tolerant towards the violation of other rights, including the political rights essential to a functioning democracy. For example, Hayek travelled several times to Pinochet's Chile to admire its free market laboratory. He wrote to Margaret Thatcher urging her to use Pinochet's model for a reform of Britain's Keynesian economy.[34] Subsequently, he visited China to assist Deng Xiaoping in transforming the Chinese economy into a market economy, but without any democratic reform. In other words, unlike socialist planned economies, authoritarian regimes ensuring economic freedom do not seem to count as examples of the totalitarian regimes that Hayek warned about in *The Road to Serfdom*.[35] Similarly, Friedman, invited to China by Deng Xiaoping, explained to an audience of officials that Hong Kong, despite having no democracy, was freer than the US, since its government interfered less with the economy.[36] In Europe, the ordoliberal ideal for the EU was formulated in terms of a 'private law society' and an 'economic constitution' rather than first and foremost as a democracy.[37] And, more recently, in response to the financial and economic crisis, the neoliberal agenda of austerity, privatization, and market liberalization 'reforms' was led by the technocrats of the 'troika' (European Commission, European Central Bank, and IMF), without much democratic deliberation, and in spite of the massive public outcry in all the countries subjected to the 'reforms'. In summary, neoliberal successes in the fight for economic freedom, free markets, and a minimal state in the name of liberty seem to have come, more than once, at the expense of political freedoms and democracy. However, it would be unfair (indeed demagogical) to suggest that all libertarians and neoliberals are authoritarians, or that libertarianism is intrinsically hostile towards democracy. Clearly, 'shock therapy', as Klein calls it, is not the

[34] N. Klein, *The Shock Doctrine: The Rise of Disaster Capitalism* (2007), at 84.

[35] F. A. Hayek, *The Road to Serfdom* ([first published 1944] 2005). See also F. A. Hayek, *The Constitution of Liberty* (1978) and F. A. Hayek, *The Fatal Conceit; The Errors of Socialism* (1988).

[36] Klein (n. 34) 185.

[37] Böhm, 'Privatrechtsgesellschaft und Marktwirtschaft', 17 *ORDO: Jahrbuch für die Ordnung von Wirtschaft und Gesellschaft* (1966) 75.

only conceivable way of pursuing a libertarian agenda.[38] Also more principled cases have been made for limiting the realm of democracy with a view to preserving individual liberty and private ownership. According to a principled libertarian view, private rights are not up for political deliberation: determining private rights and remedies is not a matter of the *volonté générale*, however defined. In other words, from a libertarian point of view, democratic private law might be—and frequently has been in fact—illegitimate.

B. Negative Liberty

The libertarian scepticism (or downright suspicion) towards a democratic contract law is best explained from their particular understanding of freedom, i.e. freedom as non-interference, in particular (but not exclusively) the absence of interventions from the government.[39] In a famous essay, Berlin warned that the ever further expansion of positive liberty (collective self-determination) will gradually reduce, and may ultimately undermine and suffocate, negative liberty (the freedom from government).[40] The argument was an echo from Benjamin Constant's vindication in the nineteenth century of the 'liberty of the moderns' (individual freedom) over the 'liberty of the ancients' (political freedom).[41] The idea is that we should be free to make our own choices (and our own mistakes), subject to our moral duty to respect the equal liberty of others, without interference by the state, *including* the interference by democratic rule. In summary, anticipating the Habermasian distinction that will be discussed further later (in Section 7.C), according to a sustained libertarian case against a democratic law of contract, contract law emphatically is a matter of 'private autonomy', not of 'public autonomy'.

C. Natural Law

It is a defining characteristic of most libertarian or neoliberal theories of private law in general, and of contract law specifically, that they regard private law as essentiality concerned with the legal protection of already existing entitlements, and the correction of wrongful interferences by others with a person's rights, by making remedies available that aim to restore the status quo ante. Thus, among the very few tasks that the 'minimal state' is allowed to fulfil from a libertarian point of view the 'enforcement of contracts' figures quite prominently.[42] Central to all libertarian theories, therefore,

[38] Still, it is the core claim of Klein's book *The Shock Doctrine* (n. 34), substantiated by many documented examples throughout the world, that libertarian economic reforms have been introduced in situations where democracy was 'off-guard' (i.e. post-revolution, post-tsunami, post-crisis, etc.).

[39] Cf. M. Foucault, *Naissance de la biopolitique: cours au Collège de France 1978–1979* (2004), at 78: 'ce qu'on pourrait appeler l'anti-étatisme ou la phobie d'Etat'.

[40] Berlin, 'Two Concepts of Liberty', in H. Hardy (ed.), *Liberty* (2002) 166.

[41] B. Constant, *De la liberté des Anciens comparée a celle des modernes* ([first published 1874] 2010).

[42] R. Nozick, *Anarchy, State and Utopia* ([first published 1974] 2006), at 302.

is the idea of pre-legal and pre-institutional, and indeed pre-societal, entitlements.[43] Characteristic is the opening sentence of Nozick's seminal book *Anarchy, State and Utopia*: 'Individuals have rights, and there are things no person or group may do to them (without violating their rights).'[44] In Nozick's view, property is an absolute, pre-positive right. Whatever the positive law says, I am morally entitled to what I own if I obtained it from the rightful owner, who, in turn, got it from the previous rightful owner, and so on. The idea of the full justification of ownership by acquisition through free exchange leads back logically to the first owner and, thus, raises the question of initial acquisition. For his answer to that question Nozick relies on the natural law theory of Locke who argued that the appropriation of a parcel of land, by improving it, does not prejudice others as long as there is 'still enough, and as good left in common for others'.[45] Nozick similarly claims that 'the crucial point is whether appropriation of an unowned object worsens the situation of others'. He concludes, surprisingly, that it usually does not, and that 'the free operation of a market system will not actually run afoul of the Lockean proviso'.[46]

Even if the 'Lockean proviso', or some similar notion, could provide a solid basis for justice in acquisition under contemporary conditions of scarcity and trade where everything has a price,[47] or if there was another convincing foundation for natural, pre-institutional entitlements, then that would still leave much of the determination of contract law open, because the notion of justice in transfer, when interpreted as formally as possible (as libertarians require), remains highly indeterminate. None of the usual limits to contract enforcement, on familiar grounds such as threats or fraud, follow naturally from the notion of justice in transfer; nor is it natural that other, equally familiar doctrines like mistake, misrepresentation, undue influence, unconscionability, and unfair exploitation should be excluded from contract law. As Raz put it (with reference to Nozick's understanding that contracts obtained through coercion and deceit should be excluded from enforceability), 'We do not find in any of Nozick's writings much of an explanation as to why some means of getting people to act are allowed, while others are not'.[48] But if there is no natural or formal way of determining what justice in transfer requires then libertarian private law essentialism becomes a chimera. Moreover, and most relevant here, this also substantially weakens the libertarian (Nozickian) case against democratic contract law. If we want to protect entitlements we will have to find some other rational way of determining the details and limits of contractual obligation. And given that we are talking about the conditions for the exercise of state power, would a democratic process not be a rational way

[43] Nozick (ibid. 199) explicitly rejects Rawls's theory of justice as a 'manna-from-heaven model'. Instead, he argues, 'things come into being already held', ibid. 219.

[44] Ibid. ix. See also the closing lines (at 333–334), which run as follows: 'The minimal state treats us as inviolate individuals, who may not be used in certain ways by others as means or tools or instruments or resources; it treats us as persons having individual rights with the dignity this constitutes.... How *dare* any state or group of individuals do more. Or less.' (emphasis in original)

[45] J. Locke, *Two Treatises of Government* (P. Laslett, ed.) ([first published 1689] 1994), Second Treatise, § 27 (at 288) and § 33 (at 291).

[46] Nozick (n. 42) 175, 182.

[47] Cf. Varden, 'The Lockean "Enough-and-as-Good" Proviso: An Internal Critique', 9 *Journal of Moral Philosophy* (2012) 410.

[48] J. Raz, *The Morality of Freedom* (1986), at 274.

of determining these matters, also from a libertarian point of view? This was conceded to some extent by another prominent libertarian.

D. Rules of Just Conduct

While many libertarians, ordoliberals, and other neoliberals have had misgivings about the priority of the democratic constitution over private law,[49] not all libertarians reject democratic private law. In Hayek's view, unrestricted government was the problem, not democracy.[50] Hayek even regarded private law as the area where democracy has its main role to play. He thought that democracy should not be about taxation and public spending,[51] but about what he called 'rules of just conduct', i.e. the rules of private law (which should include criminal law, just as in Roman times). Ideally, private law rules should be developed on a case-by-case basis by a common law judge on the basis of established custom. However, sometimes judicial law making is too slow and leaves important gaps. These gaps, then, should be filled by the democratic legislator. Still, crucially, this should not become a matter of political bargaining between different stakeholders and political parties with their various ideologies.[52] Rather, in Hayek's view 'rules of just conduct' should be formal and abstract rules that apply equally to everyone. And what the democratic legislators should do is to find rules that are best fit for that purpose, not the rules they personally prefer. In order to assure the impartiality of the legislator, Hayek developed a rather curious democratic system, which he described in some detail in his outline for a model constitution.[53] What is needed, he thought, is an 'assembly of men and women elected at a relatively mature age for fairly long periods'.[54] The members of this 'assembly of representatives' should consist of 'persons who already had made their reputation in the ordinary pursuits of life'.[55] They should not be re-eligible but should remain publicly employed, for example as a lay judge. The election should take place by asking each group of people

[49] As Habermas (n. 7) 396, phrased it for the German context: 'The end of the substantive priority of private law over constitutional law, which sealed the de facto dissolution of an ideologically maintained "private law society" (Franz Böhm), has been perceived by German civil-law jurisprudence as an "overpowering" of private law by principles of public law and as the "destruction" of the independent edifice of a unified legal system.'

[50] See Hayek, 'Postscript: Why I Am Not a Conservative', in F. A. Hayek, *The Constitution of Liberty* (1978) 341, at 348.

[51] Cf. F. A. Hayek, *Law, Legislation and Liberty: A New Statement of the Liberal Principles of Justice and Political Economy*, Vol. III *The Political Order of a Free People* ([first published 1979] 2003), at 4: 'is there really no other way for people to maintain a democratic government than by handing over unlimited power to a group of elected representatives whose decisions must be guided by the exigencies of a bargaining process in which they bribe a sufficient number of voters to support an organized group of themselves numerous enough to outvote the rest?'

[52] Generally speaking, libertarians often regard majority decisions as problematic; their ideal is unanimity. See M. Friedman, *Capitalism and Freedom* (1962), at 23: 'To the liberal, the appropriate means are free discussion and voluntary co-operation, which implies that any form of coercion is inappropriate. The ideal is unanimity among responsible individuals achieved on the basis of free and full discussion.' This seems difficult to reconcile with his support for certain authoritarian regimes.

[53] Hayek (n. 51) 113–115.

[54] Ibid. 113.

[55] Ibid.

of the same age once in their lives (e.g. in the calendar year of their 45th birthday) to select from their midst representatives that should serve in the resulting legislature for 15 years. This senate would not be a very busy body. In contrast to such a legislative body, our current legislatures, which are organized along party lines which, in turn, often represent vested interests,[56] may be well equipped for 'government' (i.e. notably the administration of public resources) but are completely unfit to enact what Hayek regarded as true legislation, i.e. 'rules of just conduct', which notably include the rules of private law.

E. Distributive Justice

The libertarian case against democratic contract law is closely related (but not limited) to their case against a distributive (in their terminology, '*re*-distributive') role for private law. Private rights are entitlements that are not up for egalitarian redistribution by Parliament. The same applies for the libertarian claim that private law should be formal, i.e. without regard to any of the specific characteristics of the parties at hand, such as their unequal bargaining power, even though it is well known that in our societies substantive inequalities are structural in certain types of contractual relationships. Neoliberal private lawyers in Europe rejecting the *Materialisierung* of private law look back with some nostalgia to the 'classical' age of late nineteenth-century contract law that was based on formal notions of party equality and freedom of contract.[57] We will discuss the libertarian case against distributive motives in contract law making in detail in Chapter 6. Here, we note that such motives constitute one of the main misgivings libertarians have about the notion of a democratic private law.

Sometimes, libertarian contract theorists simply ignore the already existing 'materialized' contract law, important parts of which are statutory, for example when they offer an account or justification only of 'general contract law' or 'the common law of contract'. However, that strategy amounts to a denial of the reality of democratic contract law as it is in place, also in common law jurisdictions. Atiyah had already made this very clear more than three decades ago, when he remarked that although the libertarian theorist 'may wish to avoid discussing statutory provisions, insisting that he wishes only to defend the common law, a theory of contract law which has no room for statutes involving such fundamental ideas as [contained in the Unfair Contract Terms Act 1977, among others] would be gravely deficient.'[58] Something very similar can be said, today, with regard to European contract law. As we will see, libertarian theories have no room for much of the EU contract law *acquis*, keeping their focus on national general contract law. Therefore, conversely, from the perspective of EU contract law,

[56] Think of a political party like 50PLUS, for example, currently represented in the Parliament of the Netherlands, which has the explicit aim of taking care of the interests of people over the age of 50.

[57] Cf. P. S. Atiyah, *Essays on Contract* (1986), Essay 6: 'The Liberal Theory of Contract Law' 121, at 121: 'The liberal theory of contract is close to, if not indeed wholly identical with, the classical theory of contract'.

[58] Ibid. 129.

libertarian contract law theories in fact amount to an agenda for a very radical reform (or, indeed, restoration).[59]

F. An Internal Market Shielded from Democracy

According to ordoliberals, the EU does not need to be democratic because its whole point is to provide us with an internal market where free competition and free movement are ensured—shielded off from democratic politics, which deals with distributive issues that should be addressed, if at all, by national governments.[60] The ordoliberal idea of an economic constitution (on which more in Chapter 4), significantly reduces the scope for democracy, especially at the EU level, and, therefore, also for a democratic European contract law. On this view, democracy is not necessary, because the internal market only serves the purpose of protecting individual freedom.[61] As Somma puts it, 'even if ordoliberalism is not necessarily linked to antidemocratic thinking and practices, it is at least indifferent towards the destiny of democracy. Politics has to impose a market order based on competition and this agenda may also include the instauration of authoritarian or totalitarian regimes.'[62]

It seems doubtful, as a matter of historical fact, that it ever was the original intent of the founders of the EU for it to become a fully blown ordoliberal private law society. Still, this does not exclude the possibility that the way in which the EU was set up, especially its system of limited functional competences combined with the fact that the exercise of those competences is constrained by the market freedoms, in practice favours neoliberal policies, in particular market liberalization. This problem has been referred to as the EU's social deficit.[63] A related problem, more relevant here, is what Marija Bartl calls the 'substantive democratic deficit' of the EU.[64] The democratic debate with regard to EU private law is constrained—and political actors are handicapped—by the fact that functional competences, such as Article 114 TFEU on market integration, reduce both the scope of the political debate, by removing various subjects, aspects, and perspectives on private law from the table,[65] and its depth, because by understanding private law questions merely as functional problems that can

[59] Libertarians require a contract law for which there probably would not even exist a legal basis in the EU's foundational treaties. Absent treaty reform, this would mean it would be best for contract law to be national. Thus, under the current European constitutional framework these theories would effectively constitute an argument against EU contract law, and for its renationalization. See further, Chapter 4.

[60] Cf. Joerges, 'What Is Left of the European Economic Constitution? A Melancholic Eulogy', 30 *European Law Review* (2005) 461, at 471; Walker, 'Legal Theory and the European Union', *EUI Working Papers*, Law No. 2005/16, 13.

[61] Less radical, Mestmäcker, 'On the Legitimacy of European Law', 58 *Rabels Zeitschrift für Ausländisches und Internationales Privatrecht* (1994) 615, at 631, arguing, nevertheless, that the legislative powers of the EU are inherently limited by the purpose of the underlying individual rights.

[62] Somma, 'Private Law as Biopolitics: Ordoliberalism, Social Market Economy, and the Public Dimension of Contract', 76 *Law Contemp. Probl.* (2013) 105, at 114.

[63] Joerges and Rödl, 'Informal Politics, Formalised Law and the "Social Deficit" of European Integration: Reflections After the Judgments of the ECJ in *Viking* and *Laval*', 15 *ELJ* (2009) 1.

[64] Bartl, 'The Way We Do Europe: Subsidiarity and the Substantive Democratic Deficit', 21 *ELJ* (2015) 23.

[65] On this problem, see also Davies, 'Democracy and Legitimacy in the Shadow of Purposive Competence', 21 *ELJ* (2015) 2.

best be solved by technical experts, it depoliticizes the legislative debate on EU private law. In particular, the problem of scope indeed seems to be related to the neoliberal influence in the EU's original set up. By contrast, functionalism (and, more broadly, instrumentalism) is rejected as teleology by most libertarians, whose understanding of private law is strictly deontological.

3. Utilitarian

A. Institutional Comparison

The first question utilitarians will raise is whether we can seriously discuss the issue of whether contract law in Europe should have a democratic basis without considering the consequences. What social costs and benefits are to be expected from a democratically enacted contract law in comparison with the available or conceivable alternatives, such as private law making by courts, legal academics, or other experts? Indeed, utilitarians, as consequentialists, will reject the notion that anything should be taken into account other than the overall balance of good and bad consequences. In particular, deontological concerns such as public autonomy or political rights should not trump considerations of welfare.

In other words, from a utilitarian point of view a democratic basis for contract law—and democracy in general, for that matter—is never an aim in itself. The aim is the maximization of utility (defined as overall happiness, social welfare, or aggregated preference satisfaction) and if a democratic basis is the best means to contribute to achieving that end then (and only then) a utilitarian will endorse it, and only for that instrumental reason. This is a marked difference from, for example, civic republican and discourse-theoretical accounts of democracy where, as we will see, freedom from domination by others (including from laws made by others), popular sovereignty, or public autonomy, is the aim of democracy. Utilitarians may be interested in democratic law making, but only for the reason—and to the extent—that individuals derive utility (happiness, welfare, satisfaction of preferences, or wealth) from it. This may be the case, for example, when a significant part of the population has a strong 'taste' for democracy or even—admittedly less likely—specifically for a democratic contract law. However, this is not the only possible instance where a utilitarian would recommend a democratic basis for contract law.

What matters is the overall amount of utility a society derives from the institutional arrangement, i.e. the net balance of its social costs and benefits. Certainly, people may obtain utility directly from the satisfaction of a preference for the institution at hand, for example when they are fans of the European Parliament. However, the overall surplus in happiness, welfare, or economic growth a society derives from its laws, including its contract law, as adopted by one institution in comparison with the foreseeable performance of alternative institutional arrangements, is likely to be much more significant. It may even outweigh a widespread distaste for a certain institution. Thus, indirect utilitarian cases can and have been made for a law maker that people do not generally like or prefer (say an expert- or judge-made law instead of an act of parliament or a referendum), because the expected welfare consequences of that institutional choice are more significant than under any possible alternative arrangement. Therefore, a straightforward welfarist argument for expert government could be that it will make people better off (in their own estimation) than any of the alternatives would. What, then, are the relevant foreseeable social costs and benefits of a democratic (European) contract law? As we will see, this depends, in part, on what one is prepared to include in the calculus.

B. The Greatest Happiness of the Greatest Number and Democratic Government

What does democracy have to offer in broad welfare terms? There is a simple answer to this question with a long pedigree in utilitarian thinking, which runs as follows. If everyone's happiness or wellbeing has equal moral weight when it comes to formulating policies and laws, and if the decisive decisional basis is subjective welfare, happiness, or wellbeing, i.e. utility in the relevant subjects' own subjective estimation, at least in principle,[66] then why not ask them? Why not organize elections where individuals can express their preferences by casting their votes? Bentham was very clear on this. In his *Constitutional Code* (1843), he wrote: 'The only species of government which has or can have for its object and effect the greatest happiness of the greatest number, is a democracy'.[67] Indeed, there exist strong historical links between democracy and utilitarianism. Think of Mill's plea for the universal franchise (to be implemented progressively)[68] and his advocacy specifically of women's suffrage.[69] Having said that, Mill's appreciation of representative democracy was mixed.[70] In particular, he was worried about 'a government of privilege in favour of the numerical majority' which may lead to the complete disenfranchisement of minorities—what de Tocqueville had called 'the tyranny of the majority'[71]—and of 'a low grade of intelligence in the representative body'.[72]

C. The Utility of Codification

In the eyes of the classical utilitarians, judge-made law appeared distinctly premodern, based on elitism rather than on any principle, let alone the principle of utility. Indeed, Bentham condemned the system of precedent as: 'acting without reason, to

[66] For some limits, see later, in Sections 3.E–3.G.

[67] J. Bentham, *Constitutional Code*, Ch. IX, republished in J. Bowring (ed.), *The Works of Jeremy Bentham*, Vol. IX (1843).

[68] J. S. Mill, *Considerations on Representative Government* ([first published 1862] 2007), ch. 8.

[69] Ibid. 130: 'I consider [difference of sex] to be as entirely irrelevant to political rights as difference in height or in the colour of the hair.'

[70] On Mill's ambivalence with respect to the principle of representative democracy, see J. H. Burns, 'Utilitarianism and Democracy', 9 *Philosophical Quarterly* (1959) 168.

[71] Mill (n. 68) 101. Cf. de Tocqueville, 'De la démocratie en Amérique' (Vol. I 1835, Vol. II 1840), in A. de Tocqueville, *Œuvres, Pléiade* (1992), at 287: 'tyrannie de la majorité'.

[72] Mill (n. 68) 100; see also at 85: 'general ignorance and incapacity', 'deficiency in high mental qualifications'.

the declared exclusion of reason and thereby in opposition to reason'.[73] He was a strong advocate of codification. In 1811, he wrote to the president of the United States, James Madison, to propose drafting a complete codification of the common law.[74] Note, however, that the reason he offered for codification was not democratic legitimacy grounded in political autonomy but rather the 'advantageous results' following from codification compared to the 'ex-post-facto' and 'unwritten, or rather uncomposed and unenacted law', i.e. the common law. He considered the common law to be an 'impostrous law' 'the perpetual fruits' of which are to be found 'in the civil branch', i.e. private law including contract law: 'uncertainty, uncognoscibility, particular disappointments without end, general sense of insecurity against similar disappointment and loss'.[75]

D. The Efficiency of the Common Law

In stark contrast to Bentham's position, in the contemporary law and economics literature the influential paradigm of the efficiency of the common law is seen. This notion has a long pedigree, running from Holmes,[76] via Posner,[77] to Baird, most recently.[78] The basic idea is that the common law is the law of experience. It develops piecemeal, on a case-to-case basis, and, therefore, matches best with the preferences of the parties directly affected. It does a much better job than enacted private law legislation, which runs a much greater risk of diverging from actual preferences.[79] Moreover, it is argued that compared, for example, to a civil code, judge-made law is much more flexible and therefore can more easily adapt to new needs and developments.[80]

Are people governed by the common law of contract indeed likely to be better off (in their own estimation) than they would be if they lived under a democratically enacted contract law? Could we perhaps run an experiment where this bold empirical claim could be tested? Or, even better, are such empirical data perhaps already available, as a result of a 'natural experiment'? Indeed, could we not compare the wellbeing of people in otherwise similar countries but with different contract laws: common law, based on judicial precedent in one country, and democratically enacted law in the other? This was suggested by a group of economists ('LLSV'), led by Shleifer, who applied this idea in a series of papers sustaining the thesis of 'the economic consequences of legal origins', according to which the economic performance of legal systems with

[73] Bentham (n. 67) ch. IX, Art. 49.

[74] Bentham, 'To James Madison from Jeremy Bentham, 30 October 1811', in J. C. A. Stagg, J. Kerr Cross and S. Holbrook Perdue (eds), *The Papers of James Madison, Presidential Series*, Vol. 3 (1996) 505.

[75] Ibid.

[76] O. W. Holmes Jr., *The Common Law* (1881).

[77] R. A. Posner, *Economic Analysis of Law* (1st ed., 1973).

[78] D. G. Baird, *Reconstructing Contracts* (2013).

[79] Other legal economists have contested this view. E. A. Posner, 'Economic Analysis of Contract Law after Three Decades: Success or Failure?' 112 *Yale L.J.* (2003) 829, for example, argues that the kind of differences between different existing or conceivable contract laws are so small, from an economic point of view, that any presumed differential economic effects could not even be tested. Similar, C. R. Sunstein, *Legal Reasoning and Political Conflict* (2nd ed., 2018), at 79.

[80] See e.g. M. A. Eisenberg, *The Nature of the Common Law* (1988), at 5.

English legal origins is significantly better than that of systems with French and other civil law legal origins.[81] The legal origins thesis attracted a lot of attention[82]—both endorsements[83] and strong criticism.[84] What Shleifer and others compared were the economic performances in gross domestic product (GDP) of countries with common law and civil law legal origins. Of course, economic performance in GDP is a much narrower basis for the comparative evaluation of legal systems than welfare or well-being.[85] Moreover, the legal origins thesis is not identical to the claim of the efficiency of the common law, but only a specific version of it. Nor does it specifically address our own question of the relationship between democratic contract law and utility (even if social utility were reduced to mere societal wealth). The reason is that much of the law in countries with civil law legal origins was, in reality, never democratically enacted. As a general point, today several countries with civil law legal origins are not democracies but authoritarian regimes. Moreover, the contract laws of prominent civil law jurisdictions are contained in civil codes that date back to times well before the arrival of the universal franchise. Indeed, the French Civil Code was famously enacted by an emperor, Napoléon Bonaparte,[86] while the other countries that became members of the French 'legal family', as the cosy euphemism goes, typically did so not through democratic endorsement, but as a result of invasion by that same emperor or through colonial rule. Indeed, the staunch defence of the civil law legal tradition by French and German academics and public authorities against the legal origins attack and its endorsement by the World Bank, was not undertaken on the ground of its democratic pedigree. In other words, the common law versus civil law divide does not coincide with the democratic versus expert made contract law divide, neither as an empirical matter nor in terms of the justifications that have been advanced in favour of each of them.[87] Therefore, whatever the merits of common law in comparison to civil law, the legal origins papers do not prove the greater economic efficiency of the common law of contract as compared to democratic contract law.

[81] See e.g. La Porta, Lopez-de-Silanes, and Shleifer, 'The Economic Consequences of Legal Origins', 46 *Journal of Economic Literature* (2008) 285.

[82] See e.g. 'Order in the Jungle', *The Economist*, 13 March 2008.

[83] The World Bank's *Doing Business: Measuring Business Regulations*, reports available at www.doingbusiness.org (last visited 4 July 2020).

[84] Association Henri Capitant des amis de la culture juridique française, *Les droits de tradition civiliste en question; À propos des rapports "Doing Business" de la Banque Mondiale* (2006); B. du Marais (ed.), *Des indicateurs pour mesures le droit? Les limites méthodologiques des Rapports Doing Business* (2006); Siems, 'Legal Origins: Reconciling Law and Finance and Comparative Law', 52 *McGill Law Journal* (2007) 55; Garoupa and Gómez Ligüerre, 'The Syndrome of the Efficiency of the Common Law', 29 *Boston University International Law Journal* (2011) 287.

[85] E.g. as defined by M. D. Adler and E. Posner, *New Foundations of Cost-Benefit Analysis* (2006).

[86] On the 2016 reform of contract law provisions in the *Code Civil* by presidential degree, see later, in Section 5.B.5.

[87] For a specific case, i.e. with regard to rules requiring the 'incorporation' of existing trade usage into commercial contracts, of a claim, substantiated with extensive empirical evidence, for the superiority of the common law (in this case, of New York) over a code (Art. 2 UCC), *within* a single common law country, see L. Bernstein, 'Trade Usage in the Courts: the Flawed Conceptual and Evidentiary Basis of Article 2's Incorporation Strategy', *Coase-Sandor Institute for Law & Economics Working Paper No. 669* (2014).

E. Experts

In the philosophical satire *The Curious Enlightenment of Professor Caritat*, the main character visits the Parliament of Utilitaria, where at that moment a debate is ongoing between members of the opposition (the Act party) and of the ruling party (the Rule party). In the debate, several leaders of the opposition reject experts as 'people who think they've got a special insight into what the people want' and as 'impostors in white coats who have usurped our wills and would do our choosing for us'. Then, the Prime Minister takes the floor and responds:

> Our great object is to produce more and more utility. We must not be deflected from that noble task by subversive ideas, such as the idea the Opposition seems to favour that you must respect the whims of actually existing persons. *Why* should you? What is there to respect? Nothing. Because (she paused dramatically) there is no such thing as *persons*. We must get rid of obsolete ideas like "personal identity", "personal dignity" and "personal integrity". People are just producers and consumers of utility.

This scene nicely illustrates, through hyperbole, that not all utilitarians are convinced that the best way of figuring out what makes people better off is by actually asking them. In fact, there exists a utilitarian line of thinking, also with a long pedigree, that is quite sceptical about involving the people in all sorts of complex choices on which they lack expertise. On these views, there exists a serious risk that the people will make the wrong choices by adopting laws that are not in the best collective interest of society, and perhaps not even in their own personal best interest (defined, for example, as their personal preferences expressed in their individual utility functions). As Held points out, even John Stuart Mill 'ultimately trusted little in the judgment of the electorate and elected' and saw an important role for professionalism and expertise.[88] More recently, Caplan argued forcefully in favour of a more important role in politics for economic (and other) experts and reducing the scope of democracy, for the reason that democracies frequently adopt policies that are harmful for most people, citing protectionism as a classical example.[89] His central claim is that 'voters are worse than ignorant; they are, in a word, *irrational*—and vote accordingly'. In Caplan's view, the problem with democracy is not that it often fails because it does not do what voters want:

> democracy fails *because* it does what voters want. In economic jargon, democracy has a built-in *externality*. An irrational voter does not hurt only himself. He hurts also everyone who is, as a result of his irrationality, more likely to be under misguided policies. Since most of the cost of voter irrationality is *external*—paid for by other people,

[88] Held (n. 33) 85 and 87.

[89] B. Caplan, *The Myth of the Rational Voter: Why Democracies Choose Bad Politics* (2007), at 1.

why not indulge? If enough voters think this way, socially injurious policies win by popular demand.[90]

It is not difficult to see how this idea could be applied to (European) contract law as well. The argument might go as follows: the electorate has no idea of what kind of contract law we need, and by adopting misguided contract law rules (or by rejecting socially beneficial ones), in complete disregard—perhaps even wholly oblivious—of an available sophisticated body of contract law expertise, voters act irrationally, i.e. demonstrably against their own interests and preferences. However, even if voters can be demonstrated to be irrational in this sense, it is not clear that this necessarily would undermine the legitimacy of—or affect the case for—a democratic contract law. As we will see, such a rationality requirement for public reasoning may well be based too much on a controversial conception of the public good, or of the person in their public role as a citizen, to be acceptable as a general condition for legitimate law. This is different, of course, if one has decided already, on utilitarian grounds, that economic rationality should define (or trump) legitimacy.

There also exists expertise with regard to expert involvement in private law making. Indeed, Schwartz and Scott developed a 'positive theory of private legislatures', such as the American Law Institute, the main drafter of the restatements of the law.[91] The American restatements were the main source of inspiration for the drafters of the UNIDROIT Principles of International Commercial Contracts (1994, 2010), the Principles of European Contract Law (2002), and the Draft Common Frame of Reference (DCFR) (2009). These, too, were drafted by privately constituted bodies, i.e. UNIDROIT, the Lando group, and the Study Group on a European Civil Code, respectively. The main conclusions reached by Schwartz and Scott were that private law making bodies 'furnish useful technical expertise to state legislatures in areas where there is a consensus on the underlying values and where the resulting statutes cannot create large winners and losers', but that 'the set of such "technical subjects" is, considerably smaller than the set of subjects that [the private law making groups] attempt to regulate'.[92] In particular, their theory suggests that private legislatures with a membership and procedures similar to that of the drafters of the American restatements will have 'a strong status quo bias and sometimes will be captured by powerful interests'.[93] Very similarly, in the academic and political debates on European contract law, the Principles of European Contract Law (PECL) and (especially) the DCFR were

[90] Ibid. 3.

[91] Schwartz and Scott, 'The Political Economy of Private Legislatures', 143 *University of Pennsylvania Law Review* (1995) 595.

[92] Ibid. Schwartz and Scott are entirely right that insights of this kind (and their contestations) should be central to teaching contract law as well. This is one of the reasons why the present book on European contract law discusses, as its first question, who can legitimately—or should ideally—be the contract law maker.

[93] Ibid. 651.

criticized for being driven by status quo bias (or outright conservatism)[94] and exposed as having engaged in controversial value choices.[95]

F. Impact Assessments

An important instance of expert involvement in contract law making are the 'impact assessments' that have accompanied the more recent legislative proposals in the field of EU contract law.[96] Impact assessments are the European equivalent of the cost-benefit analyses that were made compulsory by the American president Ronald Reagan in the 1980s as an important part of his deregulatory agenda.[97] They have been a key feature of the European Commission's 'better regulation' agenda. The objective is to promote 'evidence-based rule-making'.[98] That sounds neutral enough. Indeed, the Commission's Communication explicitly points out that:

> Better regulation is not about favouring certain policies or objectives over others. It is about being clear on the objectives, whatever they are. It is about ensuring that the policy solution is the best and least burdensome way to reach those objectives and it is about being honest about how well solutions are working. All significant impacts—whether positive or negative, quantifiable or not—should be analysed and considered.[99]

This may be true in theory. However, at least in the field of contract law, in practice the main effect of impact assessments has been a very specific one: it has framed the political debate on European contract law strongly around its potential for contributing to economic growth, understood quite narrowly as GDP. This is not surprising,

[94] See e.g. Niglia, 'Beyond Enchantment—the Possibility of a New European Private Law', 28 *Yearbook of European Law (YEL)* (2009) 60, at 91:

> The importance of this democratic issue is, despite its obscuration in orthodox analyses, self-evident. It is also self-evident that conventional scholarship, structured as it is, cannot credibly face the participatory problem. In fact, 'broader participation' would be perceived as conflicting with the practice of 'revealing' the common-rules-in-the-abstract through the work of orthodox scholars who see themselves as having almost exclusive decision-making powers based on their supposed 'expertise'.

Contrast: Grundmann, 'The Optional European Code on the Basis of the *Acquis* Communautaire—Starting Point and Trends', 10 *ELJ* (2004) 698, at 710: 'The drafts for a European Contract Law Code and—as a first step—for a common frame of reference should probably be developed in groups dominated by academics, and certainly in groups acting without a democratic legitimisation.'

[95] See e.g. Hesselink, 'The Principles of European Contract Law: Some Choices Made by the Lando Commission', 1 *Global Jurist Frontiers* (2001) 4; Sefton-Green, 'Lawmakers in the Shadows: Legal Academics in the Construction of European Private Law', in E. Fahey (ed.), *The Actors of Postnational Rule-Making: Contemporary Challenges of European and International Law* (2016) 185.

[96] E.g. the CESL proposal, and the two contract law proposals for the Digital Single Market. The former was withdrawn, the latter two were adopted in modified form in 2019. See Chapter 2.

[97] See Adler and Posner (n. 85) 3.

[98] Commission Communication 'Better Regulation: Delivering Better Results for a Stronger Union', (COM/2016/0615 final), at 3.

[99] Ibid. 6.

given that impact assessments were part of the EU's Lisbon Strategy for the internal market to become the most competitive economy in the world.[100]

Regulatory impact assessments fit very well with a consequentialist understanding of the law, in this case contract law.[101] And their focus in practice on economic impact, understood very narrowly as the potential to contribute to economic growth, matches well with a particularly narrow reading of welfarism as the basis and justification for contract law.[102] However, that understanding is based on a series of assumptions with regard to contract law making that are far from self-evident or unproblematic. Van Schagen argues that regulatory impact assessments have a thus far unnoticed 'hidden potential' for European private law.[103] In her view, they can prevent legislators from making 'poor regulatory choices' and can become an important method for improving the quality of the private law *acquis*. However, she does not offer any standard for determining and evaluating the quality of the private law *acquis*. It is clear, nevertheless, that the potential she sees is not a democratic potential. By contrast, Bartl points out the democratic risks posed by impacts assessment in European contract law making.[104] For the case of the CESL proposal (now withdrawn) she shows how their limited focus on economic growth could strongly constrain the aspects to be considered during the legislative process. For example, the inclusion of data concerning the impact on the environment (transport, packaging), urbanism (the emptying of city centres), and public health (armchair shopping) of the promotion of cross-border online sales through contract law harmonization in the name of economic growth, might have changed the political debate. Obviously, impact assessments are not intrinsically biased towards certain types of concerns,[105] but they may easily become so if used in

[100] Presidency conclusions, Lisbon European Council 23 and 24 March 2000, 5, at 14. Cf. Micklitz, 'Do Consumers and Businesses Need a New Architecture of Consumer Law? A Thought Provoking Impulse', 32 *YEL*(2013) 266, at 278: 'the Lisbon Strategy set out by the European Council in 2000, by which the *ökonomische Effizienzdenken* mutated into the dominant European ideology'.

[101] It is also connected to a widely held specific reading of the EU's law making competence concerning the internal market, which itself is strongly marked by a utilitarian, more specifically welfarist and efficiency-oriented reading of the internal market, according to which a properly functioning market is a *growing* market. On this reading of Art. 114 TFEU, the existence of a solid legal basis needs to be demonstrated with the help of impact assessments, which must show, in particular, how much the proposed harmonization measure can contribute to economic growth. By contrast, impact assessments do not fit with neoliberal understandings of contract law, contrary to what has sometimes been suggested, since neoliberals emphatically reject consequentialism, instrumentalism, and collectivist objectives, in contract law and elsewhere, as seen earlier.

[102] The Explanatory Memorandum to the contract law proposals for the Digital Single Market announced quite candidly: 'The general objective of the proposals is to contribute to faster growth of the Digital Single Market, to the benefit of both consumers and businesses.' (Proposal for a Directive on Certain Aspects Concerning Contracts for the Supply of Digital Content (COM(2015) 634 final); Proposal for a Directive on Certain Aspects Concerning Contracts for the Online and Other Distance Sales of Goods Brussels (COM(2015) 635 final). See, generally, Commission Communication 'The EU Justice Agenda for 2020: Strengthening Trust, Mobility and Growth Within the Union' (COM(2014) 144 final), especially at 2 and 7 ('justice for growth').

[103] Van Schagen 'The Hidden Potential of Regulatory Impact Assessments (RIAs) in the Private Law *Acquis*', 22 *ERPL* (2014) 69.

[104] Bartl (n. 64) 36–38.

[105] For example, the general definition given by the European Commission in its Communication 'On Impact Assessment' (COM(2002) 276 final), at 3, remains neutral with regard to different types of impact: 'Impact assessment is the process of systematic analysis of the likely impacts of intervention by public authorities.' However, the framing starts when the Commission writes, with regard to identifying impacts ('screening'), that 'impacts will as far as possible be expressed in economic, social and environmental terms although it may be difficult to group certain impacts in one or the other of these categories'.

the context of legal harmonization based on limited, functional competences. And, in any case, they are always (i.e. intrinsically) biased towards consequentialism. Indeed, in the European Commission's communication on impact assessments, human rights violations figure as 'social impacts',[106] to be traded off, in typically utilitarian vein, against—and therefore presumed to be commensurable with—other types of impact, notably 'economic' and 'environmental' impact.[107]

G. Regulatory Capture

Building on political theories of government as interest group pluralism,[108] economic ('public choice') theories of law making understand legislation as the outcome of a market process where voters and interest groups (the demand side) buy their preferred legislation from politicians and their political parties (the supply side) in return for their votes and financial and other support.[109] According to such theories, what economic actors and interest groups do—and what it is rational (in the specific sense of being in their own economic interest) for them to do—is to demand regulation commensurate to their lobbying strength,[110] while regulators seek to maximize political support. Note that the economic theory of legislation and 'regulation' is a positive theory: it aims to predict and explain legislative outcomes. In particular, it predicts that outcomes will often be inefficient.[111] This is the case, especially, when regulation provides economic actors with monopoly-like economic benefits they would not be able to obtain in a competitive market (rent-seeking through regulation).[112] The legislation then creates benefits for a few at the expense of the many, not only in the distributive sense of transferring resources from one group to another, but also in the allocative sense of preventing the creation of a state with more overall welfare.[113] The economic theory of legislation predicts that certain types of interest groups will be more successful in capturing the legislative process and ensuring favourable outcomes than others. In particular, small groups of actors sharing a homogeneous interest are likely to be effective, while larger groups with more indeterminate and mixed objectives are comparatively weak.

[106] Ibid 15.

[107] See ibid. 15, in the section on 'assessing the impacts ("scoping")', on 'the trade-offs between competing economic, social and environmental objectives'.

[108] Seminal, R. A. Dahl, *Who Governs? Democracy and Power in an American City* ([first published 1961] 2nd ed., 2005).

[109] Stigler, 'The Theory of Economic Regulation', 2 *Bell Journal of Economics and Management Science* (1971) 3, at 3 and 12; Landes and Posner, 'The Independent Judiciary in an Interest-Group Perspective', 18 *Journal of Law and Economics* (1975) 875. See, more generally, J. M. Buchanan and G. Tullock (C. K. Rowley ed.), *The Calculus of Consent: Logical Foundations of Constitutional Democracy* ([first published 1962] 2004), at 280.

[110] Stigler (n. 109). Cf. Keeler and Foreman, 'Regulation and Deregulation', in P. Newman (ed.), *The New Palgrave Dictionary of Economics and the Law* (2002) 213, at 214.

[111] Cf. Wagner, 'The Economics of Harmonization: the Case of Contract Law', 39 *CMLR* (2002) 995.

[112] D. C. Mueller, *Public Choice III* (2003), at 343.

[113] Ibid. ch. 15.

Facts of the kind predicted by this theory could indeed be observed in the context of EU contract law making, both with regard to the CFR-net[114] and the stakeholder meetings where the expert group had to present its drafts and where, for example, notaries were over-represented and well focused in their objectives, while consumers were underrepresented and much less specific in their demands (and unable internally to prioritize among these).[115]

Imperfect information leads to further inefficiencies. Even a legislator trying to enact perfectly efficient regulation will be confronted with the problem of not knowing the preferences of the public (principal-agent problem). This problem is more serious when the legislation deals with complex problems that are perceived by the public as technical and not directly relevant to their lives. As Stigler explains:

> The voter's expenditure to learn the merits of individual policy proposals and to express his preferences (by individual and group representation as well as by voting) are determined by expected costs and returns, just as they are in the private marketplace. The costs of comprehensive information are higher in the political arena because information must be sought on many issues of little or no direct concern to the individual, and accordingly he will know little about most matters before the legislature.[116]

Contract law reform is likely to be a subject where the costs of being fully informed are too high for most voters, as Wagner points out:

> As has been established beyond any doubt to anyone in the course of the recent German reform of the law of obligations, matters of private law in general and of contract law in particular are far too complex to capture the public interest. Lacking any public apprehension, politicians do not really care either as long as there are no pressure groups who push their particular concerns. Thus, to suggest that 'the people' would vote a government out of office for the reason of it inaugurating an inefficient contract law or leaving such inferior law in place, is simply absurd. People care about other things, if they care at all, and politicians behave accordingly.[117]

Thus, the problem of regulatory capture is likely to be exacerbated by imperfect information: when a piece of legislation is hugely beneficial to a few while the costs are spread out evenly over all consumers in such a way that the public will not notice, let alone be mobilized politically, then politicians will be prepared to sell that regulation

[114] The CFR-net was 'a network of stakeholder experts on the CFR' meant to ensure that the research done by the research network that was given the task by the Commission to prepare a draft Common Frame of Reference, would 'take into account the practical context in which the rules are to be applied and the needs of users'. (*Report from the Commission—First Annual Progress Report on European Contract Law and the Acquis Review* (COM/2005/0456 final)).

[115] BEUC was ultimately unsuccessful in convincing the European Parliament that the CESL was bad for consumers. The eventual withdrawal of the proposal by the European Commission after its adoption, in first reading, by the European Parliament had more to do with legal nationalism than with pressure from the European consumer organization (see Chapter 2).

[116] Stigler (n. 109) 11–12.

[117] Wagner (n. 111) 83.

for the price (e.g. financing of their political campaign) offered by the 'stakeholder representatives' (which is the European Commission's euphemism for lobbyists). Wagner argues that the risk of inefficient outcomes of the private law making process is even greater at the EU level. If private law is already not secure at the hands of the legislator, because the public does not understand and will not become mobilized, and consequently politicians do not really care, then, at the EU level the fact that the legislative process is so opaque that the outcome cannot easily be attributed to any political party or actor is added. Therefore, he concludes, especially in the EU 'it would be naive to count on the democratic process in issues of civil law'.[118]

As stated earlier, the economic theory of legislation is a positive theory. However, the argument easily slips into a normative one when it is concluded that government failure may be worse than market failure *and* recommendations are made in favour of deregulation or, more relevant here, against new EU contract law harmonization measures. However, the missing step in such reasoning is a proper discussion of the question of whether efficiency should be the only consideration concerning legislation, or whether perhaps other considerations should trump the objective of increasing overall welfare. Obviously, such other reasons are not likely to include the objective of creating new rents for powerful industries—nor should they. However, they might include concern for the losers of efficiency enhancing deregulation.[119] In contract law, this could lead, for example, to the protection of consumers and other weaker contracting parties, which could easily be framed in terms of regulatory capture but may well be justifiable in terms of both distributive and interpersonal justice, as we will see in Chapter 6.

A further major flaw of the theory is that it simply assumes that citizens act entirely strategically, as rational maximizers of their own welfare (i.e. as a *homo economicus*). However, as Habermas and many others have stressed, the model of strategic action and its corollary of exogenous and stable 'preferences' is highly implausible even as a descriptive matter.[120] It is much more likely that people, when confronted with the need to make practical decisions (i.e. about what to do) are convinced, at least sometimes, by the arguments proposed by others (i.e. change their 'preferences' or develop new ones). Specifically in the context of deliberation about generally applicable laws (including the choice to become actively involved in the societal debate), it seems implausible, as a descriptive matter, that considerations of justice will never cross people's minds or have an impact on their choices.

[118] Ibid. 82.

[119] Keeler and Foreman (n. 110) 221. Cf. I. M. Young, *Justice and the Politics of Difference* (1990), at 92.

[120] For a radical version of the idea, see Stigler and Becker, 'De Gustibus Non Est Disputandum', 67 *American Economic Review* (1977) 76, at 89 who claim that the 'the hypothesis of stable tastes yield[s] more useful predictions about observable behavior' and consequently, that '*all* changes in behavior are explained by changes in prices and incomes, precisely the variables that organize and give power to economic analysis' (emphasis in original).

H. Democracy and Preferences

A great advantage of consequentialist approaches is that they naturally direct our attention to the question of the available institutional alternatives and which one of these scores best on the efficiency or welfare scale. In particular, they raise the question of whether contract law made by judges or academic experts might yield more benefits, compared to its social costs (defined in terms of welfare or other), than a democratically deliberated and enacted contract law. However, the matter becomes more complex—and the empirical case, in terms of welfare consequences, against democratic contract law less obvious—if we consider the possibility that people might have 'a taste for democracy' (in analogy to the 'taste for fairness' admitted by Kaplow and Shavell),[121] or that they might have a preference for (i.e. derive happiness or wellbeing from) public autonomy, collective self-determination or non-domination, or experience disutility from being subject to laws designed by judges and other experts rather than by themselves together with their co-citizens. That does not seem a ludicrous hypothesis. It may well be that ultimately the only reliable way of finding out whether people have a preference for democratic private law is through the democratic process itself. One possible outcome might be, then, that preferences in this regard are not homogeneous, but differ from country to country. In all likelihood that would be the result, to a large extent, of what people are used to (e.g. whether they live in a common law or civil law jurisdiction). However, from a welfare perspective, this would not make the result any less significant, since path dependence and other cognitive biases do not per se render preferences illegitimate nor do they otherwise give reason for these to be discarded. The result would be that, on empirical grounds, welfare or efficiency oriented theorists cannot make any universal recommendations for the ideal contract law making institution.

Moreover, there is the more fundamental, ontological point of what it is exactly that theorists mean when they speak of 'preferences'. The concept is well established in the economic literature, and the law and economics scholarship inspired by it. However, by no means do preferences constitute observable facts. This is underscored by the usual recourse to the (problematic) concept of 'revealed preferences'.[122] In reality, these are a theoretical construct, with quite specific (individualistic) characteristics and connotations, based on a series of assumptions (not always made explicit)[123] with regard to individual and collective human agency. As Habermas explains, with regard to the democratic process, 'it is unrealistic to start with a model that assumes that opportunities and preferences can be treated as something given; both of these change in the political process itself'.[124]

[121] See L. Kaplow and S. Shavell, *Fairness Versus Welfare* (2002), at 21.

[122] As O. O'Neill, *Bounds of Justice* (2000), at 17, points out, if we infer preferences from choices and label the result as 'revealed' preferences, 'no *authority* is assigned to preferences in what passes for preference-based practical reasoning' (emphasis in original) and, consequently, the models of rational choice based on it are entirely fictitious.

[123] But see explicitly Mueller (n. 112) 406: 'This postulate of normative individualism underlies much of the normative analysis in public choice'.

[124] Habermas (n. 7) 336. Also J. S. Mill, a prominent utilitarian, stressed that individuals are not cognitively self-sufficient and underlined the epistemic role in identifying the common good and the constitutive effect of democracy. Cf. Brink, 'Mill's Moral and Political Philosophy', in E. N. Zalta (ed.), *Stanford Encyclopedia of Philosophy*, available at https://plato.stanford.edu/entries/mill-moral-political/ (last visited 5 July 2020).

In addition, even on a consequentialist view, where the maximization of wellbeing is the aim of democracy, it is not clear that human wellbeing is best understood ultimately as preference-satisfaction. As Raz underlines, people usually have reasons for their preferences:

> There is a view of democracy which … is best understood as premised on the belief that the good for people is to have their preferences satisfied. Its purpose is simply to assure each person that his preferences will count together with those of all others. This attempt to view utilitarianism as the necessary underpinning of democracy fails, like all versions of preference-satisfaction utilitarianism, because it misconceives individual well-being. People flourish and their lives are fulfilled and successful to the extent that they successfully engage in worthwhile activities, pursuits, and relationships. Success in the sense of preference satisfaction is only part of this story. To contribute to a person's well-being, the success has to be in a worthwhile, valuable activity, pursuit, or relationship. This is attested to by the fact that preferences are reason-based, and are held and valued by those who have them because they believe that they are preferences for what is valuable and worthwhile.[125]

4. Communitarian

A. Understanding Contract Law

The democratic legitimacy of private law is not a direct concern for communitarians. What matters is the proper definition of the common good (a perfectionist concern) rather than the participation or representation of everyone affected. This does not mean that communitarians are anti-democratic. Rather, they regard democracy as a means for achieving the common good, not as an aim in itself, and also not necessarily the only or most suitable means in all cases. The common good is not necessarily best defined by counting votes, nor through deliberation in which everyone's voice can be heard. Indeed, a more natural method for arriving at the truth in these matters, according to communitarians, is a hermeneutical one. And the proper interpretation of a community's traditions, culture, identity, or social imaginary may be best left in the hands of an authority different from Parliament or the electorate. This may be the case *a fortiori* with regard to contract law. In most advanced cultures, there exists a sophisticated body of learning concerning contract law, enshrined in legal doctrine, which has developed gradually over time—the full riches of which may be difficult for members of (the European) parliament and their electorate to grasp.

[125] Raz, *Ethics in the Public Domain* (1994), at 116. See also H. Dagan and M. Heller, *The Choice Theory of Contracts* (2017), at 54: 'the usual utilitarian move of translating everything to preferences fails here for the same reasons as elsewhere: it assumes that all things of value are commensurable and it has no plausible account of the value of preference satisfaction'.

B. Legal Culture and Legal Tradition

Communitarians regard private law as an expression of the community's tradition and culture. As the Dutch Minister of Justice put it, when explaining the government's scepticism with regard to the need for a common European sales law, 'it is characteristic of private law that it essentially reflects the social opinions and culture of a society'.[126] On this view, private law and its underlying values are local, not universal. This has two important implications for our question. First, from a communitarian perspective it is not self-evident that private law has to be formulated in a democratic process. There may be other, perhaps even better ways of capturing 'our' tradition or 'our' culture with regard to private law relationships and contracting. Secondly, if private law is going to be enacted by the legislator it will have to be limited to a codification or restatement essentially of what is already there. The legislator should not engage in a rational design and collective decision on a new set of private law rules. Thus, drawing up a codification is not primarily a political but essentially an (advanced) cultural task, one that may be best left to jurists; a legislative assembly would not fully grasp it.

C. Defining the Common Good

For a communitarian, any law making cannot but be a matter of defining the common good. Our laws should express our communal values and our self-understanding, i.e. our definition of who we are and what is good for us. Therefore, law making should not be a neutral exercise (or be constrained e.g. by a public reason requirement). Nor could it be, given that we all are always already situated,[127] and always understand the world against the background of social imaginaries.[128] Therefore, the idea of democratic law as aggregate individual choice, that utilitarians and also many liberal-egalitarians share, is too reductive and too atomistic from a communitarian point of view.[129] In the words of Taylor, 'a democratic society needs some commonly recognized definition of the good life'.[130] In other words, law—and certainly contract law with its long and rich tradition—cannot legitimately be designed afresh on a clean slate. The definition of the common good is not a matter of rational design. The idea of a fresh start totally disregards—indeed offends—the value of experience and tradition. This is why communitarians, neo-romantics, and neo-pandectists are worried about—and do sometimes resent—the idea and the practice of democratic private law making.

126 'Nieuwe Commissievoorstellen en initiatieven van de lidstaten van de Europese Unie—Brief van de Minister van Veiligheid en Justitie', 30 September 2013 (Tweede Kamer, vergaderjaar 2013–2014, 22 112, nr 1708) (my own translation). See also the reasoned opinion on the CESL from the Bundesrat of the Republic of Austria, referring to the Austrian Civil Code and its interpretations as 'an inherent part of the citizens' conception of the law'.

127 M. J. Sandel, *Liberalism and the Limits of Justice* (2nd ed., 1998).

128 C. Taylor, *Modern Social Imaginaries* (2004); C. Taylor, *A Secular Age* (2007), ch. 4.

129 On (and against) political atomism, see Taylor, 'Atomism', in C. Taylor, *Philosophy and the Human Sciences: Philosophical Papers 2* (1985) 187; and, of course, G. W. F. Hegel, *Outlines of the Philosophy of Right* ([first published 1821] 2008), at §§ 308 and 311.

130 Taylor, 'Cross-Purposes: the Liberal-Communitarian Debate', in N. Rosenblum (ed.), *Liberalism and Moral Life* (1989) 159, at 160, contrasting his own view with Dworkin's neutralist stance (on which, see earlier, in Chapter 2, Section 3.F).

D. A People and its Spirit

From a communitarian point of view, the common good is always the good of a given community. The community is understood as a unit, indeed the most fundamental unit, not as an aggregate of individuals. For law this means, in particular, that it is closely and organically connected to a specific people. Montesquieu explained, in his *The Spirit of the Laws*, how different factors, such as geography and climate, contribute to the spirit of the laws, which, in turn, explains the differences between one legal system and another.[131] For this reason, Montesquieu is often referred to as the first comparative lawyer. In the more mystical versions of this idea, the law, including contract law, expresses the spirit of a people (*Volksgeist*). Savigny famously relied on this notion. Note that a people (*Volk*) and its spirit is not understood by Savigny as a reference to a given set of citizens but as an (ideal) cultural concept.[132] Thus, from a communitarian point of view, pluralism is not a matter of differences between individuals and their opinions, but of differences between communities and their respective (legal) cultures, traditions, and spirits.

E. Organicism and Legal Evolution

In the communitarian tradition, the development of the law is understood as an organic process. On this view, legal development takes place incrementally and without being based on anyone's plan.[133] Thus, the law is often assimilated by communitarians to the natural languages and to culinary traditions. As a strong expression of this organicist understanding of the law and its development, the Historical School constituted the Romantic reaction against the systematic civil codes of France and Austria, that they rejected as emblematic expressions of the law of reason.[134]

Sometimes, a dimension of progress is added, implicitly or explicitly, to organicist accounts. This happens, in particular, when private law and its development is presented in evolutionary terms.[135] On such views, the law is not only changing gradually, but also becoming better, through a process of trial and error, whereby inferior rules

[131] Montesquieu, *De l'esprit des lois* (1748), Book I, ch. III:

> [Les lois politiques et civiles] de chaque nation doivent être tellement propres au peuple pour lequel elles sont faites, que c'est un très grand hasard si celles d'une nation peuvent convenir à une autre. ... Elles doivent être relatives au physique du pays; au climat glacé, brûlant ou tempéré; à la qualité du terrain, à sa situation, à sa grandeur; au genre de vie des peuples, laboureurs, chasseurs ou pasteurs; elles doivent se rapporter au degré de liberté que la constitution peut souffrir; à la religion des habitants, à leurs inclinations, à leurs richesses, à leur nombre, à leur commerce, à leurs mœurs, à leurs manières.

[132] See F. Wieacker, *A History of Private Law in Europe* (1995), at 311.

[133] See F. C. von Savigny, *Vom Beruf unserer Zeit für Gesetzgebung und Rechtswissenschaft* (1814), at 67: 'auf organische Weise, ohne eigentliche Willkühr und Absicht, entstehen'.

[134] See Wieacker (n. 132) 311

[135] See e.g. J. M. Smits, 'The Harmonisation of Private Law in Europe: Some Insights from Evolutionary Theory', 31 *Georgia Journal of International and Comparative Law* (2002) 79.

and doctrines are eliminated while the better ones survive. Clearly, the spontaneous evolution would be interrupted by a legislative intervention, which, therefore, on this view, could seriously impair the quality of the law. For this reason, the common law, because it allows for incremental change (from case to case) and for inductive reasoning (from existing cases and problems to principles), is often regarded as an ideal environment for legal evolution. In the notion that spontaneous order and unfettered evolution are for the better, communitarian and libertarian ideas at first sight might seem to converge.[136] For example, Smits quotes Hayek and Fried when he argues in favour of an understanding of private law more as an organism rather than as a product of explicit design. He writes:

> If private law is made subordinate to democratic decision making, it is a means to a (political) end. It is the view of private law as a matter of conscious design by some legislator. [T]here is an alternative: one can also look at private law as the result of a long process of trial and error, of spontaneous development towards the standards a community prefers. Looked at in this way, private law is much more independent from State institutions. I believe this understanding of private law is more in line with how it has developed over the ages (also in the civil law world), providing this area of the law with its own rationality independent from any public aim.[137]

However, on this view private law making would still remain a teleological exercise. What differs is only the way the good is defined ('the standards a community prefers') and the proper means to achieve the collective goal ('a long process of trial and error'). In contrast, as we saw, Hayek's understanding is not teleological, focusing on preferred or otherwise good outcomes, but deontological, concentrating on rules of just conduct.[138]

F. Doctrinal Groundwork

The idea of law as tradition and culture also explains why, according to communitarians, private law should not become the object of political compromise. For what MPs

[136] See, in particular, F. A. Hayek (n. 51), Vol. I *Rules and Order* ([first published 1973] 2003) 22 and 74. There are also agnostic organicist theories, which claim to be merely descriptive. Think, in particular, of the autopoietic theories of Luhmann, Teubner and their followers. Having said that, Luhmann was a conservative (a prominent Christian-democrat) and an advocate of technocratic and bureaucratic rule. In the words of J.-W. Müller, *Contesting Democracy* (2011), at 204: 'he offered the most coherent and sophisticated theoretical justification for why policy-making should be shielded from widespread participation and essentially left to bureaucrats'. Moreover, some of his followers seem to have a distinctly libertarian laissez-faire view of transnational law. See, in particular, e.g. G.-P. Calliess and P. Zumbansen, *Rough Consensus and Running Code: A Theory of Transnational Private Law* (2010).

[137] The reference to reason, in the last sentence, is reminiscent of Popper's evolutionary concept of objective knowledge. See K. R. Popper, *Objective Knowledge: An Evolutionary Approach* (1972). On the relevance of Popper's notion of objective knowledge for democratic theory, see Benhabib, 'Ein Deliberatives Modell Demokratischer Legitimität', 43 *Deutsche Zeitschrift für Philosophie* (1995) 6.

[138] Note that the communitarian and libertarian arguments for the common law and for legal evolution both differ from the utilitarian support for the common law on behalf of its purported efficiency, which, as we saw, is conditional (upon a net surplus, in terms of wealth or welfare).

and MEPs essentially lack, especially in comparison to legal academics, is doctrinal expertise. Both the recent national reforms of the law of obligations in Germany and France and, especially, the proposals for a Common European Sales Law were criticized for their low quality. Critics do not always define their concept of 'quality', but what they seem to have in mind in such cases is something like the proper next step forward in the legal tradition. In practice this means, in the first place, that reform proposals should take into account—or, in a stronger version, simply follow—the prevailing doctrine as determined by legal scholars (*communis opinio doctorum*). In other words, the notion of the 'quality' of enacted private law is an essentially perfectionist concept in that it relies on the idea that a private law reform must and can meet objective standards of good quality. The paradigmatic example in this regard is Savigny's opposition to a German Civil Code, in what became known as the *Kodifikationsstreit*. When, following the German victory in the Franco-Prussian war, Thibaut proposed to crown German unity with a national civil code after the example of the French *Code Civil* of 1804, Savigny famously rejected the idea as coming too soon. First, he claimed, proper preparatory work had to be done by 'legal science'. He wrote that 'an organically advancing legal science, that can be common to the entire nation' was the proper means towards the end of legal unity.[139] As we saw, Savigny believed that private law should be the expression of the *Volksgeist*, which he thought it was only for the legal elite to capture.

On this view, ideally any codification should be prepared through doctrinal work by legal scholars—in the case of a European code by a truly European legal scholarship.[140] That idea is still reflected today in the position of Zimmermann and others that 'legal science' should prepare the ground for any European private law.[141] With this they do not mean an 'expert group' designing an 'optional instrument' overnight.[142] Instead, it is the task of legal scholars to uncover 'the deeper roots of our European cultural identity'.[143] What this amounts to in practice is classical doctrinal work.[144] And that takes time. In the words of Zimmermann, 'the search for doctrinal structures which are recognizably European and teleologically satisfactory has only just begun'.[145] Also, their critique was not that the DCFR was too technocratic but that it was a dogmatic work of poor quality.[146] In other words, like Savigny in his time Zimmermann and Jansen today believe in a division of labour—and the right temporal order—between

[139] Savigny (n. 133) 126.

[140] N. Jansen, *Binnenmarkt, Privatrecht und Europäische Identität* (2004).

[141] See Zimmermann, 'Roman Law and the Harmonization of Private Law in Europe', in A. Hartkamp *et al.* (eds), *Towards a European Civil Code* (2011) 27.

[142] The expert group that prepared the CESL was given less than one year to prepare a draft.

[143] Zimmermann, 'The Present State of European Private Law', 57 *AJCL* (2009) 479, at 510.

[144] See N. Jansen and R. Zimmermann (eds), *Commentaries on European Contract Laws* (2018), a classical doctrinal commentary (of more that 2,000 pages) that discusses modern texts in the light of their historical and comparative foundations.

[145] Ibid. 512. See also Jansen, 'Dogmatik, Erkenntnis und Theorie im Europäischen Privatrecht', *Zeitschrift für Europäisches Privatrecht* (2005) 750.

[146] See Eidenmüller *et al.*, 'The Common Frame of Reference for European Private Law—Policy Choices And Codification Problems', 28 *OJLS* (2008) 659, at 707: 'The document, so far, exhibits serious structural deficiencies.' And specifically with regard to Book VI DCFR (on tort law), ibid. 682: 'its doctrinal structure proves equally complex and clumsy'.

preparatory doctrinal work and actual drafting. From this point of view, the DCFR and the CESL proposal simply came far too early.[147]

More radically, Jansen argues that 'it is an oversimplification to base private law essentially or conceptually on the state or a Parliament's or government's political will'.[148] In a study of non-legislative codifications, ranging from the Corpus Iuris Civilis in the time of the *ius commune* via the American restatements of the twentieth century through to the PECL today, Jansen concludes that 'European private law has long been developed on the basis of texts that were largely independent of any political domination. ... Thus, private law has mostly been, and still is today to a large degree, autonomous from the states' political system.'[149] The ultimate authority of a private law system, Jansen submits, derives from its substantive quality, not from collective self-determination.

G. Conservatism

Neo-romantic and communitarian politics tends to be conservative, which is not surprising given the importance communitarians tend to give to the past, with their focus on experience and tradition. In law, this is expressed in an emphasis on those parts of the law with the longest tradition, going back to Roman law (in civil law jurisdictions) or to the medieval common law and equity (in common law jurisdictions). As a result, 'new' (ie twentieth-century) legal developments, such as consumer law, are frequently ignored as marginal, or contested as disruptive. This further explains the resistance by certain communitarians to the Europeanization of private law, much of which in fact consists of consumer law, which, thus, is not only European (and, therefore, from the perspective of national traditions, not 'ours'—see Chapter 4) but also instrumental and lacking any basis in legal culture.[150] With their eagerness to accept 'the rule of the past over the present',[151] communitarian understandings of contract law represent the exact opposite of utilitarian views,[152] which are consequentialist, i.e. forward-looking, regarding the past as water under the bridge.

[147] See Zimmermann (n. 143) 512: 'The extent to which the different areas of private law have acquired (or re-acquired) a European identity differs very widely. Some are well on their way while others have barely started. All of them require genuinely European, as opposed to national, legal scholarship, based on historical and comparative study. But none of them is ready to be cast into an official European legal instrument, whatever its name may be.'

[148] N. Jansen, *The Making of Legal Authority: Non-Legislative Codifications in Historical and Comparative Perspective* (2010), at 8.

[149] Ibid. 138.

[150] Cf. Cornu, 'Un code civil n'est pas un instrument communautaire' (2002) *Recueil Dalloz* 351.

[151] Savigny (n. 133) 107: 'die Herrschaft der Vergangenheit über die Gegenwart'. On Savigny's conservatism, see Van Caeneghem (n. 6) 156.

[152] Contrast also Holmes Jr., 'Law in Science and Science in Law', in O. W. Holmes Jr., *Collected Legal Papers* (1920) 210, at 225: 'Every one instinctively recognizes that in these days the justification of a law cannot be found in the fact that our fathers have always followed it. It must be found in some help which the law brings towards reaching a social end which the governing power of the community has made its mind up that it wants.'

H. Codification as Civilianization

Historically, codification was a weapon of the people against the elite, especially against the judiciary and legal academia.[153] However, from a communitarian perspective, the ideal or principle of codification holds no universal validity or appeal.[154] Rather, it belongs merely to one legal experience, i.e. that of the civil law tradition. Therefore, pressure to codify the common law or attempts to introduce a European civil code in common law jurisdictions may not only be futile (because it would not work) or harmful (because it would interrupt evolution) but also disrespectful—indeed, an act of violence—towards the common law legal culture. The idea of a European civil code would be nothing less than an attempt to abolish the common law tradition in Europe and to 'civilianize', as Legrand put it, the laws of England and Ireland.[155] Such views seem to suggest that an enacted private law would be incompatible with the common law. However, surely the English parliament, which is sovereign (which was the stated point of Brexit), in the (admittedly rather unlikely) case that it wished to enact its own English civil code would be free to do so? In the 1960s—well before the UK's accession to the European Communities in 1973—the English Law Commission drafted such a code.[156] It is not surprising that it was never enacted,[157] but would it have been illegitimate? In fact, in the most prominent common law jurisdiction in the world, i.e. the US, virtually all states have adopted a version of the Uniform Commercial Code. Moreover, today in England core parts of private law are in fact contained in statutes. Think of the Unfair Contract Terms Act 1977 and the Consumer Rights Act 2015, which are both Acts of Parliament. And sometimes, Law Commission proposals do lead to a reform of the common law of contract, as the examples of the Law Reform (Frustrated Contracts) Act 1943 and the Contracts (Rights of Third Parties) Act 1999 exemplify. So, contract law making by the legislature is not wholly incompatible with the common law tradition after all.

5. Liberal-Egalitarian

Liberal-egalitarian political theorists and social-democratic politicians are naturally committed to democracy. Indeed, the term 'liberal democracy' is often used as a synonym for Western democracy. Beyond this general commitment, however, we find wide divergence among liberal thinkers, both with regard to democratic institutions and to democratic practices, and not only in general but also specifically with respect to private law. While most liberals believe that the democratic majority should be constrained (by individual rights or public reason), some others emphatically reject such counter-majoritarian moves on liberal grounds. The heterogeneity of liberal views on

[153] Van Caeneghem (n. 6) 152.

[154] For an instance of constitutionalization of codification principle, see e.g. Art. 107(1), Dutch Constitution: 'Civil law, criminal law and civil and criminal procedure shall be regulated by Act of Parliament in general legal codes'.

[155] Legrand, 'Against a European Civil Code', 60 *MLR* (1997) 44.

[156] H. McGregor, *Contract Code: Drawn Up on Behalf of the English Law Commission* (1993).

[157] Nor was it ever published in the UK.

democracy calls for separate discussions of some of the leading voices in liberal political and legal theory.

A. Public Reason Revisited

In *A Theory of Justice*, Rawls refers to the first of his two principles of justice, i.e. the principle of equal liberty, for the specific context of determining the justice of the political process as guaranteed by the constitution, as the 'principle of equal participation'. This principle requires that all citizens have an equal right to partake in establishing the laws that will apply to them.[158] This right is not a merely formal right. Everyone must have 'a fair opportunity to take part in and to influence the political process'.[159] This may mean, for example, that when the rich have a disproportionate influence on legislation, compensating steps must be taken 'to preserve the fair value for all of the equal political liberties'.[160] At no point in his discussion of the equal right for citizens to influence the making of the laws that will apply to them does Rawls distinguish between different types or branches of the law, e.g. public and private law. When explaining, more generally, how the principles of justice ought to be applied in practice, Rawls introduces a four-stage sequence, i.e. (1) the adoption of principles of justice in the original position, (2) a constitutional convention, (3) the legislature, and (4) adjudication.[161] The last stage he defines as 'the application of rules to particular cases by judges and administrators'.[162] This suggests a sharp distinction between law making by the legislature and law-application by courts, with no space remaining for judicial law making.[163] It is remarkable that Rawls, who lived all his life in a common law jurisdiction, at no point even mentions the common law.[164] For him, it seems, in a constitutional democracy, legitimate law is limited to democratic legislation.

In *Political Liberalism*, which is more empirically grounded (or reconstructive, one could say) than *A Theory of Justice*, rather than providing a justification for democratic government, the political conception of justice presented by Rawls already presumes its presence. More specifically, he explains, a political conception of justice as he understands it, and of which his own principles of justice as fairness are but one instance, is meant for modern constitutional democracies.[165] The most influential contribution made by Rawls's political liberalism to democratic theory is his idea of public reason. In Chapter 2, that idea was outlined briefly. We will now further explore what it entails

158 J. Rawls, *A Theory of Justice* (1971), at 194.
159 Ibid. 197
160 Ibid. 198.
161 Ibid. section 31.
162 Ibid. 175.
163 As we will see, Habermas draws a very similar distinction. Contrast Bagchi, 'The Political Morality of Convergence in Contract', 1 *ELJ* (2018) 36, at 45, who suggests that democratic contract law making in the Rawlsian sense should not necessarily exclude judicial contract law making, at least not in certain jurisdictions: 'The rules of contract must be the product of democratic process (though we should not interpret that demand too narrowly, excluding, for example, the role of courts in lawmaking in certain jurisdictions).'
164 Neither in *A Theory of Justice* nor in *Political Liberalism*.
165 J. Rawls, *Political Liberalism* ([first published 1993] 2005), at 11.

for the democratic basis of (European) contract law. If we assume with Rawls that in a constitutional democracy contract law, like any law, has to be democratic, then the next question becomes: what do we mean by that? In particular, from the point of view of Rawls's political liberalism the central question is what limits, if any, the duty of public reasoning places on the democratic debate concerning (European) contract law.

As Rawls sees it, the requirement of public reason applies exclusively to public political debates, as opposed to merely private discussions, and only when they concern 'constitutional essentials and matters of basic justice'. What it demands is that the public discussion, when such constitutional essentials and questions of basic justice are at stake, be conducted exclusively in terms of the political conception of justice.[166] This means, in particular, that in the political debates on such matters participants should not rely (ultimately) on their 'comprehensive doctrines', i.e. their general worldviews and conceptions of the individual and common good. However, as we saw in Chapter 2, Rawls understands the notion of constitutional essentials and matters of basic justice very narrowly. So narrowly, in fact, that they are unlikely to include any of the fundamental political questions central to this book, let alone the more detailed matters of contract law drafting.

That result may be a little extreme, on the theory's own terms. Suppose a new contract law was proposed and adopted, whose core doctrines, or even its entire system, was justified explicitly with reference to, say, a religious dogma, a metaphysical assumption (e.g. concerning the essence of contract law), or a controversial ultimate value. Suppose, further, that other, more public reasons are not readily available to justify even the most fundamental rules and principles of that new contract law regime. Would this still be a legitimate contract law making process and outcome for a pluralist society?[167] And would a society with such a partisan contract law still be a sufficiently just society, one where non-believers are treated with equal respect? Should a political conception of justice, such as justice as fairness, not be more demanding in addressing the fact of reasonable pluralism? On the terms of Rawls's own principles, one would think it should. However, the limitation of the public reason demand to constitutional essentials and questions of basic justice seems to exclude this as a legitimacy requirement for contract law.

B. Private Law's Empire

1. Partnership Democracy

Dworkin's holistic liberal theory includes a conception of democracy, which he develops in contrast to majoritarianism.[168] The mere will of the majority has no

[166] Ibid. 44.

[167] On the other hand, different contract law systems may each be justifiable, albeit for different but equally public reasons. In other words, the public reason requirement does not suggest any single right answers on questions of justice in contract law. See Bagchi (n. 163) 39: 'The public reasons behind contract in liberal states can be of the right sort and yet differ among states.'

[168] See R. Dworkin, *Freedom's Law: The Moral Reading of the American Constitution* (1996), at 1–28; R. Dworkin, *Is Democracy Possible Here? Principles for a New Political Debate* (2006), ch. 5; R. Dworkin, *Justice for Hedgehogs* (2011), ch. 18. On liberal majoritarianism, see Section 5.B.5.

normative value, he claims. We always need to know first whether the subject is one that a given majority is entitled to legislate on. For example, the legislation may affect a much wider (or smaller) range of people, or concern areas of life protected by human rights. More generally, Dworkin denies the viability of purely procedural conceptions of democracy. He proposes a substantive conception of democracy, which he calls the partnership view of democracy. On the partnership conception, 'democracy means that the people govern themselves each as a full partner in a collective political enterprise so that a majority's decisions are democratic only when certain further conditions are met that protect the status and interests of each citizen as a full partner in that enterprise'.[169] More concretely, this means that there must a set of individual constitutional rights in place that can trump majority decisions.[170] This, in turn, means, according to Dworkin, that legislation violating individual rights must be set aside in judicial review. Moreover, on the partnership view, democratic decision making also has to be deliberative: 'Public political discourse must have a decent argumentative texture if we are to treat it as an exchange between mutually respectful partners who disagree.'[171]

Nothing in Dworkin's definition of a partnership democracy seems to exclude private law from its scope. On the contrary, it is quite a general (indeed universal) concept of democracy, grounded as it is in human dignity.[172] Dworkin even claims democratic deliberation is best understood itself as a debate over the best interpretation of two shared principles of human dignity, i.e. that each human life has equal intrinsic value and that each person has special personal responsibility for how well her or his own life goes.[173] Still, he nowhere even considers the possibility of democratic deliberation over matters of private law. The question is: why? It cannot be an attempt at realism (e.g. because he thinks that there is no reason to expect that private law could ever be democratic), given that his theory of democracy is avowedly utopian.[174] Rather, this blind spot for the possible need for a democratic private law (as a matter of human dignity) and even for the mere possibility that the democratic partners might want to deliberate and legislate on private law seems to follow from his conception of law.

2. Interpretivism

In a sense, Dworkin's theory of law,[175] which notably covers private law, is the opposite of a democratic theory. As an interpretivist theory,[176] it understands the law, especially the constitution and the common law, not as contingent and in need of justification

[169] Dworkin, *Is Democracy Possible Here?* (n. 168) 131.

[170] Dworkin therefore rejects the notion of a conflict between constitutionalism and democracy. He believes that 'the conflict is illusory, because it is based on an inaccurate understanding of what democracy is' (Dworkin, 'Constitutionalism and Democracy', 3 *European Journal of Philosophy* (1995) 2, at 2).

[171] Dworkin, *Is Democracy Possible Here?* (n. 168) 147.

[172] Ibid. 143; Dworkin, *Justice for Hedgehogs* (n. 168) 379.

[173] Dworkin, *Is Democracy Possible Here?* (n. 168) ch. 1.

[174] Ibid. 9. By his conception of democracy, according to Dworkin, writing more than a decade ago (ibid. 131), 'America falls short of being a true democracy' and it is questionable whether it will become one any time soon.

[175] See especially, R. Dworkin, *Law's Empire* (1986).

[176] Cf. Stavropoulos, 'Legal Interpretivism', in E. N. Zalta (ed.), *Stanford Encyclopedia of Philosophy*, available at https://plato.stanford.edu/entries/law-interpretivist/ (last visited 6 July 2020).

or legitimation, but as already there and in need of interpretation. According to Dworkin, legal interpretation has to meet the demands of fit with the legal materials, and of justification in terms of the community's principles of political morality. In addition, Dworkin draws a distinction between the common law, on the one hand, and legislation, on the other, where the former is understood as the source of general, abstract rights, while the latter depends on particular regulative policies.[177] Thus, in his account, the scope for democracy somehow seems to be limited to legislation.

Dworkin nowhere further justifies the legitimacy of the common law as such. For specific cases, he finds legitimacy in 'integrity', i.e. in a legal community's commitment to its own principles as expressed in past decisions (which may differ from one community to another).[178] He illustrates this with many private law examples, including his famous example of Elmer's case, on whether a grandson can inherit from the grandfather he murdered.[179] However, he never explains why exactly a political community ought to be committed to the value of integrity. Thus, it remains unclear why a political community should understand itself as being bound by past decisions of courts. His metaphor of the chain novel, where each judge writes a new chapter of the law, may provide an adequate description of the self-understanding of the common law judge, but integrity in itself does not offer a (normative) justification for *stare decisis*. Nor is it clear whether, on Dworkin's view, the demand for integrity competes with democratic principles or derives from them (or another principle grounding democracy, such as equality), and why this should mean that a democratic community's new insights should not prevail over its established precedents. As Waldron points out, 'there is still no explanation of *why* equality requires us to accept the discipline of keeping faith even with past decisions conceived as mistaken rather than enforcing with scrupulous consistency new principles which we think are better'.[180]

3. Taking the People Seriously?

At the end of the day, Dworkin's account of democratic law making does not seem particularly centred on the people—or the 'partners', as he calls them. By contrasting two models of democracy, one that turns on majority voting and another where judges play a more important role, he reduces the question of democracy to the very narrowly institutional one of judges versus legislatures. There is no discussion in his account of civil society, the public sphere, the role of experts, or similar. And by expressing confidence in the counter-majoritarian constraints to be enforced by judges as a way to increase *democratic* legitimacy he does in fact understand democracy in a way that seems to express 'discomfort' with (Unger) or even 'distrust' of (Forst) the people. Indeed, Dworkin's liberalism is the first that comes to mind with regard to 'jurisprudence's dirty little secret'. In addition, Dworkin's partnership theory also seems to have a blind spot specifically for private law. When he writes[181] that 'people

[177] Dworkin (n. 175) chs 8 and 9. Critical, R. Bellamy, *Political Constitutionalism: A Republican Defence of the Constitutionality of Democracy* (2007) 74.

[178] Dworkin (n. 175) ch. 6.

[179] Ibid. 15.

[180] Waldron, 'The Rise and Decline of Integrity', *New York University School of Law Public Law & Legal Theory Research Paper Series Working Paper*, no. 19-49 (2019).

[181] Dworkin, *Freedom's Law* (n. 168) 26.

who take personal responsibility for deciding what kind of life is valuable for them can nevertheless accept that issues of justice—about how the different and sometimes competing interests of all citizens should be accommodated—must be decided collectively, so that one decision is taken as authoritative for all', then one would expect that claim naturally to cover private law as well. It almost reads as a plea for a democratically enacted civil code, the 'civil constitution', as Carbonnier called it. Instead, however, he understands the moral reading of private law as a task reserved to judges. It is not immediately clear how this makes the people govern themselves as partners in a collective political enterprise.

4. Constitutionalization

Liberal-egalitarian theories have provided an especially important source of inspiration for advocates of the transformation of private law by constitutional values and the judicial review of private law by constitutional courts, both at the Member State and at the EU levels (private law constitutionalism).[182] And among European private law constitutionalists, the work of Dworkin, who famously argued for 'taking rights seriously' and presented rights as 'trumps' that can overrule majority decisions,[183] has been especially influential.[184] Interestingly enough, however, Dworkin's own discussion of judicial constitutionalization and judicial review is entirely concerned with the review of statutes, not of the common law, which, however, still constitutes the bulk of general private law (contract, property, and torts). But if constitutionalization is understood first and foremost as the judicial review of legislation, i.e. as a check on majoritarianism, then of course the common law may not be in need of constitutionalization, since it is not the product of legislative majorities but already judge-made.

5. Majoritarianism

Waldron's account of democratic legitimacy is the best-known and most articulated defence of law making exclusively through majoritarian legislation. This seems to speak directly against judicial contract law making, not only judicial review and the judicial 'constitutionalization' of contract law, but also against the common law of contract, and, logically, in favour of the codification of contract law. However, Waldron's core case against judicial review has not yet inspired him to present a similar case against the common law.[185] Beyond the rejection of judicial contract law making, Waldron's defence of the dignity of legislation and his argument for a democratic jurisprudence[186] could perhaps underscore, in a more positive vein, a democratic theory of contract law. Having said that, however, his understanding of democracy is so strongly vote-centric (majoritarian) that in the case of private law it is not clear it could ensure much more than what would seem merely nominal legitimation.

[182] This is not surprising, given that liberals were also the champions of the rights revolution in the US.

[183] R. Dworkin, *Taking Rights Seriously* (1978), at xi: 'Individual rights are political trumps held by individuals.'

[184] E.g. Mak, 'Hedgehogs in Luxembourg? A Dworkinian Reading of the CJEU's Case Law on Principles of Private Law and Some Doubts of the Fox', *ERPL* (2012) 323.

[185] Cf. Waldron (n. 7).

[186] Waldron, 'Can There Be a Democratic Jurisprudence?', *NYU School of Law, Public Law Research Paper*, no 08-35 (2008).

Take the example of the recent reforms of the law of obligations and the law of contract respectively in Germany and France. In both cases, the reforms were prepared by academic experts. When Germany had to transpose a series of EU directives, most notably the 1999 Consumer Sales Directive, into national law, the Ministry of Justice concluded this was the right moment for a comprehensive reform of the law of obligations. A committee of academic experts and judges had already presented a reform proposal in 1992.[187] That expert draft became the basis for the Ministry's reform proposal.[188] In particular, the introduction of a unitary system of remedies for breach of obligation, the centrepiece of the eventual reform, was copied from the original expert proposal. The reform proposal led to a major debate in legal academia.[189] Only when the leading private law scholar Canaris decided to back the proposal[190] did the *Zivilrechtslehrervereinigung*, the society of German private law scholars, vote in favour of it. After the academic debate, the proposal was adopted within six months of its formal submission to parliament, by the *Bundestag* and *Bundesrat*, in 2001.[191] The reform entered into force in 2002.[192] In France, a group of legal academics led by Professor Catala saw the upcoming Bicentenary of the *Code Civil*, in 2004, as the right occasion for proposing a reform of the law of obligations (*le projet Catala*).[193] Soon, another group, led by Professor Terré, made a counter-proposal with a specific focus on contract law (*le projet Terré*).[194] Then, the Ministry of Justice had its own draft prepared by a small group of academics and magistrates (*l'avant-projet de la Chancellerie*).[195] In France too, the debate among legal academics was intense. In particular, the proposed abolition of the doctrine of *la cause* proved quite controversial.[196]

There exist strong similarities between these recent contract law reforms in two of the EU's largest and most influential Member States. In both countries, the reform was heavily prepared by academics.[197] In both cases, too, the expert drafting was followed

[187] See *Abschlußbericht der Kommission zur Überarbeitung des Schuldrechts, Herausgegeben vom Bundesminister der Justiz* (Bundesanzeiger, 1992). The expert committee included Hein Kötz, Dieter Medicus, and Peter Schlechtriem among other prominent academic experts. See also the earlier reports and proposals: *Gutachten und Vorschläge zur Überarbeitung des Schuldrechts* (Vol I and II) (Bundesanzeiger, 1981 and 1983).

[188] See the *Diskussionsentwurf eines Schuldrechtsmodernisierungsgesetzes*, 2001.

[189] See, especially, the contributions to W. Ernst and R. Zimmermann (eds), *Zivilrechtswissenschaft und Schuldrechtsreform 2001: zum Diskussionsentwurf Eines Schuldrechtsmodernisierungsgesetzes des Bundesministeriums der Justiz* (2001).

[190] Canaris, 'Die Reform des Rechts der Leistungsstörungen' 10 *Juristenzeitung* (2001) 499.

[191] For further details, see C.-W. Canaris, *Schuldrechtsmodernisierung 2002* (2002), IX–XI.

[192] See Grundmann, 'Germany and the Schuldrechtsmodernisierung 2002', 1 *ERCL* (2005) 129, with further references.

[193] See *Avant-projet de reforme du droit des obligations (articles 1101 à 1386 du code civil) et du droit de la prescription (articles 2234 à 2281 du code civil): Rapport à Monsieur Pascal Clément, Garde des Sceaux, Ministre de la justice* (22 September 2003).

[194] F. Terré (ed.), *Pour une réforme du droit des contrats* (2009).

[195] Ministère de La Justice, *Projet de réforme du droit des contrats* (2008).

[196] See Fauvarque-Cosson, 'The French Contract Law Reform and the Political Process', 13 *ERCL* (2017) 337.

[197] For France, see ibid. 341: 'From the very beginning, the most crucial actors were French academics, outside parliament and also outside the Ministry of Justice.'

by a minimal political process.[198] In both countries, the respective Ministries of Justice were at least formally in charge of the drafting of the final proposal and also in practice did make some serious modifications—in France, especially, in response to criticism from stakeholders (chiefly from the business world). However, in both cases, there was a total absence of a meaningful role played by their respective parliaments. In particular, in both cases the time between the government's proposal and its enactment was extremely short. And in both cases there was no room for any amendments by parliament.

However, there was one remarkable difference. In France, parliament (*Sénat* and *Assemblée nationale*) did not even get to vote on the new contract law before its entrance into force—i.e. before it started to determine the contractual rights and obligations of citizens and other contracting parties—since the reform was enacted by presidential decree, while in Germany, as we saw, both the *Bundestag* and *Bundesrat* had a vote on the reform. This raises the question of how much this matters from a legitimacy point of view. In particular, the question arises of whether in one country (France) the reform lacked a democratic basis, while in the other (Germany) the reform was democratic. From the point view of liberal majoritarianism, as defended by Waldron, it would seem, there was indeed a crucial difference between the German and the French reforms, perhaps even a categorical one. From this viewpoint, it seems the German reform was fully legitimate, while the French reform wholly lacked legitimacy.[199] (Or, if the subsequent ratification by Parliament is considered as making a crucial difference, it obtained legitimacy three years after its entrance into force.) By contrast, from the perspectives of certain other political theories the matter is likely to look quite differently. Civic republicans, as we will see, have a much less vote-centric and more talk-centric conception of democracy, where there is extensive debate in society (not merely among legal experts) and in parliament (e.g. on the merits of various proposals for amendments, and more generally on the merits of the reform, e.g. in terms of weaker party protection and freedom of contract). Therefore, they are likely to regard the difference between the French and German reforms in terms of legitimacy, as mostly formal, and therefore rather minimal. Similarly, from a Habermasian point of view a key question will be whether public opinions at the periphery of society

[198] As mentioned earlier, in France there was a political debate, not on the merits of the contract law reform, but on the legitimacy of a reform of contract law without the involvement of parliament. See also J.-P. Sueur, *Président de la commission des lois*, at the Senate session of 21 January 2014, responding to the Minister of Justice, Christiane Taubira, who had claimed that the government's plan to enact a new contract law by presidential decree did not constitute an expropriation of parliament:

> La République a voulu que la loi fût écrite non pas par des juristes, si brillants et si compétents soient-ils, mais par les représentants de la nation. C'est un processus au sein duquel tous les groupes s'expriment. Chaque parlementaire intervient dans le feu du débat et, de débat en débat, on arrive peu à peu à écrire un texte, poli et repoli au fil des navettes ... De cette manière, s'ébauche peu à peu, puis se perfectionne cette loi dont tous les mots, toutes les lignes, tous les alinéas s'appliqueront à l'ensemble du peuple français, souvent pour des décennies, voire des siècles.

Available at: www.senat.fr/seances/s201401/s20140121/s20140121011.html (last visited 6 July 2020).

[199] Cf. Waldron (n. 1) 54: 'A single elective ruler—an American President, for example—may have democratic credentials in virtue of having more popular support than any other candidate for his office. But these are not the sort of democratic credentials we associate with legislation.'

have an equal opportunity of influencing the reform or whether the reform is dominated by experts' opinions or by the lobbying of well-organized interest groups.

There was also another important difference. It concerned the substance of the reform. And it is more puzzling, at least from an egalitarian justice point of view (both interpersonal and social). In both cases, the reform was presented chiefly as a 'modernization' of the law of contract.[200] However, in France this meant a marked 'socialization', i.e. a striking move to the political left. With the extension of the role of the general duty of good faith to the pre-contractual stage (Article 1104), the introduction of the new broad category of contracts of adhesion (Article 1110), the codification of a general pre-contractual information duty (Article 1112-1), the introduction of a new doctrine of exploitation of dependence (Article 1143), and, finally, the acceptance of the doctrine of *imprévision* (Article 1195), referring to the concept of excessive onerosity, which overturned a longstanding rejection of the doctrine by the *Cour de Cassation*,[201] the reform has been characterized rightly as 'a shift towards more contractual justice'.[202] While perhaps falling short of a new manifesto for social justice in European contract law,[203] the reformed French law of contract easily qualifies as Europe's most modern social model of contract law, beating also the EU's *acquis communautaire*. Moreover, a very large part of the new provisions, especially the more social ones, were borrowed directly from the DCFR and the CESL. With some exaggeration it could be said that the greatest success, at least in terms of substantive influence, of the European civil code movement has been in France. This is ironic in two respects. First, because the reform was inspired strongly by motivations of national pride. The reform was meant to present a modern French model of contract law as a defence against foreign dominance. Secondly, because France was probably the country where the opposition against the DCFR and the CESL was strongest. Arguably, such a distinctly social and Europe-minded reform would have had less of a chance of being adopted had it gone through parliament in the usual way instead of via the shortcut of a promulgation by presidential decree. Therefore, the case of the French contract law reform very clearly illustrates—contrary, for example, to what the Social Justice Manifesto had suggested[204]—the possible tension between democratic legitimacy and social justice, and the difference between substantive and procedural justice. If the most social contract law reform in Europe was adopted by presidential decree where does this leave those who advocate a democratic contract law in the name of social justice?[205] This is a troubling question not only for liberal majoritarians

[200] Rightly sceptical with regard to the meaningfulness of claims to modernization, is Fabre-Magnan, 'What Is a Modern Law of Contracts? Elements for a New Manifesto for Social Justice in European Contract Law', 13 *ERCL* (2017) 376, at 377: 'It is not enough simply to say that something is "new" or "modern". As the manager of the *Théâtre des Funambules* said in one of the most beautiful films in the history of French cinema, "*Le public demande sans cesse du nouveau. Du nouveau, de la nouveauté. À quoi ça ressemble? C'est vieux comme le monde, ça, la nouveauté*"!'

[201] Cass. Civ, 6 March 1876, *D* 1876, 1, 193 (*Canal de Craponne*).

[202] Fauvarque-Cosson (n. 196) 348.

[203] Fabre-Magnan (n. 200).

[204] The Manifesto claimed that democratic legitimacy and weaker party protection would go hand in hand.

[205] See notably, M. W. Hesselink (ed.), *The Politics of a European Civil Code* (2006); and Hesselink, 'A Democratic Contract Law', 11 *ERCL* (2015) 81.

like Waldron, but also for civic republicans like Bellamy and for Habermasian discourse theorists, as we will see in the next sections.

In fact, there was a further twist, perhaps even more troubling from a democratic point of view. When it came to ratification, a choice had to be made between a 'lock, stock and barrel' ratification (*ratification sèche*) or a 'reform of the reform' (*réforme de la réforme*); there was a sustained attempt in the Senate to achieve the latter. It ultimately failed. However, some non-negligible modifications were made. And they all went in the same, libertarian (*libéral*, in French), political direction of more freedom of contract and less contractual justice. Moreover, strikingly the partially successful attack on the social model of the reform is attributed by observers to strong lobbying from the side of big business, in particular the financial industry.[206]

C. Promoting Sound Decisions

Perfectionists consider it the state's task to improve the lives of its citizens by some standard of goodness. Liberal perfectionists take autonomy to be that standard and, therefore, claim that the state should promote personal autonomy. If it is the state's task to promote the good of its citizens, in particular their autonomy, then what does this mean for our question of whether contract law must have a democratic basis? Liberal perfectionists are outspoken about the importance of contract law for personal autonomy and, vice versa, the importance of autonomy to contract law. They are also quite clear on the crucial role of the state in promoting autonomy. However, from the perspective of liberal perfectionism, which state institutions should be entrusted with the task of promoting personal autonomy through contract law? Do liberal perfectionists prefer one institution—or set of actors—over another, or do they perhaps even require the involvement of specific actors? The answer to this question seems to be negative.

In particular, given liberal perfectionists' understanding of autonomy as private autonomy, i.e. individual self-determination, they do not seem to require, as a matter of their liberal perfectionist principles, that generally applicable laws necessarily be the result of collective self-determination, i.e. public autonomy. Certainly, Raz has a theory of democracy, which is teleological, but it is not based on autonomy, i.e. it is not liberal perfectionist.[207] He defines democracy as follows:

> Democracy is best understood as a political system allowing individuals opportunities for informed participation in the political process whose purpose is the promotion of sound decisions. Democracy is justified inasmuch as it is necessary to serve the well-being of people. It shares the general structure of authority and relies, for its legitimacy, on its ability to deliver sound decisions.[208]

[206] See Mekki, 'La loi de ratification de l'ordonnance du 10 février 2016: une réforme de la réforme?', *Recueil Dalloz* (2018) 900; and Mazeaud, 'Quelques mots sur la réforme de la réforme du droit des contrats', *Recueil Dalloz* (2018) 912.

[207] On the relationship between liberalism, perfectionism, and teleology, see de Marneffe, 'Liberalism and Perfectionism', 43 *American Journal of Jurisprudence* (1998) 99.

[208] Raz (n. 125) 117.

Thus, Raz's understanding of democracy is teleological because it understands it as aiming to promote some good. The objective is sound decisions promoting wellbeing. The democratic legitimacy of, say, a contract law reform depends on how well it contributes to people's wellbeing, not on how much everyone to whom the new contract law will apply had a chance to influence its content. From this point of view, then, there might exist better ways of democratic law making than ones aimed at ensuring that the addressees of the laws will be able to regard themselves also as their authors (which is the Habermasian requirement for democratic legitimacy, as we will see later, in Section 7.E).

Moreover, from a liberal perfectionist point of view there may also be better ways of ensuring the promotion of personal autonomy through contract than via a democratically enacted contract law. Indeed, in their explicitly liberal perfectionist theory of contract law, which they characterize as a political theory, Dagan and Heller do not require contract law to have a democratic basis at all. This is remarkable especially in the light of the fact that their core idea is that contract law should provide an attractive menu of contract types. Given that these types will be made available as options to everyone within the jurisdiction, and that people are likely to have diverging views about which types should count as attractive—two points the authors themselves emphasize—one might expect that the most legitimate—but also the most pragmatic—way of trying to compose a menu of sufficiently attractive options in the eyes of everyone within the contract law system's prospective jurisdiction, would be to involve all of them as much as possible in the process. Instead, Dagan and Heller write:

> democracy cannot substitute for choice theory in providing the normative underpinning of liberal contract law. Considering democracy as the foundational value conflates the search for substantive moral truth with that of institutional legitimacy. It also overstates the comparative advantage—in terms of either competence or legitimacy—of legislatures vis-à-vis courts in private law matters. By whichever path we take concerning concrete neutrality, we return to choice theory.[209]

Thus, first, they reaffirm their (cognitivist realist) perfectionism where law making (in this case contract law making) is understood as a search for substantive moral truth. Presumably, whoever has found the moral truth about contract law does not need democracy. Nor, on their view, it seems, can democracy be of much assistance in bringing us any closer to that truth (epistemic inferiority of legislatures compared to courts).[210] Secondly, according to Dagan and Heller, as private law makers courts may do just as well as legislatures, and perhaps even better, both in terms of competence and of legitimacy. Competence presumably means here the capacity to design a contract law menu, i.e. knowing what the more attractive options are and what would be a sufficiently wide range of options (again, epistemic inferiority). What legitimacy should mean in this context is much less clear. If the legitimacy derives from the law

[209] Dagan and Heller (n. 125) 90.

[210] Obviously, their liberal perfectionism is uninhibited by any public reason requirement, characteristic of political liberalism, to refrain from invoking ethical truths about ultimate values and the meaning of life as a precondition for the legitimacy of a society's basic structure.

maker's capacity to design an autonomy-promoting contract law, then the concept seems redundant. If it is a distinct concept and, especially, if it is a separate demand that the law (or the law maker), including contract law (and the contract law maker), must meet, then we need to know what exactly would make contract law, its maker, or the law making process, legitimate and how that demand relates both to competence and to moral truth. Suppose legitimacy requires some form of democracy: does this mean that on Dagan and Heller's perfectionist view legitimacy may sometimes require the enactment of contract law by less than competent law makers or the implementation of propositions about contract law that are understood to be morally false? Finally, note that Dagan and Heller understand the question of whether or not contract law should be democratic as a matter of legislatures versus courts, implying that the legitimacy they think courts could give to contract law would not be specifically democratic legitimacy. Thus, they do not claim that the common law of contract is democratic; rather, they explicitly contrast judge-made law with democracy. However, as we will see presently, other liberals instead commend the judge-made common law of contract precisely for its democratic credentials.

D. The Democratic Value of the Common Law

While most liberals merely acknowledge the instrumental value of democracy as the best means for implementing liberal principles, in particular principles of liberal justice, Shiffrin, in her Tanner lectures, emphasizes the intrinsic value of democracy.[211] In her view, the intrinsic value of democratic law is that it uniquely enables us to communicate to each other our commitment to justice and our other collective moral duties.[212] It matters that we should not only treat each other as moral equals, but also publicly communicate to each other our commitment to do so, by generating and articulating democratic law. And she proposes the common law of contract as a prominent example of democratic law.[213]

Shiffrin offers three arguments for the democratic importance of the common law. First, she argues, the common law method of law making has some distinctive democratic virtues:

> common law judges are in conversation with litigants, amici, and other judges over the generations and throughout the states. The issues themselves arise from the grass roots, in a way, as problems occur. Any party who may allege a prima facie cause of action may present arguments, have them heard, and elicit a reasoned response.[214]

This contrasts favourably, she argues, with the legislature, which is responsive mostly to lobbyists and political donors. 'Thereby', she claims, 'the common law

[211] Tanner Lectures on Human Values at UC Berkeley, 2016–2017, *Speaking Amongst Ourselves: Democracy and Law*, S. V. Shiffrin, 'Democratic Law' (Lecture 1) and 'Common and Constitutional Law: A Democratic Legal Perspective' (Lecture 2).
[212] Ibid. Lecture 1.
[213] Ibid. Lecture 2.
[214] Ibid. Lecture 2, at 17.

process embodies a judicial manifestation of the equal importance of each citizen, less sensitive to affiliation and social power'.[215] This optimistic account of judicial law making seems to overlook a number of well-known aspects of the reality of civil litigation: that in civil cases judges are informed first and foremost by the parties, who have every reason to act strategically rather than deliberatively; that most ordinary citizens cannot afford litigation; that civil litigation may take many years (sometimes decades); that the citizens with the deepest pockets are most likely to come out ahead; and that civil litigation often involves corporations, which should not be considered as equals to citizens when it comes to democratic law making. Moreover, it is not entirely clear how it is ideal that citizens communicate their moral commitments towards one another through the opinions of judges. In a democratic polity, should they not address each other more directly?

Secondly, she argues that compared to legislation, the scope of the common law is broader and more trans-substantive: 'Because common law reasoning places greater pressure on courts to think comprehensively about how a concept's interpretation will fit into the legal system as a whole, there is some structural pressure for common law reasoning to generate greater trans-substantive unity than the more focused agenda enacted by statutes.'[216] From a comparative law perspective this is a somewhat surprising claim. The best-known and most important examples of legislation in the field of private law are civil codes. Civil codes and civil law reasoning more generally are usually contrasted with the common law and its method for being more systematic and based on general principles, while the common law method is usually characterized as piecemeal (or worse)[217] and focused on solving specific problems.[218]

Thirdly, she argues, common law courts may enjoy greater versatility than legislators to articulate law that responds to the circumstances of the case through 'clean-up' doctrines like good faith.[219] While it is true that, especially in civil law jurisdictions, the doctrine of good faith has indeed played such a role as a catalyst for modernization in contract law,[220] nevertheless there may be some democratic merit in periodically codifying the new rules and doctrines developed by courts on the basis of good faith, and where necessary improving them after public and parliamentary deliberation. This is exactly what happened in the Dutch (1992), German (2002), and French (2016) reforms where doctrines such as pre-contractual liability, pre-contractual information duties, contractual duties of care, the right to withhold performance, and change of circumstances—all of which had been developed by courts in the preceding decades

215 Ibid. Lecture 2, at 18.
216 Ibid. Lecture 2, at 18.
217 See the unflattering characterizations by Bentham, cited earlier, in Section 3.C.
218 See e.g. Bingham LJ in *Interfoto Picture Library Ltd v. Stiletto Visual Programmes Ltd* [1989] 1 QB 433, at 439, with reference to the general principle of good faith:

> In many civil law systems, and perhaps in most legal systems outside the common law world, the law of obligations recognises and enforces an overriding principle that in making and carrying out contracts parties should act in good faith. ... English law has, characteristically, committed itself to no such overriding principle but has developed piecemeal solutions in response to demonstrated problems of unfairness.

219 Ibid.
220 See Hesselink (n. 25).

on the basis of the general doctrine of good faith—were codified and assigned their respective proper places within the overall system of the code.

What Shiffrin really seems to have in mind, then, are the merits of general contract law (and general private law), as opposed to specific statutes each with their own narrow scope and specific regulatory objectives. However, there is no reason to think that general principles of private law are best developed on a case-by-case basis, on a narrow informational basis, by judges who all tend to belong to a specific social class (or intersection of social groups) that is much narrower and less diverse than society at large and who differ from case to case, without at any given moment the judges—or the parties to these various cases—deliberating all together and publicly. On the contrary, from a point of view both of coherence and of democratic legitimacy—the main concern of Shiffrin's Tanner lectures—public deliberation, communication, and justification by the legislator are likely, at least under equally ideal circumstances (her focus),[221] to be superior to whatever the common law method can achieve. Therefore, on its own terms, that is as a liberal-egalitarian case for the common law of contract *as* democracy, i.e. the idea that the common law method of law making makes us a more democratic society—as opposed to an argument of the kind we saw above for judge-made contract law *in spite* of its weaker democratic credentials than enacted contract law (both under ideal circumstances)—the argument is not fully convincing.

In an earlier paper, Shiffrin argued for the merits of legal standards over rules, specifically on moral and democratic grounds.[222] The idea is that a polity thrives to the extent that citizens are able to make autonomous moral judgements, that this capacity is developed through training, and that while hard-and-fast rules brings citizens into a compliance mode, standards like good faith and fair dealing invite them to deliberate, individually and collectively, about what conduct may be expected from them. While the argument, which emphasizes the constitutive benefits for society of 'making possible richer forms of moral and democratic relations than would otherwise take place',[223] sounds more republican than liberal, and also verges on perfectionism because of its rather thick understanding of citizens' moral agency, what matters most here is that the codification into specific rules of doctrines developed by courts on the basis of general standards such as good faith may constitute a democratic loss from the perspective proposed by Shiffrin. On the other hand, however, it important to realize that the use of standards in private law making is by no means specific for the common law or necessarily introduced through judge-made law. This was well illustrated by the 1992 recodification in the Netherlands, where the new civil code massively resorted to good faith and fair dealing and other open-ended standards.[224] Similarly, the main

221 See Shiffrin (n. 211) Lecture 1.

222 Shiffrin, 'Inducing Moral Deliberation: on the Occasional Virtues of Fog', 123 *Harvard Law Review* (*Harv. L. Rev.*) (2010) 1214.

223 Ibid. 1223.

224 Think also of the DCFR, which was severely criticized for its extensive use of standards, notably reasonableness. See e.g. Eidenmüller *et al.* (n. 146) 675:

> The legal uncertainty caused by the widespread use of blanket provisions is further aggravated by the frequent appearance of open-ended legal concepts in the requirements established by the DCFR's rules for triggering specific legal consequences and in the definitions of those consequences themselves. Standing out in particular is the excessive use of the term 'reasonable'. 'Reasonable' appears to be the solution to every conceivable problem.

references for the general good faith duty in the US are § 1-304 Uniform Commercial Code and § 205 Restatement (Second) of Contracts.

6. Civic Republican

Republicans are strongly committed to democracy, albeit for varying reasons and with divergent institutional implications. One strand of republicanism, going back to Aristotle and the Greek *polis*, regards the participation of citizens in democratic politics as the best way for each of them to live a good, virtuous life.[225] The role model for this 'civic humanist' interpretation of the republican ideal is the Athenian citizen. Today, such a perfectionist understanding of democratic citizenship is found mostly in the more communitarian readings of the democratic republic.[226] It is rejected by those republicans who take the Italian republics of the Renaissance and the Dutch, American, and French revolutions as their historical models.[227] These 'civic republicans' consider freedom as non-domination to be the core value of republicanism. From this point of view, democratic government is the best—or the only—political regime to ensure freedom as non-domination. Civic republicans can easily agree in principle that it follows from republican freedom as non-domination that all generally applicable laws require a democratic basis. Yet, this shared normative starting point, as we will see, leads different civic republicans in strongly divergent, at times even diametrically opposed, directions when it comes to the institutional and other practical implications of the principle of freedom as non-domination for politics and law making. One possible explanation is that civic republicanism is a teleological theory of freedom, not a deontological theory of political autonomy or agency.[228] Therefore, for civic republicans the same result, i.e. more freedom as non-domination, can be reached through different means. What works best for freedom as non-domination then becomes an empirical question. Here, I will first contrast the views of Pettit and Bellamy, respectively, on how democratic government can and must ensure freedom as non-domination, with a specific focus on what this means for private law making. Then I will discuss the more communitarian version of republicanism recently defended by Saprai.

[225] Cf. Lovett, 'Republicanism', in E.N. Zalta (ed.), *The Stanford Encyclopedia of Philosophy*, at 15, available at https://plato.stanford.edu/entries/republicanism/ (last visited 6 July 2020). See e.g. H. Arendt, *Between Past and Future* (2006), ch. 4: 'What is Freedom?' 152; Held (n. 33) 29.

[226] E.g. M. J. Sandel, *Democracy's Discontent: America in Search of a Public Philosophy* (1996), at 5.

[227] But see G. S. Wood, *The Radicalism of the American Revolution* (1991), at 368, referring to 'the revolutionaries' dream of building a classical republic of elitist virtue'.

[228] A set of theories where political autonomy is central, i.e. the discourse theories of law, democracy, and politics, will be discussed presently.

A. On the People's Terms

1. Tough luck

Pettit understands political legitimacy as a matter of the vertical relationship between citizens and the state that rules over them, as opposed to the horizontal relationships of citizens to one another, which, on this view, is the issue of social justice.[229] 'The point of legitimacy', he writes, 'is to ensure that you and your fellow citizens are not subject to an alien, controlling will'.[230] He proposes the 'tough-luck test' as a good index for political legitimacy: whether you can regard the outcome of the political process—for example in our case, of contract law making—as just tough luck, simply the result of the fact that a different view prevailed among the majority of your co-citizens, not that one or more others schemed against you or the group to which you belong.[231] In all cases where the tough luck test is met, Pettit writes, 'that the state enacts an unjust policy, by your lights, will be the result of the bad luck of your having many culpably ignorant or indifferent compatriots, not a result of its harbouring an alien will'.[232]

Pettit explains how citizens can have control over government without actively shaping its course, using the metaphor of riding a horse and allowing it leeway, without ever losing control over the horse. For this reason, he rejects Rousseauvian participatory conceptions of democratic government.[233] From the point of view of freedom as non-domination and the tough luck test, it is not necessary for all citizens to be actively engaged in shaping a 'general will'. Contestation is more important for a democracy than participation. For this reason, people must be on guard. What is needed is 'civic vigilance'.[234] Again, there is no need for everybody to be on guard about everything all the time. Specialization and organization is what is really needed. In short, 'a division of labour in the exercise of civic vigilance'.[235] For European contract law, for example, this could mean that it is more important that consumer protection groups are active and make an important impact on the debate, as BEUC certainly has done at the EU level, than that sustained but probably futile attempts be made to engage the European electorate in a broad societal and political debate on the future of European contract law.[236]

[229] P. Pettit, *On the People's Terms: A Republican Theory and Model of Democracy* (2012), at 136. This is in sharp contrast, for example, to political liberals, like Rawls, and discourse theorists, like Habermas and Forst, who understand social justice largely as legitimacy, in terms of the kind of reasons that can justify the basic structure of society (i.e. its core political and socio-economic and arrangements). Explicitly against the 'confusion' of social justice with political legitimacy in public justifiability accounts, and the undue overshadowing of the former by the latter, see Pettit, ibid. 146.

[230] Ibid. 177.

[231] Ibid. 176.

[232] Ibid. 178.

[233] See Rousseau, 'Le contrat social', Book III, ch. 15 (1762) in J. J. Rousseau *Œuvres Complètes*, Vol. III (1964) 429: 'La Souveraineté ne peut être représentée, par la même raison qu'elle ne peut être aliénée.' Note, however, that Rousseau distinguished sharply between the legislator (the 'sovereign') and the executive (the 'government'), where only the former, which interests us here, requires direct participation. See ibid. 430.

[234] Pettit (n. 229) 226.

[235] Ibid. 226.

[236] For such a (failed) attempt, see e.g. Hesselink, 'Europese Verkiezingen Moeten Over Europees Burgerlijk Wetboek Gaan', *Nederlands Juristenblad* (2004) 1169 (arguing that the then upcoming European Parliament elections of 2004 should be about a European civil code).

2. Experts as Proxies for the People

Another implication of Pettit's understanding of democratic legitimacy is that from this point of view judicial (contract) law making and other expert involvement are not per se problematic at all. What matters is that the experts genuinely work in the public interest. Then, even if citizens do not participate in the contract law making, they are still not dominated by any alien will, as long as the relevant judges or expert groups genuinely do their best to act in the public interest. Pettit formulates four specific requirements. The judges or other experts must (1) be selected on the basis of their experience, expertise, and impartiality; (2) be exposed to incentives of professional esteem; (3) be given a brief that enjoys presumptive popular support; and (4) operate under conditions of publicity with a realistic possibility of being exposed to criticism and contestation.[237] At least some of the expert groups involved in the drafting in recent contract law proposals and reforms in England (reform proposals from the Law Commission), the Netherlands (new Civil Code 1992), Germany (the 2002 reform law of the obligations), France (the contract law reform of 2016), and the EU (the 2011 CESL proposal) seem to meet these requirements. At the very least, their set-up, composition, and brief, it seems, were meant to do so.[238] In Pettit's view, genuine expert involvement is not only permissible but necessary: unelected authorities play a crucial role, as 'proxies for the people', in complementing and containing elected politicians.[239]

3. The Dual-Aspect Model of Democracy

Pettit proposes a model of democracy with a dual aspect, i.e. short and long term. According to Pettit, in any practice of popular self-government over time some decision making norms will develop that enjoy widespread acceptance.[240] And these norms will end up constraining future political debate, as 'deliberative regulation'. In spite of the apparent similarity with deliberative democracy models inspired by Habermas, there is the important difference that in Pettit's dual-aspect model of democracy, the norms are a (long-haul) by-product of (short-haul) day-to-day politics. They come about through an 'invisible-hand mechanism'. They are not the object of deliberation but the side-effect of ordinary politics.[241] Participants in the political debate will learn that they are not going to convince others with arguments that these others cannot relate to. They will have to offer considerations, in support of or against a proposal, that all others can regard as relevant: 'Those who present considerations that can only carry weight with a particular subgroup will be laughed out of court.'[242] Once this 'norm of norms' becomes established, over time, certain types of reasons will become widely understood as being off the table. This leads to the gradual emergence of more specific norms as an 'inevitable by-product' of the political debate: 'Over the

[237] Pettit (n. 229) 236–237.

[238] See e.g. Commission Decision 2010/233/EU of 26 April 2010, OJ L105/109, Setting Up the Expert Group on a Common Frame of Reference in the Area of European Contract Law, especially Art. 4 (Membership-Appointment).

[239] Pettit (n. 229) 237. See also P. Pettit, *Republicanism: A Theory of Freedom and Government* (1997), at 239: 'The committee is the enzyme of the body politic, at least in the republican conception of that body.'

[240] Pettit (n. 229) 264.

[241] Ibid. 276.

[242] Ibid. 254.

long haul, a deliberatively regulated politics will generate and regenerate a supply of publicly valorized considerations. These will serve at any particular time to keep an indefinite number of policies and processes off the table, rendering them unthinkable and invisible.'[243] Thus, while these norms were never explicitly subject to deliberation, they will nevertheless develop non-intentionally.[244]

From the point of view of the republican dual-aspect model of democracy, therefore, the debate on—in our case—contract law is not constrained by any public reason requirement according to which only justifications are permitted that no one *could reasonably* reject, with reference to an independent standard or procedure for non-rejectability such as Forst's proposed standard of generality and reciprocity.[245] Only those considerations that no one in the society at hand *would* reject—and all of them—are off the table. In other words, Pettit's account of the norms constraining the democratic debate is entirely descriptive (and perhaps predictive), not itself normative. For example, people might learn not to propose essentialist contract theories because if they did they would be laughed out of court. Or, say, Marxist theories may be off the table because such radical ideas are unthinkable or invisible among contract law makers. But this seems wrong. Whatever the merits of essentialist or Marxist contract law theories it is these substantive merits that should be decisive for their impact on law making, not the likelihood of their defeat. There is a difference between democratic deliberation and preaching to the choir. Also, contestation seems far from easy when it comes to norms that are said to be given by an invisible hand. In summary, the dual aspect model of democracy seems to carry serious risks of tunnel vision, if not outright conservatism, and tyranny over all those whose ideas happen to be regarded as off the table for no good reason.[246]

B. Political Constitutionalism

1. Democracy as Constitution

While Pettit, as we just saw, accepts judicial law making and the judicial review of statutes as legitimate, on account of the judges' expertise, impartiality, and specific brief as proxies for the people,[247] another prominent contemporary republican, who does endorse Skinner's and Pettit's understanding of freedom as non-domination, strongly rejects judicial review as an expression of what he calls 'legal constitutionalism' and

[243] Ibid. 270.

[244] The dual-aspect model of democracy, Pettit argues (ibid. 309), meets the standard for democracy of government of the people, by the people, for the people, famously set by Lincoln in his Gettysburg Address, on all three counts. See address delivered by Abraham Lincoln at the dedication of the Soldiers' National Cemetery in Gettysburg, Pennsylvania, 19 November 1863.

[245] See Chapter 2, Section 2.G.6. Pettit explicitly rejects Rawlsian public reason and Habermasian deliberative democracy models that refer to some independent standard of reasonableness. See especially, Pettit (n. 229) 254, 257, and 267.

[246] Conversely, some policies and processes (e.g. dominating or exploitative ones) may still be on the table merely because no one so far has dared to contest them or even realized they could speak out against them. See Spivak, 'Can the Subaltern Speak?' [first published 1985], in P. Williams and L. Chrisman (eds), *Colonial Discourse and Post-Colonial Theory: A Reader* (1994) 66.

[247] Other prominent republican defenders of judicial review include Michelman and Sunstein.

proposes 'political constitutionalism' in its stead.[248] Bellamy not only rejects judicial review but even the written constitution, and in particular a constitutional bill of rights,[249] because, according to the political conception of constitutionalism, 'the democratic process *is* the constitution'.[250]

Following Waldron, Bellamy argues that in pluralist societies reasonable disagreement is to be expected not only with regard to questions concerning the good life but also in matters of justice. As we saw, Rawls argued that in contemporary constitutional democracies that are characterized by the fact of reasonable pluralism of worldviews, citizens who want to live together with equal respect for each other should try to reach an overlapping consensus among their worldviews concerning a political conception of justice that is self-standing with regard to each of these comprehensive doctrines. However, Bellamy argues (with Waldron) that there is no reason to think that the burdens of judgement will affect only people's opinions and deliberations concerning values and the common good, and not also their views on justice.[251] As he points out, 'debates between libertarians and social democrats are not within a political framework of rights, they are about that framework'.[252] So, in addition to the 'circumstances of justice' (Hume, Rawls), i.e. the presence of competing claims on scarce resources between which justice must arbitrate, a society also faces the 'circumstances of politics', i.e. disagreement, even among citizens who fully respect each other as equals, on the question of what justice requires in matters where a collective decision is needed.[253] The argument concentrates on social justice and human rights, but it can easily be extended to the questions of interpersonal justice that are particularly relevant to private law. If we disagree on the ultimate value(s) that private law (or contract law) is based on, then we are unlikely to reach a unanimous view on what an autonomous conception of interpersonal justice should entail for private law relationships.

The implication is that as a society we have no uncontroversial way of knowing what justice requires. The general determination of human rights and principles of justice and their interpretation with a view to a specific case are within the circumstances of politics.[254] Under these circumstances (i.e. the circumstances of politics), the best that citizens can do is to allow each other an equal say in the matter. And the best way to ensure political equality is majority voting. To replace the view of the majority of the legislature with that of a limited elite, i.e. the majority in a constitutional court, is arbitrary and, therefore, an act of domination. The argument that judicial review is legitimated by the expertise of judges concerning the implications of the fundamental

[248] Bellamy (n. 177).

[249] Ibid. 3.

[250] Ibid. 5 (emphasis in original).

[251] Ibid. 22–23. One cause of the fact of reasonable pluralism, i.e. one reason why disagreement about comprehensive world views is not likely to go away even among reasonable people (who are neither in bad faith nor biased or opportunistic), according to Rawls, are what he calls the 'burdens of judgment'. By this Rawls means that the judgment of each of us inevitably will be determined, in part, by our own particular vantage point. Each of us has had different experiences in our lives, which will inevitably colour our general views on life and the world around us, and will burden our judgments, including on subjects under public deliberation. Each of us will assess the available evidence, balance the interests, evaluate the arguments, and interpret the question differently. As a consequence, even if everyone participating in the political debate is perfectly reasonable and guided by the utmost public spirit, different persons are still likely to disagree, especially on the most foundational questions of life and the world we live in. See Rawls (n. 165) 54.

[252] Bellamy (n. 177) 24. See also, ibid. 26.

[253] Ibid. 5.

[254] Ibid. 20.

rights protected by the constitution does not hold, given the circumstances of politics, where the burdens of judgement will inevitably lead to contrasting views on the determination and interpretation of human rights, and where an uncontroversial standard for determining the truth in these matters is unavailable.[255]

2. The Procedural Account of Public Reasoning

For the same reason, Bellamy argues, all substantive notions of public reasoning must be rejected. The requirement that only certain substantive reasons can be used in matters of basic justice is incoherent since in those matters the question of exactly what those reasons could be is what keeps citizens divided. It is both impossible and undesirable to keep controversial views on values and norms out of politics,[256] especially since we lack an epistemology for arriving at the truth in these matters. In Bellamy's view, a genuinely public form of reasoning is one where all sides are heard: 'the aim is to provide opportunities for the public to reason rather than specifying a rarefied type of public reasoning'.[257] Bellamy calls this the procedural account of public reasoning.[258] On this purely procedural understanding, judicial public reasoning cannot replace public reasoning by the citizens themselves: 'public reasoning has to be by the public'.[259]

3. Actually Existing Democracy

Bellamy debunks the notion that citizens are only motivated by selfish preferences without any concern for the interests and views of others. There is no empirical evidence in support of this view of democratic citizens. On the contrary, there is reason to believe that ordinary citizens are more sensitive than judges, who belong to society's elite, to the predicament of those individuals and groups human rights and judicial review are meant to protect.[260] In any case, the self-interested voter would not even bother to go out to vote (rational voter paradox).[261] Therefore, Bellamy argues, 'voting is more like expressing a judgement or set of value commitments'.[262] Moreover, he emphasizes the importance, in the circumstances of politics, of compromise. Compromises, he underlines, do not necessarily have to be trade-offs between interests; they can be principled.[263] More generally, just like Unger, he denounces lawyers' denigration of actually existing democracy.[264] As we saw, similar disparagement certainly also exists with regard to private law. Many private law experts (practitioners, doctrinal lawyers, and theorists alike) believe that the legislature cannot be entrusted with private law making, which—they believe—requires their own expertise.

[255] See ibid. 4: 'If there are reasonable disagreements about justice and its implications, then it becomes implausible to regard judges as basing their decisions on the "correct" view of what democratic justice demands in particular circumstances. There are no good grounds for believing that they can succeed where political philosophers from Plato to Rawls have failed.'
[256] Ibid. 169–170.
[257] Ibid. 178.
[258] Ibid. 178.
[259] Ibid. 9.
[260] Ibid. 98.
[261] Ibid. 225.
[262] Ibid. 225.
[263] Ibid. 193.
[264] Ibid. 210.

4. Implications for the Constitutionalization of Private Law

The first implication of Bellamy's political constitutionalism in the context of (European) private law would be the radical rejection of the constitutionalization of private law as it is usually understood, i.e. as a constraining force upon legislators and as an empowerment of courts (constitutional courts and other courts, depending on the institutional arrangement).[265] The example of the *Urgenda* case and similar ones are cases in point.[266] These are private law litigations where public interest groups claim that the state's violation of air pollution standards to which the state has committed under the UN Climate Convention, constitutes a tort towards members of the public and seek an injunction requiring the state to comply with these standards. In the *Urgenda* case, the Dutch supreme court (the *Hoge Raad*), with reference to the case law of the European Court of Human Rights, decided that under Articles 2 and 8 of the European Convention on Human Rights (ECHR) the Dutch state has a duty of care to protect residents in the Netherlands from the risks to their lives, health, and wellbeing as a result of climate change, and that the state would fail to fulfil its duty of care by not ensuring the reduction of emissions by at least 25 per cent by the end of 2020. From a partisan environmentalist perspective such litigation can be appreciated as being potentially highly effective—much more so than any regular political campaign—in ensuring a reduction in pollution and in protecting public health. However, in addition to such strategic reasons, court rulings of this kind have also been defended on democratic deliberative grounds as instances of public reasoning.[267] The problem with this line of argument is that, whatever the alleged quality of the reasons put forward by the litigants and the court, these remain merely the reasons of the litigants and judges, without access to the deliberation being assured for other affected parties to allow them to bring forward their own reasons and to try to influence the outcome.[268] In other words, the court seems to be an unlikely forum for truly inclusive democratic deliberation. Moreover, unlike the ordinary democratic process of legislation by coalition governments, litigation and judicial decisions allow no room for compromise: the court finds for the plaintiff or the defendant, and the winner takes all. And as Bellamy points out, 'when the winner in the Court takes all, then the judicial majority may prove tyrannous indeed'.[269]

Having said that, it is not clear that the matter is as black and white as Bellamy suggests either. Rather than providing a ground for a categorical rejection of all forms of judicial review in all circumstances, the illegitimacy of judicial review and of the judicial constitutionalization of private law more generally seems a matter of degree. Therefore, Bellamy's arguments are perhaps best understood as strongly calling for judicial deference towards majority decisions, especially in those cases where the democratic debate has already specifically addressed the constitutional dimensions of the

[265] Depending on the constitutional system, especially its mechanisms for judicial review, these may include ordinary civil courts applying the constitution.

[266] Hoge Raad, 20 December 2019, ECLI:NL:HR:2019:2006, NJ 2020, 41 note J Spier.

[267] See e.g. Burger, 'Mijn motivatie is dat ik denk dat ik gelijk heb', *De Groene Amsterdammer*, 11 April 2018.

[268] In this sense, de Boer, 'Trias Politica niet opofferen voor ambitieuze klimaatpolitiek', 73 *Socialisme & Democratie* (2016) 40.

[269] Bellamy (n. 177) 204, with regard to class actions.

matter at hand.[270] This clearly was not the case in *Urgenda*, where the failure to meet the greenhouse emission standards was not based on any positive democratic decision but rather the result of the absence of sufficient action from the side of the government, while both the ECHR and the UN Climate Convention (and the Paris Accord), on which the court relied, had democratic backing.[271]

5. Implications for Judicial Private Law Making

Bellamy's argument is directed against counter-majoritarian law making, in particular through judicial review. However, it can be turned with equal force, it would seem, against other forms of non-majoritarian law making, in particular the common law. In other words, it gives reason to question the legitimacy of judicial law making much more generally. For example, the slogan 'what touches all should surely be decided by all',[272] it seems, could be directed with equal force against other types of judicial law making, such as the common law of contract and the extensive judicial contract law making that has taken place, e.g. especially on the basis of general clauses such as good faith, in civil law jurisdictions—not to mention the Court of Justice. It is true that in the case of ordinary judicial law making strictly speaking courts do not overrule the democratic legislature, which is perhaps most problematic from the perspectives of political equality and freedom as non-domination. However, the arguments concerning public reason, deliberation, expertise, and the circumstances of politics speak just as strongly against ordinary judicial law making. Thus, it seems to follow from the point of view of political constitutionalism that judicial law making is generally inferior, to say the least, to law making by the legislator. In a republican defence of the constitutionality of democracy,[273] therefore, one would expect a general rejection of—or at least strong scepticism towards—judicial law making.

Of course, a degree of judicial law making can never be avoided. The application of general rules to concrete cases always implies some new law making. However, Bellamy's argument suggests at the very least that judicial law making should be limited wherever possible and should certainly not be normalized by the constitution, whether it is a written or an unwritten one. The arguments from political constitutionalism, therefore, seem to speak quite strongly against judicial activism, against open-textured concepts (such as 'good faith and fair dealing', 'reasonableness', 'good morals'), against the common law in general, and in favour of codification, including periodic re-codification, and legislative law reforms in general. However, remarkably, none of these positions is taken by Bellamy. Instead, he advocates analogical, case-by-case reasoning by courts as an appropriate means of overcoming reasonable disagreement

[270] See Hesselink, 'The Justice Dimensions of the Relationship Between Fundamental Rights and Private Law', in H. Collins (ed.), *European Contract Law and the Charter of Fundamental Rights* (2017) 167, at 196.

[271] Indeed, in the Supreme Court's own view it was merely upholding the democratic rule of law. See the official English summary: 'The Dutch State has argued that it is up to politicians to decide on the reduction of greenhouse gas emissions. According to the Supreme Court, however, the Dutch Constitution requires the Dutch courts to apply the provisions of the ECHR. This role of the courts to offer legal protection is an essential element of a democracy under the rule of law. The courts are responsible for guarding the limits of the law. That is what the Court of Appeal has done in this case, according to the Supreme Court.'

[272] Bellamy (n. 177) 51.

[273] This is the subtitle of Bellamy's *Political Constitutionalism* (n. 177).

within the circumstances of politics.[274] This may come across as a straightforward endorsement of the common law style judicial law making.[275] However, he presents his proposal as 'a way of skirting around political conflict'.[276] The focus on concrete precedents, according to Bellamy, helps courts and the parties to a dispute to avoid discussions about underlying conflicts of principle.

From the perspective of democratic legitimacy (republican and other) there are two problems with this proposal. First, it looks like a cover-up. In terms of democratic equality there seems to be a great risk, both because of path-dependence (if not outright conservatism) and of hegemony, in hiding from the surface fundamental conflicts where they do exist and are pertinent to the case. Some judicial precedents (say, *Lochner* or, in the EU, *Alemo-Herron*) are just plain wrong.[277] Or at least it can and—most to the point here—*should* be argued that they are. (Remember Bellamy's purely procedural understanding of public reason.) Indeed, 'skirting around political conflict' sounds like the opposite of political contestation, which has been at the core of republican political thought. While it is true that in the case of decentralized judicial law making 'there is no rational-hierarchical centralized decision-maker trying to run the system according to some common plan', the development of the law (in our case contract law) may still be in the firm hands of a relatively narrow class, excluding especially those at the periphery of society from any meaningful influence.[278] And while law making through precedent does indeed allow for incremental change, which can help in avoiding major mistakes, the doctrine of *stare decisis* also entrenches mistakes that courts have made. Moreover, and most importantly, from the republican point of view there is no reason to think that incremental change will be any less arbitrary than radical reform. Secondly, there is nothing in Bellamy's proposal ensuring the primacy of democratic legislation by keeping at least the role of judicial law making through precedent—whether by common law judges or by civil law courts on the Continent—as limited as possible. A more consonant approach towards judicial law making could mean, for example, that courts are required to refer certain key decisions to the legislator, and that legislators must actively maintain their primacy via periodical law reforms and codifications (e.g. by enshrining the codification principle in the constitution).[279]

[274] Ibid. 84.

[275] Cf. Sunstein (n. 79) ch. 3 (analogical reasoning), e.g. at 62: 'In England and America, the common law places a premium on analogical thinking.'

[276] Bellamy (n. 177) 84.

[277] See Bartl and Leone, 'Minimum Harmonisation After Alemo-Herron: the Janus Face of EU Fundamental Rights Review', 10 *European Constitutional Law Review* (2015) 140; Hesselink (n. 270).

[278] For a recent acknowledgement by the president of the Court of Appeal of the Hague, in the Netherlands, that the Dutch judiciary is far too white, see 'Rechterlijke macht moet streven naar meer rechters met migratieachtergrond', *Volkskrant*, 26 March 2018.

[279] As an example, see art. 107(1) Dutch Constitution.

C. Citizen Participation

Saprai offers elements towards republican theory of contract law.[280] However, his version of republicanism is distinctly more communitarian and perfectionist than the ones proposed Pettit and Bellamy. In his view, it is the task of the law to promote co-operation and solidarity among citizens. And contract law should be instrumental to this goal. By promoting contractual relationships, which are intrinsically cooperative, the law nurtures an attitude in citizens, and, consequently, a political climate, disposed towards cooperation and solidarity and social cohesion among citizens. As to institutions, Saprai follows Dworkin in regarding courts, being forums of principle,[281] as the proper place for debating fundamental choices concerning contract law.[282] However, when considering matters of political morality, courts should take popular views on these matters into account. This differs from Dworkin's liberal view and, according to Saprai, is what makes his approach distinctly republican: 'at least some legal categories may be linked with aspects of conventional or popular morality to serve the republican ideal of encouraging citizen participation in social and political life'.[283]

It remains an empirical question whether citizens are likely to be very interested in participating in political life by discussing the political morality of contract law questions that judges might pick up on for debate. However, even if they were, it is not clear that this kind of citizen involvement would give citizens the kind of control that, for example, Pettit (as we saw) regards as necessary for not being dominated. Indeed, in this scenario citizens' expected control and agency, even collectively, would seem rather minimal. Given the fact of value pluralism that Saprai also emphasizes, there seems to be a great risk of cherry picking by courts among popular opinions. As a result, the determination of 'popular morality' would risk becoming arbitrary and thus dominating. In any case, the suggestion that judicial contract law making 'gives ordinary citizens the opportunity to share in the collective effort of determining what exactly the law in their particular society requires',[284] does not seem to be based on any idea of collective self-determination, public autonomy, or co-authorship of the laws that apply to them, as required by Rousseauvian republicanism, for example.

7. Discourse Theory

A. A Radically Democratic Private Law

Habermas is committed to radical democracy. 'In the final analysis', he argues, 'private legal subjects cannot come to enjoy equal individual liberties if they do not themselves, in the common exercise of their political autonomy, achieve clarity about justified interests and standards. They themselves must agree on the relevant aspects

[280] P. Saprai, *Contract Law Without Foundations: Toward a Republican Theory of Contract* (2019).
[281] Dworkin, 'The Forum of Principle', 56 *New York University Law Review* (1981) 469.
[282] Saprai (n. 280) 57.
[283] Ibid. 6.
[284] Ibid. 57.

under which equals should be treated equally and unequals unequally.'[285] This radically democratic hunch provides the starting point for the legal and political theory that Habermas unfolds in *Between Facts and Norms*.[286] It is of crucial importance for our purposes to understand that the radically democratic promise must be redeemed also with regard to private law. Indeed, in Habermas's discourse theory of law and democracy, not only are legitimate private rights unthinkable without democracy but the reverse is also true: a true democracy cannot exist without a system of private rights. In other words, democracy is at the core of a legitimate system of private law and vice versa.

Therefore, the short answer to the question central in this chapter, i.e. whether (European) contract law should have a democratic basis, is emphatically—indeed, radically—affirmative. But what exactly does this entail? Habermas's theory of law and democracy is complex. It draws on different academic disciplines (law, philosophy, and the social sciences). Moreover, it introduces and relies upon a number of concepts and ideas that are not all self-explanatory (to put it mildly). At the same time, however, they bear very directly upon our question of the legitimacy of (European) contract law making. Therefore, I will now briefly introduce the core ideas and concepts insofar as directly relevant here.[287] Where helpful I will also address the work of other critical theorists who have built on Habermas's discourse theory of democracy and have elaborated it further.

B. Private Law Making Between Facts and Norms

First, we must first be clear on a point of method and scope. In this book I ask normative questions. More precisely, I discuss fundamental normative political questions of European contract law. Whilst Habermas's theory is certainly also normative, nevertheless it is deliberately not limited to that. His account understands the law as being situated 'between facts and norms', as in need both of (normative) legitimation and of (factual) effectiveness. His aim is to move beyond the rival accounts of natural law (which regards law as subject to morality) and legal positivism (which understands law as independent of morality and focuses on law's societal recognition), respectively, by emphasizing that law has both a factual and a normative side, neither of which takes precedence over the other.[288] Rather, the tension between the two is internal (albeit not essential) to law.[289] Thus, Habermas combines insights from philosophy and the social sciences. His method is neither purely normative nor merely empirical, but reconstructive.[290] In particular, his aim is 'to rationally reconstruct the self-understanding

[285] Habermas (n. 7) xiii.

[286] Ibid. See also the follow-up essays collected in J. Habermas, *The Inclusion of the Other* ([first published 1996] 1998).

[287] For a more general introduction, see Chapter 2.

[288] In other words (and against natural law), law and morality do not stand in a hierarchical but in a complementary relationship. See Habermas (n. 7) 37.

[289] Habermas considers law, unlike morality, to be contingent, an artifact.

[290] Habermas, therefore, does not offer a theory of justice as an abstract external standard for the evaluation of our laws. Having said that, throughout his book, and also in his further work, he pays much attention to law's normative side. Indeed his factual claims have been criticized for being too normative. See e.g.

of modern legal orders'.[291] Rational reconstruction means exploring the normative presuppositions of a given practice (in our case making private law), understood as rational (i.e. reason guided), and, insofar as these have remained unfulfilled, uncovering its normative potential.[292] The specific nature, scope, and method of Habermas's account should be kept in mind when considering and discussing our normative questions from a Habermasian point of view.

C. The Co-originality of Private and Public Autonomy

Central to Habermas's reconstruction of modern law—and of eminent importance to our question—is his contention that private and public autonomy are 'co-original'. The notion of co-originality expresses the idea that—both factually and normatively—it is not possible to have the one without the other. Private and public (or political) autonomy mutually presuppose each other; they are equiprimordial. More concretely, this means that popular sovereignty presupposes citizens having certain private rights (paradigmatically, the right to property), while the extent of these private rights (which define the autonomy citizens enjoy as private persons) has to be determined through collective self-legislation, i.e. through the exercise of their public autonomy. For private law, this has three implications. First, a society is not legitimately constituted unless it has a system of private law. This amounts to the constitutionalization of at least the idea—or the basic structure, to use a Rawlsian phrase—of private law. Secondly, the system of private law is not legitimate unless it has a democratic basis. And, thirdly, there exists no further, external standard for private law's legitimacy or justice.

D. The System of Private Rights

In the rational reconstruction of the self-understanding of modern legal orders that Habermas proposes, he takes as his starting point 'the rights citizens must accord one another if they want to legitimately regulate their common life by means

Koller, 'Recht Als Kategorie der Vermittlung zwischen Faktizität und Geltung', in P. Koller and C. Hiebaum (eds), *Jürgen Habermas: Faktizität und Geltung* (2016) 21, at 36. A different line of well-known criticism of Habermasian discourse theory relationship to society concerns its commitment to a specifically European understanding of modernity, where a certain type of reason-giving person is centre-stage. As post-colonial critical theorists have pointed out, from the point of view of the non-European periphery, the discourse conception of practical reason, especially its normative presuppositions of communicative action, may strike as distinctly Eurocentric. See A. Allen, *The End of Progress: Decolonizing the Normative Foundations of Critical Theory* (2016), ch 2. Although the scope of this book is limited to European contract, that critique nevertheless is relevant here too, not only because European contract law also shapes contractual relationships going beyond the EU, but also because Eurocentrism in the legitimation of EU contract law risks othering all those within the EU who do not understand themselves first and foremost as Europeans.

[291] Habermas (n. 7) 82.

[292] Thus, Habermas's account, although firmly rooted in the critical tradition of the Frankfurt school, is less pessimistic than those of his predecessors. See especially T. W. Adorno and M. Horkheimer, *Dialectic of Enlightenment* ([first published 1944] 2016); M. Horkheimer, *Eclipse of Reason* (1947).

of positive law'.[293] For 'all rights ultimately stem from the system of rights that free and equal legal subjects would mutually accord to one another'.[294] The term rights here refers quite generally to subjective rights. In his discussion Habermas mainly focuses on the most fundamental subjective rights, i.e. human rights. It is important to note, however, that in his reconstruction of the system of rights, these rights are understood in the first place as ones that citizens have against each other, i.e. as fundamentally horizontal rights.

In Habermas's reconstruction, the system of rights is not the system of purely moral rights that Kant and neo-Kantians like Weinrib and Ripstein believe can be derived, as a matter of philosophical analysis, from equal freedom, ready to be enforced by the legitimate law maker.[295] This is because unlike moral norms and rights, legal norms and subjective legal rights are not universal. The concrete content and extent of the system of rights will have to be determined, in each legal order, through its own legitimate democratic procedure. In that law making process, not only moral considerations (about universal norms) but also ethical ones (about the collective self-understanding of the society at hand) and pragmatic ones (about the best means to achieve that society's ends) have a legitimate place. Here, again, we see the tension between facts and norms at work. Subjective rights are determined by the objective law that citizens have given themselves in the legitimate democratic process established in the particular society at hand.

Moreover, Habermas understands subjective rights as negative rights, i.e. as freedom from interference by others (whether by private persons or the state) and—crucial in the discourse understanding of law—especially as freedom from reason-giving. In a pre-political society without any laws, the only way that persons who want to live together, respecting each other as free and equal, can coordinate their actions and resolve conflicts when they arise is with references to morality, whose rights and obligations are universal. This means, first, that they must be willing to offer reasons whenever conflicts arise and, secondly, that their actions must be motivated by the moral principles to which these reasons refer. However, in complex societies like our own we would be overburdened by this constant duty of moral motivation and reason-giving. According to Habermas, in modern societies it is the main function of the 'medium' of law to relieve citizens from this burden by providing for a system of subjective rights, each of which has the function of providing a sphere where the right-holder is exempted from the duty to give any reasons for her actions (it suffices to refer to her right). Moreover, unlike morality the law does not care about the motivation for norm-compliance; what matters is external compliance.

[293] Habermas (n. 7) 82.
[294] Ibid. 409.
[295] See I. Kant, *The Metaphysics of Morals* ([first published 1797] 1996); E. J. Weinrib, *The Idea of Private Law* (1995); A. Ripstein, *Force and Freedom: Kant's Legal and Political Philosophy* (2009).

E. The Democratic Principle

Having clarified Habermas's concept of rights, the next question is: what is his concept of democracy? Habermas introduces the 'principle of democracy', which establishes a procedure for legitimate law making, as follows: 'Specifically, the democratic principle states that only those statutes may claim legitimacy that can meet with the assent of all citizens in a discursive process of legislation that in turn has been legally constituted.'[296] As stated, Habermas rejects natural law. Therefore, he underlines that the democratic principle should be distinguished from the moral principle.[297] Moral reasons are internally motivating, while democratic deliberation must be externally convincing.[298] For our purposes, it is crucial to understand that, in this regard (i.e. with regard to the legitimacy requirements), there is no difference between the making of public and private law.[299] Both public law and private law owe their legitimacy to the proper implementation of the democratic principle.[300]

With its focus on the procedure of democratic deliberation and decision making and, especially, on reason-giving, Habermas's discourse theory of democracy soon became the main source of inspiration for various theories of 'deliberative democracy',[301] or, as Forst puts it, 'the rule of reasons'.[302] However, in contrast to some of these theories, which make concrete recommendations, Habermas's discourse theory of democracy remains fairly abstract. This raises the question of what exactly the democratic principle demands and permits.[303]

In Habermasian discourse theory, the concept of 'discourse' has a specific meaning that is distinct from (in particular, narrower than), for example, Foucauldian discourse analysis,[304] in that it is concerned exclusively with the justification of action (individual or collective) with reasons. In other words, discourse theory is concerned with communicative action, where people try to coordinate their actions (and resolve disputes) with others, understanding those others as responding and entitled to reasons, not also with strategic action, where people treat others as mere obstacles to the achievement of their own ends and are prepared to use illegitimate power (i.e. beyond the power of the better argument). With regard to practical discourses (i.e.

[296] Habermas (n. 7) 110.

[297] Both the moral and the democratic principle derive from the discourse principle, which is situated at a higher level of abstraction.

[298] Habermas (n. 7).

[299] Similar, Shiffrin, 'The Divergence of Contract and Promise', 120 *Harv. L. Rev.* (2007) 708, at 712 and 718.

[300] Unlike Habermas, Forst grounds democracy in justice. See R. Forst, *The Right to Justification: Elements of a Constructivist Theory of Justice* (2012), at 186: 'Democracy is the only appropriate, though never fully appropriate, political expression of the basic right to justification and of mutual respect between persons.' See also Forst, 'Legitimacy, Democracy, and Justice: On the Reflexivity of Normative Orders', in R. Forst, *Normativity and Power: Analyzing Social Orders of Justification* (2017) 131, at 135. And on a basic human right to democratic participation, see Forst, 'The Justification of Human Rights and the Basic Right to Justification: A Reflexive Approach', 120 *Ethics* (2010) 711, at 725.

[301] See e.g. A. Gutmann and D. Thompson, *Why Deliberative Democracy?* (2004), at 9.

[302] Forst, 'The Rule of Reasons: Three Models of Deliberative Democracy', in R. Forst, *The Right to Justification: Elements of a Constructivist Theory of Justice* (2012), ch. 7.

[303] As Bellamy (n. 177) 128, points out, people 'can differ in their views of private and public autonomy, and so propose different accounts of democracy and the procedural rights it entails'.

[304] See M. Foucault, *L'ordre du discours* (1971).

discourse about what to do, individually or collectively), Habermas draws a distinction between moral, ethical, and pragmatic discourses.[305] Moral discourses aim to answer questions about what we owe each other as human beings; they make (or imply) validity claims with regard to norms that have universal application, for the interaction between all human beings. Ethical discourses address questions of individual or collective self-understanding; they rely on the validity of claims concerning values for the group at hand (e.g. one's own family, club, religious congregation, or nation). Finally, pragmatic claims concern the most appropriate means for achieving given ends (collective or individual). Although these three types or reasons or rationalities, thus, can be distinguished analytically, usually they will not operate in isolation from each other since complex practical problems will often have various moral, ethical, and pragmatic dimensions at the same time—or at least can be claimed to raise a combination of these three types of questions.

According to Habermas, it is a key characteristic of modern law (including modern private law) that it is legitimately informed by both moral, ethical, and pragmatic reasons.[306] Here Habermas's position differs from most private law theories, which tend to privilege one type of discourse, for example moral discourses by Kantian liberals who regard private law entirely as a matter of the moral right (as opposed to the individual and collective good), communitarian discourses of collective self-understanding, and pragmatic discourses of means-ends reasoning and output legitimacy made by utilitarians. Having said that, moral reasons, because of their universal vocation, should have priority over ethical reasons, which properly apply only within the ethical community at hand; while ethical reasons have logical priority over pragmatic reasons, since the latter reasons presuppose the value of whatever good is pursued. At first sight, this may seem to imply that private law should still be based first and foremost on morality, with little place for legal culture and tradition and even less for pragmatic considerations of effectiveness and efficiency. However, that would be a misunderstanding. It is true that moral reasons have priority over all other considerations—or should 'trump' these, as Forst puts it, using a Dworkinian term.[307] However, for a reason to prevail as a moral reason its universal validity will have to be demonstrated in the justificatory discourse at hand. While this may be feasible for the core of human rights, such as the right to human dignity, the case for universal validity (i.e. independent of time and place) becomes less plausible when it comes to the more peripheral aspects of human rights, and even less so in a dispute, say, on contract law remedies, between proponents of specific performance and expectation damages. The validity conditions for ethical claims are less demanding than for moral claims but still pretty tough: for an ethical argument justifiably to prevail it must be capable of convincing everyone (not merely the majority) within the ethical community at hand. It is not clear for most contract law rules and doctrines—not even for some of the central or fundamental ones—that their irremovability could be justified

[305] See Habermas, 'On the Pragmatic, the Ethical, and the Moral Employment of Practical Reason', and Habermas, 'Remarks on Discourse Ethics', in J. Habermas, *Justification and Application: Remarks on Discourse Ethics* (1995), chs 1 and 2. Similar, Forst, *The Right to Justification* (n. 300) ch. 7.

[306] Habermas (n. 7) 154. In the same sense, R. Forst, *Contexts of Justice: Political Philosophy Beyond Liberalism and Communitarianism* (1994), at 126.

[307] Forst, *The Right to Justification* (n. 300) 158. See also Forst (n. 306) 126.

in such a way. Perhaps it might be argued that German contract law would no longer be German contract law without the doctrine of *Treu und Glauben* (i.e. good faith and fair dealing) or that contract law in the English common law tradition necessarily has to include the doctrine of consideration. However, would such a claim be really convincing, even on its own terms? French law recently abolished the doctrine of *cause* and it is not clear that the reform denatured French contract law beyond recognition, even though in the debate forceful arguments had been made to this effect.[308]

F. Public Sphere and Private Law

The public sphere plays a cardinal role in Habermas's account of democratic legitimacy.[309] While a political debate and, ultimately, a majority vote in parliament are indispensable for the legitimacy of the law, including private law, parliamentary deliberation and decision making cannot carry the full weight of the legitimation of the law. In modern, pluralist societies representative democracy crucially depends on the presence of a healthy public sphere that generates public opinions and feeds them into the political decision making process. The point here is not that every person should have an equal voice, but rather that every argument should have an equal chance of being considered—what Habermas calls 'subjectless communications' in a 'decentred society'.[310] Institutionalized deliberation alone—even when optimal—cannot achieve this; what is also needed is that ideas from civil society reach the law-making institutions. Therefore, the informal opinion and will-formation is not merely what precedes or informs the democratic process: it is constitutive of it.[311]

Thus, the public sphere is an autonomous space, separate from the state (and from political parties), 'essentially anarchical' as Somek puts it,[312] where public opinions are generated and circulate freely, where the forceless force of the better argument (discursive power) prevails without any distortion by the corrupting forces of money (economic power) or the executive (bureaucratic power), and where opinions from the periphery of society have a real chance of being heard, considered, and, ultimately, of being influential in the decision making process within the political institutions at the centre. The public sphere is not itself guided or limited by the need to take political decisions. Indeed, in addition to its role in yielding public opinions concerning topics already on the political agenda of the political institutions, another role of the public sphere, which is at least as important, is agenda setting: feeding problems, seen as in urgent need of a solution, into the legislative agenda, without the agenda-setting being hijacked—and the discussion being framed—by the corrupting forces

308 See e.g. J. Ghestin, *Cause de l'engagement et validité du contrat* (2006), a volume of 960 pages on the matter, written specifically with a view to preserving the doctrine at the reform.

309 See J. Habermas, *The Structural Transformation of the Public Sphere: An Inquiry Into a Category of Bourgeois Society* ([first published 1962] 1991) and Habermas (n. 7) especially ch. 8.

310 Habermas (n. 7) 299 and 301.

311 Ibid. 442.

312 Somek, 'Zur Rekonstruktion des Rechts: die Prinzipien des Rechtsstaats', in P. Koller and C. Hiebaum (eds), *Jürgen Habermas: Faktizität und Geltung* (2016) 69, at 74.

of illegitimate power.[313] Moreover, in a healthy public sphere the discussions are unregulated, informal, conducted in ordinary language,[314] and therefore accessible to ordinary people.[315] A crucial further characteristic of the public sphere is that it is fundamentally unconstrained.[316] In particular, its agenda is radically open. While liberals, in the name of state neutrality, want to keep certain questions and arguments off the public agenda thus privatizing them by relegating them to the private sphere, from the perspective of discourse theory 'there can be no agenda to *predefine* the topic of public conversation'.[317] It is important to underline that these characteristics are partly *counter-factual* idealizing elements of a *critical* theory of democracy and legitimate law making.[318] They can serve as a benchmark by which the existing law making practices can be criticized. In summary, the public sphere is where societal change and progress originate in a change of public opinion.[319]

The role of the public sphere in Habermas's account is much more limited and less demanding than Ahrendt's agonistic republican understanding of the public realm from which it derives.[320] In particular, it is not necessary that all law making be preceded by a societal debate involving all citizens. Thus, citizens do not constantly have to develop views of their own on every possible subject, such as, say, the introduction of withdrawal rights for consumers or the extension of the scope of unfair terms control to small businesses. For the democratic legitimacy of laws, including private law, it is sufficient that arguments from the various points of view of different citizens have an equal chance of influencing the legislative agenda and its outcome. However, even by this less demanding standard, in most Member States and at the EU level, it seems, private law making still suffers from a serious democratic deficit. The debate in civil society on private law, to the extent that it exists, is almost never conducted in ordinary language. On the contrary, the discussion is usually heavily dominated by the conceptual jargon of legal doctrine. As a result, citizens would need a law degree to understand a private law reform,[321] even though the main issues are not rocket science

[313] Habermas (n. 7) 359; Habermas, 'Political Communication in Media Society: Does Democracy Still Have an Epistemic Dimension? The Impact of Normative Theory on Empirical Research', in J. Habermas, *Europe: The Faltering Project* (2009) 138, at 169.

[314] Habermas (n. 7) 360.

[315] Ibid. 373.

[316] Ibid. 314.

[317] S. Benhabib, *Situating the Self: Gender, Community and Postmodernism in Contemporary Ethics* (1993), at 94 (emphasis in original).

[318] Habermas (n. 7) 360. Cf. e.g. J. Butler, *Precarious Life: the Powers of Mourning and Violence* (2004), at xvii, with regard to the actual, non-ideal public sphere: 'The public sphere is constituted in part by what cannot be said and what cannot be shown. The limits of the sayable, the limits of what can appear, circumscribe the domain in which political speech operates and certain kinds of subjects appear as viable actors.'

[319] Fraser, 'Transnationalizing the Public Sphere: On The Legitimacy and Efficacy of Public Opinion in a Postwestphalian World', in N. Fraser, *Scales of Justice: Reimagining Political Space in a Globalizing World* (2008) 76, at 92, distinguishes, in particular, two normative demands that public opinions generated in the public sphere have to meet: they must be legitimate and efficacious, where the legitimacy condition requires inclusiveness and participatory parity and the efficacy condition requires that public opinions be translated into binding laws and that the enforcement of these laws be ensured by administrative power.

[320] On the main differences between these concepts, see S. Benhabib, 'Models of Public Space: Hannah Arendt, the Liberal Tradition and Jürgen Habermas', in Benhabib (n. 317) 89, at 110.

[321] This is perhaps less true for EU private law, which is less conceptual and therefore somewhat more accessible to non-lawyers. For example, leading MEPs in the debates on consumer law directives have not always been lawyers.

and could easily be discussed in more accessible language. The disempowerment of citizens here mirrors the empowerment of legal experts. Moreover, in the area of private law there is usually not much agenda setting coming from the periphery either. With regard to EU private law, Micklitz claims that the European Commission's Green and White papers 'serve legitimizing purposes and rehearse arguments to support the option already chosen'.[322] For the EU more generally, Kukovec argues that legal discourse, *including* the discourse of inequality and weaker party protection, structurally favours those at the centre and fails to take into account the impact of EU law on those at the periphery, thus worsening their condition.[323] He discusses the rulings of the Court of Justice in *Viking* and *Laval* as cases in point,[324] but, as Daniela Caruso points out, consumer protection and other contract law examples could equally be given.[325] Finally, the voices (or silence) of people outside the EU who are affected by our contract laws, for example those who find themselves caught up in relationships of domination in global value chains constituted and governed by European contract laws, often go wholly unnoticed at the centre of European contract law making.[326]

Unlike certain other philosophers,[327] Habermas does not regard power as per se illegitimate or otherwise problematic. In particular, discursive power, i.e. the 'unforced force of the better argument'—or the 'power of justifications', as Forst calls it[328]—is wholly unproblematic, not only because it is grounded in reason but also because no one can control it. You cannot put it in a box to use it when it comes handy. In particular, discursive power cannot be appropriated by economic operators or bureaucratic institutions. However, there is a real danger when the public sphere, the only place where discursive power can be generated, is infiltrated, suppressed, or even taken over by the illegitimate power of money or bureaucracy.[329] In the private law debate, much of the corruption by economic interests takes place indirectly. Private scholars close to legal practice tend to be more familiar with the problems and needs that surface in the major law firms that they regularly do consultancy work for and that tend to have mostly large corporations and banks as their clients. Such scholarly contributions, although one-sided, are not necessarily made in bad faith. However, they reflect only very partially, if at all, the problems and the 'needs of practice' (as the phrase often goes) in the way they are perceived at the periphery of society. As to subversion by

[322] H.-W. Micklitz, 'Do Consumers and Businesses Need a New Architecture of Consumer Law? A Thought Provoking Impulse', 32 *YEL* (2013) 266, at 280.

[323] Kukovec, 'Taking Change Seriously: the Rhetoric of Justice and the Reproduction of the Status Quo', in D. Kochenov (ed.), *Europe's Justice Deficit?* (2015) 319, at 321–323.

[324] Ibid. See also, Kukovec, 'Law and the Periphery', 21 *ELJ* (2015) 406.

[325] Caruso, 'Qu'ils mangent des contrats: Rethinking Justice in EU Contract Law' in D. Kochenov (ed.), *Europe's Justice Deficit?* (2015) 367. She does not, however, seek the solution in removing the obstacles (coming from vested interests or path-dependence) to the free flow of arguments from the periphery towards the centre, thus allowing those at the periphery to make themselves heard and enhancing their agency and discursive power, but rather in the 'tracking' and 'measuring' (by others, presumably experts) of the uneven costs and benefits of contract law harmonization—a more outcome-oriented, welfarist approach.

[326] Allen (n. 290) ch. 4, questions—with reference to Spivak's famous question: can the subaltern speak?—whether those caught up in relationships of domination and subordination will always be able to demand justifications in such a way that they will be heard, and if they do not, whether their silence will be noticed. Cf. Spivak (n. 246).

[327] Notably, Foucault, 'The Subject and Power', 8 *Critical Inquiry* (1982) 777.

[328] Habermas (n. 7) 306; Forst, *Normativity and Power* (n. 300) 37.

[329] Habermas (n. 7) 362.

bureaucratic power, private law reforms are hardly ever triggered in the public sphere. They are usually initiated and drafted by the public administration or by experts on its behalf. As recent examples, the Dutch (1992), German (2002), and French (2016) reforms and the reforms initiated by the Law Commission in England, were all triggered or recommended by legal experts. Similarly, at the European level probably none of the *acquis* can be said to have been generated in the public sphere. The point here is not that the experts are not independent and impartial, but that they belong—or are close—to the political centre of society and, therefore, are not necessarily very much in touch with groups and individuals at the periphery and their perception of what the real problems are.[330]

In complex societies like our own, in addition to the general public sphere there usually also exist more specific, functionally differentiated public spheres. From a legitimacy point of view, however, it is of crucial importance that these specialized public spheres should also remain accessible to laypersons.[331] The regulatory silos that Micklitz and Svetiev have shown to play a crucial role in shaping European regulatory private law and that they hail for their legitimating force[332] in fact seem highly problematic in this regard. For although they operate deliberatively, they are wholly inaccessible to ordinary people as they include only hyper-experts. The risk here is, 'to enclave certain matters in specialized discursive arenas and thereby to shield them from general public debate and contestation', as Fraser wrote in a slightly different context.[333] The same goes, it seems, for Mak's expectation that civil courts operating at the interface between national and EU private law can 'foster a transnational public sphere, in which deliberative processes on legal-political questions of European private law can take shape'.[334] Whatever deliberation takes place there will be highly institutionalized (which strongly constrains the free flow of arguments) and will inevitably be conducted in legal jargon that only very few citizens will have access to—and most of those citizens are unlikely to be found at the socio-economic periphery of society, where, however, many justice problems are likely to occur. Could not perhaps civil law courts, in spite of being part of the legal-political institutional framework, nevertheless trigger societal and political debates on matters of justice that would not otherwise occur by dramatizing them in appealing cases? Mak argues as much, citing the example of the activist Spanish judge Fernández Seijo, who referred to the Court of Justice for preliminary rulings in both the *Océano* and the *Aziz* cases, which led to a political and societal debate on the legitimacy of evictions that would not otherwise have occurred.[335] However, this raises the legitimacy question not only of whether this is what we want our judges

[330] As we saw, for civic republicans like Pettit expertise, impartiality, and a specific brief suffice for experts to be considered 'proxies for the people'. According to Habermasian discourse theory, by contrast, when it comes to generating and circulating public opinions, no one can be a proxy for anyone, most certainly not someone at the centre for someone else at the periphery.

[331] Habermas (n. 7) 373.

[332] Micklitz and Svetiev (n. 5). See earlier, in Section 1.B.

[333] Fraser, 'Rethinking the Public Sphere: A Contribution to the Critique of Actually Existing Democracy', *Social Text* (1990) 56, at 71.

[334] Mak, 'Civil Courts as Constitutional Courts: Polity-Building Through European Private Law' (forthcoming).

[335] Mak (n. 32). Cf. F. Nicola and B. Davies, *EU Law Stories: Contextual and Critical Histories of European Jurisprudence* (2017), at 372; Fernández Seijo, 'El impacto emocional de la sentencia' *Huffpost* 20 March 2013.

to do (if we take popular sovereignty and the separation of powers seriously), but also whether they are really best placed to do the agenda-setting. As Habermas points out, 'the political sphere can fulfil its function of perceiving and thematizing encompassing social problems only insofar as it develops out of the communications taking place among *those who are potentially affected*'.[336] This applies as least as much, it seems, for the judicial branch as for the other political institutions—probably even more so. In summary, then, with regard to private law, it seems, from a Habermasian point of view the vitality of the public sphere leaves much to be desired.

There is one more important point to be addressed. Any theory of the public sphere presupposes a distinction between the public and the private. This may seem problematic at first, given the powerful feminist critique of the private/public divide, which showed that the relegation of all sorts of issues to the non-political private sphere was instrumental to the oppression of women. In the words of Benhabib, 'the struggle to make something public is a struggle for justice'.[337] However, to the extent that this critique does not amount to the total rejection of the private sphere and is concerned, rather, with the question where to trace the line between the private and public spheres and with redefining what is private and what public,[338] the feminist critique can go hand in hand with discourse theory and its proceduralist conception of democracy. For discourse theory rejects any natural or otherwise reified, pre-discursive definition of the boundary between private and public. As Fraser points out, 'only participants themselves can decide what is and what is not of common concern to them' and 'there are no naturally given, a priori boundaries here'.[339] Any claim that some matter belongs to the private sphere, and therefore should not be subject to public regulation (whether through public or private law), will have to prove itself in the democratic debate, where everyone affected has an equal chance of determining the outcome, which means, among other things, that the outcome is not legitimate to the extent that it was determined by patriarchy or other illegitimate power asymmetries. In other words, the political nature of the private/public boundary is intimately related to the co-originality of private and public autonomy.[340]

G. The Epistemic Dimension of Democracy

According to Habermas, democratic deliberation has epistemic (truth-tracking) and cognitive (learning) dimensions in that the process of reason-giving, both in the public sphere and the law making institutions, improves the quality and rationality of

[336] Habermas (n. 7) 365 (emphasis in original).
[337] Benhabib (n. 320) 94.
[338] See, famously, H. Arendt, *The Human Condition* ([first published 1958] 2nd ed., 1998), 38: 'The emergence of society—the rise of housekeeping, its activities, problems, and organizational devices—from the shadowy interior of the household into the light of the public sphere, has not only blurred the old borderline between private and political, it has also changed almost beyond recognition the meaning of the two terms and their significance for the life of the individual and the citizen.'
[339] Fraser (n. 333) 71.
[340] Habermas, *The Inclusion of the Other* (n. 286) 101.

a society's laws,[341] and results in collective learning.[342] Democratic deliberation and decision making, he argues, take place under the (counterfactual) presupposition that under ideal conditions the truth with regard to moral, ethical, and pragmatic claims will prevail with the unforced force of the better argument.[343]

Habermas's procedural theory of law combines ideas of Rousseau and Kant in that it links collective self-determination to reason,[344] thus regarding the validity standards as counterfactually presupposed (and reflexively questioned) in the democratic deliberations themselves. Habermas's 'epistemic proceduralism' may therefore be labelled as 'constitutive'.[345] This is in contrast to 'instrumental' truth-tracking theories of deliberation, that regard the democratic procedure as a way of approximating truths *external* to the procedure,[346] determined, as the case may be, by relevant moral principles or cultural traditions, or in pragmatic terms of problem-solving.[347] A prominent example in European (private) law of the latter are experimentalist theories[348] that go back to Dewey's pragmatic experimentalism[349] and aim 'to institutionalize direct problem-solving by citizens'.[350] Populists claiming that their electoral victories provide evidence of 'the general will' provide another example of an instrumental epistemic conception of democracy.[351]

[341] Habermas, 'Political Communication' (n. 313) 147.

[342] Habermas, 'Media, Markets and Consumers: The Quality Press as the Backbone of the Political Public Sphere', in J. Habermas, *Europe: The Faltering Project* (2009) 131, at 135.

[343] Habermas, 'Political Communication' (n. 313) 148.

[344] See Rousseau (n. 233) Book II, ch. 6, 380: 'Le Peuple soumis aux loix en doit être l'auteur; il n'appartient qu'à ceux qui s'associent de régler les conditions de la société.' See also Kant (n. 295) § 46 [6:313]:

> The legislative authority can belong only to the united will of the people. For since all right is to proceed from it, it *cannot* do anyone wrong by its law. Now when someone makes arrangements about *another*, it is always possible for him to do the other wrong; but he can never do wrong in what he decides upon with regard to himself (for *volenti non fit iniuria*). Therefore only the concurring and united will of all, insofar as each decides the same thing for all and all for each, and so only the general united will of the people, can be legislative. (emphasis in original)

[345] See Gledhill, 'The Ideal and Reality of Epistemic Proceduralism', 20 *Critical Review of International Social and Political Philosophy* (2017) 486.

[346] Cf. List and Goodin, 'Epistemic Democracy: Generalizing the Condorcet Jury Theorem', 9 *Journal of Political Philosophy* (2001) 277, at 295.

[347] See Estlund, 'Beyond Fairness and Deliberation: The Epistemic Dimension of Democratic Authority', in J. Bohman and W. Rehg (eds), *Deliberative Democracy* (1997) 173.

[348] See Cohen and Sabel, 'Directly-Deliberative Polyarchy', 3 *ELJ* (1997) 313. For private law, see Mak, 'Who Does What in European Private Law—and How Is It Done? An Experimentalist Perspective', *Tilburg Private Law Working Paper Series*, No. 5/2017, available at https://ssrn.com/abstract=2958146 (last visited 7 July 2020), who makes a case for 'the application of Experimentalist Governance to lawmaking in European private law', claiming that there is 'sufficient agreement on its goal' (i.e. market regulation).

[349] J. Dewey, *The Public and its Problems* ([first published 1927] 1991), at 202 described the experimental method as 'finding out the particular thing which needs to be done and the best way, under the circumstances, of doing it.'

[350] See Cohen, 'Reflections on Habermas on Democracy', 12 *Ratio Juris* (1999) 385, at 411. Cohen argues that experimentalism is superior to Habermas's discursive democracy in terms of the radical-democratic ideal of collective self-regulation. Note, however, that his own account is all about problem-solving, not about detecting problems and setting the agenda. The same applies to other experimentalist accounts that, tellingly, no longer speak of popular sovereignty or collective self-rule but of 'governance'. See e.g. Sabel and Zeitlin, 'Experimentalist Governance', in D. Levi-Faur (ed.), *The Oxford Handbook of Governance* (2012) 169. By contrast, in Habermas's proceduralist account of radical democracy, as we saw, the problem-raising role of a healthy public sphere is central.

[351] See Cohen, 'An Epistemic Conception of Democracy', 97 *Ethics* (1986) 26, at 34.

In Habermas's epistemic claims concerning the truth-tracking capacities of democratic procedure, the core-periphery dichotomy (or, better: continuum) is of central importance. Only with inclusive democratic deliberation (where a healthy public sphere plays a key role, as we have seen) can the points of view, problems, and arguments, reflecting the interests and experiences of those living at the periphery of society have a chance of influencing democratic decision making and law making at the political centre. Hayek famously regarded competition as a discovery procedure: since central planners have no way of knowing what is needed (and how much of it) throughout the country, all we have is the market price going up or down as a signal for needs, desires and preferences in society.[352] Borrowing Hayek's concept and turning it on its head it could thus be argued, from a Habermasian point of view, that democratic deliberation is a powerful and indeed indispensable discovery procedure.[353]

It should be pointed out, however, that the epistemic merits of democratic deliberation are far from uncontroversial.[354] A lot is at stake here. First, epistemic proceduralism might seem to open the door to populist decisionism, where the majority (or populist leaders) claim to know what the people really want.[355] However, that charge would not even apply to Rousseau, who distinguished the general will, which aims at the common good,[356] from the mere will of the majority,[357] let alone to Habermas, who, as said, regards public reason-giving as morally grounded in autonomy and who strongly rejects plebiscitary views of popular will and 'overly concrete notions of "the people" as an entity'.[358] In other words, according to Habermas, legal rules, including in the field of private law, are not right, good, or expedient merely because the majority says so;[359] a democratic procedure grounded in public and private autonomy and in reason-giving is much more demanding. Majority rule is necessary because a decision (e.g. on a contract law reform) has to be taken at some point.

[352] Hayek, 'Competition as Discovery Procedure', in F. A. Hayek, *New Studies in Philosophy, Economics and the History of Ideas* (1978), ch. 12; F. A. Hayek (n. 51)) 67. With specific reference to (European) contract law, see Grundmann 'European Contract Law(s) of What Colour?', 1 *ERCL* (2005) 184, at 195: 'Competition, and in particular freedom of contract, have indeed proven to be probably the most powerful discovery device.' However, markets, even when competitive, are only of limited use as a discovery procedure since market prices fundamentally fail to reflect the effects on those other than the contracting parties (externalities). Cf. Habermas, 'The Postnational Constellation and the Future of Democracy' in J. Habermas, *The Postnational Constellation: Political Essays* (2001) 58, at 95: 'markets are deaf to information that is not expressed in the language of price'.

[353] Similar (with reference to Dewey), Brunkhorst, 'Deliberative Politik—ein Verfahrensbegriff der Demokratie', in P. Koller and C. Hiebaum (eds), *Jürgen Habermas: Faktizität und Geltung* (2016), 117, at 123: 'Demokratie als problemlösender Entdeckungszusammenhang'.

[354] The idea of the wisdom of the multitude seems to go back to Aristotle (who, however, rejected democratic government). See, Aristotle, *The Politics* (1992), at 202–203. Another prominent historical root is Condorcet's jury theorem. See M. J. A. N. de Caritat, Marquis de Condorcet, *Essai sur l'application de l'analyse à la probabilité des décisions rendues à la pluralité des voix* (1785).

[355] Cf. J.-W. Müller, *What is Populism?* (2017).

[356] Rousseau (n. 233) 371: 'la volonté générale est toujours droite et tend toujours à l'utilité publique'.

[357] See ibid. 371: 'la différence entre la volonté de tous et la volonté générale'. It is surprising, therefore, that the populist Italian political movement *MoVimento 5 Stelle* chose 'Rousseau' as the name for its platform for 'direct democracy', available at https://rousseau.movimento5stelle.it (last visited 7 July 2020), understood by them merely as online majority voting.

[358] Habermas (n. 7) 185.

[359] In the same sense, Dewey (n. 349) 207: 'Majority rule, just as majority rule, is as foolish as its critics charge it with being. But it never is *merely* majority rule.'

However, as a matter of truth-seeking all questions always remain open to new, better arguments. In other words, the minority has reason to accept the majority decision if the right procedure was followed, because the procedure entails the *fallible* presumption that the better argument prevailed:

> Majority rule retains an internal relation to the search for truth inasmuch as the decision reached by the majority only represents a caesura in an ongoing discussion; the decision records, so to speak, the interim result of a discursive opinion-forming process. To be sure, in that case the majority decision must be premised on a competent discussion of the disputed issues, that is, a discussion conducted according to the communicative presuppositions of a corresponding discourse.[360] Only then can its content be viewed as the rationally motivated yet fallible result of a process of argumentation that has been interrupted in view of institutional pressures to decide, but is in principle resumable.[361]

A second highly relevant stake in the debate on epistemic proceduralism is that the claim to an epistemic dimension of democracy directly questions the viability of substantive (as opposed to merely procedural) normative political and legal theories, including substantive normative theories of contract law, *and* the related expertise of contract law theorists. For what can theorists really know about contract law as it ought to be in advance of an inclusive democratic deliberation? In particular, how can they know for the society at hand what are the most pressing justice problems that contract law ought to resolve before affected persons themselves have had the opportunity to raise them?

H. Judicial Private Law Making

Habermas follows Günther in drawing a sharp distinction between law making and law application.[362] The most dramatic implication of this view regards judicial review. Although Habermas does not generally reject the judicial review of the constitutionality of statutes (he accepts a procedural control of the law making process),[363] he does undertake a frontal attack on the reading by the *Bundesverfassungsgericht* of the German constitution as an 'objective order of values'.[364] By turning subjective rights into objective values, Habermas claims, judicial review loses all its rationality, and, thus, its normative force, since the balancing of values cannot be justified with reasons. This position led

[360] This premise was discussed earlier, in Section 7.E on moral, ethical, and pragmatic private law discourses.

[361] Habermas (n. 7) 179.

[362] K. Günther, *Der Sinn für Angemessenheit: Anwendungsdiskurse in Moral und Recht* (1988). Habermas (n. 7) 172. In the same sense, Forst, 'Justice, Democracy and the Right to Justification: Reflections on Jürgen Neyer's Normative Theory of The European Union', in D. Kochenov (ed.), *Europe's Justice Deficit?* (2015), 227, at 232–233.

[363] He regards judicial review as a second best solution. Institutionalized 'internalisation of self-reflection' by parliament on the constitutionality of its laws in a specialized committee, which could include (also) legal experts, would be his preferred solution. See Habermas (n. 7) 241. Cf. critical, Grimm, 'Justiz und Gesetzgebung. Zur Rolle und Legitimität der Verfassungsrechtsprechung', in P. Koller and C. Hiebaum (eds), *Jürgen Habermas: Faktizität und Geltung* (2016), 99, at 100.

[364] See famously the *Lüth* ruling, *Bundesverfassungsgericht*, 15 January 1956, *BVerfGE* 7, 198, NJW 1958, 257: 'das Grundgesetz, das keine wertneutrale Ordnung sein will, [hat] in seinem Grundrechtsabschnitt auch eine objektive Wertordnung aufgerichtet.'

to his famous debate with Alexy, who defended the *Bundesverfassungsgericht*'s position, claiming that the balancing of values can be rationalized in terms of the degree to which one interpretation of the constitution and its implications for the case, rather than another interpretation, would affect the core of one of the constitutional values at hand.[365]

In addition, Habermas's rejection of judicial law making seems to have further implications for modern private law. First, it casts serious doubt on the legitimacy of the common law. In common law jurisdictions, not only are court decisions in specific cases binding on that same court and other courts of the same or lower hierarchical level for new cases in the future (*stare decisis*), which effectively amounts to a form of law making (albeit not rule making), also, and more importantly, the common law (understood this time in the narrow sense, i.e. as opposed to statutory law) does not even go back to legislation (let alone democratic legislation). Contemporary precedents have their historical roots in a limited set of forms of action made available by the royal courts in mediaeval times: for contract law, especially, the action of assumpsit.[366] In other words, while courts apply the law, the law they are applying was never enacted by a democratic legislator in the first place. Put differently, in the Habermasian distinction, the opinions of judges in common law cases do not amount to discourses of law application: they quite fundamentally are always discourses of law making.

Habermas himself does not explicitly consider the possible illegitimacy of common (contract) law making. However, Baxter explicitly addresses the question.[367] He argues that from the perspective of Habermas's legal and democratic theory the common law does indeed seem illegitimate because it is insufficiently (if at all) based on the people's communicative power. He points out, quite rightly, that the arguments in litigation (certainly in private law disputes) are presented only by the parties; there is no opportunity for public input and participation.[368] However, Baxter argues, such a conclusion would be incompatible with Habermas's project which, as we saw, is explicitly reconstructive and not merely normative.[369] A similar point is made by Peterson, who argues that Habermas's discourse theory of law and democracy:

> cannot simply reject common law as undemocratic, because it aims to succeed not only as a philosophical theory of justice, but also at the level of legal theory. For Habermas, legal theory differs from philosophy of law in presupposing the basic principles and institutions of a particular legal order, which in the US includes common law.[370]

However, that seems too strong—as if the common law was not capable of codification or reform through democratically enacted statutes. It would amount to an essentializing understanding of the common law which seems unwarranted, both

[365] R. Alexy, *A Theory of Constitutional Rights* ([first published 1986] 2002).

[366] See A. W. B. Simpson, *A History of the Common Law of Contract: The Rise of the Action of Assumpsit* (1975).

[367] H. Baxter, *The Discourse Theory of Law and Democracy* (2011), at 115–118.

[368] In *The Theory of Communicative Action*, Vol. 1 (1984), at 35, Habermas, in addition, regarded litigation as purely strategic action. His view is more nuanced, in Habermas (n. 7) 234 ff.

[369] Baxter (n. 367) 118.

[370] Peterson, 'Creativity in Norm Application and Legal Adjudication: Discourse Theory on the Democratic Legitimacy of Legal Norms Developed through Common Law Adjudication and Judicial Review' (2010), available at https://ssrn.com/abstract=1570065, at 75 (last visited 7 July 2020).

empirically (e.g. in the light of the various acts of Parliament in the field of contract law in the UK and the Uniform Commercial Code in the US) and normatively (as if popular sovereignty in matters of private law was right only for one part of the world).

The situation is somewhat different in civil law jurisdictions. Whilst there too the judiciary has become an important protagonist in shaping the private law, courts nevertheless apply—and usually more than merely nominally—the civil codes enacted by their respective legislatures. Moreover, in many civil law jurisdictions there have been recodifications or reforms of private law (e.g in the Netherlands in 1992, in Germany in 2002, and France in 2016), which has reinforced to a degree (albeit rather modest from a Habermasian point of view) the democratic credentials of contract law. These reforms, as we also saw, are usually a mix of bringing judge-made legal doctrines and rules into the system of the code (codification), on the one hand, and changing some of the rules and doctrines with a view to improving them (modernization).

I. Dogmatic Reasoning and the Role of Scholars

Building on Habermas's discourse theory, Alexy argues that legal argumentation is a special case of practical argumentation and, consequently, that legal reason (or rationality) is a special case of practical reason.[371] Given that democratically enacted generally applicable laws do not determine the outcome of all disputes, we need legal argumentation as a rational way to fill the gap of uncertainty between general legal norms and specific cases.[372] Legal reasoning has in common with other types of practical argumentation that it is concerned with practical questions of what should or may be done, and thus with the correctness of normative statements. However, it is special in that legal argumentation is constrained by the legal sources of the legal order at hand, and consequently (fully) valid only within that order. The special case thesis has a wide range of dimensions and implications that do not concern us here. However, there are some specific implications that are highly relevant. In particular, if the rationality of legal reasoning entails the legitimacy of outcomes justified by legal reasons, then the direct consequence of this is the capacity of case law and legal doctrine to be legitimate sources of law. This is what is at stake, among other things, in the debate between Habermas and Alexy on the idea of legal discourse as a special case of practical discourse. In Section H we discussed the legitimacy of judicial private law making; here we will address the other main stake in the debate on the 'special case thesis', i.e. whether doctrinal legal scholarship, as a science, can contribute to legitimate law making for private law.

Alexy defines 'legal dogmatics' (*Rechtsdogmatik*) as 'a class of propositions which relate to enacted norms and case law but are not identical with a description of them, and stand in some coherent relationship, are composed and discussed in the framework

[371] R. Alexy, *A Theory of Legal Argumentation: The Theory of Rational Discourse as Theory of Legal Justification* ([first published 1978] 1989); Alexy, 'Jürgen Habermas's Theory of Legal Discourse', in M. Rosenfeld and A. Arato (eds), *Habermas on Law and Democracy: Critical Exchanges* (1998) 226; Alexy, 'The Special Case Thesis', 12 *Ratio Juris* (1999) 374; Alexy, 'Unbestimmtheit des Rechts und Rationalität der Rechtsprechung', in P. Koller and C. Hiebaum (eds), *Jürgen Habermas: Faktizität und Geltung* (2016), 85.

[372] Alexy, *A Theory of Legal Argumentation* (n. 371) 288.

of an institutionally organized legal science, and have normative content'.[373] Note that having normative content means that doctrinal propositions have a rightful (but fallible) claim, not only to being capable of being true or false but also to being binding (to some degree), and that the responsibility for elaborating them falls upon doctrinal legal scholarship (or 'legal science'). Still, legal dogmatics is not self-contained: it stands in connection with—indeed is dependent on—general practical reasoning (i.e. moral, ethical, and pragmatic arguments). As a result, the propositions of dogmatics are not irrefutable. 'They are not dogmas in the conventional sense.'[374] They are nothing more (or less) than hypotheses. According to Alexy, legal dogmatics has a number of important functions in a democratic society, including a stabilization function, a developmental function, and a burden-reducing function.[375] More fundamentally, the general practical principle of universalizability (the most fundamental principle in discourse theory) requires that the law treat like cases alike.[376] It follows, according to Alexy, that the 'dogmatization' of law is required by general practical principles.

The reconstruction of legal doctrine as institutionalized legal discourse, is based on the counterfactual presupposition of discursive rationality, i.e. of justifiability by reasons which must be redeemed by the actual practice. Therefore, the realities of doctrinal scholarship can be critically examined by this standard. Moreover, the principles of legal discourse as formulated by Alexy, understood as it is by him as a special case of general discourse, can also be critiqued by the general standard of the discourse principle D. The most prominent aspect of the reality of doctrinal scholarship that should be pointed out in this regard, it seems, is its intrinsic risk of—or structural bias towards—conservatism. The reality of doctrinal commentary-writing is that most of the text usually remains unchanged from one edition to another, sometimes over a dozen editions, except when a specific appellate court decision or a doctrinal monography sheds new light on the matter at hand. Given the great influence of doctrinal arguments, the stabilizing function of legal doctrine thus risks having an undue (because undemocratic) conservative effect of entrenching past understandings of legal texts.[377] Put differently, while Habermas is impressed by the knowledge contained in doctrinal scholarship,[378] and while doctrinal legal scholarship at times certainly does constitute an impressive cultural achievement, nevertheless, from a democratic point of view, scepticism seems warranted as to the (continuing) validity of this knowledge: do the leading commentaries really (still) contain the best understanding of the legal text at hand?

Lomfeld takes the idea of legal dogmatics as a special case of practical reason one step further. He offers a 'deliberative discourse theory of contractual rights'.[379] In

[373] Ibid. 156.

[374] Ibid. 265.

[375] Ibid. 266.

[376] For 'U', see Habermas, 'Remarks on Discourse Ethics', in J. Habermas, *Justification and Application: Remarks on Discourse Ethics* (1995), ch. 2; Habermas (n. 7) section 3.2.

[377] This point is akin to Duncan Kennedy's critique of the legitimation effect of adjudication, on which see D. Kennedy, *A Critique of Adjudication* (1997), ch. 10.

[378] See Habermas (n. 7) 80, where he explains the 'comparatively high degree of rationality' of legal norms from the fact that they 'incorporate doctrinal knowledge, that is, knowledge that has been articulated and systematized, brought to a scholarly level, and interwoven with a principled morality'.

[379] B. Lomfeld, *Die Gründe des Vertrages: eine Diskurstheorie des Vertragsrechte* (2015), at 3.

Alexian fashion, he understands legal rules as logical priority relationships between different values, and conceives of deliberation as the balancing of a plurality of values. He proposes 'a logic of reasons'[380] for this balancing exercise in the shape of a 'general deliberative grammar of the reasons of contract'. Within this framework, the entire normative debate on contract law is reduced ultimately to four conflicting core values, i.e. utility, security, justice, and freedom,[381] where justice is turned into one value to be balanced against the other three. This theory raises the question of how we can ever know what the reasons of contract might be in advance of any actual deliberation, i.e. before people in the society at hand have themselves thematized problems and solutions, and have proposed relevant ethical, moral, and pragmatic considerations (i.e. values, norms, and means to ends). Although Lomfeld emphasizes the political nature of contract law, he does not address the political process of contract law making or its legitimacy at all. Indeed, he hardly considers the possibility of drafting a contract law reform; the theory is focused almost exclusively on application discourses of the kind judges and doctrinal scholars typically engage in. The result is a rather static picture of a 'closed' value system.[382] There is no sense of how citizens could modify the grammar of contract law by supplementing its core values or by replacing some of them. If changes in the law are started by changing the discourse, it is not clear that a static, universal grammar will be helpful in making any progress. Note that Alexy also uses the metaphor of a grammar, but only with regard to forms of argument, not their substance.[383] By contrast, Lomfeld aims to structure and limit (through a 'closed' value system)[384] even the content of what people can or might want to say about (in this case) contract law. That seems directly at odds with the core commitments of the discourse theory of law and democracy.

J. The Impotence of the Mere Ought

As previously discussed, Habermas's theory of law and legitimate law making is meant to be located between facts and norms. He criticizes substantive normative theories ('the return of modern natural law') for ignoring both the pertinence of the justified charge that Hegel made to Kant, i.e. that non-situated norms are destined to remain of no practical consequence ('the impotence of the mere ought'),[385] and the sociological 'disenchantment' of the law (Weber).[386] Still, in reality Habermas's own discourse theory of

[380] Ibid. 185.

[381] Ibid. 74, 386, and passim.

[382] Ibid. 40.

[383] Alexy, *A Theory of Legal Argumentation* (n. 371) 245. See also e.g. N. Jansen, *Die Struktur der Gerechtigkeit* (1998), who proposes, as a meta-ethical theory, a comprehensive formal analysis of the structure of argumentation about justice.

[384] Lomfeld (n. 379) 40.

[385] Habermas (n. 7) section 2.2. See also Habermas, 'Treffen Hegels Einwände gegen Kant auch auf die Diskursethik zu?', in J. Habermas, *Philosophische Texte*, Vol. 3 (2009) 116, at 117: 'Kant muß sich den Vorwurf machen lassen, daß eine Ethik, die Pflicht und Neigung, Vernunft und Sinnlichkeit kategorial trennt, praktisch folgenlos bleibt.'

[386] Habermas (n. 7) section 2.1. See also, more radical, Kennedy, 'The Disenchantment of Logically Formal Legal Rationality, or Max Weber's Sociology in the Genealogy of the Contemporary Mode of Western Legal Thought', 55 *Hastings L.J.* (2004) 1031.

law and democracy remains rather thin on facts, as critics have pointed out.[387] That criticism seems justified with particular pertinence with regard to private law, especially contract law. How can democratic deliberation work in practice in the face of public apathy, and *a fortiori* with regard to such a perceived 'technical' subject as contract law? A Habermasian discourse theory of contract law that wants to make a practical impact, it seems, must provide an answer. One possible partial response to this charge could be that debates on contract law are likely to attract more public engagement if—unlike the European civil code debate and the debates on the Dutch, German, and French contract law reforms—they are about the legal response to actual social and relational injustices, or the risk thereof, rather than about the system of contract and its core doctrines.[388]

By contrast, Auer's reconstruction of the private law discourse of modernity takes private law's reality and its role in society very seriously.[389] She demonstrates how the modern individualistic understanding of private law, that reached its completion with Kant, remained effective in practice quite independently from the various specific philosophical systems that came and went in modern times.[390] Moreover, and most to the point here, she shows that even though we know now that there is no private law without a state, that the basic structure of private law is determined by state institutions (i.e. the legislator and courts), that state action has an impact on all relationships governed by private law with inevitable distributive dimensions, and that private law cannot be normatively autonomous from heteronomous values 'alien' to private law,[391] nevertheless the practice of private law has always remained committed, at least in part, to the idea of a coherent and autonomous system of private law, based on subjective rights and corrective justice. In other words, as Auer points out, counter-modern structures are immanent to our modern private law. Indeed, private law has never been—and could not be—more than 'half modern'.[392]

8. Concluding Remarks

There exists a wide divergence among the leading contemporary political theories with regard to questions of whether (European) contract law must have a solid democratic basis and what this would entail. Moreover, even within several of these strands of political thought, which stand firmly united on other fronts (as we will see in the next chapters), we found strong disagreement with regard to the question of the need for a democratic private law.

387 See e.g. Koller, 'Recht als Kategorie der Vermittlung zwischen Faktizität und Geltung', in P. Koller and C. Hiebaum (eds), *Jürgen Habermas: Faktizität und Geltung* (2016), 21.

388 Hesselink, 'The Right to Justification of Contract', 33 *Ratio Juris* (2020) 196–222.

389 M. Auer, *Der Privatrechtliche Diskurs der Moderne* (2014).

390 Ibid. 43. As she points out, this conclusion, that had been reached earlier by Pound, constitutes an important objection against substantive private law theories. Cf. Pound, 'The End of Law as Developed in Juristic Thought II', 30 *Harv. L. Rev.* (1917) 201, at 203, discussing five different strands in theory (Kantians, utilitarians, historical school, positivists, and social radicals) that all have in common that they understand the law end as ensuring individual self-assertion (as opposed to directly furthering of social progress).

391 Auer (n. 389) 67–70.

392 Ibid. 87, with reference to B. Latour, *Nous n'avons jamais été modernes. Essai d'anthropologie symétrique* (1991).

The divergence exists, in the first place, at the level of the general principle. The endorsement of a democratic contract law by utilitarians and civic republicans is conditional, as a presumably effective means for achieving the end of the maximization of welfare or for realizing freedom as non-domination, respectively. The communitarian support is weaker: democracy may be helpful in defining the common good, but there may also be better ways to do this. The rejection by libertarians is categorical, albeit not necessarily comprehensive: democracy cannot legitimately limit liberty, understood as freedom as non-interference. The endorsement from the side of discourse theory is comprehensive and categorical: every person should be able regard herself as a co-author of every law that applies to her, including contract law. Finally, liberal-egalitarian principles are indeterminate with regard to the importance of democracy relative to other concerns, especially rights, as is testified by the particularly wide and diverse range of liberal-egalitarian positions in this matter.

Also with regard to their understanding of what would amount to a democratic contract law, the political theories we saw diverge significantly. For certain theories mere majority voting in parliament suffices to ensure democratic legitimacy. Some go even further and accept a contract law that was not enacted in parliament as democratic, for example because the president of the republic, who enacted the contract law reform by decree, was democratically elected. Others have a much more demanding conception of democratic deliberation where majority voting is merely the conclusion (temporary in principle) of a society-wide debate that should consider everyone's point of view.

A particularly divisive question concerns the legitimacy of judicial law making. Two quite different arguments must be kept apart here. Some theorists claim that judicial law making is acceptable in spite of its limited democratic credentials, because other concerns and values are more important (ultimately) when it comes to contract law making (private autonomy, human rights, minority groups) and are safest in the hands of the judiciary. Others, by contrast, argue for the legitimacy of judicial law because, in their view, it is democratic. Among these latter views we can further distinguish between those who argue that judicial law making, although second best from a democratic point of view, is nevertheless acceptable as long as the legislature retains primacy, and those, on the other hand, arguing that judicial contract law making has certain specific democratic merits that legislatures lack (either presently or even under ideal circumstances), most notably that it naturally allows people themselves (under ideal circumstances) to table their very real and concrete problems and grievances. It is important to remember that this question of whether judicial contract law making is democratically legitimate does not coincide with the question about the legitimacy of the common law. During the past century, judicial contract law making has been massive in civil law jurisdictions—where almost all new doctrines were developed by courts, with hardly more than nominal basis in the civil codes, typically with reference to 'general clauses' on good faith—while in common law jurisdictions legislation (and in some cases codification) is widespread in the field of contracts. Moreover, as we have seen, the theorists defending and attacking judicial law making are themselves frequently not situated in jurisdictions on the corresponding sides of the civil versus common law divide.

As explained in Chapter 1, the objective of this book is to derive convincing reasons and arguments from the theories that can enlighten us on some of the most fundamental political questions of (European) private law. The idea is that with a deeper understanding of the various arguments we will be better placed to reach conclusions and to formulate answers to these questions. The existence of strongly divergent views on whether contract law should be democratic and what this would entail does not mean that the answer to these questions is necessarily indeterminate or that all theories are equally right. It merely shows that the question is controversial. Ultimately, it remains a matter of argumentation. Reasons are all we have got. And arguably some reasons are stronger than others.

It is difficult to see why a person ought to accept living under laws made by others. Moreover, there is no reason why private law, in particular contract law, should be any different, in this respect, from criminal law, tax law, or any other branch of the law. Therefore, the very basic principle of political autonomy, or collective self-determination, it seems, has to be the starting point in any consideration of legitimate contract law making. None of the arguments raised against this general principle or its applicability to contract law discussed in this chapter were found convincing. Therefore, fundamentally, the answer to our question of whether contract law should have a democratic basis must be affirmative. The next question is what specifically this entails.

It is important to underline that democratic legitimacy is not a binary either/or question, but a matter of degree: political autonomy and agency, i.e. for people to have a say in the law making that affects them, can be assured to different degrees in different institutional arrangements. In particular, combinations of different contract law makers are not merely theoretically conceivable: they are also the reality in most jurisdictions, both in the common law and the civil law world. Thus, the institutional division of labour may well involve several institutions legitimately participating in contract law making. Still, such a shared responsibility can exist with or without a hierarchy, normatively speaking. Thus, the question remains whether there is a first and second best relationship between contract law making institutions and whether one of them should have final authority.

From the point of view of collective self-government, it seems, judicial law making cannot but be second-best compared to law making by the legislature, at least under ideal conditions. The conclusion that in terms of legitimacy judicial law making is always second best applies as much with regard to private law as to other fields of the law. There exists no plausible justification for private law exceptionalism. Non-ideal cases, even though they are bound to be the majority, are difficult to discuss in the abstract, i.e. without knowing the specific less than ideal circumstances. As we saw, from a legitimacy point of view a sweeping contract law reform by presidential decree may be as problematic as judicial activism from a civil or a constitutional court or the Court of Justice. And in either case, the realistic and robustly warranted perspective of subsequent democratic deliberation and decision by the legislature on whether or not to ratify/codify may constitute an important mitigating factor. Still, in all non-ideal cases the ideal should provide at least some guidance in assessing private law's legitimacy and in indicating the right direction for making progress.[393]

[393] Against ideal theory, see A. Sen, *The Idea of Justice* (2009), at 15 ff, 101 ff and passim. On the need for non-ideal, partial compliance theories of private law, see Bagchi, 'Distributive Injustice and Private Law', 60 *Hastings L.J.* (2008) 105. Her focus is especially on the role for private law in the (hardly counterfactual) case when distributive justice through other institutions, such as tax and transfer, is not ensured. A similar

In addition to judges, the same also goes for the role of other experts, such as legal academics (in expert groups) and technical experts (in regulatory silos), who ultimately should be at the service of the democratic legislature when it comes to law making. Expert government is illegitimate because for the vast majority of people—i.e. everyone except the experts themselves—it means being governed by others. In advanced societies like our own a division of labour and the development of expertise are of course not only inevitable but also entirely legitimate in principle. (And, conversely, 'expert bashing' easily becomes corrosive even in an otherwise healthy public sphere.) However, when it comes to law making the role of experts should be to enlighten the general public and the democratic legislature on what is at stake, the advantages and disadvantages of various alternatives, and perhaps also on how a reform in a certain direction could look. Their legitimate role with regard to law making is to open up democratic space and to widen the debate by offering their insights, not to constrain the democratic deliberation and the political agency of non-experts. However high the perceived quality of their output may be (say, a doctrinally impeccable blueprint for reform), it could never compensate for any ensuing reduction in the possibility for citizens (and affected non-citizens) to influence the outcome, both in terms of solutions and—what is often more important—in setting the law making agenda by formulating the main problems that (in our case) European contract law should address.

A final comment on populism. If we define populists as those who claim to speak on behalf of 'the people', understood as a monolithic entity, and against 'the elite', who do not know or care what the people want,[394] then clearly populism undermines democracy for two important interrelated reasons: populist government and law making fail to ensure political autonomy and agency, because it is the populist leaders who speak in the name of 'the people', and they ignore the diversity of opinion among the people that is both a precondition and the natural result of a truly democratic polity and its institutions. Therefore, if anything, the rise in populism in recent years, both on the right and the left of the political spectrum, gives reason to strive for more, not less, democracy. The notion that in these serious times there should be less space for democracy, because fundamental rights and justice are under attack, is misguided, because what is needed now, more than ever, is that the people themselves (in the plural) must be able to protect their rights and fight against social and interpersonal injustice, through inclusive democratic debates on the main problems and the best solutions. The result may well be a radically different agenda and outcomes, including when it comes to European contract law making.

argument could be made with regard to the democratic legitimacy of private law under conditions of partial compliance. The argument could then become a case for the statutory regulation of contracts, where the judicial law making practice is particularly lacking in legitimacy, e.g. when the judiciary consists effectively of a narrow elite, or, vice versa, for judicial contract law making, where the legislature is captured by powerful economic interests while the judiciary are making a genuine attempt to also include the points of view of those at the periphery of the public sphere.

394 See e.g. Müller (n. 355).

4
National, European, or Global

1. Introduction

In Europe today, contract law can be found not only at the national level, but also at the European level and on the international level, and in some cases at the further sub-national level of regions. Over history, not least in recent decades, the vertical distribution of contract law making powers and initiatives has proved to be eminently variable. Moreover, it has also become a highly controversial matter, both in the political and the academic arenas. One of the most clamorous events, in this respect, was the defeat in 2014 of the academic and political movement for a European civil code (ECC), a Common Frame of Reference (CFR), or Common European Sales Law (CESL).[1] Another, even more radical event—whose contract law implications still remain to be determined—was the UK's 2016 Brexit decision to leave the EU.

Just as for the horizontal division of labour of contract law making powers, discussed in Chapter 3, here too the question arises whether the status quo is justifiable or whether it can reasonably be rejected and, if so, on what grounds. Do we perhaps have a moral right to a European civil code? Or, conversely, are we entitled to an entirely renationalized contract law? Should the integrity of national legal cultures be respected, or should a (re)nascent European legal culture be fostered? Are contract law rules essentially a matter of universal truth or rather of local identities? If a common European contract law could be demonstrated to boost cross-border trade and, thus, to make a significant contribution to economic growth, would that alone justify replacing national contract laws with it? Is the activist role of the Court of Justice in promoting consumer protection, often directly overruling the national supreme civil courts in bold preliminary rulings, illegitimately undermining the authority of these national courts?

The question of whether contract law should be European was at the heart of the European civil code debate that raged in Europe, especially in legal academia, for more than a decade from around the turn of the century,[2] with passionate believers and declared enemies.[3] The European civil code debate subsequently transformed into a debate on the merits of a common frame of reference, and the CESL proposal, successively. In many respects, those contract law debates were mere specific instances of the more general debates about European integration, the future of the EU, and its

[1] For a short narrative of the Europeanization of contract law, see Chapter 2.

[2] See the various contributions to A. S. Hartkamp *et al.*, *Towards a European Civil Code* (1st ed., 1994). See also the contributions to the seminal conference 'Towards a European Civil Code', organized by the Dutch EU presidency in 1997 in Scheveningen, published in 5(4) *ERPL* (1997).

[3] Contrast e.g. Lando, 'Why Codify the European Law of Contract?', 5 *ERPL* (1997) 525, with Legrand, 'Against a European Civil Code', 60 *MLR* (1997) 44.

Justifying Contract in Europe: Political Philosophies of European Contract Law. First Edition. Martijn W. Hesselink, Oxford University Press. © Martijn W. Hesselink 2021. DOI: 10.1093/oso/9780192843654.003.0004

nature and finality. However, there were also arguments relating more strictly to the (perceived) specific characteristics of private law integration or the specific nature of private law.

Meanwhile, the real Europeanization of contract law was taking place chiefly through a series of directives that went ever further to core subjects of contract law. These include, in particular, the Unfair Terms Directive 1993,[4] the Consumer Sales Directive 1999,[5] the Consumer Rights Directive 2011,[6] and the two Digital Single Market Directives of 2019, on the online and offline sale of goods (replacing the 1999 directive) and the supply of digital content, respectively.[7] These directives have in common that their substantive scope is not limited to any specific market. Together, they have brought about a major transformation of contract law in Europe.[8] In practice, the familiar categories of contract law—sometimes referred to as being based on the life cycle of a contract—such as formation, validity, interpretation, contents and effects, performance or non-performance, and remedies, are being increasingly pushed to the background by withdrawal rights, unfair terms control, and remedies for non-conformity.[9] These key new doctrines will soon apply to most internal market transactions with consumers. In addition, an important 'radiating' effect is to be expected, in particular towards contracts involving small and medium-sized enterprises (SMEs).[10]

Thus, the central question to this chapter, i.e. whether contract law should be European, is not an abstract question. It is concretely situated in the reality of the ongoing Europeanization of contract law and asks after its justification. In other words, with respect to the contract law *acquis* the question is a critical one. Moreover, the Europeanization of contract law has been a process, i.e. dynamic and heading in a certain direction. Therefore, if a sufficient justification for any further Europeanization is found wanting, then—unless the current state of European contract somehow happened to be immune to the same criticism—the unjustifiability of any further Europeanization would lead to the conclusion that the dynamic must be inverted, i.e. that EU contract law must be undone, in part or in its entirety. In other words, the

[4] Directive 93/13/EEC of 5 April 1993 on unfair terms in consumer contracts, OJ 1993 L 95 ('Unfair Terms Directive').

[5] Directive 1999/44/EC on certain aspects of the sale of consumer goods and associated guarantees, OJ 1999 L 171.

[6] Directive 2011/83/EU on consumer rights, OJ 2011 L 304 ('Consumer Rights Directive').

[7] Directive (EU) 2019/770 on certain aspects concerning contracts for the supply of digital content and digital services, OJ 2019 L 136; and Directive (EU) 2019/771 on certain aspects concerning contracts for the sale of goods, OJ 2019 L 136.

[8] Also part of the same transformation are Directive 2008/48/EC on credit agreements for consumers, OJ 2008 L 133 ('Consumer Credit Directive'), Directive 2008/122/EC on the protection of consumers in respect of certain aspects of timeshare, long-term holiday product, resale and exchange contracts, OJ 2009 L 33 ('Timeshare Directive'), and Directive (EU) 2015/2302 on package travel and linked travel arrangements, OJ 2015 L 326 ('Package Travel Directive'), which although more sector-specific in scope, share the same horizontal characteristics (notably the private law remedies).

[9] See further Hesselink, 'Private Law, Regulation, and Justice', 22 *ELJ* (2016) 681.

[10] A first example is provided by Directive (EU) 2019/633 on unfair trading practices in business-to-business relationships in the agricultural and food supply chain, OJ 2019 L 111. Although this directive provides only for administrative enforcement and, therefore, does not directly affect private law, it was heavily inspired by both the Unfair Terms Directive and the Unfair Commercial Practices Directive, and is therefore likely to have an impact in particular on the validity of contract law clauses as well. In this sense, see M. P. de la Cuesta de los Mozos, 'SMEs in the (Food) Global Value Chain: a European Private Law Perspective' (2020) (doctoral thesis on file at EUI, Florence).

most obvious response to any conclusion of non-justifiability of Europeanization, it seems, would not be to keep the *acquis* as in stands, but to renationalize contract law.

As noted earlier, national and European contract law are not the only two conceivable alternatives. Contract law could also be located at the global level. Indeed, there exist several instances of world-wide international conventions in the field of contract law, the best-known of which is the UN Convention on Contracts for the International Sale of Goods (CISG) (1980). In addition, there is also soft law, most notably the UNIDROIT Principles of International Commercial Contracts (2016). Moreover, beyond positive law, instances of exploitation in global value chains, for example, raise the question of whether justice demands a global contract law response. On the other hand, contract law could also be subnational. An recent example of regional private law is the *Codi Civil de Catalunya*.[11]

Moreover, all sorts of combinations are possible too. Such a compound is, in fact, the current situation in Europe. It follows directly from a combination of the principle of conferral (Article 5 TEU), the absence of general private law making competence (Article 114 TFEU), the fact that the internal market competence is shared by the Union with the Member States (Article 4(2) TFEU), and the practice of minimum harmonization. However, this, in turn, raises a new set of questions: should we regard the respective national private law systems, on the one hand, and the existing EU private law, on the other, as separate systems (dualism), or as one single multi-level system (European monism), or should the private law of EU origin simply be understood, in each country, as part of their respective national systems of private law (national monism)?

This chapter critically discusses six normative political accounts of the Europeanization of private law, in terms of efficiency (justice for growth), liberty (the private law society), regulation (the silos view), identity (nationalism, Europeanism, and cosmopolitanism), non-domination (demoicracy), and discourse theory (the post-national condition), respectively. As we will see, not only the answers but also the understanding of the main question differs from one political theory to another. While the main focus here will be on contract law, the field that has been at the centre of European private law debate, much of the analysis will be of relevance also for most other branches of European private law.

2. Utilitarian

A. Justice for Growth

Virtually the entire *acquis communautaire* in the area of contract law is based, at least in part, on Article 114 TFEU and its predecessors. Therefore, EU contract law consists essentially of measures for the approximation of laws that 'have as their object the establishment and functioning of the internal market'. This means that the *raison d'être*, at least officially, for European contract law is the objective of establishing a European

[11] The codification of Catalan civil law started in 2002 and completed in 2018, with the adoption of Book 6 On Obligations and Contracts.

internal market and ensuring its proper functioning. In other words, the nature of EU contract law is functional and its function is internal market building. The basic idea is that by removing obstacles to the proper functioning of the single market, such as, for example, difference in the degree or type of consumer protection, a more level playing field can be created among sellers and service providers across the EU.[12]

From the wording of the Treaty, it seems to follow that market building is the aim, not a means to any ulterior end.[13] This point is underlined by libertarians, as we will see. However, on a more utilitarian (consequentialist) reading the internal market, like any other market, is itself a mechanism for achieving the aim of increasing the welfare of society. On this view, the harmonization of laws, including contract laws, will lead to the integration of the various national markets into one single, comprehensive European internal market. This, in turn, will make Europeans better off, because businesses will be able to sell their products more easily across national borders while consumers will be offered a wider range of products and at lower prices. Thus, everyone will be able to 'reap the benefits' of the internal market, as the European Commission put it.[14] Positive market integration (i.e. the introduction of new market-wide institutions and instruments) complements negative integration (i.e. the removal of national rules and institutions constituting trade barriers incompatible with the market freedoms) and provides the economic rationale for the contract law *acquis*.[15]

It is this latter understanding of market integration as an engine for economic growth that has been at the heart of the idea of an internal market right from the beginning. The Single European Act (SEA) of 1986 had the deliberate aim of providing new impetus to the economies of the Member States, which had been suffering from the economic recession of the early 1980s.[16] For this purpose, the SEA set as its main objective the establishment of an 'internal market' by 1992.[17] A key instrument for achieving this objective was the introduction of Article 100a EEC Treaty, the future Article 114 TFEU, which allowed for qualified majority voting. The objective gained renewed impetus with the adoption of 'the Lisbon strategy' by the European Council in 2000, where the EU set itself 'a new strategic goal for the next decade', i.e. 'to become the most competitive and dynamic knowledge-based economy in the world, capable of sustainable economic growth with more and better jobs and greater social cohesion'.[18] On this reading, the harmonization measures introduced with a view to

[12] However, as the CJEU ruled in Case C-376/98, *Germany v. Parliament and Council* (EU:C:2000:544) and Case C-491/01, *British American Tobacco (Investments) and Imperial Tobacco* (EU:C:2002:741), 'a mere finding of disparities between national rules' does not suffice for providing a solid legal basis; a harmonization measure 'must genuinely have as its object the improvement of the conditions for the functioning of the internal market'.

[13] However, the Second Preliminary Recital to the Treaty of Rome (1957), already mentioned the resolve of the high contracting parties 'to ensure the economic and social progress of their countries by common action to eliminate the barriers which divide Europe'.

[14] See generally, Commission's 'Consumer Policy Strategy 2002–2006' (COM(2002) 208 final) (hereinafter Commission's 'Consumer Policy Strategy'). Specifically with regard to contract law, see the (meanwhile withdrawn) CESL-proposal, Recital (6): 'Differences in national contract laws therefore constitute barriers which prevent consumers and traders from reaping the benefits of the internal market.'

[15] For the classical statement, see J. Tinbergen, *International Economic Integration* (2nd ed., 1965), at 76.

[16] D. Chalmers, G. Davies, and G. Monti, *European Union Law* (4th ed., 2019), at 18.

[17] See Art. 13 SEA.

[18] Presidency Conclusions, Lisbon European Council, 23 and 24 March 2000.

completing the internal market, including those affecting contract law, serve the ulterior purpose of increasing the economic prosperity of Europeans. In other words, on this view the purpose of European contract law is to contribute to economic growth.

In this light, it came as no surprise that the European Commission decided, in 2002, to switch, in its legislative proposals in the field of consumer law, from minimum harmonization, which allows the Member States to maintain a higher level of consumer protection than the minimum required by the directive,[19] to full harmonization, where the minimum also becomes the maximum.[20] Only full harmonization, it was thought, could offer European sellers the level playing field that was needed to meet the Lisbon objectives.[21] This new policy was successfully implemented in the Unfair Commercial Practices Directive of 2005. It was also at the basis of the European Commission's proposal in 2008 for a directive on consumer rights, but this turned out to be so controversial that the Commission had to withdraw towards a policy of 'targeted' full harmonization.[22] The Consumer Rights Directive (CRD) was eventually adopted in 2011. Although its name suggests that it might be taking consumer rights seriously, its true concern was to assist consumers in becoming confident cross-border shoppers, which, in turn, was expected to contribute to economic growth.[23] The most striking example, however, of the economic growth rationale was the 2011 Proposal for a Common European Sales Law (CESL), which, the explanatory memorandum claimed, would make a significant contribution to the EU's recovery from the economic crisis.[24] Thus, the focus was squarely on economic growth.[25] Indeed, in the vision of the European Commission, justice itself should be at the service of growth, as expressed in its remarkable slogan 'justice for growth'.[26] Similarly, the explanatory memorandum to the contract law proposals for the Digital Single Market

[19] The notion of minimum harmonization was inspired by the ideas of differentiated integration and a multi-speed Europe that go back to the Tindemans Report 1974. See 'European Union, Report by Mr Leo Tindemans, Prime Minister of Belgium, to the European Council', *Bulletin of the European Communities*, Supplement 1/76, 20 ('A New Approach'). Cf. Walker, 'Sovereignty and Differentiated Integration in the European Union', 4 *ELJ* (1998) 355.

[20] See the Commission's 'Consumer Policy Strategy' (n. 14) 12.

[21] Cf. Micklitz, 'Do Consumers and Businesses Need a New Architecture of Consumer Law? A Thought Provoking Impulse', 32 *YEL* (2013) 266, at 278: 'The crucial turning point towards maximum harmonization resulted from the Lisbon Strategy set out by the European Council in 2000, by which the *ökonomische Effizienzdenken* mutated into the dominant European ideology.'

[22] Speech of the Vice-President of the European Commission V. Reding, 'An Ambitious Consumer Rights Directive: Boosting Consumers' Protection and Helping Businesses', Madrid, 15 March 2010.

[23] See the Consumer Rights Directive (n. 6), preliminary Recital (5). See, more generally, the Commission Communication 'A European Consumer Agenda—Boosting Confidence and Growth' (COM(2012) 225 final): 'Improving consumer confidence in cross-border shopping online by taking appropriate policy action could provide a major boost to economic growth in Europe. Empowered and confident consumers can drive forward the European economy.'

[24] See Commission Staff Working Paper, Impact Assessment, accompanying the document Proposal for a Regulation of the European Parliament and of the Council on a Common European Sales Law, SEC(2011) 1165 final, at 7, which contains the following astounding claim: 'The value of the trade foregone by those who are dissuaded due to differences in contract law amounts to some tens of billions of euros.'

[25] In its Annual Growth Survey, Progress Report on Europe 2020 (COM(2011) 11 final), at 5, the European Commission had already announced its proposal for an optional contract law instrument. See also Recital (16) of the proposal, which underlined the 'potential for growth in cross-border trade, especially in e-commerce'.

[26] See the Commission's Communication 'The EU Justice Agenda for 2020: Strengthening Trust, Mobility and Growth Within the Union' (COM(2014) 144 final), especially at 2 and 7.

announced with striking candour: 'The general objective of the proposals is to contribute to faster growth of the Digital Single Market, to the benefit of both consumers and businesses.'[27] This aim is radically different from the stated reasons for civil codes (and recent re-codifications) to have been adopted in the Member States.

Another direct consequence of the Lisbon Strategy was that henceforward legislative proposals were consistently accompanied by 'impact assessments'. What this boils down to, as we saw in Chapter 3, is essentially an American style 'cost benefit analysis' primarily in economic terms. This was the case, for example, for the CRD, the CESL proposal, and the Digital Single Market proposals. The underlying policy assumption was, again, not merely that economic growth is good per se and that European contract law should contribute to achieving it, but also that economic growth is the primary (or even exclusive) aim of European contract law. The claims made in those impact assessments with regard to expected benefits often seem highly exaggerated. Therefore, it is not surprising that they have been contested frequently. In fact, with regard to the CESL proposal the European Parliament undertook its own 'health check' of the Commission's impact assessment.[28]

The result of this framing, however, was that the question of whether Europe should adopt a regulation on a common European sales law or its successor proposals for two contract law directives for the Digital Single Market, seemed to have become an entirely empirical question with regard to their expected net economic benefits. Opponents were also expected to argue in this same welfare-economic vein, for example by pointing to certain negative externalities of the encouragement of cross-border sales, such as the costs to the environment when goods travel further.[29] That result should not come as a surprise under such an essentially utilitarian approach. It will also not worry those who are convinced that welfare, defined narrowly, should indeed be the basis of public choice, including choices with regard to contract law. However, those who do not regard wealth maximization as the main objective of contract law may beg to differ. In this regard, the latest Commission proposals may not constitute a truly 'new deal'[30] as announced,[31] at least not for contract law, but they certainly came with a new tone, i.e. a shift from the language of 'justice for growth' to 'better protection' of and 'more fairness' to consumers.[32]

[27] Proposal for a Directive on Certain Aspects Concerning Contracts for the Supply of Digital Content (COM(2015) 634 final), at 2.

[28] 'Common European Sales Law, Appraisal by the EP Impact Assessment Unit of the European Commission's impact assessment, Commission proposal for a Regulation of the European Parliament and of the Council on a Common European Sales Law', January 2013, PE 496.736.

[29] E.g. M. Bartl, 'Legitimacy and European Private Law' (2012) (doctoral thesis, on file at EUI, Florence), at 32.

[30] Proposal for a Directive Amending Directive 93/13/EEC, Directive 98/6/EC, Directive 2005/29/EC and Directive 2011/83/EU as regards better enforcement and modernisation of EU consumer protection rules (COM(2018) 185 final).

[31] Commission Press Release of 11 April 2018, 'A New Deal for Consumers: Commission Strengthens EU Consumer Rights and Enforcement' (IP/18/3041).

[32] Ibid.

B. Decentralization and Regulatory Competition

While the idea of the harmonization of laws with a view to positive market integration leads to the European centralization of contract law making, there are also other welfare economic theories pointing in the exact opposite direction of decentralization. These tend to be inspired by the (American) paradigm of the economics of federalism, according to which centralized government and uniform law are problematic because of the principal-agent problem. One such claim, which has been present in the European private law debate since its inception, consists of the argument that the preferences of citizens, including with regard to private law rules, differ along national lines, while being sufficiently homogeneous within each nation, and therefore national legislators are best placed to respond to those preferences, and, consequently, uniform private law cannot but thwart the expectations and preferences of citizens.[33] This claim was directed, especially, against the idea of a European civil code, which, according to this hypothesis concerning the preferences of European citizens, would inevitably contain rules that correspond to no one's preferences, while the risk of this would be proportionately smaller if contract law was enacted at a lower level of law making.[34] However, although citizens in Europe are likely to have diverging preferences with regard to contract law rules, it is not clear that these preferences differ chiefly along national lines. Indeed, the hypothesis of homogeneous national preferences seems to suffer from a strong nationalist bias.[35] In reality, there exists some preliminary evidence suggesting that preferences among similar market operators in different Member States are more convergent than the hypothesis claims.[36] Another aspect of the nationalist bias is that the status quo of the current national borders is taken for granted even though it seems hardly plausible that all European Member States, from Malta to Germany, currently have an efficient size. However, if the public choice argument against the Europeanization of private law is indeed based on the principal-agent problem and the distance between law maker and citizen, then why

[33] See e.g. Ogus, 'Competition Between National Legal Systems: A Contribution of Economic Analysis to Comparative Law', 48 *ICLQ* (1999) 405; Van den Bergh, 'Forced Harmonization of Contract Law in Europe: Not to Be Continued', in S. Grundmann and J. Stuyck (eds), *An Academic Green Paper on European Contract Law* (2002) 249.

[34] Faure, 'Economic Analysis of Tort Law and the European Civil Code', in A. S. Hartkamp *et al.*, *Towards a European Civil Code* (4th ed., 2011) 977, at 985.

[35] The problem with the assumption of homogeneous national preferences is that it derives from empirical data collected almost invariably by national statistics institutes. These, however, were themselves paradigmatic products of nationalism. See E. J. Hobsbawm, *Nations and Nationalism: Programme, Myth, Reality* (1990). This is acknowledged by G. Hofstede, *Cultures and Organizations* (1994), at 12. The European Commission, when arguing for full harmonization in its Consumer Rights Directive proposal, produced its own statistics concerning the preferences of European citizens and barriers to cross-border trade. See e.g. *Consumers Attitudes Towards Cross-Border Sales and Consumer Protection* (Flash Eurobarometer 282, March 2010); *Business Attitudes Towards Cross-Border Sales and Consumer Protection* (Flash Eurobarometer 224, July 2008). Obviously, an important objective of the Eurobarometers has been, in a very similar vein, the construction (or suggestion) of a European public opinion and, thus, of a European *demos*.

[36] Vogenauer and Weatherill, 'The European Community's Competence to Pursue the Harmonisation of Contract Law—An Empirical Contribution to the Debate', in S. Vogenauer and S. Weatherill (eds), *The Harmonisation of European Contract Law, Implications for European Private Laws, Business And Legal Practice* (2006) 105.

not first question the size of certain existing Member States?[37] Perhaps efficiency gains could be made from splitting up certain countries that are too large, or from bundling a few small countries, say the Benelux, and subjecting them to the same contract laws. In summary, when it comes to increasing the welfare of citizens in Europe, it is not clear that regulatory competition among different legal models with a view to being adopted, as legal transplants,[38] by national contract law makers, is necessarily superior, purely from the perspective of efficiency, to a more centralized European contract law making.

Still, the ideas of decentralized approximation and regulatory competition do not intrinsically depend on any nationalist bias, as is shown by the example of the US, from which most of the theory of regulatory competition derives (especially with reference to company law). For example, in our case of contract law different models could be proposed and followed by different jurisdictions (i.e. the Member States) without any (strong) form of centralized coordination. Thus, a more plausible version, at least on its own terms, of regulatory competition in the field of private law, which is also based on a hypothesis concerning citizens' preferences concerning the law but which is not biased by nationalism, can be found in the case for a free choice of law for private parties, made on the ground that this would allow them to pursue their objectives in the way most congenial to their own preferences. This idea, which became highly controversial in the context of the political debates on the 'Bolkestein' Services Directive ('country of origin principle') and, more recently, on posted workers, will be discussed in more detail in Chapter 8. What is relevant here, however, is that this argument also goes against uniform contract law. For the latter would remove the choice from private parties. And this would be bad from an efficiency perspective, on this view, considering the presumably heterogeneous preferences concerning contract law held by economic actors in Europe, plus the risk that it would stifle innovation and competition among national law makers and keep them from attempting to offer economic agents the most efficient contract law.

As will also be discussed further in Chapter 8, even if regulatory competition led to a net economic benefit, the distribution of the ensuing benefits might be very uneven: there may be not only economic winners but also losers. Indeed, in their zeal to reduce costs for businesses national law makers may try to beat the competition by reducing certain rights, for example those of socially more vulnerable groups. Thus, regulatory competition may lead to a race to the bottom. From an efficiency point of view that would not necessarily be a problem as long as losses sustained by some groups in society are exceeded by the gains accruing to others. It is not clear, however, that this justification can reasonably be expected to be acceptable to those who will be losing out.

Moreover, in either version the idea of regulatory competition is based on the assumption that citizens have exogenous and stable 'preferences' with regard to contract

[37] This idea is explored in A. Alesina and E. Spolaore, *The Size of Nations* (2003), which provides an economic analysis of the size of countries. For an egalitarian version of the idea of more rational boundaries in Europe, see this map with 28 equally sized EU Member States, available at https://brilliantmaps.com/eu-28-equal/ (last visited 9 July 2020).

[38] Cf. A. Watson, *Legal Transplants: An Approach to Comparative Law* (1974).

law and would thus be able to rank their relative preferences for various rule alternatives, without the need for democratic deliberation based on reasons and arguments. However, as we have seen in Chapters 2 and 3, that hypothesis is highly problematic, not only empirically but also from the perspective of legitimate law making.

3. Libertarian

A. The Ordoliberal Reading of the EU

There exists another reading of the EU and its main institutions, which at first sight might seem rather similar to the one we just saw, because it is also an economic reading. In reality, however, it is quite distinct. This is the ordoliberal idea of the EU and its 'economic constitution'. Ordoliberals regard free, competitive markets as an aim in itself, not merely as a means for boosting economic growth. Indeed, they reject the political aim of maximizing welfare,[39] just as much as the objective of achieving social justice, which they regard as a mirage.[40] Society has no aims, law should not be instrumentalized, and it is the single but highly important task of private law merely to provide a legal order, an 'economic constitution', within which individuals are free to take their own initiatives (or not).[41] What ordoliberals strive for is a private law society, not (or at least not necessarily) an affluent society. Therefore, although many private law scholars combine so-called 'economic' arguments borrowed from both welfare economics and libertarianism, these are actually quite distinct ideas, chiefly because libertarians reject a collectivist, instrumental conception of private law. (The same applies for much of the critique of a 'neoliberal' EU private law, which also tends to lump the two together.[42])

In the ordoliberal view, although private law is constitutive of competitive markets, the market, its institutions, and free competition are not themselves instrumental to any political or societal objectives, whether they are economic growth, full employment, or an equal distribution of income. Ordoliberals reject the pursuit by the government of such economic objectives because if the economic constitution is placed at the service of growth, social justice, and the like, its main coordination function will be distorted; private law should be formal and purpose-independent. What the law should do, in the ordoliberal view, is to provide legal order, i.e. a structure or framework that is entirely formal (i.e. not at the service of any substantive objectives). In doing so, it allows individuals and businesses to pursue their own objectives resting assured that the public institutions will maintain the legal order through the enforcement of the

[39] See e.g. F. A. Hayek, *Law, Legislation and Liberty; A New Statement of the Liberal Principles of Justice and Political Economy*, Vol III *The Political Order of a Free People* ([first published 1979] 2003), at 201: 'the whole of the so-called "welfare economics", which pretends to base its argument on inter-personal comparisons of ascertainable utilities, lacks all scientific foundation.'

[40] Ibid. Vol II F. A. Hayek, *The Mirage of Social Justice* ([first published 1976] 2003).

[41] Cf. E.-J. Mestmäcker, *Legal Theory Without Law; Posner v. Hayek on Economic Analysis of Law* (2007).

[42] There is a loss of clarity when welfare and libertarian arguments for free markets are merged into a vague concept of neoliberalism. Moreover, unlike the tags of 'libertarian' and 'ordoliberal', the label of 'neoliberal' is used mostly in a pejorative sense, by opponents: not many theorists or politicians proudly self-identify as neoliberals.

rules of the game, i.e. by protecting property, enforcing contracts, and maintaining competition by combating cartels.[43] So, from the ordoliberal perspective the EU's essential task is quite naturally to provide and enforce such a formal framework for the internal market, and this leads to their reading of the founding European treaties, in particular the Treaty of Rome, as an economic constitution. By contrast, ordoliberals strongly reject European integration by intervention, i.e. positive integration, through consumer protection directives, for example, as a deplorable 'conditional planning programme'.[44] They praised the EEC Treaty as a treaty which provided a framework for a common market, but they were very critical of the SEA and especially of the Maastricht Treaty because these contained too many non-market elements. Indeed, it was argued, 'the Maastricht Treaty paves the way for a rent-seeking Union'.[45]

German theorists, including many opponents of ordoliberalism, tend to consider the ordoliberal reading of the EU's founding treaties and of the first decades of European integration as the orthodox view,[46] even though this reading has been much less influential (if not entirely absent) in most other EU Member States, including other founding members.[47] Indeed, integration through law seems to be a much more diffuse process than the consistent implementation of one quite specific German post-war economic view of society. Doubtlessly prominent ordoliberals were influential in the founding years of the EU, but many other actors were too, and most of them had quite different ideals. Therefore, as a matter of historical reconstruction the ordoliberal understanding may not be the most plausible reading of Europeanization.[48] This, of course, does not in itself disqualify ordoliberalism as a normative foundation for the EU. It merely means that, at least today, we should understand the ordoliberal idea of a European 'economic constitution' as a proposal for reform—and a rather radical one

[43] M. Foucault, *Naissance de la biopolitique: Cours au Collège de France (1978–1979)* (2004), at 121, points out that a key difference between classical liberalism and ordoliberalism is that while the former's main focus was on exchange, the latter concentrates on competition. Hayek, however, was less worried about monopolies than the Freiburg school and more about arbitrary interference by antitrust authorities. See F. A. Hayek, *The Constitution of Liberty* ([first published 1960] 2009), at 231.

[44] Streit and Mussler: 'The Economic Constitution of the European Community: From "Rome" to "Maastricht"', 1 *ELJ* (1995) 84, at 6 and 13.

[45] Streit and Mussler, 'Reply to the Comments by Leigh Hancher and Claus-Dieter Ehlermann', 1 *ELJ* (1995) 89, at 90.

[46] See E.-J. Mestmäcker, *Die Wirtschafsverfassung in der Europäischen Union* (1993), 1; J. Basedow, *Von der Deutschen zur Europäischen Wirtschafsverfassung* (1992), at 26; Grundmann, 'Information, Party Autonomy and Economic Agents in European Contract Law', 39 *CMLR* (2002) 269, at 278; Joerges, 'What Is Left of the European Economic Constitution? A Melancholic Eulogy', 30 *European Law Review* (2005) 461; Cseres, 'Competition and Contract Law', in A. S. Hartkamp *et al.*, *Towards a European Civil Code* (4th ed., 2011) 205, at 208; Herresthal, 'Constitutionalisation of Freedom of Contract In European Union Law', in K. S. Ziegler and P. M. Huber (eds), *Current Problems in the Protection of Human Rights: Perspectives from Germany and the UK* (2013) 89, at 90; Habermas, 'Democracy, Solidarity and The European Crisis', Lecture delivered on 26 April 2013 in Leuven. Cf. Walker, 'Legal Theory and the European Union' (2005) *EUI Law Working Paper No. 2005/16*, at 13; Somma, 'Private Law as Biopolitics: Ordoliberalism, Social Market Economy, and the Public Dimension of Contract', 76 *Law Contemp. Probl.* (2013) 105, at 105.

[47] See Rutgers, 'The European Economic Constitution, Freedom of Contract and the DCFR', *ERCL* (2009) 95, doubting, for example, that A. M. Donner, the Dutch president of the Court of Justice at the time, had ordoliberalism on his mind when the Court deliberated and decided in Case 26/62, *Van Gend en Loos* (EU:C:1963:1) and Case 6/64, *Costa/ENEL* (EU:C:1964:66).

[48] In the same sense, see L. Raiser, *Die Zukunft des Privatrechts* (1971), at 25–26.

at that. Indeed, probably most of the *acquis communautaire* and also the competences on which it was based would have to be revoked.[49]

Given that strong formal subjective private rights and freedom of contract are key elements of the economic constitution for a private law society, it is not surprising that German theorists have also read this normative underpinning specifically into the contract law of the EU.[50] On this reading, contract law is part of the depoliticized institutional framework—in this respect not different from the European Central Bank—that assures the proper functioning of a market with free competition. Indeed, the European constitutionalization of freedom of contract by the European Court of Justice would constitute a distinctly libertarian move.[51]

B. The European Economic Constitution and the European Civil Code

One puzzling aspect of the ordoliberal reading of the Rome Treaty as a European economic constitution is the near total absence in that treaty of any private law provisions. In a treaty establishing a 'private law society' one would have expected the exact opposite. In fact, the most concrete private law provision in the treaty was Article 222 EEC, pursuant to which the treaty in no way prejudices the property regimes of the Member States, i.e. a provision that rather than protecting private property deliberately leaves open nationalization measures by Member States. Indeed, the one thing one would expect as a core part of an ordoliberal economic constitution is a civil code, with constitution-like status, containing formal rules of general private law. And in the case of a European economic constitution, one would expect a European civil code, perhaps with the status of primary EU law, like EU competition law. However, neither the EEC treaty nor consecutive treaties have ever even demanded the introduction of a European civil code. On the contrary, as has often been pointed out, the founding treaties lack any general legal basis for a European civil code.[52]

[49] See e.g. Mestmäcker, 'On the Legitimacy of European Law', 58 *Rabels Zeitschrift für Ausländisches und Internationales Privatrecht* (1994) 615, at 635, with regard to the then new competences in the Maastricht Treaty: 'As far as Community legislation, and particularly harmonisation of law, is concerned, they go far beyond the limitations suggested by the principles of a constitutional charter based upon the guarantee of economic liberties.'

[50] See, as a prominent example, Grundmann, 'The Structure of European Contract Law', 4 *ERPL* (2001) 505, at 515: 'the thinking of the ordoliberal school which is still the theoretical basis of the business regulation concept in the Community'.

[51] Arguably, the Court's reading in Case C-426/11, *Alemo-Herron and Others v Parkwood Leisure Ltd* (EU:C:2013:521) of the freedom to conduct a business protected by Art. 16 of the Charter of Fundamental Rights of the European Union, as a 'fundamental right ... cover[ing], inter alia, freedom of contract', is partisan in the sense that it is difficult to see how any interpretation not based on a libertarian understanding of liberty could ever yield such an outcome. Indeed, it is not dissimilar, in this respect, to the US Supreme Court's laissez-faire ruling in *Lochner v. New York*, 198 U.S. 45 (1905). For criticism of *Alemo-Herron*, see e.g. Weatherill, 'Use and Abuse of the EU's Charter of Fundamental Rights: On the Improper Veneration of "Freedom of Contract"', 10 *ERCL* (2014) 167; Bartl and Leone, 'Minimum Harmonisation After *Alemo-Herron*: The Janus Face of EU Fundamental Rights Review', 11 *European Constitutional Law Review* (2015) 140; and Hesselink, 'The Justice Dimensions of the Relationship Between Fundamental Rights and Private Law', 24 *ERPL* (2015), 425.

[52] See e.g. Hesselink, Rutgers, and De Booys, 'The Legal Basis for an Optional Instrument on European Contract Law: Short Study for the European Parliament on the Different Options for a Future Instrument

Collins has argued for a European civil code as an indispensable element of a European economic constitution.[53] He underlines the fundamental constitutive role of private law in society. In particular, he refers to three 'constitutional qualities' of private law: its persistence, providing continuity and support for civil society often even in times of radical change in the political constitution; its contribution to social justice, in particular its distributive role; and the way it articulates citizens' rights. He concludes that, therefore, the work towards a European civil code or a European code of contract law could provide 'a vital contribution to the construction of a European economic constitution'.[54] This argument resonates to a certain extent with Carbonnier's characterization of the civil code as '*la constitution civile—la véritable*'.[55] The latter characterization was not limited to the civil code's economic role and in any case referred to the French Code (as a *lieu de mémoire*), not a European one. Still, when Collins refers to the constitutional qualities of private law 'through which it constructs and reinforces the foundations of civil society'[56] that is in fact quite similar to Carbonnier's argument that the civil code is materially a constitution because 'en lui sont récapitulées les idées autour desquelles la société française s'est constituée au sortir de la Révolution et continue de se constituer de nos jours encore':[57] both regard the civil code as the constitution of civil society. As we will see, strongly cultural and identity-laden readings of private law as a civil or economic constitution are also conceivable and have been given. However, a somewhat more neutral, self-standing civil constitution for Europe, which does not rely so strongly on controversial ultimate values or identities, also seems a possibility.[58] Thus, according to Collins, an economic constitution 'endeavours to promote a consensus of values regarding fairness and social justice for a community' and thus 'provides a cement of social and economic principles and structures around which a community may build more permanent institutional structures, including its political institutions'.[59]

The main lesson to be learned, then, is that it is difficult to imagine any economic constitution without a key role for private law in it. Or, to put it differently, an understanding of the European economic constitution that does not deal with private law is necessarily a very incomplete one. For how can we understand, appreciate, or criticize

on a Common Frame of Reference (CFR) in EU Contract Law, in Particular the Legal Form and the Legal Basis for Any Future Optional Instrument', available as *Centre for the Study of European Contract Law Working Paper No. 2007/04*, available at SSRN: https://ssrn.com/abstract=1091119 (last visited 9 July 2020), with further references.

[53] Collins, 'The European Economic Constitution and the Constitutional Dimension of Private Law', *ERCL* (2009) 71.

[54] Ibid. 92.

[55] See J. Carbonnier, 'Le Code civil', in P. Nora (ed.), *Les lieux de mémoire*, Vol. II (1986) 293, at 309. See also J. Carbonnier, *Droit Civil: Introduction* (25th ed., 1997), at 82.

[56] Collins (n. 53) 86.

[57] Carbonnier, 'Le Code civil' (n. 55).

[58] Cf. Oliver Wendell Holmes (dissenting) in *Lochner v. New York*, 198 U.S. 45 (1905): 'a constitution is not intended to embody a particular economic theory'.

[59] Collins (n. 53) 73–74. Contrast Nicola and Mattei, 'A "Social Dimension" In European Private Law? The Call for Setting a Progressive Agenda', 41 *New England Law Review* (2006) 1, who argue that 'any project for European private law should go beyond coalitions around social justice', which is a notion that only serves for 'giving a human face to capitalist exploitation', and call instead for a radical progressive agenda.

an economic system's foundational principles if we do not know in which ways private entitlements are secured and which main rules of conduct between private parties will be enforced? However, the idea of an economic constitution also clearly turns our attention to a likely source of tension and conflict. Inevitably, the European economic constitution will differ, at least on some points, from national economic constitutions. In this respect, an economic constitution is not different from a political constitution. And if the economic constitution claims supremacy (or primacy), as constitutions tend to do, then the private law principles and rules that are part of the economic constitution will also claim primacy. This raises the question: where should the economic constitution be located—on the national or the European level, or both? Just as for the ordoliberal version, it seems to be true that a less politically partisan economic constitution is not intrinsically European. Still, whatever is meant to be—or best understood as—the economic constitution of the EU's internal market, it seems, will have to be located on the European level. In any case, it seems difficult to imagine that the whole of private law, or its most basic principles, remain located exclusively in a different economic constitution, i.e. the national one. In other words, the very idea of an economic constitution seems to point towards the Europeanization of the main principles, rules, and doctrines of private law, not because of efficiency or identity reasons, but because it is impossible to properly constitute an economic system without defining private rights and the basic rules of interpersonal conduct. Obviously, the implications of this are not limited—or even chiefly related—to contract law.

C. Market Integration and Deregulation

In a visionary essay pre-dating the foundation of the EEC by almost two decades, Hayek advocated a 'single market' of different states (taking shape through a federation), which he expected to be intrinsically deregulatory. The reason why, in his view, market integration would inevitably have a deregulatory effect, is that market regulation presupposes the existence of common ideals and common values: 'in a federation, certain economic powers, which are now generally wielded by the national states, could be exercised neither by the federation nor by the individual states, [which] implies that there would have to be less government all round if federation is to be practicable.'[60] Therefore, he claimed, an essentially libertarian regime ('liberal' in his terminology) is an economic precondition for political union and vice versa, both of which he welcomed: 'the abrogation of national sovereignties and the creation of an effective international order of law is a necessary complement and the logical consummation of the liberal program.'[61] Even though Hayek's forecast strongly resonates with some of the main political difficulties in which the EU has found itself in recent years, and with the claims of those critics who regard the EU as essentially a 'liberalization machine'[62] and an intrinsically neoliberal project,[63] his core claim of inevitability

[60] Hayek, 'The Economic Conditions of Interstate Federalism' (1939), in F.A. Hayek, *Individualism and Economic Order* (1948), ch. XII, 255, at 264.
[61] Ibid. 269.
[62] W. Streeck, *Buying Time: The Delayed Crisis of Democratic Capitalism* (2nd ed., 2017), ch. 3.
[63] C. Lapavitsas, *The Left Case Against the EU* (2019).

seems exaggerated. And if an internal market is not intrinsically and inevitably neo-liberal (as is underscored, to give merely one salient example, by the introduction of consumer protection through EU market integration measures, where none existed before in many Member States), then a deregulatory agenda for the EU would still need a separate normative argument in order to be justified. And since the libertarian programme is not affirmed by citizens generally, as Rawls would put it, its pursuit through basic institutions of the internal market would give the EU a distinctly sectarian character.[64]

4. Communitarian

A. Private Law Identities

Given the fact that we are dealing here with the territorial boundaries of legal systems (as opposed, e.g., to their personal or substantive scopes), it may seem natural to focus on what we value in relation to these different territorial units, in other words, on our geographical senses of belonging. Surely, if I strongly identify with Europe then the idea of one comprehensive European legal system will be more attractive to me than if I regard myself first and foremost as a national citizen of my own Member State, or indeed consider myself predominantly to be a world citizen. Therefore, when it comes to evaluating and justifying different possible territorial scopes and borders for legal systems, territorial allegiances would seem to be prima facie relevant.[65]

There exists in fact a long-standing tradition, going back to Montesquieu, Herder, and Hegel, according to which the law, including private law, should be closely related to the identity, spirit, and traditions of the people to whom it is meant to apply.[66] Indeed, the relationship between law, on the one hand, and culture, tradition, and identity, on the other, is at the heart of contemporary neo-romanticism and communitarianism.

However, if private law making in Europe is a matter of defining the common good of the community and if tradition and identity should play a decisive part in this process then one question arises immediately: what is the relevant community whose traditions and identity should be decisive? With regard to private law there seem to be at least three prima facie relevant traditions and identities, i.e. the national, the European, and the cosmopolitan ones, each of which is at the heart of an articulate

[64] Cf. J. Rawls, *Political Liberalism* ([first published 1993] 2005), at 179.

[65] See Taylor, 'The Politics of Recognition', in A. Gutmann (ed.), *Multiculturalism: Examining the Politics of Recognition* (1992) 25, at 58: 'Political society is not neutral between those who value remaining true to the culture of our ancestors and those who might want to cut loose in the name of some individual goal of self-development.' Clearly, the same could be said specifically of remaining true to a legal culture.

[66] Montesquieu, *De l'esprit des lois* (1748), Part III, Book 14, ch. 1: 'S'il est vrai que le caractère de l'esprit et les passions du cœur soient extrêmement différents dans les divers climats, les lois doivent être relatives et à la différence de ces passions, et à la différence de ces caractères.' See also B. Pascal, *Pensées* (1670), fragment Misère' n°9/24: 'on ne voit rien de juste ou d'injuste qui ne change de qualité en changeant de climat, trois degrés d'élévation du pôle renversent toute la jurisprudence. Un méridien décide de la vérité, en peu d'années de possession les lois fondamentales changent. . . . Plaisante justice qu'une rivière borne! Vérité au-deçà des Pyrénées, erreur au-delà.'

and coherent political view that can be—and has been—applied also to the question of which geographical unit should be responsible for private law making, i.e. nationalism, Europeanism, and cosmopolitanism.[67] We will now briefly visit each of these three instances of what could be called 'legal communitarianism'.[68]

B. National Identity

1. Nationalism

Nationalism is the political principle according to which the political and the national unit ought to be congruent.[69] Consequently, we can speak of 'legal nationalism' when it is argued (or taken for granted) that the boundaries of the legal system should coincide with the national borders.[70] Similarly, we can refer to someone as a 'private law nationalist' when she affirms that it is natural or preferable for private law to be national. Clearly, from the nationalist perspective, Europeanization (and also globalization) amounts to a loss: loss of relevance of the nation state, loss of importance for national law, and loss of prestige for the national civil code—or, as the case may be, the common law—as an important expression of national identity.[71] Therefore, nationalism, which set out in the nineteenth century as a progressive international movement (think of Lord Byron fighting for Greek independence) today seems more conservative (or even reactionary at times). Even the Brexit vote, which was definitely about changing the status quo, was less concerned with building a nation than with undoing Europeanization. Think, for example, of the Great Repeal Bill.[72]

[67] In general, communitarians tend to focus on subnational communities. However, in private law (as a result of the historical success of nationalism), regional law is less prominent. Still, Catalonian and Scots law provide important examples of regional (i.e. sub-(former)Member-State) private laws in Europe.

[68] See further Hesselink, 'How Many Systems of Private Law Are There In Europe? On Plural Legal Sources, Multiple Identities and the Unity of Law', in L. Niglia (ed.), *Pluralism and European Private Law* (2013) 199, at 217–224, on which this subsection draws.

[69] See E. Gellner, *Nations and Nationalism* (2nd ed., 2006), at 1. Similar, Hobsbawm (n. 35) 9; J. Leerssen, *National Thought in Europe; A Cultural History* (2006), at 14. Cf. Hesselink, 'The Case for a Common European Sales Law in an Age of Rising Nationalism', 8 *ERCL* (2012) 342. For a comprehensive study of private law nationalism, see G. Comparato, *Nationalism and Private Law in Europe* (2014).

[70] See e.g. J. S. Mill, *Considerations on Representative Government* ([1862] 2007), at 209: 'it is in general a necessary condition of free institutions that the boundaries of governments should coincide in the main with those of nationalities'.

[71] See e.g. Cornu, 'Un code civil n'est pas un instrument communautaire', *Dalloz* (2002) 351: 'La loi des Français se pense et s'écrit en français. Le code civil français forme un tout. C'est notre coutume générale.... Irréductible à une réglementation, le code civil est un monument du droit français parmi nos références primordiales.' See also the reasoned opinion that was submitted by the Federal Council of Austria in response to the European Commission's proposal for a CESL which speaks of 'the Austrian private law regime and, in particular, the Code of Civil Law and its interpretations as an inherent part of the citizens' conception of the law', available at www.ipex.eu/IPEXL-WEB/scrutiny/COD20110284/atbun.do (last visited 10 July 2020). In 2013, the Dutch minister for safety and justice wrote to the Dutch Parliament, in reply to questions concerning the CESL-proposal: 'The legal norms of the Dutch Civil Code ... are the coherent and cognizable expression of the Dutch societal views.' (Vergaderjaar 2013–2014, 22 112, nr. 1708, my translation)

[72] See the White Paper, 'Legislating for the United Kingdom's withdrawal from the European Union' (Cm 9446, March 2017), presented to Parliament by the Secretary of State for Exiting the European Union. Somewhat surprisingly, rather than to repeal EU law the aim of the bill seemed to be to keep most of it, including presumably, most of the contract law *acquis*, 'converting EU law into UK law'.

2. European Union

In the nationalist view of Europeanization, the Member States never gave up their sovereignty. This view coincides, of course, with the position of several Member State constitutional courts concerning the CJEU's long-standing claim (i.e. since *Costa/ENEL*)[73] as to the primacy of EU law and to the Court's own final say in interpretative matters including with regard to the limits of EU law.[74] They will also vindicate the Union's duty, introduced by the Lisbon Treaty, to respect the 'national identities' of the Member States (Article 4(2) TEU). Similarly, nationalists will underline that European citizenship is merely derivative: pursuant to Article 20 TFEU it depends on national citizenship. And they will endorse the *Bundesverfassungsgericht*'s view that there is no such thing as a 'European people' (*Volk*) of which the European Parliament could be the representative.[75] The *pouvoir constituant* of 'We the People' appertains exclusively to the nation. Indeed, in the nationalist view, EU law is not fundamentally different from international law: both apply inside the national borders because, to the extent that, and in the way in which, national law (in particular the national constitution) allows for it. Leaving aside secessionist and irredentist claims, this matches with the classical Westphalian conception of the world, as revised in Wilsonian terms: sovereign nation states have exclusive internal jurisdiction and can be bound externally only by their consent to an international treaty, while individuals derive their rights ultimately from their own respective national legal orders, as national citizens. In its strongest version this leads to national monism: there is no other law than national law. In a weaker, much more recurrent but also more problematic version, it leads to dualism: foreign and international law do exist, but are applicable on the national territory only to the extent recognized by the constitution (with respect to international law) or by conflict rules of private international law (with respect to foreign private law). Similarly, nationalists in Europe regard the Council (i.e. both the European Council and the Council of the European Union) as the most legitimate EU institution. In other words, the nationalist's perspective on EU decision-making is naturally intergovernmentalist (and anti-supranationalist).

[73] Case 6/64, *Costa v. ENEL* (EU:C:1964:66).

[74] See A.-M. Slaughter, A. Stone Sweet, and J. H. H. Weiler (eds), *The European Court and National Courts—Doctrine and Jurisprudence: Legal Change in Its Social Context* (1998). In its Judgment of 5 May 2020 (*PSPP*), the German FCC held that the CJEU exceeded the judicial mandate conferred upon it by Art. 19 TEU because its interpretation of the Treaties was 'simply not comprehensible and thus objectively arbitrary'. K. Pistor, 'Germany's Constitutional Court Goes Rogue', *Project Syndicate*, 8 May 2020, denouncing the 'angry, self-righteous tone' of the judgment, warns that the FCC itself, 'contemptuous of the rule of law within the EU and cavalier about its own limitations' is an institution 'now out of control'. See also M. Poiares Maduro, 'Some Preliminary Remarks on the PSPP Decision of the German Constitutional Court', *Verfassungsblog*, 6 May 2020, who rejects the FCC's approach to the relationship with EU law as 'parochial', for failing to see that it is 'part of an engagement of [their own] legal order with other national legal orders, that have different constitutional needs that are equally deserving of accommodation'.

[75] See *BVerfGE* 123, 267 (*Lissabon*), at 372: 'Das Europäische Parlament ist ... kein Repräsentationsorgan eines souveränen europäischen Volkes.' Contrast J. Habermas, *Europe: The Faltering Project* (2009), at 86, who rejects the idea that there is no European *demos*, arguing that it is due to the tenaciousness of the Romantic background philosophy of the Historical School. Habermas sees no reason why a European *Volksgeist* could not be construed, although he acknowledges that a European identity would necessarily be a weaker one. See further, later.

3. How Many Systems?

From the nationalist perspective, there are just as many legal systems in Europe as there are nations. Accordingly, from a nationalist point of view, the Europeanization of private law is a process that affects and modifies the national systems of private law of each of the Member States. In this perception, although the bulk of private law is of domestic origin, today an increasing part of it is of European extraction. The focus is on how to integrate these 'foreign' elements into the original national system without upsetting it too much. For example, a nationalist reading of cases such as *Messner*,[76] where the Court of Justice referred to 'general principles of civil law', would probably lead to the conclusion that the Court was referring only to general principles common to national civil laws and that these principles, therefore, apply as national law in the Member States. So, on this view no general principles of EU private law exist.[77]

4. ECC, DCFR, CESL

It is not difficult to find differences between national contract law systems. Comparative law provides plenty of examples. And these differences can easily be read—especially if we understand the nation, not as primordial but as 'un plébiscite de tous les jours'[78]—as expressions of different national traditions, cultures, or *mentalités*. On such a communitarian view of private law, legal differences between countries are not mere historical accidents. On the contrary, they are meaningful. They are expressions of legal communities as they really are. These expressions can be found not only in the different 'styles' of legal systems (the rationality and abstractness of the *BGB* being typically 'Germanic', etc.), but also in 'national models of social justice in private law',[79] or different national conceptions of the person (in this case, of the typical contracting party) and of the contractual relationship,[80] which explain different outcomes (e.g. the presence or absence of precontractual information duties or relief for change of circumstances). Brushing over these differences or setting them aside would not only mean a major loss, but also be entirely illegitimate. In this respect, the worst thing that could have happened would have been a European civil code replacing the national private laws of the Member States.

Clearly, from a nationalist perspective the CESL, if it had been enacted, would have become a national regime, rightly called the *second* national regime, which could never have stood the comparison with the first, autochthonous national contract law regime. Had the European Commission proposed a European legislator's 'toolbox' for

[76] See Case C-489/07, *Pia Messner v. Firma Stefan Krüger* (EU:C:2009:502).

[77] Indeed, this view matches well with the fact that the Court itself in these cases does not speak explicitly of EU principles. See further Hesselink, 'The General Principles of Civil Law: Their Nature, Roles and Legitimacy', in D. Leczykiewicz and S. Weatherill (eds), *The Involvement of EU Law in Private Law Relationships* (2013) 131.

[78] E. Renan, *Qu'est-ce qu'une nation?: Conférence faite en Sorbonne, le 11 Mars 1882* (2nd ed., 1882), at 27.

[79] Micklitz distinguishes the English model (liberal and pragmatic), the French model (rational and political), the German model (liberal and authoritarian/paternalistic), and the European model (enabling and restricting). See Micklitz, 'Social Justice and Access Justice in Private Law', in H.-W. Micklitz (ed.), *The Many Faces of Social Justice in Private Law* (2011).

[80] Sefton-Green, 'Cultural Diversity and the Idea of a European Civil Code', in M. W. Hesselink (ed.), *The Politics of a European Civil Code* (2006) 71, contrasting the French and the English understandings of the relationship between the parties to a contract.

contract law—the other much discussed alternative[81]—then the attitude from private law nationalists towards it would probably have been formal: it is not binding law so it can be safely ignored.[82]

5. Critics

Critics will point to nationalism's bad name, not only because of its inextricable link, in our memory, to the darkest episodes in recent European history, but also because today it is easily associated with renewed xenophobia and populism. However, it would be demagogical to suggest that neo-nationalism will inevitably lead us down the dangerous path towards new violent clashes between European countries, or nations turning against some of their own citizenry deemed not true nationals. National communities may be imagined,[83] but they are not imaginary. According to a Eurobarometer (2004), 87 per cent of people in Europe think of themselves mostly as national citizens.[84] Moreover, various national differences do exist (nationalism has been successful), also in private law, and these differences mean something important to many people in Europe.[85] Nationalism, whether in its general appearance or in the specific instance of private law nationalism, cannot be dismissed out of hand, for example for being based on ignorance or fear.[86] Nationalism is a sense of belonging that is important to very many people in Europe. With the exception of fundamentalist versions, it would count as a reasonable doctrine, it seems, that should have its proper place, for example, in today's democratic societies characterized by what Rawls calls reasonable pluralism.[87]

A difficulty for legal nationalism, nonetheless, is that as a description it is difficult to match with the current state of postnational law and postnational society at large. The world has changed and the nationalist vision, especially in its stronger versions, simply seems to deny the new reality. Nor is it likely that the processes of Europeanization and globalization can be reversed. Even the UK saw its post-EU future immediately in terms of 'Global Britain'.[88] Therefore, it seems that those rejecting new steps towards

[81] Commission, 'Green Paper on Policy Options for Progress Towards a European Contract Law for Consumers and Businesses' (COM(2010) 348 final).

[82] On such formalist patterns of entrenchment, see Caruso, 'The Missing View of the Cathedral: The Private Law Paradigm of European Legal Integration', 3 *ELJ* (1997) 27.

[83] See B. Anderson, *Imagined Communities* (revised ed. 2006), at 6–7. They are imagined because even the members of the smallest nation will never know most of their fellow members, but they are conceived nevertheless as communities of 'deep, horizontal comradeship'.

[84] See Eurobarometer 61 (July 2004), B 94. In more recent barometers, this question is no longer asked.

[85] See N. MacCormick, *Questioning Sovereignty: Law, State and Practical Reason* (1999), at 183: 'There is at least a prima facie case for some kind of right to respect for national identities as a part of respect for persons, for implicit in respecting human individuals is respect for whatever goes into their individuality.' Contrast Nussbaum, 'Patriotism and Cosmopolitanism', *Boston Review*, 1 October 1994, who regards the nationalist sentiment as 'a morally irrelevant characteristic'.

[86] Contrast Lando, 'Liberal, Social and "Ethical" Justice In European Contract Law', 43 *CMLR* (2006) 817, at 822–823 who claims that 'contract law is not folklore'. But see the critical response by Sánchez Lorenzo, 'What Do We Mean When We Say "Folklore"? Cultural and Axiological Diversities as a Limit for a European Private Law', 14 *ERPL* (2006) 197.

[87] See Rawls (n. 64) 36.

[88] See the speech of Prime Minister Theresa May of 17 January 2017, 'The Government's Negotiating Objectives for Exiting the EU': 'But the great prize for this country—the opportunity ahead—is to use this moment to build a truly Global Britain.'

the further Europeanization of contract law on the nationalist ground that the core of private law should remain national will also have to address the question of what is so attractive about the status quo of European private law. Indeed, it would seem that a consistent private law nationalist would argue in favour of abolishing most of the *acquis* by revoking, for example, the unfair terms, consumer sales, and consumer rights directives—in other words, the full renationalization of private law.[89]

C. European Identity

1. Europeanism

For Europeanists, Europe comes first.[90] They consider themselves, in the first place, Europeans and, quite apart from what the Treaty says, they regard their national citizenship as merely of secondary importance. They believe in Europe, in the European project, in an ever closer Union. Their ultimate dream is a federal European state, the United States of Europe.[91] Of course, like nationalism, Europeanism also comes in many different degrees and varieties.[92]

It is the Europeanists in particular who emphasize the dynamic nature of the EU and the role its laws play in bringing about the change they regard as progress. From this perspective, further Europeanization is obviously most welcome. The nation state is a thing of the past; the emphasis is on the post-national condition.[93] European integration may be regarded as good for a variety of reasons but they usually include a rejection of nationalism (or a fear of neo-nationalism). This, Europeanists have in common with cosmopolitans, as we will see. Indeed, many committed Europeanists think of the EU as being based essentially on cosmopolitan values.[94]

2. European Union

According to Europeanists, the Member States of the EU have limited their sovereignty. They fully endorse the CJEU's position in *Costa/ENEL* and its own claim to

[89] As H. Kelsen, *General Theory of Law and State* ([first published 1945] 2007), at 387 pointed out already, 'the ultimate consequence of the primacy of national law is State solipsism'.

[90] See e.g. S. Zweig, *Die Welt von Gestern: Erinnerungen eines Europäers* ([first published 1942] 2017), at 463, one of the heroes of Europeanism wrote at a particularly dramatic moment: 'Europa, unsere Heimat, für die wir gelebt'.

[91] See e.g. G. Verhofstadt, *The United States of Europe; Manifesto for a New Europe* (2006). See also the *Sofia Declaration of The Spinelli Group and the Union of European Federalists* (Sofia, 22 February 2018): 'Faced with euroscepticism and even resurgent nationalism, unification of Europe is the greatest duty of our generation. ... European citizens share a community of fate. ... Only through a common sense of belongingness will European citizens gain back the ability to decide on their destinies.' For a recent plea for a radical shift from *telos* to *demos*, see Bartl, 'From Europe-As-Project to a Real Political Community', *Social Europe*, 24 April 2019, arguing that the EU should transform itself into 'a political community, where the question of direction or destination becomes meaningless'.

[92] For some further details and literature, see Hesselink (n. 69). See generally J. McCormick, *Europeanism* (2010).

[93] J. Habermas, *The Postnational Constellation: Political Essays* (2000).

[94] See T. Risse, *A Community of Europeans? Transnational Identities and Public Spheres* (2010), at 47. On the tension between the cosmopolitan values ascribed to the EU and the communitarian explanation of how they have emerged, see Castiglione, 'Political Identity in a Community of Strangers', in J. T. Checkel and P. J. Katzenstein (eds), *European Identity* (2009) 29.

ultimate authority (*Kompetenz-Kompetenz*).[95] They point to the declaration concerning primacy that was annexed to the Lisbon Treaty as an acknowledgement of the legitimacy of their claim.[96] Attributed competence, subsidiarity, and proportionality are tolerated as principles, but the democratic principles of Articles 9–12 TEU, underlining the role of the European Parliament, are considered to be more important. Of the scenarios for the EU's future proposed by the Commission in 2017, they would opt wholeheartedly for scenario 5: 'doing much more together'.[97]

3. How Many Systems?

In a Europeanist perception, all the private law in the EU constitutes one single, gradually integrating system (European monism). The focus is on the interplay between the different levels of law making, increasing coherence within the overall multilevel system, and the gradual convergence of its components. On this view, a steadily growing part of European private law is regulated at the EU level, while a considerable part of it is still regulated at the national level (and a minor part at the global level—think, e.g., of the CISG) of *one and the same* system. There is no urgent need to find any precise formal answers as to which legal argument belongs to what level within the system. Obviously, Europeanists welcomed the Court's discovery of 'general principles of civil law' as a European model of interpersonal justice between private parties. If one regards all private law in the EU as one single, gradually integrating system and strives for coherence and convergence, then the idea of general principles does not represent a problem but, instead, a welcome solution. From the Europeanist perspective, there is no great need to draw any formal distinctions between national and European principles. Rather, the focus will be on the substantive convergence of the various versions—Member State and Union—of the *same* principle. And for this purpose, the flexible and malleable nature of principles represents an advantage. Borderlines are helpful for those who want to separate but represent an obstacle for those who wish to unite.

4. ECC, DCFR, CESL

From the Europeanist perception, the idea of a common frame of reference that could guide us through a process of gradual and progressive convergence, and a legislator's toolbox, was exactly what was needed.[98] The strategy vis-à-vis this text (and its

[95] Case 6/64, *Costa v. ENEL* (EU:C:1964:66). After the German FCC's ruling of 5 May 2020 (*PSPP*), the CJEU issued a press release (no 58/20), with a reminder that 'in order to ensure that EU law is applied uniformly, the Court of Justice alone—which was created for that purpose by the Member States—has jurisdiction to rule that an act of an EU institution is contrary to EU law. ... Like other authorities of the Member States, national courts are required to ensure that EU law takes full effect. That is the only way of ensuring the equality of Member States in the Union they created.' The press statement (20/846) by European Commission President Von der Leyen was even more outspoken: 'The final word on EU law is always spoken in Luxembourg. Nowhere else.'

[96] Treaty of Lisbon, Final Act, Annex, nr. 17, Declaration concerning primacy, recalling that, in accordance with the well-settled case-law of the CJEU, EU primary and secondary laws have primacy over the law of Member States, and referring to Opinion 11197/07 (JUR 260) on the primacy of EC law of the Council's legal service to the same effect.

[97] Commission, 'White Paper on the Future of Europe: Reflections and Scenarios for the EU27 by 2025' (COM(2017) 2025).

[98] Another important contribution to the European legal identity was expected from the European Law Institute, which was founded in 2011. For its mission, see 'The European Law Institute Manifesto', available at www.europeanlawinstitute.eu (last visited 11 July 2020): 'By its endeavours, ELI seeks to contribute to the

precursors and successors) was to discuss its substantive quality and to emphasize the need to go beyond formal limits towards the further Europeanization of private law. The CESL proposal, although disappointing for its narrow scope (in comparison to a European civil code) was welcomed for its potential as a catalyst for further convergence. Benefits such as spill-over effects, a toolbox, a common frame of reference or persuasive authority beyond its formal status of a law applicable only when the parties have chosen it, and a source of inspiration for general principles of civil law were eagerly anticipated. And the withdrawal in 2014 of the proposal by the European Commission came as a severe blow. Having said that, the whole terminology used by the European Commission of tools and problem fixing may sound too pragmatic to anyone holding a more romantic and evolutionary understanding of the law. Indeed, the specific contribution to the European private law debate of scholars such as Zimmermann and Jansen (the new Historical School) has been to claim that although the (re-)Europeanization of private law is desirable in itself, it is just too early for a European civil code: a European tradition with the same level of doctrinal sophistication as was achieved on the national level has to develop first.[99] And that takes time—much more time than the CFR and CESL processes allowed for.[100]

5. Critics

Critics of Europeanism point out that Europeanists are deceiving themselves. The idea of a European community or union may be good in theory but it has proved to be deficient in practice. In particular, the democratic deficit, which still exists (and at a crucial moment even increased, as a result of the technocratic response to the economic crisis),[101] is highly problematic because only a few people will value Europe higher than democracy. After decades of 'permissive consensus', they argue, the elite project of creating Europe by stealth, has had to face, from the referendums on the constitutional treaty onwards, repeated outbreaks of popular dissent,[102] culminating (for now) in Brexit. Euro-optimists, by contrast, will argue that what we have been witnessing in recent years, as a result of the financial, refugee, and Brexit crises, may actually be the birth of Europe. As Haltern points out, a sense of identity, belonging, and togetherness cannot be born without drama.[103] Nations are built on sacrifice (think of monuments

formation of a more vigorous European legal community, integrating the achievements of the various legal cultures, endorsing the value of comparative knowledge, and taking a genuinely pan-European perspective.' Cf. the speech of Viviane Reding, 'The European Law Institute—Tracing the Path Towards a European Legal Culture Opening of the European Law Institute', 17 November 2011'; Vassilios Skouris, 'Towards a European Legal Culture, ELI Inaugural Congress' June 2011, both available at www.europeanlawinstitute.eu (last visited 11 July 2020).

[99] See e.g. Zimmermann, 'Savigny's Legacy: Legal History, Comparative Law, and the Emergence of a European Legal Science' (1996) *Law Quarterly Review* 576; N. Jansen, *Binnenmarkt, Privatrecht und europäische Identität* (2004), at 72 ff.

[100] For a major contribution, see N. Jansen and R. Zimmermann (eds), *Commentaries on European Contract Laws* (2018), a volume of over 2,000 pages, exploring for PECL and DCFR and similar 'reference texts' to what extent they 'constitute a manifestation of a common core of European contract law'.

[101] See J. Habermas, *The Crisis of the European Union: A Response* (2012).

[102] See Checkel and Katzenstein, 'The Politicization of European Identities', in J. T. Checkel and P. J. Katzenstein (eds), *European Identity* (2009) 1.

[103] Haltern, 'On Finality', in A. von Bogdandy and J. Bast (eds), *Principles of European Constitutional Law*, (2nd ed., 2010), ch. 6.

to the unknown soldier) and perhaps one day the EU27 (or EU28, if Scotland re-joins) will look back at Brexit as the moment when our relationship became serious (a real point of no return) and brought a sense of togetherness and belonging that no European Constitution with hymns and flags could have achieved. And they will eagerly point out that in 2018, on average 71 per cent of the population in all 28 EU Member States felt that they were citizens of the EU.[104]

D. Cosmopolitan Identity

1. Cosmopolitanism

Cosmopolitans, like nationalists, are critical of Europeanization, but for the opposite reason. Their wish is not to go back to the nation state but rather to move forward to the approximation of laws at the global level. They take the world as the relevant community. Since Kant wrote, in *Toward Perpetual Peace*, that 'the idea of a cosmopolitan law is not fantastic and overstrained, but a necessary complement to the unwritten code of constitutional and international law',[105] there have been many different strands of legal cosmopolitanism, ranging from more ethical identity-oriented to a stronger focus on moral universalism.[106] Cosmopolitans want to move beyond sovereignty. Ultimate authority does not lie in the nation state nor does international law derive from agreements between sovereign nations (the Westphalian model). Rather, they argue, it is the other way around: the sovereignty of nation states and its limits derive from international law. In its strongest, Kelsenian form this leads to one, hierarchically organized global system of law. In more contemporary versions there is a global constitutional framework of principles that have ultimate authority.[107] In the cosmopolitan view, there exists only one internal perspective, i.e. from inside the world community.[108] This change in perspective is adopted in global constitutionalism, which, in this respect, is monist in the Kelsenian tradition.[109]

2. European Union

From the cosmopolitan perspective, Europeanization, like any type of regional convergence, may be regarded as a first step in the right direction. MacCormick's idea of Europe as 'pluralism under international law', i.e. a monistic framework,[110] could be

[104] Standard Eurobarometer 90 (Autumn 2018). As noted earlier, in recent Eurobarometers there is no longer a question on the relative importance of national and EU citizenship, which may be somewhat misleading.

[105] I. Kant, *Zum ewigen Frieden* (1795), B 46, at 360: 'so ist die Idee eines Weltbürgerrechts keine phantastische und überspannte Vorstellungsart des Rechts, sondern eine notwendige Ergänzung des ungeschriebenen Kodex sowohl des Staats- als Völkerrechts'.

[106] See generally G. W. Brown and D. Held, *The Cosmopolitanism Reader* (2010).

[107] Kumm, 'The Cosmopolitan Turn in Constitutionalism: On the Relationship Between Constitutionalism in and Beyond the State', in J. L. Dunoff and J. Trachtman (eds), *Ruling the World? Constitutionalism, International Law and Global Governance* (2009) 258–324.

[108] Cf. Habermas (n. 101) 54. Of course, since the global system will have many subsystems, there will be internal perspectives specific to each of these subsystems. However, these specific smaller-scale perspectives will still be internal to the broader perspective, somewhat like being in a room means being also inside the house.

[109] Explicitly so ibid. 58.

[110] As acknowledged by MacCormick (n. 85) 117.

attractive in the eyes of a cosmopolitan. However, European integration may also become an obstacle to cosmopolitan aspirations. A Europe that increasingly focuses on internal integration and closes itself off from the rest of the world (a 'fortress Europe'), risks becoming an impediment to global convergence and unity, and to global justice.

3. How Many Systems?

Cosmopolitan private lawyers can proudly point to the fact that more than a century ago comparative law and the legal unification projects were originally set up with a view to world harmony and peace. Think of the Hague Conference of Private International Law, first convened in 1893 at the initiative of Asser (Nobel Peace Prize 1911) and currently based in the Peace Palace in the Hague; the International Congress for Comparative Law, organized by Lambert and Salleilles, during the 1900 World Exhibition in Paris; and the International Institute for the Unification of Private Law (UNIDROIT) in Rome, which was set up in 1926 as an organ of the League of Nations.[111] Another example is Schlesinger's famous Cornell research project which aimed to establish 'general principles of law recognized by civilized nations' in the sense of Article 38(1)(c) of the Statute of the International Court of Justice.[112] Specifically in the field of contract law, and in particular, sales, they can also point to the fact that Europeanization means a step backwards rather than forwards. A historical line running from Rabel's *Recht des Warenkaufs*, via the Hague conventions (LUF and LUVI) and the CISG directly to the UNIDROIT Principles, was interrupted by the European *Alleingang* from the Principles of European Contract Law (PECL) to the Draft Common Frame of Reference (DCFR) to the CESL proposal.[113]

Legal cosmopolitanism is often inspired by a belief in universality, akin to modern forms of natural law thinking.[114] Are the answers to questions of sales law really a matter of national culture, a cosmopolitan private lawyer will ask, or is there some more general progress in thinking about sales that could be put to the benefit of all? Perhaps some universal private law principles and values could be uncovered.[115] At least, it seems, cosmopolitans could argue for a 'natural law light', in the form of a

[111] Cf. Lambert, 'Conception générale et définition de la science du droit comparé, sa méthode, son histoire; le droit comparé et l'enseignement du droit', in K. Zweigert and H.-J. Puttfarken, *Rechtsvergleichung* (1978) 30, at 37:

> L'action unificatrice [du droit comparé] se bornera à effacer progressivement les diversités accidentelles entre législations régissant des peuples de même civilisation, s'appliquant à des milieux économiques analogues, à raréfier le nombre des divergences législatives qui n'ont pas leur raison d'être intime dans la constitution politique, morale ou sociale des peuples, qui ne sont dues qu'à des hasards de la formation historique, ou à des causes passagères et superficielles.

[112] See Schlesinger, 'Research on the General Principles of Law Recognized by Civilized Nations', 51 *American Journal of International Law* (1957) 734 and R. B. Schlesinger (ed.), *Formation of Contracts: A Study of the Common Core of Legal Systems* (1968). This search for universal (natural law) principles subsequently inspired Bussani and Mattei's regional (Europeanist) project of establishing the 'common core of private law in Europe'. See Bussani and Mattei, 'The Common Core Approach to European Private Law', 3 *Columbia Journal of European Law* (1997/1998) 339.

[113] In addition, there is the claim concerning the existence of a *lex mercatoria* which supposedly has grown organically and informally within the international community of business people. See e.g. www.trans-lex.org. See earlier K.-P. Berger, *The Creeping Codification of the Lex Mercatoria* (1997).

[114] Cf. J. Finnis, *Natural Law and Natural Rights* (1980), at 150.

[115] Cf. Collins, 'Cosmopolitanism and Transnational Private Law' 8 *ERCL* (2012) 311.

reversal of the burden of proof concerning the universality of private law principles. At first sight, the 'global law' paradigm may seem akin to private law cosmopolitanism.[116] However, in reality most contributions to that debate are not identity driven. With their focus on the *lex mercatoria* and private ordering, they understand the law not only as post nation-state, but often also as post state *tout court*. And when they point to cohesive transnational business or professional communities developing their own standards, especially when these claims are not merely descriptive (as in Luhmann's systems theory) but also normative (as in Teubner's version of systems theory),[117] then they are often hardly distinguishable from the classical libertarian laissez-faire discourse.[118]

The ultimate consequence of the cosmopolitan view would be to regard all the private law in the world as one single system, to be studied from the inside.[119] Combined with a formalist view of rules, system, and hierarchy, such a cosmopolitan view might not seem utopian even in the eyes of the most ardent private law cosmopolitan, but rather almost dystopian. However, in a less formalist approach the idea of interpreting EU and national private law in the light of the CISG and the UNIDROIT principles, as they have been applied across the world, with a view to working towards the further development of common principles of private law, may seem much less outrageous.

4. ECC, DCFR, CESL

The CISG is a great success, in the light not only of the number of ratifications but also of the number of cases in which it has been applied, especially for businesses concluding their contracts without any legal assistance. Similarly, the UNIDROIT principles have found their way into international arbitration.[120] Compared to these, the European unification projects look like smaller brothers, and, in any case, instances of European isolationism, the small private law equivalent of *Kadi*.[121] Therefore, as far as its formal role as the applicable law in cross-border sales contracts is concerned, cosmopolitans looked upon the proposal for a CESL with a critical eye. However, in a less formal sense, the CESL could have been beneficial also from a cosmopolitan perspective. In its informal role as a source of inspiration, toolbox, or common frame of reference it would have meant an important step in moving beyond national private law. It could have become a proto-cosmopolitan model of just conduct among

[116] Key contributions include G. Teubner (ed.), *Global Law Without a State* (1997), at 3–28; G.-P. Callies and P. Zumbansen, *Rough Consensus and Running Code: A Theory of Transnational Private Law* (2010); N. Walker, *Intimations of Global Law* (2014); and H. Muir-Watt *et al.* (eds), *Global Private International Law: Adjudication Without Frontiers* (2019).

[117] Contrast Luhmann, 'Law as Social System', 83 *Northwestern University Law Review* (1988–1989) 136; N. Luhmann, *Das Recht der Gesellschaft* (1993) with G. Teubner, *Recht als autopoietisches System* (1989).

[118] See especially Callies and Zumbansen (n. 116). On classical global market thinking, see (critically) K. Polanyi, *The Great Transformation: The Political and Economic Origins of Our Time* ([first published 1944] 2001).

[119] Cf., for public law, Kumm (n. 107).

[120] See S. Vogenauer and J. Kleinheisterkamp, *Commentary on the UNIDROIT Principles of International Commercial Contracts* (2009).

[121] Joined cases C-402/05 P and C-415/05 P, *Yassin Abdullah Kadi and Al Barakaat International Foundation v. Council and Commission* (EU:T:2005:332).

private parties.[122] Such a role would have been facilitated by the fact that the text of the CESL was much closer to the CISG and the UNIDROIT Principles than the DCFR was. Indeed, when European contract law, after decades of drafting work, seemed close to yielding its first concrete result, Ole Lando, one of the founding fathers of the European contract law movement, argued for a 'Global Code' of contract law as the natural next step.[123]

5. Critics

Critics of global law argue that today the idea of cosmopolitan private law, with a view to universal justice, still sounds rather utopian, or simply misguided. What about day-to-day dispute resolution between the parties to a contract? Most contracts are purely domestic: why should these necessarily have to be resolved according to universal principles? Another line of criticism (coming from civic republicans) is that one global legal system with only one internal perspective leaves no room for contestation, which is crucial given the fact that universalist claims may be driven by power (e.g. economic power pushing for deregulation) rather than ideals and that even ideals will differ from one individual or group to another, and therefore universal hierarchies (of laws, principles, values) can easily lead to domination and exclusion.[124]

E. Multiple Identities

The previous discussions were only very rough sketches of nationalist, Europeanist, and cosmopolitan sympathies and how these might shape different views on where contract law making in Europe should be located, i.e. on the national, European, or global level, respectively. Readers may find more than one of these views attractive, maybe even all three to some extent. This would not be surprising given the fact that most people hold a sense of multiple belongings. Moreover, geographical links represent merely one of many dimensions of our complex identities. Very different aspects of our identities may be relevant—and in potential conflict—in different contexts, or even in the very same context.[125] It is entirely natural for one person to have very different, often conflicting, allegiances at the same time. Derrida declared: 'I feel European *among other things*.'[126] Most of us would experience great difficulty in reducing our different senses of belonging to only one.

[122] Cf. Hesselink (n. 69). See also Hesselink, 'Unjust Conduct in the Internal Market: On the Role of European Private Law in the Division of Moral Responsibility Between the EU, its Member States and their Citizens', 35 *YEL* (2016) 410.

[123] Lando, 'Tradition Versus Harmonization in the Recent Reforms of Contract Law', in the Xiamen Academy of International Law, *Collected Courses 2010*, Vol. 3 (2011) 83, at 87. See also Bonell, 'The CISG, European Contract Law and the Development of a World Contract Law', 56 *AJCL* (2008) 1, who refers, in particular, to the role that UNIDROIT principles could play.

[124] See N. Krisch, *Beyond Constitutionalism: The Pluralist Structure of Postnational Law* (2010), at 81 ff.

[125] See A. Sen, *Identity and Violence; The Illusion of Destiny* (2006), at xii; J. H. H. Weiler, *The Constitution of Europe: 'Do the New Clothes Have an Emperor?' And Other Essays on European Integration* (1999), at 328; M. Sandel, *Democracy's Discontent* (1996), at 343; and MacCormick (n. 85) 182.

[126] J. Derrida, *L'autre cap* (1991), at 80: 'je me sens européen *entre autres choses*' (emphasis in original). See also T. Judt, *Postwar, a History of Europe Since 1945* ([first published 2005] 2010), at 798, writing in 2005: 'The European Union in 2005 had not superseded conventional territorial units and would not be

Statistics show that most people in Europe today count a European sense of belonging among the different aspects of their identities, albeit usually not with a prominent place. Although Europeanists are only a small minority, nationalists are not the majority either. According to a 2017 Eurobarometer survey on the different levels of citizenship, 35 per cent define themselves solely by their nationality, 54 per cent first by their nationality and then as European, 7 per cent first as European citizens and then by their nationality, while 2 per cent see themselves as Europeans only.[127] On the basis of an earlier (and similar) version of these data, Checkel and Katzenstein concluded:

> The number of unambiguously committed Europeans is simply too small for the emergence of a strong cultural European sense of belonging. The number of committed nationalists is also too small for a hegemonic reassertion of national sentiments. The remaining part of the population holds primarily national identifications that also permit an element of European identification.[128]

Fligstein refers to this latter group of people who in certain circumstances think of themselves as Europeans, as 'situational Europeans'.[129]

Under these conditions, it seems, the enactment of a European civil code replacing national private laws, would be experienced, with some reason, as an act of violence against all those (the vast majority) who identify primarily or even exclusively with their nation. However, the total rejection of the Europeanization of contract law merely on nationalist grounds (i.e. the ground that contract law is essentially national) equally seems to constitute an act of intolerant cultural monism and a questionable projection of one's own identity onto others. Perhaps the availability of an optional European contract law, as in the withdrawn CESL proposal, would have done justice, in the area of contract law, to the reality that the majority of people in Europe regard themselves as situational Europeans.

An important question about national, European, and indeed cosmopolitan identities is whether the relationship between these is of a 'zero sum' or a 'positive sum' nature. If one can be, say, Parisian and French, Tuscan and Italian, British and English (or a woman and German) at the same time, then perhaps also national and European identities 'do not wax or wane at each other's expense'.[130] Indeed, the acquisition of European citizenship does not seem to have diminished in any sense the value of national citizenship. See explicitly Article 9 TFEU: 'Citizenship of the Union shall be additional to and not replace national citizenship.' Similarly, the CESL was not meant to replace national contract law. See the Explanatory Memorandum: 'The proposal for an optional second contract law regime has the advantage that, without replacing the

doing so for the foreseeable future.... What was new, and thus rather hard for outside observers to catch, was the possibility of being French *and* European, or Catalan *and* European—or Arab *and* European.'

[127] Standard Eurobarometer 88 (Autumn 2017).

[128] Checkel and Katzenstein, 'Conclusion—European Identity in Context', in J. T. Checkel and P. J. Katzenstein (eds), *European Identity* (2009), 213 (specific percentages omitted).

[129] Fligstein, 'Who Are the Europeans and How Does This Matter for Politics?', in J. T. Checkel and P. J. Katzenstein (eds), *European Identity* (2009) 132, at 154.

[130] Checkel and Katzenstein (n. 94) 9–10.

national contract laws in the Member States, it allows parties to use one single set of contract law rules across the EU.'[131] The proposed regulation, therefore, would merely have added a common European sales law, as an option available for cross-border relationships, to the pre-existing national regime. Nor would it have replaced the global sales law of the CISG: for business-to-business contracts the CESL would have represented merely one additional option (and not even the default option). As this example of sales law shows, the sum of private law identities—national, European, and cosmopolitan—could also be positive.

F. Identity and Public Justification in a Pluralist Society

If different people have different senses of belonging, which on the one hand can have strong implications, also in the field of private law (think only of a European civil code as a symbol of European unity), but on the other go in diametrically opposing directions (i.e. for or against a European civil code), then can identity, in this case private law identity, ever solve the question of the proper level for contract law making: national, European, global (or maybe sub-national)? And, most importantly, can it do so without one section of society (typically the majority) imposing its identity on the others (typically the minority), which would inevitably (and rightly) be experienced by the latter as an act of violence? However, if private law is severed from community, tradition, and identity, will we not end up with a private law that belongs to no one? And can it even be done: if we cannot rely on tradition, is it even possible to draft a private law that is neutral with regard to different identities? We will consider the viability of the different proposals made in this regard by liberal-egalitarians and by discourse theorists. As we will see, ethical neutrality is not the same as starting entirely from scratch, on a *tabula rasa*.[132] If a certain tradition cannot legitimately be invoked by the legislator in a pluralist society as the basis for introducing a fundamental rule, principle, or doctrine of private law, this does not mean that all rules, principles, and doctrines that have been accepted in (and in this sense 'belong to') a certain legal tradition should be rejected for that reason. It is not the case that an ethically neutral system of private law can only consist of rules and doctrines that have not been accepted, tested, and valued anywhere. As we will see, political liberalism and discourse ethics reject tradition and identity as a *reason* for justifying generally applicable laws, not the factual resemblance of certain proposed rules to those belonging to a certain tradition. What is required, on these views, is neutrality of reasons, not of outcomes.

[131] Commission Proposal for a Regulation on a Common European Sales Law (COM(2011) 635 final), at 11.

[132] Cf. O. Neurath, 'Protocol Sentences', in A. J. Ayer (ed.), *Logical Positivism* (1959) 199, at 201: 'No *tabula rasa* exists. We are like sailors who must rebuild their ship on the open sea, never able to dismantle it in dry-dock and to reconstruct it there out of the best materials.' Hugh Beale citing this metaphor once added: 'although the CFR-process is probably as close as you can get to a dry-dock'.

5. Liberal-Egalitarian

A. A Matter of Justice?

Most liberal political theories are anti-perfectionist,[133] which means that the coercive powers of the state cannot be used to implement a conception of the individual or common good, for the reason that in a liberal democracy, by definition, different and opposing reasonable conceptions held by citizens are to be expected and welcomed. Thus, a liberal society, qua liberal society, does not hold a view on the merits of European ideals, national identity, or cosmopolitan values as grounds for or against the further Europeanization of contract law. Rather, from the perspective of political liberalism (and most other versions of liberal-egalitarianism), the question of whether contract law should be national or European is an aspect of the more general question of whether European integration raises any issues of justice, which, in turn, is a specific instance of the even broader question of whether boundaries and their significance can be a matter of justice. Can the gradual reduction, in a variety of ways, of the significance of national borders within the EU be said to be just or unjust? Do individuals within the EU have a right to the preservation, or the removal, of borders between the Member States? Can Brexit (whatever it will turn out to mean exactly, if it reaches an end state) constitute justice or an injustice towards British (e.g. Scottish) or non-British (e.g. Irish) citizens? It is against the background of these more general questions that we can appreciate, from a political-liberal perspective, whether the Europeanization of contract law is a matter of justice.

B. The Law of Peoples

For Rawls, justice across boundaries means justice between peoples. In other words, he understands transnational justice as international justice. The central focus in *The Law of Peoples*, which provides an extension of political liberalism to foreign policy, international relations, and international law, is on democratic peace and stability.[134] In his focus on peace among peoples as the main concern of transnational justice, rather than on the (cosmopolitan) rights of individuals, Rawls explicitly follows Kant.[135] We need liberal democratic 'peoples', according to Rawls, because these make a 'liberal democratic peace' possible,[136] since constitutional democracies will not wage wars against one another. As a result, it becomes crucially important how Rawls defines and understands 'peoples'[137] and the role and significance of boundaries. In Rawls's view, 'liberal peoples have three basic features: a reasonably just constitutional democratic government that serves their fundamental interests; citizens united by what

[133] Liberal perfectionism (e.g. Raz) is of course perfectionist, contrary to political liberalism (e.g. Rawls, Nussbaum) and comprehensive liberalism (e.g. Dworkin).

[134] J. Rawls, *The Law of Peoples* (1999).

[135] Ibid. 10. See I. Kant, *Zum ewigen Frieden: Ein philosophischer Entwurf* (1795).

[136] Rawls (n. 134) 56.

[137] In *A Theory of Justice* (1971), at 331–333, Rawls still referred to 'nations' rather than 'peoples' and the 'law of nations' instead of the 'law of peoples'.

Mill called "common sympathies";[138] and finally, a moral nature'.[139] As a result especially of the first basic feature, the notion of 'peoples', who are the only actors to whom international justice applies, includes only those peoples that happen to have a state of their own.[140] Thus, in Rawls's conception, the principles of international justice do not apply to individuals, to groups that are not a people as defined, to international organizations such as the WTO, nor indeed—crucial for our purposes—to the EU. If the peoples in the EU decided one day to become one people or a single federal union,[141] then the principles of justice as fairness, including the difference principle, would become applicable to the EU, including, it seems, to its distribution of competences (some of which are shared competences). Rawls explicitly addresses this possibility, albeit as a mere hypothetical,[142] i.e. in disregard of the actual existence of the EU for which the Member States had already given up part of their sovereignty several decades earlier.[143] Until such a decision, the relationship between one EU Member State and another is not different, in Rawls's view, from that with any other liberal democracy. Rawls speaks of a 'division of labour between the Law of Peoples, which is to serve as a scheme of norms for international law and practice, and the decisions of free and equal citizens in liberal societies'.[144] As a consequence, on this view, as long as the EU has no people thus defined, the question of whether contract law should be European will not become a matter of justice.

C. Cosmopolitan Justice

Rawls's conception of justice beyond national borders, in particular, the focus on 'peoples' central to his *ius gentium* approach, has been rejected by other liberal egalitarians as 'rules for a vanished Westphalian world'.[145] The 'law of peoples' is not merely incomplete. Rather, it leaves no moral space for addressing the questions of global injustice (poverty) and intra-state injustice (minority rights) that are among the most pressing questions of political morality today.[146] Several authors have argued that the principles of justice should be applied at the global level, directly to individuals,[147] and that

[138] Rawls refers to Mill (n. 70) 206.
[139] Rawls (n. 134) 23.
[140] Or had one but were unjustly deprived of it.
[141] Rawls (n. 134) 53.
[142] Rawls and Van Parijs, 'Three Letters on the Law of Peoples and the European Union', 7 *Revue de philosophie économique* (2003) 7.
[143] Cf. Sangiovanni, 'Solidarity in the European Union: Problems and Prospects', in J. Dickson and P. Eleftheriadis (eds), *The Philosophical Foundations of European Union Law* (2012) 384, at 388: 'Rawls does not confront the EU as it is.'
[144] Rawls and Van Parijs (n. 142). Cf. Beitz, 'Rawls's Law of Peoples', 110 *Ethics* (2000) 669, at 677, contrasting what he calls Rawls's 'social liberalism' with his own 'cosmopolitan liberalism'.
[145] Buchanan, 'Rawls's Law of Peoples: Rules For a Vanished Westphalian World', 110 *Ethics* (2000) 697. Similar, Pogge, 'The Incoherence Between Rawls's Theories of Justice', 72 *Fordham Law Review* (2004) 1739, at 1758; M. C. Nussbaum, *Frontiers of Justice* (2006) 234, at 245.
[146] Beitz (n. 144) 680; Buchanan (n. 145) 717–721; T. W. Pogge, *Realizing Rawls* (1989), at 247; A. Sen, *The Idea of Justice* (2009), at 141–143; W. Kymlicka, *Contemporary Political Philosophy: An Introduction* (2002), at 289.
[147] Pogge (n. 146) 1744.

international law and institutions should also be assessed in their light.[148] Buchanan argues that there exists a global basic structure[149] which determines in part the prospects not only of individuals but also of peoples in Rawls's sense, and that appropriate principles of justice for this global basic structure are required.[150]

However, one difficulty with the cosmopolitan monist idea of global justice, compared to the Rawlsian dualist two-stage social contract approach is that it fundamentally questions the legitimacy of *all* boundaries and states. As Nussbaum aptly remarks with regard to the remaining role of the nation state:[151]

> Pogge and Beitz set out to question the finality and closed character of domestic state structures. But they do not tell us how far they really want to go. Are we standing back so far from current events that the very concept of the state will have to be reinvented, and considered against other options for arranging people's lives? But it is hard to arrange human lives in a complete vacuum.

Specifically, we could add, it is difficult to enforce contracts in a world devoid of states.

D. Liberal Nationalism

There is a strong (primordialist) nationalist bias in Rawls's theory of international justice in the sense that it suggests that it is natural for political boundaries to coincide with the boundaries of 'peoples' whose existence is considered prior to justice. Beyond Rawls's mere bias towards the nation state, among liberal-egalitarians (or social-democrats) the explicit project of liberal nationalism also exists.[152] Liberal nationalists claim that the degree of loyalty required for viable democratic politics and the level of solidarity needed for successful redistributive policies cannot realistically be found in political units beyond the nation state.[153] It is explicitly based on the idea that the successful implementation of liberal-egalitarian principles depends on nation building, not cultural or even ethnic, but merely civic, i.e. based on a 'thin' national identity, which amounts to not much more than 'we the people' or the 'assemblée nationale' (as it was originally understood, i.e. in mere opposition to the King).[154] As Kymlicka explains, 'nation-building need not take the form of promoting a particular conception of the good life ... The liberal nationalist state remains an anti-perfectionist state, which leaves the evaluation of the merits of competing conceptions of the good life to individual choice (and revision) in civil society.'[155]

[148] Beitz (n. 144) 686 and 694–695.
[149] Buchanan (n. 145) 704.
[150] Ibid. 706.
[151] Nussbaum (n. 145) 266.
[152] Rawls explicitly endorses Tamir.
[153] Y. Tamir, *Liberal Nationalism* (1993); D. Miller, *On Nationality* (1995); D. Miller, *Citizenship and National Identity* (2000); MacCormick (n. 85) especially chs 10 and 11. See earlier Mill (n. 70) 206.
[154] Hobsbawm (n. 35).
[155] Kymlicka (n. 146) 264–266.

However, if we are looking for a non-ethnic and non-cultural, 'thin' and more 'civic' national identity, then would Europe not be at least an equally appropriate community as a basis for this type of civic solidarity?[156] Civic European nationalism would not easily become violent or intolerant exactly because, compared to some Member States, Europe has a relatively weak ethnic and cultural homogeneity, and is based rather on common political principles, justice, and legal obligations. European civic nationalism thus is likely to be benign. The main risk would not be internal but external, i.e. a fortress Europe, for example, if it leads to isolationist positions concerning justice, which might also be seen in private law.

A similarly (primordialist) liberal nationalist bias seems to underlie Bagchi's argument against 'prematurely transnational' contract law.[157] Her argument is primordialist in that it takes national communities as prior to the legal system (among other institutions) rather than as an important product of it. If, by contrast, nations are understood as artefacts, construed by women and men on a daily basis[158]—not only by football supporters cheering at World Cup matches, but also by academics and politicians when debating the future of private law—then an argument against the Europeanization of private law in the name of national, political, and legal culture is not politically neutral: it is an act of nationalism.[159] After all, some of the 'nation states' were themselves not much older when they co-founded the EU than the Union is today. At the same time, however, her argument is specifically liberal (hence, liberal-nationalist), and not communitarian, in that her concern is with different national understandings of justice, rather than with diverging national identities and values. In other words, her claim is that reasonable disagreement about justice to an important degree aligns with national boundaries, and that differences in national contract laws are morally significant in that they depend on different national, economic, and political arrangements, which in turn should be understood, at least in part, as local attempts at implementing universal moral rights and principles, in this case the formal right to contract and the right to substantive limits to contractual freedom. Her core argument is that contract law diversity 'is morally imperative from within the demands of liberalism itself'—'that is, liberalism offers a limited common mandate for contract. For the rest, it affirmatively mandates disunity.'[160] However, it would seem that this does not imperatively lead to contract diversity along national lines, neither empirically nor morally. Not empirically, since enormous socio-economic and political differences exist within certain EU Member States, which would suggest, on Bagchi's account, a case for sub-national diversity of contract law. Not morally, because existing national boundaries seem morally arbitrary and their political reaffirmation is not a moral imperative.

[156] Cf. Habermas's constitutional patriotism, discussed later in Section 7.A.

[157] Bagchi, 'The Political Morality of Convergence in Contract', 24 *ELJ* (2018) 36.

[158] See Anderson (n. 83).

[159] See Hesselink (n. 69) 345. Cf. Weiler (n. 125) 340: 'At a societal level, nationhood involves the drawing of boundaries by which the nation will be defined and separated from others. The categories of boundary-drawing are myriad: linguistic, ethnic, geographic, religious etc. The *drawing* of boundaries is exactly that: a constitutive act, which decides that certain boundaries are meaningful both for the sense of belonging and for the original contribution of the nation.' (emphasis in original)

[160] Bagchi (n. 157) 46.

E. No Right Answer

Thus, it is not clear that either of these liberal-egalitarian approaches can resolve the issue.[161] They propose liberal versions of nationalism, Europeanism, and cosmopolitanism in taking respectively the national, European, or global basic structure as the main locus for distributive justice, but they do not resolve the question of how (or indeed whether) to choose among these. Thus, liberal versions of nationalism, Europeanism, cosmopolitanism, dualism, and pluralism remain on the table as a basis for determining distributive issues, including our question of which law maker(s)—national, European, international, or a combination of these—should (or at least legitimately can) be responsible for contract law making.

Dworkin, discussing the question 'who are the people?', underlines that there exists no right answer to these questions.[162] He submits:

> There is no non-historical right answer to the question: on what principle should people be divided into political communities? We cannot find an answer in the ideal of democracy itself because that ideal presupposes a political community and cannot be used to define one. Nor in the emotionally powerful but terminally vague idea of national self-determination—the supposed right of ethnocultural groups to govern themselves. There is no concept of nonpolitical nationhood precise enough to make sense of that right, and even if there were, there is no satisfactory answer to the question why any individual member of any group so defined has a duty to associate himself with the rest of them. ... Those who live a mile inside California's border with Nevada or France's border with Germany are governed rather differently from those who live a mile on the other side, and no abstract principle of political philosophy can justify that difference. Most attempts to draw supposedly more rational lines only create new uncomfortable minorities to replace newly comfortable old ones.[163]

Thus, private law disputes, for instance, are governed by the *Code Civil* and the *Bürgerliches Gesetzbuch*, respectively, on the two sides of France's border with Germany, and if that reality were to be superseded by the introduction of a European civil code that would certainly make certain people more comfortable but many others quite uncomfortable.

In conclusion, then, there do not seem to exist any principles of international justice that could provide an answer to the question whether there should be any boundaries between groups of people and, if so, where these boundaries should be, and what their significance, implications, and degree of porosity should be. But if no just and unjust borders exist then, it would seem, there is also no answer in justice to the question of the distribution of law making competences in Europe between the Member States

[161] Critical for this reason of political liberalism, Kymlicka (n. 146) 255.

[162] In the same sense, J.-W. Müller, *Was ist Populismus? Ein Essay* (2016), at 132: 'Somit sehen sich liberale Demokraten im Gegensatz zu den Populisten mit einer der schwierigsten philosophischen Paradoxien der Demokratie überhaupt konfrontiert: Fragen der demokratischen Inklusion lassen sich nicht demokratisch Entscheiden. Denn wer sagt, die Grenzen der Demokratie sollten vom Demos bestimmt werden, muss ja erst einmal feststellen, wer zum Demos gehört—... was ja gerade die Frage war.'

[163] R. Dworkin, *Justice for Hedgehogs* (2011), at 380–382.

and the EU, both in general and specifically with regard to contract law, because that latter question seems only a specific instance of the former general question.

F. The Status Quo as the Default

Rawls writes: 'there *must* be boundaries of some kind'.[164] There are only two conceivable alternatives to national borders. One is a world-state without any internal boundaries; the other is the state of nature, i.e. a world without any state. A world-state is probably undesirable from a liberal perspective, because of the risk that it will become a 'soulless despotism' and the 'graveyard of freedom'.[165] In any case, for the foreseeable future it does not seem a realistic prospect. Therefore, if we want to avoid the anarchy implied in the second alternative and—most relevant here—if we want contracts to be enforceable by the institutions of some state, we are left with no choice but to accept existing national boundaries at least as the default. The reason why there must be boundaries, then, is the Kantian reason that there must be some society with outer limits—some 'we the people'—that protects property and enforces other private rights. The current location of the boundaries, and what they represent in terms of the possibility to migrate, for example, may be very unsatisfactory for some individuals and groups, but it would be unjust to everyone if there were no state to protect anyone's rights. In Kantian terms, that would be a state of unfreedom.[166] We could rephrase this in less ethical sounding terms by saying that there would be no moral autonomy for anyone.

Dworkin suggests that we should accept historical boundaries as the default:

> Still, the boundaries created by accidents of history remain the default.... If we rule out a one-world global democracy with one vote for everyone in every continent (which is impossible and would in any case raise all the old questions when the necessary subdivisions were created), we rarely find a persuasive argument for correcting what history has achieved.[167]

This conclusion, although often unsatisfactory, seems indeed inevitable at least as a general rule. The situation is not dissimilar to the familiar property law rule according to which it is up to the plaintiff to demonstrate that she has a stronger title than the possessor.

However, this still does not settle our question. Indeed, the implications for our question, if there are any, seem rather limited. For, if we have to take existing national

[164] Rawls (n. 134) 39. Put differently, there has to be some specifically delineated foreground to background justice. Cf. Rawls (n. 64) 272, footnote 9.

[165] Kant, 'Toward perpetual peace' (1795), in M. J. Gregor (ed.), *Practical Philosophy: The Cambridge Edition of the Works of Immanuel Kant* (1996) 312, at 335.

[166] Cf. A. Ripstein, *Force and Freedom: Kant's Legal and Political Philosophy* (2009), at 226–227. Cf. also Nussbaum (n. 145) 257 (referring to Grotius).

[167] Dworkin (n. 163) 382. Having said that, Dworkin also appreciates the wisdom of a shift to larger and more diverse political communities, such as the EU, from smaller and more homogeneous ones, like the European nations. See explicitly ibid. 381.

borders as the default because otherwise moral autonomy, which includes at least some private rights, is impossible, this certainly does not exclude that a nation state limit its sovereign rights (as an expression of the political autonomy of its citizens) with a view to constituting 'a new legal order of international law' (*Van Gend en Loos*) such as the EU,[168] and as a result of which contract law could also become, in part or in its entirety, the competence of that new legal order, as has been the case within the EU. More specifically, most of the existing EU contract law *acquis* builds upon that limitation of national sovereignty in that it is based on the internal market competence that the EU and the Member States share.[169] The Directives on Unfair Terms (1993), Consumer Sales (1999), and Consumer Rights (2011) are so well established and entrenched by now that they definitely belong to the status quo in contract law in Europe.[170]

G. The EU's Basic Structure as Subject of Justice

In an exchange of letters with Rawls, Van Parijs pointed to the substantive importance of the question of whether and where boundaries between peoples should be drawn; he challenged Rawls's dichotomic view specifically with reference to the EU.[171] Van Parijs argued that at the stage of integration that Europe had reached by then (i.e. in 1998, a year after the signing of the Treaty of Amsterdam), the question had become whether, within Europe, the difference principle applies directly to European citizens,[172] or whether instead there merely exists a duty of assistance of European nations towards each other in case one of them should become a 'burdened society',[173] and that in this debate Rawls's book, *The Law of Peoples*, brought ammunition to the latter position. Following Sen, who argues against Rawls that 'international justice is simply not adequate for global justice',[174] it could be added *a fortiori* that international justice is simply not adequate for European justice.

Van Parijs seems right that today arguably the EU has a basic structure of its own.[175] It would roughly consist of what the ordoliberals—and Collins in a much less

[168] Case 26/62, *Van Gend en Loos* (EU:C:1963:1): 'a new legal order of international law for the benefit of which the states have limited their sovereign rights, albeit within limited fields, and the subjects of which comprise not only the Member States but also their nationals'.

[169] The legal bases of certain directives and regulations in the field of contract law have been contested, e.g. the Doorstep Selling Directive, in light of its weak impact on the internal market, and the CESL proposal, because it was doubted that the introduction of an optional EU contract law would have harmonized (i.e. modified) the existing national laws. It is, however, clear that Art. 114 TFEU provides a solid legal basis for EU legislation of various types in the area of contract law.

[170] The reality of existing EU contract law, which is already socially and economically embedded and thus goes well beyond mere aspiration, is largely ignored by Bagchi (n. 157).

[171] Rawls and Van Parijs (n. 142).

[172] As we saw, the difference principle demands that any differences within a society work to the benefit also of the least well off.

[173] Burdened societies are societies that live under unfavourable conditions as a result of which they are unable to maintain basic liberal institutions, such as the protection of human rights.

[174] Sen (n. 146) 143.

[175] See Hesselink, 'Unjust Conduct in the Internal Market' (n. 122), where I argue that the objection that a European polity does not exist gets things backward. If the EU's internal market has a basic structure that exercises an important distributive role, which seems undeniable today, then to that extent a European *demos* (not an *ethnos*) by necessity has to exist too. In the same sense, Forst, 'A Critical Theory of Transnational

politically partisan version—would call the EU's 'economic constitution'. From the Rawlsian perspective of justice as fairness this would imply, among other things, that the distribution of competences between the EU and the Member States would be directly subject to the principles of justice, including, in particular, the difference principle. Thus, the answer to the question of whether contract law should be national or European would come to depend to an important degree on what would be best for those Europeans who are least well-off. This perspective would shift attention towards the interests of citizens at the periphery of the EU, including those, mostly in the south, who were hit hardest by both the 2008 financial crisis and the 2020 Covid-19 crisis.[176] On this view, the response to those crises at the EU level, including any failure to properly respond as a Union, including in the field of European contract law (e.g. think of rules on *force majeure* and change of circumstances), would not be a matter of mere empathy and charity but rather of equal respect and justice.

6. Civic Republican

A. The Liberal Undermining of Republican Legitimacy

According to Scharpf, the legitimacy of Western constitutional democracies rests on normative arguments deriving from two traditions in political philosophy, i.e. liberalism and republicanism.[177] By contrast, the EU, he claims, appears to be 'the extreme case of a polity conforming to liberal principles which, at the same time, lacks practically all republican credentials'.[178] Scharpf understands liberalism as prioritizing the individual through the protection of rights and the (related) demand for unanimity for any interference with these rights, and republicanism as prioritizing the polity though majoritarian decisions that promote the common good. In the EU, he argues, republican legitimacy is undermined by the transformation by the Court of Justice of market freedoms into subjective rights (with direct effect and primacy), on the one hand, and by the difficulty in Europe of taking collective action promoting the common good because of high consensus requirements and the virtual impossibility of overturning 'judicial legislation' by the Court, on the other. This has the effect, he argues, of:

> transforming the hierarchical relation between European and national law into a hierarchical relationship between liberal and republican constitutional principles.

(In-)Justice: Realistic in the Right Way' (forthcoming), arguing that the requisite institutional form of justification depends on the degree of subjection ('demoi of subjection').

176 With regard to contract law, see Caruso, 'Qu'ils mangent des contrats: Rethinking Justice in EU Contract Law', in D. Kochenov, G. de Búrca, and A. Williams (eds), *Europe's Justice Deficit?* (2015), and more generally, see Kukovec, 'Law and the Periphery', 21 *ELJ* (2015) 406.

177 Scharpf, 'Legitimacy in the Multilevel European Polity', 1 *European Political Science Review* (2009) 173, at 175.

178 Ibid. 176. Contrast A. Kocharov, *Republican Europe* (2017), who argues that the constitutional design of Europe presents both liberal and republican elements.

> Subjective rights derived from (the interpretation of) European law may, in principle, override all countervailing national objectives, regardless of their salience as manifestations of democratic self-determination.[179]

What is needed, according to Scharpf, is a rebalancing between autonomy and community.[180] In Scharpf's view, the European institution best placed to strike a fairer balance between the two would be the European Council.

This account relies on a version of the no *demos* thesis that could be labelled as the 'weak *demos* thesis', i.e. that Europeans lack a collective identity and sense of common solidarity strong enough to legitimate Europe-wide majority rule by the European Parliament in political matters characterized by high stakes and strong disagreement.[181] It is only if one rejects a potential legitimating role for the European Parliament (on which see further later, in Section 7.A) that the conflicts between national legislatures and the European Court of Justice—aptly referred to by Joerges as 'diagonal conflicts'—come to turn on democratic self-determination.[182]

Scharpf's diagnosis of the 'liberal undermining of republican legitimacy' is based on a rather perfectionist and communitarian understanding of 'republicanism', while it understands 'liberalism' in a sense that this book refers to as libertarian (or neoliberal), i.e. a concern chiefly for negative liberty (freedom as non-interference).[183] At the same time, his account of EU law, especially its interpretation by the CJEU, seems rather one-sided and, as a consequence, unduly grim. For example, his claim that 'the overall pattern is shaped by an institutional constellation in which political legislation must be negotiated in the shadow of judicial decisions which, for structural reasons, have a liberalizing and deregulatory impact',[184] totally ignores the presence of a vast consumer law *acquis*, notably including control over unfair terms, that critics have rejected as socialist,[185] but that the Court consistently understands as 'intended to substitute for the formal balance established by the contract between the rights and obligations of the parties real balance re-establishing equality between them'[186]—hardly a liberalizing and deregulatory impact, one would think.

In the name of republican legitimacy, Scharpf undertakes an attack on two core doctrines of EU law, i.e. direct effect and primacy. Both were indeed originally the result of judicial legislation by the Court of Justice, in *Van Gend en Loos* (1963) and *Costa/ENEL* (1964), respectively, but have long since been recognized by the Masters of the Treaties, i.e. the EU Member States.[187] His main targets are the market freedoms, which

[179] Scharpf (n. 177) 193.
[180] Ibid. 198.
[181] Ibid. 177.
[182] See Joerges, '"Deliberative Political Processes Revisited": What Have We Learnt About the Legitimacy of Supranational Decision-Making', 44 *JCMS* (2006) 779, at 794.
[183] Scharpf (n. 177) 175.
[184] Ibid. 186
[185] Brandner and Ulmer, 'The Community Directive on Unfair Terms in Consumer Contracts: Some Critical Remarks on the Proposal Submitted by the EC Commission', 28 *CMLR* (1991) 647, at 669: 'instrumental in establishing within the [EU] the system of control and regulation underlying the socialist law of contract'.
[186] See e.g. Joined Cases C-70/17 and C-179/17, *Abanca Corporación Bancaria* (EU:C:2019:250).
[187] Explicitly in Lisbon Treaty, Annex, Declaration 17 concerning primacy.

the Court has indeed turned into subjective constitutionalized rights.[188] However, his criticism of direct effect and primacy is much more general and fundamental:

> The root of the problem is a basic asymmetry in how the Court defines the balance between the legitimate concerns of member-state autonomy and the legitimate requirements of European community. It has its origin in the very first decision postulating the direct effect of European law in *Van Gend en Loos* (1963). Combined with its nearly simultaneous assertion of the supremacy of European law, this construction has permitted the Court to define and expand subjective rights against member states, and thus to shift the balance between the rights and obligations of citizens or subjects that had been established in national polities.[189]

For our purposes here, this raises the question of what it would mean for European contract law if the doctrines of direct effect and primacy were abolished, say, in the next treaty reform. Only a small portion of EU law in the field of contract law consists of regulations which are directly applicable in the legal orders of the Member States. These include most notably the Air Passengers Regulation and the Rome I Regulation.[190] If the doctrine of direct effect was abolished, this would mean that private parties could no longer directly rely in their litigation on the provisions in these regulations.[191] Or, to be more precise, EU law would no longer require such direct effect. National law, depending on the constitution at hand, could still consider EU regulations as directly effective on their territory. Member States with monistic constitutions, like the Netherlands, would be more likely to do so than countries with dualist constitutions, like Germany and most other Member States. This would bring Rome I back to the situation where it was before it was turned from an international treaty into an EU regulation, and would provide the Air Passengers Regulations (at most) with a similar status—one akin to that of the CISG, for example. However, the bulk of the existing contract law *acquis* consists of EU directives and, therefore, lacks direct effect in the first place. Directives have to be transposed into national law, which means that the abolition of the direct effect doctrine would have no great direct impact on European contract law.[192] However, what about the doctrine of harmonious interpretation, which plays an important role in the effectiveness of EU contract law? Would that have to be abolished too? This brings us to implications of the doctrine of primacy, to which it is closely connected, since the principle of harmonious interpretation presumes the primacy of EU law.

Pursuant to the doctrine of the primacy (or supremacy) of EU law, provisions of national law that are incompatible with EU law must be set aside and remain

[188] Scharpf (n. 177) 192–193. See earlier F. Scharpf, *Governing in Europe* (1999).

[189] Scharpf (n. 177) 192.

[190] Regulation (EC) 261/2004, establishing common rules on compensation and assistance to passengers in the event of denied boarding and of cancellation or long delay of flights, OJ 2004 L 46; Regulation (EC) 593/2008 on the law applicable to contractual obligations ('Rome I') OJ 2004 L 177.

[191] See C-26/62, *Van Gend en Loos* (EU:C:1963:1): 'Independently of the legislation of Member States, Community law ... not only imposes obligations on individuals but is also intended to confer upon them rights which become part of their legal heritage.'

[192] Nor does Scharpf claim so, of course. The point here is to determine what his general republican theory of EU legitimacy (or, rather: illegitimacy) means for the contract law *acquis* and its legitimacy.

inapplicable.[193] In other words, in case of a conflict between a provision of national law and a provision of EU law, the latter takes precedence. For example, national courts are not allowed to engage in weighing the substantive importance of the EU measure and its objectives against the national measure and its particular aims, and find for the latter; the priority rule is entirely formal. Were it to be abolished, it seems, the implications could be quite radical. In a case of conflict between the national provisions transposing an EU directive (e.g. the consumer rights directive or the one on unfair terms) and another provision of national law, Member State courts could simply set aside the provision of EU origin on account, for example, of the autochthonous national provision being posterior or simply protecting a weightier interest (or, in the case of full harmonization: better protecting the same interest). This would also strongly reduce the practical relevance of the preliminary ruling procedure, for what would be the point of determining the incompatibility of national law with EU law if EU law no longer had precedence? A national court might just as well engage directly in an interpretation of EU law most in conformity with the remainder of its own system of national law. This would be likely to lead to a large reduction in the number of cases brought before the CJEU. This, in turn, would dwarf the Court's current role as a protagonist. The abolition of the primacy of EU law would also strongly diminish the impact of EU law on the national private law systems of the Member States. Therefore, the implications for European private law could be quite drastic indeed. At the same time—most relevant here—it is not immediately clear—at least not for contract law—what the specifically republican (as opposed to merely nationalistic) benefit would be, even if we understand republicanism, not as freedom as non-domination (as civic republicans like Skinner, Pettit, and Bellamy do), but as the promotion of the common good through majoritarian decisions. In other words, there does not seem to be an obvious distinctly republican argument against the primacy of EU private law over national private law. This could perhaps be different if the ordinary legislative procedure,[194] which applies when adopting directives, and where the European Parliament plays a key role as co-legislator, somehow also structurally 'shift[ed] the balance between the rights and obligations of citizens or subjects that had been established in national polities' in a liberalizing and deregulatory direction. However, as we saw (and as discussed more fully in Chapter 6), in the core area of European contract law, i.e. consumer law, for most Member States the opposite has been the case.

B. European Demoicracy and its Private Law

Nicolaïdis argues that the EU should be understood as a 'demoicracy', by which she means 'a Union of peoples, understood both as states and as citizens, who govern

[193] See Case C-6/64, *Costa v. ENEL* (EU:C:1964:66), at 594: 'the law stemming from the Treaty, an independent source of law, could not, because of its special and original nature, be overridden by domestic legal provisions, however framed, without being deprived of its character as community law and without the legal basis of the community itself being called into question'.

[194] Pursuant to Art. 289 TFEU, the ordinary legislative procedure consists in the joint adoption by the European Parliament and the Council of (in this case) a directive on a proposal from the Commission. The procedure is defined further in Art. 294 TFEU.

together but not as one'.[195] The basic idea is that we should move beyond considering democracy in the singular, i.e. in terms of one single *demos*, either at the national level or at the supranational level, and thus transcend the question of more or less Europe.

Still, if the notion of demoicracy is meant as a 'third way' between the 'European *demos*' and the 'no *demos*' theses,[196] then it certainly it is not a middle way[197] since it leans strongly towards nationalism. The endorsement of the 'no European *demos*' thesis, in both its empirical and its normative meaning, is the starting point for European demoicracy.[198] And the idea of national peoples, with a national identity, not only remains unquestioned but is even reaffirmed, and national identity essentialized, by the fact that these peoples (*demoi*) are at the centre of the theory. Indeed, this nationalist conception of peoples even seems primordialist in that it is a non-statist concept of a people, the members of which may deliberate with each other across borders, directly, i.e. without the need for going through the interference of their state institutions, but still qua members of a people, not in their individual capacity, for example as a person with multiple identities, allegiances, or even citizenships.[199] According to Nicolaïdis, the two (interrelated) core norms of demoicracy are transnational non-domination and mutual recognition. 'The EU is an anti-hegemonic, not an anti-national, project', she argues.[200] Originally founded in order to overcome threat of war, today the EU's key republican role remains the prevention of 'soft domination' by one people of another, i.e. the subjection to the arbitrary power of others. At the same time, supremacy claims risk turning the EU itself into an instrument of domination. Hence, the case for horizontal, mutual recognition. Although the notion of non-domination clearly refers to neo-republican thinking, she underlines that the demoicratic theory of the EU should not be reduced to it (nor, for that matter, to liberalism, on which it also draws).[201]

Nicolaïdis' understanding of the EU as a demoicracy is not meant as a mere ideal theory—an external standard by which to evaluate the Union—but explicitly also, or even primarily, as a convincing account and a defence of what the EU, properly understood, already is today,[202] even though there certainly is room for demoicratic improvement.[203] For this latter, practical purpose she formulates 10 guiding principles

[195] Nicolaïdis, 'European Demoicracy and its Crisis', 51 *JCMS* (2013) 351. The term was introduced first, with reference to the EU, by van Parijs, 'Should the European Union Become More Democratic?' in A. Follesdal and P. Koslowski, *Democracy and the European Union* (1998) 287.

[196] Nicolaïdis (n. 195) 352.

[197] Explicitly, ibid. 353.

[198] See ibid. 351 and 356, where it is simply assumed: 'the lack of a European demos means that European citizens will not and should not accept to be bound by a majority of Europeans'. On this view, it seems, the failure of the CESL was the right demoicratic outcome, in spite of the large majority vote for it (almost 2/3) in the European Parliament.

[199] For this reason, Nicolaïdis' theory of Europe would perhaps fit more properly into the section on communitarianism. It is discussed here, nevertheless, because, as we will see, she herself draws in part on civic republicanism (especially on the notion of non-domination), and because prominent contemporary republicans, most notably Bellamy, build upon her theory of demoicracy.

[200] Nicolaïdis (n. 195) 358.

[201] Nicolaïdis, 'The Idea of European Demoicracy', in J. Dickson and P. Eleftheriadis (eds), *The Philosophical Foundations of European Union Law* (2012) 247, at 263: 'a demoicratic theory should combine background theories of democracy—e.g. republicanism and liberalism—and should not be reduced to one or the other'.

[202] Nicolaïdis (n. 195) 352: 'a demoicracy is what the EU has become over time'.

[203] Ibid. 355.

for European demoicratic politics. The implementation of these principles in the field of European private law making (which she does not herself address) would have potentially quite radical implications. Not only does Guiding Principle 10 (Diversity), according to which 'the commitment to diversity in a demoicracy should serve as a mental beacon to resist the pull to oneness—be it one people, one state, one voice on the world stage or one story for the EU' and to 'counter the messianic discourse calling for oneness',[204] when applied to private law, seem to imply a firm rejection of a European civil code (and probably also of a common frame of reference or principles of European contract law). More importantly, pursuant to Guiding Principle 5 (Equivalence), 'in a demoicracy, shared projects (for example, single market, single space, single money) do not require harmonized standards, but minimal compatibility and maximal recognition',[205] which seems to question directly the desirability and legitimacy of harmonization and, thus, of the private law *acquis communautaire* which, as said, is almost entirely based on Article 114 TFEU. On this view, the *acquis* should be replaced, it seems, by a radically private international law oriented approach. As Nicolaïdis writes explicitly: 'European policies and laws should deal with tensions between home and host country jurisdiction through conflict-of-laws approaches and managed mutual recognition.'[206] Thus, it seems, under the guiding principles proposed by Nicolaïdis, paradigmatic examples of a demoicratic European private law should no longer be the unfair terms, consumer sales, and consumer rights directives, but rather the Rome I and Brussels I Regulations (perhaps even re-transformed into treaties between the Member States).[207]

C. A Republican Europe of Sovereign States

The idea of demoicracy has been picked up and further elaborated by civic republicans as the best way to ensure freedom as non-domination in Europe. In particular, Bellamy's vision of a republican Europe of sovereign states, as a realistic utopia, explicitly builds on the idea of the EU as a demoicracy.[208] However, he gives it a sovereigntist twist that transforms it beyond recognition, straying far afield from the third way, and landing it decidedly in the intergovernmentalist camp. Indeed, Bellamy's starting point is that there is no need for the EU 'to detract from the sovereignty of the

[204] Ibid. 365.
[205] Ibid. 363.
[206] Ibid. 364.
[207] The proposal by S. Hennette *et al.*, *Pour un traité de démocratisation de l'Europe* (2017), for a new parliamentary assembly for the Eurozone that should democratize the governance of the euro and thus promote fiscal and social justice, also has distinctly demoicratic traits. The authors expect that the new assembly could bring to a halt the austerity policies that are supported only by a minority of Europeans. Crucially, in their proposal, the membership of the assembly should be drawn from the national parliaments of the Member States of the Eurozone. Pursuant to Art. 4 of the proposed treaty, 80% of the members are nominated on a pro rata basis by national parliaments and 20% by the European Parliament. The reason they offer (ibid. 9–10) for this choice is that the governance of the euro 'goes to the heart of the social pacts of the Member States' and that the national parliaments alone enjoy the necessary legitimacy for democratizing the powerful intergovernmental network that currently governs the euro.
[208] See explicitly, R. Bellamy, *A Republican Europe of States: Cosmopolitanism, Intergovernmentalism and Democracy in the EU* (2019), at xvi.

member states and their peoples'.[209] He embraces the no-*demos* thesis,[210] rejects the primacy and direct effect of EU law and, more generally, the constitutionalization of the founding treaties by the Court of Justice,[211] as well as the idea of the EU as a multi-level system of governance.[212] On this proposed republican view, Bellamy writes, 'the normative goal of an EU conceived as an association of sovereign democratic states is to ensure fair terms of cooperation between them'.[213]

However, it is far from clear what exactly this would entail for EU law, including EU private law. Specifically, what would the contract law of a republican Europe of sovereign states look like? Take the example of contract law, where all recent directives, not only on B2C but also on B2B contracts,[214] were adopted through the ordinary legislative procedure. From now on, should the ordinary legislative procedure (formerly referred to as the 'community method') be abandoned altogether and directives be adopted by the Council alone? That would mean giving up the current role of the European Parliament with its influential IMCO (Internal Market and Consumer Protection) and JURI (Legal Affairs) committees. And once European law is adopted in this way, should it then no longer be interpreted autonomously and harmoniously, with the possibility of references for preliminary rulings to the Court of Justice? And as we saw when discussing Scharpf's view, the abolition of direct effect and primacy could have even more far-reaching consequences, including in the field of private law. In response, Bellamy would probably claim that the national private law systems thus would no longer be 'dominated' by the EU, and that national courts would be liberated from domination by the CJEU. However, it would also mean the partial or perhaps even total de-Europeanization of private law through the reduction of the *acquis* and its relevance. Indeed, it is far from clear that there still would be any contract law *acquis* (or indeed any other *acquis communautaire*) as we know it left, nor that there would be anything else to replace it. The most likely outcome, it seems, would be the renationalization of private law. Indeed, because of its strong emphasis on national sovereignty as a precondition for democracy and as the only way to prevent domination (internal and external) and its related understanding of the EU as an ever closer union of peoples,[215] 'republican nationalism' may be more appropriate as a label for this view than Bellamy's own term 'republican intergovernmentalism'. In any case, it is difficult to distinguish the agenda and foreseeable practical outcomes of this version of private law republicanism from those of private law nationalists.

[209] Ibid. xiv. However, a survey three months before the European Parliament elections in 2019, found that a majority of Europeans (54%) would like to see the European Parliament's role strengthened. See *Spring Eurobarometer 2019, Eurobarometer Survey 91.1 of the European Parliament*, 8.

[210] Bellamy (n. 208) 119. Similar, Kocharov (n. 178) 12: 'There is no such European polity today.'

[211] Bellamy (n. 208) 22 and 200.

[212] Ibid. 42.

[213] Ibid. 174.

[214] As two recent examples of the former, see Directive (EU) 2019/770 on contracts for the supply of digital content and digital services, OJ 2019 L 136; and Directive (EU) 2019/771 on certain aspects concerning contracts for the sale of goods, OJ 2019 L 136. And as instances of the latter, think of Directive 2011/7/EU on combating late payment in commercial transactions, OJ 2011 L 48; and Directive (EU) 2019/633 on unfair trading practices in business-to-business relationships in the agricultural and food supply chain, OJ 2019 L 111.

[215] Bellamy (n. 208) 69.

D. Interference with Private Law Sovereignty

As we saw earlier,[216] Saprai's version of republicanism is strongly communitarian. From his discussion of contract law beyond the nation state, in particular its Europeanization, it becomes clear that his view is also strongly nationalist.[217] For example, claiming that 'French contract law expresses vividly the importance of keeping one's word' he speculates that this 'may reflect something deep in the French psyche that goes well beyond the domain of politics and social justice'.[218] Still, his private law nationalism is not primordialist. His focus is on states, not nations. And he argues that a state's private law identity can contribute to building and strengthening the national identity of the political community of a state.[219]

One of the most striking features of Saprai's argument is that he consistently adopts an international law approach to the EU, as a result of which the Europeanization of contract law appears as an external interference with national contract law.[220] In particular, he denies that the Member States of the EU have given up part of their sovereignty by transferring law making competences to the EU,[221] allowing them, among other things, to enact secondary EU law (mostly directives) that goes to the heart of contract law now—a process that, to date, has been going on for almost three decades.[222] Thus, Saprai's view of transnational private law is avowedly Westphalian.[223]

Saprai's starting point in his discussion of EU private law is the value of national sovereignty.[224] He sees a strong link between value pluralism in contract law and state sovereignty. He argues: 'The value of state sovereignty in this context resides in the

[216] In Chapter 2.

[217] See P. Saprai, *Contract Law Without Foundations: Toward a Republican Theory of Contract Law* (2019), ch. 10 ('Contract Law Beyond the State'); Saprai, 'The Convergence of Contract Law in Europe and the Problem of Legitimacy: A Common Lawyer's Perspective', 12 *ERCL* (2016) 96.

[218] Saprai, *Contract Law Without Foundations* (n. 217) 210. Similarly, he suggests, ibid., that 'whether a state chooses to lay down a mitigation doctrine [as English law does and French law does not] expresses something about the national character of that state'.

[219] Ibid. 211: 'a sense of national identity is forged, reflected, and expressed by the rules, principles, and doctrines that constitute national private law'.

[220] Ibid. 221: 'the attempt to harmonize the general law of contract in Europe involves an interference with state sovereignty which is the freedom of a state to decide for itself how to interpret and balance the irreducible plurality of values that shape contract law rules and doctrines'.

[221] See ibid. 216, explicitly rejecting 'the idea in this context that Member States of the EU consented to give away their sovereign rights over contract law by signing up and ratifying various EU treaties'.

[222] The Unfair Terms Directive was adopted in 1993. Saprai acknowledges that the EU 'clearly does have competence' in spheres such as consumer law. However, to the extent that his argument is directed against 'the Commission programme for the harmonisation of the general law of contract' (ibid. 216), it is moot, since the Commission never proposed any general contract law rules. Even the CESL-proposal did not concern general contract law, since (1) its substantive scope was limited to sales while (2) its personal scope was restricted to B2C and B2SME.

[223] Explicitly, ibid. 213, where he 'assumes the Westphalian primacy of the sovereign state'. For a critical account of the Westphalian doctrine of sovereignty on private law, especially the ensuing depoliticized understanding of private international law, see Muir Watt, 'Private International Law Beyond the Schism', 2 *Transnational Legal Theory* (2011) 347.

[224] Throughout he assimilates European contract law to human rights in international law, relying strongly on the sovereigntist account of international human rights law presented by Tasioulas, 'Human Rights, Legitimacy, and International Law', 58 *American Journal of Jurisprudence* (2013) 1. At times, Saprai even claims that sovereign states have a 'moral right to national self-determination' (*Contract Law Without Foundations* (n. 217) 213), suggesting that states themselves have moral agency.

freedom of states to decide how they interpret and balance the values that shape contract law. This matters because the contract law rules and doctrines chosen by Member States play an important role in constituting and expressing national character or identity.'[225] However, given the fact of value pluralism, that Saprai underlines, it is not immediately clear why the value of state sovereignty should somehow trump all other values.[226] One could think that perhaps the value of European unity is more important than the value of the Member States, or that EU-wide consumer protection in contracts is of more value than national sovereignty in contract law making. However, in Saprai's account, although value pluralism provides the foundation for his 'republican' and 'protestant' theory of contract, the value of sovereignty somehow seems to be prior to—or ranking higher than—all others. So, when Saprai argues that 'the presence of interpretative and value pluralism justifies the existence of positive law, and they also explain why state sovereignty is a powerful objection to the EU contract law harmonization programme', then, while the former point is easily granted, the latter remains obscure.

A central premise to his account is a strong version of the no EU *demos* thesis. 'The main objection to attempts to harmonize contract law in Europe' he argues, 'is the absence of any political community, even a "bare" or "de facto" political community'.[227] As we saw earlier, most people would agree that a thick ethical community of Europeans is currently lacking. However, for a thin civic community of European citizens, which may indeed be 'bare' and 'de facto' and exist next to the much thicker national (and in some cases, like Belgium, sub-national) political communities of each of the Member States, the no *demos* thesis seems less self-evident. Overall, Saprai's strongly ethical, identity-oriented understanding of private law republicanism is hardly distinguishable from the private communitarianism that was discussed earlier. When he concludes that 'there is an insufficiently robust sense of European identity embraced by the people of Europe' to justify the harmonization of European contract law,[228] it is difficult to see which specifically republican (as opposed to merely communitarian) dimension that argument adds to the European contract law debate. There is a striking contrast in this regard with the position of Pettit, whose civic version of neo-republicanism concentrates on freedom as non-domination:

> While the republican state represents an indispensable means of furthering people's non-domination, there is nothing sacred from the republican point of view about the state or about the state's sovereignty. Given the existence of multinational bodies of various kinds, there are some domestic issues on which it may be better from the point of view of promoting freedom as non-domination to give over control to those

[225] Saprai, *Contract Law Without Foundations* (n. 217) 205.

[226] Ibid. 209, simply postulates that: 'states should, on the whole, be free to decide how to interpret and balance ... the various competing values that fashion contract law rules and doctrines'. He claims that thus freedom has 'an intrinsic value', but does not clarify why it should trump all other values, in particular the 'moral values which play a role in contract law, such as fairness, the prevention of exploitation, trust, freedom and so forth' that he refers to (ibid. 206).

[227] Ibid. 204. Saprai borrows the idea of a 'de facto' political community from Dworkin. See R. Dworkin, *Law's Empire* (1986), at 209.

[228] Saprai, *Contract Law Without Foundations* (n. 217) 220.

> bodies and thereby to restrict the local state. The more distant the agency is from a given issue, it is true, the less well informed it will be on certain aspects. But, equally, the more distant the agency is from an issue, the more likely it is to represent an impartial arbiter. That being so, it may be quite a good thing from the republican point of view that various domestic issues should be taken out of the realm of local decision-making and given over to international adjudication.[229]

There seems to be nothing in the nature of contract law for it to be excluded from the scope of this civic republican consideration.

7. Discourse Theory

A. European Civic Solidarity

For a long time, Habermas has been one of the most outspoken pro-European public intellectuals. Even in times of increasing disaffection with the EU, Habermas still continues to argue explicitly for 'more Europe'.[230] A long-standing reason for his support for further European integration has been his understanding of European union based on European solidarity as the only way to preserve the main achievements of the welfare state in a globalizing world.[231] More recently, another reason has been that we need a political union to tame the financial markets. Many citizens and observers, who regard the EU as structurally flawed towards managerialism and technocracy and as an intrinsically neoliberal project, advocate a return to national democracy.[232] Habermas, by contrast, rejects the 'nostalgic option' of the withdrawal behind the 'Maginot line' of national sovereignty.[233] Instead, he argues, we should enhance the role of the European Parliament relative to that of the Council.[234] Likewise, Habermas has been a severe critic of the German Constitutional Court's case law on the European treaties. In particular, he rejects as nationalistic the claim the *Bundesverfassungsgericht* has made consistently, from its Maastricht ruling onward,[235] that no European *demos* (*Volk*) exists of which the European Parliament would be the direct representative.[236]

229 P. Pettit, *Republicanism: A Theory of Freedom and Government* (1997), at 13.

230 In Habermas, 'Three Reasons for More Europa', in J. Habermas, *The Lure of Technocracy* (2015), ch. 6, he offers three grounds for more Europe. The first one relates to German history, the other two (the need to regulate international financial markets and the need, because of the euro, for a political Union) somewhat surprisingly seem no less technocratic than classical market-functionalism.

231 Habermas, 'The Lure of Technocracy: A Plea for European Solidarity', in J. Habermas, *The Lure of Technocracy* (2015), ch. 1; Habermas (n. 75) 56–58. Note that for exactly the same reason of distributive justice, as we saw, liberal nationalists support the nation-state.

232 See e.g. Streeck (n. 62).

233 Habermas, 'Demokratie oder Kapitalismus? Vom Elend der nationalstaatlichen Fragmentierung in einer kapitalistisch integrierten Weltgesellschaft', *Blätter für deutsche und internationale Politik* 5/2013, 59, at 61.

234 Ibid. 65.

235 See also Grimm, 'Does Europe Need a Constitution?', 1 *ELJ* (1995) 282.

236 See Habermas (n. 75) 86. See also 'Democracy, Solidarity and the European Crisis, Lecture delivered by Professor Jürgen Habermas on 26 April 2013 in Leuven'. The 'no *demos* thesis', i.e. the claim that Europeans identify insufficiently with the EU and feel insufficient solidarity with each other for a democracy to function fully, including when it comes to decisions with distributive dimensions, is essentially an

In the field of private law, there was the original idea of a political common frame of reference.[237] The European legislature would follow it (pursuant to an inter-institutional agreement between European Commission, Council, and Parliament[238]) unless they had good reason not to do so ('comply or explain'), and it would play an increasing role in the doctrinal debate and in legal education on general European principles of European private law (or a loose European system of private rights), as part of the EU's civic identity. This idea of a political common frame of reference could still be considered today.[239] It would, of course, be crucial that the drafting and further development of such a common frame of reference came about through a sufficiently inclusive and deliberative process. And probably such a European common frame of reference—or the basic structure of a European system of private rights and obligations—should be less doctrinal and more accessible for non-experts than the DCFR, and more focused on real issues of injustice, especially as experienced at the periphery of European society.

Still, whether or not it will be possible to construct a civic European identity grounded in shared constitutional ideals that European citizens will embrace as constitutional patriots,[240] it seems only fair to say that in order to engender allegiance, such a 'civic' Europeanist identity—including a European private law identity—would probably have to be so thick and postnational that it would end up coming very close to a (communitarian) Europeanist (or Euronationalist) sense of belonging.

B. A European Public Sphere

Given the fact that not only national identities but also all other collective identities are constructs,[241] the real question is what kind of Europe we want to build

empirical claim. This claim has been challenged by Risse, 'No Demos? Identities and Public Spheres in the Euro Crisis', 52 *JCMS* (2014) 1207, who points to the fact that the majority of European citizens, as we saw, have developed dual identities and argues that this Europeanization of national identities is sufficient to sustain selective distributive policies at the EU level.

[237] On the plan for—and work on—a common frame of reference in the first decade of this century, see Chapter 2.

[238] See Institutional Agreements, Framework Agreement on Relations between the European Parliament and the Commission, OJ 2010 L 304/47.

[239] The letter from six Member States to the then incoming Juncker Commission, that asked for (and obtained) the withdrawal of the CESL proposal, recommended that the Commission should return to its original plan of a common frame of reference. See letter of 18 November 2014 from the Ministers of Justice of Austria, Finland, France, Germany, the Netherlands and the UK to Vera Jourová, the Commissioner for Justice, Consumers and Gender Equality (unpublished, on file with the author).

[240] Sceptical: Kumm, 'Why Europeans Will Not Embrace Constitutional Patriotism', 6 *International Journal of Constitutional Law* (2008) 117, at 135, arguing that the 'no demos' thesis gets the problem the wrong way around: it is the current institutional arrangements that prevent the European Parliament from becoming a protagonist in European politics and a true representative of European citizens: 'Current institutional structures perpetuate the very obstacles that are invoked as a reason not to establish meaningful electoral politics at the heart of the European political process.... Parliament deserves to emerge as an independent and strong agenda setter'.

[241] J. Habermas, *Die postnationale Konstellation; Politische Essays* (1998), at 37. In the same sense, Gellner (n. 69) 54; Hobsbawm (n. 35) 10. K. W. Deutsch, *Nationalism and Its Alternatives* (1969), at 3, phrases it more ironically when he refers to the nation as 'a group of persons united by a common error about their ancestry and a common dislike of their neighbors.'

together.[242] What is needed for further constructing a civic European identity[243] is a European public sphere. This public sphere can come about if the national public spheres open themselves up towards each other.[244] This would also make the usual argument of the linguistic obstacle become mute.[245] On this view, the idea that there needs to be a separate European space with its own single language (probably English) is misguided;[246] a 'transnationalization' of the public sphere will suffice.[247] In recent years, indeed we seem to be witnessing already some instances of 'transnational deliberation',[248] especially with regard to subjects that European citizens really care about. During the euro-crisis there was an intense cross-European debate on whether Greece should be bailed out, where the same arguments (and also stereotypes, such as lazy Greeks and commandeering Germans) came up and circulated in the different national debates in different languages, for and against austerity, pro- and anti-Europe, and so on.[249] Very much the same has been seen in relation to other highly controversial recent political events that have affected all Europeans, such as the refugee crisis, the Brexit vote, and the question of European solidarity in response to the Covid-19 pandemic. In each of these cases, arguments and emotions have circulated rapidly, via social media, across the political and linguistic boundaries between the Member States.[250]

[242] See Habermas, 'Ist die Herausbildung einer Europäischen Identität nötig, und ist sie möglich?', in J. Habermas, *Der gespaltene Westen* (2004) 68, at 81.

[243] Habermas, 'Why Europe Needs a Constitution', *ELJ* (2001) 15.

[244] Habermas (n. 75) 87. According to C. Taylor, *Modern Social Imaginaries* (2004), at 178, 'the public sphere always extended in some aspect beyond national borders'.

[245] Kymlicka, 'Citizenship in an Era of Globalization: A Commentary on Held', in I. Shapiro and C. Hacker-Cordon (eds), *Democracy's Edges* (1999) 112, at 121, for example, is sceptical that post-national democracy could work, whether global or in the EU. He argues that true democracy is difficult without a common language: 'democratic politics is politics in the vernacular'. Therefore, he believes, the nation-state will remain the primary locus for exercising democratic citizenship.

[246] Habermas (n. 75) 182–183. Contrast van Parijs, 'Thatcher's Plot—and How to Defeat It', *Social Europe*, 29 November 2016: 'There cannot be a European demos unless people are able to communicate cheaply and effectively with one another despite the diversity of their native languages. This requires the democratization of a common lingua franca.'

[247] Habermas (n. 75) 183. Habermas and Derrida, 'February 15, or What Binds Europeans Together: A Plea For a Common Foreign Policy, Beginning in the Core of Europe', 10 *Constellations* (2003) 291, at 295–297.

[248] Cf. Habermas, 'Ist die Herausbildung einer Europäischen Identität nötig, und ist sie möglich?', in J. Habermas, *Der gespaltene Westen* (2004), 68, at 82. See also MacCormick (n. 85) 154, on Europe-wide deliberation (against the *BVerfG*).

[249] For empirical evidence, specifically with regard to the euro crisis, see Risse (n. 236) 1208, finding that the euro crisis has led to the growing Europeanization of national public spheres.

[250] This does not mean that each of these views and reasons is equally good. Habermas is extremely critical of the German self-image as 'good Europeans', which, in light of Germany's 'unabashed national economic egoism' with regard to the governance of the euro must be characterized as 'profane *mauvaise foi*'. See Habermas, 'Are We Still Good Europeans?', *Social Europe*, 13 July 2018.

C. The Constitution of European Private Law: The *Pouvoir Constituant Mixte*

Even though European civic solidarity seems possible in principle[251] (even if more fragile than ever before in the history of the EU, in the light of the rise of nationalism following the euro, refugee, Brexit, and Covid-19 crises), and an emerging European public sphere can be discerned (partly as a result of the same crises), it is far from obvious, from a normative point of view, that the deliberate construction of a civic European identity, the strengthening of EU institutions, and, more generally, political Union, can be justified in terms not susceptible to reasonable disagreement. And given that national identity and national solidarity can easily be constructed in similarly civic terms we are likely to remain with two equally legitimate but conflicting identity claims. In particular, the idea of civic identity does not seem to bring us much further in answering the question of the right distribution of competences between the EU and its Member States, including—the most relevant for present purposes—in the field of contract law.

In a more recent essay, Habermas tried to move beyond this impasse, arguing that we should regard Europe as belonging, at the same time, to the citizens and the peoples of Europe.[252] In other words, the EU is based on a *pouvoir constituant mixte*.[253] While still rejecting communitarian claims based on assertions of thick national identity ('the reactive impulse to cling to naturalized ethnonational features'), Habermas now acknowledges that citizens do have justifying reason to vindicate the achievements, in terms of freedom and justice, of their respective Member States and—crucially—their claims to remain the guardians of this—what we might call the national civic *acquis*.[254]

Habermas finds evidence in Article 10(1) and (2) TEU for this dual legitimation of the EU, where European citizens are represented in their dual capacities of EU citizens and citizens of their respective Member States, which stand in a non-hierarchical relationship to each other:[255]

[251] Solidarity is to be distinguished from charity. See Habermas, 'Why the Necessary Cooperation Does Not Happen: Introduction to a Conversation Between Emmanuel Macron and Sigmar Gabriel on Europe's Future', *Social Europe*, 20 March 2017.

[252] Habermas (n. 101).

[253] Habermas, 'Citizen and State Equality in a Supranational Political Community: Degressive Proportionality and the *Pouvoir Constituant Mixte*, 55 *JCMS* (2017) 171.

[254] As he puts it, ibid. 173–174:

> It is not as if democracies could preserve their democratic substance unaffected by involvement in the systemic dynamic by digging themselves in behind their national frontiers. Unless a new balance of power is struck between politics and the market, the citizens of national democracies are in danger of being reduced to the status of serfs behind democratic façades. However, at the same time these citizens have good normative reasons to engage in the transnationalization of democracy only under the proviso that their nation-states, in their role as future member states, remain *guarantors of the levels of justice and freedom already achieved*. In the supranational polity, the higher political level should not be able to overwhelm the lower one. (emphasis in original)

[255] Still, as far as the *pouvoir constituant* is concerned, i.e. the EU constitutional framework from the perspective of its democratic legitimacy, the fact remains that treaty change can be initiated only by the Member States, not by the European Parliament.

> (1) The functioning of the Union shall be founded on representative democracy. (2) Citizens are directly represented at Union level in the European Parliament. Member States are represented in the European Council by their Heads of State or Government and in the Council by their governments, themselves democratically accountable either to their national Parliaments, or to their citizens.

More generally, the idea of a *pouvoir constituant mixte* seems indeed a plausible reconstruction of the EU, in particular its democratic legitimacy.[256] Still, the question arises of what this means in practice for law making in the EU, in particular in the field of private law.

At the end of the day, from a Habermasian point of view, the most legitimate way of dealing with the question of the proper distribution of private law making competences between the Member States and the EU seems to be through inclusive (re-) (constitutive) democratic debate in which each of us must be able to partake, in our double capacity as both national and European citizens.[257] Discourse theory being a fundamentally procedural theory, there is little we can say in terms of legitimate substantive outcomes, in our case with regard to the ensuing distribution of contract law making competences. Still, the idea a *pouvoir constituant mixte* seems to match well with an understanding of private law in Europe as a multi-level system, based in part on competences shared by the Member States and the EU, and where perhaps minimum harmonization should be the default with a view to securing the private law justice *acquis* (interpersonal and distributive) already achieved by national law makers. Thus, the Habermasian reconstruction would offer a plausible justification, not only of the general European constitutional framework, but also specifically of the current constitution of European private law. Having said that, it is not clear, from the perspective of the idea of a system of private rights and obligations with a moral core,[258] that a functional competence directed specifically at market building (Article 114 TFEU) should be the proper entrance point for dealing with questions of contract law and contractual justice at the EU level.[259]

D. Transnational Justice

In his critical discourse theory of transnational justice, Forst does not reserve any specific place or attention for the EU. When discussing contexts of justice, he consistently contrasts domestic societies with the global context, without even mentioning the equally transnational, intermediate level of the European context. This is all the more surprising, because if the circumstances of justice in the Rawlsian and Humean sense do indeed 'obtain to an important degree at the global level'[260] as Forst suggests,

256 C. Eckes, 'The Paradox of EU External Relations: Taking Back Control' (inaugural lecture, University of Amsterdam 2018), recently endorsed the idea with a specific focus on European external relations.
257 See Hesselink, 'Democratic Contract Law', 11 *ERCL* (2015) 81, at 123–125.
258 On Habermas's understanding of the system of rights, see also Chapters 2 and 3.
259 Hesselink (n. 122) 410.
260 R. Forst, *The Right to Justification: Elements of a Constructivist Theory of Justice* (2013), at 254.

then this would seem to be the case *a fortiori* at the European level. Specifically, Forst argues for a duty of justice

> as a duty (of those who have suitable means at their disposal and who benefit from existing injustices) to establish a just global structure in which individual members would first of all have fair opportunities to cooperate in developing rules and institutions that would be effective enough to combat (internal and external) political and economic injustices.[261]

A similar duty of justice, it would seem, should exist also—indeed, in particular—at the European level, with regard to the EU, i.e. a duty to establish a just European basic structure.[262]

According to Forst, what is needed is 'a discursive, moral-political construction of co-original principles of local and global justice'.[263] This may well be true. However, to this should be added, in the context of the EU, a similarly discursive, moral-political construction of co-original principles of national and European (and global) justice. For this, we would need, among other things, a critical theory of European injustice and justice in contract.[264] Put differently, the EU should also be a context of justice, i.e. a 'concrete context of justification and responsibility'.[265] In other words, any injustices in the internal market do not just *happen*, they are also *done*. And a contract law for the internal market has to be justified by its authors in justice terms.[266]

8. Concluding Remarks

Should contract law be national, European, or global? The most outspoken and unequivocal answer to this fundamental political question of contract law we find in the nationalist, Europeanist, and cosmopolitan theories. From the point of view of the private law nationalist, there is no reason for contract law to be either European or global, not even in part, let alone entirely. Similarly, for the Europeanist there is no advantage in leaving or making part of contract law become national or global. And private law cosmopolitanism is a similarly maximizing principle: a cosmopolitan's acceptance of a multi-level system, where private law is located at the global level and also partly at the European and national levels, will always be the result of a compromise with other principles (held by others or herself). Thus, in their purest forms, private law nationalism, Europeanism, and cosmopolitanism are mutually exclusive. At the same time it is a fact that none of these three senses of belonging is held generally by everyone. Indeed, as Eurobarometers have shown consistently over the last decades, most Europeans identify both with their respective Member States and with the EU. In the

[261] Ibid. 234.

[262] See Hesselink (n. 122). Similar, it seems, Forst (n. 175), arguing that the requisite institutional form of justification depends on the degree of subjection ('demoi of subjection').

[263] Forst (n. 260) 240.

[264] For a first attempt, see Hesselink, 'The Right to Justification of Contract', 33 *Ratio Juris* (2020), 196.

[265] Forst (n. 260) 257.

[266] In this sense, see Hesselink (n. 122).

face of this reality, one could, of course, still maintain that it is simply true that our own nation should come first, or, on the contrary, that nationalism in Europe was a historical accident that we are now overcoming by (re)discovering European unity, or that in truth we are all world citizens. However, if we believe that the fact of pluralism requires us to move beyond such intransigence, the question is what compromise between the three should be acceptable, or what procedure should be adopted for deciding for a multi-level system of contract law, and how much and which parts should be located at the national, European, and global levels, respectively. It seems that to that question of the distribution of contract law making competences over these different levels, neither of these three principles has an answer other than their respective maximizing claims.

At first sight, a way out of the impasse seems to be the reference to another kind of principle or value, such as justice, freedom (understood as non-interference, as self-determination, or as non-domination), or efficiency.[267] However, here we run into the opposite problem that these principles and values yield much less determinate answers. Indeed, it turns out that for each of them different versions have been proposed that align with nationalism, Europeanism, and cosmopolitanism, respectively. Thus, we find liberal-egalitarians all agreeing that justice should be the key consideration, but then liberal nationalists and Europeanists disagreeing on where egalitarian principles ought to be realized. Similarly, we find civic republicans who argue for demoicracy, i.e. for political deliberation and decision-making in the respective democracies of the Member States, while other civic republicans believe that reinforcing the European Parliament is the only safeguard for preserving freedom as non-domination. And utilitarians disagree even on what should in principle be an empirical matter, i.e. whether a national, European, or global contract law would yield the highest net surplus in terms of economic growth (or the greatest total amount of welfare by another standard, e.g. preference satisfaction). Finally, Habermas underlines the dual origin—the co-originality—of the EU's legation, which means that the EU belongs both to the nations and to the individual citizens of the EU, and that, therefore, the question of what should be done by the EU and what by the Member States should be decided by citizens in Europe in both their capacities, i.e. as a citizen of the Member State and as an EU citizen; however, it is not immediately clear what this means for contract law, not only in terms of outcomes, but even in terms of procedure.[268]

[267] Views on the vertical distribution of law making competences over different levels of government that refer to a different value or principle, are based on the expectation that that different value or principle is best realized at that particular level. In other words, they are conditional upon the plausibility of that expectation.

[268] Similarly, at first sight externalities may seem to constitute a sufficiently neutral reason, in principle, to justify 'moving up' one level of law making, e.g. from the national to the European or from the European to the international (the principle of subsidiarity). However, we immediately run into the practical difficulty of establishing how serious the externalities need to be (i.e. the question of proportionality). For, in a globalized and highly interconnected world virtually any law can be demonstrated to have externalities. This is certainly true for contract law, that may affect people all over the world, via the effect of private international law and by other means. Moreover, it cannot be taken for granted (i.e. remains a matter to be assessed empirically) that moving law making up to a higher, more general level will ensure that more (let alone all) affected persons will get to have a say.

Therefore, the main contribution made by this chapter, perhaps, has been the modest one of providing a better explanation of why and how the question of the Europeanization of contract law has been so divisive and why neither the status quo, nor fully undoing the Europeanization of private law, nor indeed a move fast forward towards a European civil code, seem today to be alternatives commanding widespread support. This brings us to the familiar distinction between more empirical conceptions of legitimacy, referring to the actual support by citizens for their institutions—in our case for contract law and contract law making institutions—and more normative conceptions, emphasizing whether citizens have reason to support their institutions. Perhaps the fact that not only libertarians, liberal-egalitarians, utilitarians, communitarians, civic republicans, and discourse-theorists disagree with each other but are also internally divided, suggests that any change in political boundaries or the smaller versions of it discussed here—i.e. the redistribution of law making competences over the national, European, and global levels (and the connected shifts in sovereignty)—should not be abrupt, but rather take place gradually, in order to keep as many affected citizens on board as possible.

Indeed, if we understand the EU as fundamentally,[269] from its inception,[270] a peace project,[271] and if the only peace that counts is a just peace, then the EU's first concern, with precedence over everything else, including the internal market, should be the prevention of conflict[272]—not only another civil war among European nations,[273] but also less catastrophic forms.[274] This has a number of implications for what the EU should and can legitimately do, both internally and externally. In the first place, the EU cannot pursue policies that are so fundamentally unjust that they put social peace at risk, either between or within its Member States. The governance of the euro, in particular the ruthless austerity politics, and most visibly the Greek crisis seem a case in

[269] This is not an essentialist claim. Prior to the World Wars, a European union would also have been conceivable and peace might then not have been such a central concern. Similarly, today the EU legitimately has additional objectives. In other words, the claim of the EU's peacekeeping *telos* is not even (at least not necessarily) a monistic one. Moreover, the characterization of the EU as a project does not exclude an understanding of the EU as having a demos. It may well be a peace-seeking demos: Europeans coming together, as peoples and as individuals, with a view to overcoming war and preventing other conflicts among themselves.

[270] Recall the first paragraphs of the Schuman declaration (9 May 1950):

> World peace cannot be safeguarded without the making of creative efforts proportionate to the dangers which threaten it. The contribution which an organized and living Europe can bring to civilization is indispensable to the maintenance of peaceful relations. ... Europe will not be made all at once, or according to a single plan. It will be built through concrete achievements which first create a de facto solidarity. ... With this aim in view, the French Government proposes ... that Franco-German production of coal and steel as a whole be placed under a common High Authority, within the framework of an organization open to the participation of the other countries of Europe. The pooling of coal and steel production ... will change the destinies of those regions which have long been devoted to the manufacture of munitions of war, of which they have been the most constant victims.

[271] See e.g. A. Heller, *Paradox Europa* (2019), at 20, and Heller, 'Achtung, Europa!', keynote lecture, Viadrina Institut für Europa-Studien, 10 April 2019.

[272] Art. 3 TEU: 'The Union's aim is to promote peace, its values and the well-being of its peoples.'

[273] This is how Romain Rolland understood World War I. See R. Rolland, *Au-dessus de la mêlée* (1914): 'Le principe dont nous partons est que la terrible guerre qui déchire aujourd'hui le cœur de notre Europe constitue, par définition, une guerre civile.'

[274] Cf. Kocharov (n. 178) ch. 6: 'Union law as the pacifier of conflicts'.

point; the response to the economic consequences of the Covid-19 pandemic risked becoming another tragic example. Secondly, if a plausible claim can be made by the EU to better credentials for peace than its Member States, both individually and collectively before EU was founded,[275] and if the EU's most important mission is peace, then it cannot jeopardize peace by pushing integration in a direction or at a speed that risks undermining that core objective. This calls for prudence not only but most importantly for political institutions that ensure that citizens across the EU are on board and can feel comfortable with the European project, because they have a realistic sense that they are taking part in shaping and steering it.

[275] In 2012, the Nobel Peace Prize was awarded to the European Union, which 'for over six decades contributed to the advancement of peace and reconciliation, democracy and human rights in Europe'.

5
Binding Force and Remedies

1. Introduction

In Chapters 3 and 4 I discussed the question of who are the legitimate or ideal contract law makers in Europe. The next question is: do contemporary normative political theories limit themselves to the procedural question of how contract law can legitimately—or should ideally—come about, or do they also have something to say on what (European) contract law should look like in substance, either ideally or minimally? The first and most fundamental question in this regard is whether there should be any contract law at all. In other words, should contracts in Europe have legally binding force and, if so, what should this binding force entail, in particular in terms of remedies for breach of contract? This question is the subject of the present chapter. Subsequently, in the next two chapters, we will see whether the generally binding force and the general availability of contract law remedies should be qualified or limited by contract law, with a view to protecting vulnerable parties (Chapter 6) or the wider public (Chapter 7), respectively.

A. Self-legislation

Pursuant to Article 1103 of the French Civil Code, 'contracts which are lawfully formed have the binding force of legislation for those who have made them'.[1] The powerful 'force of legislation' formula derives from the Article's famous predecessor, i.e. Article 1134(1) of the 1804 Code Napoléon, which remained almost unchanged by the 2016 reform.[2] Most other recent civil codes no longer specifically proclaim the binding force of contract. Instead, they consider it implied in the system of contract law.[3] Thus, it could be said that all the contract law rules together spell out, in great

[1] Translation by J. Cartwright, B. Fauvarque-Cosson, and S. Whittaker (2016). The French original: 'Les contrats légalement formés tiennent lieu de loi à ceux qui les ont faits'.

[2] On this formula, see Aynès, 'Le contrat, loi des parties', *Cahiers du Conseil Constitutionnel*, no. 17 (2005): 'Un texte fort: à l'époque de la sacralisation de la loi, voici que le législateur dote la convention de la même force que la loi. . . . Le juge devrait être la bouche qui prononce les paroles du contrat, si celui-ci tient lieu de loi. . . . Le contrat est un processus de création de normes; et celles-ci ne présentent avec les normes légales qu'une différence de format. Le contrat fabrique la loi à l'échelle des relations entre individus.' For the US, cf. Fuller, 'Consideration and Form', 41 *Colum. L. Rev.* (1941) 799, at 799: 'When a court enforces a promise it is merely arming with legal sanction a rule or lex previously established by the party himself. This power of the individual to effect changes in his legal relations with others is comparable to the power of a legislature. It is, in fact, only a kind of political prejudice which causes us to use the word "law" in one case and not in the other, a prejudice which did not deter the Romans from applying the word lex to the norms established by private agreement.'

[3] For the common law, see *Paradine v. Jane* [1647] EWHC KB J5: 'when the party by his own contract creates a duty or charge upon himself, he is bound to make it good', that stated strict liability for breach of contract, which was mitigated, subsequently, by *Taylor v. Caldwell* [1863] EWHC QB J1.

Justifying Contract in Europe: Political Philosophies of European Contract Law. First Edition. Martijn W. Hesselink, Oxford University Press. DOI: 10.1093/oso/9780192843654.003.0005

detail, the nature, degree, scope, and modalities of the binding force of contract. Similarly, at the EU level, most directives in the field of contract law simply presume the presence, at least in a general sense, of legally binding force of contract in the legal orders of the Member States.[4] By contrast, the Court of Justice of the European Union (CJEU) explicitly acknowledged the binding force of contract (in a tax law case) as a 'general principle of civil law'.[5]

B. State Coercion

The notion of binding force evokes the coercive nature of contract law: it binds people to their agreements even—indeed, especially—when they themselves no longer wish to honour their contractual engagements. It coerces people to do something they do not want to do. The strength of the legally binding force of contract may be formidable. If a person fails to comply with their contractual obligations then ultimately a bailiff may show up at their residence or place of business, if necessary accompanied by a police officer, and seize their assets. In other words, contract law is a public institution backed up by the state's coercive power. This raises the question of what justifies the legal enforcement of contracts. Why should contracts be legally binding at all? Why is it that we sometimes even speak of 'the sanctity of contract',[6] as if breach provoked divine punishment?

Even if there exist good social and moral reasons for promise-keeping and standing by our agreements, does this mean that contracts should also be enforceable in law? Most of our other moral and social obligations are not legally enforceable at all. If we lie to a friend or deliberately send a tourist in the wrong direction, then normally no legal consequences will follow. So, why is it that if somebody turns their back on their agreement this should become a concern for society as a whole, as organized in the state and its institutions? Why should the state's power be employed to ensure that breaches of contract are remedied? Why should a private agreement be enforced by the public authorities? And why should public resources be employed, via the public enforcement of agreements, to sponsor the practice of contract performance? In summary, it seems we need a specifically political reason why state institutions should interfere in cases of breach of contract.

[4] The CESL proposal also did not stipulate the binding force of contract. By contrast, the DCFR makes it explicit, in Art. II.-1:103 (Binding effect) (1): 'A valid contract is binding on the parties'.

[5] Case C-277/05, *Société thermale d'Eugénie-les-Bains v. Ministère de l'Economie, des Finances et de l'Industrie* (EU:C:2007:440). Cf. Hesselink, 'The General Principles of Civil Law: Their Nature, Roles and Legitimacy', in D. Leczykiewicz and S. Weatherill (eds), *The Involvement of EU Law in Private Law Relationships* (2013) 131.

[6] See e.g. TransLex-Principles, *Principle No. IV.1.2—Sanctity of Contracts*, available at www.trans-lex.org/919000/_/sanctity-of-contracts/ (last visited 27 May 2020). Cf. N. Nassar, *Sanctity of Contract Revisited: A Study in the Theory and Practice of Long-Term International Commercial Transactions* (1995).

C. Legal, Moral, and Social Binding Force

The concept of contractual obligation remains obscure unless we clarify the relationship between social, moral, and legal obligations. Theories that merely concentrate on personal morality or the virtue of corrective justice, without more, do not—and by definition cannot—explain the specifically *legal* binding force of contract. Indeed, many corrective justice and other essentialist theories of contract law do not answer or even address the question. They simply assume, postulate, or bootstrap the legally binding force of contract. Once they have established the morally binding force of a promise or agreement, they seem to take the legally binding force of contract for granted. Thus, they regard breach of contract as not merely a morally but also a legally relevant wrong for which the state must provide remedies.[7] By contrast, political theories, including theories of political morality, can and do explain the legal enforcement of contracts, albeit, as we will see, in quite divergent ways.

D. Rights, Remedies, and Enforcement

There will be no legal response to a breach of contract unless the innocent party exercises one of the remedies provided to her by the law; thus contract enforcement is an instance—indeed a paradigmatic example—of the private enforcement of the law. The relationships between contractual rights, remedies, and their enforcement are both complex and contested, as a matter both of positive law, legal theory, and indeed legal terminology, and are often intertwined.

While entirely standard in common law jurisdictions, the use of the term 'remedies' in civil law jurisdictions is only quite recent. Its diffusion (or transplantation) was a direct consequence of the Europeanization (and wider: transnationalization)[8] of private law discourse and the important influence of common law actors and their thinking in the relevant debates. The publication of the Lando Principles of European Contract Law, with their chapters dedicated specifically to remedies, played a key role.[9] They represented a major conceptual shift. Until then, none of the civil codes used the language of 'remedies' when spelling out the legal consequences of the failure by a party to perform adequately her obligations under a contract.[10] Today, the new French law of contract opts for *sanctions* (which has slightly more punitive, rather than restorative, connotations, in both French and English).[11] However, the official comment

[7] But see A. Ripstein, *Force and Freedom: Kant's Legal and Political Philosophy* (2009).

[8] The shift was preceded (and inspired) by the United Nations Convention on Contracts for the International Sale of Goods (CISG) (1980), with its core sections on 'Remedies for Breach of Contract by the Seller' (Part III, Ch. II, S. III) and 'Remedies for Breach of Contract by the Buyer' (Part III, Ch. III, S. III).

[9] See especially ch. 8 on 'Non-performance and remedies in general' and ch. 9 on 'Particular Remedies for Non-Performance'. See also DCFR, Book III, ch. 3 on 'Remedies for Non-Performance'.

[10] The German law of obligations, even at the reform where breach of duty (*Pflichtverletzung*) became the central organizing concept, did not adopt the language of 'remedies' for breach.

[11] See Art. 1217(2) French Civil Code (new).

refers to these sanctions as *remèdes*, a term which also recurs nowadays in the doctrinal debate.[12]

Judicial injunctions for the specific performance of a contractual obligation are given particular force (and effectiveness) in certain civil law jurisdictions, such as France, Belgium, and the Netherlands, through the civil procedure device of *astreinte*, i.e. the threat of a high penalty on failure to comply with a court order (in this case, the injunction to perform a contractual obligation) payable *to the plaintiff* (and not to the state, as would perhaps be the more natural response to contempt of court).[13] This procedural dimension makes the relationship between contractual rights, remedies, and enforcement—and hence the binding force of contract—even more complex (and contested).

EU law adds further legal complexities with the interplay between the principle of the procedural autonomy of the Member States, the principle of effectiveness (*effet utile*) of EU law, and the right to an effective remedy,[14] in particular the question of horizontal effect, i.e. whether EU legislation can lead to setting aside a national remedy, introducing a new EU remedy, or reinterpreting existing national ones. This question arises in particular in the contractual context, including breach of contract.

In legal theory, at least since Bentham and his pupil Austin, there is the vexed question of how essential the threat of the use of force is to legal obligation,[15] and in political theory, at least since Kant, the relationship between political obligation, force, and freedom has been a central theme,[16] while, as Derrida points out, the idiom of the enforceability of the law or of a contract does not even have an equivalent in French (nor, for that matter, in several other European languages).[17]

[12] With regard to Art. 1217, see *Rapport au Président de la République relatif à l'ordonnance n°2016-131 du 10 février 2016 portant réforme du droit des contrats, du régime général et de la preuve des obligations*: 'Cet article énumère en son premier alinéa l'ensemble des *sanctions* à la disposition du créancier d'une obligation non exécutée.... le dernier alinéa règle l'articulation entre ces différentes *remèdes*' (emphasis added).

[13] As M. Fabre-Magnan, *Droit des obligations*, Vol 1 n. 681 (4th ed., 2016), explains, discussing 'les moyens de pression pour forcer à l'exécution', the nature of the *astreinte* is not compensatory but comminatory, i.e. its purpose is not to compensate the creditor but to pressurise and threaten the debtor and, thus, to force him to perform.

[14] See Art. 47 CFREU (Right to an effective remedy and to a fair trial): 'Everyone whose rights and freedoms guaranteed by the law of the Union are violated has the right to an effective remedy before a tribunal in compliance with the conditions laid down in this Article.' With regard to the Unfair Terms Directive, see Van Duin, 'Metamorphosis? The Role of Article 47 of the EU Charter of Fundamental Rights in Cases Concerning National Remedies and Procedures Under Directive 93/13', 6 *Journal of European Consumer and Market Law* (2017) 190. Similar questions may arise with regard to remedies for breach of contract within the scope of EU law.

[15] On Austin's understanding of law as 'commands backed up by threats', see H. L. A. Hart, *The Concept of Law* (2nd ed., 1994), ch. II. For a neo-Benthamite account, see F. Schauer, *The Force of Law* (2015). Critical, Green, 'The Forces of Law: Duty, Coercion, and Power', 29 *Ratio Juris* (2016) 164, arguing that the force of law consists in three different things, i.e. the force of duty, the force of coercion, and the force of power: 'Coercion is a very important member of the trio, but it is what it is, and not one of the other two things.'

[16] See most recently, Ripstein (n. 7).

[17] J. Derrida, *Force de loi* (1994), at 17, writes (based originally on a presentation addressing an American audience):

> Il y a dans votre langue un certain nombre d'expressions idiomatiques qui m'ont toujours paru assez précieuses pour n'avoir aucun équivalent strict en français.... La première est « to enforce the law » ou encore « enforceability of the law or of contract ». Quand on traduit en français « to enforce the law », per exemple par « appliquer la loi », on perd cette allusion directe, littérale a la

No assumptions are made—nor are any *a prioris* taken—on any of these vexed questions at the outset of this chapter. Rather, these issues will all come back during the discussion. And, as we will see, some of them are more central to some political theories and debates (especially between libertarians and liberals) than to others.

E. Limits to Binding Force

No political theory advocates legally binding force for absolutely any agreement or promise. All theories, even the most libertarian ones, and, for that matter, all existing legal systems, place some limits on the 'freedom of contract', as it is usually called. In particular, agreements may be held unenforceable or invalid either for reasons relating to the way in which they came about ('defects of consent') or because of the nature or content of the contract ('illegality and immorality', 'public policy'). All existing legal systems police contractual consent and contractual content to some extent, albeit such control is supported to quite different degrees, and for rather divergent reasons, by the different political theories. Thus, the questions of the binding force and of the freedom of contract are intimately interrelated, both in theory and in practice. Indeed, the question of whether contracts should ever be legally binding at all is nothing but the most extreme version of the more general question of the extent to which contracts should be binding. And if we know what justifies the binding force of contract then we may also be more confident in answering the question of how far this binding force of contract should extend.[18]

Still, although these two questions are interconnected they can also be distinguished, and it makes sense, for analytical and practical reasons of exposition, to discuss them separately. In this book, two important limits to the freedom of contract will be addressed. Chapter 6 looks at the question of whether the characteristics of the contracting parties, in particular their unequal bargaining power, should influence the binding force of contracts (or of certain clauses therein). Then, Chapter 7 turns to the parties' freedom in choosing the content and object of contractual obligations. This is the question of the extent to which legal systems can legitimately subject the legal enforceability of an agreement to an evaluation of the substantive merits of the content, object, and performances agreed to—and perhaps still accepted—by the parties. In particular, I will discuss how different political theories evaluate the doctrines that exist in most legal systems concerning invalidity for reasons of 'immorality' and 'public policy'.

force qui vient de l'intérieur nous rappeler que le droit est toujours une force autorisée, une force qui se justifie ou qui est justifiée à s'appliquer, même si cette justification peut être jugée d'autre part injuste ou injustifiable.'

[18] However, this does not necessarily mean that finding one or more foundational principles for the binding force of contract will provide us with the key to answering all questions of contract law, as monist theorists expect. For example, it has been suggested that the design of non-mandatory ('default') rules, which constitute the bulk of contract law, may require a very different explanation. This will be discussed in Chapter 8.

F. Differentiation

So far, I have referred to the binding force of contract and to the legal enforcement of contractual obligations in a unitary way. However, in practice the binding nature of contracts is very much a matter of degree. In fact, contract enforcement, in theory and in practice, can come in many different varieties (and combinations). The legal order may coerce contracting parties actually to perform the promised act—or even, in certain countries, commit the act in their stead (e.g. in the case of an obligation to transfer property)[19]—(performance in kind) or it may oblige the contracting parties merely to compensate the damage they have caused, or indeed it can release the innocent party from its side of the contractual bond.

These various different remedies, such as specific performance, damages, withholding performance, termination, and price reduction, have been recognized to different degrees and with a great variety of modalities in different jurisdictions.[20] In particular, there is the traditional difference between the common law jurisdictions, where specific performance is an exceptional remedy, available only where damages are inadequate, and the civil law jurisdictions, where specific performance is not even considered a remedy for breach but a primary right, following directly from the contract, indeed constituting the core of the contractual obligation (*obligatio*, being bound).[21]

EU consumer contract law ensures a particularly strong right to specific performance in consumer sales. If the goods are not in conformity with the contract, the consumer has a right to have the goods brought into conformity by repair or replacement (i.e. specific performance), as the primary remedy.[22] In addition, legal systems also differ on the degree to which the determination of the appropriate response to breach of contract is left in the hands of the parties (e.g. through rescission, limitation, and penalty clauses),[23] or remains for the state to determine, whether *ex ante*, through contract law rules in the code, for example though a hierarchy of remedies or

[19] See e.g. Art. 6:300 Dutch Civil Code.

[20] See H. Beale *et al.*, *Cases, Materials and Text on Contract Law* (*Ius Commune series*) (2019), ch. 22.

[21] See e.g. Art. 241(1) German Civil Code (*BGB*): 'By virtue of an obligation an obligee is entitled to claim performance from the obligor'.

[22] See Art. 3(3), Directive 1999/44/EC on certain aspects of the sale of consumer goods and associated guarantees, OJ 1999 L 171. See also Art. 13(2) and Art. 14, Directive (EU) 2019/771 on certain aspects concerning contracts for the sale of goods, OJ 2019 L 136, which will replace Directive 1999/44/EC as of 1 January 2022. Moreover, the Court of Justice has given a wide interpretation to the consumer's right to repair or replacement, and thereby to the binding force of contract, by ruling that this right is not limited by any exception for 'absolute disproportionality', i.e. a strong disproportion between the benefit of the specific performance (repair or replacement) to the consumer and its cost to the seller. See Joined Cases C-65/09 and C-87/09, *Gebr Weber* and *Putz* (EU:C:2011:396). The Court's reasoning is formulated in terms of strong binding force (at para. 46): 'Even assuming that the non-conformity of goods does not result from the fault of the seller, the fact remains that by delivering goods not in conformity the seller fails correctly to perform the obligation which he accepted in the contract of sale, and must therefore bear the consequences of that faulty performance.' However, Art. 13(2) and (3), Directive 2019/771, introduces an exception for absolute disproportionality and, to that extent, weakens the binding force of consumer sales contracts.

[23] Critical of such clauses, on liberal and democratic grounds, Shiffrin, 'Remedial Clauses: the Overprivatization of Private Law', 67 *Hastings L.J.* (2016) 407: 'private parties should not decide their own cases and the public has a special interest in deciding what remedies are appropriate for breaches of legal duty'.

by subjecting the choice to a proportionality requirement, or *ex post*, through judicial control.[24]

Finally, the binding force itself may be moderated or varied in response to, for example, a radical change of circumstances via doctrines such as *Wegfall der Geschäftsgrundlage*,[25] *eccessiva onerosità sopravvenuta*,[26] *imprévision*,[27] and frustration of contract,[28] which were adopted throughout Europe in the course of the past century. The EU contract law doctrine that releases airlines from the obligation to pay compensation for flight cancellation in the case of 'extraordinary circumstances' is akin to these doctrines.[29] They gained particular relevance when the Covid-19 pandemic, and the responses to it by public authorities, upset the regular performance of a wide range of contracts across the economy.

There is the further question of whether contract enforcement should be monolithic in quite a different respect. As we saw in Chapter 2, there exist many different types of contracts: spot contracts and relational contracts; consumer contracts and commercial contracts; contracts for essential services and contracts for trivial goods; and so forth. This raises the question of whether the binding force (its intensity and modalities) should be the same for all these different types of contracts. And if the answer is negative, then perhaps the reasons for granting binding force are also different, at least in part, depending on the type of contract at hand.

[24] In this respect, the 2016 reform of French contract law constituted a major shift. While the old code enshrined judicial termination (and discretion) as the main principle, today, the new Art. 1224 places extra-judicial unilateral termination on an equal footing. This modernization, which brings the new code in line with other modern European codes, was justified by the legislator with 'economic' (i.e. utilitarian) considerations: 'Cette innovation s'inscrit dans une perspective d'efficacité économique du droit.' (*Rapport*).

[25] The doctrine was adopted by the *Reichsgericht* in the 1920s. At the reform in 2002 it was codified, in § 313 *BGB*.

[26] Art. 1467 Italian *Codice Civile*. The Italian Civil Code of 1942 was the first to codify the doctrine.

[27] See Art. 1195 French Civil Code (new). Cf. the official motivation for the recent French reform that finally introduced provisions on *imprévision* in 2016 (in Ch. IV, S. 1, SS. 1 called 'force obligatoire'). *Rapport:*

> L'article 1195 constitue quant à lui l'une des innovations importantes de l'ordonnance, puisqu'il introduit l'imprévision dans le droit des contrats français ... La France est l'un des derniers pays d'Europe à ne pas reconnaître la théorie de l'imprévision comme *cause modératrice de la force obligatoire du contrat*. Cette consécration, inspirée du droit comparé comme des projets d'harmonisation européens, permet de lutter contre les déséquilibres contractuels majeurs qui surviennent en cours d'exécution, conformément à l'objectif de justice contractuelle poursuivi par l'ordonnance. (emphasis added).

[28] The English doctrine of frustration of contract is interpreted narrowly (*Ocean Tramp Tankers Corp v. VO Sovfracht, The Eugenia* [1964] 2 QB 226). In the recent case *Canary Wharf v. European Medicines Agency* [2019] EWHC 335 (Ch), the High Court ruled that the lease for the premises was not frustrated by the withdrawal of the UK from the EU. Neither the UK's transition from Member State to third country nor the EMA's shift of headquarters from London to Amsterdam constituted a frustrating event. (Subsequently, the case was settled. See Evans, 'EU agency settles Canary Wharf Brexit dispute with WeWork deal', *Financial Times*, 4 July 2019.)

[29] The (autonomous) interpretation of the latter concept in Art. 5(3) Regulation (EC) No 261/2004, establishing common rules on compensation and assistance to passengers in the event of denied boarding and of cancellation or long delay of flights, OJ 2004 L 46, has been the object of profuse litigation before the CJEU. See e.g. Case C-257/14, *Van der Lans* (EU:C:2015:618). The CJEU does not seem to limit the scope of the doctrine to cases where the extraordinary circumstances render proper performance impossible, but also seems to cover, at least potentially, cases of mere excessive onerosity.

G. Withdrawal Rights

More fundamentally, if the laws of the Member States of the EU, as required by EU law, grant consumers rights to withdraw unilaterally from their contracts without having to provide a reason in certain contexts, such as online and off-premises sales,[30] and if, conversely, the EU limits the possibility for service providers to interrupt the provision of certain 'universal services' (water, electricity, the internet) to vulnerable consumers even in the case of breach of contract by the consumer,[31] then shouldn't that make us rethink the whole notion of binding force? Today, should the law still recognize, as a general principle, that contracts have 'the binding force of legislation' for those who concluded them—to cite once again the famous formula from the French Civil Code?

H. The Core Political Question

This brings us back to the core question of this chapter. Should contracts in Europe have legally binding force? And if so, what do we mean by that? As in the other chapters, in this chapter I will critically discuss the answers to our main question provided by different contemporary political theories. And here too it will be seen that the theories will differ not only in the answers provided but also in their understandings of the question, in particular on which aspects of it—and which of the specific sub-questions raised in this introduction—they consider particularly relevant.

2. Utilitarian

A. Party Preference and Mutual Benefit

There is a straightforward utilitarian argument in favour of the binding force of contract. Contracts should be enforced, in principle, because this is likely to make both contracting parties better off, since they both wanted the contract, as evidenced by their agreement, and in the absence of externalities this is all that matters.[32] A society that provides legal remedies in the case of a breach of contract is better off overall, because there is more preference satisfaction in it.[33] Contract enforcement will perhaps not be able to avoid making some people worse off (and therefore will be Pareto inefficient), but at least the winners will gain more than is lost by any losers, compared to a society where the state would not make contracts become legally enforceable. Thus, the general binding force of contract would seem to meet the requirement of Kaldor-Hicks efficiency, which, as we saw in Chapter 2, is the usual standard in cost-benefit

[30] See Directive 2011/83/EU on consumer rights, OJ 2011 L 304 (hereinafter 'Consumer Rights Directive').

[31] See Art. 14 TFEU and Art. 36 CFREU (access to services of general economic interest).

[32] R. Cooter and T. Ulen, *Law & Economics* (6th ed., 2012), at 283; S. Shavell, *Foundations of Economic Analysis of Law* (2004), at 293. On contractual externalities, see Chapter 7.

[33] H. Dagan and M. Heller, *The Choice Theory of Contracts* (2017), at 62, rightly refer to the utilitarian account as 'a collectivist understanding of contract'.

analysis. That this is indeed the case ultimately remains an empirical claim but it is a highly plausible one. In the words of Adam Smith, 'Commerce and manufactures can seldom flourish long in any state . . . in which the faith of contracts is not supported by law'.[34] Therefore, any society where markets play some role in the production and exchange of the goods and services that people value is likely to need some degree of reliable contract enforcement. The existence of certain specific commercial sectors and communities that rely primarily (or even exclusively) on business reputation rather than contract enforcement[35] does not undermine this very basic empirical claim.[36]

Therefore, on a utilitarian account contracts should be enforced because—and to the extent that—the agreement, which normally may be taken as a proxy for the preferences of the parties, may be expected to be mutually beneficial (yield a joint surplus), which, in the absence of externalities, will increase overall happiness, welfare, and preference satisfaction in society. At first sight, there might seem to be a problem with this argument since, although both parties may have wanted the performance of the contract at the moment of its conclusion, this is no longer the case, by hypothesis, when one party fails to perform its contractual obligation and the other seeks a remedy for breach. The latter party will not be made better off, in her own estimation, if the court forces her to specifically perform her contract or to pay damages in lieu of it. It may even be the case that this party will be made much unhappier by the contract enforcement than the plaintiff will be made happier by it. So, why should the parties' *ex ante* preferences be decisive rather than their preferences *ex post*? This brings us to the distinction between fact and rule utilitarianism, which was introduced briefly in Chapter 2. The reason why, for a utilitarian, contracts should be binding is that a world where it is possible to count on the enforceability of contracts is likely to be a world where there is more preference satisfaction than a world in which parties are released from their contractual obligations whenever they happen to have second thoughts. Only when contracts are enforceable, because of a rule that creates contractual rights and obligations,[37] can each party make a credible commitment to the future performance of its side of the deal.[38] As a result, there will be more economic deals, which makes the society better off overall, even though there will always be some deals that leave one party disappointed.

[34] A. Smith, *An Inquiry Into the Nature and Causes of The Wealth of Nations* (1776), Book V, ch 3.

[35] See Macaulay, 'Non-Contractual Relations in Business: A Preliminary Study', 28 *Am. Sociol. Rev.* (1963) 1; Bernstein, 'Opting Out of the Legal System: Extralegal Contractual Relations in the Diamond Industry', 21 *J. Legal Stud.*) (1992) 115; H. Collins, *Regulating Contracts* (1999), ch. 5.

[36] See e.g. Schwartz and Scott, 'Contract Theory and the Limits of Contract Law', 113 *Yale L.J.* (2003) 541, at 546: 'a modern commercial economy can function well with little more than honest courts and a set of enforcement rules. The rest is of second-order importance'.

[37] Cf. the opening sentence of J. Bentham, *Principles of the Civil Code* (1843): 'Every thing which the legislator is called upon to distribute among the members of the community, may be reduced to two classes: 1st, Rights. 2d, Obligations.'

[38] Cooter and Ulen (n. 32) 286.

B. The Theory of Efficient Breach

According to the utilitarian idea of the binding force of contract, therefore, my contractual promise is binding, not because I have a moral obligation to keep my promise, but exclusively because it creates happiness or welfare.[39] A contract or a promise is not in itself a reason for legal obligation. For the binding force of contracts we should not look for facts in the past (those are mere 'water under the bridge'), but to the consequences that the contract enforcement is most likely to have in the future. This also means that contracts should not be enforced in cases where a plausible empirical case can be made that the refusal to grant specific performance of a contract would lead to a net gain in welfare in society. This latter idea constitutes the rationale for the well-known theory of 'efficient breach' that was proposed by Posner and others[40] and became the object of an intense debate in the 1980s and 1990s.[41] According to this theory, contracts should not be specifically enforced—i.e. a party should not be forced actually to perform its side of the bargain—if breach would be 'efficient'. Breach is efficient, on this view, whenever the breaching party could fully compensate its contractual partner and still be better off than it would be if it fully performed its contractual obligation.[42] This may be the case in the presence of either a fortunate contingency (a windfall, e.g. a subsequent better offer made by a third party) or an unfortunate one (a setback, e.g. an unexpected rise in production costs). Thus, if after the conclusion of a contract a more profitable opportunity comes up, for example where a second offer is made on a seller's house which is higher than the one the seller has already accepted, then—the argument goes—the courts should not make an unwilling seller perform his contractual obligations if the seller could compensate the entire damage that his contract partner (i.e. the first buyer) would sustain as a result of the breach, and still be better off by selling it and transferring the property to the second buyer.

However, as others have pointed out, invoking the Coase theorem,[43] in an ideal world without transaction costs inevitably everything (in our example, the house) will always end up in the hands of those who value it most. So, what law makers in the real world should do in order to facilitate efficient allocation is to make sure that transaction costs remain as low as possible.[44] In the example of the house, when the first

[39] Much of the literature follows the American terminology of 'contractual promises' (for the acts, with 'promisor' and 'promisee' for the agents), rather than 'contractual obligations' (for the acts, with 'debtor' and 'creditor' for the agents), which is more often used in Europe, especially on the Continent. The UNIDROIT Principles of International Commercial Contracts introduced the terms 'obligor' and 'obligee' (see at p. 31) to refer to the two sides of a contractual obligation, followed by the Principles of European Contract Law (see e.g. Art. 9:102 PECL, on specific performance). I will use the three sets of terms interchangeably.

[40] See earlier Birmingham, 'Breach of Contract, Damage Measures, and Economic Efficiency', 24 *Rutgers Law Review* (1970) 273.

[41] R. Posner, *Economic Analysis of Law* (1973); more nuanced, R. Posner, *Economic Analysis of Law* (5th ed., 1998).

[42] For Pareto efficiency actual compensation is required. For Kaldor-Hicks efficiency whether or not compensation actually takes place is immaterial (because it only affects distribution); potential compensation suffices. However, in the debate no one actually advocates the no-remedy solution of neither specific performance nor expectation damages.

[43] Coase, 'The Problem of Social Cost', 3 *Journal of Law and Economics* (1960) 1. Critical, R. Unger, *What Should Legal Analysis Become?* (1996), at 24: 'the egregious and elastic category of transaction costs'.

[44] Cf. Coase (n. 43) 15, on transaction costs specifically with regard to contracting.

buyer discovers that there is a second buyer who values the house more than she does, she would presumably resell the house to the second buyer. However, that would require two transactions, whereas if the court refused to order specific performance by the seller to the first buyer then the seller could make the house become the second buyer's property in one single transaction. Two transactions are more costly than one (think of the costs of notaries or solicitors and taxes). So, social waste can be avoided if the law accepts breach by the seller and only allows a claim in damages from the first buyer.[45] However, it may be retorted, in such cases the court will have to determine the damage sustained by the first buyer. And this will be a difficult and potentially very costly task. We may assume that the first buyer valued the house more than the price she paid for it, for otherwise she would not have bought it at all, but how much? What amount of consumer surplus did she anticipate? Markets are generally more efficient than public officials in determining prices, as was illustrated spectacularly by the failure of planned economies. So if we reject the efficient breach theory and uphold the claim for specific performance, then we will make the first and the second buyer sort out among themselves what compensation the first buyer requires for giving up the house. This means that the remedy of specific performance should be awarded after all. However, to this argument there is a new rejoinder: the first buyer and the second buyer both know that a unique gain can be obtained if they reach a deal and they also both know that this benefit can only be obtained if they actually reach an agreement. Under those circumstances, neither of the parties will be prepared to make the first move and yield part of the gain to the other. Game theory suggests that this bilateral monopoly situation may lead to protracted and costly negotiations.[46]

Finally, there is also a wider economic perspective. In addition to the micro-economic gains or losses there may also be macro-economic implications.[47] If contracts no longer create legal entitlements to the actual performance of whatever was bargained for, but only the assurance of being compensated adequately in the case of breach by the other party, it is likely that people will become much less willing to enter the market and conclude transactions. This reasoning may be understood (or

[45] Ulen, 'The Efficiency of Specific Performance: Toward a Unified Theory of Contract Remedies', 83 *Michigan Law Review* (1984) 341. Note that notary fees and taxes do not necessarily amount to social waste: they are likely to make certain people better off (i.e. notaries and those on whom the tax revenue will be spent). Whether there will be social waste depends on whether the potential alternative uses of the resources are likely to be more productive of utility (opportunity costs). This may be less likely in the case of tax revenues (especially in the case of a redistributive tax scheme, as a result of the decreasing marginal utility of money) than in the case of notary fees.

[46] Schwartz and Markovits, 'The Myth of Efficient Breach: New Defenses of the Expectation Interest', 97 *Virginia Law Review* (*Va. L. Rev.*) (2011) 1939, have argued that a contract should be understood as giving the promisor a duty to either perform or compensate (the 'dual performance hypothesis'). Therefore, the party who makes a transfer to the other instead of performing does not breach. Hence, the 'myth of efficient breach'. The idea that contract provides a party with a choice to perform or pay damages goes back to Holmes, but was already dismissed as unrealistic by F. Pollock, *Principles of Contract* (3rd ed., 1881), at 19 (as quoted by P. S. Atiyah, *Essays on Contract* (1986), at 60): 'A man who bespeaks a coat of his tailor will scarcely be persuaded that he is only betting with the tailor that such a coat will not be made and delivered within a certain time. What he wants and means to have is the coat, not an insurance against not having a coat.' Equally critical, Shiffrin, 'Must I Mean What You Think I *Should* Have Said?', 98 *Va. L. Rev.* (2012) 159, at 176: 'It involves attributing to the parties the rather crabbed motives of rational maximizers, an attribution true of some contractors on some occasions but not true of all.'

[47] Friedmann, 'The Efficient Breach Fallacy', 18 *J. Legal Stud.* (1989) 1.

reinterpreted) as an indirect utilitarian argument to the effect that ultimately society has more to gain from granting contracting parties an enforceable right to specific performance.

C. Success or Failure?

Note that this debate, which I have presented in some detail, turns entirely on claims about facts. Both sides advance verifiable hypotheses as to which solution would be most efficient, i.e. welfare enhancing. For neither side is the fact that the seller made a promise and that the second buyer wants to 'steal' the house that the first buyer thought she had already bought decisive or indeed even relevant at all.[48] Similarly irrelevant, from the welfare perspective, is the distribution of the social gain. The question is not whether it would be fair for the first buyer to receive a fair share of the windfall, or whether it is morally acceptable for a seller to turn his back on the buyer, snap his fingers at the bargain, and walk away with an extra profit. From a welfare point of view, the distributional effect is purely incidental. It is a mere side-effect of the most efficient allocation of resources. Unlike under the entitlement theories discussed later, the utilitarian analysis remains entirely limited to the factual question of which system of contract remedies is likely to be most conducive to an increase in social welfare (or, in a more reductive version, social wealth). Applying Rawls's expression to our case, 'it is by this construction that many persons are fused into one'.[49] Indeed, this example of the law and economics debate on efficient breach illustrates very clearly what Rawls meant when he famously pointed out that 'utilitarianism does not take seriously the distinction between persons'.[50] Needless to add that the efficient breach theorem is also on a direct collision course—and vice versa—with the strong right that EU law grants consumer buyers in case of non-conformity of the goods with the contract.[51]

Eric Posner argues that economics has failed to explain contract law.[52] The reason is that there is a mismatch between the degree of specificity required for economic hypotheses to be testable and the level of generality at which contract law rules are formulated. For the same reason—and most relevant here—economics also provides little normative guidance for reforming contract law:

> Models that have been proposed in the literature either focus on small aspects of contractual behaviour or make optimal doctrine a function of variables that cannot realistically be observed, measured, or estimated. The models do give a sense of the factors that are at stake when the decision maker formulates doctrine, and might give

[48] Cf. Barnett, 'A Consent Theory of Contract', 86 *Colum. L. Rev.* (1986) 269, at 281 and 291–292, who speaks of 'efficient thefts'.
[49] J. Rawls, *A Theory of Justice* (1971), at 25.
[50] Ibid.
[51] This was especially true for the CJEU's rejection in *Weber and Putz* (n. 22) of an exception for absolute disproportionality. However, as already mentioned, meanwhile this ruling has been overruled by the EU legislature, with Art. 13(2) and (3), Directive (EU) 2019/771 (n. 22).
[52] Posner, 'Economic Analysis of Contract Law After Three Decades: Success or Failure?' 112 *Yale L.J.* (2003) 829.

> that decision maker a sense of the trade-offs involved, but in the absence of information about the magnitudes of these trade-offs—and the literature gives no sense of these magnitudes—the decision maker is left with little guidance.[53]

This does not mean that the economic theory of contract fails to explain—or that utilitarianism fails to justify—the binding force of contract at the most general level. It can certainly provide a general explanation for the general enforceability of contracts, i.e. for the presence of some remedies in the case of breach of contract. Other things being equal (an important limitation to which we will come back in the next two chapters), there is good reason, it would seem, to enforce contracts simply because they are welfare enhancing. Our society would probably be worse off (in everyone's estimation) if contracts were never legally enforced. As Posner writes: 'A free market can function only if people can trade, and trading almost always requires the making of binding promises. But ... there are many different rules of contract law that will be equally good at enabling people to make binding promises. Specific performance is about the same as damages'.[54] In summary, economic theory does not provide a decisive general argument for or against certain types of remedies, or for or against a right of withdrawal, or on the vexed question of whether core terms should be excluded from unfairness control, but it does provide a plausible argument (and an attractive one, in the eyes of many) for the very general principle of the binding force of contract.

D. Beneficial Practice

In more recent times, a different consequentialist theory (which is utilitarian, in a wider, non-welfarist sense) has gained support. According to this Humean view, the binding force of contract is best explained as the support lent by society to an overall beneficial practice. Hume argued that the obligation to keep a contractual promise is not a natural duty but a conventional one. The idea that the will, or its expression, could by itself create an obligation is as absurd as the Roman Catholic doctrine of transubstantiation. Promissory obligations are a human invention, created in the public interest, in particular of commerce: 'promises have no force, antecedent to human convention'.[55] Except in certain specific communities and sectors of trade, where reputation suffices as a ground for keeping promises and agreements, it is likely (as an empirical matter) that fewer contracts will be concluded if they are not backed up by legal

[53] For a response to Posner's 'trashing piece', see Ayres, 'Valuing Modern Contract Scholarship', 112 *Yale L.J.* (2003) 881, who, however, concedes the potential strength of Posner's 'evolutionary critique' that modern economic analysis of contract law may have run its course.

[54] Ibid. 865.

[55] See D. Hume, *A Treatise of Human Nature: Being an Attempt to Introduce the Experimental Method of Reasoning into Moral Subjects* (1739), Section V (Of the obligation of promises). This view is rejected by Scanlon, 'Promises and Contracts', in P. Benson (ed.), *The Theory of Contract Law: New Essays* (2001) 86, at 87, who argues that social practices and conventions play no essential role in explaining why breaches of promises are wrong.

enforceability. Given that the conclusion and performance of contracts is an overall beneficial practice, this provides a sufficient reason for a society to enforce contracts.[56]

This reading has distinct implications. As Murphy argues, if indeed the point of contract law is to support a beneficial practice of contracting then surely specific performance is the most obvious default remedy and a doctrine of efficient breach becomes difficult to explain. There clearly is a contradiction between the explanation of the binding force of contract as serving the purpose of making it possible for the parties to make credible commitment, on the one hand, and a remedial system that allows (indeed provides incentives for) 'efficient breach', i.e. for reneging that very same commitment, on the other. Since actual performance is what most parties seem to expect, granting specific performance as the standard remedy seems to be the best way to support that practice.[57]

Still, what the conventionalist account has in common with the welfarist account is that they both understand the legal enforcement of contract and its remedial system as being instrumental to the furthering of some social good, rather than as a response to the interpersonal wrong of breach of contract. Murphy writes: 'The first order of business, when thinking about remedies, and rationales for them, is the health of that background practice.'[58] However, against this view Kymlicka argues that utilitarians reach the right outcome for the wrong reason. What is wrong, on the utilitarian view, with breaching promises and contracts is that this undermines the possibility for social cooperation. It is wrong, not primarily towards the promisee or contracting partner, but towards society at large. In the utilitarian account, the wrong done to the specific partner with whom the contract created a special relationship does not play any decisive role. Discussing promises, Kymlicka writes:

> On the rule-utilitarian view, the wrong done in not paying the boy who mowed my lawn is the increased doubts caused in others concerning the institution of promising. But surely that is a misinterpretation. The wrong is done to the boy who had a special claim to the promised money. The wrong is present whatever the long-term effects on others.[59]

Clearly, this criticism applies just as much to the welfarist as to the conventionalist views of contract law, which are both rule-utilitarian in this wide sense.

[56] See the related argument by Durkheim that the division of labour requires contract enforcement: E. Durkheim, *De la division du travail social* ([first published 1930] 5th ed., 1998), at 374: 'En effet, les relations contractuelles se développent nécessairement avec la division du travail, puisque celle-ci n'est pas possible sans l'échange dont le contrat est la forme juridique.' See also Fuller and Perdue Jr, 'The Reliance Interest in Contract Damages' (Part 1 and Part 2) 46 *Yale L.J.* (1936–1937), 52 and 373, at 61: 'When business agreements are not only made but are also acted on, the division of labor is facilitated, goods find their way to the places where they are most needed, and economic activity is generally stimulated.'

[57] Murphy, 'The Practice of Promise and Contract', in G. Klass, G. Letsas, and P. Saprai (eds), *Philosophical Foundations of Contract Law* (2014), ch. 9.

[58] Ibid. 179.

[59] W. Kymlicka, *Contemporary Political Philosophy: An Introduction* (2nd ed., 2002), at 28.

3. Liberal-Egalitarian

A. The Values of Autonomy and Individuality

One very straightforward reason for enforcing contracts could be along the lines that contracts are the expression of the autonomy of the parties. Personal autonomy is a central value or right in various versions of liberalism. It refers to individual self-government, i.e. to living one's life according to one's own reasons and motives, and to making one's own choices while assuming responsibility for them. Although there exist various different liberal conceptions of individual autonomy, what the concept usually refers to in its various versions is a certain ideal of the person.[60] And the general ideal of the autonomous person seems to match well, at first sight, with the nature of contractual obligation as an essentially self-imposed obligation, i.e. as self-legislation.[61] Still, as we will see, not all liberal-egalitarian political theories seem to require contract law as we know it, with its usual remedies.

Even though the law of contract and philosophical speculation about its normative foundations long pre-date the arrival of liberalism,[62] contract law and liberal principles are usually thought to be closely related to one another. Given that contracts, as expressions of individual autonomy, have been of central importance to many liberal political theories, it will not come as a surprise that liberal theories of contract law abound in the contemporary debate. Indeed, beyond their unison rejection of utility (or welfare) as the ultimate foundation of contract, the debate on the normative foundation of contractual obligation sometimes seems strictly intra-liberal. While it is a key objective of this book to broaden our horizons towards other, competing political philosophies of contract law, if we want to do justice to the wealth of contemporary liberal-egalitarian accounts of contractual obligation and critically assess their main differences, inevitably this section will have to be somewhat longer than the others in this chapter. As mentioned in Chapter 1, this will be compensated quite naturally by the fact that other theories claim more space with regard to the questions they deem more important, for example the question of a democratic basis for discourse theory, and the question whether contract law should be national, European, or global for communitarians, as we saw in Chapters 3 and 4.

B. Contract as Self-Authorship

The central idea in the political philosophy of Raz is that individuals should be the authors of their own respective lives and that the state should actively support self-authorship by making available a sufficiently broad range of valuable and attractive alternative ways of life to choose from.[63] Dagan translated this Razian idea into the

[60] G. Dworkin, *The Theory and Practice of Autonomy* (1988), at 3 and 6.

[61] The classical expression of this idea is found in the French Civil Code in (what is now) Art. 1103. See also e.g. Art. 1322 Italian *Codice Civile* (*Autonomia contrattuale*).

[62] On normative contract theory before liberalism, see J. Gordley, *The Philosophical Origins of Modern Contract Doctrine* (1991).

[63] J. Raz, *The Morality of Freedom* (1986), at 424 ff.

claim that the state should provide a suitable range of sufficiently diverse contract types as a way for people to shape their own lives.[64]

Building on Dagan's earlier papers, in *The Choice Theory of Contracts*, Dagan and Heller offer a comprehensive liberal view of contract law.[65] Their main focus is on what contract law is for (its *telos*), in particular the good it can bring, which they argue is individual autonomy, understood as self-determination and self-authorship through choice.[66] As they phrase it in the opening lines of the book, 'as free people, we do not live each on our own island, isolated in perfect independence. We want and need each other to achieve life's worthy goals. Contract law provides a powerful means to achieve these goals. Through contract, we can recruit others to help write the stories of our lives.'[67] Thus, their theory is a teleological one: the aim of contract law is to enhance autonomy, from which it derives its value.[68] Indeed, autonomy is contract law's 'ultimate value'.[69] Because they regard it as the state's task to promote this value (through contract law), their theory is also a perfectionist one in that it is committed to the implementation of an objective account of the human good,[70] in this case the notion that an autonomous (self-determined, self-authored) life is a life better spent.[71]

In their presentation of the choice theory of contract, Dagan and Heller pay remarkably little attention to the binding force of contract. Even if one understands contractual obligation as essentially voluntary and self-imposed, it remains an *obligation* nevertheless, a case of self-*binding*. The closest they come to an explicit reference to the binding force of contract is their recurrent metaphor of enlistment: 'Contract serves autonomy by enabling people legitimately to enlist others in advancing their

[64] Dagan, 'Pluralism and Perfectionism in Private Law', 112 *Colum. L. Rev.* (2012) 1409; Dagan, 'Autonomy, Pluralism, and Contract Theory', 76 *Law Contemp. Probl.*) (2013) 19. Raz's own understanding of contractual obligation is structured rather differently. Starting from the Millian harm principle (see J. S. Mill, *On Liberty* ([first published in 1859] 1974), at 68–69), Raz, 'Promises in Morality and Law', 95 *Harv. L. Rev.* (1982) 916, at 937–938, argues that:

> it follows from the harm principle that enforcing voluntary obligations is not itself a proper goal for contract law. To enforce voluntary obligations is to enforce morality through the legal imposition of duties on individuals. In this respect it does not differ from the legal proscription of pornography. Compensating individuals for harm resulting from reliance on voluntary obligations is, on the other hand, a proper goal for the law.

However, exceptionally it may be the case that expectation damages, or even specific performance, are the most effective way of protecting detrimental reliance. By contrast, Kimel, who subscribes to Raz's version of liberalism and also to the harm principle, nevertheless argues in favour of the expectation interest (D. Kimel, *From Promise to Contract: Towards a Liberal Theory of Contract* (2005), at 102). Still, he also rejects specific performance as the standard remedy, on the basis of the idea (introduced as an interpretation of the harm principle) that the least intrusive measure for preventing harm must be chosen.

[65] Dagan and Heller (n. 33) xi.

[66] Throughout, for Dagan and Heller (ibid) the concepts of 'autonomy', 'self-determination', and 'choice' (which they use interchangeably) refer to the private individual, and not to public autonomy, collective self-determination, and collective or public choice.

[67] Ibid. 1.

[68] See ibid. 40: 'Contract is not worth keeping in and of itself. Rather, its value derives from its contribution to our autonomy, which is valued for its own sake.'

[69] Ibid. 5.

[70] Cf. Wall, 'Perfectionism in Moral and Political Philosophy', in E. N. Zalta (ed.), *Stanford Encyclopedia of Philosophy*, available at https://plato.stanford.edu/entries/perfectionism-moral/ (last visited 28 May 2020).

[71] To this extent, their theory also seems to be a metaphysical one, making claims about objective goods (without, however, addressing meta-ethical questions concerning moral realism *v.* non-realism and cognitivism *v.* non-cognitivism).

own projects, and thus it expands the range of meaningful choices people can make to shape their own lives.'[72] Perhaps the militaristic connotation suggests strong binding force. However, remarkably, their emphasis is not on self-conscription but on enrolling others.[73] They also strongly criticize both libertarian transfer theorists and neo-Kantians for understanding contract law as fundamentally duty-imposing: 'Rather than vindicating existing rights', they write, 'contract law is first and foremost *power-conferring*.'[74] That may well be right as far as their rejection of natural rights is concerned. However, put this way it is also misleading. They emphasize contract law's empowering virtue without clarifying the very specific nature of the power that contract law confers, namely the power to *bind* oneself, i.e. to impose an *obligation* on oneself. In other words, also under choice theory, it seems, contract law is duty-imposing—in the familiar language, contracts remain a source of obligations[75]—even though choice theory understands contractual duties as self-imposed.[76] However wide the range of contract types the parties can choose from,[77] and whichever contract type they autonomously choose, and however self-empowering that choice may be, contract law holds them bound to that choice just as much as when there was only one single type. Nominate contracts are no less binding than innominate ones and the question remains: why? The (implicit) response from Dagan and Heller seems to be: you *bound* (not merely empowered) yourself through your own choice. However, if your past choice is the justification for your present obligation, then how exactly does their liberal theory of contractual obligation differ from a libertarian one, other than by adopting a much more substantive understanding of individual free choice?

Similarly, and somewhat unusually for a contract theory, the book does not discuss remedies for breach of contract. However, in a series of follow-up papers Dagan and Heller remedied this omission. As one of the three principles that they argue contract law in a liberal society must follow, they formulate the maxim that the law 'should

[72] Dagan and Heller (n. 33) 47.

[73] See ibid. 41: 'The value that contract serves is autonomy: law empowers individuals, as Fried argued, to make agreements that facilitate their ability legitimately to enlist one another in pursuing private goals and purposes'. Interestingly, however, the language of enlistment is entirely absent from C. Fried, *Contract as Promise: A Theory of Contractual Obligation* (1981), at 2: instead he speaks of 'joint ventures'. That Fried should shun such instrumental language is not surprising as he emphasizes, at 8, that other persons are not available for us to use, because they share our moral power of self-determination: 'thus to use them as if they were merely part of external nature is to poison the source of the moral power we enjoy'.

[74] Dagan and Heller (n. 33) 37 (emphasis in original). See also ibid. 10: 'despite several decades of sustained effort, rights-based theories of contractual autonomy, and the ambitious reform programs they advance, have failed. It is time to move on'. This sweeping statement also seems to exclude the existence of a general moral right to contract, based on a right to moral autonomy, as proposed, for example, in the various versions of moral constructivism (e.g. by O'Neill or Forst), on which see further later. However, Dagan and Heller, ibid. 40, also write that 'contract law confers the power to create new rights which are crucial to people's autonomy, and therefore contract should not be understood in pure conventionalist terms. It is . . . a convention that a liberal state is *obliged* to establish given its obligation to respect people's autonomy' (emphasis added). It is difficult to see how this obligation can be other than deontological. The autonomy a society ('the state') needs to respect, it seems, is moral autonomy or, as Forst puts it, second-order ethical autonomy, to which we have a moral right. See further later, in Section 7.B.4.

[75] See e.g. the French Civil Code, Title III 'Sources of Obligations', and Art. 1101: 'A contract is a concordance of wills of two or more persons intended to create, modify, transfer or extinguish obligations'.

[76] Where they mention obligations, the emphasis is immediately on their content, and on the state's obligation to supply it. See e.g. Dagan and Heller (n. 33) 47.

[77] This core feature of their theory will be discussed in Chapter 8.

take seriously the autonomy of the parties' future selves'.[78] In their view, this principle is expressed in particular in the law of remedies, in particular in the common law's rejection of a general right to specific performance. 'This traditionally strong preference for monetary recovery is not, as mistakenly presented by some critics, an embarrassment to contract law, but rather a salutary testament to contract law's underlying liberal commitments.'[79] However, both this principle and its specific application seem a little ambiguous. First, the best way to take seriously the autonomy of the parties' future selves is by rejecting the binding force of contracts altogether (at least for executory contracts, as Atiyah called them).[80] That clearly would reduce the autonomy of the parties' present selves, but the point is that choice theory provides no guidance on how to balance the interests of the present and future selves of the contracting parties, which contract law has to undertake, by hypothesis, in the parties' stead. Secondly, once we give up on the right to specific performance it is not clear how liberal principles can justify a right to recover the expectation interest (rather than, say, some fraction of that amount) as the proper trade-off between the autonomy of the contracting parties' present and future selves. Moreover, on its own terms, one would expect the choice theory's approach to remedies to be less monolithic, given its aim to move beyond general contract law. The various contract types could differ, not only in terms of rights and obligations, but also when it comes to their respective remedial regimes. Contract types could vary, for example, between a narrower and a wider range of available remedies—specific performance, damages (reliance, expectation, punitive), right to withhold performance, termination, price reduction—and a more or less free choice among the remedies (hierarchy of remedies or not) depending on the contract type; or between contract types with generous excuses for non-performance (frustration of contract; excuse due to an impediment (*force majeure*) and change of circumstances (*imprévision*)) and stricter liability regimes (*Paradine v. Jane* style);[81] or with and without withdrawal rights. In other words, remedial regimes could be an attractive aspect of the menu of contract types.

As we will see, not all liberal-egalitarians will accept the value of autonomy as a justification for the binding force of contract. In particular, political liberals have difficulty with endorsing the notion that autonomy is a value that the state should promote.[82] As stated previously, among most people in many contexts personal autonomy is probably not a very controversial value (although it is not difficult to see how it could easily conflict with other values).[83] Similarly, many people will regard the free

[78] Dagan and Heller, 'Freedom, Choice, and Contracts', 20 *Theoretical Inquiries in Law* (2019) 595, at 629.

[79] Ibid. 632–633; Dagan and Heller, 'Why Autonomy Must Be Contract's Ultimate Value', 20 *Jerusalem Review of Legal Studies* (2019) 148.

[80] These are contracts creating obligations to perform at some point in time in the future, as opposed to exchanges on the spot.

[81] *Paradine v. Jane* [1647] EWHC KB J5.

[82] Also Gardner, while characterizing himself politically as 'an undaunted 1960s-style liberal', nevertheless rejects the notion that 'the basic architecture of private law is *essentially* an architecture of freedom' (emphasis in original) and argues instead that the most durable features of private law have a more ecumenical set of rationales (J. Gardner, *From Personal Life to Private Law* (2018), at 198–199, discussing the view of Dagan among others).

[83] What is controversial, however, is the degree to which autonomy and individuality should be presumed to exist or to be realistically achievable in our societies today. See e.g. ibid. 199: 'late modern private law has tended to assume that people already possess such autonomy more than it has helped to nurture or protect

choice among contract types as a good. Still, it is not self-evident that it should be the state's task actively to promote this particular value, and to do so through contract law. Therefore, it is not clear that a wide range of contract types should be enforced by the state *in the name of* autonomy, nor that the state should generally enforce contracts, including against people who do not value autonomy as much as Dagan and Heller do, if no other reason were available. In other words, as Rawlsian political liberals will point out, the notion of autonomy as self-authorship on which the theory is based is probably too thick to be reasonably acceptable to all members of a society characterized by reasonable pluralism.[84]

There is more: if the binding force of contracts is good because it enables us to live more autonomous lives than we ever could without binding contracts, then perhaps the implication is that contracts should play an ever more important role in our lives. Instead of depending on choices made by public authorities with regard to health service, education, transport, telecommunications, etc., perhaps we should be able to choose our own health insurer and the terms that best suit us, etc. In other words, if we regard contracts as essentially autonomy enhancing we may be more inclined towards the privatization of public services. Again, people are likely to differ on whether that would be a good idea (and whether it would be so for this reason—welfarists will regard efficiency gains as the decisive ground). Therefore, implementing a liberal perfectionist agenda with the help of contract law, and the general promotion of contractualization (i.e. binding force for ever more contracts) as one of its core tenets may be problematic in a society characterized by a pluralism of worldviews.[85]

C. The Public Justification of Contractual Obligation

1. Autonomy: Political not Ethical

As discussed earlier, the controversial liberal ideal of private autonomy as self-authorship is not available for the liberal neutral state, as the ultimate ground for enforcing contracts because that would make the state become sectarian. As Larmore puts it, 'the liberal state can intervene in an area of social life only if the state has a neutrally justifiable goal that requires that intervention ... This ideal demands that so long as some view about the good life remains disputed, no decision of the state can be justified on the basis of its supposed intrinsic superiority or inferiority.'[86] Clearly, the liberal-perfectionist goal of promoting self-authorship is not neutrally justifiable in this sense, since it is based on the assumption that a self-authored life is a better spent life. Therefore, from the perspective of the political liberalism proposed by Larmore, Rawls, and Nussbaum, among others, it seems, the good of private autonomy cannot provide a sufficient reason for justifying the binding force of contract. Are there

them in securing it'. See also J. Butler, *Precarious Life* (2004), at 27: 'Individuation is an accomplishment, not a presupposition, and certainly no guarantee.'

[84] On thinner (i.e. less ethical and more moral) notions of autonomy, see later in this section.

[85] As Charles Larmore points out, in a pluralist society liberal theories proclaiming ideals of autonomy and individuality have become part of the problem (C. Larmore, *The Morals of Modernity* (1996), at 131).

[86] C. E. Larmore, *Patterns of Moral Complexity* (1987), at 46.

any other reasons, grounded in a conception of justice that is 'autonomous' or 'self-standing' with regard to the various conceptions of the good life prevailing in our pluralist society, that can justify contractual obligation? Put somewhat differently, is the absence of legally binding force of contract incompatible with a society where people mutually respect each other as human beings entitled to equal human dignity?

As we saw in Chapter 2, Rawls's political conception of the person implies that his political liberalism does not address the private person but the public citizen,[87] i.e.—for our context—not the person who concludes contracts but the citizen who deliberates and co-decides on making contract law. In other words, from the point of view of justice as fairness full autonomy is realized by citizens in public life not by private parties in their contracts.[88] As Rawls points out, justice as fairness 'hopes to satisfy neutrality of aim in the sense that basic institutions and public policy are not to be designed to favor any particular comprehensive doctrine',[89] whether utilitarianism, Catholicism, or liberal perfectionism. In particular it 'does not seek to cultivate the distinctive virtues and values of the liberalisms of autonomy and individuality'.[90] Does political liberalism's neutrality of aims entail that it has no reason to offer for the justification of the enforcement of contracts by the state?[91] Rawls himself never claimed that the two principles of justice central to justice as fairness required the enforcement of contracts.[92] It is a controversial question among Rawlsian theorists whether such a right to contract can nevertheless be construed. Different attempts have been made.

[87] J. Rawls, *Political Liberalism* ([first published 1993] 2005), at 29. See also C. Larmore, *The Autonomy of Morality* (2008), ch. 6. See further, Hesselink, 'Private Law Principles, Pluralism and Perfectionism', in U. Bernitz, X. Groussot, and F. Schulyok (eds), *General Principles of EU Law and European Private Law* (2013) 21.

[88] Rawls (n. 87) 77–78:

> Here I stress that full autonomy is achieved by citizens: it is a political and not an ethical value. By that I mean that it is realized in public life by affirming the political principles of justice and enjoying the protections of the basic rights and liberties; it is also realized by participating in society's public affairs and sharing in its collective self-determination over time. This full autonomy of political life must be distinguished from the ethical values of autonomy and individuality, which may apply to the whole of life, both social and individual, as expressed by the comprehensive liberalisms of Kant and Mill.

[89] Ibid. 194.

[90] Ibid. 200.

[91] Towards the end of his life Rawls himself became disillusioned with the welfare state and favoured more radical left-wing politics, believing that just liberal principles 'could only be achieved in either "a property-owning democracy" characterized by universally high levels of education and "the widespread ownership of productive assets", or in a market-socialist regime' (Rogers, 'John Rawls: A Leading Political Philosopher in the Tradition of Locke, Rousseau and Kant, He Put Individual Rights Ahead of the Common Good', *The Guardian*, 22 November 2002). The latter, especially, might require only a comparatively minimal role for binding force of contract.

[92] The role of the institutions that belong to the basic structure of society is, according to Rawls, to secure just background conditions for individual transactions and agreements, i.e. (among other things) contracts (see Rawls (n. 49) 265). This suggests that Rawls presumed that in a just society there will at least be some enforceable contracts since otherwise it is not clear what justice would provide a background for, or, put differently, whether there would be anything in the foreground. Another way of looking at this could be to focus on the reconstructive aspect of Rawls's theory. His theory is meant for our Western democratic societies, not for every society. Perhaps we should assume that Rawls understands his theory as meant as an external test for the justice of institutions in *such a society*, i.e. a society with some form of democracy, market economy, and enforceable contracts, which does not mean that different societies, without binding force of contracts are, for that reason and to that extent, unjust.

2. Contracts and Promise Keeping

The question here is not whether in a sufficiently just society contract law has to comply with principles of social justice—that contentious question will be discussed in Chapters 6 and 7—but whether a society, in order to be just (i.e. in order to comply with the principles of justice) needs to have a system of contract law. Under justice as fairness, a society may be under a duty to create new institutions when the basic structure of society is unjust for the reason that it is incomplete. This seems to follow from what Rawls calls the 'natural duty to support and to further just institutions' pursuant to which we have to 'assist in the establishment of just arrangements when they do not exist'.[93] However, this does not answer, but merely raises, the question of whether the basic structure of a society without a law of contract would be incomplete for that reason. According to Rawls, a society is not unjust merely if it lacks the conventional practice of promise-keeping.[94] But if there is such a practice and its convention is just, then the principle of fairness requires that (in the absence of circumstances justifying breach) one keep one's promise. Therefore, to the extent that contractual agreements contain promises, as defined by a prevailing convention, then, according to Rawls, we are under a moral obligation to keep contractual promises as well. However, this still does not mean that justice also requires the public enforcement of contracts, let alone that it should do so via the remedies of expectation interest or specific performance. Therefore, Rawls's account of promising does not imply an account of the legally binding force of contract.[95]

3. Contract Enforcement as Distributive Justice

In a famous article in the 1930s, Fuller and Perdue questioned the naturalness of the remedy of expectation damages. They pointed out that when we award damages for loss of profit, 'we "compensate" the plaintiff by giving him something he never had' and that 'the loss which the plaintiff suffers (deprivation of the expectancy) is not a datum of nature but the reflection of a normative order'.[96] Indeed, they argued, in passing from compensation for detrimental reliance to compensation for loss of profit 'we pass from the realm of corrective justice to that of distributive justice'.[97] From this perspective, depending on the principles of distributive justice, to award expectation remedies (expectation damages and specific performance) to be paid by a poor defendant to a rich plaintiff might be considered problematic, while the case would be entirely different if the remedy was mere reliance protection. Would a legislator, generally or in certain cases, be allowed to opt for reliance protection only? Or would that (i.e. non-distribution) be problematic as a matter of distributive justice? Here we see another potential road through which binding force (if it protects the expectation interest) could be justified: it might be required as a matter of distributive justice. However, it is not clear what kind of theory of *distributive* justice would *require* (as opposed to merely permit) the legally (as opposed to merely morally) binding force of contract

[93] Rawls (n. 49) 293–294.
[94] Ibid. 303–304.
[95] Whether it requires accommodation is a separate question that will be addressed later, in Section 3.D.
[96] Fuller and Perdue Jr (n. 56) 53.
[97] Ibid. 56.

through the remedies of expectation damages or specific performance. Under such a theory, a society (or its basic structure) would be (*pro tanto*) a *distributively unjust* one if it refused expectation damages or specific performance in the case of breach of contract. Justice as fairness does not seem to be such a theory of justice, as nothing in the two principles of justice suggests that they require such a binding force of contract.

4. Maximum Justice

A variant to this approach would be to regard both or one of the Rawlsian principles of 'justice as fairness' as maximizing principles. If the difference principle, enshrined in Rawls's second principle of justice, requires that the position of the least well-off be maximized, this may well require the kind of economic growth that can only be obtained by markets that depend on contract enforcement. However, it has been argued convincingly that the Rawlsian difference principle should not be understood as a maximizing principle.[98] Therefore, under justice as fairness, such an instrumental need for contract enforcement does not seem to exist. Indeed, Rawls pointed out more than once that justice as fairness is compatible with socialism.[99] Similarly, if the first principle required maximal liberty, it could be argued, then maybe it should also maximize the self-respect enhancing protection of personal property, which then arguably (as discussed next, in Section 3.C.5) should include a right to transfer property as well, and hence a right to contract. However, Rawls made it very clear, in response to criticism from Hart,[100] that the first principle is not a maximizing principle either. It merely requires an *adequate* set of basic liberties.[101]

5. Basic Liberties

According to Kymlicka, the entire distinction between political and comprehensive liberalism is overstated. He writes: 'Both are committed not only to public rights, but to ensuring the conditions in private life needed to actually exercise these rights. Both are committed, in other words, not only to the legal recognition of liberties, but also to enabling their exercise.'[102] Leaving to one side the question of whether this would necessarily undermine the idea of political liberalism,[103] if this is true, as it seems to be, and if owning private property is one of the basic liberties, as Rawls himself claims, then Rawlsian political liberalism might indeed require some legally binding force of contract, simply because without a regime in place that ensures the enforceability of contracts people are not (or are insufficiently) enabled to exercise their private property right.

Kordana and Tabachnick have made a similar point, arguing that a 'right to contract', i.e. the availability of at least some contract options, follows from Rawls's first

[98] Scheffler, 'Distributive Justice, the Basic Structure and the Place of Private Law', 35 *OJLS* (2015) 1.
[99] Rawls (n. 49) 228.
[100] Hart, 'Rawls on Liberty and its Priority', 40 *University of Chicago Law Review* (*U. Chi. L. Rev.*) (1973) 534.
[101] Rawls (n. 87) 291 and 331.
[102] Kymlicka (n. 59) 239.
[103] It would still be meaningful, and morally relevant, it seems, to distinguishing between different ways in which the main institutions of a society can address a person (and vice versa), and the limitations this may entail for political justification, especially of its laws, including—most relevant here—the law of contract.

principle of justice, i.e. the principle according to which each person is to have a right to equal basic liberties.[104] These basic liberties are understood by Rawls as the political liberties that are necessary for participating, on an equal footing, in setting up and maintaining fair institutions. According to Rawls, these liberties include a right to at least some personal property, because without any individual property citizens are likely to lack the material bases for self-respect that are needed to participate in the political process.[105] Kordana and Tabachnick argue that from the inclusion of personal property in the set of basic liberties, it follows logically that a 'right to contract', understood as 'having at least some contract options open', should also be included. For, what does a personal property right (as a basis for self-respect) amount to if it includes only a right to use and not also a right to alienate one's property and exchange it for something else?

However, as Kordana and Tabachnick, point out, nothing very specific follows from the recognition, as a matter of justice, of some freedom—connected with some binding force—of contract. Clearly, the first principle does not require any specific contract rights or remedies. Those are reserved, they argue, entirely for the second principle.[106] In particular, the first principle of justice would not necessarily demand the recoverability of expectation damages or specific performance as remedies for breach. From the perspective of the first principle of justice, especially the right to own personal property which, on a minimally substantive understanding, would include some right to effective alienation of that property, it does not follow that these strong remedies are required. In any case, it does not seem to demand the enforcement of wholly 'executory' (Atiyah), i.e. or merely 'obligatory' (civil law) contracts. If this is true, then a full system of contract law would not be required under Rawlsian justice after all. A sufficiently just societycould, then, still live with 'the death of contract' and limit itself to sanctioning past (actual) exchanges (via property law and 'real' agreements) and, for the case of promises or agreements for future performances, protecting the reliance interest through non-contractual liability (tort and restitution).[107] And in any case, it would be compatible both with the endorsement and the rejection of all the remedial choices made by EU contract law, including withdrawal rights and a strong right to specific performance (repair or replace) for consumers.

6. Contract as Fairness

Klijnsma also argues that Rawlsian justice as fairness requires the presence in a just society of some form of contract law.[108] However, in his reading of Rawls's theory—in contrast to the one proposed by Kordana and Tabachnick—the binding force of contract (i.e. the need for some contract enforcement) does not follow from the principles of justice, but from a characteristic of the kind of citizens who could accept the principles as political principles in an overlapping consensus. Under the thin conception

[104] Kordana and Tabachnick, 'Rawls and Contract Law', 73 *Geo. Wash. L. Rev.* (2005) 598.

[105] Rawls (n. 49) 53.

[106] This may be incorrect. As Klijnsma argues, the horizontal effect of fundamental rights may be (also) a first principle matter. See later in this section.

[107] See G. Gilmore, *The Death of Contract* ([first published 1974] 2nd ed., 1995), at 995.

[108] J. Klijnsma, *Contract Law as Fairness: A Rawlsian Perspective on the Position of SMEs in European Contract Law* (2014), at 62–63; Klijnsma, 'Contract Law as Fairness', 28 *Ratio Juris* (2015) 68.

of the person adopted by Rawls, these are individuals with two moral powers, i.e. a capacity for a sense of justice and for a conception of the good.[109] According to Klijnsma, the binding force follows from the first moral capacity, i.e. a capacity for a sense of justice. As a result, the binding force of contract remains entirely *subject to* the principles of justice, both the first and the second principle. This means, of course, that the principle of binding force required by justice as fairness can only be very general; it leaves open all the familiar questions that an actual legal system has to face when it tries to formulate a system of contract law, and which all remain subject to the principles of justice.[110] In other words, on this view the question is not whether a just society should enforce contracts, but rather whether a society constituted of persons who cannot conclude any legally binding contracts can still be regarded as the kind of 'well-ordered society' to which the principles of justice are meant to apply and give normative guidance.

7. The Capability to Contract

Nussbaum presents her version of the capabilities approach as an ideal, partial theory of justice. It is an ideal theory grounded in human dignity in that it prescribes a set of 10 central capabilities every human being is entitled to.[111] It is partial because it requires only a threshold level of capability fulfilment, as a social minimum, and remains agnostic about what should happen beyond the threshold level.[112] Nussbaum situates her theory of justice within the Rawlsian frame of political liberalism, as a competitor to Rawls's own theory of justice as fairness, claiming that an overlapping consensus could be reached on the canon of core capabilities, or a version of it, that should be ensured by institutions, in particular the basic structure of society, or, as she puts it, the responsibility-bearing structure.[113]

Does Nussbaum's capabilities approach include or require a right to contract? It is not clear that a right to the legal enforceability of private agreements, or the binding force of contract as a general principle, would necessarily figure among the minimum core social entitlements required for 'truly human functioning' in a life with human dignity.[114] In the list of 10 'central human capabilities' she proposes,[115] and which is

[109] Rawls (n. 87) 19.

[110] This does not follow necessarily, since the principles of justice apply only to those institutions that are part of the 'basic structure of society'. However, Klijnsma argues separately that contract law is indeed part of the basic structure and that, therefore, both principles of justice apply to contract law.

[111] M. C. Nussbaum, *Women and Human Development: The Capabilities Approach* (2000).

[112] Ibid. 6.

[113] Ibid. 5; M. C. Nussbaum, *Frontiers of Justice: Disability, Nationality, Species Membership* (2006), at 311. Brooks, 'Capabilities, Political Liberalism and Private Law', 104 *Archiv für Rechts- und Sozialphilosophie* (2018) 556, at 569, argues that re-stating Rawlsian primary goods as capabilities 'offers a more robust perspective from which to consider the private law in light of political liberalism than currently available from Rawls'. However, he discusses 'the private law' only quite generally, without addressing any specific branch, basic principle, or doctrine, such as the binding force of contract. Moreover, his claims that 'a sphere of private law helps enable the flourishing of each citizen's two moral powers by providing a space for their individual development' and that 'one important link between political liberalism and private law is that the latter can foster the exercise of our moral powers and development of individual freedom', suggest that his re-reading of primary goods as core capabilities expresses a much thicker conception of the good life, that would seem to turn political liberalism into a comprehensive doctrine.

[114] Nussbaum, *Frontiers of Justice* (n. 113) 74, borrows the phrase from Marx.

[115] Ibid. 76–78; Nussbaum (n. 111) 78–80; M. C. Nussbaum, *Creating Capabilities* (2013) at 33–34.

meant to provide 'the underpinnings of basic political principles that can be embodied in constitutional guarantees',[116] she lists, as number 10, 'control over one's environment', defined, sub B ('material'), as 'being able to hold property (both in land and movable goods), and having property rights on an equal basis with others'. Arguably, and in analogy to the argument made by Kordana and Tabachnick with regard to Rawls's two principles of justice discussed earlier, in Section 3.C.5, the capability to hold property and to have property rights also includes a right to alienate property since the ability to hold property would be meaningless unless it also included the ability to sell whatever one owns (or at least some of it) on to others.

In addition, moving from ideal to non-ideal (or partial compliance) theory,[117] Tjon Soei Len argues that in the world we live in people depend on market access for their capabilities and that, therefore, the state should ensure the legally binding force of contract, i.e. the public enforceability of market transactions.[118] Anderson made a similar point. In her view, to be capable of functioning as an equal citizen in a democratic state—which, she argues, is the point of justice—includes the capability to participate in the economy (which she understands as being wider than the mere market). And this, in turn, requires, among other things, 'the right to make contracts and enter into cooperative agreements with others'.[119]

However, as we will see in Chapters 6 and 7, from the capabilities point of view, the more important point is that contractual enforcement has to be selective.[120] In particular, since contract enforcement can be both capability enhancing and capability depriving, it has to meet standards of minimum contract justice (informed by the central capabilities as a standard for minimum justice), which should be understood not as external to contractual relationships but as constitutive of them.[121] Most relevant here, the nature of the legally binding force of contract and its implications in terms of remedies (not only remedies for breach, but also e.g. a right of withdrawal), either in general or in specific contexts,[122] should similarly be subject to the standard of minimum justice immanent to contract law.[123]

[116] Nussbaum (n. 111) 74.

[117] L. K. L. Tjon Soei Len, *Minimum Contract Justice: A Capabilities Perspective on Sweatshops and Consumer Contracts* (2017) focuses explicitly on partial compliance, leaving to one side whether under ideal conditions all human beings should a have right to contract, and addressing the question of whether such a right can be construed for human beings whose core capabilities depend to a large extent on market access.

[118] Ibid. 46. See also Tjon Soei Len, 'Equal Respect, Capabilities and the Moral Limits of Market Exchange: Denigration in the EU Internal Market', *Transnational Legal Theory* (2017) 1.

[119] Anderson, 'What Is the Point of Equality?', 109 *Ethics* (1999) 287, at 318.

[120] Indeed, ultimately Tjon Soei Len does not make a normative argument for binding force, but rather takes it as an empirical premise of her partial and non-ideal theory of minimum justice in contract. See Tjon Soei Len (n. 117) 50.

[121] Ibid. 54. See also Deakin, '"Capacitas": Contract Law and the Institutional Preconditions of A Market Economy', 3 *ERCL* (2006) 317, who argues that it is the task of contractual regulation 'to protect and enhance the capability of the individual, understood as the substantive freedom to realise, through participation in the market, a range of desired end-states and activities'.

[122] For the context of services, see Tjon Soei Len, 'Consumer Protection, Sexual Services and Vulnerability: Exploring Social Justice in European Contract Law', 11 *ERCL* (2015) 127.

[123] According to Nussbaum the 10 capabilities on her list cannot be balanced and traded-off against one another. This follows from their incommensurability and from the fact that hers is an ideal theory about the threshold level of these capabilities that the state should provide each citizen with as a minimum. Cf. Robeyns, 'The Capability Approach' in E. N. Zalta (ed.), *Stanford Encyclopedia of Philosophy*, at 25, available at https://plato.stanford.edu/entries/capability-approach/ (last visited 29 May 2020). See Nussbaum (n.

8. Mine and Thine

Ripstein offers a strongly Kantian reading of Rawls. In particular, he ascribes to Rawls's theory of justice the consequences that follow from Kant's theory of right.[124] Ripstein underlines that the Kantian strategy for legitimizing the enforcement of rights, including contractual rights, is of a public nature. A Kantian and Rawlsian perspective is a public perspective: 'The plaintiff is asking the court to grant her a remarkable power: the power to exact a claim against the defendant's resources, and thus to interrupt the defendant's power to use those resources as he or she sees fit.'[125]

According to Kant, under natural law the borderlines between your equal freedom and mine, and between what belongs to me and what to you (*Mein und Dein*) follows from pure practical reason, i.e. from *a priori* principles, notably the categorical imperative.[126] However, if we move from the state of nature to a civil condition, Kant says, we need 'public laws' of 'private right', i.e. a system of private law, to sort out disputes concerning what is mine and what is yours.[127] The state is both allowed and required to determine what belongs to whom, because if the state fails or refuses to do so, the result will be that the strongest person will prevail; weaker parties will be at the mercy of the stronger ones, which is a condition of heteronomy, not of equal freedom.[128] Ripstein refers to Rawls's 'basic structure' as the 'coercive structure'.[129] He explicitly argues that state coercion in enforcing private rights is not heteronomous but autonomous: we impose the binding force of contract on ourselves.[130] Following Kant, Ripstein finds the justification of the binding force of contracts in voluntary agreement.[131] The united will of the parties—their *consensus ad idem*, not a mere correspondence of promises or concurrence of expressed preferences—justifies contractual enforcement. Contracts are 'arrangements through which separate persons get together to vary their respective obligations'.[132] And since arrangements between private persons are expressions of their respective freedom the enforcement of contracts is consistent with that freedom.[133]

111) 81: 'The list is, emphatically, a list of *separate components*. We cannot satisfy the need for one of them by giving a larger amount of another one. All are of central importance and all are distinct in quality.' (emphasis in original). However, in non-ideal theories such as the one proposed by Tjon Soei Len, weighing and trade-offs among different capabilities as components of minimum contract justice seems inevitable. The problem is akin to those encountered in case of conflicting fundamental rights, especially in horizontal disputes such as contract cases.

[124] Ripstein, 'Private Order and Public Justice: Kant and Rawls', 92 *Va. L. Rev.* (2006) 1391, at 1400, footnote 25, is well aware that such a strongly Kantian reading of Rawls is controversial.

[125] Ibid. 1414.

[126] I. Kant, *Groundwork of the Metaphysics of Morals*, ([first published 1785] 2012); I. Kant, *The Metaphysics of Morals* ([first published 1797] 1996).

[127] Kant, *The Metaphysics of Morals* (n. 126) 6:256–6:257.

[128] Ibid. 6:312.

[129] Ripstein (n. 124) 1437; Ripstein, 'Liberty and Equality', in A. Ripstein (ed.), *Ronald Dworkin* (2007), at 82–108 and 106, footnote 20.

[130] Ripstein (n. 124) 1429. Surprisingly, Ripstein does not refer, in this regard, to Habermas's argument based on co-originality of private and public autonomy (discussed later), which Habermas explicitly derives from Kant.

[131] Ripstein (n. 7) ch. 5.

[132] Ibid. 112.

[133] Ibid. 112.

Contract as agreement, as a meeting of the minds, or as a bilateral juridical act expressing both parties' consent, is fully in line with orthodox contract doctrine in countries belonging to the civil law tradition, where American-inspired reference to contract as promise has always seemed descriptively and analytically beside the point. However, it is not clear that the analysis brings us much further in justifying contractual obligation in societies such as our own, which are characterized, as Rawls puts it, by the 'fact of reasonable pluralism'.[134] The reason is that thus the justification of the binding force of contract ultimately depends on its consistency with freedom. Here we run into the same problems as we saw with regard to liberal-perfectionist theories of contract as choice, discussed earlier, in Section 3.B, and the libertarian ones of contract as consent, that we will see later, in Section 4.C. It is true that Kant's and Ripstein's concepts of freedom are different from those of Dagan and Heller, and Nozick and Barnett, respectively. Ripstein understands freedom neither as self-authorship or self-determination (positive freedom) nor as non-interference (negative freedom), but as 'independence', i.e. as being one's 'own master'.[135] However, whether that notion refers to a value, a conception of the person, a comprehensive doctrine, or an ontological postulate, it is based on a controversial truth of the kind that, in a society characterized by the fact of reasonable pluralism and committed to a non-metaphysical conception of justice,[136] will have difficulty in justifying generally applicable laws.[137] Moreover, also on its own terms the argument seems flawed, because it is essentially definitional. The question still remains why consent only and always would make an arrangement become consistent with freedom as non-domination.[138] Ripstein does not explain why other factors could not also make the contractual arrangement become non-dependent or why certain consensual acts could not in fact nevertheless be dependent.

9. Contract Law in a Regulatory State

In a series of papers, Bagchi situates contractual obligations broadly within the Rawlsian frame of political liberalism.[139] For her, there is no doubt that private law is 'among the pillars of the basic structure of society'.[140] However, her argument is more wide-ranging. She explores the rightful place of contract law in a liberal state. Bagchi argues that a liberal regulatory state has two competing interests in contract regulation, i.e. promoting the justice of public institutions and allowing space for private

[134] Rawls (n. 87) 3.

[135] Ripstein (n. 7) 5 and *passim*.

[136] See Rawls, 'Justice as Fairness: Political Not Metaphysical', 14 *Philosophy and Public Affairs* (1985) 223.

[137] In the same sense, Scheffler (n. 98) 19: 'Ripstein's account is instructive and appealing, although it provides a heavily Kantian interpretation of Rawls's theory, and one that I suspect Rawls himself would have seen as relying, to a degree he wished to avoid, on a particular comprehensive doctrine.'

[138] Ripstein (n. 7) 42, reserves the term 'domination' for the wrong of interfering with someone's freedom as independence.

[139] Bagchi, 'Distributive Injustice and Private Law', 60 *Hastings L.J.* (2008) 105; Bagchi, 'Separating Contract and Promise', 38 *Florida State University Law Review* (2011) 709; Bagchi, 'Contract as Procedural Justice', 7 *Jurisprudence* (2016) 47; Bagchi, 'The Political Morality of Convergence in Contract', 24 *ELJ* (2018) 36; Bagchi, 'Interpreting Contracts in a Regulatory State', 54 *University of San Francisco Law Review* (2020) 35–86.

[140] Bagchi, 'Interpreting Contracts in a Regulatory State' (n. 139). See also Bagchi, 'Distributive Injustice and Private Law' (n. 139); Bagchi, 'Distributive Justice and Contract', in G. Klass, G. Letsas, and P. Saprai (eds), *Philosophical Foundations of Contract Law* (2014) 193.

moral agency. Her core claim is that 'a liberal state plausibly responds to the competing moral demands that it faces by only conditionally and partially delegating its authority over transactions to the parties to exchange. That is, private parties share authority over their transactions with the state, and private parties are the junior partners in this arrangement.'[141] It is not entirely clear how she understands moral agency in this context and how well her understanding fits with the Rawlsian frame. If we understand moral agency as the ability to make moral judgements about what we owe to each other, to distinguish right from wrong, and to act on the basis of those judgements, then it is not clear that contracting and state enforcement of contracts is necessary to ensure moral agency in this sense. What it might do instead is to further ethical agency. We can define ethical agency as the ability to make ethical judgements about the good life, to distinguish a good from a bad life, and to act on the basis of those judgements. Clearly, contract enforcement furthers—indeed seems indispensable to—certain conceptions of the good life, in particular those according to which a life goes better to the extent that it is self-authored. However, it is not clear, at least within the Rawlsian frame, that it should be the task of the state to promote us living such lives, rather than other ways of life, and certainly not that such a task should be entrenched in the basic structure of society.[142] Indeed, Rawlsian political liberalism is based on a political conception of human agency that, while being morally grounded, addresses us only as citizens.[143] Still, as we saw, Rawls understands a citizen, i.e. 'a normal and fully cooperating member of society',[144] as a person having two moral powers. While, as we saw, Klijnsma derives the binding force from the first moral power, i.e. a capacity for a sense of justice, Bagchi's notion of 'moral agency' can perhaps be understood as an interpretation of the second moral power, i.e. a capacity for a conception of the good.[145] The idea would be, not that the binding force of contract is indispensable for living a self-authored life, as liberal perfectionists such as Dagan and Heller would have it, but that it is impossible to pursue any conception of the good (including one that rejects self-authorship as a value) unless the state will enforce contracts in principle.[146]

A distinct feature of Bagchi's liberal theory is that it is an imperfect procedural theory of justice in contract.[147] While pure procedural theories understand a promise (or corresponding declarations of will, in the civil law expression) as a necessary and sufficient requirement for contractual obligation, without any regard, in principle, for the outcome (*qui dit contractuel dit juste*), and while perfect procedural theories regard contractual agreement as the best proxy for an exogenous standard (typically,

[141] Bagchi, 'Interpreting Contracts in a Regulatory State' (n. 139).

[142] As we saw earlier, in contrast to comprehensive liberalism, political liberalism is agnostic about the application of liberal principles beyond the basic structure of society, and also rejects, for political purposes, i.e. as far the basic structure of society is concerned, anything going beyond the narrow (or 'thin') political-liberal conceptions of the person (as a citizen with two moral powers) and of the good life (having access to primary goods). On the distinction, cf. Lewin, 'Liberalism, Comprehensive vs. Political', in J. Mandle and D. Reidy (eds), *The Cambridge Rawls Lexicon* (2014), at 447.

[143] See Rawls (n. 87) 109: 'The moral agent here is the free and equal citizen as a member of society, not the moral agent in general.'

[144] Ibid. 18.

[145] Ibid. 19.

[146] That would bring her view quite close to Forst's idea of a moral right to ethical autonomy, which will be discussed later.

[147] Bagchi, 'Contract as Procedural Justice' (n. 139).

welfare), which cannot be improved upon by another procedure (such as judicial intervention), imperfect procedural theories assume that the determination of contractual obligation by the parties themselves inevitably will be only one part of the attempt to ensure sufficiently just outcomes.[148] The implication is that a liberal state committed to justice has a task in implementing background duties, notably including duties of justice. These background duties are immanent to existing legal norms: 'The state has already backed them with its political authority. Voluntary commitments in contract are undertaken in the shadow of these "political" duties.'[149] Put differently, the conditional delegation of authority over their contracts to private parties gives states only content-dependent reasons for enforcing contractual obligations.[150] Put differently again, on this view the legally binding force of contract law is always conditional upon interpersonal and distributive justice.[151]

10. Justice in Transactions

As we saw, Fuller and Perdue argued that the law of contract, by awarding expectation damages as compensation for breach, gives the plaintiff something they never had. Benson addresses this criticism head on, arguing that through the conclusion of a contract, by mutual assent, the parties transfer ownership rights to one another.[152] In other words, he understands contract formation as a mode of acquisition.[153] As a result, any breach of a contractual obligation becomes an interference from the 'promisor' (the obligor) with the right of the 'promisee' (the obligee), and, consequently, expectation remedies (i.e. specific performance, expectation damages) do nothing more than to correct that injury by compensating for the loss resulting from the interference. Benson writes: 'Breach becomes the equivalent of attempting to "take back" or "withhold" what, as a matter of rights, one has *already* given over to the other. It interferes with the other's ability to take or receive in fact what, in accordance with the terms of the agreement, is rightfully already hers.'[154] With such a proprietary understanding of contractual rights one would naturally expect specific performance to be the primary legal response to breach, simply as a means for recovering what is rightfully hers, akin to the *rei vindicatio* in property law. However, Benson understands private law as essentially compensatory.[155] This allows him to support the familiar

[148] This view draws on the distinction introduced by Rawls (n. 49) 74–76, between pure, perfect, and imperfect procedural justice, and where justice as fairness is presented as a theory of pure procedural justice.

[149] Bagchi, 'Interpreting Contracts in a Regulatory State' (n. 139).

[150] Ibid.

[151] This has important implications in particular for contract interpretation. In the regulatory state it is the task of courts interpreting contracts, actively to bring the contract within the limits set by background duties, in particular duties of interpersonal and distributive justice. Bagchi draws a parallel, in this regard, with the canon of constitutional avoidance in American statutory interpretation. In the EU context, a similar analogy could be drawn with the doctrine of harmonious interpretation, according to which national courts must interpret national law as much as possible in conformity with EU law. See e.g. Case C-106/89, *Marleasing v. La Comercial Internacional de Alimentación* (EU:C:1990:395); Case C-240/98 to Case C-244/98, *Océano Grupo Editorial SA v. Rocio Murciano Quintero (and Others)* (EU:C:2000:346); Case C-555/07, *Seda Kücükdeveci v. Swedex GmbH & Co. KG* (EU:C:2010:21), at para. 56.

[152] P. Benson, *Justice in Transactions: A Theory of Contract Law* (2019).

[153] See ibid. 20: 'contract formation may properly be viewed as a form of transactional acquisition.'

[154] Ibid. 8.

[155] Ibid. 255 and 322.

common law principle of adequacy, according to which the remedy of performance in kind should be made available only if expectation damages would not adequately compensate the promisee (the obligee).[156]

Benson arrives at these conclusions through a careful reconstruction of the common law of contract. However, that is only part of the justification. He presents his theory of contract law as offering a public basis of justification in the Rawlsian sense.[157] Taking as his starting point, like Rawls did, the fact of reasonable pluralism of worldviews and ultimate values that characterizes liberal democracies, he aims to complement Rawls's own principles of political justice, that apply to the basic structure of society, with principles applicable to private transactions between individuals, that can be justified, in a similar way, with a public justification (or 'public reasons', as Rawls called it), i.e. without reference to controversial values and worldviews. However, crucially, Benson argues, the principles meant for the justification of the welfare state cannot be applied mechanically to contract law. On the contrary, he claims, a public justification for contract law 'has to be specifically worked out anew for contract law'.[158]

It is for this purpose that he proposes his theory of contract law as a transfer of ownership between the parties ('justice in transactions'). While it is clearly *possible* to understand contract as transferring proprietary rights between the parties at the moment of conclusion of the contract, the question remains why we *should* understand it that way. The reason Benson offers is ultimately metaphysical rather than normative. It draws on Hegelian philosophy of mind. Hegel understood the human mind as 'an individual that is aware of its individuality as absolutely free will'.[159] By placing my will in an external thing I can make it my property. But once I have done so, another exercise of my free will becomes indispensable for changing this state of affairs: 'only with my will can the thing pass to another, whose property it similarly becomes only with his will'.[160] And this is what contract does through its binding force: 'The comparatively "ideal" utterance (of contract) in the stipulation contains the actual surrender of a property by the one, its changing hands, and its acceptance by the other will. The contract is thus thoroughly binding: it does not need the performance of the one or the other to become so'.[161] It is this concept of the 'ideal utterance' of the transfer that Benson picks up.[162] He argues that 'the contractually relevant and effective interaction takes place in this realm of ideation prior to and independently of actual performance.' He believes that this 'purely representational and inherently transactional

[156] Ibid. 265 ff. Frankly, this argument requires, in addition, the endorsement of some form of libertarian default to the effect that any interference by the state with the negative freedom of individuals is in need of justification; otherwise the adequacy principle might just as well operate in the opposite direction. This libertarian move is not unfamiliar among liberal-egalitarians, as we saw, for example, in the case of Dagan and Heller. However, within the Rawlsian scheme there exists no pre-institutional entitlement to negative liberty. The basic liberties, that are protected by the first principle of justice and do have lexical priority over the second principle (which includes the difference principle), are narrowly defined, specific, and political (no general priority for 'liberty').

[157] Ibid. On the idea of public justification, see J. Rawls, *Justice as Fairness: A Restatement* (2001), at § 9.

[158] Benson (n. 152) 13.

[159] G. W. F. Hegel, *Hegel's Philosophy of Mind*, translation by W. Wallace, A. V. Miller (2007), at § 488.

[160] Ibid. § 492.

[161] G. W. F. Hegel, *Philosophy of Mind*, translation by W. Wallace, A. V. Miller (1971), at 493.

[162] Benson (n. 152) 324.

mode of contractual acquisition' is defensible as part of a public basis of justification in the Rawlsian sense.[163] However, it seems, as in the case of Ripstein's recourse to Kantian metaphysics, so too Benson's reliance on Hegelian metaphysics, in particular his conceptions of mind, free will, and ideal utterances, are too much of what Rawls would refer to as a controversial comprehensive doctrine (albeit not a conception of the good) to be acceptable in a pluralist society as a public basis for justification of the legally binding force of contract.[164]

11. Overlapping Consensus, the Circumstances of Politics, and the Fact of Oppression

In summary, what we find is a reasonable pluralism of Rawlsian contract theories. Each of the Rawlsian accounts discussed proposes what seems a reasonable conception of justice (or the application thereof) for contract. And as such they all seem serious candidates for an overlapping consensus on a self-standing conception of justice in contract.

However, each of these Rawlsian approaches struggles to justify contractual obligation without their account becoming a comprehensive doctrine (perfectionist or metaphysical). They all try to navigate between the Scylla of going beyond mere political principles of justice and the Charybdis of being insufficiently determinate to be of any assistance to a society trying to answer fundamental political questions. On the one hand, there is the constant danger of sliding into the terrain of comprehensive doctrines, either by falling into perfectionism (proposing an ultimate value for society or for contract law) or by adopting a metaphysical stance, whether about human nature (a thick conception of the person) or about contract (suggesting essential characteristics). On the other, there is the continuing risk of theories remaining so general and abstract that they will not yield even a minimally determinate answer to the fundamental political questions societies face today, including, in our case, the fundamental political question of the justifiability of the legally binding force of contract.

Perhaps this state of affairs tells us something more in general about the viability of political liberalism as a project. Indeed, this result was perhaps to be expected in the light of Waldron's point about 'the circumstances of politics', i.e. the fact of persisting disagreement among reasonable people not only on conceptions of the good but also on core questions of justice.[165] In particular, as he argues, the Rawlsian 'burdens of judgement' (i.e. the way we balance different considerations and assess evidence is shaped inevitably by our different life experiences)[166] affect questions of justice just as much as questions about ultimate values—if not more. This seems to be reflected in the wide variety of contract theories proposed within the Rawlsian framework.

[163] Ibid. 325.

[164] This does not exclude the possibility of 'fit' (in the Dworkinian sense) with the existing legal materials—far from it. Benson's Hegelian approach is quite similar, in certain respects, to orthodox doctrine prevailing in certain civil law jurisdictions, such as Germany, the Netherlands, and Portugal, which grant a central role to the concept of the—perhaps indeed purely representational—'juristic act', in particular the 'bilateral juristic act' that we otherwise usually refer to as 'contract'.

[165] J. Waldron, *Law and Disagreement* (1999), at 102. See also R. Bellamy, *Political Constitutionalism: A Republican Defence of the Constitutionality of Democracy* (2007), at 5.

[166] J. Rawls (n. 157) 35. The idea of the burdens of judgement goes directly against the ideal of Hercules central to R. Dworkin, *Law's Empire* (1986).

Specifically, on the fundamental political question of the binding force of contract, not only do they differ in their reasons but—crucially—they also lead to fundamentally divergent outcomes.

Is it possible perhaps to reach an overlapping consensus among the different Rawlsian contract law theories? This would be a second-order overlapping consensus among all those contract theories proposing political principles of contract justice that are self-standing with regard to (i.e. do not presuppose) any view about ultimate values, human nature, or the nature of contract law (or so they claim). And would such a second-order overlapping consensus among Rawlsian contract theories alone be easier to find than if non-Rawlsian ones were involved as well? These, however, seem the wrong questions to ask from the Rawlsian point of view. It is important to underline that the Rawlsian idea of public justification (with its cognates of reflective equilibrium and overlapping consensus) is not a binary matter, but is best understood as a matter of degree—of a more and less wide consensus on matters that are more or less fundamental. The idea of public justification is to 'seek to moderate divisive political conflicts'[167] and to 'narrow disagreement at least regarding the more divisive controversies'.[168] The same is implied also in his idea of political philosophy as reconciliation.[169]

So, has the disagreement been narrowed down or moderated on the fundamental political question of the binding force of contract? In particular, are the differences among the Rawlsian contract theories significantly smaller than the differences with and among contract theories that are part of comprehensive doctrines or otherwise rely on metaphysical truths or refer to controversial worldviews or ultimate values? Perhaps they are. First, in terms of reasons, the Rawlsian theories make greater effort to avoid referring to ultimate values, teloi, and thick conceptions of the person and of human agency. Secondly, in terms of outcomes, the Rawlsian theories (with the notable exception of Benson) seem to be much less willing to make very specific policy recommendations, in this case with regard to remedies for breach, than comprehensive doctrines feel free doing. This may seem a disadvantage from the point of view of policy makers seeking guidance in legislative or judicial reform in the field of (European) contract law reform. But perhaps that is all we can reasonably justify towards each other in a pluralist society, as opposed to imposing our views with violence. This brings us to a second fact that Rawls underlines in addition to the fact of reasonable pluralism. This is what he calls 'the fact of oppression':

> a continuing shared adherence to one comprehensive doctrine can be maintained only by the oppressive use of state power, with all its official crimes and the inevitable brutality and cruelties, followed by the corruption of religion, philosophy, and science. If we say a political society is a community when it is united in affirming one and the same comprehensive doctrine, then the oppressive use of state power with these attendant evils is necessary to maintain political community. Let us call

[167] Rawls (n. 166) 28: 'Of course, it is too much to expect complete agreement on all political questions. The practicable aim is to narrow disagreement at least regarding the more divisive controversies.'
[168] Ibid. 28–29.
[169] Ibid. 37–38.

> this the fact of oppression. In the society of the Middle Ages, more or less united in affirming the Catholic faith, the Inquisition was not an accident; its suppression of heresy was needed to preserve the shared religious belief. The same holds, we suppose, for any comprehensive philosophical and moral doctrine, even secular ones. A society united on a form of utilitarianism, or on the moral views of Kant or Mill, would likewise require the oppressive sanctions of state power to remain so.[170]

To be sure, any oppression following from a society's adoption of utilitarianism, liberal perfectionism, or religion as the foundation of contract law would be utterly unlikely, on its own, to come anywhere near the brutalities of the Inquisition. However, to make all law students in a pluralist society believe that their contract law is based on one ultimate value is likely to require more than persuasion. At the least, it would take some form of indoctrination. Vice versa, if a political community were found united in affirming one and the same value as the normative foundation of their contract law this should give us reason to worry about the state of their democracy. Therefore, the absence of a consensus in Europe on a thick principle of binding force or a capacious right to contract that would strongly constrain, morally speaking, the legitimate contract law maker should not be understood as a failure. On the contrary, the fact of reasonable contract law pluralism is a sign of the vitality of its liberal democratic institutions and practices.[171]

D. Accommodating Moral Agency

Shiffrin proposes a very different liberal justification for the binding force of contract. Her argument is subtle. She does not argue that contract law should be based on the value of autonomy, a moral right to contract, or the virtuous or otherwise valuable practice of promise keeping. Nor does she claim that in a liberal society neutrality requires that the state abstain from any act that would support people in keeping their promises. The law, she argues, should neither directly reflect nor entirely ignore morality.[172] Instead, she advocates an intermediate position: that in a liberal society the law should accommodate people who wish to live up to their commitments. Thus, state neutrality may require that contract law not be explicitly anti-moralistic or incompatible with moral principles. Shiffrin argues that both political liberalism (on account of state neutrality) and comprehensive liberalism (as an expression of autonomy) require the accommodation of those who find it important to regard the legal obligation of contracting parties as also a moral obligation, in particular the moral duty to keep one's promises. This approach differs, in particular, from Fried's theory (discussed later, in Section 4.D) in that it does not make any claims as to contract law's rationale

[170] Ibid. 34.

[171] Cf. Rawls (n. 87) xxiv–xxv: 'This pluralism is not seen as disaster but rather as the natural outcome of the activities of human reason under enduring free institutions. To see reasonable pluralism as a disaster is to see the exercise of reason under the conditions of freedom itself as a disaster. Indeed, the success of liberal constitutionalism came as a discovery of a new social possibility: the possibility of a reasonably harmonious and stable pluralist society.'

[172] Shiffrin, 'The Divergence of Contract and Promise', 120 *Harv. L. Rev.* (2007) 708.

being the enforcement of our moral obligations to keep our promises. The political-liberal state is prevented from making such natural-law-like claims. Instead, Shiffrin makes the much more modest claim that the state should accommodate people who hold—and regard as an objective moral truth—a comprehensive doctrine (as Rawls would call these) that requires them to keep promises. In other words, the accommodationist approach calls for contract law to make room for moral agents, not to reflect morality. This type of accommodation is similar to other cases where citizens reciprocally allow each other some space for choices that they do not share.[173] Shiffrin focuses specifically on ways in which contract law expects less of the promisor and more of the promisee than morality does.[174] The best example is the doctrine of efficient breach. If enshrined in law, this doctrine would make it more difficult for people to want to keep their promises and it might even make them feel abnormal if they did. As she puts it:

> how could a moral agent think both that breach of promise is, all things considered, wrong and also that it makes sense for us, as a community of moral agents, to create a system in which we attempt to encourage, however mildly, breach of promise (all the while holding out the possibility of deploying our moral condemnation of breach)?[175]

At first sight this seems a powerful argument. A liberal state cannot enforce contracts on account of the asserted true value of personal autonomy. However, neither should the state refrain from enforcing contracts—or from enforcing them in a certain way, such as through specifically enforced performance—for the reason that it would risk establishing a certain moral conviction. Just as the establishment of atheism in the guise of *laïcité* is not neutral, so too is the state not neutral if it fails to accommodate people who aim to live up to what they regard as their moral duties to honour their promises and to be faithful to their agreements, wherever this is possible without violating any principles of justice. However, what about people who genuinely believe that it is not decent, or even plain wrong, to keep someone to their promises, especially if that would risk getting the other person into trouble (unfortunate contingency) or causing them to lose a very attractive new opportunity (fortunate contingency), for example because they believe that this would be socially wasteful? Empirical evidence shows that businessmen often prefer business solutions over legal solutions and are reluctant to stand on their contractual rights.[176] Does a law that tells them that in case of breach their contracts can be enforced with strong remedies risk bringing them into a conflict of conscience? The idea of accommodation to some extent already seems to assume that promises should be kept and, therefore, it focuses on remedies. But what if promise keeping—or, more to the point, keeping other people to their promises—is

[173] Shiffrin gives the examples of allowing people from minority religions not to work on their holidays (where colleagues will have to step in); not making people who drink too much alcohol pay more for their health insurance or be given lower priority for organ transplant; where meat-lovers eat in a vegetarian restaurant with their vegetarian friends; or where in an ordinary restaurant vegetarian friends split the bill with their-meat-eating friend thus sponsoring their (presumably more expensive) meat consumption. See further on accommodation also Shiffrin, 'Egalitarianism, Choice-Sensitivity, and Accommodation' in R. J. Wallace *et al.* (eds), *Reason and Value: Themes from the Moral Philosophy of Joseph Raz* (2004) 270.

[174] Shiffrin (n. 172) 719.

[175] Ibid. 732–733.

[176] Macaulay (n. 35).

already a controversial ideal?[177] Then, the state will have to choose between different groups of moral agents and their respective moral convictions; it cannot accommodate these contradicting moralities at the same time. However, it is not clear that the state would be allowed to make such choices in a political community based on politically-liberal principles. So it is not entirely clear after all that accommodation can explain the legally binding force of contract for a pluralist society committed to principles of political liberalism.[178]

Specifically with regard to remedies for breach of contract, Shiffrin warns against what she calls 'the overprivatization of private law', referring to the contemporary trend in the US towards greater enforcement of remedial agreements—in particular, liquidated damages.[179] In Europe, recent decisions by the UK Supreme Court, restricting the scope of the penalty rule pursuant to which penalty clauses are unenforceable, seem to display a similar trend.[180] From a comparative law perspective, this is perceived as a gradual approximation to the civil law, where penalty clauses have long been enforceable in principle. However, according to Shiffrin the common law's traditional hostility towards such clauses 'enforces important values central to the rule of law, including that private parties should not decide their own cases and that the public has a special interest in deciding what remedies are appropriate for breaches of legal duty'.[181] She offers what she calls a 'distinctive, liberal, and democratic perspective' on contract and contractual breach. However, again, although there may be important reasons in justice (both interpersonal and distributive) for a rule requiring the reduction of excessive penalties (and perhaps also for an expansive interpretation of such a rule),[182] it is not clear that liberal or democratic principles require a ban on penalty clauses, let alone on all remedial clauses. Put differently, while it may be true, as

[177] Shiffrin (n. 172) 717, assumes that the basic principles of promissory commitment are uncontroversial. However, it is not self-evident that promise-keeping is a moral, as opposed to a merely ethical obligation. The binding force of a promise (its strength, its modalities, the gravity of breach) seems to depend on the pre-existing personal relationship between promisor and promisee (which may be shaped in part by the norms of the community to which they belong) and seems questionable, and perhaps even difficult to make sense of, between total strangers (think of a 'promise' made to a random person). In Shiffrin, 'Promising, Intimate Relationships, and Conventionalism', 117 *Philosophical Review* (2008) 481, at 498, she offers a transcendental argument for the moral power to promise, claiming that our capacity to conduct our relationships in a minimally morally decent way—which she takes to be a both relatively uncontroversial and non-contingent (especially not dependent on convention)—depends on our having the power to promise. However, it is not clear that her conception of minimally morally decent interpersonal relationships is thin enough for it to be as uncontroversial as needed for getting the transcendental argument off the ground.

[178] Bagchi, 'Separating Contract and Promise' (n. 139) 712, argues *contra*, Shiffrin that where contract begins promise ends:

> In making a private promise, a promisor ordinarily creates a sufficient reason to perform the content of her promise: the very fact of her promise. To the extent she simultaneously creates a second sufficient reason—liability in the case of breach—the first reason does no work, or there is no way for the independent sufficiency of the first reason to manifest itself objectively.

Therefore, she argues, the best we can do to support the private practice of promise is to *minimize* the overlap between private promises and publicly enforceable contracts.

[179] Shiffrin (n. 23).

[180] *Cavendish Square Holding BV v. Talal El Makdessi and ParkingEye Ltd v. Beavis* [2015] UKSC 67.

[181] Shiffrin (n. 23) 407.

[182] Courts may reduce a contractual penalty if it is 'disproportionately high' (§ 343 German *BGB*), 'manifestly excessive' (Art. 1231-5 (2) French Civil Code), or 'grossly excessive' (Art. III.-3:712 DCFR), or reduction is 'obviously required by standards of reasonableness and fairness'(Art. 6:94 (1) Dutch *BW*).

she claims, that 'the judiciary's special role in crafting and meting out remedies should not be outsourced',[183] when it comes to the binding force of contract, liberal principles, let alone political-liberal ones, do not seem to warrant a categorical distinction between primary and secondary contractual obligations.

4. Libertarian

A. Spontaneous Order and Binding Force

Many libertarians, ordoliberals, and neoliberals simply assume binding force of contract without justifying it. This is surprising, given that contract enforcement constitutes a strong interference with the liberty of the party in breach. For example, Friedman regards the enforcement of contracts as a core task for government but he does not explain or justify this strong interference with liberty. Like many other libertarians (and other economists), Friedman also postulates the binding force of contract rather than explaining or justifying it, as if it were a natural fact. In particular, he fails to explain why the state should interfere with someone's liberty merely because in the past she promised or agreed to do something that today she no longer wishes to do. Friedman seems to assume that contract enforcement does not amount to coercion, or that contractual obligations will always be performed without the need for enforcement: 'The possibility of co-ordination through voluntary co-operation rests on the elementary—yet frequently denied—proposition that both parties to an economic transaction benefit from it, *provided the transaction is bi-laterally voluntary and informed*. Exchange can therefore bring about co-ordination without coercion.'[184] This proposition holds true, of course, only to the extent that neither of the parties change their minds between the moment of conclusion of the contract and the moment the contract is supposed to be performed. In other words, Friedman seems to overlook the need for an explanation as to why wholly executory (or 'promissory') contracts should be enforced, i.e. why the state should force somebody to do something merely because she promised or agreed to do so in the past. Put differently, why should libertarians support the policing by the state, with all its force, of people's changes of heart? Another passage seems to suggest that those who breach their contracts must even be regarded as enemies to our freedom: 'First, the scope of government must be limited. Its major function must be to protect our freedom both from the enemies outside our gates and from fellow-citizens: to preserve law and order, to enforce private contracts, to foster competitive markets.'[185]

Similarly, Hayek repeatedly cites the freedom and the binding force of contract as the foundations of an open and free society. However, he never expresses himself more specifically as to why it should be the task of the state to enforce contracts, and how this state coercion is compatible with a spontaneous order. For there is nothing free or

[183] Shiffrin (n. 23) 442.
[184] M. Friedman, *Capitalism and Freedom* ([first published 1962] 3rd ed., 2002), at 13 (emphasis in original).
[185] Ibid. 2.

spontaneous about contract enforcement. The enforcement of a contract by state authorities is a major interference with the freedom of any individual who does not want (or no longer wants) to perform a contract that she concluded. Why should the unpaid seller be allowed to call in the bailiff and publicly sell some of the buyer's assets in order to satisfy her claim? In a spontaneous order, why should a free person be forced by the public authorities to perform her contract and, ultimately, to give up some of her own assets. Why not leave the problem of breach of contract to be solved entirely by the free market, for example through business reputation? Hayek writes:

> At least in all those instances where the coercion threatened is avoidable, the law merely alters the means at my disposal and does not determine the ends I have to pursue. It would be ridiculous to say that I am obeying another's will in fulfilling a contract, when I could not have concluded it had there not been a recognized rule that promises must be kept, or in accepting the legal consequence of any other action that I have taken in full knowledge of the law.[186]

But most market regulation can be avoided too, by staying clear of that particular market sector. The same applies to progressive taxes: it suffices not to earn much money, etc.

B. Justice in Transfer

In contrast to Friedman and Hayek, Nozick explicitly addresses the issue. The 'minimal state' that Nozick advocates is allowed to fulfil very few tasks; among these figures the 'enforcement of contracts'.[187] He does not further elaborate how and under what circumstances contracts must be enforced. However, in his entitlement theory contracts clearly play a crucial role in relation to 'the principle of justice in transfer'. Nozick describes this principle as follows:

> How may a person acquire a holding from another who holds it? Under this topic come general descriptions of voluntary exchange, and gift and (on the other hand) fraud, as well as reference to particular conventional details fixed upon in a given society. The complicated truth about this subject (with placeholders for conventional details) we shall call the principle of justice in transfer.[188]

He then proceeds by giving the following full statement of his theory of distributive justice:

> (1) A person who acquires a holding in accordance with the principle of justice in acquisition is entitled to that holding.

[186] F. A. Hayek, *The Constitution of Liberty* ([first published 1960] 2002), at 134.
[187] R. Nozick, *Anarchy, State and Utopia* ([first published 1974] 2006), at ix.
[188] Ibid. 150.

(2) A person who acquires a holding in accordance with the principle of justice in transfer, from someone else entitled to the holding, is entitled to the holding.
(3) No one is entitled to a holding except by the (repeated) applications of 1 and 2.[189]

It is not clear, however, what exactly might amount to an 'injustice in transfer'. Nozick here refers to fraud, and elsewhere also to 'force' (coercion or threats).[190] And although a great variety of different rules on defects of consent, including fraudulent non-disclosure[191] and economic threats,[192] could be imagined, and while Nozick fails to elaborate his ideas on fraud and threats any further, most likely he would interpret the notion of 'injustice in transfer' narrowly.[193] When discussing voluntary exchange he writes, for example: 'A person's choice among differing degrees of unpalatable alternatives is not rendered nonvoluntary by the fact that others voluntarily chose and acted within their rights in a way that did not provide him with a more palatable alternative.'[194] That seems to exclude from the definition of injustice in transfer various existing doctrines such as fraudulent non-disclosure, economic threats, or unfair exploitation.[195]

What is crystal clear, however, is that, in accordance with Nozick's principle of justice in transfer, the binding force of contract is considered a just principle. Yet, in the Nozickian scheme, 'justice in transfer' (i.e. the justice of the binding force of contracts) depends strongly on 'justice in acquisition'. This is problematic, as we saw in Chapter 2, because the 'Lockean proviso',[196] according to which occupation provides a sufficient moral ground for entitlement, is itself highly questionable. For it is simply not true that nobody's freedom is reduced if I enclose a piece of land that used to be common.[197]

189 Ibid. 151.

190 Ibid. 232.

191 See for French law Art. 1137(2) of the French Civil Code (new). See also Art. 3.2.5 UNIDROIT Principles, 4.107 PECL, and II.–7:205 DCFR.

192 The *Cour de cassation* held, in 2002 (with reference to Art. 1112 French Civil Code (old) on threats), that 'seule l'exploitation abusive d'une situation de dépendance économique, faite pour tirer profit de la crainte d'un mal menaçant directement les intérêts légitimes de la personne, peut vicier de violence son consentement' (Cass. Civ. I, 3 April 2002, 00-12.932). The case law on *violence économique* was codified and its scope was widened by Art. 1143 French Civil Code (new): 'There is also duress [i.e. *violence*] where one contracting party exploits the other's state of dependence and obtains an undertaking to which the latter would not have agreed in the absence of such constraint, and gains from it a manifestly excessive advantage.'

193 Libertarians regard fraud as a kind of theft. See Kinsella, 'A Libertarian Theory of Contract: Title Transfer, Binding Promises, and Inalienability', 17 *Journal of Libertarian Studies* (2003) 11, at 17. This is akin to Aristotle's notion of corrective justice.

194 Nozick (n. 187) 264. Contrast M. J. Sandel, *Liberalism and the Limits of Justice* ([first published 1982] 2nd ed., 1998), at 114–115: 'Ruling out coercion alone cannot justify a contract any more than ruling out, say, class privilege also can justify a meritocracy. In both cases, too much is left to contingencies arbitrary from a moral point of view. Once we are bothered by the most conspicuous obstacles to individual autonomy, we are bound on reflection to reject heteronomous influences wherever they appear.' Contrast also P. Pettit, *On the People's Terms: A Republican Theory and Model of Democracy* (2012), at 59–69, on 'invasion'.

195 For the latter, see e.g. Art. II.–7:207 DCFR and Art. 51 CESL proposal. See also the doctrines of 'excessive benefit or unfair advantage' in Art. 4:109 PECL and on 'gross disparity' in Art. 3.2.7 UNIDROIT Principles.

196 Nozick (n. 187) 174–182.

197 See Kymlicka (n. 59) 116–121. See also K. Marx, *Capital: An Abridged Edition*, ([first published 1867] 1995), at 363–364, pointing out that 'the methods of primitive accumulation' in reality were 'anything but idyllic': 'In actual history it is notorious that conquest, enslavement, robbery, murder, briefly force, play the great part. In the tender annals of Political Economy, the idyllic reigns from time immemorial.'

Since there do not seem to be any justified claims to pre-institutional entitlement,[198] original acquisition cannot be the basis for any moral claims. This logically leads to a domino effect since justice in transfer is made explicitly dependent by Nozick on justice in acquisition. Therefore, if the justice of the original acquisition fails then, according to Nozick, all subsequent transfers can no longer be justified either. In other words, the binding force of a contract to sell something that was not justly acquired somewhere upstream can never be just. In addition, there does not seem to be any reason to make relative entitlements (and interpersonal justice) depend entirely on absolute, *erga omnes* entitlement. The Nozickian idea of contract enforcement seems to confuse contract law with property law. It may very well be that you owe me expectation damages if you fail to deliver something that you sold to me but that in the meantime came to—or always did—belong to someone else.[199]

However, even if the protection of entitlement itself is the aim, and if original acquisition could justify original entitlement, then it is still not self-evident that 'voluntary exchange' should create any moral or legal entitlements. Indeed, the idea that 'voluntary exchange' should be the ground for 'justice in transfer' seems entirely definitional.[200] And the assumption that 'voluntary exchange' should be understood formally (i.e. without any remedies for defect of consent, e.g. in the case of unfair exploitation) does not seem warranted either. It could easily be understood in a much more substantive sense, i.e. in that an exchange is only voluntary when both parties had a sufficiently broad range of attractive alternative options to choose from.[201]

C. Contract as Consent

Barnett's theory of contract as consent is avowedly libertarian.[202] He explicitly refers to Nozick's theory of entitlement.[203] And 'contract as consent' is meant explicitly as a theory of justice in transfer: 'contract law is that part of a system of entitlements that identifies those circumstances in which entitlements are validly transferred from

[198] L. Murphy and T. Nagel, *The Myth of Ownership: Taxes and Justice* (2002).

[199] In some jurisdictions, contracts to sell someone else's property, and more generally contracts for impossible obligations (such as selling the moon) are void. This is different, for example, in the Netherlands and the DCFR, where in such cases there may be liability for breach of contract. See Art. II.–7:102 DCFR (Initial impossibility or lack of right or authority to dispose) and Art. 3.1.3 UNIDROIT Principles (Initial impossibility).

[200] The same is not true for Benson's non-libertarian transfer theory that we saw earlier.

[201] See e.g. the liberal perfectionist (Dagan) and the political liberal capabilities (Tjon Soei Len) accounts discussed previously. A Nozickian could, of course, always argue that individuals are free to set up, through their consensus (indeed through contract), a 'utopian' society (that they would always remain free to leave), where they could jointly subject themselves to a very different, more demanding contract law. On the atomistic contractarian 'framework for utopias', see Nozick (n. 187), ch. 10, especially at 312 and 320.

[202] However, consent as the basis of contract precedes—and exceeds—contemporary libertarianism. See R. Zimmermann, *The Law of Obligations: Roman Foundations of the Civilian Tradition* (1996), at 559: 'Consent forms the basis of the modern law of contract'. The modern law of contract was developed essentially by the natural lawyers, in this case, in particular, by Pufendorf (cf. Zimmermann, ibid. 568). See Pufendorf, 'On the Law of Nature and of Nations (1672)', in C. L. Carr (ed.), *The Political Writings of Samuel Pufendorf* (1994), Book III, ch. 4, at 166: 'But the things which I owe another from pacts and agreements, these I owe for the reason that he has acquired a new right against me from my own consent.'

[203] Barnett (n. 48) 291–292.

person to person by their consent'.[204] Indeed, it is exactly this element of consent that Barnett proposes as the moral component that distinguishes morally valid from invalid transfers: 'legal enforcement is morally justified because the promisor voluntarily performed acts that conveyed her intention to create a legally enforceable obligation by transferring alienable rights. Within an entitlements approach, contractual obligation, as distinct from other types of legal obligation, is based on that consent'.[205] However, Barnett does not really explain why consent is a necessary and sufficient condition for a valid transfer of entitlement.[206] The theory seems definitional.[207] If we accept that there are boundaries between people that everyone should respect, and that these boundaries are expressed, in part, in property rights, why does it follow that consent is necessary and sufficient to justify a change in the boundaries? No explanation is given; this is simply postulated. Moreover, on its own libertarian terms it remains unclear how past consent can justify present contract enforcement, which may include coercion. Why does past consent remove the charge of present theft? And why indeed does it turn present breach into a form of theft?[208] The answer remains definitional, i.e. that with past consent there is no present interference with liberty. It vindicates the basic structure of modern contract law, at least the civil law, without, however, offering a justification for it.[209] In summary, unlike Benson's account that we saw earlier, the libertarian version of the transfer theory of contract is a Münchhausian bootstrapping theory of contract.

D. Contract as Promise

As its subtitle 'a theory of contractual obligation' already announces, Fried's *Contract as Promise* offers a direct answer to our central question in this chapter, i.e. what justifies the binding force of contract.[210] In this very influential essay from 1981,[211] Fried argues that the moral duty to keep promises constitutes the moral basis for the legally binding force of contract.[212] If we voluntarily engage in the practice of

[204] Ibid. 270.

[205] Ibid. 300.

[206] By contrast, Bagchi, 'Contract as Procedural Justice' (n. 139) 67 68, considers the 'logic and clarity' of this theory 'highly appealing' and Barnett 'persuasive about the justificatory force of consent at a foundational level'.

[207] See e.g. Barnett (n. 48) 319: 'A consent theory of contractual obligation views certain agreements as legally binding because the parties bring to the transaction certain rights and they manifest their assent to the transfer of these rights.' Why should assent make the contract binding? No reason is given.

[208] Cf. D. Boaz, *Libertarianism: A Primer* (1997), at 81: 'Failure to live up to a contract is a form of theft. If Smith borrows $1,000 from Jones, agrees to pay back $1,100 a year later, and doesn't do so, he is in effect a thief. He has stolen $1,1000 that belongs to Jones. If Jones sells Smith a car, guaranteeing that it has a working radio, and it doesn't, then Jones is a thief: he has taken Smith's money and not delivered what he contracted to deliver.'

[209] The theory is consistent in that it rejects the consideration requirement. See Barnett (n. 48) 313. As Bagchi (n. 139) 'Contract as Procedural Justice', at 67, points out, Barnett's is a 'pure procedural theory', because it regards consent as a necessary and sufficient condition for the legally binding force of contract.

[210] Fried (n. 73).

[211] In contemporary Anglo-American literature, sometimes it seems as if there was no contract theory before Fried. See e.g. Dagan and Heller (n. 33) 19: 'Modern liberal contract theory starts with Charles Fried.'

[212] See Fried (n. 73) 1: 'The promise principle, which in this book I argue is the moral basis of contract law, is that principle by which persons may impose on themselves obligations where none existed before.'

promise-keeping with a view to benefiting from it, then we owe others, who rely on the same practice, a duty to keep our promises.[213] As Fried explains, while liberty prohibits the forced recruitment of individuals for purposes they do not support,[214] contracts uniquely make it possible for each of us to make others serve our own purposes without interfering with their freedom.[215] This conception of contractual obligation as 'essentially self-imposed'—i.e. where people 'make nonoptional a course of conduct that would otherwise be optional' and 'impose on themselves obligations where none existed before'[216]—resonates with the idea of contracts as self-legislation. This is famously expressed in (now) Article 1103 French Civil Code, pursuant to which contracts 'have the binding force of legislation for those who have made them'. However, surprisingly, Fried argues for expectation damages, not specific performance, as the primary way in which the law should remedy a breach of contract. One would expect that to keep someone to their promise means to make them do as promised.[217]

Fried served as the Solicitor General in the Reagan administration from 1985 to 1989.[218] However, *Contract as Promise* already had an explicitly political aim. As he explained, the book was directed against the critical legal studies movement (CLS), which was all the rage at the time.[219] In the late 1970s, CLS had mounted a vigorous attack from the political left against the formalism and conservatism of the dominant 'technical' legal scholarship.[220] One of their core targets had been the will theory. Indeed, Fried's project is best understood as a contemporary version of the classical 'will theory', that was developed by nineteenth-century German legal scholars, but known in the US mostly through the work of Williston.[221]

As many observers have pointed out,[222] it does not follow necessarily from any moral duty of promise keeping that contracts should also be legally binding. In fact, Fried himself acknowledged that his account of the legally binding force of contracts as

[213] Ibid. 17. Fried repudiates the common law doctrine of consideration, which indeed seems inconsistent with the promise principle. See ibid., ch. 3, especially at 26, where he concludes that 'the doctrine of consideration offers no coherent alternative basis for the force of contracts, while still treating promise as necessary to it..

[214] See C. Fried, *Modern Liberty and the Limits of Government* (2007), at 174.

[215] Fried (n. 73) 8.

[216] Ibid. 1, 2, and 13.

[217] Cf. Atiyah (n. 46) 124: 'if the law was really based on the theory of the moral obligation to perform a promise, then surely specific performance would be the more obvious and primary remedy of the law'.

[218] Cf. Fried (n. 214) 163: 'Thinking back now, I recognize the energy that brought me to law, to write about freedom of contract, to work in the Reagan administration.'

[219] See the Preface to Fried (n. 73) x. See also the Postscript (2nd ed., 2015) 137: 'The critical legal theorists disputed, indeed mocked, the pretensions of standard contract doctrine as providing a neutral framework for discerning and implementing the terms of agreements freely arrived at. ... Against these intellectual and cultural themes, Contract as Promise sought to assert the coherence of standard contract doctrine as providing the structure by which actors could determine for themselves the terms of their interaction and cooperation.'

[220] See Kennedy, 'Form and Substance in Private Law Adjudication', 89 *Harv. L. Rev.* (1976) 1685.

[221] See Fried (n. 73) 5–6: 'This is my version of the classical view of contract proposed by the will theory.' Cf. Barnett, 'Contract Is Not Promise; Contract Is Consent', in G. Klass, G. Letsas, and P. Saprai (eds), *Philosophical Foundations of Contract Law* (2014), ch. 3, at 42: 'Fried's "contract as promise" thesis was a welcome and much-needed defense of the traditional view of contract as protecting the "will" or choices of private parties.'

[222] See e.g. Raz (n. 64) 921, who refers to this conflation of promises and contracts, of promissory obligations and contractual obligations, as monism and specifically to Fried as a 'monist'.

morally binding promises relies on bootstrapping.[223] And in more recent publications he admitted that in *Contract as Promise* he had failed to demonstrate why the moral duty to keep promises should be legally enforceable: 'the great difference between the moral regime of promise and the legal regime of contract is that the law (i.e. the state) threatens, and in the end will use, force to compel compliance'.[224] He now argues that the use of legitimate force by the state is a matter of justice.[225] In particular, Fried now presents the legal enforcement of contracts as a matter of involving third parties who may have their own motivations, interests, and agendas.[226] This latter view, as Fried acknowledges,[227] was influenced strongly by Shiffrin's work, discussed earlier.

5. Communitarian

A. Solidarity and Community

In contrast to liberals and libertarians, who tend to focus on the conclusion of contracts through free or autonomous choice, communitarians emphasize the ensuing relationships as the main characteristic of contract. On this view, contracts are relationships where collaboration, solidarity, good faith, mutual respect, and care for each other's interests play a central role. Thus, not individual liberty or personal autonomy, but mutual solidarity and community are the main values on which contractual obligation is based.[228] The classical statement of this idea is Demogue's characterization of a contract as a kind of microcosm where everyone must work together to achieve a common goal.[229] Similarly, Durkheim claimed that contracts are the pre-eminent juridical expression of cooperation.[230] Just as the classical solidarism at the turn of the twentieth century constituted a critique of classical liberal individualism (including the individualistic premise of social contract theory),[231] so too contemporary neo-solidarism

[223] Fried (n. 73) 12.

[224] Fried, 'The Ambitions of Contract as Promise', in G. Klass, G. Letsas, and P. Saprai (eds), *Philosophical Foundations of Contract Law* (2014), ch. 2, at 34.

[225] Ibid. 34.

[226] Ibid. 41. Fried now explicitly characterizes his theory as a 'Kantian' 'comprehensive' doctrine of both the right and the good.

[227] Fried, 'The Convergence of Contract and Promise—Responding to Seana Valentine Shiffrin, *The Divergence of Contract and Promise*', 120 *Harv. L. Rev.* (2007) 708.

[228] See e.g. B. Lurger, *Vertragliche Solidarität, Entwicklungschancen für das Allgemeine Vertragsrecht in Österreich und in der Europäischen Union* (1998); Jamin, 'Plaidoyer pour le solidarisme contractuel', in G. Goubeaux *et al.* (eds), *Etudes offertes à Jacques Ghestin: Le contrat au début du XXIe siècle* (2001).

[229] R. Demogue, *Traité des obligations en général*, Vol. VI (1931), at 9, nr 3: 'Les contractants forment une sorte de microcosme; c'est une petite société où chacun doit travailler pour un but commun qui est la somme des buts individuels poursuivis par chacun, absolument comme dans la société civile ou commerciale'. Sceptical J. Carbonnier, *Droit civil*, Vol. IV *Les obligations* (22nd ed., 2000), at 114 (227): 'L'outrance peut perdre une idée juste. On s'étonnera qu'à une époque où le mariage s'était peut-être trop transformé en contrat, d'aucuns aient rêvé de transformer tout contrat en mariage.'

[230] Durkheim (n. 56) 93: 'le contrat est, par excellence, l'expression juridique de la coopération'.

[231] R. Demogue, *Traité des obligations en général*, Vol. I (1923), at 19–20, nr 10: 'L'état d'obligé peut-il être considéré comme exceptionnel? Les civilistes le disent volontiers. D'après eux l'état de liberté est l'état naturel de l'homme. Cette idée qui rappelle inconsciemment l'état de nature de Rousseau et place comme idéal que chacun en société soit aussi libre qu'auparavant dans le prétendu état de nature, est tout à fait inexacte. L'état naturel en société est la solidarité, la liberté peut simplement être considérée comme souhaitable dans

constitutes a direct attack on the neo-atomism typical of neo-liberalism.[232] And just like a century ago, today too there are more 'sentimental' (*fraternité* oriented) versions of solidarism (and of socialism) and ones that aim to respond to the reality of pervasive structural, contractual, and societal inequalities.[233]

The difference with libertarian and most liberal contract theories is not merely about the justification and normative source of the binding force of contracts but concerns also—indeed foremost—the degree to which whatever was agreed to by the parties at contract formation is binding. While libertarian and liberal theories have great difficulty in accepting, explaining, and justifying existing doctrines that allow for contractual adaptation in the case of supervening events,[234] for communitarian contract theories based on solidarity this comes quite naturally. Indeed, from their point of view, these doctrines should not even be properly understood as providing for an exceptional mitigation of the binding force of contract. Rather, this is what a contractual relationship is all about: standing together and collaborating, especially when the going gets tough, for example when it suddenly becomes much more difficult for one of the parties to do what they had agreed upon. So, while libertarians and liberals, who understand contractual obligation as the legally binding force of whatever the parties freely committed to at formation (and where libertarians and liberals differ on whether the relevant freedom should be formal or substantive), must regard a doctrine like change of circumstances as an exception to—or mitigation of—one party's contractual obligation, communitarians can see this simply as an application of the duty for the other party to collaborate which—even when not explicitly stipulated in the contract—is at the heart of the contractual relationship and indeed of the binding force of contract properly understood.

B. Embedded Contracts

Quite different from the theories emphasizing solidarity and community among parties to the contract, are the communitarian theories that emphasize the embeddedness of contracts in the wider community and, as a consequence, the relevance of community standards for the determination and interpretation of a contractual relationship and the ensuing rights and obligations of the contracting parties. Collins, for example, emphasizes that 'contractual relations always remain "embedded" in the social practices and norms from which they arise.'[235] The best known example of a theory to which the social embeddedness of contract is central is the relational contract theory

une certaine mesure.' See also E. Gounot, *Le principe de l'autonomie de la volonté en droit privé: contribution a l'étude critique de l'individualisme juridique* (1912).

[232] Against atomism, see C. Taylor, *Philosophy and the Human Science* (1985), ch. 7 'Atomism'.

[233] See Jamin (n. 228) 471, who argues in favour of 'le solidarisme contractuel dont l'objectif est de restaurer la primauté du social au sein même de l'économie de marche et non à sa marge. Il ne s'agit donc nullement d'affirmer une quelconque fraternité de nature sentimentale entre les parties'.

[234] See e.g. § 313 German *BGB* (*Wegfall der Geschäftsgrundlage*), Art. 1467 Italian *Codice Civile* (*eccessiva onerosità sopravvenuta*), Art. 1195 French Civil Code (*imprévision*).

[235] Collins (n. 35) (1999), at 25.

of Macneil,[236] who argued that 'what is essential to any sound theoretical approach to contracts of any kind is a *Grundnorm* recognizing the embeddedness of all exchange relationships'.[237]

The emphasis on contractual embeddedness, and the rejection of the strong focus (especially by liberals and libertarians) on contract formation—where 'as much as possible of the content of the relation, both structure and detail, is forced into a pattern of mutual assent'[238]—matches well with the general communitarian scepticism with regard to the possibility and value of individual rational choice and self-determination.[239] Communitarians point to the social and cultural preconditions of choices.[240] They reject formal notions of autonomy, choice, and consent, and emphasize instead that choices are made, and consent is always given, in a certain context. If the self is never 'unencumbered' and 'always already situated',[241] then shouldn't the social context be just as important as the contract?

There is a strong parallel between the idea of the embeddedness of contracts and Polanyi's famous argument about the embeddedness of the economy. In *The Great Transformation* (1944), Polanyi famously argued that the laissez-faire idea of autonomous, self-regulating markets 'directed by market prices and nothing but market prices'[242] is a fantasy, because the market is always embedded in wider society and its socio-political practices and institutions.[243] Notably, these include contract law, which ensures the legal enforceability of contracts on which markets rely. Similarly, contracts can never be autonomous instruments of self-regulation, because they too are necessarily embedded in relational and societal contexts, including economic relations and institutions. This resonates strongly with the communitarian and liberal critique of the

[236] See I. Macneil, *The Relational Theory of Contract: Selected Works of Ian Macneil* (D. Campbell, ed.) (2001). See also D. Campbell, H. Collins, and J. Wightman, *Implicit Dimensions of Contract: Discrete, Relational, and Network Contracts* (2003).

[237] Macneil, 'Reflections on Relational Contract', 141 *Journal of Institutional and Theoretical Economics* (1985) 541, at 542. See also Macneil, 'Contract Adjustment of Long-Term Economic Relations Under Classical, Neo-Classical and Relational Contract Law', 72 *Northwestern University Law Review* (1978) 854, at 857: 'In real life, even the most apparently discrete transaction is deeply embedded in social relations.'

[238] Macneil, 'Restatement (Second) of Contracts and Presentation', 60 *Va. L. Rev.* (1974) 589.

[239] See e.g. C. Taylor, *Hegel and Modern Society* (1979), at 157 on 'situating freedom'.

[240] Sandel, 'The Procedural Republic and the Unencumbered Self', 12 *Political Theory* (1984) 81, at 86–87:

> For the unencumbered self, what matters above all, what is most essential to our personhood, are not the ends we choose but our capacity to choose them. ... Only if my identity is never tied to the aims and interests I may have at any moment can I think of myself as a free and independent agent, capable of choice. This notion of independence carries consequences for the kind of community of which we are capable. Understood as unencumbered selves, we are of course free to join in voluntary association with others, and so are capable of community in the cooperative sense. What is denied to the unencumbered self is the possibility of membership in any community bound by moral ties antecedent to choice; he cannot belong to any community where the self itself could be at stake. Such a community—call it constitutive as against merely cooperative—would engage the identity as well as the interests of the participants, and so implicate its members in a citizenship more thoroughgoing than the unencumbered self can know.

[241] Sandel (n. 194).

[242] K. Polanyi, *The Great Transformation: The Political and Economic Origins of Our Time* ([first published 1944] 2nd ed., 2001), at 45.

[243] Ibid. For a reappraisal, with a particular focus on the law's social functions in the post-national constellation, see C. Joerges and J. Falke (eds), *Karl Polanyi, Globalization and the Potential of Law in Transnational Markets* (2011).

libertarian understanding of contracts as essentially pre-institutional self-regulation. Still, it is important to note (but often overlooked) that Polanyi's own analysis was a historical reconstruction and to that extent not normative. However, the notion can also be understood—and has been in recent debates on European (private) law—in a more evaluative or normative sense, where the disembeddedness of contractual relationships is considered to be bad or otherwise problematic. And the arguments quite naturally become communitarian when it is claimed or suggested that contractual relationships ought to be embedded in social norms, traditions, culture, or 'imaginaries'. As a salient example of the idea of disembedded contracts, think of posted workers, who work temporarily in a foreign country but remain under a contract with their employer in their country of origin. It has been suggested that the practice of posted workers, whose employment relationships and situations are not (fully) governed by the laws of the host state, has a disembedding effect on the national system of labour law, disrupting industrial relations and social cohesion.[244]

The general critique of communitarianism, especially coming from the liberal side, has been that identity and the adherence to a community or culture should ultimately be a matter of individual choice. Critics claim that because community values and traditions may be oppressive, especially for minorities, individuals should at least be guaranteed exit options from community standards.[245] The critique can be applied to the idea of contractual embeddedness and the relational contract theory as well: should the strength and modalities of the legally binding force of contracts (and its limits), including the differentiation in this regard between spot contracts for commodity sales and long-term contracts such as franchising (e.g. with regard to a right to unilateral termination), be a matter of the direct interpretation of the context in which the contract is embedded,[246] rather than of the choices the contracting parties have made in that regard? Or, indeed, should perhaps different sets of rules for different contract types be established through democratic deliberation rather than through cultural interpretation? Ultimately, the question of the normative force of community standards, when it comes to the binding force of contract, is not categorically different from the question of whether contract enforcement can be justified by, for example, a religious duty to keep promises, under which breach of contract might amount to a sin, which certain religious communities may wish—and could feel under a duty—to make legally enforceable.[247] Such an understanding would of course be directly at

[244] As Van Hoek, 'Re-Embedding the Transnational Employment Relationship: A Tale about the Limitations of (EU) Law?' 55 *CMLR* (2018) 449, at 463, points out: 'from the perspective of the host State, "islands of foreign law" can be as disruptive of the embedding of the local labour market as "extralegal zones"'.

[245] See M. C. Nussbaum, *Sex and Social Justice* (1999), ch. 1; A. Sen, *Identity and Violence: the Illusion of Destiny* (2006), at 32.

[246] Art. 3:12 Dutch Civil Code defines the standard of 'reasonableness and equity' (objective good faith), which is pervasively present in the Code, in a way that could be regarded as communitarian: 'In determining what reasonableness and equity require, reference must be made to generally accepted principles of law, to current juridical views in the Netherlands, and to the particular societal and private interests involved' (translation by P. P. C. Haanappel and E. Mackaay, *New Netherlands Civil Code Patrimonial Law* (1990). How is it determined what 'the current juridical views in the Netherlands' are and why should these be decisive?

[247] For promises made in God's name or under oath, see e.g. *Catechism of the Catholic Church*, at no. 2147 ('Promises made to others in God's name engage the divine honor, fidelity, truthfulness, and authority. They must be respected in justice. To be unfaithful to them is to misuse God's name and in some way to make God

odds with an idea of contracts also as a means of individual emancipation from prevailing cultural norms.

C. Contract as Collaborative Community

Markovits proposes a theory of contract as respectful community.[248] At first blush, it has all the characteristics of a communitarian theory. Not only do some of the most central notions in his theory include community, recognition, collaboration, and social solidarity, he also considers communal relationships to be objectively valuable. Still it would be a mistake to think that Markovits's contract theory is communitarian in any thick, value-loaded sense. It is true that he presents his theory explicitly as an alternative to the dominant liberal, libertarian, and utilitarian contract theories, which are based on individualistic values,[249] and proposes instead respectful community and collaboration both as 'attractive moral and political values' and as the 'essence' of contractual obligation. However, at the same time he explicitly rejects 'thick', substantive conceptions of contractual community and collaboration, such as Macneil's relational contract theory, and proposes 'thin' and formal understandings of both collaboration and community.[250] The idea is that his Kantian communitarianism offers a conception of the good that is thin enough to be acceptable, for example, from the point of view of liberal neutrality, as required by both comprehensive and political liberalism.[251] In the liberal versus communitarian debate this would firmly place him on the liberal side.[252] Yet, there is good reason nevertheless to discuss his theory chiefly as a communitarian one.[253] Not only because of its anti-individualism, or because a thin community still remains a community, but also because it is not clear that his notions of community

out to be a liar') and no. 2152 ('A person commits perjury when he makes a promise under oath with no intention of keeping it, or when after promising on oath he does not keep it. Perjury is a grave lack of respect for the Lord of all speech').

248 Markovits, 'Contract and Collaboration', 113 *Yale L.J.* (2004) 1417.
249 Ibid. 1419–1421.
250 He aims to highlight this difference by distinguishing 'collaboration' from 'co-operation', reserving the former term for the thin and formal conception and the latter for the thick, substantive conception. See ibid. 1462. This is a bit puzzling. The reverse choice might have been more obvious since 'to labour' seems more intense and engaging than 'to operate'. See also the PECL, DCFR, and CESL proposals which contain, as a matter of general contract law, a duty to cooperate. In the DCFR, Art. III.–1:104: (Co-operation) defines the general duty to cooperate (for any obligation, not merely the contractual ones), as follows: 'The debtor and creditor are obliged to co-operate with each other when and to the extent that this can reasonably be expected for the performance of the debtor's obligation.' In addition Art. IV.E.–2:201 DCFR provides specifically for contracts of commercial agency, franchise and distributorship, as follows: 'The parties to a contract within the scope of this Part of Book IV must collaborate actively and loyally and co-ordinate their respective efforts in order to achieve the objectives of the contract.'
251 Markovits (n. 248) 1513. Cf. Rawls (n. 49) 395 on a 'thin theory of the good'. See more generally on the difference between thick and thin conceptions in ethics, B. Williams, *Ethics and the Limits of Philosophy* ([first published 1985] 2011), at 153–154, and Väyrynen, 'Thick Ethical Concepts' in E. N. Zalta (ed.), *The Stanford Encyclopedia of Philosophy*, available at https://plato.stanford.edu/entries/thick-ethical-concepts/ (last visited 30 May 2020).
252 On this debate, see Chapter 2.
253 See also Dagan and Heller (n. 33) 146, who refer (critically) to it as 'Markovits' communitarian contract theory'.

and collaboration are as thin as liberal neutrality—whether of the comprehensive (e.g. Dworkinian) or political (Rawlsian) kind—would require.

Markovits claims that contracts 'establish a relation of recognition and respect—and indeed a kind of community—among those who participate in them' and explains the reasons for making and keeping contracts in terms of 'the value of this relation'.[254] In other words, contractual relationships must be understood as objectively valuable, i.e. an objective good, that must be supported by the state. This does not make the theory perfectionist in a narrow sense. It does not claim that people are more virtuous, or that their lives otherwise go objectively better, to the extent they conclude and perform contracts, and that for this reason the state should recognize them as valid and enforce them by providing remedies. Still, it does claim that contractual relationships are intrinsically valuable and cites this as the reason for contractual obligation and enforcement. This makes it perfectionist in a wider sense of offering an objective account of the good as a basis for politics.

Just like the theories of Fried, Shiffrin, and Benson we saw earlier, so too is Markovits's a 'special case' theory,[255] in that it understands contracting as a special case of promising.[256] Put differently, after the libertarian and liberal-egalitarian versions we saw earlier now we encounter a communitarian reading of contract as promise. What these otherwise quite divergent theories have in common is that they claim that (1) promises are morally binding, (2) contracts are (or include) promises, and (3) the state must, in principle, enforce contractual promises. The distinct feature of Markovits's theory of promise and contract is that it invokes the Kantian categorical imperative, in particular in its second formula, i.e. the formula of the end in itself (or the formula of humanity).[257] As Markovits underlines, this formula contains two distinct commands, first, never to treat others merely as a means, and, secondly, always to treat them also as an end.[258] And it is the second element, often overlooked, that provides the moral basis for contractual obligation, according to Markovits's theory. He writes: 'The possibility of community is undermined both when a person *uses* another as a means to her ends, by manipulating him in ways that he cannot accept, and when a person *excludes* another from the ends of actions that apply to him, by pursuing (in such contexts) ends in which he cannot possibly share.'[259] And while a lie (including a lying promise) is an example of the former wrong, the latter wrong is exemplified by the breach of a promise, for example breach of a contractual promise. For a person may fail to treat another as an end when, without using the other, she pursues ends in which the other cannot share.[260] And a breach of contract is a prominent example of this particular wrong. Markovits argues, plausibly, that the parties to a broken promise

[254] Markovits (n. 248) 1420.

[255] There exist interesting parallels between Alexy's special case theory of practical discourse (which we saw in Chapter 3), claiming that legal reason is a special case of practical reason, and the theories claiming that contracting is a special case of promising.

[256] Markovits (n. 248) 1435: 'I move on to fill out this general theory of promises for the special case of contract'.

[257] See Kant, *Groundwork* (n. 126) 4:429: 'So act that you use humanity, in your own person as well as in the person of any other, always at the same time as an end, never merely as a means.'

[258] Markovits (n. 248) 1424.

[259] Ibid. 1428 (emphasis in original).

[260] Ibid. 1430.

become more distant than strangers: by pursuing ends that induce separation rather than community they *become estranged*.[261] As he writes, 'the breaching promisor does not just unmake but instead actively *betrays* the community established by the promise. She pursues ends, through her breach, that do not just depart from but instead *contradict* her promisee's ends.'[262]

Do we really have a moral (as opposed to merely ethical) duty not to become estranged from (certain) others? Clearly, estrangement can amount to loss and pain, and to that extent may be bad, sometimes even dramatically bad, but is it wrong?[263] Similarly, the betrayal may make the promisor a bad person, but does it also constitute a wrong towards the promisee? Doesn't betrayal always refer to an ethical community (of family, friendship, partnership or other) whose member(s) or values are betrayed? More generally, therefore, is it (morally) wrong to breach a promise or is it merely (ethically) bad? Markovits does not distinguish between ethical and moral duties, or between ethical and moral reasons.[264] He writes:

> Promises render persons practically open to one another. Without promises, their wills would remain isolated (just as their minds would remain isolated without truthful communication). Moreover, when promises are broken, persons' wills become isolated (just as their minds become isolated when they lie). But when persons make and keep promises, they may overcome their isolation and enter into respectful relations with each other. Promise-making and promise-keeping arise, as Hannah Arendt observes, 'directly out of the will to live together with others in the mode of acting and speaking'.[265]

Surely, this appreciation of promises is based on a particular conception of the good—which may be widespread, but not for that reason alone necessarily thin—i.e. the idea that a life together with others is a better one than an isolated life.[266] Indeed, the reference to Arendt's communitarian perfectionist version of republicanism (also referred to as civic humanism) is telling. Similarly, when Markovits writes that 'the morality of promise and contract engages one of the most basic values in our practical lives, and this value underwrites every element of promissory and contractual obligation',[267] then, at least in a pluralist society, the question arises: whose values and whose

[261] Ibid. 1431 and 1433.

[262] Ibid. 1433 (emphasis in original).

[263] If becoming estranged means wronging the other, what should we make of J. Prévert's *Les feuilles mortes*: 'Et la mer efface sur le sable les pas des amants désunis'?

[264] On that distinction, see Chapter 2.

[265] The reference is to H. Arendt, *The Human Condition* ([first published 1958] 2nd ed., 1998), at 246, where she writes that the moral precepts engendering the readiness to make promises and to keep them, 'arise directly out of the will to live together with others in the mode of acting and speaking'.

[266] There is a difference between controversial moral claims (concerning the right) and ethical ones (relating to the good). They answer to different questions. However, what is presented as a moral claim may well be controversial as a moral claim because in reality it is an ethical one.

[267] Markovits (n. 248) 1514. Similar, Habib, 'Promises', in E. N. Zalta (ed.) *Stanford Encyclopedia of Philosophy*, available at https://plato.stanford.edu/entries/promises/ (last visited 30 May 2020): 'Few moral judgements are more intuitively obvious and more widely shared than that promises ought to be kept.' However, the question is: are these truly *moral* judgements (in the narrow sense, i.e. as opposed to ethical judgements)?

practical lives? Isn't the duty to keep promises at heart a duty that depends on promissory culture and the person one wishes to be within that culture? The point here is not that there exist cultural differences, for example with regard to the language that may give rise to a promise that, once it is made, however, is morally binding by universal standards.[268] The question is, more fundamentally, whether the duty to keep promises is a moral one, part of the right (i.e. of what we owe to each other as human beings), which refers to universal standards, as opposed to an ethical duty, as part of the good (i.e. of the kind of person I understand myself to be, my identity), which refers to the local standards of one's relevant community, in this case its promissory culture (does it allow divorce? does it reject adultery or embrace polyamory?). To be sure, being entirely formal Markovits's conception of community leaves the parties to each contract free to give it the substance they choose, and this choice may be strongly influenced by the culture in which the parties are embedded. But is not, more fundamentally, the question of whether I should keep my promise also ultimately a matter of who I want to—or feel I have to—be towards you and what you and I want our community (of you and me, perhaps embedded in a wider one) to be, to mean, and to entail?[269]

In summary, doesn't Markovits's account of the value of contractual community and collaboration amount to a rather thick conception of the good after all? And therefore, as suggested earlier, isn't his theory indeed appropriately categorized as a communitarian view? Markovits himself underlines the link of contract (properly understood) with liberalism (properly understood). When he writes that he aims 'to connect the collaborative ideal to the most fundamental ambitions of liberal social institutions and thereby to reassert the centrality of contract, understood in collaborative terms, within the liberal legal order',[270] the question may ultimately be a semantic one of proper labelling: communitarian liberalism versus liberal communitarianism. If, by contrast, we take the idea of thin and formal Kantian community seriously, then, in effect, the theory may come close, as far as private law relationships are concerned—and in a way not dissimilar to the theories of Weinrib and Ripstein—to libertarianism. For example, when Markovits writes that 'collaboration is not, of course, devoid of all normative content—no guide to action possibly could be—but its normative commitments are all thin and formal in precisely the ways that the liberal vision of politics requires',[271] then this seems to bring us back to pre-materialized understandings of freedom, equality, and justice in contract law. Or at least, materialization would lack justification on this view. However, as we saw above, (neo-)formalism cannot justifiably claim to be the default, leaving the burden of justification to materialization.

[268] The reasoning would be similar to the ECHR's margin of appreciation doctrine with regard to human rights, which in turn is akin to the Rawlsian concept of burdens of judgement.

[269] For Aristotle, promise-keeping is a matter of virtue. See *Nicomachean Ethics*, at Book IV ch. VII, 1127a–1127b. However, one does not have to be an Aristotelian to understand promises in terms of the good. Think also of the (controversial) claim made by M. Weber, *The Protestant Ethic and the Spirit of Capitalism* ([first published 1930] 1992), about the role played of Calvinist ethics in the development of capitalism, and more generally the work on varieties of capitalism and on the cultural differences between markets.

[270] Markovits (n. 248) 1475.

[271] Ibid. 1514.

With regard to remedies for breach, Markovits's theory takes a rather surprising turn. He argues that the party in breach of contract does not wrong the other as long as she pays expectation damages. He writes:

> a breaching promisor need not even estrange herself from her promisee, but may, in spite of the breach, continue to treat her promisee as an end in himself. She does so by paying compensatory damages that secure her promisee's expectations in the shared ends that the contractual collaboration involved. A simple breach of contract, without more, therefore does not constitute a wrong that the collaborative theory of contract recognizes.[272]

It is not clear, however, why it should count as respectful to reduce the other party's ends to their monetary value. In what sense do parties continue to collaborate if one of them replaces what she agreed to do or to give, with a sum of money? Rather than being formal this amounts to a very specific material understanding of community: collaborative community reduced to its monetary value.

The collaborative theory of contract focuses only on natural persons, excluding 'organizations' from its scope.[273] That is certainly consistent, since organizations, as Markovits rightly points out, 'cannot engage the values of respect and community that underwrite the collaborative ideal'.[274] He aims to reassure us that this limitation 'does not undermine the collaborative view's claim to capture the essence of contract or indeed its practical importance'.[275] Yet, in reality the practical implications of this limitation are quite radical: it excludes from the theory's personal scope not only most B2B but also most B2C contracts, which means the bulk of contracting in the real world. For a theory that claims to be 'no mere academic conceit but . . . instead immanent in our actual legal practice',[276] this does seem problematic. A particularly low degree of fit—i.e. only for C2C contracts and some B2C (where the B is not a legal person)—may not be important for a purely normative (applied) political or moral theory, but it is important for a legal theory that aims to present what is already immanent in the practice of contract law.

D. Legal Tradition

A third strand of communitarian contract theory emphasizes the importance of legal tradition, in particular the fact that in Europe both the civil law and the common law have long acknowledged the legally binding force of contract. In the civil law tradition, the binding force of contract evolved, in the course of history, from a limited set

[272] Ibid. 1509. Schwarz and Markovits (n. 46) build upon this notion, finding overlapping consensus on this point with welfare economics.

[273] Interestingly, this goes in exactly the opposite direction to Schwartz and Scott, 'Contract Theory and the Limits of Contract Law' (n. 36), who limit their theory (and their understanding of contract law proper) explicitly to contracts between 'firms'.

[274] Markovits (n. 248) 1467.

[275] Ibid.

[276] Ibid. 1474.

of legal actions for specific types on contracts (e.g. sales, rent) and one more general but quite formal cause of action (the *stipulatio*) in classical Roman law, into the general principle, elaborated originally by medieval canon lawyers, that agreements of any kind are binding: *pacta sunt servanda*.[277] Similarly, in the common law, originally there existed only a very limited set of forms of action. The writ of assumpsit, which first made informal contracts enforceable, became the basis for the modern binding force of contract.[278] In the light of this gradual, historical development, it is argued, the idea that the question of whether (and how and to what extent) contract should be binding could even be raised in the abstract, and be answered on a clean slate, seems absurd. Communitarians may disagree as to the degree to which the historical development should matter as a guide to and justification for contemporary law making, but they will agree on the fact that tradition should have some normative force and cannot simply be ignored by the law makers of the day, whether they are legislatures or courts.[279]

A practical question with regard to the historical school of jurisprudence and neopandectism is: what aspect of history should we focus on—which elements do we place in the foreground and which others in the background?[280] Does it matter that *pacta sunt servanda* was not a principle of Roman law (which did not generally enforce contracts, only specific types, which admittedly included the rather broad *stipulatio*) but of canon law,[281] i.e. a Christian principle? And does it make any difference that the contemporary remedies for hidden defects in sales, such as price reduction, which do go back to Roman law, were developed originally with regard to goods sold on the market, which, at the time, notably included slaves (hence, hidden defects such as *morbus*)?[282]

A more fundamental question concerns the binding force of history. Why should tradition be binding? How can it provide a justification—as opposed to a mere explanation—of the law as it currently is and—as a logical consequence—a normative argument against change?[283] In the civil law tradition, in the case of non-performance of an obligation, the creditor is entitled, in the first place, to receive actual performance of the obligation, the duty to compensate damages being merely a possible secondary obligation, while in the common law tradition the default remedy for breach of contract is expectation damages. Does this mean that neither of these systems

[277] Zimmermann (n. 202) 576.

[278] A. W. B. Simpson, *A History of the Common Law of Contract: The Rise of the Action of Assumpsit* (1975).

[279] Specifically for the theory of *Rechtsgeschäft* (juridical act), see W. Flume, *Allgemeiner Teil des bürgerlichen Rechts*, Vol. II: *Das Rechtsgeschäft* (4th ed, 1992), at VII–VIII: 'Die überlieferte Lehre vom Rechtsgeschäft ist das Zeugnis einer hohen Rechtskultur. Indem wir sie so verstehen, sollten wir an der Lehre weiterarbeiten.'

[280] On the role of foreground and background (and their reversal) in demonstrating historical continuity and discontinuity, specifically with regard to private law, see Monateri, 'Black Gaius: Quest for the Multicultural Origins of the "Western Legal Tradition"', 51 *Hastings L.J.* (2000) 479.

[281] See Zimmermann (n. 202) 543.

[282] Ibid. 311.

[283] See Holmes Jr, 'The Path of the Law', 10 *Harv. L. Rev.* (1897) 991, at 1001: 'It is revolting to have no better reason for a rule of law than that so it was laid down in the time of Henry IV. It is still more revolting if the grounds upon which it was laid down have vanished long since, and the rule simply persists from blind imitation of the past ... why should any merely historical distinction be allowed to affect the rights and obligations of business men?'

could change, or that convergence, for example in the shape of a European principle or rule, should be unacceptable?[284] Or, what about short notification periods for non-conformity in sales? They have a very long pedigree. But is that a sufficient reason to keep them generally, or against abandoning them, say, for contracts for the supply of digital content and digital services to consumers?[285]

The strength of traditionalist theories is that they point our attention to the wealth of concrete experience (and tested reasons) contained in our contract law traditions. It would be insane to try to design a totally new contract law from scratch, on a clean slate. Moreover, this would also be impossible. Rather than unencumbered selves, we are all already situated,[286] formed by our own respective legal traditions,[287] especially, of course, those of us with an education in law. However, theories of contract law formulated in terms of legal culture, legal tradition, or *Volksgeist*,[288] such as neo-pandectist, neo-romantic, and other contemporary communitarian theories of private law, cannot tell us *how much* tradition should count, *which* elements of our tradition we should retain, and which other aspects we can let go of or even emphatically should reject. Clearly, we cannot receive the *ius commune*, or follow the precedents of the common law, *in toto*. Surely, we need to reflect critically upon what to preserve and what to abandon. And that reflection is more likely to be informed by other merits of the rule at hand rather than its pedigree.

6. Republican

A. Non-domination as a Prerequisite for Binding Force

From a republican perspective, there is no reason for prima facie suspicion towards the public enforcement of private contracts. The reason is that from the republican point of view of freedom as non-domination, interference is not per se problematic—only domination is. Indeed, the public enforcement of contracts might enhance freedom understood as non-domination and its enjoyment. Legitimate laws may constitute, as Pettit puts it, 'a non-mastering interferer'.[289] Indeed, legitimate laws may even be productive of freedom, understood as non-domination.[290] And the legally binding force of contract represents a key example of this.[291] On the other hand, however, from

[284] The PECL, DCFR, and CESL have quite similar systems of remedies, offering a free choice, in principle, with exceptions.

[285] Cf. Directive (EU) 2019/770 on contracts for the supply of digital content and digital services OJ 2019 L 136, Recital (11) (with reference to the full harmonization character of the Directive): 'Member States should not provide for ... an obligation for the consumer to notify the trader of a lack of conformity within a specific period.'

[286] Sandel (n. 194).

[287] Legrand, 'European Legal Systems are not Converging', 45 *ICLQ* (1996) 52.

[288] F. C. von Savigny, *Vom Beruf unserer Zeit für Gesetzgebung und Rechtswissenschaft* (1814).

[289] P. Pettit, *Republicanism: A Theory of Freedom and Government* (1997), at 35.

[290] Ibid. 41, cites W. Blackstone, *Commentaries on the Laws of England* (1765): 'laws, when prudently framed, are by no means subversive but rather introductive of liberty'. In the same sense, Bellamy (n. 165) 160: 'law, and hence interference, can be productive of liberty'.

[291] Cf. Bellamy (n. 165) 157: 'To argue government ought not to interfere with the freedom of the market ignores the fact that this liberty is structured by the establishment, through governmental action, of property rights and contract law.'

the republican point of view (and contrary to certain libertarians, as we saw) consent does not suffice as a justification—not even prima facie—for the binding force of contract. The reason is that contractual consent on its own does not ensure that the ensuing contractual relationship will be one without domination of one party by the other: 'Whether a relationship sprang originally from a contract or not, whether or not it was consensual in origin, the fact that it gives one party the effective capacity to interfere more or less arbitrarily in some other's choices means that the one person dominates or subjugates the other.'[292] Pettit explicitly addresses contract law. He writes:

> the law of contract as it emerged in the nineteenth century suggested that if a contract is entered freely, then the conduct that occurs under the terms of the contract is unimpeachable. Such a suggestion must be entirely unacceptable to a republican. The striking feature of a contract, even a free contract—a contract that is not the product of coercion or manipulation, for example—is that it may give one party a power of domination over the other.... From a republican point of view, then, the free contract cannot serve the role of automatic legitimator—even prima facie legitimator—of what happens under the terms of the contract. The idea of free contract loses the authorizing capacity that it was given in the classical liberal tradition.[293]

This does not mean, however, that Pettit rejects contractual obligation altogether. On the contrary, modern societies and their economies are unthinkable without it.[294] So what might a republican contract law look like? 'In any contract, no matter how freely undertaken', Pettit writes:

> one party gives a certain hostage to the other: they expose themselves to the damages that the other may seek in the event of their not performing as promised; if you like, one party runs the risk of domination by the other. That being so, the republican state which wants to promote non-domination is bound to expect contract law, not just to facilitate voluntary agreements among different agents, but to play a regulative role in disallowing contracts that involve terms under which one party has the possibility of dominating the other.[295]

It is important to note that Pettit addresses contract law in his discussion of 'economic prosperity'. This suggests that he regards binding force and freedom of contract as being of contingent and instrumental—as opposed to foundational—importance in a society governed by republican principles, in particular by freedom as non-domination. On Pettit's republican view the legally binding force of contract carries the structural risk of publicly facilitating and reinforcing relationships of domination, in which one party becomes dependent on the arbitrary will of another. However, given the benefits people derive from contract in modern society, rather than being fundamentally opposed to the public enforcement of private contracts, the proper

[292] Pettit (n. 289) 62.
[293] Ibid. 164.
[294] Ibid. 164–165.
[295] Ibid.

republican response should be to regulate it with a view to preventing domination from occurring. In other words, from a republican point of view the two questions of the binding force and the freedom of contract—that I discuss separately, in the present chapter and the next—are two sides of the same coin. Rather than accepting certain exceptions to the binding force of contract and understanding these as limitations to the freedom of contract, republicans accept the binding force of contract always only as conditional upon the contractual relationship (and not merely its formation) for both parties being free from domination.

B. Contractual Obligations without Foundations

1. Republican Anti-foundationalism

Saprai offers what he calls a 'republican' theory of contract law.[296] His version of republicanism is distinct from the ones proposed by Skinner, Pettit, and their followers in that he does not understand freedom as non-domination as the core republican value, whether for society at large or specifically as the normative foundation of contractual obligation. Rather, the main characteristic of Saprai's theory is that it is 'antifoundationalist'. By this he means that it rejects the notion that contract law is based on—or ought to reflect—a single moral principle, most notably the promise principle. Instead, Saprai advocates 'normative pluralism' in contract law. This entails, in the first place, that contract law should be understood as being based on a plurality of values: not only promise-keeping, but also, for example, corrective justice, fairness, and altruism.[297] As a result, the normative basis of contract law will always be a composite of different values ('value pluralism'). A second aspect of normative pluralism is the idea that each of these values, and their bearing on contract law problems, may be interpreted in a plurality of plausible ways, none of which can be said to be the single right interpretation ('interpretative pluralism').

2. Trust-based Cooperation

When balancing and interpreting the various relevant values, Saprai argues, courts should be guided by the moral convictions prevailing in society. A direct consequence of normative pluralism, thus understood, is that in different jurisdictions different composites of values and their various interpretations can—and will legitimately—prevail. This leads Saprai to the further implication of limiting his more specific claims for the normative foundation of contract law to one jurisdiction only, to wit England. Thus, he argues for English contract law specifically that its constitutive purpose is the promotion of trust-based cooperation.[298] The reason why English contract law should promote cooperation based on trust is that trust-based cooperation is intrinsically valuable, and that it cultivates republican virtues indispensable for a thriving political community, in particular political participation, which is 'the tie that binds society together'.[299] It is not immediately clear why the intrinsic—and presumably

[296] P. Saprai, *Contract Law Without Foundations: Toward a Republican Theory of Contract* (2019).
[297] Ibid. 96.
[298] Ibid. 8 and 64.
[299] Ibid. 63.

objective—republican value of trust-based cooperation should be specific for England. However, the more important point to retain is that in Saprai's view, more generally, the constitutive purpose of contract can differ from one jurisdiction to another. Consequently, contract law without foundations seems radically anti-essentialist.

3. Radical Anti-foundationalism?

As we will see when discussing Habermasian discourse theories of contract law, one possible response to the plurality of values, with potential relevance for contract law, could be a radically procedural one. On such a view, the legitimacy of the public recognition and enforcement of contracts would come to depend on the legitimacy of the procedure through which the contract law at hand, and its specific balance and interpretation of values and principles, came about. However, Saprai does not go down that procedural route. Together with his firm rejection of contract law monism this raises the question of the radicalism of Saprai's anti-foundationalism. Does he mean that contract law ultimately has no discernible foundation at all, i.e. that ultimately there is no identifiable reason that justifies the legally binding force of contract? If that is not how the title of his book is meant to be understood, then a pressing question arises: how can we know what ought to be contract law's values and their interpretation? Put in more practical terms: by what normative standard can we evaluate and criticize whatever compound of contract law values that courts happen to find as the contingent foundation of the contract law at hand? This question is pressing, both from a legitimacy and from an epistemic point of view.

As to legitimacy, Saprai rejects a strong focus, found in the legal-positivist tradition in particular, on the coercive nature of contractual obligation. Such a 'top-down model' of contract law, he argues, risks making us lose sight of the valuable relationships contract law sustains.[300] Instead, Saprai's theory is concerned primarily with justifying, not contract law's binding force—the focus of this chapter—but its existence as a separate field of law, as part of a broader republican theory of differentiation in law. This concern is republican, in his view, in that it aims to involve ordinary people, in a 'bottom-up' manner, in matters of principle in contract law making. Central to Saprai's republican legal taxonomy is what he calls 'a republican view of local priority', which, he says, 'requires judges to interpret existing or conventional legal categories in light of contingent public or popular views about moral principles and categories that they implicate'.[301] What this seems to boil down to is a surprisingly uncritical, positivistic, majoritarian (but not necessarily democratic) view of why we have contract law as a separate branch of the law with its familiar core doctrines.[302] This does not seem to offer a basis for critiquing the core principles of contract law or for proposing a reform, for example of the kind that led in the UK to the Consumer Rights Act 2015. According to Saprai, this practice of differentiation in law 'serves the purpose

[300] Ibid. 94.

[301] Here Saprai follows Dworkin, whom he regards as a republican. This is somewhat surprising since Dworkin is usually referred to (including by himself) as a liberal. Indeed, he is widely regarded as one of the leading philosophers of liberal-egalitarianism.

[302] Indeed, H. L. A. Hart, *Law, Liberty, and Morality* (1963), at 20 would refer to this as 'positive morality' (the moral convictions actually shared by people), as opposed to 'critical morality' (moral principles used to evaluate and criticize social institutions, including positive morality).

of involving ordinary citizens in legal and political decision-making about matters of principle'.[303] However, the expected agency and control of citizens, even collectively, seems rather minimal. According to Saprai 'courts should take these popular views seriously'.[304] Although, even if this were to lead to some citizen involvement, they would never be involved as authors, but at best as sources of inspiration only. Contrary to Rousseauvian republicanism, Saprai's version does not seem based on an ideal of collective self-determination and citizens' co-authorship of the laws that apply to them. Fundamentally, it takes contract law as already being there. Therefore, ultimately the theory does not justify the legally binding force of contract. In this sense it is indeed radically non-foundational.

In addition, as stated earlier, there is the epistemic question of the respect in which this view amounts to a normative theory: what knowledge or insight does it offer regarding the normative foundations of contract law? The 'bottom-up republican' approach sounds more like an *ex post* assessment. Normatively this bears the risk of becoming an apology for whatever the law makers of the day (in Saprai's understanding mostly courts) will decide, while, epistemically, it is doubtful whether the theory has any predictive force, i.e. whether anything can be said, even on core contract law questions, in advance of actual bottom-up contract law making.[305] Put differently, if the theory offers neither substantive nor procedural guidance as to what contract law makers and interpreters ought to do, then in what sense is it a normative (i.e. prescriptive) theory, as opposed to a mere descriptive account (however accurate and valuable for that reason) of, in this case, the values that seem to inform the making and interpretation of contract law in England?

4. Communitarian Republicanism

Overall, Saprai's republican contract theory has distinctly perfectionist and communitarian features. According to Saprai, trust-based cooperation is an intrinsically valuable good which the state, at least in England, should promote through its law of contract. While this metaphysical claim about objective values expresses ethical (or 'moral') realism, the call for state promotion of an objective good makes the theory also perfectionist. At first sight, there might seem to exist a tension between Saprai's perfectionism and his claim about 'the pervasive fact of "normative pluralism" in contract law'.[306] However, upon closer examination, his understanding of the fact of pluralism is quite different from that of Rawls. As we saw, the Rawlsian notion of the fact of pluralism refers to the (permanent) condition of constitutional democracies where different citizens refer to different worldviews and ultimate values with regard to the same political question. For Saprai, by contrast, the fact of pluralism means that

303 Saprai (n. 296) 42.

304 Ibid. 54.

305 Ibid. 10, Saprai grants (or rather claims) that on his view the pertinent values and their interpretation are underdetermined. However, the question is whether and how they are ever going to be determinable *ex ante*.

306 Ibid. 71. See also, ibid. 72: 'the unarguable fact of normative pluralism in contract law'. The claim that the fact of normative pluralism is 'unarguable' suggests that the fact of value pluralism itself should be understood as a (metaphysical) *a priori*. This too differs from Rawls, who regards the fact of reasonable pluralism as contingent upon the conditions prevailing in Western constitutional democracies. (Similarly, Habermas's theory aims to reconstruct the post-metaphysical condition of modernity.)

a plurality of values objectively bear on contract law. Specifically, in his view, contract law doctrine is shaped not only by promise, but also by 'other normative concerns, such as the prevention of exploitation, altruism, fairness, corrective justice, the protection of reliance, and so on'.[307] Although there exists no single right answer with regard to the ranking and balancing of these values, according to Saprai a legitimate contingent balance of such values can be reached locally. By contrast, according to Rawls, the proper response to the fact of reasonable pluralism is that the basic structure of society should be justifiable by principles of justice, which are self-standing with regard to the various ultimate values citizens may adhere to.[308]

At the same time, Saprai regards contract law, at least for England, as being instrumental to the promotion of cooperation between citizens, which, in its turn, can foster a climate conducive to active citizenship.[309] Thus, in classical civic republican vein, he considers contract law as a seedbed of civic virtue. The underlying idea is not primarily the consideration that citizens' lives go better to the extent that they actively contribute to the good of the polity. The real reason for the furtherance of trust-based cooperation through contract seems rather to be the promotion of the common good.[310] However, even if one accepts the premise that it is the task of the law to promote the common good, then it is still not clear on the theory's own, communitarian 'republican' terms that the promotion of trust-based cooperation requires contract law as we know it.[311] Social solidarity, cooperation and cohesion could be promoted just as well, and perhaps better, one would think, through other institutions, such as communes, kibbutzim, and (other) commons. Unlike the latter examples, typical contractual relationships involve only two parties, are concluded for strategic (i.e. self-serving) reasons, and are only in some cases meant to last for an indefinite time. These characteristics seem unhelpful when it comes to 'helping to foster a sense of neighbourliness or community which is an essential precondition for the existence of any state'.[312] However, whatever the plausibility of these essentially empirical claims, the more important point here is that they unequivocally express a very communitarian conception of republicanism, which to that extent is quite distinct from Pettit's civic republicanism we just saw.

[307] Ibid. 5.

[308] Similarly, Saprai's version of republicanism, as he points out, has 'a distinctly protestant bent' (ibid. 7). Even though this characteristic does not seem to be meant in the narrow sense of protestant faith (whether Calvinist, Lutheran, or other), but rather as an attitude, it nevertheless reflects quite a thick, ethical (pre-) conception—or, rather, ideal—of the person, both as a citizen and as a contracting party, that in a society characterized by value and interpretative pluralism, one would think, simply cannot be taken for granted as being either descriptively accurate or generally shared as an aspiration.

[309] See ibid. 6–7.

[310] Ibid. 66.

[311] In other words, Saprai's claim, ibid. 66, that 'the pursuit of [trust-based cooperation] through contract is *indispensable* for creating a sense of social solidarity, achieving successful social cooperation, and so forth' (emphasis added), seems implausible.

[312] Ibid. 66.

7. Discourse Theory

A. *Pacta Sunt Servanda*: the Wrong Paradigm?

Habermas reconstructs the modern history of private law thinking in terms of three successive paradigms. He presents the struggle between the 'liberal' and 'social' paradigms as a dispute concerning the limits of private autonomy, and proposes a contemporary third paradigm: the idea that this struggle can be overcome if one realizes that private and public autonomy are two sides of the same coin. The question, then, becomes how much—and what kind of—private autonomy we want to accord each other through our collective deliberation.[313] Although the likely outcome of such an inclusive deliberation would seem to be the recognition of legally binding force of contracts in some measure, it is not clear, from the Habermasian perspective, that we need to acknowledge any general principle to that effect. For example, from this reconstructive perspective it may be questioned whether in consumer contracts we should still speak of a general principle of *pacta sunt servanda*, given that after the introduction of the withdrawal rights by the European legislator, consumers have been able to walk away from their contracts without even giving any reason.[314] Thus, today a general principle of *pacta sunt servanda*, formulated quite generally, even when followed by a large number of important exceptions, may sound too much like a nostalgic or reactionary attempt at re-establishing the classical liberal paradigm. It recalls the famous Article 1134(1) of the French Civil Code of 1804, pursuant to which contracts 'have the binding force of legislation for those who have made them',[315] thus assimilating the contracting parties to sovereigns. This programmatic provision expressed the liberal *élan* of the French revolution by proclaiming and assuming the equality of all citizens. However, arguably today it would be naive (if not in blatant bad faith) to proclaim such a very general principle, totally ignoring the fact that many contracts today are concluded, not by free and equal citizens but by uninformed and dependent consumers. Significantly, the Common European Sales Law (CESL) proposal did not contain the binding force of contract among its three general principles.[316] In contrast, however, the CJEU held that 'in accordance with the general principles of civil law, each contracting party is bound to honour the terms of its contract and to perform its obligations thereunder'.[317] So, apparently—and perhaps somewhat anachronistically—the CJEU today still regards the binding force of contract as one of the European general principles of private law. Given that 'the justified critique the welfare paradigm levels

[313] J. Habermas, *Between Facts and Norms: Contributions To a Discourse Theory of Law and Democracy* (1996), at 391.

[314] Cf. Canaris, 'Wandlungen des Schuldvertragsrechts—Tendenzen zu seiner "Materialisierung"', 200 *Archiv für die Civilistische Praxis* (2000) 273, at 344: 'Wenn eine Partei einen Vertrag nach ihrem freien Belieben widerrufen kann, ... liegt darin selbstverständlich eine Einschränkung der formalen Vertragsfreiheit und des mit dieser auf das engste verbundenen Grundsatzes *pacta sunt servanda*.'

[315] Translation (n. 1). For a political history of Art. 1134 CC, see Jamin, 'Une brève histoire politique des interprétations de l'article 1134 du Code Civil', 178 *Dalloz* (2002) 901.

[316] The general principles contained in Part I, Chapter 1, Section 1 (general principles) CESL proposal were: freedom of contract (Art. 1), good faith and fair dealing (Art. 2), and co-operation (Art. 3).

[317] Case C-277/05, *Société thermale d'Eugénie-les-Bains v. Ministère de l'Economie, des Finances et de l'Industrie* (EU:C:2007:440), at para. 24.

against bourgeois formal law precludes a return to the liberal paradigm',[318] from a Habermasian point of view this proclamation of a general principle holding each contracting party 'bound to honour the terms of its contract', comes across as the ideological denial of an irreversible paradigm shift. The same applies, it would seem, to the conservation of the 'force of law' formula in the recent 'modernization' of the French Civil Code.[319]

In the words of Habermas, private and public autonomy are co-original. This means that enfranchised citizens mutually grant each other private rights while at the same time also determining their limits. Rights and democracy are equiprimordial: subjective rights are a precondition for democracy while democracy is a precondition for subjective rights. Thus, one would expect the ensuing system of rights to include some contractual rights, meaning that an inclusive societal debate would be likely to yield some binding force of at least some contracts. However, because of its procedural nature Habermas's theory (or rather, his proposed reconstructive paradigm) of private law deliberately remains open-ended. It yields hardly any specific answers, in our case with regard to the binding force of contract, and certainly no final ones, given that (as seen in Chapter 3) what counts ultimately is the forceless force of the better argument and that even democratic legislation should be understood only as a caesura, demanded by practical considerations, in an ongoing debate.[320] The total absence of legal recognition and enforcement of contracts would probably be difficult to reconcile with the system of rights and, therefore, seems unlikely to be the outcome of an inclusive deliberative process where everyone's point of view is considered. In particular, claims to the effect that the respect for a moral right to ethical autonomy requires some binding force would be difficult to reject with non-ideological reasons. However, on questions of remedies (such as specific performance, expectation or reliance damages, termination, price reduction), rights of withdrawal, rights to the unilateral termination of a long-term contract, for example, it seems, from a Habermasian point of view, nothing concrete can be conjectured, as a matter of private law theory, in advance of deliberation by the private law subjects *themselves* in their capacity of citizens.[321] Private law theorists have no privileged access to right answers concerning ideal contract law because they lack universal access to the dispersed relevant experiences of all citizens, who include not only the few close to the core of political decision-making but also the many at the periphery.

[318] Habermas (n. 313) 407.

[319] In the 2016 reform, the principle was re-codified, almost verbatim, as Art. 1103 CC, in spite of the reform's explicit objective to modernize general contract law. Cf. Art. 8, Loi no. 2015-177 du 16 février 2015 relative à la modernisation et à la simplification du droit: 'moderniser [le] droit commun des contrats'.

[320] Habermas (n. 313) 179.

[321] Remember the radically democratic hunch (ibid. xiii): 'in the age of a completely secularized politics, the rule of law cannot be had or maintained without radical democracy. . . . In the final analysis, private legal subjects cannot come to enjoy equal individual liberties if they do not *themselves*, in the common exercise of their political autonomy, achieve clarity about justified interests and standards'.

B. Contexts of Autonomy

Forst does not specifically discuss the binding force of contract law, or indeed private law in general. However, from his discussion of autonomy we can derive a number of implications for contract law, in particular concerning justifications for legally binding force of contracts and remedies for their breach.

1. Private Autonomy?

The concept of private autonomy plays a central role in many theories and arguments about contracts, in particular the justification of their binding force. Thus, it is frequently argued—or simply assumed—that contract law is essentially based on private autonomy.[322] Or, that a certain legal rule, reform, or court ruling 'undermines' private autonomy[323] or, on the contrary, 'respects' it.[324] However, in the various doctrinal, political, and theoretical arguments, the concept of private autonomy has been understood in quite divergent ways. As to its ontology, private autonomy has been referred to as a principle,[325] a right, an ideal, a value, and a mere ideology.[326] Similarly, concerning its scope, private autonomy has been understood as pertaining to the moral, political, and legal domains. And within the legal context, its role is said to go well beyond (substantive) private law, extending not only into private international law ('party autonomy'),[327] but also into constitutional law.[328] Thus, private autonomy has been regarded both as being prior to and as being a consequence of the law. Similarly, private law has been understood, variously, as protecting (or respecting or warranting), being based on (or justified) by limiting,[329] and being limited by private autonomy. When private autonomy is defined, as we have seen in this chapter, key elements may include references to self-constitution, self-determination, self-realization, self-authorship, self-mastery, or agency-freedom—concepts that are similar but by no means identical.[330] Often the notion of autonomy is considered to be closely related to 'freedom' or 'liberty'. However, these concepts too have notoriously been understood in many

[322] Cf. e.g. Comparato, 'Private Autonomy and Regulation in the EU Case-Law', in H.-W. Micklitz, Y. Svetiev, and G. Comparato (eds), *European Regulatory Private Law—the Paradigms Tested*, EUI Working papers, LAW 2014/04, 4, at 4.

[323] See e.g. Eidenmüller *et al.*, 'The Common Frame of Reference for European Private Law—Policy Choices and Codification Problems' 28 *OJLS* (2008), 659, at 707: 'a massive erosion of private autonomy'.

[324] See e.g. the Opinion of Advocate-General Poiares Maduro in Case C-438/05, *Viking Line* (EU:C:2007:292), at para. 49: 'the horizontal effect of the provisions on freedom of movement and respect for private autonomy'.

[325] E.g. Fuller (n. 2) 799: 'Among the basic conceptions of contract law the most pervasive and indispensable is the principle of private autonomy.'

[326] Kennedy, 'From the Will Theory to the Principle of Private Autonomy: Lon Fuller's "Consideration and Form"', 100 *Colum. L. Rev.* (2000) 94. See also H. Kelsen, *Introduction to the Problems of Legal Theory* ([first published 1934] 1992), at 40–41.

[327] A. Mills, *Party Autonomy in Private International Law* (2018).

[328] According to the German Federal Constitutional Court, private autonomy is 'constitutionally warranted' by Art. 2(2) of the Basic Law. See *BVerfGE* 89, 214, 51 (*Bürgschaft*): 'Art. 2 Abs. 1 GG gewährleistet die Privatautonomie'.

[329] *BVerfGE* 81, 242 (*Handelsvertreter*): 'Vorschriften des Privatrechts, die zwingendes Recht enthalten und damit der Privatautonomie Schranken setzen'.

[330] Cf. Gutmann, 'Some Preliminary Remarks on a Liberal Theory of Contract', 76 *Law Contemp. Probl.* (2013) 39, at 40.

different ways. Thus, some definitions of private autonomy place more emphasis on the 'freedom from' interference (negative liberty) or from domination (republican liberty), while others focus on the 'freedom to', i.e. to empowerment (positive liberty). In summary, the undifferentiated use of the concept of private autonomy risks confusing, rather than clarifying, our understanding of what grounds might justify political choices with regard to the binding force of contract. The unitary concept may be too ambiguous[331] and—most importantly—insufficiently nuanced for our present purposes. When critically examining public discourses on the binding force of contract in European contract law a more differentiated approach may be called for.

2. Types of Personal Autonomy

Forst distinguishes, as aspects of the freedom that members of a political community must grant and guarantee each other, five different conceptions of autonomy, i.e. moral, ethical, legal, political, and social autonomy.[332] At first sight, a discussion of conceptions of autonomy as dimensions of political liberty may seem out of place in a discussion of the private law question of the binding force of contract. However, what we are discussing here is not the personal morality of promise keeping, but the public enforcement of private agreements by political institutions (the institutions of the *polis*, i.e. the political community). Just as for other political questions, so too for the fundamental political question of the legally binding force of contracts, including their public recognition as well as the backing by the state authorities of selected private responses to breaches of contract ('remedies'), a multi-dimensional single concept of political liberty, distinguishing different conceptions of individual autonomy, may clarify our understanding.

As Forst points out, a discussion of *conceptions* of autonomy presupposes an underlying *concept* of the autonomous person, that he defines as follows: 'a person acts autonomously—that is, as a self-determining being—when she acts intentionally and on the basis of reasons. Autonomous persons in this sense are accountable agents, accountable for themselves to both themselves and others; they can reasonably explain and justify their actions'.[333] Crucially, different intersubjective contexts require different kinds of justifications. And a person is autonomous to the extent she can recognize good reasons, and act upon them in each of these contexts. This applies to contract too. A person may be confronted with the question of the binding force of contract in quite different practical contexts. In other words, Forst's approach to autonomy confronts us with the fact that a discussion of the normative question concerning the binding force of contract ('ought contracts to be binding?') has different aspects, and, crucially, will require different kinds of answers, in different practical contexts. And a general principle of binding force of contract and general contract remedies are only fully justifiable—in the sense that no one could reasonably reject them—if they are compatible with the personal autonomy of persons in each of these practical contexts.

331 Cf. J. Busche, *Privatautonomie und Kontrahierungszwang* (1999), at 13 ff.
332 R. Forst, *The Right to Justification: Elements of a Constructivist Theory of Justice* (2007), ch. 5.
333 Ibid. 129.

Each dimension of personal autonomy has its own corresponding justificatory context, pertinent type of reason, and aspect of personhood: moral, ethical, public, legal and social autonomy, contexts, reasons and persons, respectively.[334] Each of these types of autonomy may play a role in discourses contesting and justifying (European) contract law, including in particular the binding force of contract. In other words, citizens (and non-citizens) may contest political choices with regard to binding force and remedies in (European) contract law referring to different types of autonomy, or may reasonably be understood as referring to one type of autonomy rather than another. Similarly, contract law makers, in their justificatory grounds, may refer—or be understood as referring—to different conceptions of autonomy. In each of these cases the appropriateness of the conception of autonomy for the context at hand may itself become the subject of critique.[335] Indeed, this is to be expected.

3. Moral Autonomy

Moral autonomy means to respect others (and ourselves) equally as persons[336]—as beings with human dignity[337] (in Kantian terminology: as aims in themselves)—by acting on reasons that take every affected person equally into account. Indeed, moral discourses aim to be convincing to *any* other person. They respond to the question of what we owe to each other as human beings.[338] They therefore address practical questions from a universal perspective. In the context of moral questions, we cannot presume that others share our values, and we should beware of projecting our own values onto others.[339] Instead of invoking ethical values, in the moral context we should appeal to moral norms.[340] Thus, an agent is morally autonomous when she is moved, in the moral context, only by reasons of action that can convincingly claim universal validity. This means that in response to moral objections she convincingly justifies her actions with reasons that no affected person could reasonably reject, i.e. reasons that are both general and reciprocal.[341] Moral autonomy thus refers to the moral person,

[334] Moreover, as we will see, there is also a different type of heteronomy (i.e. the opposite of autonomy) corresponding to each type of autonomy. Cf. I. Kant, *Critique of Practical Reason* (1788), at 5:33 (Theorem IV).

[335] The critique may be both immanent and transcendent. R. Forst, *Normativität und Macht: Zur Analyse sozialer Rechtfertigungsordnungen* (2015), at 15–16.

[336] Empirically, persons are not equal. On the contrary, they are quite diverse in all sorts of ways. Their universal equality is entirely moral. Hence, for example, the inevitably moral basis of any discourse on distributive justice, discrimination, and exploitation.

[337] Kant, *Groundwork* (n. 126) 4:437: '*Autonomy* is thus the ground of the dignity of a human and of every rational nature.'

[338] Cf. T. M. Scanlon, *What We Owe to Each Other* (1998).

[339] Forst (n. 332) 66.

[340] This does not entail that these ethical values should be regarded as false. As R. Forst, *Contexts of Justice: Political Philosophy Beyond Liberalism and Communitarianism* (1994), at 38–39, underlines:

> it is important to see that the reasons sufficient for answering a person's ethical questions do not become ethically false per se for this person if they do not turn out to be an acceptable basis for general norms. It just means that there are different ethical conceptions and morality is not the medium to demonstrate their *ethical* truth or falsehood. A form of life does not become false because its general realization cannot be morally demanded. Just as ethical reasons are not necessarily general reasons in a moral sense, moral reasons are not sufficient to determine the good life. (emphasis in original)

[341] Forst (n. 332) 130.

i.e. to persons in the context of moral justification, where moral claims are made and considered. The moral context is not abstract (or even transcendental) but 'the very concrete context in which persons respect each other as human beings, whatever else they may or may not have in common with regard to other contexts such as a culture, a state, a family, and so on'.[342]

In the context of the justification or contestation of European contract law, including with regard to the binding force of contract and contractual remedies, both the addressees of the law and the law makers may invoke moral autonomy as a justifying reason. However, given that moral autonomy is based on a very thin conception of the person—i.e. it refers only to characteristics that hold true for all human beings—its justificatory or contestatory pertinence in the context of debates concerning (European) contract law will be rather limited. Thus, respect for moral autonomy may perhaps require that a society give some binding force to some contracts, if a right to conclude at least some contracts cannot be denied by anyone anywhere, i.e. if the morally autonomous person is someone who concludes legally binding contracts, at least potentially. Whether she actually will have the social, economic, and other resources to do so would be a question of social autonomy (discussed later). In other words, the moral right to contract would be entirely formal. Or, put differently, we would have a moral right to the availability of the contractual form.[343] It seems implausible, however, that moral autonomy would also demand a certain type of remedy for breach of contract (e.g. specific performance) rather than another one (e.g. expectation damages or even mere reliance damages). By contrast, the moral core of human rights, it seems, may also be justifiably invoked in contract law contexts, for example when arguing that a certain contract law rule or outcome violates a person's human dignity. Thus, the horizontal effects of human rights may place important limits to the binding force of contract, as will be discussed in Chapter 7.[344]

4. Ethical Autonomy

Ethical autonomy refers to the good of leading an authentic life, faithful to one's own deepest truths. The ethically autonomous person adequately gives and responds to reasons that are required in ethical contexts. These are the reasons that a person considers to be constitutive (not necessarily through her own choice) of her identity. The identity may be individual and/or collective, shared with the other members of the relevant ethical community. As Forst puts it:

> ethical questions are those a person must answer as somebody who is 'constituted' by relationships, communities, values, ideals that serve as the (reflectively affirmed) 'fixed points' or 'strong evaluations' of her life; they are questions concerning 'my life', the life one is responsible for as its (at least partial) author. A person is ethically autonomous when she determines what is important for herself on the basis of reasons that

[342] Ibid. 130.

[343] This would be in analogy to a right to 'the legal form', i.e. a formal right to law. However, Habermas (n. 313) 111, introduces the idea of 'the legal form' as part of a functional explanation, not a normative justification, of law: 'The legal form is in no way a principle one could "justify," either epistemically or normatively.'

[344] At the same time, a 'human right to contract' seems far-fetched. See the discussion on a capability to contract, earlier, in Section 3.C.7.

> most fully and adequately take her identity into account, as the person she has been, as she is seen, as she wants to be seen, and to see herself in the present and the future; ethical reflection is retrospective and prospective at the same time.[345]

People differ on what an ethically autonomous, authentic life requires.[346] For some people obedience to their god will be central to living a good life, for others it may mean living a life that is original or even eccentric (Mill).[347] However, each person is morally required to respect other people's ethical autonomy. One person, therefore, cannot legitimately project her own values, including her own understanding of the ethical value of autonomy, onto other persons. That would violate the (moral) requirement of reciprocity.[348] This means, for example, that values of individuality (Mill),[349] certain rather ethical versions of 'Kantian' 'moral' autonomy, or Razian self-authorship cannot provide a public justification for generally applicable laws, including (European) contract law, in particular its core principle of the binding force of contract.

It is important, in this regard, to note the crucial distinction Forst draws between first-order conceptions and a second-order conception of ethical autonomy. First-order conceptions propose personal autonomy as a conception of the good life. Think, for example, of Raz's claim that an autonomous, self-authored life, lived by one's own lights, in accordance with the ideal of 'self-creation',[350] is a better life than the life of someone 'who drifts through life unawares'.[351] By contrast, according to the second-order conception, people have a moral right to live their lives according to a first-order conception (where first-order ethical conceptions understanding the good life as an autonomous life are just one set of ethical doctrines among many others, including notably more communitarian ones). It is this second-order autonomy that, pursuant to the right to justification, cannot be reasonably denied to anyone. As Forst writes:

> the leading insight is that one of these first-order answers can be absolutely sufficient for an autonomous and a good life, but that, given that there can be reasonable disagreement about the right answer, the political community cannot choose one of the first-order conceptions as the basis for answering the question concerning the extent to which law and politics should guarantee the exercise of ethical autonomy.[352]

For (European) contract law, it follows that although it is very well conceivable that a coherent system of contract law can be derived from the value of 'private autonomy',

345 Forst (n. 332) 131.

346 This may be seen as a conceptual truth in the sense that we would not speak of identities if they were all identical. Still, that we have different identities, values, and conceptions of the good life may be nothing more than an empirical fact. Hence, Rawls's idea of the fact of reasonable pluralism.

347 See Mill (n. 64) 130, 132.

348 Forst (n. 332) 5. In the same sense Rawls, 'The Idea of Public Reason Revisited' (1997), in J. Rawls, *Political Liberalism* ([first published 1993] 2005) 442.

349 See Mill (n. 64), ch. III, e.g. at 127: 'In proportion to the development of his individuality, each person becomes more valuable to himself, and is, therefore, capable of being more valuable to others.'

350 Raz (n. 63) 370.

351 Ibid. 382.

352 Forst (n. 332) 132–133.

as has been shown in the various monist liberal perfectionist and libertarian theories of contract discussed earlier, a contract law proclaimed as expressing, protecting, or promoting the (first-order) ethical value of autonomy in this way would violate the moral right to (second-order) ethical autonomy because it would fail to respect fully all those citizens who adhere to different values, i.e. to different ethical doctrines than those claiming a good life is an autonomous, self-authored life. Thus we see the direct relevance, for the questions that concern us here, of the crucial difference between the second-order understanding of (formal) ethical autonomy (i.e. to act in accordance with one's own values, whatever they are), which is grounded in moral autonomy, and first-order (substantive) ethical understandings of autonomy based on a certain conception of a valuable life (e.g. individualism) or of human nature (e.g. rationalism).[353] If indeed generally applicable laws have to be justified by reasons that meet the requirements of reciprocity, at least where the basic structure of society is concerned, as Forst claims, and if at least the basic structure of contract law is part of the basic structure of society, as was argued previously, then this has important implications for the justification of contractual obligation.[354] In particular, first-order ethical contract theories, claiming that contracts should be legally enforced because this makes the lives of their addressees go better, cannot justify the legally binding force of contract.[355]

5. Legal Autonomy

Legal autonomy refers to the autonomy of legal persons, i.e. of human agents (individually or collectively, as juridical persons) as the addressees of laws, in our case (European) contract law.[356] Legal personality is the legal expression of legal autonomy. It ensures legal agency, i.e. the capacity to have legal rights and obligations. Thus, the legally autonomous person offers—and responds to—appropriate legal reasons in legal contexts. Legal discourses, offering legal reasons, address practical questions from the perspective of a specific political community and its laws. These discourses are concerned with the legal rights and obligations that derive from the generally applicable legal rules of the legal system.[357] They address the other as a legal person. Within the confines of their territorial and personal scope, legal rules are generally applicable. They do not distinguish between individuals and groups, for example in accordance with their individual or collective values. Legal discourses offer arguments with regard to the proper application and interpretation of legal rules, rights, obligations, and remedies. An important set of legal discourses are constitutional discourses, about constitutional rights and—most relevant for private law—their horizontal effect. Some of these rights (i.e. the human rights in contrast, for example, to certain

[353] Ibid. 132.

[354] From a Forstian point of view, not only ethical theories referring to ultimate values, but also a moral theory relying on a controversial metaphysical conception of the moral person as the apex principle for a system of contract law, can be morally vetoed, as a justification of the binding force of contract, for failing to provide reciprocal reasons, as demanded by the right to justification.

[355] See Hesselink, 'The Right to Justification of Contract', 33 *Ratio Juris* (2020) 196.

[356] Forst (n. 332) 102.

[357] See the closely related distinction, and the normative reasons for it, between discourses of law making and discourses of law application. Habermas (n. 313) § 4.2.3.

'freedoms' protected by the EU Charter)[358] have an important moral core. In those cases, it is the moral core of the right that has priority over other legal considerations and arguments. Disputes concerning the proper interpretation of a human right are (at their core) moral disputes.[359]

As we have seen, sometimes the law explicitly protects 'private autonomy' or 'party autonomy', thus turning it into a legal concept.[360] It may even be elevated to a constitutional concept (i.e. in the case of constitutional protection), the content of which, however, often remains uncertain or indeterminate. Similarly, 'the freedom of contract' is sometimes constitutionalized.[361] The binding force of contract has not received a similar explicit constitutional recognition, except that of course freedom and binding force of contract are closely connected,[362] and that in some countries (but not in all; think of Germany, where the civil code is explicitly subjected to the post-war basic law) the civil code is sometimes considered to have a quasi-constitutional status (think of Carbonnier's often cited reference to the French Civil Code as 'la constitution civile, la vraie').[363] And as we saw, in some countries—notably France—the binding force of contracts—indeed the quasi-legislative status—is explicitly spelled out in the civil code (and was even recently re-codified). From the Forstian point of view, it is critical that such legal notions as 'private autonomy' and 'party autonomy' should not be reinterpreted, in their application, as more ethical notions, for example in the sense of promoting self-authorship, but should ensure that contract law remains available to persons not sharing a liberal-perfectionist conception of the good life, to promote their own respective (individual or community) values, ideals, and conceptions of the good.

Indeed, Forst understands the conception of legal autonomy as ensuring that no one will be forced to live according to a specific (i.e. first order) conception of ethical autonomy. As he writes: 'respecting legal autonomy implies respecting the freedom of persons to live according to their ethical convictions'.[364] In other words, there is an important, direct link between legal autonomy and ethical autonomy (i.e. the second-order ethical autonomy, which is based on moral autonomy): through the concept of legal personhood, law provides a 'protective cover' that equally protects everyone's ethical identity:[365]

> Legal autonomy implies that a legal person is accountable and responsible only to the law, not to certain ethical values. Since positive law regulates only the external

[358] See Hesselink, 'Private Law and the European Constitutionalisation of Values', *Amsterdam Law School Research Paper No. 2016-26.*

[359] Human rights (rights we have by virtue of our humanity) do not always fully overlap with—and are usually a narrower but sometimes a wider set than—catalogues of fundamental rights or constitutional rights.

[360] See e.g. Art. II-1:102 DCFR.

[361] On the constitutionalization of freedom of contract, see Chapter 7.

[362] It is the freedom to conclude legally binding contracts, that received constitutional protection.

[363] See Carbonnier, 'Le code civil', in P. Nora (ed.), *Les lieux de mémoire*, Vol. II (1986) 293, at 309.

[364] Forst (n. 332) 133.

[365] The concept of a protective cover builds upon Hannah Arendt's conception of legal personality as a protective mask, based on the original meaning in Latin of *persona*, i.e. a theatrical mask. See H. Arendt, *On Revolution* ([first published 1963] 2006), at 96–97. Cf. Forst (n. 340) 68.

> behavior of persons and abstracts from the motivation of their actions, it opens a space of personal arbitrariness in which persons have the right 'not to be rational', understood in the sense of ethical nonconformity.[366]

Thus, 'as a protective cover, law is a reflection of the fragility of ethical identities'.[367] For the specific context of (European) contract law, this means that legal persons should not be expected or encouraged in (or through) their contractual relationship to pursue or promote certain ethical values, such as self-authorship or welfare maximization. Conversely, persons (including contract law scholars and theorists) should not try to implement their values through contract law. For, 'persons do have a right to have their ethical identity respected equally, yet they do not have a right to have their ethical views become the basis of general law'.[368]

6. Political Autonomy

Political autonomy means the autonomy of a person as a citizen, especially as a co-author responsible for generally applicable laws.[369] It refers to the political values of collective self-determination (popular sovereignty) and self-legislation, free from domination, for example, by a tyrant (whether enlightened or not), that have been central to republican understandings of autonomy, especially Rousseau's idea of self-legislation.[370] It can be exercised only jointly, in concert with the other members of one's political community.[371] Together with other citizens, a politically autonomous agent decides and justifies with—and responds to—reasons that are appropriate for the political context, i.e. public reasons (as opposed to private reasons): 'While legal autonomy means that a person is responsible *before* the law, political autonomy means that a person is, as part of a collective, responsible *for* the law.'[372] This requires the formal and material existence of equal rights and opportunities for citizens, in institutionalized procedures of public justification, to share the political power of shaping the laws that apply to them. Thus, core to political (or public) autonomy is the democratic deliberation on—and the enactment of—generally applicable laws. And these include private law as much as public law.[373]

Political autonomy is especially relevant for the questions that were discussed in Chapters 3 and 4, on who is or are legitimate contract law makers in Europe. As we saw, both justificatory and contestatory discourses concerning the legitimacy of a particular contract-law-making institution, relative to potential alternatives (or the lack thereof), may invoke the value of political autonomy as the normative basis for their

[366] Forst (n. 332) 134. See also Forst (n. 340) 233.
[367] Forst (n. 340) 233.
[368] Forst (n. 332) 134.
[369] Ibid. 102, 133–135.
[370] Rousseau, 'Le contrat social' (1762), in J. J. Rousseau *Œuvres Complètes*, Vol. III (1964). See also Kant, 'Metaphysical First Principles of the Doctrine of Right', in I. Kant, *The Metaphysics of Morals* ([first published 1797] 1996), at § 46 (6:314). Cf. Forst (n. 332) 135.
[371] Forst (n. 332) 136.
[372] Ibid. 135 (emphasis in original).
[373] Thus, Forst does not understand political autonomy in the ethical sense, advocated by republican perfectionists, of what a person, being a political animal, should do to live a fulfilling life. Cf. Aristotle, *Politics*, at 1253a1.

argument. And if it is true for all generally applicable rules that its addressees must be able to regard themselves also as their authors,[374] then all contract law rules are subject to that principle too. Therefore, political choices concerning European contract law, especially the fundamental ones under discussion in this book, including the question of the general binding force of contract and remedies for breach, will need to involve all affected persons and therefore—or in that general sense—have to be democratic. Another way of putting this is by saying that individual self-legislation through contract—in the phrase used by the French Civil Code, contracts 'have the binding force of legislation for those who have made them'[375]—and collective self-legislation cannot exist without one another. Or, more pointedly: the binding force of the social contract and of private contracts mutually presuppose each other. This is the Habermasian point about co-originality.[376]

7. Social Autonomy

Finally, social autonomy means having the socio-economic means to be autonomous in the four other senses, i.e. having the means for moral, ethical, political, and legal autonomy.[377] It refers to the social and material preconditions for being an equal citizen, which includes a justifiable distribution of resources. The assurance of these conditions—i.e. the prevention of social exclusion—is the responsibility all citizens together.[378] The idea is akin to 'the social bases of self-respect', one of the 'primary goods' in Rawls's theory of justice,[379] and also to the 'basic capabilities' in the theories of Nussbaum and Sen,[380] albeit that the latter are more ethical ('thicker'), i.e. more tied up with specific conceptions of the good life (in Nussbaum's case Aristotelian), than the former.

In private law, this is expressed in the idea of *Materialisierung*, a more substantive understanding of private autonomy, of freedom of contract, and of the equality of the parties, where real alternatives are available, as opposed to a merely formal private law, that treats the parties as equal even where they patently are not, whether in the relational or the social sense.[381] Social autonomy is what libertarians have no place for. It is also what Marx thought could never be achieved in a market system—it could happen only if the workers became the owners of the means of production. Thus, from

[374] Habermas (n. 313) 120.

[375] Art. 1103 French Civil Code, translation (n. 1).

[376] Cf. Habermas (n. 313) 104: 'The co-originality of private and public autonomy first reveals itself when we decipher, in discourse-theoretic terms, the motif of self-legislation according to which the addressees of law are simultaneously the authors of their rights.' Note, however, the difference with Habermas in that for Forst both 'private' and 'public' autonomy (indeed all types of autonomy, i.e. moral, ethical, political, legal, and social) are morally grounded in the single right to justification, while Habermas, as we saw in Chapter 3, reconstructs the equiprimordiality of private and public autonomy more empirically from the encounter of the discourse principle with the 'legal form'. On this difference, see Forst (n. 332) 304, footnote 38; Forst, 'The Justification of Basic Rights: A Discourse-Theoretical Approach', 45 *Netherlands Journal of Legal Philosophy* (2016) 7, at 20.

[377] Forst (n. 332) 136.

[378] Ibid.

[379] Rawls (n. 49) 348.

[380] A. Sen, *The Idea of Justice* (2009), at 269 ff; Nussbaum, *Creating Capabilities* (n. 115).

[381] For a historical reconstruction of the idea of the 'materialization' of private law norms, see M. Auer, *Der privatrechtliche Diskurs der Moderne* (2014).

a Forstian point of view, the justifiability of the legally binding force of contract and of the availability of remedies for breach of contract are subject to the social autonomy of contracting parties that would be bound by it. In other words, the binding force of contract should be upheld only in a system of sufficiently materialized private law. Persons should be bound by a contract only in circumstances of sufficient social autonomy.

The implications of this demand for European contract law will be discussed further in Chapter 6, on contractual inequality and weaker party protection. For now it suffices to recall that the binding force of contract, and the system of contract remedies, are fully justifiable—i.e. reasonably non-rejectable—only if they are compatible with the autonomy of persons in each practical context, including the socio-economic one. In other words, from the point of view of the right to justification, social autonomy, as an aspect of full autonomy, must be immanent to any general principle of binding force of contract or a right to contract.

C. Contract as Deliberation

Lomfeld proposes a 'discourse theory of contractual rights' that understands 'contract as deliberation'.[382] He argues that the contracting parties, in addition to their promises of contractual performances, also make a second-level promise of reasons for the binding nature of these promises.[383] The binding force of contract arises through this reference to reasons.[384] In other words, every contract promises reasons for its own legally binding force.[385] In this sense, 'every contract is a social contract'.[386] The reasons for contract are fundamentally plural. Therefore, any contract law is grounded in a plurality of reasons.[387] As we saw in Chapter 3, Lomfeld offers a universal grammar of the reasons for contract. This grammar presents all the reasons for contract as referring to ethical values and argues that political deliberation (by the legislature or the courts) consists of the balancing of these conflicting values.

Lomfeld draws on Habermas's theory of communicative action.[388] He aims to follow the procedural legal paradigm by offering a framework for the deliberation on contracts' reasons.[389] He also invokes the Forstian right to justification.[390] His theory shares some of the main characteristics of Habermasian and Forstian discourse theory; however, there are also important differences. As we saw, both Habermas and Forst draw an analytical distinction, normatively grounded in Kantian deontology, between different types of reasons that are appropriate for different deliberative and justificatory contexts. By contrast, Lomfeld understands all reasons bearing on contract law as referring to ethical values. By ethical values he means 'every normative principle

[382] B. Lomfeld, *Die Gründe des Vertrages: Eine Diskurstheorie des Vertragsrechte* (2015); Lomfeld, 'Contract as Deliberation', 76 *Law Contemp. Probl.* (2013) 1.
[383] Lomfeld, 'Contract as Deliberation' (n. 382) 16.
[384] Lomfeld, *Die Gründe des Vertrages* (n. 382) 56.
[385] Ibid. 389.
[386] Lomfeld, 'Contract as Deliberation' (n. 382) 18.
[387] Lomfeld, *Die Gründe des Vertrages* (n. 382) 73.
[388] Lomfeld, 'Contract as Deliberation' (n. 382) 12.
[389] Ibid. 10.
[390] Ibid. 16

evaluating individual or social actions' without 'preset hierarchies' among them.[391] Thus, when Lomfeld writes that 'only a deliberative framework is capable of capturing the political battle between competing ethical principles',[392] then it is not clear how we should understand the deliberation. Will it be a Schmittian political battle[393]—an 'agonistic' struggle[394] among the proponents of different ethical values for as large as possible a scope of influence for their favourite value? Even if such an account of political battle were largely correct as a descriptive matter, should it be accepted as the normative foundation for contract law? Shouldn't the procedure ensure that the point of view of everyone affected (including notably those at the periphery) has an equal chance of influencing the contract law making process? And, at least on certain questions, shouldn't certain types of reasons (e.g. reasons referring to human rights and justice) categorically count more than others? Indeed, in some cases shouldn't individuals have a moral veto right against certain balances of values? To be sure, a Schmittian war of contract law values, where everyone wants their own value to prevail[395] and in which no price is too high,[396] is probably not what Lomfeld intends. However, will it be possible to avoid it altogether without a more deontological underpinning for a discourse theory of contract?

8. Concluding Remarks

A. The Politics of Binding Force

The question about the legally binding force of contract is an eminently political one. It is about what a society ought to do, through its public institutions, about private contracts. In particular, what private remedies, if any, should it make available to the innocent party, backed up with public force, in the case of breach of contract? Given the state's formidable power and its claim to a monopoly for the legitimate use of force, the legal recognition of contracts as binding and enforceable—as well as its rejection—requires a convincing political justification.

Unsurprisingly, different contemporary political theories understand and answer in radically divergent ways the normative questions of whether and why contracts should have legally binding force, and what this force should entail in terms of remedies for breach. For some theories, the binding force of contract is about enforcing duties of interpersonal morality. For others, the contractual obligation is teleological: political communities enforce contracts with a view to achieving some good, whether individual or collective. This immediately raises fundamental questions concerning the

[391] Ibid. 8
[392] Ibid. 2.
[393] C. Schmitt, *Der Begriff des Politischen* ([first published 1932] 9th ed., 2015).
[394] C. Mouffe, *The Return of the Political* (1993), at 1: 'for an agonistic pluralism'.
[395] See C. Schmitt, *Die Tyrannei der Werte* (3rd ed., 1960), at 41: 'Wer Wert sagt, will geltend machen und durchsetzen.' In this sense, the theory is surprisingly similar to monist theories that also have no answer to the question of how they should be combined with other theories, other than that ideally the reign of their own core value over contract law should be as extensive as possible
[396] Ibid. 60: 'Wertlogisch muß immer gelten: daß für den höchsten Wert der höchste Preis nicht zu hoch ist und gezahlt werden muß.'

general relationship between law, morality, ethics, and social norms—and, thus, the nature of law, in this case the law of contract.

In addition, as we saw, most political theories strongly underdetermine the contract law rules on binding force and remedies, not only the technical details but also the main principles with regard to the appropriate remedies for breach. As a general matter, this suggests that what is a big political question for contract law and its theory is not necessarily as important an issue for society, its politics, and its theory. It also suggests that from the perspective of political principles, the legitimate (European) contract law maker may have a large degree of discretion in determining the legally binding force of contracts and appropriate remedies for breach.

B. *Pacta Non Sunt Servanda*?

The most radical version of the question of the binding force of contract discussed in this chapter was whether it would be acceptable for a society not to ensure any binding force of contract at all. If we limit that question to societies of the kind we live in, then a legitimate immediate response would be the counter-question of whether a society without any legally binding force of contract would still be our kind of society. Beyond this point, however, we can ask whether the absence of legal recognition of any contracts or the total absence of any remedies for breach of contract would make that society, to that extent, an unjust or perhaps an intolerably bad one. Very concretely, if the legitimate law maker decided to abolish the binding force of contract in general, or to replace remedies protecting the expectation interest (in particular, specific performance and expectation damages) with mere reliance protection, could this be justified with convincing reasons? Perhaps it could. Maybe a society that acknowledged and sanctioned exchanges made on the spot, but did not recognize (through expectation remedies) contractual 'obligations' or 'promises' to give or do something in the future, would not necessarily be an unjust or otherwise failing society. Much would depend on its other social, economic, and political institutions.

C. Overlapping Consensus and Reflective Equilibrium

Of course, this radical question about the justifiability of the total absence of any *pacta sunt servanda* principle is merely a hypothetical one. In all legal systems in Europe contracts have legally binding force, with remedies protecting the expectation interest. And much of EU law—ranging from tax law to financial law to consumer law—would simply be unintelligible if the binding force of contracts was not recognized as a 'general principle of civil law'.[397] Similarly, all the normative political theories we saw seemed to demand, or permit, at least some binding force for at least some contracts, albeit for very divergent reasons. What we find, therefore, is a consensus—a very broad and inclusive one—not only among reasonable legal systems but also among

[397] Case C-277/05, *Société thermale d'Eugénie-Les-Bains v. Ministère de l'Economie, des Finances et de l'Industrie* (EU:C:2007:440).

reasonable political theories, with regard to a general principle of legally binding force of contract, understood in the minimal sense of a principle against the absence of any legally binding force. In Rawlsian terms, we could refer to this state of affairs as an overlapping consensus, perhaps to be combined with a reflective equilibrium to the extent that such a principle matches, upon reflection, with our own normative intuitions.

It is important to note, however, that any overlapping consensus on a general principle will bring us only so far. If the principle is to do any useful work with regard to practical questions it will have to be interpreted. However, different citizens (and officials) are likely to interpret it quite differently. The reason is that, when interpreting, they will seek coherence with the other elements, beyond the principle, of their respective political views. But these wider worldviews, and their core values, will often point in divergent directions. We can see this practical problem very concretely with regard to the principle of the binding force of contract. If we try to interpret it in order to determine its meaning and implications then immediately we are confronted with the various welfarist (utilitarian), liberal perfectionist, traditionalist (e.g. neo-pandectist), and libertarian theories, among others, and with all the controversies among them, with regard, for example, to the justifiability of rights of withdrawal, expectation damages, a right to specific performance, efficient breach, penalty clauses, and notification periods.

D. A Moral Right to Some Binding Force

A different take would be to argue for a moral right to the legal recognition and enforceability of at least some contracts. We saw several different arguments going in that direction. On such a view, the right to at least some binding force of contract follows from our moral right to autonomy. If we respect each other as different persons (as free and equal; as ends, not merely means for our own ends) then we must acknowledge each other some agency to live our lives in accordance with values, a worldview, or a life plan of our own. In Forst's terminology, this is the moral right to second-order ethical autonomy (i.e. the right to have a first-order ethical conception). The argument would be that if we set up the main institutions in our society in such a way that not everyone has a right, at least in principle, to the public enforcement, in one way or another, of at least some of their agreements, then to that extent that society is not sufficiently just, because its basic institutional structure is insufficiently justifiable. People in that society would have a moral right to 'veto', as Forst would put it, the public decision to totally abolish any legally binding force of contract, or the categorical refusal to (re-)introduce, or to extend it to everyone.

However, as mentioned earlier, it is an open question whether a society that only gave reliance damages in case of the breach of a wholly executory contract (i.e. one that include 'promises' or 'obligations' to perform in the future) would necessarily be an unjust society. Much would depend on the other institutions and practices in that very different society. Still, from a moral point of view, it seems, any such right, if recognized, would have to amount to more than a merely formal right to contract. The right would have to be more substantive, and be understood in the sense of reasonable access to contract. A system of contract rights could not be set up legitimately if some people were excluded from concluding any contracts or from legally enforcing them. Mere theoretical access to contract and to contract remedies would effectively amount to upholding a privilege in the guise of a general principle. Put differently, and anticipating the discussion in Chapter 6, from a moral point of view there are important contract justice limits—both distributive and interpersonal—*immanent* to any general principle of binding force of contract.

In any case, any moral right to contract inevitably would strongly underdetermine the outcome of many choices the legitimate (European) contract law maker has to make, including most choices concerning remedies. The reason is that, just as with regard to a principle of binding force based on an overlapping consensus, so too any right to contract grounded in the second-order ethical autonomy demanded by moral autonomy will have to remain so general and abstract that it is hardly possible to derive any determinate reasons for any morally required legal response to breach of contract. Many different regimes of remedies for breach of contract seem permissible from the point of view of a right to contract that is compatible with the respect we owe each other in a pluralist political community. Put differently, the moral right to contract, if it exists, seems unlikely to constrain the legitimate (European) contract law maker significantly in its specific choices concerning the legal implications of contractual obligation.

E. Incommensurable Values and Contract Systems

This brings us to what we may refer to as the 'monistic sting' (in analogy to the 'semantic sting'),[398] i.e. the widespread fixation among contract theorists on finding the ultimate value or principle on which contract law is truly founded. The appeal of monistic contract theories is that they are able to derive a complete system of contract law from one single value, whether efficiency, liberty, autonomy, solidarity, or tradition. The normative force of the foundational value starts off from the top as a general justification of contractual obligation (i.e. the legally binding force of contract) and then reaches all the way down into the details of various doctrines concerning the formation, interpretation, validity, performance, and non-performance of contracts. The trouble with these normative contract systems, however, is that they are like Kuhnian paradigms or Luhmanian social systems: each perceives the other systems only on its own terms. To give just one example among many, from the welfarist point of view a right to specific performance looks inefficient, while libertarians reject efficient breach as a form of theft. These two views are not on speaking terms, so to speak, because together with their respective foundational values comes a complete package of doctrines and rules, sometimes in the tiniest details, while the foundational values themselves, and thus the contract law systems based on them, are often in direct conflict with one another or even incommensurable. That is the reason why essentialist and other monistic normative contract theories based on an ultimate value or ultimate

[398] Dworkin (n. 166) 45, with reference to Hart and his followers.

truth, as the basis for public decisions on contract law, will inevitably run into problems in pluralist societies. If we accept a certain value as the ultimate foundation of contractual obligation then, for reasons of consistency, we will have to accept the entire contract law system based on it, as a blueprint. Indeed, from the point of view of each of the monist theories a democratic compromise with other monist theories is perceived necessarily as mere partial compliance and to that extent a lost opportunity. There exist, of course, disputes internal to each of the paradigms, but these are about the proper application of the principle or the best implementation of the value, that, however, remains understood as a given, i.e. beyond dispute. Conversely, if we reject a particular value as the normative basis of our contract law, then we cannot derive any normative argument from that value system (as such) because we do not recognize its normative force. This is what monists' contract law theories have in common with other axiomatic and dogmatic systems: once the axiom or dogma falls, all its theorems or doctrines fall with it, and the system collapses.[399] It also raises the stakes in the question of what justifies the legally binding force. In this debate, the winner takes all.

In summary, the kind of first principles that do yield concrete contract law outcomes concerning specific remedies, and so on, are not ones that in a pluralist society we could agree upon as principles underlying our main institutions, while the kind of principles that we could agree upon will necessarily be only very general and will not yield concrete contract law outcomes. This is a direct consequence of the fact of reasonable pluralism, in this case applied to contract law (reasonable contract law pluralism), and of the performative nature and the epistemic dimension of collective (democratic) deliberation. Exactly which contract law doctrines and rules are justifiable towards all persons affected by them cannot be determined by theorists (in this case the private law theorists). The reason is—to borrow an expression from Hayek—theorists' 'incurable ignorance' as to how the world—including its contract law questions—looks from the perspective of others, including notably those at the periphery of political society: we inevitably lack other people's 'local knowledge'. Hayek claimed that the only way we can figure out what people want is to refer to prices set by free markets. However, a more attractive alternative may be a free market of ideas: a free flow of reasons that will have to be fully taken into account by the democratic law maker. Atiyah remarked: 'the law must reflect diverse and conflicting values. Given this diversity, there is no hope of reducing the whole body of contract, or even its main outlines, to a single principle.'[400] With a small modification, we can conclude: the law must reflect diverse and conflicting points of view; it is therefore illegitimate to reduce the whole body of contract, or even its main outlines, to one single value.

F. The Sanctity of Contract as Ideology

There is a further political dimension. The idea of a general principle of binding force of contract, or a right to contract, contributes to placing the contractual aspects of

[399] See Swaminathan, 'Mos Geometricus and the Common Law Mind: Interrogating Contract Theory', 82 *MLR* (2019) 46.
[400] Atiyah (n. 46) 149.

certain relationships in the foreground. This is in contrast to approaches that point to the other dimensions of these same relationships as perhaps being more important than the contractual ones. Being a current account holder with a bank, a policy holder at an insurance company (financial services), a passenger of a train or airline company (transport), a patient of a doctor or hospital (medical services), having a mobile phone plan with a communications provider (telecom services), or paying every month for the supply of gas and electricity (energy) is perhaps not usually perceived, at least not in the eyes of one of the parties, as being in the first place a contractual relationship.

Moreover, the emphasis on a general principle of binding force of contract also reinforces the idea of the continued importance and relevance of general contract law. However, today specific sets of rules for consumer contracts, and the regulation of specific market sectors (telecom, transport, energy, financial services, etc.), which often include private law aspects as well, may have become at least as relevant to the persons affected by them. This has led certain theorists to question the relevance of general private law today and in the future. Such questions of legal taxonomy are far from neutral. On the contrary, placing general contract law in the foreground means emphasizing interpersonal aspects, while an emphasis on regulatory objectives places instrumentalism in the foreground. In other words, there is also a risk of ideological use of a general principle of binding force of contract or a general right to contract.

G. The *Acquis*

What does all this mean for the *acquis communautaire* on binding force and remedies: can it be justified? As we saw, some salient elements of the *acquis* include: a general principle of binding contractual obligation acknowledged by the CJEU; pervasive withdrawal rights for consumers; a strong right for consumers to specific performance (repair or replacement) in sales; and a narrow definition of acceptable excuses for airlines in the case of denied boarding or delay. Each of these is heavily contested. However, it is not clear that any one of them could be rejected with reasons that could reach the threshold of a vetoing right to contract, or principle of binding force, compatible with the respect we owe each other in the pluralist political community of European citizens.

Take the example of the withdrawal rights that consumers have pursuant to the Consumer Rights Directive, which allow them to withdraw from certain contracts without giving any reason and without incurring any costs.[401] Clearly, these withdrawal rights are at odds with several of the contract theories we saw. For example, a libertarian may regard any right unilaterally to withdraw from a contract as pure theft, because the state coercively removes from the seller an entitlement she already had, based on the consent freely given by both contracting parties (the fact that one of them can be labelled as a 'consumer' making no difference, on this view). From a welfare perspective, it may be—and has been—argued that mandatory withdrawal rights are inefficient and that, therefore, sellers should be allowed to offer consumers the

[401] See Art. 9, Consumer Rights Directive (n. 30). Consumers have similar withdrawal rights in a number of other contexts (timeshare, online credit).

opportunity to waive them in exchange for a discount. And certain communitarians may regard withdrawal rights as a blunt tool, typical of the instrumentalism characteristic for the *acquis communautaire* and not up to doctrinal standards of sophistication characterizing the national legal cultures of the EU Member States.

Do these libertarian, utilitarian, and communitarian normative points of view provide a normative basis to veto, as it were, a democratic decision in favour of introducing consumer rights of withdrawal? Do sellers claiming that withdrawal rights cannot reasonably be justified towards them have a point? This does not necessarily seem to be the case. Rather such a veto, if accepted, would seem to privilege their own controversial value, worldview, or conception of the essential nature of contract law over others—which seems disrespectful to the moral autonomy of others, who have an equal right to their own second-order ethical autonomy.

However, the reverse also seems true: a contract law without consumer rights of withdrawal for situations where consumers are under high pressure or unable to see and feel what they are buying does not seem—for that reason—necessarily unjustifiable toward consumers. First, because other legal doctrines and remedies (or market forces, if this can be demonstrated) may be able to do the same job (i.e. of doing justice) equally well. And, secondly, because even a contract law where consumers cannot walk away from a contract in these types of situation may still be justifiable towards them. This may be the case because having a right of withdrawal in consumer contracts may not be a matter of justice (social or interpersonal) within the scope of the basic structure of contract law (which arguably is part of the basic structure of society) that should be withheld (morally speaking) from the discretion of the legitimate law maker.

Thus, on the limited informational basis following inevitably from my own specific point of view (burdens of judgement), the conclusion would be that there do not seem to be obvious reasons why certain elements of the *acquis communautaire* on the binding force of contract and remedies, on the level of general rules at which they were adopted, cannot be reasonably justified towards those to which it applies. However, in order to prevent any misunderstanding, it should be repeated that this was nothing more than a (preliminary) critical analysis, not an expert evaluation (or measurement) of the justice of the *acquis*. To be more precise, this was a hypothetical account of the demand for justification of the *acquis communautaire* concerning the binding force of contract, the possible response by European law makers to that demand, and the ensuing deliberation among European citizens (and other affected persons) on the justifiability of this aspect of European contract law.

6
Weaker Party Protection

1. Introduction

Should the law protect weaker parties in contracts? The question is hardly a hypothetical one. On the contrary, weaker party protection is a central element of contemporary contract law in Europe. The laws of all Member States contain various types of weaker party protection in contracts, ranging from general rules against unfair exploitation or abuse of circumstances to more specific sets of rules protecting certain categories of contracting parties, such as workers, tenants, and consumers. Weaker party protection is even more central to EU contract law. Indeed, the bulk of contract law rules emanating from the EU are consumer protection rules. In contrast, most leading contemporary contract law theories, especially the essentialist ones, have no place for weaker party protection or, at best, only a very peripheral one. While all six questions under discussion in this book are fundamental political questions of European contract law, the present one is probably most widely regarded as politically salient, among legal scholars and politicians alike. In particular, the question of whether to protect weaker parties in contracts—and how much—is usually strongly associated with the political divide between the left and the right, not only historically but still today. As we will see, a discussion in terms of prominent contemporary political theories can bring more nuance and depth to the debate.

The question of whether and how contract law should protect weaker parties, central to the present chapter, is closely related to the questions of the binding force and the freedom of contract, discussed, respectively, in the previous and the next chapters (Chapters 5 and 7). The link between binding force and weaker party protection can be expressed in terms of remedies. When weaker party protection consists in the right to invalidate the contract (or a term in it) or to withdraw from the contract, the weaker party protection directly limits the binding force of the contract. Conversely, when weaker party protection brings additional remedies for breach of contract against the stronger party, such as a robust right for consumers to repair or replacement, then to that extent it reinforces the binding force of the contract. As to the relationship between weaker party protection and freedom of contract, rules that aim to protect weaker parties are usually mandatory and, thus, limitative of freedom of contract relative to the hypothetical baseline of unrestricted contractual freedom. Still, it makes good sense to discuss weaker party protection separately, not only because there is more to it than its binding force and freedom of contract dimensions, but especially because it has such a prominent place—socially, economically, morally, conceptually, numerically, and more—in contemporary European contracting and contract law.

Justifying Contract in Europe: Political Philosophies of European Contract Law. First Edition. Martijn W. Hesselink, Oxford University Press. © Martijn W. Hesselink 2021. DOI: 10.1093/oso/9780192843654.003.0006

A. Relational and Social Vulnerability

The notion of weaker party protection refers to inequality between the contracting parties. The inequality may relate to a variety of different characteristics of the parties, for example their wealth, power, education, skills, or experience. Moreover, the inequality may be relational (e.g. where the contract creates dependence) or social (e.g. where the contract results from dependence), or a combination. As we will see, relational weakness (e.g. a lack of bargaining power) frequently results from social weakness (e.g. belonging to a vulnerable group, or being situated at the intersection of several such groups). Finally, the inequality may relate either to the bargaining situation (unequal bargaining power, 'contracts of adhesion')[1] or to the stage of contract performance. While inequality is a factual matter the normative question is what, if anything, contract law should do about it. Should it reduce the inequality or compensate for it, or should it even ignore the inequality, either because it is not a problem or because the problem is best solved by other branches of the law or by other political and economic institutions?

B. Categorical and Contextual Protection

There are two main ways in which contract law might protect weaker parties: through categorical protection or through contextual protection. In the case of categorical protection, members of certain classes of contracting parties, such as employees, tenants, consumers, and patients, are deemed structurally or typically weaker than the other side of the contract and are granted legal protection.[2] Categorical protection is formal: whether a certain party will be protected in a given case will depend entirely on whether she falls within the definition of the category, not on any substantive considerations of whether she is in actual need of protection in the context at hand.[3] Categorical protection is quite visible and, therefore, has attracted most political attention. However, weaker party protection is not limited to the categorical protection of certain groups of contracting parties. For example, pursuant to the new Article 1143 of the French Civil Code, there is duress, and the contract can be annulled, 'where one contracting party exploits the other's state of dependence and obtains an undertaking to which the latter would not have agreed in the absence of such constraint, and gains

[1] Kessler, 'Contracts of Adhesion—Some Thoughts About Freedom of Contract', 43 *Colum. L. Rev.* (1943) 629. See Art. 1171 French Civil Code (new).

[2] See e.g. Case C-618/10, *Banco Español de Crédito SA v. Joaquín Calderón Camino* (EU:C:2012:349), at para. 39, with regard to Directive 93/13/EEC on unfair terms in consumer contracts, OJ 1993 L 95 (hereinafter 'Unfair Terms Directive'): 'the system of protection introduced by Directive 93/13 is based on the idea that the consumer is in a weak position vis-à-vis the seller or supplier, as regards both his bargaining power and his level of knowledge'.

[3] As an example, see Case C-340/16, *Landeskrankenanstalten-Betriebsgesellschaft—KABEG v. Mutuelles du Mans assurances—MMA IARD SA* (EU:C:2017:576), where the Court held that the plaintiff, who was regarded as not needing protection, could nevertheless invoke Art. 8 of the Brussels I Regulation (Regulation 1215/2012 on jurisdiction and the recognition and enforcement of judgments in civil and commercial matters, OJ 2012 L 351), in spite of the fact that its Recital (13) states, as the rationale for the Regulation, that 'in relation to insurance, consumer and employment contracts, the weaker party should be protected by rules of jurisdiction more favourable to his interests than the general rules'.

from it a manifestly excessive advantage'. The provision resembles Article II.–7:207 of the Draft Common Frame of Reference (DCFR) and Article 51 of the withdrawn Common European Sales Law (CESL) proposal. And several national contract laws in Europe contain similar provisions. While these doctrines focus on unfair exploitation at the conclusion of a contract, provisions like Article 1195 French Civil Code (new), which was strongly inspired by Article III.–1:110 DCFR and Article 89 CESL proposal, on change of circumstances, comes to the rescue of the contracting party when a change of circumstances after the conclusion of the contract 'renders performance excessively onerous'. Such doctrines, and others, protect contracting parties, who are in a vulnerable position in a contextual ('substantive' or 'material') way, focusing on the actual vulnerability of one of the contracting parties, as opposed to categorical (or 'formal') protection, where the vulnerability is assumed. Categorical protection, via the formal definition of groups to be protected, is easier and cheaper to administrate, especially in the case of standardized mass contracting, but will inevitably be both over- and under-inclusive, while, vice versa, the determination of actual, substantive worthiness of protection will be more precise but inevitably more time-consuming and costly.

C. Distributive Justice

The protection of certain groups in society against others—and the absence thereof—may have distributive implications. Distributive patterns are most salient in the case of categorical protection, with rules favouring employees, tenants, and consumers and their interests over those of employers, landlords, and traders, respectively. Even though the latter may be able to pass on some—or even most—of the cost of protection to the former, some distributive impact will usually occur.[4] This may well be a redistribution within the group of consumers, tenants, or employees (possibly even perverse, i.e. from the weakest to the stronger). Therefore, weaker party protection, and especially categorical protection, raises issues of distributive justice. Who should be made better off—employees or employers, landlords or tenants, consumers or traders, patients or doctors, and which sub-groups among the former, i.e. the average consumers, patients, and tenants or the most vulnerable ones?

D. The *Acquis Communautaire*

Much of the existing EU contract law (the *acquis communautaire*) aims at the protection of weaker parties or, more precisely, at the harmonization of the protection

[4] Cf. Kennedy, 'Distributive and Paternalist Motives in Contract and Tort Law, with Special Reference to Compulsory Terms and Unequal Bargaining Power', 41 *Maryland Law Review* (1982) 563, at 567–568:

> How much the economy produces, just in terms of the raw output of things that just about everyone wants some of, and also how well each person does in the economic struggle within civil society—both of these are in part a function of the set of property, contract and tort rules (with legislative and administrative elaborations) within which the struggle takes place.

warranted to certain weaker parties in certain situations in the laws of the Member States. Think, as an early example, of the Commercial Agency Directive of 1986, which protects self-employed commercial agents who may be in a very vulnerable position in a number of situations including notably in the case of unilateral termination of the contract by the principal.[5] The EU is also committed to the protection of workers. Pursuant to Article 153 TFEU, the Union supports and complements the activities of the Member States in a broad array of fields, including the protection of workers' health and safety and their protection when their employment contract is terminated.[6] In addition, EU law protects minorities and other groups against discrimination specifically in certain contractual contexts.[7] Finally, there is unequal treatment of men and women in work, whether in employment or self-employment.[8] However, the bulk of European weaker party protection in contracts concerns the many measures taken with a view to consumer protection.

E. The Level of Protection

Pursuant to Article 114(3) TFEU, when the European legislator adopts measures for the approximation of the laws of the Member States that have as their object the establishment and functioning of the internal market and are concerned with consumer protection, the legislator must seek a 'high level' of protection.[9] Moreover, pursuant to Article 12 TFEU, consumer protection requirements must be taken into account in defining and implementing other EU policies and activities. In *Mostaza Claro*, the Court of Justice of the European Union (CJEU) referred to Article 6(1) of the Unfair Terms Directive as 'a provision which, taking into account the weaker position of one of the parties to the contract, aims to replace the formal balance which the latter establishes between the rights and obligations of the parties with an effective balance which re-establishes equality between them'.[10] Legal objectives and considerations of this kind raise the normative question of how much inequality between the contracting

[5] Directive 86/653/EEC on self-employed commercial agents, OJ 1986 L 382, Arts 17–21.

[6] See also the European pillar of social rights that was solemnly proclaimed in 2017, e.g. its Art. 12 (Social protection): 'Regardless of the type and duration of their employment relationship, workers, and, under comparable conditions, the self-employed, have the right to adequate social protection.'

[7] See especially Directive 2004/113/EC implementing the principle of equal treatment between men and women in the access to and supply of goods and services, OJ 2004 L 373.

[8] See, respectively, Directive 2006/54/EC on equal opportunities and equal treatment of men and women in matters of employment and occupation (recast), OJ 2006 L 204, and Directive 2010/41/EU on equal treatment between men and women engaged in an activity in a self-employed capacity, OJ 2010 L 180. Obviously, women are not generally weaker contracting parties than men. However, they may sometimes be in a more vulnerable or precarious situation, which may raise inequality issues, e.g. with regard to formal versus substantive understandings of equality, that are akin, at least in part, to the ones under consideration in this chapter.

[9] The provision actually states that the Commission, when proposing such measures, 'will take as a base a high level of protection' but it seems odd that the requirement should apply only to the Commission proposals, and not also to the measures as adopted ultimately by Parliament and Council.

[10] Case C-168/05, *Elisa María Mostaza Claro v. Centro Móvil Milenium SL* (EU:C:2006:675), at para. 36. See also, with reference to Directive 1999/44/EC on certain aspects of the sale of consumer goods and associated guarantees, OJ 1999 L 171, Joined Cases C-65/09 and C-87/09, *Gebr. Weber and Putz* (EU:C:2011:396), at para. 75:

parties a society should tolerate. In other words, given that inequality is a matter of degree, the fundamental political question of consumer protection is not only a question of whether and whom to protect, but also how much protection should be provided.

F. Minimum and Full Harmonization

In relation to the protection of consumers, initially the European Community's aim was to ensure a minimum level of protection to which individual Member States were free, in principle, to add further protection (minimum harmonization).[11] However, at the turn of the century, the European Commission announced a shift in its policy from minimum to full harmonization measures, where the level of consumer protection prescribed by a directive constitutes both the minimum and the maximum from which the Member States are not allowed to deviate.[12] The 2005 Unfair Commercial Practices Directive was a salient example of this new policy.[13] Full harmonization met with strong opposition from Member States and consumer organizations, which denounced the fact that inevitably with full harmonization European integration would lead to a reduction in the level of consumer protection in certain Member States. In response, the Commission promised, as a compromise, that the full harmonization would always be 'targeted'. This policy of 'targeted full harmonization' was first introduced in the final version of the Consumer Rights Directive that was adopted in 2011.[14] However, the two latest consumer contract law directives that were proposed in 2015, specifically with a view to the digital single market, and adopted in 2019, in one case with an expanded scope, had already returned to the full harmonization objective.[15] The political opposition illustrated how controversial the full harmonization of consumer protection has been. In contrast, from the other side of the Atlantic, much of EU consumer protection law—even measures aiming merely at minimum

> Article 3 aims to establish a fair balance between the interests of the consumer and the seller, by guaranteeing the consumer, *as the weak party to the contract*, complete and effective protection from faulty performance by the seller of his contractual obligations, while enabling account to be taken of economic considerations advanced by the seller. (emphasis added)

[11] See e.g. Art. 8, Unfair Terms Directive (n. 2): 'Member States may adopt or retain the most stringent provisions compatible with the Treaty in the area covered by this Directive, to ensure a maximum degree of protection for the consumer.'

[12] See Commission Communication, 'Consumer Policy Strategy 2002–2006' (COM(2002) 208 final) 12: 'There is a need to review and reform existing EU consumer protection directives, to bring them up to date and progressively adapt them from minimum harmonisation to "full harmonisation" measures.' See also Commission Communication, 'EU Consumer Policy Strategy 2007–2013: Empowering consumers, enhancing their welfare, effectively protecting them' (COM(2007) 99 final), at 7.

[13] Directive 2005/29/EC concerning unfair business-to-consumer commercial practices in the internal market (hereinafter 'Unfair Commercial Practices Directive'), OJ 2005 L 149, preliminary Recitals (14) and (15).

[14] Art. 4, Directive 2011/83/EU on consumer rights, OJ 2011 L 304 (hereinafter 'Consumer Rights Directive'): 'Member States shall not maintain or introduce, in their national law, provisions diverging from those laid down in this Directive, including more or less stringent provisions to ensure a different level of consumer protection, unless otherwise provided for in this Directive.'

[15] See Art. 4, Directive (EU) 2019/770 on contracts for the supply of digital content and digital services, OJ 2019 L 136; Art. 4, Directive (EU) 2019/771 on certain aspects concerning contracts for the sale of goods, OJ 2019 L 136.

harmonization or the introduction of an optional instrument—is perceived as being extremely interventionist.[16] The publication in 2017 of the European Commission's White Paper on the future of Europe[17] explicitly put the question of minimum versus targeted full harmonization on the general political agenda: in Scenario 4 ('Doing less more efficiently'), 'new standards' for consumer protection were said 'to move away from detailed harmonization towards a strict minimum', while in Scenario 5 ('Doing much more together'), 'the single market' will be 'strengthened through harmonisation of standards'.[18]

G. Average and Vulnerable Consumers

There is a tendency in EU law towards defining and distinguishing different types of consumers. In particular, 'average' and 'vulnerable' consumers have been singled out. For example, the unfair commercial practices directive takes as a benchmark 'the average consumer, who is reasonably well-informed and reasonably observant and circumspect',[19] while the universal service directive, which defines the minimum set of services of electronic communication to which all end-users should have access (and which includes, notably, protection against immediate disconnection from a telecoms network on the grounds of an unpaid bill),[20] contains specific provisions for the protection of 'consumers with low incomes or with special social needs'.[21]

Another distinction, highlighted especially in recent literature, is the one between weaker parties at the periphery of the EU and those at its core: is it acceptable that a high level of consumer protection in rich Member States comes at the expense of the interests of poor people in poor countries, for example consumers who can only afford to pay low prices, or sellers whose businesses would not survive if they had to meet

[16] See e.g. the American contributions to a University of Chicago symposium on the CESL proposal, especially Bar-Gill and Ben-Shahar, 'Regulatory Techniques in Consumer Protection: A Critique of European Consumer Contract Law', 50 *Common Market Law ReviewCMLR* (2013) 109; Bernstein, 'An (Un)Common Frame of Reference: An American Perspective on the Jurisprudence of the CESL', 50 *CMLR* (2013) 169; Epstein, 'Harmonization, Heterogeneity and Regulation: CESL, the Lost Opportunity for Constructive Harmonization', 50 *CMLR* (2013) 2073. Cf. Caruso, 'The Transformation of Europe in US Legal Academia and Its Legacy in the Field of Private Law', in M. Maduro and M. Wind (eds), *The Transformation of Europe: Twenty-Five Years On* (2017) 149.

[17] Commission White Paper, 'On the Future of Europe. Reflections and Scenarios for the EU27 by 2025' (COM(2017) 2025).

[18] Ibid., Annex 2.

[19] See Arts 5–8 and preliminary Recital (18), Unfair Commercial Practices Directive (n. 13). Cf. B. Duivenvoorde, *The Consumer Benchmarks in the Unfair Commercial Practices Directive* (2014).

[20] The universal service obligation was an element in 'the market liberalization of service sectors, such as electronic communications, post and transport', i.e. the privatization of public services. See Commission Communication, 'A Quality Framework for Services Of General Interest in Europe' (COM(2011) 900 final), at 3. See Art. 14 TFEU and Art. 36 CFREU. Cf. Rott, 'The Low-Income Consumer in European Private Law', in K. Purnhagen and P. Rott (eds), *Varieties of European Economic Law—Liber Amicorum for Hans Micklitz* (2014) 675.

[21] Directive 2002/22/EC of 7 March 2002 on universal service and users' rights relating to electronic communications networks and services, OJ 2002 L 108 (hereinafter 'Universal Service Directive'), as amended by Directive 2009/136/EC, OJ 2009 L 337.

increased consumer protection standards?[22] Clearly, each of these distinctions has its own distributive implications, favouring different social groups.

H. Small Businesses

In the case of the categorical protection of certain groups, definitions, not substantive considerations concerning individual vulnerability, are decisive for who will be protected and who will not. So, who are actually protected as consumers by European legislation? For some time, the definition varied from one new legislative measure to another but in more recent times most EU legislation has consistently employed the same, narrow definition of a consumer, i.e. a natural person acting for purposes outside his trade, business, or profession.[23] This definition excludes notably professional parties such as sole traders and other small businesses, in spite of the fact that certain small businesses may seem just as worthy of protection as consumers,[24] for example when they lack bargaining power, or specific expertise (e.g. an estate agent buying an alarm system for his office),[25] or are generally inexperienced (e.g. a start-up), and the reality—relevant from a distributive point of view—that the choice of an individual to become self-employed (as opposed to working under a labour contract that comes with various legal protections) may depend strongly on the labour market conditions.[26] This raises another normative question: whether certain professional contracting parties in certain situations should be entitled, as a matter of justice, to a protection similar to that granted to consumers. In other words, in addition to the possibility of protection *as* consumers, a legal system could decide to protect certain businesses in certain situations *just like* consumers. For example, the recent French contract law reform introduced general protection against terms in standard form contracts creating a significant imbalance in the rights and obligations of the parties (not concerning the main subject-matter or the adequacy of the price),[27] thus

[22] See Caruso, 'Qu'ils mangent des contrats: Rethinking Justice in EU Contract Law', in D. Kochenov, G. de Búrca, and A. Williams (eds), *Europe's Justice Deficit?* (2014) 367; and, more generally, Kukovec, 'Law and the Periphery', 21 *ELJ* (2015) 406.

[23] See e.g. Art. 2(1), Consumer Rights Directive (n. 14).

[24] See *Cavendish Square Holding BV v. Talal El Makdessi* and *ParkingEye Ltd v. Beavis* [2015] UKSC 67 (per Neuberger and Sumption, Carnwath agreeing), at para. 38, with regard to contracts containing penalty clauses: 'Some of those who enter into such contracts, for example professionals and small businesses, may share many of the characteristics of consumers which are thought to make the latter worthy of legal protection'.

[25] See Cass. Civ. (1) 28 April 1987, *D* 1988, 1. Here the French *Cour de Cassation* ruled that in such a case a professional is a consumer for the purposes of that contract because they are 'in the same state of ignorance' as (other) consumers. However, in later cases the *Cour de Cassation* reversed its position and focused on whether the contract at hand had a direct relationship to the business carried on by the party seeking protection (see e.g. Cass. Civ. (1) 30 January 1996, *D* 1996, 228). Cf. the distinction made in *R&B Customs Brokers Ltd v. United Dominions Trust Ltd* [1988] 1 WLR 321 by Dillon LJ, between 'transactions which are clearly integral parts of the business concerned' and 'transactions which are at highest only incidental to the carrying on of the relevant business'.

[26] See Commission, 'Annual Report on European SMEs 2016/2017. Focus on Self-Employment', indicating a strong correlation between the likelihood of choosing self-employment and local unemployment rates.

[27] See Art. 1171 French Civil Code (new).

effectively extending the scope of application of the 1993 Directive on Unfair Terms from business-to-consumer (B2C) contracts to business-to-business (B2B) contracts.[28] In contrast, the EU legislator, so far, has refrained from extending consumer protection to small businesses,[29] even though nothing in Article 114 TFEU, the usual legal basis for consumer protection measures, seems to speak against it. However, recently the EU legislature has started adopting rules effectively aiming at the protection of SMEs in certain specific economic sectors (e.g. food supply chains, online platforms).[30]

I. Global Law: Laissez-Faire?

While weaker party protection is a key feature of national and EU contract law, at the global level we do not encounter any contract law rules protecting weaker parties.[31] Or, to put it the other way around, the lack of weaker party protection is a distinct characteristic of contract law located at the international level. The Vienna Sales Convention (CISG), for example, does not distinguish between sellers and buyers with stronger and weaker bargaining power, or between large and small businesses, protecting the latter against the former. The UNIDROIT Principles of International

[28] The CESL proposal adopted an intermediate solution, providing a lower degree of protection than the one granted consumers. Contrast the definition of 'unfair', as a term that 'grossly deviates from good commercial practice, contrary to good faith and fair dealing' in Art. 86 (Meaning of 'unfair' in contracts between traders), with the familiar standard (from the Unfair Terms Directive (n. 2) of a term that 'causes a significant imbalance in the parties' rights and obligations arising under the contract, to the detriment of the consumer, contrary to good faith and fair dealing' in Art. 83 (Meaning of 'unfair' in contracts between a trader and a consumer).

[29] The CESL proposal was meant to also apply to B2B contracts where at least one of the parties was an SME (B2SME). However, at first reading the European Parliament adopted as its position that the scope should be limited to B2C contracts. See European Parliament Legislative Resolution of 26 February 2014 on the Proposal for a Regulation of the European Parliament and of the Council on a Common European Sales Law, OJ 2017 C 285 (COM(2011)0635—C7-0329/2011—2011/0284(COD)), Art. 7.

[30] See, in particular, Regulation 2019/1150 on promoting fairness and transparency for business users of online intermediation services, OJ 2019 L 186, preliminary Recital (2): 'increasing dependence'; 'superior bargaining power [of online platforms], which enables them to, in effect, behave unilaterally in a way that can be unfair'. The Regulation contains a number of provisions policing the platforms' terms and conditions, that—as is characteristic of regulations—will be directly applicable to contractual relations. See also Directive 2019/633 on unfair trading practices in business-to-business relationships in the agricultural and food supply chain, OJ 2019 L 111. Although this Directive provides only for administrative enforcement and, therefore, does not directly affect private law, it was heavily inspired by both the Unfair Terms Directive and the Unfair Commercial Practices Directive, and therefore may well end up having an impact in particular on the validity of contract law clauses as well. In this sense, see M. P. de la Cuesta de los Mozos, 'SMEs in the (Food) Global Value Chain: A European Private Law Perspective' (2020) (doctoral thesis on file at EUI, Florence).

[31] This does not mean that weaker parties contracting with stronger contracting parties outside the EU will necessarily remain unprotected. Much of the EU contract law providing mandatory protection to weaker parties has tried to ensure its application also in contracts with a party from outside the EU. See e.g. Art. 6(2), Unfair Terms Directive (n. 2). For the Commercial Agency Directive (n. 5), see Case C-381/98, *Ingmar GB Ltd v. Eaton Leonard Technologies Inc* (EU:C:2000:605). However, these attempts do not protect against the loss (e.g. by non-EU residents) in cross-border cases of weaker party protection granted by non-EU systems. By contrast, when a choice is made for the law of an EU Member State in a contract with a consumer from a non-EU country affording better consumer protection than the chosen law, then Art. 6 Rome I Regulation 593/2008, OJ 2008 L 177, ensures that the consumer will continue to enjoy his non-EU consumer protection. This follows from Art. 2, Rome I Regulation (universal application).

Commercial Contracts do contain rules on gross disparity[32]—referring explicitly to the parties' unequal bargaining position[33]—and on hardship,[34] but these are not legally binding rules, only soft law. In other words, the consideration of all contracting parties as equals (formal equality) and non-intervention ('freedom of contract') are key characteristics of the contract law at the global level as it exists today.[35] So, from the perspectives of the political theories that require the protection of weaker parties in contracts, this means either that the project of global law must change radically or that contract law (at least for certain parties) must remain national or European. This explains perhaps why, as we saw in Chapter 4, libertarians in particular have been enthusiastic about the project of global law.

J. (De)Codification

The categorical protection of consumers further raises a systematic question for law makers, i.e. whether consumer law should develop into a special law, and maybe even be severed entirely from the civil code into a consumer code, following the example of the French *Code de la Consommation*. For Germany, it has been claimed by some observers that the inclusion in 2001 of consumer protection law in the civil code has been a failure and should be undone.[36] An important dimension of that question, from the point of view of justice, is the ontological question of whether today consumer protection law is still best understood in the first place as private law.[37] Another, more political, dimension is what to make of a civil code—and a private law—today that does not consider weaker party protection as one of its core tasks.

K. Epistemic Dimensions

It is not only the substance and degree of weaker party protection that is controversial. The familiar language of 'weakness' and 'protection' has also been questioned and rejected for being unduly patronizing and stigmatizing.[38] This critique, relying

[32] Art. 3.2.7, UNIDROIT Principles of International Commercial Contracts 2016.

[33] Ibid., Art. 3.2.7(a) refers to dependence, economic distress, urgent needs, improvidence, ignorance, inexperience or lack of bargaining skill. Cf. ibid. 110: 'unequal bargaining position'.

[34] Ibid., Arts 6.2.1–6.2.3.

[35] Another way of putting this, is that global contracts, including most global value chains, are left almost entirely to self-regulation. See e.g. G.-P. Calliess and P. Zumbansen, *Rough Consensus and Running Code: A Theory of Transnational Private Law* (2010).

[36] See especially, Micklitz, 'Do Consumers and Businesses Need a New Architecture of Consumer Law? A Thought Provoking Impulse', 32 *YEL* (2013) 266. Critical, Hondius, 'Against a New Architecture of Consumer Law—a Traditional View', in K. Purnhagen and P. Rott (eds), *Varieties of European Economic Law—Liber Amicorum for Hans Micklitz* (2014) 599.

[37] Hesselink, 'Post-Private Law?', in K. Purnhagen and P. Rott (eds), *Varieties of European Economic Law—Liber Amicorum for Hans Micklitz* (2014) 31.

[38] For the view that moral discourse disparages strength, see F. Nietzsche, *On the Genealogy of Morals* ([first published 1887] 2013), at 32: 'losing our fear of man, we have also lost the hope in man, respect for man, the will to be man'; at 8 denouncing 'the morality of pity'. At 32, warning that 'our greatest peril lurks in the European drift towards egalitarianism', he argues that 'there is no reason for blaming the great birds of prey for taking the little lambs', because 'to demand of strength that it should not express itself as strength,

in part on feminist and postcolonial studies, points out the important epistemic dimensions of the language of weaker party protection. How must I understand myself and my interaction with others if the law labels me as weak and presents itself as my protector? Does it not unduly divide the world into people who are weak and those who are strong? Indeed, is it not the self-proclaimed strong and able who engage in the 'othering' of the weak and deficient? And does the personal weakness frame not unduly distract from structural inequalities in society, with important impacts also on contracting? In other words, there seem to be, not only epistemic dimensions, but also specifically epistemic injustice dimensions to weaker party protection in contracts.[39]

L. The Core Normative Question

As in the other chapters, I will critically discuss the central normative question here—i.e. whether contract law should protect weaker parties—from the perspectives of different contemporary political theories. Each will provide its own view of the cathedral. This means not only that each theory answers the question quite differently, but also that the same question looks rather different from the point of view of each of these theories. This does not necessarily mean that one reading of the question is misguided or that some of its arguments must be wrong. It may simply be due to the fact that in pluralist societies citizens will inevitably understand the same political questions and their implications differently, depending on their respective backgrounds and life experiences—what Rawls called the 'burdens of judgment'. Having said that, in pluralist societies, when it comes to the 'unforced force of the better argument',[40] political theories are more likely to become—and perhaps are more deserving of becoming—effective political ideas to the extent that they refrain from projecting their own ultimate values and metaphysical truths onto others. And in the democratic process and—ultimately—the vote, compromises are more likely to carry the day than uncompromising views. Therefore, as in the other chapters, in addition to a critical discussion of each of the different political views on their respective own terms

that it should not be a wish to overpower, a wish to conquer, a wish to become master, a lust for enemies, resistance and triumphs, is just as absurd as to requires of weakness that it should express itself as strength'.

[39] See M. Fricker, *Epistemic Injustice: Power and the Ethics of Knowing* (2007). The term 'epistemic injustice' refers to the injustices done to people when their understanding (of themselves, their surroundings, what matters) is inhibited by dominant ways of looking at the world. This may occur where voices are structurally granted lower authority (testimonial injustice), and where legal categories and taxonomies foreground or background the ways specific groups in society experience their interaction with the law (hermeneutical injustice). The foreground taken by consumer groups may be an example of the first, the law's use of the language of 'weakness' of the latter, a type of epistemic injustice. As an instance of the latter, Tjon Soei Len, 'Hermeneutical Injustice, Contract Law, and Global Value Chains', 16 *ERCL* (2020) 139, demonstrates for the case of exploitation in global value chains (GVCs), how the depiction by the law of consumers as weaker parties deserving legal protection, 'obscures from collective understanding the ways in which consumers can be complicit in exploitation', thus undermining the hermeneutical interest of workers subject to exploitative production conditions in GVCs 'in properly understanding [their] own experience of mistreatment', which, in turn, severely impairs their capability of standing up against the exploitative practices.

[40] J. Habermas, *Between Facts and Norms: Contributions to a Discourse Theory of Law and Democracy* (1996), at 306.

(immanent critique), for each theory I will consider whether some of their reasons seem too sectarian to become an ingredient for a compromise in a democratic law-making process among citizens treating each other with equal respect. As explained in Chapter 1, the objective here is not to propose, as a matter of theory, a good or fair compromise. Theorists do not have any privileged access to the relative importance of values, and, therefore, have little more to say about compromises among these than any other citizen. Nor do they inhabit a point of view from where, unburdened by their own life experiences and with a full vision of what is at stake for others, they could remain neutral in controversial matters of justice. Moreover, Kennedy's point with regard to the individualism-altruism continuum, i.e. that it has no obvious extremes and, therefore, also no self-evident middle ground,[41] is even more important if we understand fundamental political questions of contract law as being multi-dimensional. Finally—crucially for the emancipation of marginalized and oppressed groups in society—political compromises should also be fundamentally open to contributions so far 'unheard of',[42] i.e. ones that go well beyond received views on values and justice. So, rather than attempting to bring closure, the aim here will be to open up the academic and political debates on weaker party protection, to move beyond positivism and essentialism, and to broaden and deepen the discussion by showing its complexity.[43]

2. Libertarian

Libertarians are fundamentally opposed to mandatory weaker party protection in contracts. Here are three distinct libertarian lines of attack.

A. Theft

For Nozickians, their rejection of mandatory rules and policies aiming at protecting weaker parties follows from their rejection of redistribution. Individuals are not resources for others: 'the state may not use its coercive apparatus for the purpose of getting some citizens to aid others', Nozick argued.[44] More specifically, redistribution transferring resources from individuals with more natural talents, etc. to the less privileged violates the principle of self-ownership. It would amount to making some individuals the (partial) owners of the person, activities, and work of other individuals. In other words, from the libertarian point of view there is nothing wrong, in principle, with stronger parties using their strength for obtaining a more favourable contract.[45] On the contrary, from the libertarian point of view weaker party protection

[41] Kennedy, 'The Political Stakes in "Merely Technical" Issues of Contract Law', 10 *ERPL* (2002) 7.
[42] R. Forst, *Normativity and Power: Analysing Social Orders of Justification* (2017), at 5.
[43] See further, Chapter 1.
[44] R. Nozick, *Anarchy, State and Utopia* ([first published 1974] 2006), at ix.
[45] Similar arguments are made with regard to EU rules on discrimination by private parties. See e.g. Safjan and Mikłaszewicz, 'Horizontal Effect of the General Principles of EU Law in the Sphere of Private Law', 18 *ERPL* (2010) 475.

constitutes a form of theft: something that belongs to one contracting party is taken from her against her will.

1. The Wilt Chamberlain Example

To explain why redistribution, on the libertarian view, is a practice whereby the government illegitimately takes something that belongs to one person in order to give it to someone else, it is worth considering an example famously used by Nozick involving Wilt Chamberlain, an American basketball player who became legendary in the 1960s. Translated into the present day European context, we could consider a football star like Cristiano Ronaldo. Ronaldo trained very hard to become a professional footballer. This choice engaged a lot of effort, sacrifice, and risk-taking.[46] And his fans freely decided to spend their money on buying tickets for the match and the merchandizing products sold by his sponsors.[47] So, if at the end of the day he has become very rich because he made life choices which have enabled him to carry out an activity that happens to be very popular with other people, then in what way is it unjust that he is so rich while others (including many of his fans and of his childhood friends) have remained (or become) very poor? According to libertarians, if someone who is entitled to something (a good, a performance) transfers it to you, typically in exchange for something else, then henceforward you are the one who is entitled to the good or the performance. So, if the transaction takes place with mutual consent (i.e. both parties prefer the new allocation of goods to the previous one) and if the transaction only involves things that belong to the parties (e.g. money and a ticket for the football match) then why should the distributive outcome of this transaction combined with the cumulated effect of a series of similar transactions, give third parties (or society as whole) reason to object? True, some football stars become extremely wealthy, even in times and places struck by severe economic crises, such as the difficulties experienced by Ronaldo's country (Portugal) following the financial crisis, but this is because they are good at football and some people love football so much that they are willing to spend a large portion of their modest income on a season ticket or the subscription to a commercial tv channel where they can see live football matches. They could have decided to spend their money on something else (or not spend it at all and keep it as savings) but they chose to buy a football ticket or pay per view to see the match on tv. And many other people apparently did the same. What can be wrong with that?

Just as Ronaldo is good at football, you may be good at bargaining. Perhaps you have a particularly convincing sales talk and other highly effective bargaining skills (not involving any lies or threats). Or, you happen to enjoy superior bargaining power (short of monopoly). Or, indeed, you combine the two and you use your resources

[46] Genetic predisposition may play its part as well. However, Ronaldo is known as a player who trains relentlessly. Messi, perhaps the best player of recent times, does not seem to be the typical example of someone who won the jackpot in the genetic lottery, given that a growth hormone deficiency at age 11 almost ended his football career even before it started. The case of Maradona may be different.

[47] Nozick's slogan 'From each as they choose, to each as they are chosen' (Nozick (n. 44) 160) is not dissimilar to the two classical laissez-faire statements of justice in (and through) contract: 'qui dit contractuel dit juste' (A. Fouillée, *La Science Sociale Contemporaine* (1880), at 410) and 'The value of all things contracted for, is measured by the appetite of the Contractors: and therefore the just value, is that which they be contented to give' (T. Hobbes, *Leviathan* ([first published 1651] 1985) at 208).

to develop and put into place certain marketing techniques (off-premises selling, online selling) that are particularly profitable. You may also have the resources to have a skilled lawyer draft a set of standard terms that, although massively tilted in your favour, nevertheless look innocuous or obscure enough not to alarm your customers, and that you manage to slip into all your contracts in small print, as a matter of course, and without any cheating. In summary, you are a stronger contracting party. According to libertarians there is nothing wrong with your benefiting from this strength. This directly follows from the principles of entitlement and self-ownership. You own your talents and the skills that make you a good saleswoman, and it is your own market position that yields your greater bargaining power. So, if the state were to adjust the inequality or compensate for its consequences by offering weaker parties a way out of their contracts (e.g. by introducing a right of withdrawal), or 're-establishing equality' between the parties by ensuring 'an effective balance between the rights and obligations of the parties'—as is the objective of the Unfair Terms Directive 1993, according to the CJEU[48]—then the state illegitimately takes something that belongs to you and transfers it to someone else. Applied to contract law, the libertarian argument based on entitlement, including what Nozick calls self-ownership, leads to the claim that weaker party protection is a form of illegitimate redistribution. In other words, morally speaking, on this view it is a form of theft. According to Nozick, the non-consensual transfer of resources from individuals with more natural talents, etc. to the less privileged violates the principle of self-ownership, because it leads to the (partial) ownership of a person, his activities, and his work by other individuals—a form of slavery.[49]

2. Social Institutions

There are two problems with this argument, a descriptive one and a normative one. As to the former, libertarian accounts of this type conveniently remove from the picture the important fact that the popularity of basketball and football players are social products. Ronaldo's fortune would not exist unless other people are free from work at the weekend to go and see a match; there are publicly maintained roads leading to the stadium; there is freedom to broadcast the match (and the commercials) on television and other media; there is a market for jerseys with his branding; there are no heavy state subsidies in place for different sports or activities that might render football less popular; and his villa is protected by the police.[50] In summary, his popularity, income, and fortune are deeply imbedded in the practices of our society and heavily dependent on its institutions. These institutions are not natural facts, but contingent social products.[51] Ronaldo could have been born in a planned economy or under an authoritarian

[48] Case C-168/05, *Elisa María Mostaza Claro v. Centro Móvil Milenium SL* (EU:C:2006:675).

[49] See Nozick (n. 44) 290–292 for 'the tale of the slave'.

[50] Cf. Anderson, 'What is the Point of Equality?', 109 *Ethics* (1999) 287, at 321–322:

> From the point of view of justice, the attempt, independent of moral principles, to credit specific bits of output to specific bits of input by specific individuals represents an arbitrary cut in the causal web that in fact makes everyone's productive contribution dependent on what everyone else is doing. ... Michael Jordan could not make so many baskets if no one kept the basketball court swept clean.

[51] Nozick (n. 44) 95 rejects this argument. He says:

regime that banned football as an immoral activity.[52] That would certainly have been unjust, but that raises the issue of just institutions. Ronaldo, like anyone else, arguably has a moral claim towards society to live under sufficiently just institutions. However, the direct consequence of this is that his own claim to his own earnings is subject to the same institutions.[53] This brings us to the second problem with the argument, i.e. that it relies entirely on a notion of natural property rights, in particular on some pre-institutional moral entitlements to pre-tax income. The same applies to your superior bargaining skills and power: whether you should be allowed to exploit these as you wish in order to conclude the best possible deals and retain the proceeds, depends on whether sufficiently just institutions in our society would allow this. But do you have a natural, pre-institutional right to your being in the position to conclude contracts as a comparatively stronger party? And do you really 'own' your superior bargaining position as a matter of self-ownership in any morally relevant sense? In particular, in the sense that the contract law of your society should simply enforce any contract you managed to conclude as a result of your favourable bargaining position?[54]

3. Pre-institutional Entitlements

Most of the libertarian claims, whether articulate like those of Nozick or 'everyday libertarian',[55] rely on a notion of pre-institutional entitlement that leads to the idea of *re*-distribution.[56] However, given that neither of Nozick's two purportedly 'Lockean' ideas, i.e. of original occupation (for sales) and of self-ownership (for services), is very convincing as a moral basis for pre-institutional entitlement, the libertarian claims seem to lack a convincing moral basis.[57] As Murphy and Nagel argue persuasively in *The Myth of Ownership*, pre-institutional (and pre-tax) entitlements lack any moral significance:

> Property rights are the product of a set of laws and conventions, of which the tax system forms a part. Pretax income, in particular, has no independent moral significance. It does not define something to which the taxpayer has a prepolitical or natural right, and which the government expropriates from the individual in levying taxes on it.[58]

> So the fact that we partially are 'social products' in that we benefit from current patterns and forms created by multitudinous actions of a long string of long-forgotten people, forms which include institutions, ways of doing things, and language ..., does not create in us a general floating debt which the current society can collect and use at will.

Not at will of course, but a legitimate, progressive income tax: why not?

[52] Closer to reality, he could have been jailed for tax evasion, which might have ended his career. Cf. Jones, 'Ronaldo Agrees To Pay €19m Fine To Settle Tax Fraud Case', *The Guardian*, 22 January 2019.

[53] Cf. R. Dworkin, *Justice for Hedgehogs* (2011), at 2: 'any distribution is the consequence of official law and policy: there is no politically neutral distribution'.

[54] Cf. J. Rawls, *A Theory of Justice* (1971), at 122: 'to each according to his threat advantage is not a principle of justice'.

[55] Cf. L. Murphy and T. Nagel, *The Myth of Ownership: Taxes and Justice* (2002), at 15.

[56] See e.g. D. Boaz, *Libertarianism: A Primer* (1997), at 76.

[57] It even seems doubtful that Locke's ideas can be rightly claimed as proto-libertarian. See the 'Introduction' by Peter Laslett to J. Locke, *Two Treatises of Government* (P. Laslett ed.) ([first published 1690] 2009), at 105: 'If not complete communism, certainly redistributive taxation, perhaps nationalization could be justified on the principles formulated by Locke in his Two Treatises.'

[58] Murphy and Nagel (n. 55) 74.

This idea can easily be extended to the realm of contract law. Thus, we could speak of the myths of the binding force and of the freedom of contract. There is no justified pre-institutional moral claim to 'the' binding force or 'the' freedom of contract.[59] Whatever moral claims people have to their contractual bargain depends on just institutions. Therefore, it cannot be a pertinent moral argument against weaker party protection that it violates the moral right of the stronger parties to self-ownership or the stronger party's moral right to freedom of contract, because such a right or freedom does not exist in any morally relevant sense unless it follows from the society's sufficiently just institutions, including notably its contract law. As Murphy and Nagel point out, 'most conventions, if they are sufficiently entrenched, acquire the appearance of natural norms'.[60] Similarly, the freedom of contract has acquired the appearance of a natural, pre-institutional norm. In summary, weaker party protection in contract law, rather than limiting freedom of contract, may be seen as distributing it more fairly.[61]

4. Redistribution by Stealth?

Friedman argued that if we want redistribution then we must have the courage to submit it to a political debate (and ultimately a vote in Parliament) rather than trying to conceal it from the public through all sorts of other measures and rules (including the rules of private law).[62] The argument is distinct from the argument against redistribution through private law rules because of its alleged inefficiency, which will be discussed in Section 3.A.2. At first sight, the argument may seem to have some force since an important aspect of the justification of laws seems to be that the true reasons for those laws must be made public. However, when it comes to weaker party protection in contract law this is not a diffuse and non-transparent way to redistribute income, but plausibly may rather be seen as a very direct and straightforward way to prevent perverse redistribution.

[59] See Murphy, 'The Practice of Promise and Contract', in G. Klass, G. Letsas, and P. Saprai (eds), *Philosophical Foundations of Contract Law* (2014), ch 9.

[60] Murphy and Nagel (n. 55) 9.

[61] After W. Kymlicka, *Contemporary Political Philosophy: An Introduction* (2nd ed., 2002), at 149: 'The inheritance tax does not *eliminate* the freedom to use the property, rather it *redistributes* that freedom.'

[62] M. Friedman, *Capitalism and Freedom* (2002), at 166, essentially advocates 'distribution according to product', i.e. in accordance with market outcome, without 're-distribution' (ibid. 174). In other words, he implicitly accepts the idea of pre-institutional entitlements. As one argument he claims that 'it enables distribution to occur impersonally without the need for "authority"—a special fact of the general role of the market in effecting co-operation and co-ordination without coercion' (ibid. 168). However, as we saw in Chapter 5, this impersonal distribution will only take place to the extent that contracts will not have to be enforced, i.e. when they are not only concluded voluntarily but also performed without coercion. Friedman does accept governmental action to alleviate poverty, i.e. 'to set, as it were, a floor under the standard of life of every person in the community' (ibid. 191). However, that could never become an argument, it seems, for the protection of weaker contracting parties, because Friedman formulates two conditions. First, any governmental programme should aim *directly* at helping the poor and it should not distort the market (ibid. 191). With regard to the former he writes: 'The program, that is, should be designed to help people as people not as members of particular occupational groups or age groups or wage-rate groups or labor organizations or industries' (ibid. 191). This also excludes, it seems, the categorical protection of consumers, small businesses, etc.

5. Incurable Ignorance

From a Hayekian point of view, the main reasons for rejecting redistribution—and consumer protection motivated by distributive concerns—are slightly different. Rather than the violation of the moral entitlements of sellers (or of other consumers—see the argument from cross-subsidization later, in Section 3.A.2) the problem, in his view, is that social justice is a mirage.[63] Weaker contracting parties are certainly unfortunate but that is not the result of any unjust conduct by anyone. Moreover, even if we wanted to, we would not be able to figure out who should be protected against whom, because of our incurable ignorance. The relevant information is dispersed among individuals. Therefore, by definition, law makers will disregard all the facts of which they are not aware.[64] Finally (and most importantly), redistributive measures of this kind would set us on the road to serfdom: redistribution will inevitably lead to totalitarianism because once we start redistributing there will be no natural end to state planning. As we saw in Chapter 2, these essentially empirical claims either lack an empirical basis, because welfare states have not turned into dictatorships en masse, or are seriously overstated, because obvious injustices are not hard to spot and finding the right remedy is usually not rocket science.[65]

The Hayekian idea of the market as a spontaneous order and as discovery device was central to an article by Brandner and Ulmer published in 1991, which was directed against the Commission's proposal for what became the Unfair Terms Directive of 1993.[66] The authors argued that with the introduction of protection against unfair terms specifically for consumers, 'the harmonisation of European law would thus have become instrumental in establishing within the EC the system of control and regulation underlying the socialist law of contract'.[67] Specifically in relation to core terms, they argued:

> In a free market economy parties to a contract are free to shape the principal obligations as they see fit. The relationship between the price and the goods or services provided is determined not according to some legal formula but by the mechanisms of the market. Any control by the courts or administrative authorities of the reasonableness or equivalence of this relationship is anathema to the fundamental tenets of a free market economy. It would partially abrogate the laws of the market and hence prevent the offerors of goods or services from acting in accordance with those laws; the consumer would no longer need to shop around for the most favourable offer, but rather could pay any price in view of the possibility of subsequent control of its reasonableness.

[63] See F. A. Hayek, *Law, Legislation and Liberty: A New Statement of the Liberal Principles of Justice and Political Economy*, Vol. II *The Mirage of Social Justice* ([first published 1973] 2003).

[64] On the 'incurable ignorance of everyone', see F. A. Hayek, *Law, Legislation and Liberty: A New Statement of the Liberal Principles of Justice and Political Economy*, Vol. I *Rules and Order* ([first published 1973] 2003), at 13.

[65] See generally A. Sen, *The Idea of Justice* (2009).

[66] Brandner and Ulmer, 'The Community Directive on Unfair Terms in Consumer Contracts: Some Critical Remarks on the Proposal Submitted by the EC Commission', 28 *CMLR* (1991) 647.

[67] Ibid. 649.

The article was immensely influential. Among other things, it led to the introduction of the current Article 4(2) into the Directive. The text of that provision was copied almost literally from the essay.[68] In other words, the exclusion of the price and other core terms from unfairness control, even of consumer contracts, and with it the exclusion of any distributive motives from the protection against unfair terms,[69] was a direct consequence of a sustained libertarian attack.[70]

B. Paternalism

1. Eternal Minors

Traditionally, most legal systems have limited the enforceability of contracts concluded by minors and by people suffering from a mental illness. The reason why the validity of contracts concluded by these two categories of persons can be challenged (by themselves or by certain others, on their behalf) in most legal systems is that they are considered by the law not to be able to judge which contracts are in their own best interest.[71] Under the doctrine of 'legal incapacity', therefore, the judgement of a person is replaced, in her own best interest, by the judgement of another person, i.e. her parents or tutor. Some observers have denounced consumer protection because in their view it turns grown-ups into incapacitated adults or eternal infants.[72] On this view, consumer protection, and perhaps more generally weaker party protection in contract law, is just as paternalistic as the doctrine of legal incapacity, except that in the case of grown-up adults who do not suffer from any mental illness paternalism is wholly unjustified,[73] indeed offensive. This is the second well-known libertarian

[68] Ibid. 655: 'This raises the question whether the control is to extend to the terms specifying *the principal obligations entered into a contract and, in particular, to the reasonableness of the price in relation to the value of the goods and services provided.*' (emphasis added)

[69] Cf. Wilhelmsson, 'Varieties of Welfarism in European Contract Law', 10 *ELJ* (2004) 712: 'As the Directive does not aim at regulating the balance between performance and price, leaving it to be determined by the market mechanism, it explicitly excludes attempts to achieve internally redistributive goals from its scope.'

[70] Also Nozickian libertarians would reject fairness control of contract prices and core terms. They would argue, in terms of self-ownership, that a 'fair' or 'just' price rule simply amounts to theft. See explicitly against the fair price theory, Nozick (n. 44) 64.

[71] Originally, women also lacked legal capacity. In the Netherlands, for example, the legal incapacity of married women was abolished only in 1956.

[72] See P. Malaurie, L. Aynès, and P. Stoffel-Munck, *Les obligations* (2005), at 423: 'le droit de la consommation tend à faire du consommateur un incapable majeur ou un éternel mineur.' See also J. Carbonnier, *Droit civil, Les obligations* (2000), at 3: 'le consommateur est un majeur que son contrat replace en état de mineur'. See also Kant, in *Naturrecht Feyerabend* (G. Feyerabend, *Kant's Natural Right, Read in the Winter Semester of the Year 1784* (2003), at 53), with regard to the doctrine of *laesio enormis*: 'The *laesio enormis* of the Roman Law therefore belongs to a civil law that regards its members as under-age minors. The opinion that the law has to provide for the citizens and their happiness like a father is totally opposed to the first principle of right, the freedom of the citizen.'

[73] Today, it is not even clear that paternalism is still justified in the case of adults living with a mental illness. See the Convention on the Rights of Persons with Disabilities, Committee on the Rights of Persons with Disabilities, General comment No. 1 (2014), Art. 12 (Equal recognition before the law), para. 9:

> All persons with disabilities, including those with physical, mental, intellectual or sensory impairments, can be affected by denial of legal capacity and substitute decision-making. However, persons with cognitive or psychosocial disabilities have been, and still are, disproportionately affected by substitute decision-making regimes and denial of legal capacity.

argument against weaker party protection, i.e. as a paternalistic—and therefore illegitimate—interference by the state with the liberty of individuals.[74] As Friedman put it, 'those of us who believe in freedom must believe also in the freedom of individuals to make their own mistakes.... Humility is the distinguishing virtue of the believer in freedom; arrogance, of the paternalist.'[75] If justified, unlike the self-ownership argument, which is exclusively libertarian, this paternalism critique could be just as problematic for liberal-egalitarians as for libertarians. For, although certain liberal perfectionists would find this criticism, if pertinent, not necessarily problematic,[76] most other liberals (e.g. Rawlsians and Dworkinians) would, because in their view paternalism also constitutes an insult to the capacities of morally autonomous agents.[77]

2. Facilitation, Accommodation, and Exploitation

So, is weaker party protection in contract law indeed a form of paternalism? Paternalism is the interference of one person with another person, against the latter's will, with a view to making her better off or protecting her from harm.[78] In the case of soft paternalism, the interference takes place in the name of a person's presumed own preferences and intentions (i.e. the ones it is presumed she would have were she not affected by certain cognitive biases or a weaknesses of the will), while in the case of hard paternalism a person's own choice is overruled because, while she knows exactly what she wants, she does not know what is good for her (i.e. she has preferences that are not in her own best interest). However, weaker party protection constitutes neither hard nor soft paternalism.

The reason, as Shiffrin points out, is that the element of interference against a person's will is totally absent, by definition, in cases of weaker party protection in contract. In the cases both of categorical protection (of workers, tenants, and consumers) and of individual contextualized protection under such doctrines as unconscionability, unfair exploitation, good faith and fair dealing, and change of circumstances, it is the person who is supposedly interfered with, herself, that invokes the doctrine.[79] In legal systems having such doctrines the legal sanction or remedy in all these cases is that the contract is 'voidable' or 'annullable' at the protected party's own request ('relative nullity').[80] Whether the contract is invalidated, therefore, remains entirely in the

[74] Friedman (n. 62) 34:

> The paternalistic ground for governmental activity is in many ways the most troublesome to a liberal; for it involves the acceptance of a principle—that some shall decide for others—... which he rightly regards as a hallmark of his chief intellectual opponents, the proponents of collectivism in one or another of its guises, whether it be communism, socialism, or a welfare state.

[75] Ibid. 188.

[76] See Raz, *The Morality of Freedom* (1986), at 422, for liberal perfectionism's 'ready embrace of various paternalistic measures.'

[77] See Shiffrin, 'Paternalism, Unconscionability Doctrine, and Accommodation', 29 *Philosophy and Public Affairs* (2000) 205, at 220. Civic republicans reject paternalism because the paternalist's interference according to his own arbitrium, not that of the other, is an example of domination. See P. Pettit, *On the People's Terms: A Republican Theory and Model of Democracy* (2012), at 59.

[78] For definitions, see e.g. Dworkin, 'Paternalism', in E. N. Zalta (ed.), *The Stanford Encyclopedia of Philosophy*, available at https://plato.stanford.edu/entries/paternalism/ (last visited 5 June 2020); F. H. Buckley, *Fair Governance: Paternalism and Perfectionism* (2009).

[79] See Shiffrin (n. 77).

[80] The case of the Unfair Terms Directive (n. 2) is different: unfair terms are 'not binding on the consumer' (Art. 6), which does not have to be raised by the consumer, but must be determined by the court of its own

hands of the protected party herself. Also, at any time before the annulment (at her own request) she remains entirely free to perform voluntarily and thus to discharge an existing legal obligation.[81] Moreover, and this is an even more important argument made by Shiffrin, doctrines like unconscionability—and I would add, more generally, weaker party protection—do not have to be (and are not best explained as being) inspired by other-regarding motives. The motivating reason for weaker party protection may be entirely self-regarding. As stated previously, it is a core characteristic of paternalistic action that it is motivated by the (perceived) interests of the persons that one is interfering with, i.e. by the intent to make them better off or protect them from harm. However, there is another possible motivation for weaker party protection that seems at least as plausible.[82] On this view, the aim of these doctrines is not the protection by the state of vulnerable parties against their own misguided decisions, but to prevent the law from being implicated in exploitative practices. Therefore, the doctrine should not be regarded as an instance of weaker party protection, but as a case where the state refuses to lend citizens its assistance in an endeavour (in this case, the unfair exploitation of one contracting party by the other) that it regards as unworthy of support—i.e. as a case of self-protection against collusion. Given that we have no right (natural or other) to the state's support for all our projects,[83] the state is allowed to exercise its own judgement as to which of our projects it will facilitate. So, doctrines that protect weaker parties may be motivated and explained by the self-regarding concern not to facilitate or assist harmful, exploitative, or immoral action. Shiffrin sets up the state against the exploitative contracting party. However, in reality what we are talking about, of course, is the society as whole as represented typically in the democratic legislature, which does not want to get its hands dirty with the business of enforcing contracts with weaker parties without providing them with proper protections.

motion, as a long string of cases of the CJEU has made clear. However, there too the protection (i.e. the non-bindingness) cannot be imposed on the consumer against her will. See Case C-243/08, *Pannon GSM Zrt. v. Erzsébet Sustikné Győrfi* (EU:C:2009:350), at para. 33: 'the term in question may be applicable, if the consumer, after having been informed of it by that court, does not intend to assert its unfair or non-binding status'.

[81] See M. A. Eisenberg, *Foundational Principles of Contract Law* (forthcoming), ch. 4, at 46: 'If the doctrine of substantive unconscionability is paternalistic at all, it is a very diluted form of paternalism. Under that doctrine the government forbids nothing and commands nothing. It simply says to the promisee, "If you can accomplish your ends without our assistance, fine. But don't ask us to help you recover a pound of flesh." '

[82] As we will see later, there are further possible (non-paternalistic) motivations for the protection of weaker parties in contract law, including distributive motives.

[83] And certainly such a right could not be grounded in liberty as it is usually understood by libertarians. See Shiffrin (n. 77). This is now acknowledged by Fried, 'The Ambitions of Contract as Promise Thirty Years On', 45 *Suffolk University Law Review* (2012) 461.

3. Utilitarian

A. Double Distortion

Welfare economists argue that if consumer protection law and general contract law doctrines like unconscionability and unfair exploitation are meant—and can be justified only—as weaker party protection, then they should be rejected because redistribution through private law is inefficient.

1. The Size of the Cake, Not Its Division

As a general matter, a fair distribution of welfare is not an aim of utilitarianism and welfare economics, or at least not a direct aim. Rather, the various utilitarian theories are neutral, in principle, concerning the distribution of welfare.[84] Policies aiming merely at the redistribution of resources from one group in society to another, therefore, have no direct justification in utilitarianism. Such policies would only lead to a different division of the cake whereas utilitarian theories, such as normative welfare economics, aim for an increase in the size of the cake, i.e. a larger total amount of welfare (or even mere wealth, depending on the theory), in whoever's hands these resources might end up. Utilitarianism would also lack a standard for what would amount to a fair distribution. Or, more precisely, it lacks a separate standard, because if a certain distribution was likely to lead to more happiness or preference satisfaction (i.e. an increase in the total amount of welfare) then that distribution would be supported by utilitarians on that ground (i.e. a net gain in social welfare). This could be the case—as, for example, Kaplow and Shavell acknowledge—when people happen to have a 'taste for fairness'.[85] To the extent that individuals have altruistic preferences or are happier (better off in their own estimation) when living in egalitarian societies,[86] this provides an indirect utilitarian reason for pursuing redistributive and other egalitarian policies. These reasons are indirect in that they are not based on distributive principles of justice or a right to economic equality, or to balanced contracts, but on the principle that the total amount of utility (defined as happiness, welfare, or preference satisfaction) should be maximized. Another way in which distribution of wealth becomes relevant in utilitarian discourse, which is often underlined by utilitarians in response to liberal-egalitarian critique, is that utilitarians have reason for supporting a degree of socio-economic equality on the basis of the (empirical) fact of the diminishing marginal utility of resources:[87] given that the happiness, welfare, or preference satisfaction derived from possessing one additional euro is likely to be greater for a beggar than for a millionaire, overall utility increases if the euro goes to the beggar. In summary,

[84] As we saw, not all consequentialists are utilitarians (focusing on happiness) or welfarists (Pareto or Kaldor/Hicks). For example, Liam Murphy's Humean conventionalism focuses entirely on socially beneficial consequences, which include explicitly distributive consequences and also non-discrimination, the non-violation of rights, etc.

[85] L. Kaplow and S. Shavell, *Fairness Versus Welfare* (2002), at 21.

[86] For empirical evidence showing that the levels of suicide, drug addiction, violent crime, etc. are significantly lower in egalitarian societies like Norway than in societies characterized by great inequality in wealth, see R. Wilkinson and K. Pickett, *The Spirit Level: Why Equality is Better for Everyone* (2010).

[87] Murphy and Nagel (n. 55) 55.

utilitarians of all stripes are interested in redistribution—and would favour the protection of weaker parties in contracts as a means to that end—only to the extent that this would lead to an increase in social (i.e. aggregate) utility, or, where welfare is reduced to wealth, to economic growth.[88]

2. A Waste of Resources

If a society pursued a fair distribution nevertheless, as a separate aim (e.g. on the Rawlsian ground of improving the condition of the least well-off), then the first concern of a welfare economist would still remain that the distributive aim should be achieved in the most efficient way, i.e. involving the lowest amount of social costs. The obvious reason is that in this way there will be more left to redistribute: the less wasteful its distributive mechanism, the more a society can improve the condition of the poor.

Legal economists tend to be highly critical of redistribution through private law because, they argue, it would lead to a lower overall amount of welfare available for distribution (if that is what people want), than there would be if redistribution were organized through the tax and transfer system (i.e. income tax and social security). Therefore, when private law is used for distributive purposes this harms the position of those who are meant to benefit from redistribution because they will obtain less than if redistribution took place through tax and transfer.[89] This is a troubling claim. If pertinent, it would give anyone who cares about distributive justice (e.g. Rawlsians and all others who want to improve the condition of the least well-off in society),[90] reason to reject the pursuit of distributive justice through contract law, e.g. via weaker party protection. In other words, a rational egalitarian, the argument goes, would not pursue her distributive objectives through private law.

Redistribution through private law, they argue, is 'inefficient' in a number of respects.[91] First, there is the problem of imprecise targeting: redistribution through private law rules is likely to be both over- and under-inclusive. Consumer protection rules benefit rich consumers as much as poor consumers, or even more (think of the typical consumers of luxury goods or simply the fact that wealthy persons can consume more), while the sellers against whom they are protected are sometimes comparatively poor (e.g. the owner of a small shop, or of a larger one which is close to insolvency). In contrast, a progressive income tax system can target those social groups that should be affected by the redistribution more precisely and directly.

[88] This idea is expressed most strongly in the concept of Kaldor/Hicks efficiency which requires only a potential, not actual, Paretian superiority, and merely possible, not actual, compensation of the losers by the winners.

[89] The assumption here is that redistribution through tax and transfer is actually going to happen. This may well be a counter-factual (and in some cases the reference to it is made in bad faith). As R. M. Unger, *What Should Legal Analysis Become?* (1996), at 48, points out, 'as a strategy for limiting inequality, tax-and-transfer has ordinarily had disappointing results'. Moreover, there may be personal and social loss following from the reduction of citizens to disempowered clients of the welfare state. See Habermas (n. 40) § 9.1.3.

[90] See later, in Section 4.A.

[91] See e.g. R. Cooter and T. Ulen, *Law and Economics* (6th ed., 2012), at 7–8 and 106–108; Kaplow and Shavell (n. 85) 33–34; Eidenmüller, 'Party Autonomy, Distributive Justice and the Conclusion of Contracts in the DCFR', 5 *ERCL* (2009) 109. See also, from a different angle, Kennedy (n. 4), who argues for paternalism.

Moreover, sellers will respond to the increased cost resulting from the consumer protection measure by increasing their own prices, as a result of which the redistribution from buyers to sellers is likely to fail.[92] Also, assertive and sophisticated consumers (e.g. consumer law students) are more likely to invoke consumer protection rules than the weakest consumers who may need the protection most; in that case the perverse effect will be that poor consumers will end up subsidizing the protection enjoyed by the richer consumers.[93] Worse, as a result of a price rise the poorest consumers may be priced out of the market because they can no longer afford the product at the new price. These various price effects—and price elasticity in general—are hard to predict. Finally, the weaker party protection, although aimed at redistribution, may have unintended distortive incentive effects on the parties—for example with regard to the level of precaution to be taken during performance—which are added to the distortion of incentives for efficient labour/leisure choices that income tax already creates. Hence: double distortion.[94]

All these claims are empirical claims that would have to be proven by evidence. However, they seem plausible enough. So, at the end of the day, legal economists argue, with redistribution that takes place, in part, through private law the poor will receive *less* than what they might obtain via redistribution exclusively through the tax and transfer system. In other words, redistribution through private law (e.g. weaker party protection) makes the poorest in society (i.e. the target group for Rawlsian distributive justice—see later, in Section 4.A.3) *worse off*, in their own estimation, than in a system of contract law with efficient incentives combined with a well-targeted tax and transfer system. As stated, that is a troubling claim, that, it would seem, should give pause to anyone who cares about distributive justice.

3. What Money Can't Redistribute

At first sight, the double-distortion argument seems compelling. However, on closer examination, it fatally relies on the identification of welfare with wealth.[95] As Walzer points out, 'distributive justice must stand in some relation to the goods that are being distributed'.[96] The problem with the 'efficiency' argument against weaker party protection is that only those aspects of human welfare susceptible of monetization can be 'redistributed' through the tax and transfer system. In contrast, the loss of dignity that a person suffers cannot be undone by a tax break. The only solution to that problem is to prevent an unfair distribution of the reasons for self-respect from occurring in the first place, for example by protecting vulnerable contracting parties against unfair exploitation through the remedy of annulment of certain contracts types or contract clauses concluded in certain contexts of unequal bargaining.[97] Take the *Aziz* case, as a striking

[92] Kennedy (n. 4).
[93] Ibid. 614; H. Eidenmüller, *Effizienz als Rechtsprinzip* (2005), at 295–306.
[94] Kaplow and Shavell, 'Why the Legal System is Less Efficient than the Income Tax in Redistributing Income' 23 *J. Legal Stud.* (1994) 667; Kaplow and Shavell, 'Should Legal Rules Favor the Poor? Clarifying the Role of Legal Rules and the Income Tax in Redistributing Income', 29 *J. Legal Stud.* (2000) 821.
[95] See Lewinsohn-Zamir, 'In Defense of Redistribution Through Private Law', 91 *Minnesota Law Review* (2006) 326.
[96] M. Walzer, *Thick and Thin: Moral Argument at Home and Abroad* (1994), at 26. See generally M. Walzer, *Spheres of Justice* (1983).
[97] See Calabresi, 'The Pointlessness of Pareto: Carrying Coase Further', 100 *Yale L.J.* (1991) 1211.

example. There, it made a crucial difference for Mr Aziz and his family whether their eviction from their home in the midst of the economic crisis could be *prevented*, by declaring the contract term on which the bank's right to initiate mortgage enforcement proceedings was based to be unfair and therefore not binding on the consumer, rather than for them merely to receive some financial support once they were out on the street.[98] How could the injustice done to Mr Aziz and his family through the eviction possibly be redistributed (and efficiently at that) by the tax and transfer system?

It is true that it would be highly inefficient for a society to try to achieve its distributive justice objectives solely through private law. And a society that nevertheless pursued this route would indeed probably do an injustice to its poorest members.[99] However, from this it does not follow that private law's contribution to distributive justice is entirely dispensable: in certain situations receiving a public money handout as compensation is simply not the same thing—not even in welfare terms[100]—as preventing the injustice. In those situations, the private act that would cause the unjust distribution has to be prevented in order to prevent social injustice.[101]

Formulated in the language of welfare economics, if we recognize, as an empirical matter, that people care about their dignity, and include this in the calculus of preference satisfaction—i.e. count what could be called, as a variant of Kaplow and Shavell's 'taste for fairness', a 'taste for human dignity'—then it is not so obvious that tax and transfer is more efficient than private law in assuring distributive justice after all. There will be more preference satisfaction among Europeans, it seems, if unfair contracts continue to be banned and if strong parties (professional sellers, employers, and principals) continue to be prevented from exploiting weaker parties (consumer buyers, employees, and commercial agents). Would it really be the same for a person who was exploited if she was told: 'Don't worry, the tax authorities will get back at them big time'? Note that this argument relies on notions internal to welfare economics; it does not question the moral basis of the welfare principle (even if limited to preference satisfaction) or claim that individual rights should trump efficiency concerns.[102]

There is no intrinsic reason why utilitarians—i.e. those who promote the policies and laws with the best overall societal consequences—should limit their conception of good outcomes to wealth maximization or preference satisfaction as expressed in 'willingness to pay'. Several broader standards of human wellbeing, and of good and bad consequences of government policies and laws, are available to consequentialists. For example, Domurath considers 'housing welfare', understood as the access to

[98] See Case C-415/11, *Mohamed Aziz v. Caixa d'Estalvis de Catalunya, Tarragona i Manresa (Catalunyacaixa)* (EU:C:2013:164), at para. 61, where the Court rejects mere monetary compensation as insufficient because it 'does not make it possible to prevent the definitive and irreversible loss of [the family home]'.

[99] Indeed, I am not denying, of course, the important task for the social security system in ensuring that nobody remains homeless after eviction; nor am I arguing that the austerity measures as they were adopted in response to the economic crisis were defensible in terms of justice.

[100] Cf. Lewinsohn-Zamir (n. 95).

[101] More generally, for those who understand the Rawlsian difference principle as a maximizing principle, any rule of the legal system should contribute to improving the condition of the least well off, wherever it can. In this sense, with a specific focus on the underlying property law scheme, see Blankfein-Tabachnick and Kordana, 'Kaplow and Shavell and the Priority of Income Taxation and Transfer', 69 *Hastings L.J.* (2017) 1.

[102] Arguments to that effect will be presented in Section 4.

a residential property, to be a societal 'welfare goal' and, taking mortgage default as a proxy for a welfare loss in this sense, argues that consumer protection in mortgage contracts is needed in order to prevent such welfare losses.[103] A more general objective account of well-being is proposed by Lewinsohn-Zamir.[104] She convincingly argues that private law actually does a *better* job than the tax and transfer system in redistributing when it comes to goods other than the satisfaction of actual preferences. The latter may be biased by cognitive limits or social circumstances ('adaptive preferences') in such a way that choices based on them will actually *reduce* one's wellbeing. Moreover, private law counts not only end results ('source-independent' aggregate amounts) but also how they came about, for example whether they were obtained as of right or as charity; as humiliation or as a reward.[105] As she puts it, 'private law rules assist in forming notions of entitlement, which enhance the objective and subjective value of the things that are distributed'.[106] A legal rule, for example, that legitimizes unfair contractual terms or unfair exploitations may have serious negative welfare consequences for many people because these unfair terms may undermine their self-respect and self-esteem, which not only instantaneously reduces their wellbeing, but will also reduce the confidence with which they are likely to embark on new projects.[107] Thus, private law rules may have important 'educational effects' with regard to a sense of entitlement, fair dealing, and appropriate relationships between people.[108]

B. Efficient Weaker Party Protection

1. Market Failure

The general rejection by welfare economists of weaker party protection as a means for the redistribution of welfare through contract law does not necessarily mean that they would reject most of the contract law doctrines protecting weaker parties. On the contrary, they could support a great deal of it. However, they would do so on a

[103] I. Domurath, *Consumer Vulnerability and Welfare in Mortgage Contracts* (2017); Domurath, 'Mortgage Debt and the Social Function of Contract', 22 *ELJ* (2016) 758.

[104] Such a perfectionist version of consequentialism, which in certain respects comes quite close to Raz's liberal perfectionism, may ultimately prove difficult to reconcile with a reasonably pluralist society (even though Lewinsohn-Zamir underlines that the objective account may itself be quite pluralistic, including, for example, autonomy and liberty as objective values, bringing her approach quite close to Nussbaum's version of the capabilities approach whose list of capabilities is explicitly meant to be acceptable to people adhering to otherwise diverging comprehensive doctrines), but that is not a problem for a consequentialist who, characteristically, is only concerned with maximizing the total amount of good outcomes. However, from that perspective to overlook important welfare consequences, as a result of a narrow fixation on 'preference satisfaction' or wealth maximization, would be a grave error that totally undermines the normative appeal that it has for consequentialists.

[105] Cf. T. Judt, *Ill Fares the Land* (2010), at 169: 'what if we factored into our estimates of productivity, efficiency, or well-being the difference between a humiliating handout and a benefit as of right?'. See also, ibid. 27: 'Contrary to a widespread assumption that has crept back into Anglo-American political jargon, few derive pleasure from handouts ... It is, quite simply, humiliating.'

[106] Lewinsohn-Zamir (n. 95) 397.

[107] This impact on well-being is exacerbated if formal contract law is enacted in the name, not of efficiency, but of a Kantian *entitlement* theory of private law, as proposed by Ripstein, on which more later, in Section 4.A.2.

[108] Lewinsohn-Zamir (n. 95) 392.

very different ground, i.e. market failure. An imperfect market allocates resources sub-optimally and thus leaves a potential for an increase in social welfare unused. Therefore, repairing market failures may be a legitimate policy from a welfarist perspective. In the words of Bar-Gil:

> the interaction between consumer psychology and market forces creates a behavioral market failure. This failure reduces welfare and hurts consumers. Market solutions exist, but their reach is limited. They mitigate the problem but cannot ameliorate it. The persistence of a market failure opens the door for considering the potential role of legal intervention.[109]

Thus, consumer protection could be justified for the reason that it makes society as a whole better off because with consumer protection a surplus can be achieved. Remember that the reason why contracts should be enforced in the first place, according to normative welfare economics, is that presumably contracts that are freely concluded will increase the welfare of the parties to the contracts and hence (in the absence of externalities) the total amount of welfare in a society.[110] However, when consumers end up in contractual relationships that do not correspond to their preferences (not even *ex ante*), failing to make them better off or even reducing their welfare, then from a welfarist utilitarian point of view this is problematic.

This may be the case when consumers enter a contract on the basis of incorrect or incomplete information (information asymmetry) or when they do possess the right information but, because of some cognitive biases, are nevertheless unable to process it properly and, as a result, reach decisions that do not correspond to their enlightened preferences ('bounded rationality').[111] On the latter point there exists an increasing body of empirical literature. In all these cases, contracts might be concluded that are not in fact welfare enhancing. The law can respond to such market failures in different ways. For example, it can ban certain contract clauses, introduce pre-contractual information duties, or establish rights of withdrawal. All of these techniques indeed have been adopted, in specific contexts, by the European legislator. The Unfair Terms Directive bans certain clauses. The Directives on Doorstep Selling, Time Sharing, Package Travelling, and Financial Services introduced both extensive information

[109] O. Bar-Gill, *Seduction by Contract: Law, Economics, and Psychology in Consumer Markets* (2012), at 667.

[110] See Chapter 4.

[111] Very critical of the limitation of consumer law to this narrow rationale, is Micklitz (n. 36) 273:

> The triumph of consumer law has sealed the fate of consumer protection law. The normative *Leitbild* of the informed consumer opens the way for a dematerialization of consumer law which correlates with a re-formalization. The scholarly concentration on consumer law which can be observed not only in Germany heralds a de-politicization of a whole field of law. The Law and Economics movement, which is becoming more and more successful in Germany, fits in seamlessly to the dismantlement of the protection model.

See also D. Kahneman, *Thinking Fast and Slow* (2011), at 413, pointing out that 'a pernicious implication of the rational-agent model in its extreme form is that customers are assumed to need no protection beyond ensuring that the relevant information is disclosed.'

duties and rights of withdrawal; the same applies prominently for the Consumer Rights Directive.[112]

Today, among welfare economists the economic rationale for banning unfair terms seems to be relatively well established.[113] Because consumers cannot assess at reasonable cost the implications of the standard terms that sellers are offering them, if unfair terms are not prohibited, consumers will assume that the proposed terms are unfair, just as a buyer on the second-hand car market will assume the cars offered him will generally be 'lemons' (i.e. cars with a hidden defect).[114] As a consequence, competition on quality is impossible for sellers (the buyer cannot single out the offerors of fair terms), sellers will compete on price and, as a result, sellers offering fair terms will be priced out of the market. Hence, the need for market regulation through unfair terms control. Withdrawal rights have also been defended on efficiency grounds.[115] The economic case for pre-contractual information duties, on the other hand, is much more controversial: it has been claimed, in terms of efficiency, that they do more harm than good, because they are of no real assistance to consumers while they raise costs for sellers.[116]

Note that here, again, the debate is not about what consumers are morally entitled to or what rights they should have, and not even about what rules would match best with the sense of justice of European citizens, but rather about which specific consumer contract rules, if any, would be most efficient, frequently (but by no means necessarily) defined in the narrow sense of wealth maximization, i.e. economic growth in terms of GDP.

2. Divergent Consumer Protection Rules as Market Obstacles

Finally, another possible non-redistributive welfarist rationale for consumer protection exists. Indeed, this is the one that provides the official basis for most of the existing EU consumer law.

[112] Busch, 'The Future of Pre-Contractual Information Duties: From Behavioural Insights to Big Data', in C. Twigg-Flesner (ed.), *Research Handbook on EU Consumer Contract Law* (2016), ch. 10, and O. Ben-Shahar and C. E. Schneider, *More Than You Wanted to Know: the Failure of Mandated Disclosure* (2014), at 5, point to mandated disclosure's 'ecumenical ideology', i.e. beyond utilitarians.

[113] See e.g. Hermalin, Katz, and Craswell, 'Contract Law', in A. M. Polinsky and S. Shavell (eds), *Handbook of Law and Economics*, Vol. I (2007) 3, at 97; Katz, 'Standard Form Contracts', in P. Newman (ed.), *The New Palgrave Dictionary of Economics and the Law*, Vol. 3 (2002) 1902; Kötz, 'Der Schutzzweck der AGB-Kontrolle; Eine Rechtsökonomische Skizze', in J. Basedow, K. Hopt, and R. Zimmermann (eds), *Undogmatisches: rechtsvergleichende und rechtsökonomische Studien aus dreißig Jahren* (2005) 221; Eidenmüller (n. 93) 295–306; Schäfer and Leyens, 'Judicial Control of Standard Terms and European Private Law', in P. Larouche and F. Chirico, *Economic Analysis of the DCFR: The Work of the Economic Impact Group within CoPECL* (2010) 97; Wagner, 'Mandatory Contract Law: Functions and Principles in Light of the Proposal for a Directive on Consumer Rights', 3 *Erasmus Law Review* (2010) 47.

[114] Akerlof, 'The Market for "Lemons": Quality Uncertainty and the Market Mechanism', 84 *Quarterly Journal of Economics* (1970) 488.

[115] Wagner (n. 113); Ben-Shahar and Posner, 'The Right to Withdraw in Contract Law', 40 *J. Legal Stud.* (2011) 115; Eidenmüller (n. 91).

[116] Ben-Shahar and Schneider, 'The Failure of Mandated Disclosure', 159 *University of Pennsylvania Law Review* (2011) 647. Contrast Bar-Gill (n. 109), who is quite pragmatic about the choice for disclosure duties: 'This is not because disclosure always works or because disclosure is always the optimal form of regulatory intervention. Rather, it is because disclosure mandates are the least intrusive form of regulation and, thus, the form of regulation most likely to be adopted.'

Originally, in the 1980s, European consumer law was conceived as a matter of weaker party protection and consumer rights,[117] even though right from the beginning the legal bases for these protective measures were the successive Treaty provisions on the construction and completion of the internal market, i.e. Article 114 TFEU and its predecessors. With the change in the political climate, and after the CJEU's *Tobacco* judgment had made clear that EU legislation based on the market building provisions must genuinely have as its object the removal of market obstacles,[118] the European Commission increasingly justified its proposals explicitly in terms of obstacles to the functioning of the internal market. Thus, achieving Europe-wide minimum levels of consumer protection was no longer presented as a beneficial aim in itself but rather as a means for achieving the aim of creating a level playing field for sellers in Europe, in particular for creating a single market that was not segregated along national lines and was expected to result in lower prices for consumers. Quite naturally—from the perspective of creating a level playing field for European sellers—the next step became to move from minimum to full (or maximum) harmonization, where individual Member States were no longer allowed to provide their consumers with protection which went further, as this would still distort the market.

Clearly, if, as a result of different levels of consumer protection in different Member States and a lack of transparency as to the actual level of consumer protection in a foreign country, consumers and businesses are comparatively less inclined towards cross-border transactions, this indeed may be regarded as a market failure or at least as an obstacle to the smooth and 'proper' functioning of a market, in particular the internal market of the EU. The question then becomes whether this is indeed the case, which is an empirical one. Enter the impact assessments. For, as we saw in Chapter 3, in order to demonstrate the required economic benefits, ever since the Lisbon summit European Commission proposals have been accompanied by extensive 'impact assessments', which are the European equivalent of the US government's cost-benefit analyses. Clearly, this is a very specifically utilitarian (i.e. welfarist) way of framing the debate on the need to protect weaker parties in contracts. Although the Consumer Rights Directive 2011 refers, in its title, to consumer *rights*, which rather suggests a liberal-egalitarian underpinning, both the explanatory memorandum that accompanied the 2008 proposal and the preliminary recitals to the directive as it was adopted in 2011 justified the new consumer rights in essentially utilitarian terms—not as an aim but as a means for increasing consumer confidence with a view to boosting economic growth: consumer rights as cross-border market building. This same instrumental approach to contractual rights (and indeed to consumers)[119] was present, in an even more pronounced way and with the specific objective of contributing to solving

[117] The original Treaty Establishing the European Economic Community (Rome Treaty, 1957) did not refer to consumer protection. European consumer policy did not start until the 1970s. After the Paris Summit (1972) had concluded that there was a need for consumer protection, a Council resolution on a preliminary programme for 'a consumer protection and information policy' was adopted in 1975. The 1985 doorstep-selling directive (85/577/EEC), introducing a right of withdrawal, is usually regarded as the first consumer protection measure in contract law.

[118] Case C-376/98, *Germany v. Parliament and Council* (EU:C:2000:544).

[119] Cf. Micklitz (n. 36) 293: 'The White Paper on the completion of the Internal Market has politicized the consumer.... It is incumbent upon him to support, promote, and expand the Single European Market.'

the economic crisis, in the Commission's proposal for a common European sales law (2011, withdrawn in 2014). In the words of Viviane Reding's favourite slogan when she was the Vice-president of the Commission: 'justice for growth'.[120] The latest development has been a specific focus on the 'digital single market'. As explained in the first preliminary recital to the 2019 Directive on contracts for the supply of digital content and digital services:

> the growth potential of e-commerce in the Union has not yet been fully exploited. The Digital Single Market Strategy for Europe tackles in a holistic manner the major obstacles to the development of cross-border e-commerce in the Union in order to unleash this potential. Ensuring better access for consumers to digital content and digital services, and making it easier for businesses to supply digital content and digital services, can contribute to boosting the Union's digital economy and stimulating overall growth.[121]

In summary, economic growth remains the first aim of EU consumer contract law.[122]

3. Growth and Justice

Welfare economists will support consumer protection only when and to the extent that this leads to an increase in social (i.e. aggregate) welfare (which some—but not all—will reduce to economic growth), and for that reason alone, not, for example, because they think that consumers have a right to—or are worthy of—protection or because resources have to be redistributed from professional sellers and service

[120] See, generally, Commission Communication, 'The EU justice agenda for 2020: strengthening trust, mobility and growth within the Union' (COM(2014) 144 final), especially at 2 and 7. The Explanatory Memorandum to the Digital Single Market proposals announced quite candidly: 'The general objective of the proposals is to contribute to faster growth of the Digital Single Market, to the benefit of both consumers and businesses.'

[121] Directive (EU) 2019/770 on certain aspects concerning contracts for the supply of digital content and digital services (n. 15), Recital (1). See also Directive (EU) 2019/771 on certain aspects concerning contracts for the sale of goods (n. 15), Recital (4):

> E-commerce is a key driver for growth within the internal market. However, its growth potential is far from being fully exploited. In order to strengthen Union competitiveness and to boost growth, the Union needs to act swiftly and encourage economic actors to unleash the full potential offered by the internal market. The full potential of the internal market can only be unleashed if all market participants enjoy smooth access to cross-border sales of goods including in e-commerce transactions. The contract law rules on the basis of which market participants conclude transactions are among the key factors shaping business decisions as to whether to offer goods cross-border. Those rules also influence consumers' willingness to embrace and trust this type of purchase.

[122] Interestingly, the European Commission objected against the 'suspension' by several Member States of consumer rights to reimbursement for flights cancelled during the COVID-19 pandemic. Here, it was the Member States that pushed the agenda of containing the recession, with no regard for consumer rights, while the Commission wanted to protect those rights. In other words, while the Commission was concerned about the subjective rights of consumers in their horizontal contractual relationships with airline companies, the Member States were interested more in the macro-economic effects on growth (or, rather, contraction). See Commission Communication, 'Commission Notice, Interpretative Guidelines on EU passenger rights regulations in the context of the developing situation with COVID-19' (C(2020) 1830 final); Commission Recommendation of 13 May 2020, OJ 2020 L 151, 'On Vouchers Offered to Passengers and Travellers as an Alternative to Reimbursement for Cancelled Package Travel and Transport Services in the Context of the COVID-19 Pandemic' (C(2020) 3125 final).

providers towards consumers. As mentioned earlier, what matters on the utilitarian view is the size of the cake, not its division.[123] Indeed, certain welfare economists might even support policies that make consumers and other weaker parties *worse* off if this would lead to an increase in social welfare. Remember that Kaldor-Hicks efficiency allows for interpersonal trade-offs and does not even require that the winners actually compensate the losers; the only thing needed is that the winners *could* compensate the losers and still be better off—whether compensation actually takes place is irrelevant. However, not everyone shares this view of the law as entirely instrumental to maximizing welfare—indeed, not even all economists do. For example, Kahneman, the 2002 Nobel laureate in economics, points out that 'Humans, more than Econs, also need protection from others who deliberately exploit their weaknesses'.[124] Indeed, even the European Commission seems to have started to change its tune: a 'New Deal for Consumers' aiming to deliver a fairer single market' and 'strengthening consumer rights' sounds different from the old language of ensuring that consumers can 'reap the benefits of the internal market'.[125]

4. Liberal-Egalitarian

A. Division of Responsibilities

Social-democratic politicians generally support the protection of workers, tenants, consumers, and other structurally weaker parties to contracts. However, among liberal-egalitarians, the philosophical current most closely related to social democracy, there is a persistent idea that there should be a division of responsibility as a result of which private law should not have any task in ensuring social justice.

In common with the libertarian view we saw previously, this view rejects a distributive task for private law and wants to limit the role of private law to ensuring existing entitlements (corrective justice), typically understood formally. However, the crucial difference is that the liberal-egalitarian idea is one of a division of labour—i.e. *other* institutions should be responsible for distributive justice—while libertarians, as we saw, totally reject the entire idea and practice of distributive justice—i.e. *no* institution should be responsible for redistribution. In this sense, the liberal-egalitarian view is closer to the welfare economic stance, according to which any distributive objectives should be pursued through the tax-and-transfer system. The key difference here is, of course, that for welfarists the reason for the institutional division of labour is its overall beneficial consequences (efficiency through a reduction of the social cost of redistribution) rather than moral reasons.

[123] Here, as on any question, indirect utilitarianism could support other stated aims for consumer protection as long as, at the end of the day, these policies would increase social welfare. However, as has been pointed out, taken to its extreme indirect utilitarianism would be self-defeating.

[124] Kahneman (n. 111) 413.

[125] Commission Press Release IP/18/3041 of 11 April 2018, 'A New Deal for Consumers: Commission Strengthens EU Consumer Rights and Enforcement'. The European Parliament may still be on the old track. Cf. N. Iacob and F. Simonelli, *How to Fully Reap the Benefits of the Internal Market for E-Commerce? Study for the Committee on the Internal Market and Consumer Protection*, European Parliament (2020).

1. Institutional Division of Labour

The idea of an institutional division of labour between private law and other institutions gained prominence—and became controversial—when Rawls, in an essay explaining that it is the task of the institutions belonging to the 'basic structure of society' to assure distributive justice, referred to the rules of contract law in a way that gave reason to believe that he thought contract law should not in fact have such a distributive task.[126] In the essay, Rawls made four points concerning the importance of background justice.[127] First, we cannot tell merely from the interaction of the contracting parties whether, from a social point of view, their contract is just and fair, because the fairness depends on the underlying social conditions. Secondly, even if everybody acts fairly and complies with the rules of contract law, then background justice will still be gradually undermined. Thirdly, it is impossible to draft private law rules, that individuals can reasonably be expected to follow, in such a way that background justice will be preserved, because private law rules cannot be too complex or require too much information to be applied. Then, as a fourth point, Rawls introduces the institutional division of labour. He writes:

> To conclude: we start with the basic structure and try to see how this structure itself should make the adjustments necessary to preserve background justice. What we look for, in effect, is an institutional division of labor between the basic structure and the rules directly applying to individuals and associations and to be followed by them in particular transactions. If this division of labor can be established, individuals and associations are then left free to advance their ends more effectively within the framework of the basic structure, secure in the knowledge that elsewhere in the social system the necessary corrections to preserve background justice are being made.[128]

From Rawls's discussion of background justice, and in particular this passage, many observers have drawn the conclusion that he rejected a distributive justice role for contract law.[129]

Contract law determines the rights and obligations of contracting parties. If no other institutions, such as the tax and transfer system, were available to assure distributive justice, then in a society that wants to achieve distributive justice the rules determining contractual rights and obligations should indeed take into account all the distributive implications of each transaction. For, there would be no *re*-distribution; only *initial* distribution through contracts. Such contract law rules would indeed be highly complex because they would have to consider many different variables. It is not only contract law that would thus be overburdened. Society would almost certainly also fail to achieve distributive justice, because the aim of social justice cannot be

[126] Rawls, 'The Basic Structure as Subject', in J. Rawls, *Political Liberalism* ([first published 1993] 2005), lecture VII. An earlier version of the essay was published in 14 *American Philosophical Quarterly* (1977) 159.

[127] Ibid. 266–269.

[128] Ibid. 268.

[129] See e.g. Kronman, 'Contract Law and Distributive Justice', 89 *Yale L.J.* (1980) 472; Kordana and Tabachnick, 'Rawls and Contract Law', 73 *Geo. Wash. L. Rev.* (2005) 598; Gutmann, 'Some Preliminary Remarks on a Liberal Theory of Contract', 76 *Law Contemp. Probl.* (2013) 39.

attained through the *exclusive* means of contract law.[130] In other words, if it fell upon contract law alone to provide background justice, then clearly a (sufficiently) just distribution would most probably not be achieved.[131] What Rawls did not seem to realize, however, is that certain private law rules and doctrines that can prevent distributive injustice do in fact satisfy the requirements of simplicity and practicality no less than other familiar rules and doctrines of private law, while at the same time also being very effective in directly preventing social injustices from occurring. Rawls writes with regard to the undesirable distributive consequences of market transactions:

> There are no feasible rules that it is practicable to require economic agents to follow in their day-to-day transactions that can prevent these undesirable consequences. These consequences are often so far in the future, or so indirect, that the attempt to forestall them by restrictive rules that apply to individuals would be an excessive if not an impossible burden.[132]

This is certainly true most of the time. And that is why we need a fair tax and transfer system to take care of a fair distribution of income. However, sometimes the consequences are immediate and direct, as in the cases of unfair exploitation (or unconscionability), unfair standard contract terms, or a radical change of circumstances (*imprévision* or hardship). There, the only burden that would be imposed on a contracting party is that she would be prevented, respectively, from exploiting the other party, from invoking the unfair term, or from enforcing the contract under radically altered circumstances. In those cases, surely, the attempt to forestall the social injustice by restrictive rules that apply to individuals would be neither an impossible nor an excessive burden.[133]

Therefore, Rawls's suggestion that an institutional division of labour must be established between the basic structure of society and the rules applying directly to particular transactions seems flawed.[134] From the fact that private law cannot maintain background justice on its own it does not follow that, therefore, it should make no contribution at all. Rather, those doctrines and rules of private law that can make such a contribution in a way that is fair, reasonable, and practicable to impose upon individuals (and their associations, e.g. firms), should be regarded, to that extent, as part of the basic structure of society.[135] In particular, those rules that have a direct impact on the 'essential primary good of self-respect',[136] such as rules banning exploitative

[130] This would be something like a Nozickian state where justice would follow exclusively from the (repeated) application of the 'principle of justice in acquisition' and the 'principle of justice in transfer', but where—in radical opposition to Nozick's theory—the 'principle of justice in transfer' alone would be assigned with the task of implementing the (separate) principles of distributive justice (say the two Rawlsian principles of justice as fairness).

[131] See Scheffler, 'Egalitarian Liberalism as Moral Pluralism', 79 *Proceedings of the Aristotelian Society, Supplementary Volumes* (2005) 229, at 240.

[132] Rawls, *Political Liberalism* (n. 126) 266.

[133] For examples of such rules, see the Introduction at the start of this chapter.

[134] See further, Hesselink, 'Unjust Conduct in the Internal Market: on the role of European Private Law in the Division of Moral Responsibility Between the EU, Its Member States and Their Citizens', 35 *YEL* (2016) 410, on which this section draws.

[135] In the same sense, albeit on somewhat different grounds, J. Klijnsma, *Contract Law as Fairness: A Rawlsian Perspective on the Position of SMEs in European Contract Law* (2014), at 34 ff.

[136] Rawls, *Political Liberalism* (n. 126) 284.

contracts, seem to be among the ones whose presence in most societies would be required by principles of social justice, simply because it seems difficult to imagine how other institutions, notably tax and transfer, could adequately compensate for the loss of self-respect, as was illustrated previously, in Section 3.A.3, with reference to the *Aziz* case. Rather than a division of labour, on Rawlsian grounds a collaboration seems to be warranted among all those institutions that are best placed to maintain background justice. The basic structure of society should be such that each of these institutions make the coordinated contribution that it is most fair, reasonable, and practicable to expect from them in the light of the ways in which these institutions tend to affect the freedom of individuals to organize their day-to-day transactions.

2. Division of Moral Labour

Ripstein combines Kant's theory of right with Rawls's theory of justice in an argument against distributive justice through private law and in favour of a formal understanding of private rights. He argues that there exists a division of moral responsibility, between the (public) responsibility of society as a whole for justice and the (private) responsibility of individuals for their own lives, and that this division implies a further division of responsibility among individuals: people are not individually responsible for how well the lives of other individuals go.[137] Individuals have no obligation, except when voluntarily undertaken, to assist others in achieving their objectives. In particular, people have no direct claim to the resources of other people. For this reason, private disputes between individuals concerning entitlements (i.e. about what belongs to whom) should not be instrumentalized as a sort of 'windfall opportunity' for achieving the essentially public aim of distributive justice: 'Under the division of responsibility, insofar as such social aims are legitimate public purposes, they can be pursued by society as a whole. Private disputes must be resolved between the parties in ways that preserve each party's special responsibility for his or her own life.'[138] That is why, in Ripstein's view, private law should be formal and not take into account the material conditions of the parties to a civil dispute, such as their respective economic power, vulnerability, skills, and experience.[139] In other words, Ripstein's argument is aimed directly against weaker party protection in contracts. Note, however, that although this formal understanding of private law is compatible with the formal understanding of liberty that libertarians advocate, Ripstein's view differs crucially from that of libertarians like Nozick in that it does not claim that it is unjust for the state to redistribute. Ripstein merely argues that horizontal, private relationships should not be the locus for re-distribution. Private law should be about what is rightfully mine and what yours, not about how much it is just for you and for me to have. It is an argument for a division of labour based on a division of moral responsibility, not one against a fair distribution of opportunities along liberal-egalitarian lines. Note also that this

137 Ripstein, 'Private Order and Public Justice: Kant and Rawls', 92 *Va. L. Rev.* (2006) 1391, at 1393. Ripstein invokes Rawls, 'Social Unity and Primary Goods', in A. Sen and B. Williams (eds), *Utilitarianism and Beyond* (1982), at 159, where he wrote that justice as fairness includes 'a social division of responsibility' between society and the individual.

138 Ripstein (n. 137) 1398.

139 A. Ripstein, *Force and Freedom: Kant's Legal and Political Philosophy* (2009), ch. 2 and *passim*. In the same sense, E. J. Weinrib, *The Idea of Private Law* (1995). Similar, Gutmann (n. 129).

argument differs from the one that we just saw according to which an institutional division of labour is required chiefly as a matter of practicability.

Ripstein is probably right that private disputes should not be used as windfall occasions to reach a somewhat more just distribution, for the simple reason that if this were permitted it is not clear why we would still apply ordinary private law doctrines to such disputes.[140] For, if it were a legitimate aim of private law to improve the distribution of wealth in a society, then if a very poor person sells an ordinary good, say a pair of sneakers, to a very rich person for a normal price, then why should the poor person ever be forced to hand over the sneakers after the buyer has paid the price? Or, conversely, if the poor person is the buyer, why should she even be obliged to pay the price? Why not use the windfall occasion for maximal redistribution? From the distributive perspective, for the state to force poor people to pay money to rich people might just seem perverse. Indeed, from that same perspective it should be the rich that should be obliged to give money directly to the poor, and the windfall occasion of a dispute over a contract would become wholly dispensable.[141] However, if this is true—i.e. if contract law should not be redistributive—then contract enforcement should also not structurally make matters worse. In other words, contract law should not be perversely redistributive either. In particular, contract enforcement should not unjustly reproduce or magnify existing unjust distributions of wealth and power. We have no natural right to the state's support of all our projects.[142] Nor, as we saw in Chapter 5, can we claim a pre-institutional entitlement to expectation remedies for breach of contract; contract law systems that protect the expectation interest change the pre-existing distribution of resources and bring about a situation in which the promisee comes to have something that she did not have before. And there does not seem to be any reason—in justice or other—why society should place contract enforcement at the service of perverse redistribution.[143] This seems especially true since, as we saw when discussing the *Aziz* case, sometimes the best or even the only way to prevent an unjust redistribution from occurring is by refusing to enforce a certain contract or contract clause.[144]

As stated, invoking the division of moral responsibility Ripstein argues not only against distributive justice through private law but also for a formal understanding

[140] Similar, Unger (n. 89) 116–117 (critical): 'if, out of respect for the ideal of human concern, we were to use the doctrine of economic duress in contract law to void all contracts concluded between members of different social classes, we would find ourselves with a roving mandate to subvert and reconstruct the social order.'

[141] In other words, while Nozick's example of the basketball star Wilt Chamberlain, discussed earlier, in Section 2.A.1, fails to demonstrate that redistributive tax is theft, it could still in fact underscore the idea of a division of moral responsibility between the state and individuals to the effect that the state is responsible for setting up an institutional framework that assures (background) distributive justice, while individuals do not have any moral responsibility in their private dealings to achieve the difference principle.

[142] Shiffrin (n. 77) 224.

[143] In the same sense Bagchi, 'Distributive Justice and Contract', in G. Klass, G. Letsas, and P. Saprai (eds), *Philosophical Foundations of Contract Law* (2014) 199, who argues that 'we should interpret interpersonal entitlements in such a way that they do not exacerbate distributive injustice'.

[144] Shiffrin (n. 77) 235, observes with regard to the US doctrine of 'unconscionability', which is roughly similar to the doctrine of unfair exploitation in Art. II.-7:207 DCFR, that it 'works directly to staunch the flow of resources from the disadvantaged to those who are better off, both by voiding exploitative contracts and by deterring their formation. These are some of the very effects that the redistributive transfers brought about by the tax system would aim in part to reverse'.

of interpersonal justice and of private law. For present purposes this would mean—in radical opposition to the *acquis communautaire* as it stands today and to most Member State private laws—that European private law should be a system of formal rights. However, is it really true that the special responsibility of individuals for their own lives and the related division of responsibility between society and individuals requires a formal private law? After all, it is not an easy task to take responsibility for your own life while being exploited. In reality, a more substantive (or 'material') system of private law does not fundamentally change the division of moral labour. It does not introduce a general duty to promote the good of other people. Contracts still merely create enforceable private rights and obligations between private parties and contract law still only consists of rules of conduct between the parties to a contract. Sure enough, the rights and obligations are different under a more material than under a more formal private law, but they remain correlative rights and obligations. In particular, the spheres of free choice may be smaller (or within equally large spheres the freedom may be less comprehensive, i.e. more conceivable options are unavailable), but my entitlement still stops where yours starts and at no point is it the case that you have a right to my performance while I am not under an obligation towards you to perform. If you invoke an unfair term, or a contract that we concluded as a result of your unfair exploitation of my dire situation, then, once I have annulled the clause or the contract, respectively, you are simply not entitled to any right stipulated in that clause or contract and, correspondingly or 'correlatively' (as Weinrib would say), I am under no obligation to do or give whatever was stipulated in the invalid clause or contract.

Weinrib argues that in civil disputes the reason why one party has to pay, give, or do something must also be the reason why the other is entitled to receive the money, thing, or service. This principle of what he calls 'correlativity' is indeed an important principle of civil justice.[145] However, it does not follow from this principle that there is no place for distributive justice in contract law, nor that contract law necessarily has to be formal. What does follow is that whatever distributive justice requires in contract law must at the same time also be just between the parties to the dispute. But that is exactly what happens in those cases where distributive justice through contract law is appropriate, for these are the cases where an unjust redistribution among the parties can be prevented from occurring, i.e. where without the intervention one party would be unjustifiably enriched at the expense of the other.[146] The example of unfair exploitation (or unconscionability) illustrates this correlativity very well.[147] It is unjust for one contracting party to exploit the other's predicament (interpersonal justice), but a society is also unjust to the extent that it accepts different distributive shares in terms of wealth, happiness, preference satisfaction, reasons for self-respect, other primary goods, or capabilities for human flourishing, resulting from unfair exploitations

[145] E. J. Weinrib, *Corrective Justice* (2012), ch. 1.

[146] Gordley regards such cases as instances exclusively of corrective justice, on a very substantive understanding of corrective justice which includes, in particular, a fair price requirement. See e.g. Gordley, 'Contract Law in the Aristotelian Tradition', in P. Benson (ed.), *The Theory of Contract Law: New Essays* (2001) 265.

[147] See e.g. Art. 1143 French Civil Code (new), that was inspired by Art. II.-7:207 DCFR and Art 51 CESL proposal.

(distributive justice). We could also combine these two elements of justice into a third one by stating that a society is unjust (social justice) to the extent that it supports exploitative practices by rendering exploitative contracts legally enforceable that unjustifiably make certain parties worse off to the benefit of others.[148]

3. The Most Vulnerable Contracting Parties

Once it is accepted that at least the basic structure of contract law is part of the basic structure of society and, therefore, within the scope of Rawlsian justice as fairness, and that an *a priori* innate right to a formal contract law is incompatible with Rawlsian political liberalism, then, from a Rawlsian perspective, a core concern becomes to ensure that socio-economic inequalities in society resulting from contract law, or existing ones exacerbated by it, also work to the benefit of the least well off. This is required by the difference principle, which is part of the second principle of justice as fairness. This, in turn, directs our attention squarely towards the most vulnerable in society.

From this perspective, the focus in recent EU private law measures on average consumers, who are reasonably well informed and reasonably circumspect, is problematic. Such idealized accounts, as Onora O'Neill puts it, 'conceal that justice to the weak demands more than justice to the strong'.[149] It is the sub-average consumers who seem to be most deserving of weaker party protection. So, any consumer protection measures allowing sellers and other traders to take average consumers as the benchmark for their market conduct seem to violate the second principle of justice as fairness, meant by Rawls as a standard for a sufficiently just society. It is true that EU contract law also provides special protection to particularly vulnerable consumers, but the substantive scope of these provisions is much more limited. For contract law, it includes only the 'essential services'.[150] However, the difference principle is not about preserving a bare minimum, it is about maximizing the minimum, or, if the difference principle is not understood as a maximizing principle, at least making sure that if consumer protection contributes to inequalities this will nevertheless also benefit the least well off. And this does not seem to be ensured by consumer protection measures that *exclude* sub-average consumers from their protective scope.

From a Rawlsian perspective, another potential problem with EU consumer protection is that other contracting parties may be just as worthy of protection as consumers, or even more so, in their contracts with stronger sellers and service providers. This may be the case, in particular, for certain small businesses in their contracts with large businesses, in very much the same contexts where consumers are protected, for example in the case of unfair terms. Klijnsma has shown that in these cases the current

[148] A different way of putting this is that considerations of distributive justice inform the determination of interpersonal duties. See Bagchi (n. 143) 201.

[149] O'Neill, 'Constructivisms in Ethics', in O. O'Neill, *Constructions of Reasons: Exploring Kant's Practical Philosophy* (1989) 206, at 210.

[150] With regard to unfair commercial practices, pursuant Art. 5(3) and preliminary Recital (18) to the Unfair Commercial Practices Directive (n. 13), only where a commercial practice is specifically aimed at a particular group of consumers (the example given is that of children), is it 'desirable that the impact of the commercial practice be assessed from the perspective of the average member of that group'. This excludes protection of the most vulnerable against commercial practice not specifically targeting a group of particularly vulnerable consumers.

limitation of weaker party protection to consumers may constitute a violation of the difference principle.[151]

Moreover, and even more troubling, consumer law in some cases may result in protecting consumers against weaker parties. This may be the case when sellers or service providers belong to a social group that is less well off than the consumers are. For the case of sex workers, for example, Tjon Soei Len shows how the rules aiming at consumer protection might exacerbate the vulnerable position of women providing sexual services on the EU internal market.[152]

In addition, there is the important question of distributive justice between Europeans at the core and those at the socio-economic periphery.[153] The high level of consumer protection required by Article 114(3) TFEU and ensured (allegedly) by the various consumer protection directives, from which consumers in rich Member States are benefiting, may come at the expense—in the absence of additional measures for protection—of the interests of people in poorer Member States, e.g. consumers who can afford to pay only low prices or sellers whose businesses cannot survive if they have to meet high consumer protection standards.

Finally, probably the most vulnerable in society are those who are at the intersection of various vulnerable social groups.[154] To the extent that they are the least well off they should receive special attention and be the first target of weaker party protection in contract. So far, however, a political discourse on intersectionality in European contract law is entirely lacking.

So, in conclusion, then, it seems that Rawlsian justice may demand much more in terms of justice than EU contract law is currently delivering. In Rawlsian terms, there seems to be a justice deficit in EU contract law, especially with regard to the weakest contracting parties, i.e. the most vulnerable in society when engaged in contracting.

B. Justice through Market Access

As already stated, much of recent EU private law was explicitly motivated by a wish to improve consumer confidence in cross-border shopping with a view to increasing economic growth ('justice for growth'), which is an essentially utilitarian agenda (albeit a rather reductive version of it, equating social welfare with GDP), that, characteristically, is not specifically concerned with distribution. However, Micklitz has argued that there is another possible reading of these EU measures and others: as expressing

[151] Klijnsma (n. 135).

[152] Tjon Soei Len, 'Consumer Protection, Sexual Services and Vulnerability: Exploring Social Justice in European Contract Law', 11 *ERCL* (2015) 127.

[153] See Kukovec, 'Taking Change Seriously: the Rhetoric of Justice and the Reproduction of the Status Quo', in D. Kochenov, G. de Búrca, and A. Williams (eds), *Europe's Justice Deficit?* 319 (2014), at 323: 'As structural subordination of various actors of the periphery in the economic and legal structure has not been recognised, the definitions of a weak party in legal vernacular follow a pattern that does not include the weaker parties in terms of the centre–periphery hierarchy.'

[154] Crenshaw, 'Demarginalizing the Intersection of Race and Sex: A Black Feminist Critique of Antidiscrimination Doctrine, Feminist Theory and Antiracist Politics', 1 *University of Chicago Legal Forum* (1989) 139.

a European conception of justice, that Micklitz labels as 'access justice'.[155] On this view consumers, and their cross-border purchases, are not merely instrumental to the aim of growth. Rather, the aim is that *all* consumers can 'reap the benefits' of the internal market. Clearly, if access justice is to be understood as an aim in itself (and not merely as an instrument for growth) and also to be understood, as Micklitz envisages, in a substantive sense, as opposed to the mere formal opportunity to enter the market, then access justice is indeed a distributive notion.[156] As Micklitz explains:

> access justice means more than a formal guarantee to workers and consumers that they may have a theoretical chance in participating in the market and reaping the benefits of the market.... The legal system is responsible for establishing tools which transform the theoretical chance into a realistic opportunity, thereby eliminating all sorts of barriers which hinder the assertion of the claim to access.[157]

These tools will inevitably come at a cost. And the social costs of implementing policies that assure access to the market for those who would be denied access under a more formal notion will inevitably also be borne by those citizens who have more resources, skills, and talents and would already be able to enter the market under a more formal guarantee of access, and therefore will not benefit from these policies. In other words, they will have an impact on the distribution both of opportunities and of resources.

The anti-discrimination and anti-exclusion rationale of access justice will appeal to liberal-egalitarians. If individuals who previously had no access to markets now gain access and, in particular, if they (or at least some of them) belong to the least well-off groups in a given society, then that society arguably becomes a more just one from the perspective of the Rawlsian difference principle, which, as we saw, requires that when a society makes institutional choices with differential outcomes for different groups, these choices must also work to the benefit of the least well off. Thus, access justice could be regarded as an implementation through private law of opportunity-egalitarian principles, notably the Rawlsian difference principle.[158] A characteristic of opportunity egalitarianism is, as Roemer puts it, that while opportunities must be equalized before the competition starts, 'after it begins, individuals are on their own'.[159] The same applies, it seems, to access justice as understood by Micklitz.

However, Ben-Shahar argues that measures of the kind that Micklitz claims can be justified as access justice may lead to outcomes that should trouble opportunity

[155] Micklitz, 'Social Justice and Access Justice in Private Law', in H.-W. Micklitz (ed.), *The Many Faces of Social Justice in Private Law* (2011) 3; H.-W. Micklitz, *The Politics of Justice in European Private Law: Social Justice, Access Justice, Societal Justice* (2018), at 2, 12–30, and *passim*.

[156] Explicitly in this sense, Micklitz, *The Politics of Justice* (n. 155) 2.

[157] Micklitz, 'Social Justice and Access Justice in Private Law' (n. 155) 37.

[158] In this sense, Klijnsma (n. 135) 76. Of course, inclusiveness could also be read as a typically communitarian notion. Interestingly, Micklitz, *The Politics of Justice* (n. 155) 23, explains that he borrowed the concept of 'Zugangsgerechtigkeit' originally from a document of the German Catholic Church, and wonders whether 'there is something "catholic" about access justice'. Quite literally, one would think there definitely is, given the etymological roots of the word "catholic"—and the self-understanding of that Church—as being all-embracing.

[159] J. E. Roemer, *Equality of Opportunity* (1998), at 2.

egalitarians, because they may turn out to be regressively redistributive.[160] For example, this is the case when in practice the least well-off in society fail to use their access rights while, through higher prices, they end up cross-subsidizing the use made of these general rights by the more sophisticated and better-off consumers. The empirical evidence presented by Ben-Shahar mainly concerns cases where the elite benefits more from free access than the poor. However, these cases of free museums, public parks, or highways, of which the elite are the principal beneficiaries, are not necessarily troubling from the perspective of, for example, the Rawlsian difference principle. For that possibility is intrinsic to the difference principle and an entirely foreseeable outcome of it. Justice as fairness was meant by Rawls as a conception of justice for specifying the fair terms of social cooperation among citizens.[161] The difference principle compares the situation of the least well off in society, as a group, before and after the introduction of a certain measure. It does not ask how much other groups benefit from the same measure or whether the measure increases inequality.[162] In other words, over-inclusiveness is not a problem from the Rawlsian opportunity-egalitarian perspective.[163] Therefore, to the extent that consumer protection benefits sophisticated and assertive consumers more than vulnerable consumers—which seems plausible enough as an empirical claim—that does not hurt the theory of access justice, read as an opportunity-egalitarian theory, as long as at least some vulnerable consumers also benefit from the consumer protection rules gaining increased access to the market. The only cases truly troubling from the perspective of access justice, understood as an opportunity-egalitarian theory, are those where sellers charge consumers a price increase for the enhanced consumer protection as a result of which their products are no longer available to the poorest consumers, thus foreclosing access to those markets for those poorest and making them worse off. Although such cases are certainly conceivable (they are predicted by basic economic models), Ben-Shahar has not yet found much empirical evidence of their occurrence in the private law context.

A more fundamental question is whether mere 'access justice' suffices for European private law to be even minimally just.[164] Although Micklitz's analysis was originally mostly descriptive of EU private law, subsequently he has defended it explicitly also as a normative concept.[165] But is it really enough for individuals to have access to the market (even access understood in a substantive sense) and to be able to choose from a broad variety of products and services? What if that market is in fact a jungle, without any guarantees for at least minimal contractual justice. It is not clear why the market should not be further regulated in an opportunities-preserving way, with adequate safety nets. Is a society whose contract law enforces exploitative contracts, or

[160] Ben-Shahar, 'The Paradox of Access Justice, and Its Application to Mandatory Arbitration', 83 *U. Chi. L. Rev.* (2016) 1755.

[161] Rawls, *Political Liberalism* (n. 126) 3.

[162] See e.g. ibid. 6: '[the difference principle] says that the social and economic inequalities are to be adjusted so that, *whatever the level of those inequalities*, whether great or small, they are to the greatest benefit of the least advantaged members of society' (emphasis added).

[163] See Klijnsma (n. 135) 78.

[164] For a fuller discussion, see further Hesselink, 'Private Law, Regulation, and Justice', 22 *ELJ* (2016) 681, expanded as Hesselink, 'Droit privé, réglementation et justice', 32 *Revue internationale de droit économique* (2018) 159, on which this section draws.

[165] Micklitz, *The Politics of Justice* (n. 155) 19 and 24.

contractual claims that are contrary to good faith and fair dealing, or contracts whose performance has become excessively onerous because of an exceptional change of circumstances, an even minimally just society under any egalitarian notion that is concerned with showing equal respect to citizens? A just society, it seems, will have to do more than provide equal access to the market and other equal opportunities.[166] In addition to background justice, there is a need also for foreground justice and in addition to *ex ante* and *ex post* fairness there is a need for fairness *during* the contractual relationship, i.e. interpersonal fairness as a social justice concern. Of course, all this could be included in a very broad definition of access justice, under which the presence of safety nets during market participation is part of the reassurances that contribute to facilitating access, but then the distinctive nature of the concept of access justice would be lost. The difference between mere access justice and full interpersonal justice would collapse. Moreover, reducing interpersonal justice to access justice would not do justice to interpersonal justice either.

In summary, as a complete and exhaustive theory of justice in European private law the access justice theory would seem flawed, because it disregards the interpersonal justice dimension of private law, which includes, but is not limited to, the important corrective (or restorative) justice of correcting and preventing wrongs.[167] However, in a recent restatement of the theory, Micklitz has clarified that access justice should not be understood as a complete and exhaustive theory of private law justice in the EU. He emphasizes that access justice is not meant to replace established understandings of justice at the national level.[168] Rather, 'it stands side-by-side national patterns of social justice'.[169] Thus, Micklitz seems to regard access justice at the EU level and national models of justice at the Member State level as complementary. At first sight, this may seem to match well with an understanding of European private law as a multi-level system based on shared competences.[170] However, upon further examination it also raises new questions. First, coordination problems are bound to arise. Given that shared competences do not imply an obligation for either the Member States or the EU to legislate, a legislative gap, and consequently a justice deficit, can easily arise. This may occur, for example, when neither the EU nor the Member States (either none of them or, more likely, not all of them) take responsibility for injustices arising from negative or positive integration and their respective deregulatory or re-regulatory effects.[171] Secondly, conflicts are to be expected too. Presumably, access justice is meant to have priority over national conceptions in case of a conflict between the two, following (or mimicking) the primacy of EU law over national law. However, this would be highly problematic since, as Micklitz himself emphasizes, compared to national

[166] For a critique of distributive justice as mere inclusion, Somek, 'From Workers to Migrants, from Distributive Justice to Inclusion: Exploring the Changing Social Democratic Imagination', 18 *ELJ* (2012) 711, who, however, seems to misread Rawls's justice as fairness as an *ex post* approach, while Rawlsian justice is opportunity-egalitarian.

[167] A similar point is made by Dagan, 'Between Regulatory and Autonomy-Based Private Law', 22 *ELJ* (2016) 644.

[168] Micklitz, *The Politics of Justice* (n. 155) 12.

[169] Ibid. 19.

[170] On such conceptions, see Chapter 4.

[171] Not only deregulation but also reregulation can lead to injustices, especially in the case of full harmonization, e.g. when minimal weaker party protection becomes the maximum.

conceptions access justice is only a thin conception of justice.[172] So, if mere access justice is meant to exhaust the EU's responsibility for justice in private law then this may well still leave or create a justice deficit, because of EU law's primacy over national law, for example in the case of a consumer law directive aiming at full (and exhaustive) harmonization.

C. The 'Materialization' of Autonomy and Equality

As we saw in Chapter 5, both liberal perfectionists and comprehensive liberals regard personal autonomy as the value on which contract law should be based. Pursuant to the 'principle of private autonomy', individuals themselves can shape their own legal relationships in accordance with their free will or choice.[173] However, if personal autonomy is understood as the equal opportunity for each of us to make our own choices and to live accordingly, i.e. to live our lives in accordance with our own conceptions of what amounts to a good life, then clearly the degree to which we are able in fact to live such autonomous lives depends on the range of potentially valuable alternatives that are actually available to us. Actual freedom, therefore, requires more than the formal freedom of not being hindered when choosing; it requires the presence of valuable options to choose from. According to this argument, private autonomy should be understood in a substantive sense. And accordingly, the definition and determination of private rights should also be substantive, or 'material'.

It is such a substantive understanding of private autonomy that was at the basis of the gradual transformation of private law by courts and legislators in the course of the twentieth century in Germany and other European countries. Wieacker, borrowing the concept from Weber,[174] famously referred to this trend as '*Materialisierung*' when he wrote that the German courts had converted the foundation of private law from a formal morality of freedom into a substantive morality of social responsibility.[175]

[172] Micklitz, *The Politics of Justice* (n. 155) 24.

[173] The view that public institutions should promote autonomy because the autonomous life is the best life, are sometimes also referred to as 'Kantian'. For example, Rawls, *Political Liberalism* (n. 126) 78, when referring to 'comprehensive liberalism', e.g. at 78 and 99: 'Kant's doctrine is a comprehensive moral view in which the ideal of autonomy has a regulative role for all of life'. Critical of this reading of Kant, Pogge, 'Is Kant's *Rechtslehre* Comprehensive?', 36 *Southern Journal of Philosophy* (1997) 161, and Ripstein (n. 139) 11: 'Whatever its appeal, it is not Kant's view.'

[174] Weber identified legal formalism with rationalism and was critical of a material/substantive concept of law. With regard to contractual fairness, see M. Weber (G. Roth and C. Wittich, eds), *Economy and Society* Vol II ([first published 1922] 1978), at 886:

> New demands for a 'social law' to be based upon such emotionally colored ethical postulates as 'justice' and 'human dignity' and directed against the very dominance of a mere business morality, have arisen with the emergence of the modern class problem. They are advocated not only by labor and other interested groups but also by legal ideologists. By these demands legal formalism itself has been challenged. Such a concept as economic duress, or the attempt to treat as immoral, and thus as invalid, a contract because of a gross disproportion between promise and consideration, are derived from norms which, from the legal standpoint, are entirely amorphous and which are neither juristic nor conventional nor traditional in character but ethical and which claim as their legitimation substantive justice rather than formal legality.

[175] Wieacker, 'Das Sozialmodell der klassischen Privatrechtsgesetzbücher und die Entwicklung der modernen Gesellschaft' [1953], in F. Wieacker, *Industriegesellschaft und Privatrechtsordnung* (1974) 9, at

According to the more substantive understanding, private rights should arise only in the presence of substantive equality and freedom of both parties. If one party was free in a merely formal sense, then, to that extent, the act (e.g. her assent to a contract) was not autonomous but heteronomous, i.e. effectively determined by the other party (*Fremdbestimmung*). Such a more substantive notion of party autonomy has been endorsed explicitly by the German Constitutional Court. It was articulated very clearly in the famous *Bürgschaft* case, where a young woman without a job or an education had signed a personal guarantee to a bank for the benefit of her father's business for an amount that she could not realistically expect ever to pay back during her life. The court held:

> In contract law, a just balance of interests results from a concurrence of wills among the contracting parties. Both bind themselves and in doing so protect their own individual freedom of action. If one contracting party has such a strong presence that he can factually determine the contract's content unilaterally, this means that the other party loses autonomy. . . . [I]n cases of typical types, where one party to a contract may be recognised as being structurally weaker, and if the consequences for the weaker contracting party are significantly imbalanced, the civil law order must react and make correction possible, this follows from the fundamental guarantee of private autonomy (Article 2(1) GG) and the principle of the social state (Article 20(1), Article 28(1) GG).... If the content of a contract is significantly onerous and obviously unreasonable as a balance of interests, a court may not content itself with the conclusion that: 'contract is contract'. On the contrary, it must clarify whether the provision is the consequence of structurally unequal bargaining strength, and where appropriate make correction within the framework of the general principles of the civil law.[176]

The CJEU, in the *Mostaza Claro* case, on the validity of an arbitration clause in a consumer contract, similarly rejected a formal notion of equality when it explained the aim of Article 6(1) of the Unfair Terms Directive:[177] 'This is a mandatory provision which, taking into account the weaker position of one of the parties to the contract, aims to replace the formal balance which the latter establishes between the rights and obligations of the parties with an effective balance which re-establishes equality between them.'[178] This idea of re-establishing substantive equality between the parties as an aim of contract law can easily be explained by a substantive understanding of private autonomy as the normative basis of contractual obligation, which, in turn, is

23–24. For a reconstruction of 'materialization' in terms of the private law discourse of modernity, see M. Auer, *Der privatrechtliche Diskurs der Moderne* (2014).

[176] *Bundesverfassungsgericht*, 19 October 1993, *BVerfGE* 89, 214, at paras 56–59. Translation from B. S. Markesinis, H. Unberath, and A. C. Johnston, *The German Law of Contract: A Comparative Treatise* (2nd ed., 2006), case 81. 'GG' is *Grundgesetz*, i.e. Basic Law.

[177] Case C-168/05, *Mostaza Claro* (n. 10) para. 36. The French language version speaks of 'l'équilibre formel' and 'l'équilibre réel', the German version of 'formale Ausgewogenheit' and 'materielle Ausgewogenheit'.

[178] This is consistently held by the CJEU. More recently, see e.g. Case C-266/18, *Aqua Med sp. z o.o. v. Irena Skóra* (EU:C:2019:282), at para. 27; Case C-383/18, *Lexitor Sp. z o.o v. Spółdzielcza Kasa Oszczędnościowo—Kredytowa im. Franciszka Stefczyka and Others* (EU:C:2019:702), at para. 29.

typical of certain liberal perfectionist and comprehensive liberal-egalitarian views.[179] If personal autonomy and individual liberty are understood as the equal opportunity for each of us to make our own choices and to live our lives by our own lights, then clearly the degree to which we really are able to live such an autonomous and self-authored life depends crucially on the range of potentially valuable alternatives that are actually available to us. Actual freedom, therefore, requires more than not being hindered when choosing; it requires the presence of valuable options to choose from,[180] and the absence of substantial party inequality that would compromise any genuinely free choice among the available options. In other words, on a 'materialized' view, substantive equality and substantive freedom go hand in hand.

Materialization was vindicated explicitly on liberal perfectionist grounds by Dagan and Dorfman, who argue that 'private law should openly embrace the liberal commitment to self-determination and substantive equality. A liberal private law establishes frameworks of respectful interaction conducive to self-determining individuals. These frameworks are indispensable for a society in which individuals recognize each other as genuinely free and equal agents.'[181] Their account is perfectionist in that they claim that private law is intrinsically valuable because it secures 'just relationship', which, on their view, is intrinsically valuable.[182] This goes further than a comprehensive liberal-egalitarian view according to which, whatever the value of contractual and other private law relationships, it should be the task of private law to preserve substantive autonomy and equality within such relationships whenever they are entered into.

Although cases like the *Bürgschaft* case and doctrines like unconscionability and unfair exploitation may thus be justified on the basis of a substantive (or 'materialized') version of private autonomy, another way of looking at the same doctrines, which is also liberal-perfectionist, albeit of a different kind, is to regard these cases

[179] The Court's concern with imbalance between contracting parties is not limited to consumer contract law. For competition law, see e.g. Case C-453/99, *Courage Ltd v. Bernard Crehan* (EU:C:2001:465), at para. 33:

> In particular, it is for the national court to ascertain whether the party who claims to have suffered loss through concluding a contract that is liable to restrict or distort competition found himself in a *markedly weaker position* than the other party, such as seriously to compromise or even eliminate his freedom to negotiate the terms of the contract and his capacity to avoid the loss or reduce its extent, in particular by availing himself in good time of all the legal remedies available to him. (emphasis added)

For private international law, see Case C-340/16, *Landeskrankenanstalten-Betriebsgesellschaft—KABEG v. Mutuelles du Mans assurances MMA IARD SA* (EU:C:2017:576), at para. 28:

> In the same way as matters relating to workers and consumers, and as is clear from recital 13 of Regulation No 44/2001, a matter relating to insurance is characterised by a certain *imbalance between the parties* that the provisions of that section aim to *correct* by enabling the *weaker party* to benefit from rules of jurisdiction more favourable to his interests than the general rules provide for. (emphasis added)

[180] Raz (n. 76). For private law, see Dagan, 'Pluralism and Perfectionism in Private Law', 112 *Colum. L. Rev.* (2012) 1409.

[181] Dagan and Dorfman, 'Just Relationships', 116 *Colum. L. Rev.* (2016) 1395. See also H. Dagan and M. Heller, *The Choice Theory of Contracts* (2017), at 87, with reference to relational equality: 'contract law—like private law more generally—should be guided by substantive, rather than formal equality'.

[182] See, critical, Gardner, 'Dagan and Dorfman on the Value of Private Law', 117 *Colum. L. Rev* (2017), 179, at 196.

as instances of justified paternalism.[183] On that view, contract law removes certain options because the choices by individuals of these options are incompatible, in the eyes of the law, with human flourishing and an autonomous life. Kimel, for example, writes that: 'certain options can have the effect of reducing one's overall autonomy, or one's chances of leading an autonomous life, even if chosen freely. Discouraging or even preventing a person from choosing such an option can quite straightforwardly be justified as means of protecting her autonomy'.[184] This reasoning provides a different liberal-perfectionist explanation for weaker party protection, especially for cases where the protection cannot be waived by the protected parties (*ex ante* or *ex post*), e.g. in exchange for a lower price. As we saw earlier, however, most other liberal-egalitarians—and not only they—reject paternalism as an impermissible interference with an agent's moral autonomy. Moreover, liberal perfectionist principles, like the ultimate values and principles of any other perfectionist doctrine, are unlikely to be acceptable to other citizens as the foundation of our generally applicable laws, in this case European private law. Liberal perfectionism as a comprehensive ethical doctrine, although enjoying significant support in Western democracies, nevertheless is far from generally accepted—a point that political liberals would emphasize (and not only they).[185]

This raises a question which is troubling for those of us who tend to look favourably upon the transformation, during the course of the twentieth century, of private law from a formal to a more substantive outlook, but who also think that a democratic compromise on the basic structure of contract law should be justifiable as much as possible by public reasons. The question is whether the 'materialization' of private law fatally depends, for its justification, on liberal perfectionist principles, in particular the ideal of the autonomous person (understood in the ethical sense) and the idea that a human life is more valuable to the extent that it is self-authored, and the assertion that contractual relationships characterized by substantive freedom and equality are intrinsically valuable. Not necessarily, it seems. For as we just saw, the rejection of private law formalism does not depend on the endorsement of liberal perfectionism. Nor does it seem impossible, as we will see, to find basic principles of contract justice that can also be justified by other than partisan reasons, and that hold independently of whether contractual relationships have intrinsic value.

[183] Shiffrin, whose view was discussed previously, does not argue that paternalism cannot explain the unconscionability doctrine. Her argument is rather that paternalism cannot justify it, because paternalism offends the autonomy of moral agents, and that there is another (morally more appealing) explanation of weaker party protection (on which, see Section 2.B.2).

[184] D. Kimel, *From Promise to Contract: Towards a Liberal Theory of Contract* (2005), at 130.

[185] See C. Larmore, *The Morals of Modernity* (1996), at 131; Nussbaum, 'Perfectionist Liberalism and Political Liberalism', 39 *Philosophy and Public Affairs* (2011) 3.

5. Communitarian

A. Fraternity

Communitarians have argued, with regard to distributive justice, that when there is solidarity within a community there is less need for state assistance. Sandel, for example, when critically discussing Rawls's 'circumstances of justice', i.e. the circumstances in which the two principles of justice will play their role, points out that there is no need for justice where there is fraternity. He argues that a situation of justice, where the difference principle takes care of a fair distribution, is not necessarily morally superior to a situation where distribution takes places without justice but out of fraternity:

> When fraternity fades, more justice may be done, but even more may be required to restore the moral status quo. Furthermore, there is no guarantee that justice and its rival virtues will be perfectly commensurable. The breakdown of certain personal and civic attachments may represent a moral loss that even a full measure of justice cannot redeem.[186]

'In some cases', he claims, 'justice is not a virtue but a vice'.[187] A similar argument, it seems, could also be directed against interpersonal justice and weaker party protection in contracts. Thus, a communitarian could argue that the legal protection of weaker parties by contract law is a typical liberal attempt to remedy pathologies resulting from excessive individualism.

B. Solidarity

Others, however, have argued in the opposite direction, claiming that contract law should express the values of community and solidarity, replacing the individualist values of private autonomy and liberty that are usually ascribed to it.[188] On this view, a general duty of good faith and fair dealing, requiring that the contracting parties take each other's interests into account, should be regarded as the central duty of contract law. Moreover, on this view, solidarity best explains why contract law prevents various types of contractual unfairness (unfair exploitation, unfair terms), gives relief in case of bad luck (*force majeure*, change of circumstances), and protects certain groups who are structurally in a weaker position than their counterparties (workers, tenants, consumers, patients). All these rules and doctrines can easily be interpreted as expressions of contractual and social solidarity.[189]

[186] M. J. Sandel, *Liberalism and the Limits of Justice* (2nd ed., 1998), at 33.
[187] Ibid. 34.
[188] See e.g. B. Lurger, *Vertragliche Solidarität, Entwicklungschancen für das allgemeine Vertragsrecht in Österreich und in der Europäischen Union* (1998); Jamin, 'Plaidoyer pour le solidarisme contractuel', in G. Goubeaux *et al.* (eds), *Études offertes à Jacques Ghestin; Le contrat au début du XXIe siècle* (2001); Markovits, 'Contract and Collaboration', 113 *Yale L.J.* (2004) 1417, at 1421.
[189] In contrast, Markovits, 'Good Faith as Contract's Core Value', in G. Klass, G. Letsas, and P. Saprai (eds), *Philosophical Foundations of Contract Law* (2014), ch. 14, although considering collaboration, community,

In reality, these contemporary solidaristic views are more properly referred to as neo-solidaristic. For the idea that solidarity is the core value of contract law already has a long pedigree. According to Durkheim, 'le contrat est, par excellence, l'expression juridique de la coopération'.[190] And Demogue famously argued that a contractual relationship should be understood as a microcosm where everyone works together towards a common goal: 'Les contractants forment une sorte de microcosme; c'est une petite société où chacun doit travailler pour un but commun qui est la somme des buts individuels poursuivis par chacun, absolument comme dans la société civile ou commerciale'.[191] The first wave of contractual solidarism took place more than a century ago, against the backdrop of the birth of sociology, which studied society as something more than a mere collection of individuals, and the related discovery of 'the social',[192] and the social question, starting with the workers' movement, that eventually led to the transformation of private law.[193] Writing in 1952, Wieacker concluded:

> Solidarity is the hallmark of today's society ... The impact of the solidarity of the social state went far beyond the enactment of public laws restricting private rights. The courts were quick to see that contracts, damages, and ownership in the market economy of the social state are not merely a private matter between participating individuals.

Thus, solidarity also stood for reform as opposed to revolution. As a value, it appealed not only to social-democrats but also to Christian-democrats. Indeed, in the words of the Catechism, 'solidarity is an eminently Christian virtue'.[194]

However, as we saw in Chapter 3, many communitarians see great difficulty in locating fraternity and solidarity at the European level. What would be the community

and good faith as the core values of contract law, explicitly understands good faith in a 'thin' (ibid. 281) sense of subjective good faith, not as a principle of substantive fairness (ibid. 280), arguing that 'it does not establish affirmative duties of other-regard so much as articulate respect among parties who remain at arm's length' (ibid. 280). Indeed, in his view, the structure of good faith 'corresponds to the formal equality' enshrined in contract law. Thus, Markovits's understanding stands in the tradition of attributing subjective states of mind to people and of legal fictions such as 'terms implied in fact' (explicitly at ibid. 281). Contrast the definition of 'good faith and fair dealing' in the DCFR, Art I.-1:103 (Good faith and fair dealing), para. 1: 'The expression "good faith and fair dealing" refers to a standard of conduct characterised by honesty, openness and consideration for the interests of the other party to the transaction or relationship in question.'

[190] E. Durkheim, *De la division du travail social* ([first published 1930] 5th ed., 1998), at 93; see also at 374: 'Il est donc nécessaire que . . . la solidarité contractuelle soit, autant que possible, mise à l'abri de tout ce qui peut la troubler'.

[191] R. Demogue, *Traité des obligations en général*, Vol. II *Effets des obligations* (1931), Part VI, at 3 (9). Critical, J. Carbonnier, *Droit civil*, Vol. IV *Les obligations* (22nd ed., 2000), at 114 (227): 'L'outrance peut perdre une idée juste. On s'étonnera qu'à une époque où le mariage s'était peut-être trop transformé en contrat, d'aucuns aient rêvé de transformer tout contrat en mariage.'

[192] Cf. Jamin (n. 188). See Kennedy, 'Three Globalizations of Law and Legal Thought: 1850–2000', in D. Trubek and A. Santos (eds), *The New Law and Economic Development. A Critical Appraisal* (2006) 19, on 'the social' as the second globalization of legal thought, and Habermas (n. 40) ch. 9, on the second, social-welfare paradigm of law.

[193] F. Wieacker, *A History of Private Law in Europe* (1995), at 485.

[194] *Catechism of the Catholic Church*, Part 3, S. 1, Ch. 2, Art. 3 (social justice), at no. 1939: 'The principle of solidarity, also articulated in terms of "friendship" or "social charity", is a direct demand of human and Christian brotherhood.'

of people among whom the state would promote solidarity? Therefore, from a communitarian point of view, the question under discussion here, i.e. whether contract law should protect weaker parties, is closely related to the question of whether contract law should be European: if contract law must protect weaker parties then this may mean that it cannot be European, simply because at the European level the kind of solidarity that is indispensable for achieving it, is lacking. Many of the discourses we hear today, especially from the disillusioned left, which has become sceptical of the European potential for solidarity and regards the EU as an intrinsically 'neoliberal project' ('the EU as a liberalisation machine'), go in this direction.[195] They point to the lack of solidarity in the financial, refugee, and Covid-19 crises, expressed in the rejection by many Member States and citizens of refugee quotas and a transfer Union, and advocate withdrawal (often nostalgic) into national solidarity. Versions of this thought can be found also in contract law discourse with regard to weaker party protection. This led, for example, to the rejection of full harmonization directives, and of the CESL that would have bypassed Article 6 Rome I, which guarantees European citizens in cross-border contracts the level of consumer protection assured by the law of their home country.[196] The fact that the level of consumer and other weaker party protection in the CESL (undisputedly) was significantly higher than the average level in the Member States did not provide a sufficient basis, in their view, for cross-border European solidarity among consumers. The eventual failure to reach a political consensus on pan-European black and grey lists of terms respectively deemed and presumed to be unfair, during the protracted negotiations on the Consumer Rights Directive, merely seems to underscore this communitarian point. However, it could just as well be argued, from the same normative perspective, i.e. communitarianism, but with a different community of reference, i.e. the European one, that these crises and failures show that we have to move forward towards a federal Union of strong solidarity among European citizens and Member States.[197]

C. Social Imaginaries

The concept of 'social imaginaries' plays a central role in Taylor's discussion of modernity.[198] The concept is also relevant for certain communitarian understandings of

[195] See W. Streeck, *Gekaufte Zeit: Die vertagte Krise des demokratischen Kapitalismus* (2013), at 141: 'die Europäische Union als Liberalisierungsmaschine'.

[196] See e.g. on behalf of the European consumer organization BEUC, Goyens, 'Why the Optional Instrument is the Wrong Way for Consumers', *European Voice*, 16 June 2011. See also Pachl, 'The Common European Sales Law—Have the Right Choices Been Made? A Consumer Policy Perspective', 19(1) *Maastricht Journal of European and Comparative Law* (2012) 180–194.

[197] On the general debate, see Chapter 3.

[198] C. Taylor, *Modern Social Imaginaries* (2004); C. Taylor, *A Secular Age* (2007), ch. 4. In developing the concept, he drew in particular on B. Anderson, *Imagined Communities* (1983) and B. Baczko, *Les imaginaires sociaux: mémoires et espoirs collectifs* (1984). However, Vanheeswijck, 'The Philosophical Genealogy of Taylor's Social Imaginaries: A Complex History of Ideas and Predecessors', 78 *Journal of the History of Ideas* (2017) 473, explains how its deeper roots can be found in Taylor's lifelong struggle to overcome the pre-eminence of epistemology in modern philosophy and modern culture, in particular 'epistemological foundationalism', i.e. the understanding of epistemology as the foundational philosophical discipline able to test the validity of all truth claims.

weaker party protection in European contract law. What Taylor means by this notion is 'the ways people imagine their social existence, how they fit together with others, how things go on between them and their fellows, the expectations that are normally met, and the deeper normative notions and images that underlie these expectations'.[199] It is this 'background understanding',[200] 'a shared understanding of how our society works',[201] that enables our practices by making sense of them.[202] Social imaginaries are distinct from theories in that they are not the exclusive domain of a small group of experts, but are shared by much larger groups of people, if not the whole society.[203] The idea is that for each group there is one such social imaginary at a time. This makes sense. For how could the social imaginary otherwise give guidance to our action? At the same time, the same background understanding may be compatible with a variety of competing theories trying to make more theoretical sense of it.[204] When we try to work out the social imaginary, we do this in the first-person plural: 'we're trying to get clear what a language could be by which we can express our self-understanding related to that plural self.'[205] In the social imaginary, positive understandings, about how things usually go, are interwoven with normative ones, about how they ought to go.[206]

The concept of social imaginaries is akin to the idea of *Sittlichkeit* (*ethical life*),[207] which is central to Hegel's understanding of history, politics, and law, and the relevance of which to our society today Taylor has aimed to demonstrate since his early work.[208] According to Taylor, 'Hegel is important today because we recurrently feel the need for a critique of the illusions and distortions of perspective which spring from the atomistic, utilitarian, instrumental conceptions of man and nature'.[209] As Taylor explains, *Sittlichkeit* refers to the moral obligations we have to an ongoing community of which we are part.[210] Thus, the crucial characteristic of *Sittlichkeit* is that it 'enjoins us to bring about what already is',[211] thus connecting *Sein* and *Sollen* (is and

199 Taylor, *Modern Social Imaginaries* (n. 198) 23.

200 Ibid. 25

201 Bohmann and Montero: 'History, Critique, Social Change and Democracy. An Interview with Charles Taylor', 21 *Constellations* (2014) 3.

202 Taylor, *Modern Social Imaginaries* (n. 198) 11 and 165.

203 Ibid. Contrast, Komárek, 'European Constitutional Imaginaries: Utopias, Ideologies and the Other' University of Copenhagen Faculty of Law Legal Studies Research Paper Series, paper no. 2020-88, *iCourts Working Paper Series*, No. 172; 2019 *IMAGINE Paper* No. 1 (2019), who understands 'European constitutional imaginaries' as 'ideas that stand behind various conceptualisations of the EU constitution, produced by EU constitutional lawyers and theorists'.

204 In this sense, the present book can be said to be exploring a specific dimension (the political-theoretical) of a specific aspect (private law) of our social imaginary (i.e. of Europeans today). See further, Chapter 9.

205 Bohmann and Montero (n. 201).

206 Taylor, *A Secular Age* (n. 198) 172.

207 The standard translation for Hegelian *Sittlichkeit* is 'ethical life'. See e.g. G. W. F. Hegel, *Outlines of the Philosophy of Right*, Part III, translation by T. M. Knox, revised by S. Houlgate (2008). Alternative translations include 'ethical order' and 'ethical substance'. See Redding, 'Georg Wilhelm Friedrich Hegel', in E. N. Zalta (ed.), *The Stanford Encyclopedia of Philosophy* available at https://plato.stanford.edu/entries/hegel/ (last visited 8 June 2020).

208 C. Taylor, *Hegel* ([first published 1975] 2008) and C. Taylor, *Hegel and Modern Society* ([first published 1979] 2015).

209 Taylor, *Hegel and Modern Society* (n. 208) 70. The main romantic counter-illusion is that we can do without reason. Hegel instead insisted on the essential role of reason.

210 Ibid. 81.

211 Ibid. 81.

ought) in the typically Hegelian fashion that is also reflected in Taylor's concept of social imaginaries. It is based on an understanding of human beings as participants in a larger community life in which they are immersed. On this view, 'the rational state will restore *Sittlichkeit*, the embodiment of the highest norms in an ongoing public life'.[212]

There are at least two implications to be drawn from Taylor's Hegelian communitarianism, and in particular the concepts of ethical life and social imaginaries, for our question of whether contract law should project weaker parties. First, the law, in order to be legitimate, should not be out of step with the background understandings prevailing in society. From this perspective, the hyper instrumentalism of EU contract law seems problematic. Not only the atomistic conception of human beings as consumers individually seeking to reap the benefits of the internal market,[213] but also the instrumentalization of consumer protection for the purpose of constructing an internal market,[214] even merely economic growth, treating the economy as objectified reality,[215] comes across as deeply misguided, and indeed alienating, from the perspective of an understanding of society as a larger community life in which everyone participates as a member. From this communitarian point of view, EU consumer law, which addresses human persons consistently as consumers, i.e. as 'any natural person who is acting for purposes which are outside his trade, business, craft or profession',[216] seems staggeringly disembedded,[217] while the market-building rationale seems difficult for most people to make sense of. It is important to emphasize, however, that, contrary to what is often thought, the Hegelian conception of society is not intrinsically conservative.[218] The interactions between society and its members, and between the factual and the normative sides of social imaginaries, are dynamic and they go in both directions. This dialectic could even become revolutionary. While Taylor rejects vanguard politics,[219] it is central to his understanding of social imaginaries that they can undergo a revolution.[220]

This brings us to the second implication. It may well be that more convincing accounts of weaker party protection—and perhaps even more far reaching ones—match

212 Ibid. 92.

213 See e.g. Commission Proposal for a Directive on Consumer Rights of 8 October 2008 (COM(2008) 614/3), at 2: 'If consumers are precluded access to competitive cross-border offers they do not fully reap up [*sic*] the benefits of the internal market in terms of more choice and better prices.' Cf. Taylor, *Hegel and Modern Society* (n. 208) 91: 'Only an exaggerated atomism could make the condition of alienated men seem the inescapable human norm.'

214 As previously stated, Art. 114 TFEU, providing a legal basis for approximation measures 'which have as their object the establishment and functioning of the internal market', has been the legal basis for all European consumer contract law legislation. Cf. Taylor, *Hegel and Modern Society* (n. 208) 87, emphasizing 'the importance of Hegel's insistence that the end sought by the highest ethics is already realized. It means that the highest norms are to be discovered in the real, that the real is rational, and that we are to turn away from chimaeric attempts to construct a new society from a blueprint.'

215 Cf. Taylor, *Modern Social Imaginaries* (n. 198) ch. 5 ('The Economy as Objectified Reality') and at 72, on how the economy came to be seen as 'the dominant end of society'.

216 Art. 2, Consumer Rights Directive (n. 14).

217 Cf. Taylor, *Modern Social Imaginaries* (n. 198) ch. 4 ('The Great Disembedding') and at 62–63: 'Embeddedness is both a matter of identity and of social imaginary: the ways we are able to think or imagine the whole of society.'

218 Ibid. 28.

219 Ibid. 124.

220 Indeed, the whole point of *Modern Social Imaginaries* is to demonstrate how modernity brought and constituted a revolution in our social imaginary. See ibid. 159 and *passim*.

better with background understandings prevailing today in Europe. Chalmers argues, with reference to Taylor's concept of social imaginaries, that 'the imaginary set out by EU law has profoundly alienating qualities because it sets out a vision of human association based exclusively around shared or common activities', and thereby totally ignores that people may come together for all sorts of reasons, which do not have to be functional at all.[221] To this we could add that even when they come together for joint projects, there is no need to assume that their first objective is to create some joint economic surplus. In other words, and specifically for our question, people may conclude contracts, and the law may want to protect weaker parties in contractual relationships, for other than purely instrumental reasons.

Bartl links up the idea of social imaginaries to the transformation of European private law. She presents successive transformations over the past two centuries as responses to different imaginaries of economy, politics, and society, and shows how these imaginaries 'have analogues in supportive legal imaginaries, rules and practices'.[222] Specifically with regard to European consumer law, she describes a transition in the EU 'from the imaginary of the market as a political project to the imaginary of the market as means of rationalisation'. She explicitly adopts Taylor's definition of social imaginaries. However, it is not clear that the ways people imagine their social existence—their background understanding, i.e. their shared understanding of how their society works and enables their practices by making sense of them—is as strongly focused on the economy as Bartl suggests. Indeed, it seems implausible that most EU citizens hold any 'core internal market imaginary' at all. While Taylor explicitly uses the term to trace and critique economic reductionism,[223] Bartl instead seems to go along with the neoliberal narrative that understands society essentially as a market. However, as Taylor points out, social imaginaries can be false—a 'cover-up'.[224] In particular they can be ideological, 'full of self-serving fiction and suppression'.[225] Ultimately, this may be a matter of semantics. For Bartl's interest seems to be in a potentially subversive role for the law and legal discourse in bringing change in the shared pre-understandings by offering different 'imaginaries' as to the role of the law in society, as a result of which 'a far broader shift in social imaginary may ensue'. Indeed, such a shift may well be a shift away from narrowly socio-economic narratives, including in the context of weaker party protection in contracts, towards 'the larger life in which people are immersed'.[226] As a minimum,

221 Chalmers, 'The Unconfined Power of European Union Law', 1 *European Papers* (2016) 405.

222 Bartl, 'Socio-Economic Imaginaries and European Private Law', in P. F. Kjær (ed.), *The Law of Political Economy: Transformations in the Function of Law* (2019).

223 Taylor, *Modern Social Imaginaries* (n. 198) 77:

> our coming to see our society as an economy, an interlocking set of activities of production, exchange and consumption, which form a system with its own laws and its own dynamic.... Conceiving of the economy as a system is an achievement of eighteenth-century theory, with the physiocrats and Adam Smith, but coming to see the most important purpose and agenda of society as economic collaboration and exchange is a drift in our social imaginary that begins in that period and continues to this day.

Similar, Chalmers (n. 221). Generally, on market reductionism, see Judt (n. 105) 34 and *passim*.

224 Taylor, *Modern Social Imaginaries* (n. 198) 183.

225 Ibid. 183.

226 Taylor, *Hegel and Modern Society* (n. 208) 78 and 91.

clearly this would require the abandonment of narrowly functional legal bases for EU law.[227]

D. Historical Roots

Finally, with regard to weaker party protection, communitarians also can point to tradition. However, that reference too would be inconclusive, since historical roots and precedents are available pointing in either direction. The egalitarian tradition goes back to the Roman law doctrine of *laesio enormis*, that, although focusing on an objective imbalance between price and value, was originally introduced by emperor Diocletian in order to protect impoverished farmers against the new rich patricians who wanted to buy land beyond Rome's city walls, and to the *iustum pretium* principle, as defined especially in the late scholastic tradition.[228] Indeed, when Wieacker signalled the trend of materialization this was in fact, as he pointed out, a trend towards *re*-materialization, back to the ethical foundations of the *ius commune* and natural law.[229] Of course, most contemporary attempts at restoring the substantive equality of the parties can easily be placed in that tradition. However, the laissez-faire tradition also has a venerable pedigree. Hobbes famously wrote, squarely against the scholastic natural law tradition, that 'the value of all things contracted for, is measured by the appetite of the contractors: and therefore the just value, is that which they be contented to give'.[230] And the adages 'qui dit contractuel dit juste' and 'volenti non fit iniuria' became emblematic for the spirit of the nineteenth century.[231] As Monateri pointed out, since the argument from tradition is based on 'the desire to see continuity', placing one historical line in the foreground and relegating others to the background, it is easy to adopt the delegitimating move of reversing the positions.[232] The question of weaker party protection in contract illustrates this point well. In the presence of divergent traditions, it seems impossible to make a reasonable choice among them *qua* traditions, i.e. for the reason of adopting the rule that best expresses or fits with 'our' tradition (whoever is meant by 'us'). To this critique must be added, of course, the general question, discussed in Chapter 5, of why tradition should be granted decisive normative force in the first place, thus overriding other, contemporary considerations, including, in particular, reasons of justice.

227 See Davies, 'Democracy and Legitimacy in the Shadow of Purposive Competence', 21 *ELJ* (2015) 2, and Davies, 'The Competence to Create an Internal Market: Conceptual Poverty and Unbalanced Interests', in S. Garben and I. Govaere (eds), *The Division of Competences Between the EU and The Member States* (2017) 74, especially section VI, on 'establishing a disembedded market'.

228 See R. Zimmermann, *The Law of Obligations: Roman Foundations of the Civilian Tradition* (1996), at 255–268; J. Gordley, *The Philosophical Origins of Modern Contract Doctrine* (1991), at 109–111.

229 Wieacker (n. 175) 23–24: 'Unter Führung des Reichsgerichts hat die Rechtsprechung ... die formale Freiheitsethik, die der deutschen Privatrechtsordnung zugrundelag, in eine materiale Ethik sozialer Verantwortung zurückverwandelt; "zurückverwandelt", weil sie damit, meist unbewußt, zu den ethischen Grundlagen, des älteren europäischen Gemein- und Naturrechts zurückkehrte.'

230 Hobbes (n. 47) 208.

231 Fouillée (n. 47) 410. The adage 'volenti non fit iniuria' goes back (or is related, in the tort law context) to Digest, Book 47, 10, 1, 5 (Ulpian): 'nulla iniuria est quae in volentem fiat'.

232 Monateri, 'Black Gaius; A Quest for the Multicultural Origins of The "Western Legal Tradition"', 51 *Hastings L.J.* (2000) 479, at 507.

6. Civic Republican

A. Domination by Contract

A powerful argument directly against unequal bargaining and in support of weaker party protection comes from civic republicanism. Pettit explicitly addresses contract law and points out the dangers to freedom deriving from the doctrine of freedom of contract:

> The development of the doctrine saw freedom of contract invoked in defence of some fairly appalling contractual arrangements, as people ignored the consequences for domination—as they ignored the asymmetries of power established under the contract—and argued that a contract that was not actively coerced was free. This development is highly questionable from the point of view of anyone who is worried about domination. It could never have materialized, in all likelihood, had people remained focused on that evil, in particular, had they continued to think that freedom required the absence of domination, not just the absence of interference.[233]

This view seems to constitute a general argument against the enforceability of any contract resulting from unequal bargaining. Indeed, Pettit explicitly addresses unequal bargaining. He writes:

> A law of contract is obviously going to have a place, and an important place, in any modern society; it is a prerequisite for economic activity and prosperity. . . . That being so, the republican state which wants to promote non-domination is bound to expect contract law, not just to facilitate voluntary agreements among different agents, but to play a regulative role in disallowing contracts that involve terms under which one party has the possibility of dominating the other.[234]

Note that this state control of terms, as Pettit phrases it, does not seem to be limited to standard terms, as in the (minimum harmonization) Unfair Terms Directive 1993, for example, but much more generally, perhaps somewhat like the famous General Clause (§ 36) in the Nordic Contracts Acts.[235] Among the strategies for achieving non-domination that Pettit discusses, the first is 'the strategy of reciprocal power', i.e. 'to make the resources of dominator and dominated more equal'. This sounds very similar to the restoration of equal bargaining power as undertaken by the CJEU in *Mostaza Claro* and by the German Constitutional Court in the *Bürgschaft* case.

[233] P. Pettit, *Republicanism: A Theory of Freedom and Government* (1997), at 62.

[234] Ibid. 164–165. See also at 54, about exploitative contracts as illegitimate interferences with a person's freedom as non-domination.

[235] Cf. e.g. C. von Bar and E. Clive (eds), *Principles, Definitions and Model Rules of European Private Law: Draft Common Frame of Reference (DCFR) Full Edition* Vol. I (2009), at 640 and 643; Wilhelmsson and Willett, 'Unfair Terms and Standard Form Contracts', in G. Howells *et al.* (eds), *Handbook of Research on International Consumer Law* (2010) 168.

B. Beyond Market Freedom

A central aim of the neo-republican project is to recover, 'as a kind of archaeologist, bringing buried intellectual treasure back to the surface', freedom as it was understood before liberalism.[236] Republican freedom as non-domination is distinct from both libertarian negative liberty ('freedom from') and liberal perfectionist positive liberty ('freedom to'). A key dimension of this project is a challenge to the market-centred conception of freedom, shared by libertarian advocates and Marxist critics alike.[237] In the words of MacGilvray, both sides of the debate on free markets share:

> a folk intuition that says that in a truly free society ... economic growth would be promoted by private rather than public means, failing businesses would be allowed to fail, people would have to live with the consequences of their bad decisions or bad luck, those in need would be left to their own devices, and so on. The contrary policies can be defended only by appealing to some other value or set of values: justice, solidarity, prosperity, stability, sustainability, or charity, for example. Yet the idea that freedom means *market* freedom—freedom to do what you want with what is yours and to enjoy the rewards or suffer the consequences—profoundly shapes debates about public policy even when other values prevail in a given case.[238]

For European private law, in Chapter 5 we saw that both advocates and critics of 'neo-liberalism' understand the contract law of the EU as driven essentially by a free market rationale and understand the debate as one about whether values other than freedom are needed to tame the market. Instead, republicans submit that the solution is to be found in a very different understanding of freedom, i.e. freedom as non-domination.

There is certainly a lot of merit in de-reifying the concepts of freedom used by both advocates and critics of 'free markets', especially when this helps in understanding contract law being considered, in a positive or negative role, as more than a mere market institution. Still, an understanding of contract law exclusively in terms of freedom as non-domination would be no less reductive than the libertarian and liberal-perfectionist accounts of liberty. Put differently, a dominant role in the debate for the republican value of freedom as non-domination seems difficult to match with a pluralist society seeking democratic compromises. Moreover, as Forst points out, to the extent that republicanism is a political theory of freedom, not a theory of justice, it answers only the question of when we are free, not what we owe each other. A society whose basic institutions ensure us freedom as non-domination is not necessarily also a just society.[239]

236 Q. Skinner, *Liberty Before Liberalism* (1998), at 112.
237 E. MacGilvray, *The Invention of Market Freedom* (2011), at 183.
238 Ibid. 181–182.
239 See Forst, 'A Kantian Republican Conception of Justice as Nondomination', in A. Niederberger and P. Schink (eds), *Republican Democracy: Liberty, Law and Politics* (2013) 154.

C. The Eyeball Test

In *On the People's Terms*, Pettit picks up this challenge and elaborates a republican social justice theory.[240] 'The republican theory of social justice', according to Pettit, 'requires that people should enjoy freedom as non-domination in their relationships with one another, whether as individuals to individuals, as groups to groups, or as groups to individuals.'[241] In other words, it covers not only distributive justice but also interpersonal justice, including, in particular, it would seem, contractual justice. The republican standard for social justice is relational equality understood in a very substantive way.[242] The core idea in this theory is the 'eyeball test': social relationships are undominated when people are uninhibited to look one another in the eye: 'They can look others in the eye without reason for the fear or deference that power of interference might inspire; they can walk tall and assume the public status, objective and subjective, of being equal in this regard with the best.'[243]

This rather demanding test has important implications, it seems, for contract law. For in many contractual relationships the parties cannot look each other in the eye. These are relationships of domination (economic, social, emotional, or other), where the state, therefore, on the republican view, would have a task in redressing the contractual inequality to the point that meets the eyeball test, because, 'the state has to guard people against private domination—that is, the requirement of social justice'.[244] What exactly does the eyeball test demand from contract law? In the first place, it seems, it provides a justification for the categorical protection of weaker parties, such as employees, tenants, and consumers, where these relationships are considered to be structurally imbalanced. However, the test seems to require more. It seems to demand general doctrines, like unfair exploitation and unconscionability, to be in place and to be applicable also in B2B contracts, in particular perhaps in long-term contracts where the risk of private domination seems to be bigger. Think also of global supply and value chains where, in many sectors, domination and exploitation seem endemic. Similarly, the eyeball test seems to require a doctrine protecting contracting parties against private dominations resulting from a change of circumstances, again not only in B2C but also in B2B contracts. Moreover, in all these cases the test provides not only a criterion for when weaker party protection is required but also for the amount of protection the rules should provide. Weaker party protection is not strong enough, according to the republican theory of social justice, unless it actually restores inequality to the point where one party to the contractual relationship no longer dominates the other.

240 Pettit (n. 77) ch. 2.

241 Ibid. 76.

242 On the 'interactional character' of equal freedom as non-domination, see Petit, ibid. 91. That the republican reading of equality cannot be a merely formal one, is underlined also by R. Bellamy, *Political Constitutionalism: A Republican Defence of the Constitutionality of Democracy* (2007), at 70: 'In general, formal equality of treatment promotes rather than reduces substantive inequalities.'

243 Pettit (n. 77) 84.

244 Ibid. 3.

7. Discourse Theory

A. The Procedural Paradigm of Private Law

Habermas criticizes the conception of materialization within what Habermas calls the 'social welfare' paradigm, according to which private autonomy was limited by the requirements of social justice. This idea that weaker party protection (e.g. of consumers) means the limitation of party autonomy by the requirements of social justice was famously formulated and elaborated by Raiser.[245] It can also be found in the more recent 'Manifesto on social justice in European contract law'.[246] The idea, according to Habermas:

> insinuates a false assumption: that the domain in which the classical idea of private autonomy had validity was *curtailed* by the competing, politically enforced claim of social justice. ... In fact, however, the changes in private law are explained by a *changed paradigmatic understanding* of the same normative concept of private autonomy. ... The idea of private autonomy, expressed in the right to the greatest possible degree of equal liberty, did not change at all.[247]

Thus, Habermas is critical not only of the classical liberal paradigm but also of the welfare-state paradigm of law that, on this account, succeeded it. Certainly, we should not go back to the formal notion of freedom of contract, where it was simply assumed that the contracting parties were free and equal,[248] since this assumption is no longer empirically correct (if it ever was).[249] However, the response by *Materialisierung*, if it is limited to mere *compensation* for inequality, without otherwise affecting the system of (in this case) private law, may also have the downside that it may limit the freedom of individuals if the state paternalistically makes choices for weaker contracting parties without involving them. Habermas gives the example of labour law, but he might as well have chosen consumer law. A contract law that is based on formal equality, but compensates for actual inequality by providing freedom of contract except in contracts with certain categories of weaker parties, does not treat people as free and equal citizens.

The only way out of this dispute between the formal liberal and the welfare-state materialist paradigm concerning the preconditions for the exercise of private autonomy,

245 L. Raiser, *Die Zukunft des Privatrechts* (1971), at 32.

246 Study Group on Social Justice in European Private Law, 'Social Justice in European Contract Law: a Manifesto', 16 *ELJ* (2004) 656:

> The unification of contract law in Europe also poses profound questions about the values that should underpin the market order. ... A unified law will have to strike a balance between, on the one hand, the weight attached to individual private autonomy as expressed in the idea of freedom of contract, and on the other hand, principles which respect other equally important demands for social solidarity.

247 Habermas (n. 40) 400 (emphasis in original). Similar, Shiffrin (n. 77) 213: 'the failure to enforce unconscionable contracts does not, in fact, violate an autonomy right.'

248 Habermas (n. 40) 407: 'the justified critique that the welfare paradigm levels against formal law precludes return to the liberal paradigm'.

249 Ibid. 402: 'vulnerable to empirical criticism'.

according to Habermas, is a procedural approach where free and equal citizens give themselves a legitimate private law:

> Both views lose sight of the internal relation between private and *political* autonomy, and thus lose sight of the democratic meaning of a community's self-organization. The still-unresolved dispute between these two parties is focussed on specifying the material preconditions for the equal status of legal persons as addressees of the legal order. These persons are autonomous, however, only insofar as they can at the same time understand themselves as authors of the law to which they are subject as addressees. ... Under postmetaphysical conditions, the only legitimate law is one that emerges from the discursive opinion- and will-formation of equally enfranchised citizens. The latter can in turn adequately exercise their public autonomy, guaranteed by rights of communication and participation, only insofar as their private autonomy is guaranteed. A well-secured private autonomy helps 'secure the conditions' of public autonomy just as much as, conversely, the appropriate exercise of public autonomy helps 'secure the conditions' of private autonomy. This mutual dependency, or circular reinforcement, is manifested in the genesis of valid law.[250]

So, what is needed is a political process that is fully informed by the interests and points of view of all, including those at the periphery, in which citizens together give themselves—in our case—a law of contract. Clearly, as a fundamentally proceduralist theory, discourse theory will not provide any substantive directions on contractual inequality.[251] However, the expectation is that an inclusive democratic law-making procedure, which is not dominated by the illegitimate power of money (lobbying) and bureaucracy (experts rule), where only the force of the better argument counts, would lead to more thoroughly egalitarian rules and doctrines, also for private dealings among citizens. The idea is that it is unlikely that a process where everyone's interests are considered will lead to a contract law licensing some people, through 'freedom of contract', to exploit others. Discourse theory has been criticized for this optimism by liberal-egalitarians who do not trust such a procedural approach and require more substantive principles (such as the difference principle) and rights. In any case, it is clear that from a Habermasian perspective both the question of binding force of contract (discussed in Chapter 5) and the present question of weaker party protection are closely and fundamentally connected to the question of whether contract law must

[250] Ibid. 408 (emphasis in original).

[251] Cf. ibid. xiii, 'In the final analysis, private legal subjects cannot come to enjoy equal individual liberties if they do not *themselves*, in the common exercise of their political autonomy, achieve clarity about justified interests and standards. They themselves must agree on the relevant aspects under which equals should be treated equally and unequals unequally.' (emphasis in original). Canaris, 'Wandlungen des Schuldvertragsrechts—Tendenzen zu seiner "Materialisierung"', 200 *Archiv für die civilistische Praxis* (2000) 273, at 291 is critical of Habermas's terminology, especially of his reservation of the term 'proceduralist' for his new paradigm, as if the classical formal understanding of private law was not proceduralist. Moreover, Canaris argues, a merely procedural approach to justice is not viable: 'weil zu Unrecht die Verzichtbarkeit von verfahrensunabhängigen inhaltlichen Gerechtigkeitspostulaten insinuiert oder gar behauptet wird.' However, Habermas's point is not that substantive justice claims should be ignored—on the contrary. His point is merely that justice claims will look different from different points of view and that everyone's point of view on justice should have an equal chance of influencing whatever is decided in the name of justice about generally applicable rules of contract law.

have a democratic basis, that was central to Chapter 3. The reason is, as already stated, that for Habermas private and public autonomy are co-original and mutually reinforce each other.

Habermas's criticism of the social-welfare-paradigm of *Materialisierung*, although justified with regard to his reading of it, nevertheless does not seem to apply to the German Constitutional Court's understanding of *Materialisierung* in its *Bürgschaft* judgment. There, as we saw, the court did not justify the 'materialization' of private law in terms of compensation for inequality, but rather in terms quite similar (if not identical) to those advocated by Habermas: i.e. undersigning a personal guarantee under the constraining conditions at hand did *not* in fact constitute an autonomous act, but merely a heteronomous one (*Fremdbestimmung*). Similarly, in *Mostaza Claro* and following cases, the CJEU understands the consumer protection against unfair terms provided by the 1993 Directive not as compensation for inequality but as replacing merely formal with effective equality. Similarly, the paternalism charge, as we saw, does not apply to weaker party protection in contract law in all those cases (i.e. the vast majority) where the protection depends on the weaker party's own choice to exercise the remedy.

Habermas makes an important point when he observes:

> after the formal guarantee of private autonomy has proven insufficient, and after social intervention through law also threatens the very autonomy it means to restore, the only solution consists in thematizing the connection between forms of communication that *simultaneously* guarantee private and public autonomy *in the very conditions from which they emerge.*[252]

This point is akin to the one made earlier, when critically discussing Ripstein's Kantian formalism. It combines the notion that contract law is a matter of interpersonal justice with the idea that contract law rules, which inevitably will have distributive consequences (in terms of the material bases for freedom, equality, and human dignity), should not be perversely redistributive. Contract enforcement should not make matters worse by reproducing or exacerbating existing unfair distributions, and sometimes the best—or even only way—to prevent distributive injustices is by refusing to enforce certain contracts or contract clauses. What exactly this entails—i.e. all the concrete questions of weaker party protection: who should be protected when against whom and how?—must be determined by generally applicable rules of contract law that the people give themselves.

B. The Ambivalence of Modern Private Law

In the 1980s, Habermas engaged in the reconstruction of the philosophical discourse of modernity, essentially as a response to the critique of the Enlightenment's project of modernity, in particular its commitment to reason, coming from postmodern and

[252] Habermas (n. 40) 409 (emphasis in original).

poststructuralist philosophers (notably Foucault and Derrida).[253] More recently, in a profound study Auer offers a reconstruction specifically of the private law discourse of modernity.[254] The concrete empirical focus of her study is on property law, but a very similar story can also be told about contract law. She distinguishes two different private law modernities.[255] The first modernity ('the turn to the subject')[256] placed the autonomous subject at the centre of private law, which came with the idea of subjective rights, i.e. the understanding of private law as a closed system (of subjective rights, understood as mutually exclusive spheres of freedom), and with a sharp private/public law divide. The second modernity ('reflexivity as deconstruction'),[257] by contrast, directed reason towards itself.[258] This led to various successive strands of critique, with the idea that society makes the subject, not the other way around (sociological turn), the deconstruction of rights,[259] and the rejection of the autonomy of private law (private law is public law and inevitably distributive). In addition, not only as a matter of theory but also in practice in society, modernity turned against itself (reflexivity as negative dialectics): it is immanent to modernity that it produces outcomes that undermine the conditions for its own existence,[260] such as the massive substantive inequalities following from classical private law's presumption of formal equality.[261] Although the two discourses of modernity came up consecutively, the latter did not succeed in wholly defeating the project of the first. Although there is no turning back to the private legitimations of Locke and Kant,[262] nevertheless the categories of subjective rights, system, and the private/public divide have not been replaced. As a result, contemporary private law discourse is characterized by both discourses and, especially, the irresolvable tension between the two, which is immanent to the system of private law.[263] Borrowing an expression from Latour, Auer concludes that our private law has always remained 'half modern'.[264]

[253] J. Habermas, *The Philosophical Discourse of Modernity: Twelve Lectures* (1990).

[254] Auer (n. 175).

[255] Following the sociological reconstruction by A. Nassehi, *Der soziologische Diskurs der Moderne* (2006).

[256] Auer (n. 175) 13–45.

[257] Ibid. 46–73.

[258] See T. Adorno and M. Horkheimer, *Dialectic of Enlightenment* ([first published 1944] 1997): 'the Enlightenment *must examine itself*, if men are not to be wholly betrayed.'

[259] See D. Kennedy, *A Critique of Adjudication: Fin de Siècle* (1997), at 331: 'Rights then function as no more than interests (perhaps with an explanation point)'.

[260] U. Beck, *Risk Society: Towards a New Modernity* ([first published 1986] 1992).

[261] Auer (n. 175) 77.

[262] See earlier Auer, 'Subjektive Rechte bei Pufendorf und Kant: Eine Analyse im Lichte der Rechtskritik Hohfelds', 208 *Archiv für die civilistische Praxis* (2008) 584, arguing that the Hohfeldian insight—i.e. that freedom cannot, on its own, justify subjective rights with corresponding duties (because it does not follow from someone's freedom—or 'privilege'—to do something that others have a duty to refrain from hindering the exercise of that freedom; it merely follows that the first person is not under a duty towards anyone not to do that something; as a result, unlike rights, freedoms may clash (Hohfeld, 'Some Fundamental Legal Conceptions as Applied in Judicial Reasoning', 23 *Yale L.J.* (1913) 16)—leads to the collapse of the Kantian justification for private law as a system of rights, understood as mutually exclusive spheres of freedom.

[263] Auer, therefore, rejects Habermas's idea of successive private law paradigms (liberal, social, procedural). For this reconstruction of private discourse, see Habermas (n. 40) section 7.3. Similar, Kennedy (n. 192) (classical, social, policy).

[264] Auer (n. 175) 87. See B. Latour, *Nous n'avons jamais été modernes. Essai d'anthropologie symétrique* (1991).

Interestingly, subjective rights, system, and the private/public law divide have been strikingly absent from EU private law.[265] Indeed, the private law of the EU does not even have a general concept of the legal subject, only specific definitions of consumers, customers, passengers, SMEs, etc.[266] Auer's diagnosis of contemporary private law suggests that attempts at restoring a private-public law divide at the EU level,[267] to make it more systematic,[268] may seem to be in vain. However, the same applies, it would seem, for endeavours to severe consumer law from general private law, for example by placing it at a distance, in a separate code.[269] In both cases the reason is that the various tensions (between form and substance, system and critique) are immanent to contemporary private law and, therefore, here to stay.[270]

C. Weaker Parties' Right to Justification

From the point of view of the right to justification, as Forst understands it, 'the first thing is to become an *agent of justice*, not just a *recipient of justice*'.[271] The worst injustices—also in the context of contractual inequality and weaker party protection, it would seem—are those where the affected parties have no real chance of raising their objections with a view to achieving change. Thus, Forst stresses:

> it is essential to see the political point of justice and free oneself from the false picture, which highlights only the quantity of goods (as important as that surely is). In accord with a second, more appropriate picture, which conveys the fundamental impulse against arbitrariness, justice—which always includes an analysis of injustice—must aim at intersubjective relations and structures, not at a subjective or supposedly objective provision of goods. Only in this way, by considering the first question of

265 See Hesselink, 'Contract Theory and EU Contract Law', in C. W. Twigg-Flesner (ed.), *Research Handbook on EU Consumer and Contract Law* (2016) 508.

266 For early discussions of the implications, see Alpa, 'The Meaning of "Natural Person" and the Impact of the Constitution for Europe on the Development of European Private Law', 10 *ELJ* (2004) 734; Hesselink, 'European Contract Law: A Matter of Consumer Protection, Citizenship, or Justice?', 15 *ERPL* (2007) 323.

267 For a recent attempt, see Cherednychenko, 'Rediscovering the Public/Private Divide in EU Private Law', *ELJ* (2019) 1.

268 See notably Research Group on the Existing EC Private Law (*Acquis* Group) (eds), *Principles of the Existing EC Contract Law (Acquis Principles)* (2007). Cf. ibid. 19: 'The *Acquis* Principles provide a systematic analysis of Community legislation in the area of contract law and thus give an overview of the *acquis communautaire* in this field of law.'

269 See e.g. the *Code de la consommation* (1993) in France, and the Consumer Rights Act 2015 in the UK. See also in the US the project for a Restatement of the Law, Consumer Contracts. Very critical of the integration in 2001 of consumer contract law into the German Civil Code, see Micklitz (n. 36).

270 Negative dialectic is not intrinsically pessimistic. It even has a 'utopian reach' (Zuidervaart, 'Theodor W. Adorno', in E. N. Zalta (ed.), *The Stanford Encyclopedia of Philosophy*, available at https://plato.stanford.edu/entries/adorno/ (last visited 8 June 2020)). See T. W. Adorno, *Negative Dialectics* (1973), at 11: 'Regarding the concrete utopian possibility, dialectics is the ontology of the wrong state of things. The right state of things would be free of it: neither a system nor a contradiction.' Auer's diagnosis of reflexivity as negative dialectic mainly concentrates on immanent self-endangerment and immanent countermodernity. However, one wonders what (if anything) might private law in the right state look like, being neither a system nor a contradiction?

271 R. Forst, *The Right to Justification: Elements of a Constructivist Theory of Justice* (2007), at 245 (emphasis in original).

> justice—the justifiability of social relations and the distribution of the 'power of justification' within a political context—is a radical conception of justice possible: one that gets to the roots of social injustice. This insight is at the center of a critical theory of justice, whose first 'good' is the socially effective power to demand, question, or provide justifications, and to turn them into the foundations of political action and institutional arrangements. This 'good,' however, cannot be 'delivered' or 'received,' but must be discursively and collectively constituted. Only a critical theory of relations of justification can show whether and to what extent this is possible or impeded.[272]

Forst specifically focuses on distributive justice. However, the argument equally applies, it would seem, to other types of justice, in particular interpersonal justice, and to the question of how distributive and interpersonal justice, both shaping intersubjective relations, should relate to one another. This also means that the question of whether the current state of weaker party protection, including the EU *acquis* on weaker party protection, meets the standards of justice, is a matter in the first place of robust institutions where citizens can contest—and ultimately veto—core elements of contract law, such as its main principles of weaker party protection, when these are not justifiable towards them with reasons no one can reasonably reject.

Still, as we saw in Chapter 2 and in contrast to Habermas's discourse and democratic principles, the right to justification, which according to Forst every person enjoys as the most basic human right, is not entirely procedural. It demands, in particular, that justificatory discourses meet the two standards of reciprocity and generality. Reciprocity means here that those offering the justification do not claim any privileges for themselves (reciprocity of content) or project their own values and higher truths onto others (reciprocity of reasons), while generality connotes here that no one's objections should be disregarded.[273] These requirements apply strictly to questions about the basic structure of society which, as we saw, may include questions concerning the basic structure of contract law, such as the fundamental political questions central to this book, including the present one on weaker party protection. In particular, the positive conclusion that the reasons offered in justificatory discourses, with regard to either positive law or reform proposals (avoiding any status quo bias), are ones that no one could reasonably reject seems to be one that cannot be reached as a matter of theoretical analysis. But what about the negative conclusion? It seems less hazardous to suggest with regard to certain reasons, and the contract law rules (in positive law or reform proposal) allegedly justified by them, that they fail to meet the requirements of generality and reciprocity. In particular, it seems possible, and relevant from the point of view of the right to justification, to point out reasons offered by political theories that seem particularly sectarian, which directly raises issues of reciprocity, or rules that seem entirely to disregard the interests of certain groups, which raises doubts as to whether their point of view has been considered at all.

[272] Ibid. 4–5. Critical, A. Allen, *The End of Progress: Decolonizing the Normative Foundations of Critical Theory* (2016), ch. 4, arguing that Forst 'puts too much responsibility for upholding relations of dominance on those who are subordinated to the power of others.'

[273] Forst (n. 271) 49.

Throughout this chapter, we encountered several instances of justificatory discourses that seem problematic from the point of view of reciprocity of reasons.[274] For example, the rejection of certain (or all) types of weaker party protection on the sole ground that contract law should be instrumental to the exclusive aim of maximizing the total amount of wealth in society, can only be defended on the basis of a conception of human welfare that is so reductive that many people will not find it reasonably acceptable. Similarly, the idea of 'self-ownership' is probably too controversial a notion to justify a general licence for exploitative practices. Also, the notion of an 'innate right to freedom', defined as independence from the choice of others, although purportedly entirely 'formal' and therefore seemingly neutral, may still be too 'thick' and controversial to be acceptable as a political ground for either extending or limiting weaker party protection. The same may be true for notions of party autonomy, understood as a basis for a self-authored life of human flourishing: even though probably many people will be sympathetic to that notion, those, for example, who believe that we were created in the image of God have reason to disagree. Similarly, although a broad range of ideologies and religions could probably reach a degree of overlapping consensus on solidarity as a founding value for society, including with regard to contract law, it nevertheless remains a value that other reasonable worldviews find totally unacceptable as the basis for any generally applicable laws, including the law of contract. Finally, the claim that a certain level—or certain types—of weaker party protection must be preserved as part of 'our' tradition may sound as oppressive rather than liberating to those groups and individuals who are struggling to emancipate themselves from a dominant tradition. For each of these ethical arguments it seems to be the case that, while they are not (or not necessarily) immoral themselves, they also do not reach the threshold of non-rejectability that would justify their demands for or against a certain rule of consumer protection.[275] Similarly, we also saw examples, especially in positive EU law, that raise generality concerns, such as rules that take the average consumer as a benchmark (at the cost of consumers who are less well-informed and circumspect) or contract law rules that seem focused mostly on the interest of consumers at the socio-economic centre of the EU, disregarding the interests of consumers and businesses at the European periphery and perhaps also not fully considering their objections.

The central focus of a critical and realist discourse theory of justice should be on instances of injustice, i.e. acts and norms that can be rejected generally-reciprocally. On this view, maximal justice does not mean the full implementation of an ideal theory, in our case, of contract law, but (counterfactually) the elimination of all injustices, in

[274] Note that also the right to justification itself—and deontological understandings of justice in general—may strike, for example, non-protestants as very austere, and as not neutral at all, but rather an expression of a particular conception of the person and of the human condition. See also Allen (n. 272) ch. 4, especially at 144:

> Might the freestanding conception of practical reason that serves as the foundation for Forst's theory of justice turn out not so freestanding at all? Might it not implicitly presuppose the superiority of the particular Western, post-Enlightenment form of life in which it is rooted and thus rely on the very kind of historical truth claim that Forst claims to eschew?'

[275] See Forst (n. 271) 71: 'In the case in which a judgment that refers to ethical values claims moral validity—that it cannot be reasonably rejected and is morally obligatory—the threshold of reciprocal and general justification remains decisive. Only if it can reach that threshold can such a claim be justified.'

our case the total absence of any contract norms and acts (i.e. rules of contract law and contractual relationships) that cannot be justified with reasons no one can reasonably reject. This means, in turn, that the right to justification, as the normative core of a realist and critical theory of contract law, turns our attention most urgently to the worst instances of injustice that contract law can and should prevent (or bring to an end, as the case may be).[276] Thus, economic and other types of exploitation and domination through contract become a prime concern. As Forst points out, exploitation is a moral concept that expresses the violation of personal autonomy and human dignity;[277] the same applies to domination. From the point of view of the right to justification of contract, it is a priority for contract law to prevent—or put an end to—the injustice of exploitative contractual relationships and of domination through contract, by providing the victims with adequate remedies. Conversely, from the point of view of justice, relationships that are not structurally exploitative give less reason for concern, as long as effective mechanisms are in place to respond to incidental situations of subjection.[278]

Very concretely, this means that at the most general level, the binding force of contract will probably not incur any major difficulties of justifiability, since contractual relationships are not intrinsically (perhaps not even typically) relationships of domination.[279] At the same time, however, adequate doctrines, such as a general doctrine on the voidability of a contract in the cases of exploitation and domination, have to be in place in order to ensure that contractual relationships do not turn into situations of subjection.[280] By contrast, it is not clear that the right to justification of contract would necessarily require the kind of undifferentiated, categorical consumer protection we are familiar with today in Europe. From the perspective of justice (both social and interpersonal), the EU's consumer law *acquis* is both over- and under-inclusive. Consumer protection rules benefit rich and powerful consumers as much as poor and vulnerable ones, or even more, while the sellers against whom they offer protection may sometimes be comparatively poor or vulnerable.[281] Indeed, more likely priority

[276] See Hesselink, 'The Right to Justification of Contract', 33 *Ratio Juris* (2020) 196, on which this section draws.

[277] Forst (n. 42) 125. For this reason, the adjective 'unfair' in the legal concept of 'unfair exploitation' in Art. II.-7:207 DCFR and Art. 51 CESL proposal formula seems redundant: exploitation is intrinsically unfair.

[278] See Forst (n. 42) 168 (principle of political proportionality).

[279] Bagchi, 'How Well Do We Treat Each Other in Contract?', 9 *William and Mary Business Law Review* (2018) 351, argues that 'the experience of domination is driven in part by the necessity, inequality, and competition enjoined by markets, and partly by the very structure of authority created by legally binding promise'. However, especially if we understand domination as a normative, agency-oriented concept rather than as a purely empirical one referring to psychological experience, then the suggestion that structurally contracts are relationships of domination seems too strong, since at least in some cases (and perhaps in many) the authority created by legally binding contracts may be legitimate, i.e. justifiable with general and reciprocal reasons.

[280] As an example of such provision, see e.g. Art. II.-7:207 DCFR (Unfair exploitation). Art. 51 (Unfair exploitation) of the withdrawn Proposal for a Regulation of the European Parliament and of the Council on a Common European Sales Law (COM(2011) 635 final), was almost identical to this provision.

[281] Perhaps the objective of 'a high level of consumer protection' (Art. 114(3) and Art. 169(1) TFEU) could be regarded as a proxy for substantive interpersonal justice. In an ideal world without dispute resolution costs, substantive interpersonal justice probably would be served best exclusively through more contextualized rules rather than via the categorical protection of 'consumers', but in times where governments try to limit the costs of civil justice—a policy that may be based on the distributive objective of increasing access to justice—the operation of such rules would perhaps be too costly. Therefore, it could be suggested, we may have to settle for a more standardized and categorical approach, even if this comes at the cost (in

candidates, where the law must prevent contractual injustices, seem to be cases of multiple domination[282]—best known in feminist theory as intersectionality[283]—where different dimensions of structural domination overlap and mutually reinforce each other. This includes racial, gender, and other types of discrimination, to which could be added, for contractual relationships, individual factors such as economic distress, urgent needs, improvidence, ignorance, inexperience, or lack of bargaining skills.[284]

8. Concluding Remarks

Some contracting parties are stronger than others. They may have more power—economic or other—or better bargaining skills, or more experience than other contracting parties, who are comparatively vulnerable, inexperienced, or dependent. This relative strength may have an important impact on the contractual terms, the contractual relationship during performance, and the situation in which the parties find themselves after the contract has ended. Thus, unequal bargaining, unbalanced contracts, relationships of dependence, and loss of wealth or dignity are all possible consequences or aspects of the reality of being a weaker contracting party. Societies have to decide how to deal with (pre-)contractual inequality. One possibility is the introduction of weaker party protection in contract law. As we have seen, this is not merely a theoretical possibility. In Europe, today, there are many instances of weaker party protection in contract law. These include not only the contextualized protection of individuals against unfair exploitation, unfair terms, and the consequences of a radical change of circumstances, but also—and especially—the categorical protection of certain groups, such as employees, tenants, consumers, and victims of discrimination. Most of these rules and doctrines, although they were often controversial at their introduction, are well-established today. A significant proportion of them consist of EU law or are based on it. This means that the normative discussion with regard to the desirability and justice of weaker party protection in European contract law takes place against the background of existing weaker party protection. In practice, therefore, the question of whether in certain contractual contexts the law should protect weaker parties against stronger ones becomes a question about the repeal, reduction,

terms of justice) of over-inclusiveness (protecting also consumers with relevant expertise, experience, or power) and under-inclusiveness (failing to provide adequate protection to particularly vulnerable consumers). However, under-inclusiveness seems highly problematic from the point of view of distributive justice, e.g. in terms of the Rawlsian difference principle. See Hesselink (n. 164).

[282] See Forst (n. 271) 246; Forst, 'A Critical Theory of Transnational (In-)Justice: Realistic in the Right Way', in T. Brooks (ed.), *The Oxford Handbook of Global Justice* (2020) 451.

[283] Crenshaw (n. 154).

[284] These are the individual factors mentioned in Art. II.-7:207 DCFR and Art. 51 CESL proposal, cited earlier, in n. 280. Frequently, such relational 'weaknesses' and vulnerabilities are the consequence of belonging to a group—or the intersection of various groups—that are in a socially vulnerable or 'weak' position. From the point of view of the right to justification of contract, it seems, the familiar language of 'weaker party protection' has unduly stigmatizing connotations. Put differently, as a matter of epistemic justice in contract, the use of this terminology could reasonably be rejected by contract law's addressees. Cf. Forst, 'A Critical Theory . . . ' (n. 282) 464: 'One owes it to victims of domination not to treat them as "weak" and miserable human beings in need of "help."'

modification, improvement, or expansion of certain existing types of weaker party protection.

In this chapter, we saw that there are some quite divergent normative approaches and answers to this question, ranging from the total rejection of weaker party protection to strong support for it. Some political theories require weaker party protection as a matter of justice (distributive, interpersonal, or both); others understand it as a question of substantive autonomy; while still others support certain remedies and doctrines but not for the reason that the parties benefiting from them are weaker. In the light of the wide range of arguments for and against various types and degrees of weaker party protection, the EU legislator's strong emphasis in recent years on consumer law's capacity to contribute to economic growth in the internal market as a justification for consumer protection, appears particularly narrow. Moreover, the consistent limitation in EU law of most of the weaker party protection rules and remedies categorically to consumers seems arbitrary from the perspective of most, if not all, of the political theories we discussed.

We also saw that some of the answers given to our questions were based on values and conceptions of the person, the good life, and justice, that are so partisan and controversial that they seem unlikely to be acceptable to citizens committed to treating each other with equal respect, as the basis for generally applicable laws of contract. In other words, an overlapping consensus among the leading contemporary political theories discussed here, on justice in weaker party protection, does not seem to be within reach. On the contrary, there exist disagreements—sometimes even very strong ones—between a number of these theories on almost every important aspect of weaker party protection. Worse, while several theories do agree that the question of weaker party protection in contract law is an important question of justice, they strongly disagree on what answer should follow from justice considerations. This means that in pluralist societies like our own, where each of these political theories—and others—in general, and their implications for weaker party protection in contract, specifically, do or could command substantial support, the relevant contract law rules will have to be a compromise between several—and perhaps, to a degree, all—of these theories (plus others that were not discussed here), without any of them being able, as such, justifiably to claim the moral high ground.

Still, the very strong focus on consumers in EU private law does seem problematic. Not only because it unduly celebrates consumerism and materialism, but also because it distracts attention from justice. Interpersonal and distributive justice in contractual relationships cannot be reduced, without loss, to consumer rights and remedies. Certainly not if the agile 'average consumer', who is reasonably well informed and circumspect, is the benchmark. The strongly reductive economic instrumentalism in the EU's approach to contract law risks preventing us from concentrating on the worst injustices in contracts, such as exploitation and domination. Even if, for reasons of legal basis, the EU legislature necessarily had to limit its role in private law to the improvement of the functioning of the internal market—which, however, is simply untrue because the Treaties can, and perhaps should, be changed—then still it would not be clear why combating injustices in the internal market, such as exploitation and domination in contracts, in whichever market sector and whatever the status of the contracting parties, should not be a key priority. An internal market that tolerates exploitation or domination is hardly functioning properly, even—or perhaps especially—when that market is a growing market. Perhaps the highest priority from the point of view of justice should be given to the predicament of the most vulnerable contracting parties. These are likely to be persons—or their businesses—who find themselves at the intersection of various vulnerabilities that may severely impair their chances of avoiding exploitative contracts of whatever kind. There is little doubt that EU directives and regulations directly targeting the worst injustices in the internal market would have a solid legal basis in Article 114 TFEU. Finally, it may be time to change the terminology. The language of weakness and protection not only lacks respect towards the human beings addressed by the law in this way. At least for the cases where the real aim of the rule is—or ought to be—in fact contractual justice, the law may also be doing them an epistemic injustice when it fails to call injustices by their real name. It is true that the language of consumer 'protection' and 'weakness' is deeply entrenched in European contract law, but a crucial step towards real change may well be a change in the discourse.

7
Public Policy and Good Morals

1. Introduction

A. Freedom of Contract and Binding Force

Once it is established whether good reasons exist, as a general matter, for the public recognition and enforcement of private contracts,[1] the next question is which contracts the law should recognize. Must a court simply enforce any contract presented to it by one of the parties, or may—and perhaps should—the law take a more limitative view? In the latter case, which limits might—or should—there be? And what might be the reasons, if any, that could justify such a limitation? This question is usually referred to as the question of the 'freedom of contract': can a society legitimately limit the freedom of the parties to conclude contracts as they please?[2] As familiar as it is, this terminology is, however, somewhat misleading. Not many contracts are forbidden in the strong sense that those who conclude them will be imprisoned or fined. Contract law, in particular, does not prohibit the parties from concluding the contract or from performing it. What it does, instead, is to refuse the legal recognition, enforceability, and, thus, facilitation, of certain contracts. In such cases, the contract is called 'invalid'.[3] So, in reality, the question of freedom of contract is not so much about being allowed by the state to conclude a certain kind of contract as it is about being forced by public institutions to honour it: if I fail to live up to what I agreed to do in the contract and if my counterpart brings this contract to a court of law then will the court enforce the contract, i.e. will it provide the other party with some sanction or remedy against me, such as an order to pay damages or to actually comply with the contract? In other words, the question of freedom of contract can be understood as an aspect of the question of the binding force of contract: which agreements are binding in law? Does the legal system withhold from certain contracts the binding effects that it is generally

[1] The question that concerned us in Chapter 5.

[2] The language of freedom is adopted, for example, in Art. II.–1:102 (1) DCFR, (Party autonomy): 'Parties are free to make a contract or other juridical act and to determine its contents, subject to any applicable mandatory rules.'

[3] H. L. A. Hart, *The Concept of Law* (2nd ed., 1994), at 27–28, refers to contract law as a set of 'power conferring' rules: it confers upon the parties the power to create legally binding obligations. From this point of view, a limitation on the freedom of contract constitutes merely a limitation to that power. A political society does not confer an unlimited power upon private parties; it circumscribes that power, in particular for reasons of public policy. Frankly, the language of power conferral and facilitation, in its turn, risks obscuring the fact that the empowerment is one to bind oneself, and to that extent to limit one's own freedom. It also rather optimistically foregrounds the opportunity-creating character of contract law even though many valid contracts are hardly empowering. Klass, 'Three Pictures of Contract: Duty, Power and Compound Rule', 83 *New York University Law Review* (2008) 1726, argues that contract law is a 'compound' in that it functions both to create powers and to impose duties, which seems descriptively more accurate.

Justifying Contract in Europe: Political Philosophies of European Contract Law. First Edition. Martijn W. Hesselink, Oxford University Press. © Martijn W. Hesselink 2021. DOI: 10.1093/oso/9780192843654.003.0007

inclined to provide? Or, in the normative version that concerns us here, what limits regarding their substance (i.e. content or object) may or should a political community place on the contracts it enforces, and why?

B. Private and Public Interests

A legal system may have different reasons for limiting the freedom of contract. These reasons belong primarily to one of two types. The first is to protect the interests of one of the contracting parties, especially weaker contracting parties; the second is to protect the interests of others, either specific individuals or groups external to the contract or the general public. Cases of the first type were discussed in Chapter 6. In the second type of cases, which are central to the present chapter, both contracting parties may be perfectly happy with their contract; however, the law nevertheless refuses to enforce it. This may be the case especially when a contract, although mutually beneficial to the parties, has unacceptable negative effects on certain third parties or the public at large. A good example of such negative externalities are agreements between businesses which aim to restrict competition. Cartels may be very lucrative for the parties that are part of them, but this benefit comes at the expense of the interests of competitors (who have difficulty in entering or remaining in the market) and consumers (who pay higher prices). Therefore, Article 101 TFEU renders such agreements void. As we will see, other reasons of public policy may relate to public morality.

Although it is easy to distinguish these two different sets of cases analytically, in the abstract, important overlaps also exist. Thus, the invalidity of a contract may be explained and justified sometimes both with a view to protecting the interests of one of the parties and also with a view to protecting the public interest. Think of surrogacy contracts, which may be declared invalid in order to protect the interests of the potential surrogate mother or the child, or to prevent moral decline in society at large. Another example is usury, which has been forbidden, throughout history, both on religious grounds and in order to protect those who are preyed on by loan sharks. The overlaps may be more or less significant, depending on the normative point of view. This may be the case, in particular, where contracts are invalidated for paternalistic reasons.

C. Legal Sanction

The different reasons for invalidity of the contract are usually reflected in the type of invalidity the law provides for. In the case of protective rules, as we saw in Chapter 6, the sanction is typically relative nullity: the contract can be annulled, with retroactive effect, by the party who is meant to be protected by the rule.[4] If that party chooses not

[4] However, the CJEU interprets the rule in Art. 6 of the Unfair Terms Directive, according to which unfair terms should be 'not be binding on the consumer', in a sense that comes very close to absolute nullity. A court must examine, of its own motion, whether the contractual term is unfair, and when this the case it must not apply the term, 'except if the consumer opposes that non-application' (Case C-243/08, *Pannon GSM Zrt. v. Erzsébet Sustikné Győrfi* (EU:C:2009:350), at para. 35). The main remaining difference with

to annul the contract (extrajudicially or via judicial interference, depending on the legal system) then the contract remains valid and, therefore, fully binding on both parties. By contrast, in the cases that we are turning to in this chapter, the nullity is absolute. The public interest requires that the question whether the contract is valid or void should not to be left in the hands of the parties. The nullity is automatic ('*de plein droit*') whether the parties like it or not. To this nullity in contract law, the rules of civil procedure usually add the requirement that courts must declare the nullity of their own motion (*ex officio*), i.e. without any need for one of the parties to raise it in their litigation.

Absolute nullity means that neither of the parties can rely on the contract. What if one of the parties has already performed her side of the contract? Can she rely on the invalidity and claim restitution? In several systems, she may be barred by the principle '*nemo auditur turpitudinem suam allegans*', pursuant to which one cannot invoke one's own wickedness.[5] However, for EU competition law, the Court of Justice famously decided in *Courage and Crehan* that a party to a contract that is automatically void because it restricts competition in the sense of Article 110 TFEU (in this case a beer tie) can rely on the violation of that provision to obtain 'damages' from the other party.[6]

D. Immorality and Illegality

All European legal systems do indeed limit the freedom of contract. They do not recognize and enforce every agreement whatever its content; they refrain from facilitating just any transaction. In particular, they have long refused to recognize and enforce contracts if they were considered immoral. This is true not only for civil law systems, where contracts that are—or whose *causa* is—held to be 'against good morals' (*contra bonos mores*) are invalid.[7] The common law also refuses to enforce contracts that are 'immoral' or 'contrary to public policy'.[8] Of course, contracts may be invalid because a specific statute makes them invalid. And the statute may do so for moral (or ethical) reasons or other reasons of public policy, in particular for socio-economic objectives. These cases are usually referred to as cases of illegality.

Some salient examples of sales contracts that have been declared void by national contract laws because they are considered to be contrary to good morals or public

absolute nullity, in addition to the right to oppose, then, is that the other party, i.e. the professional seller or service provider, cannot invoke the unfairness of his own standard terms, which seems only of rare practical interest.

[5] For a comparative overview, see H. Beale *et al.*, *Cases, Materials and Text on Contract Law; Ius Commune Casebooks for the Common Law of Europe* (2019), ch. 17.5. For a nuanced rule, see Art. 15.104 (Restitution) Principles of European Contract Law.

[6] Case C-453/99, *Courage and Crehan* (EU:C:2001:465). The Court also made clear that national private law cannot bar such a damages claim 'on the sole ground that the claimant is a party to that contract', but only when that party 'bears significant responsibility for the distortion of competition'.

[7] See e.g. § 138(1) German Civil Code (*sittenwidriges Rechtsgeschäft*); and Art. 1343 Italian Civil Code (*causa illecita*). For the Roman law origins, see R. Zimmermann, *The Law of Obligations: Roman Foundations of the Civilian Tradition* (1996), at 706–715.

[8] See e.g. H. Beale (ed.), *Chitty on Contracts* (33rd ed., 2019), ch. 16 ('Illegality and public policy').

policy, include the sale of weapons, soft and hard drugs, alcohol, *Mein Kampf*, pornography, human organs, human blood, human milk,[9] voting rights, passports, political offices, and court rulings. As examples of service contracts that have been held contrary to public policy, think of sexual services (prostitution), gestational services (surrogacy), laser tag games, and dwarf tossing. Other types of contracts or clauses, beyond sales and services, that have been held immoral, include polygamous PACS ('*pacte civil de solidarité*', a form of civil union in France),[10] penalty clauses (in common law jurisdictions),[11] and terms excluding liability for intentionally (or grossly negligently) caused personal injury or death. We will return to several of these examples in the course of this chapter.

The law maker may offer different specific reasons why the contract should be void. This raises the question of whether freedom of contract can be limited for absolutely any reason of 'public policy' or 'public morality', i.e. arbitrarily as a matter of sheer political will, whether of the parliamentary majority or of the particular judges on the bench, or whether there are reasons, for example of justice, that limit the law maker's discretion in deciding on limitations to the freedom of contract. In a sense, this question is the mirror image of the question of what justifies the binding force of contract: here the question is what justifies the refusal of binding force.

In most European countries, in the course of the twentieth century, a shift took place in the interpretation of the legal notions of good morals, from traditional Christian values towards modern constitutional values. For example, in Germany the 'general clauses' in the civil code on 'good morals' (especially § 138 *BGB* for contracts and § 826 *BGB* for torts), together with those referring to 'good faith' (chiefly § 242 *BGB*), are regarded today as the 'gateways' (*Einfallstore*) through which constitutional values enter private law.[12] Thus, in more recent decades limitations to the freedom of contract have been motivated by the need to uphold the fundamental values enshrined in the Constitution. At the same time there have also been attempts, at both the Member State and the EU levels,[13] at what may be regarded in a sense as the reverse, i.e. the constitutionalization of freedom of contract itself.

There has been a parallel development in views on which institution is best placed for determining the immoral nature of a certain type of contracts: the courts or the legislature. In most European jurisdictions, the instances of invalidity of contracts because of their 'immorality' (i.e. for being contrary to 'good morals' or 'public policy'—an open-ended standard or general clause to be interpreted by courts) have fallen sharply in the past century relative to instances of invalidity for 'illegality' (i.e. based on statutory prohibitions).

[9] Cf. Cohen, 'Regulating Milk: Women and Cows in France and the United States', 65 *AJCL* (2017) 469.

[10] See Art. 515-2 French Civil Code.

[11] See *Cavendish Square Holding BV v. Talal El Makdessi and ParkingEye Ltd v. Beavis* [2015] UKSC 67, at para. 7 and para. 243 (per Hodge): 'The rule against penalties is a rule of contract law based on public policy.'

[12] Another term is *Einbruchstellen* (break-in points). See e.g. *BVerfG*, 15 January 1956, *BVerfGE* 7, 198 (*Lüth*): 'Deshalb sind mit Recht die Generalklauseln als die "Einbruchstellen" der Grundrechte in das bürgerliche Recht bezeichnet worden.'

[13] For the latter, see especially Case C-426/11, *Alemo-Herron and Others v. Parkwood Leisure Ltd* (EU:C:2013:521), on which further later, in Section 4.E.

Finally, an analytical question, not merely of doctrinal interest but also with normative implications and therefore relevant here, is what exactly it is that the law is assessing the immorality of: the contract, its 'cause', its object, its content, the intent of the parties (one or both of them), or their objectives. In French law, for example, there was a recent shift, from the 1804 Civil Code, where a contract could be invalid because its object or *cause* was illicit, notably for being contrary to good morals or public order, to the 2016 Civil Code reform, following which it became a requirement for the validity of a contract that its content should be lawful.[14]

E. Commodification versus Market-inalienability

An important dimension of the contemporary political debate on the invalidity of contracts against good morals or public policy has been the critique of commodification, i.e. the contestation of the market alienability of certain goods and services which, it is claimed, ought not to be exchanged for money.[15]

In the nineteenth century, Marx famously denounced the treatment of workers as commodities.[16] The contemporary use of 'commodification' as a wider concept goes back to Polanyi, who analysed the 'great transformation', where labour, land, and money, that had been understood hitherto as deeply embedded in society, came to be regarded as fungible, indeed as commodities.[17] Another striking case of commodification, that would have been unthinkable until the 1990s, has been the commodification and marketization, through privatization, of public services, such as the provision of energy, public transport, telecoms, water, education, and healthcare, and in some countries even police and military services. Personal data are a contested commodity with particular relevance for EU contract law. A recent directive applies to the supply of digital content and digital services in exchange for personal data, thus turning the commodified personal data into a currency.[18]

The notion of 'commodification' gained particular force and prominence in the feminist critique of the commodification of the female body, especially in the cases of sex work and gestational services. As we will see, there has been strong disagreement on these questions among feminist theorists on both moral and pragmatic grounds.

[14] See Art. 1128 (new) French Civil Code. As M. Fabre-Magnan, *Contrat et engagent unilatéral* (2010), at 424 points out, the new formula is largely tautological.

[15] See Radin, 'Market-Inalienability', 100 *Harv. L. Rev.* (1987) 1849; M. J. Radin, *Contested Commodities: The Trouble with Trade in Sex, Children, Body Parts, and Other Things* (1996).

[16] Marx, 'Economic and Philosophical Manuscripts' (1844), in K. Marx, *Early Writings* (1992), at 322: 'the worker sinks to the level of a commodity, and moreover the most wretched commodity of all'.

[17] K. Polanyi, *The Great Transformation: The Political and Economic Origins of Our Time* ([first published 1944] 2001), ch. 6.

[18] See Directive 2019/770 on Contracts for the Supply of Digital Content and Digital Services, OJ 2019 L 136, preliminary Recital (24):

> Digital content or digital services are often supplied also where the consumer does not pay a price but provides personal data to the trader. Such business models are used in different forms in a considerable part of the market. While fully recognising that the protection of personal data is a fundamental right and that therefore personal data cannot be considered as a commodity, this Directive should ensure that consumers are, in the context of such business models, entitled to contractual remedies.

Commodification is a form—or has an aspect—of objectification, which brings up the object-subject dichotomy, a much-debated issue in metaphysics. This, in turn, raises the question of contract law's conception of the person, in particular, how thick or thin the personhood of contracting parties must be understood to be. If I conclude a contract involving my body, is there a point where it becomes difficult to distinguish between the subject of the contracting party and the object of the contract? It also raises the question of how to understand non-human animals. Are they properly understood as objects that we can buy and sell, either alive (as pets) or dead (as meat)? As we will see, different philosophical theories understand and answer these questions quite divergently.

Under Roman law, certain categories of things were already considered '*extra commercium*'.[19] And the concept of '*choses hors commerce*' had remained part of French law until the reform of 2016.[20] By contrast, in extending the scope of the market, commodification directly expands the scope of contract law too (and vice versa). And the contestation of market alienability in practice often means questioning the legal recognition and enforcement of certain transactions as contractual, with the usual remedies for breach of contract (expectation damages, specific performance). Therefore, the doctrine of invalidity of contracts contrary to good morals or public policy not only determines the moral limits to the market but also the correlated scope of contract law.

F. Donation

Both commodification and market-inalienability refer to exchange for money. In many cases, gratuitous voluntary transactions are regarded as much less problematic than a sales or service contract with the same object. In some cases, donations are even considered positively good from the point of view of morality (interpersonal or political) and public policy. Think of the difference between selling your kidney and donating it. In the case of donation there is much less reason than in the case of sales (which usually occur under conditions of extreme poverty) to worry whether the contract was freely entered into, except, perhaps, in the case of donation between relatives, where there may be undue emotional pressure. Also, organ donation—far from being immoral and contrary to public policy—is usually considered a noble act and a practice that is socially desirable and therefore also publicly institutionalized. Indeed, as we will see, one recurrent argument against the legal recognition and enforceability of contracts for the sale of human organs is that the existence of an organ market with a known market price, would risk undermining the morally and socially desirable practice of donation.

[19] These included *res publicae* (e.g. public roads, stadiums, theatres), *res sacrae* (e.g. temples), *liberi homines* (free men, as opposed to slaves, who were considered commodities). Any contract for the sale of one of these 'things' was void. Cf. Zimmermann (n. 7) 241–245.

[20] See former Art. 1128 French Civil Code: 'Il n'y a que les choses qui sont dans le commerce qui puissent être l'objet des conventions.' This matter is now covered by Art. 1162 (new), the general provision on contracts against public policy. Cf. M. Fabre-Magnan, *Droit des obligations*, Vol. 1 (2007), § 422. See also the German legal concept of 'Verkehrsunfähigkeit'.

While the distinction between commodification and non-commodification (as well as market-alienability versus market-inalienability) coincides with the one between sales (and service) versus donation, it does not necessarily also correspond with the contractual versus non-contractual divide. In other words, being outside the scope of the market does not necessarily mean also being outside the scope of contract law. For while in common law jurisdictions gifts are not considered enforceable contracts (because they lack consideration), in the civil law tradition donations are in fact recognized as legally binding contracts. This legal recognition is expressed in their well-established place in the civil codes amidst other specific contracts such as sales and rent.[21] Usually, law prescribes some requirements as to form (in writing or even a notarial recording),[22] especially for an undertaking to make a donation (as opposed to donations where the good is handed over instantly), in order to ensure donative intent. Still, a dispute between a donor and a donee is considered a genuine contract dispute that may end up being resolved through the law of contract, which notably provides remedies for breach of contract.[23]

G. The Internal Market and its Moral Limits

The importance of freedom of contract in EU contract law has proved highly contentious. In its 'Action Plan' of 2003, the European Commission stated, in relation to its plans for a common frame of reference: 'In this context contractual freedom should be the guiding principle; restrictions should only be foreseen where this could be justified with good reasons'.[24] The 'Manifesto on Social Justice in European Contract Law' questioned why this should be the case, and inquired:

> Why should the principle of freedom of contract have such a privileged position, so that proposals for constraint must satisfy the heavy burden of proof that they can be justified with good reasons? Why not reverse the burden, so that those who wish to deregulate market transactions should have the burden of explaining the potential advantages to be gained by the parties to these transactions from the absence of mandatory rules?[25]

21 See e.g. German Civil Code, Book 2 (Law of obligations), division 8 (Particular types of obligations), title 4 (Donation), which consists of 19 provisions. See also DCFR, Book IV (Specific contracts and the rights and obligations arising from them), Part H (Donation), which contains 31 provisions. For the definition, see Art. IV.H.–1:101 (2) DCFR: 'A contract for the donation of goods is a contract under which one party, the donor, gratuitously undertakes to transfer the ownership of goods to another party, the donee, and does so with an intention to benefit the donee.'

22 See e.g. Art. 518 German Civil Code (notarial recording), Art. 931 French Civil Code (notarial recording); Art. IV.H.–2:101 DCFR (writing).

23 In the DCFR, see Section 2 (Remedies of the donee). In principle, the general rules for breach of contract apply, but there are exceptions. See Art. IV.H.–3:201. In particular, the right to specific performance is severely restricted. See Art. IV.H.–3:202 (Restricted right to enforce performance).

24 Commission Communication, 'A More Coherent European Contract Law: An Action Plan' (COM(2003) 68 final), at 62.

25 Study Group on Social Justice in European Private Law, 'Social Justice in European Contract Law: A Manifesto', 10 *ELJ* (2004) 653, at 663.

A classical illustration of the question of the limits of cross-border freedom of contract in the European context is provided by the *Omega* case.[26] In that case, the Court of Justice of the European Union (CJEU) had to decide whether a prohibition order issued by the mayor of Bonn forbidding a laser tag parlour from allowing people to play at killing each other was compatible with European law, in particular the free movement of goods and (especially) services. The Court held that restrictions were permissible on the ground of public policy, and that it was not necessary, in the present context, for this to be a European-wide notion of public policy, accepted in all Member States. The *Omega* case dealt with administrative law; it was not a contract case. However, it is not difficult to imagine that a very similar question could arise with regard to contract law. In the case at hand, Omega Spielhallen had offered the laser tag game to the public, making use, on the basis of a franchising contract, of a format developed by British company Pulsar. Thus, two types of contracts were involved: the franchise contract between the English franchisor and the German franchisee; and the service contracts between consumers and the laser dome. As already mentioned, most legal systems contain a doctrine pursuant to which contracts are invalid when they are illegal or immoral or contrary to public policy. Here the game was forbidden by the mayor and the interdiction was held by the Court of Justice to be compatible with European law. In all likelihood, then, any invalidity of the franchise and the consumer contracts in Germany, if this was determined under the general clause § 138 *BGB*, would also have been upheld by the Court, and for the same reasons. Therefore, one way of looking at our question, especially with regard to the EU, where the internal market has been so central, is as a question concerning the moral limits to the internal market. How should EU contract law respond to contested commodities? Should certain goods (and services) remain outside the internal market ('*choses hors commerce*')? And is it justifiable that major divergences continue to exist between Member State laws as to what money can't buy?[27]

The Principles of European Contract Law (PECL) dedicate a provision to 'contracts contrary to fundamental principles', Article 15:101 PECL.[28] The Draft Common Frame of Reference (DCFR) contains a very similar provision.[29] Pursuant to Article II.–7:301 DCFR (contracts infringing fundamental principles), a contract is void to the extent that it infringes a principle recognized as fundamental in the laws of the Member States of the EU and nullity is required to give effect to that principle. The wording of Article II.–7:301 DCFR raises the question of what exactly is meant by a principle 'recognised as fundamental in the laws of the Member States'. In particular,

[26] Case C-36/02, *Omega Spielhallen- und Automatenaufstellungs-GmbH v. Oberbürgermeisterin der Bundesstadt Bonn* (EU:C:2004:614).

[27] Cf. M. Sandel, *What Money Can't Buy: The Moral Limits of Markets* (2012).

[28] O. Lando *et al.*, (eds), *Principles of European Contract Law, Part III, Prepared by the Commission on European Contract Law* (2003).

[29] On the intended use of the DCFR, see the 'Comments' to Art. I.–1:101 (Intended field of application), in C. von Bar and E. Clive (eds), *Principles, Definitions and Model Rules of European Private Law: Draft Common Frame of Reference (DCFR), Full Edition* (2009), at 85: 'One of the main purposes of the DCFR is to act as an optional source of rules, concepts and terminology for those drafting legislative instruments and contracts. It is hoped that the rules may also prove useful to judges, arbiters, legal practitioners, researchers and law teachers.'

if the DCFR were the applicable law,[30] what would happen if a contract infringed a principle recognized as fundamental in the law of one Member State but not in others? This question is not easily solved. Take, as an example, a contract for sexual services (prostitution) which probably infringes a principle recognized as fundamental in the laws of the majority of Member States but which (under certain circumstances) is accepted as a regular economic activity in some Member States. Contrast, for example, the Netherlands, where the providers of sexual services are subject to the ordinary tax rules, usually as self-employed persons, with the situation in France where their clients may be subject to criminal punishment. If contracts for sexual services were considered valid under the DCFR, this would hardly be acceptable to Member States where such contracts are considered immoral and contrary to recognized fundamental principles. However, if they were invalid, then citizens of some Member States would no longer be able to do in their own country (more precisely: their agreement to do so would no longer be legally enforceable) what is regarded there as perfectly acceptable.[31] This is the dilemma between a maximalist ('moralist') approach where the highest common denominator counts, and a minimalist ('moral dumping') approach that focuses on the lowest common denominator.[32] One way out of this dilemma would be to leave the answer to this question to the national courts in the Member States, in analogy to the CJEU's ruling in *Freiburger Kommunalbauten* concerning the notion of unfairness.[33] But then we would be back at square one. In contrast to the PECL and DCFR, the Common European Sales Law (CESL) proposal explicitly removed invalidity for immorality from its substantive scope of application, thus relegating the matter to the applicable national law.[34]

H. Regulation

Contract law is not the only branch of the law dealing with private transactions which are held to be contrary to public policy or public morality. On the contrary, in many cases (e.g. sale of arms or hard drugs, sex work, commercial surrogacy) criminalization has been the more salient legal response. And even within contract law, the doctrine of contracts against good morals or public policy, with its binary consequence of validity or invalidity, is not the most frequent contemporary approach. Today, various

[30] Moreover, Art. VII.–6:103 DCFR (Illegality) adds that in the case where such a contract has already been performed there is no claim for restitution under the chapter on unjustified enrichment to the extent that the restitution would contravene the policy underlying the principle.

[31] For the sake of the argument, here the DCFR is taken as a draft European civil code intended to replace national laws. On the DCFR, see further Chapter 2.

[32] The Comment to Art. 15:101 PECL (at 211) suggests that a minimalist approach is intended, where only the violation of principles recognized in (almost) all Member States will make the contract invalid.

[33] Case C-237/02, *Freiburger Kommunalbauten GmbH Baugesellschaft & Co. KG v. Ludger Hofstetter and Ulrike Hofstetter* (EU:C:2004:209).

[34] See Recital (27): 'the invalidity of a contract arising from . . . illegality or immorality' remains 'governed by the pre-existing rules of the national law'. Critical, Hesselink, 'How to Opt into the Common European Sales Law? Brief Comments on the Commission's Proposal for a Regulation' 20 *ERPL* (2012) 195.

different types of market regulation find a middle ground between laissez-faire and criminalization, and between the validity and invalidity of the contract.[35]

Still, that does not make the fundamental political question of whether contract law should limit the freedom of contract for reasons of public policy or public morality any less important—quite the contrary. It merely shows that contemporary contract law's approach has evolved from a binary to more nuanced one. This has happened especially—but by no means exclusively—in the case of paternalistic concerns, where the regulator is not confident that the parties to certain types of contracts, which are typically concluded by persons having only very limited alternative options, are making choices that are in their own best interest. Typical instances of contemporary market-regulatory private law responses include: duties to inform or to warn; age limits for validity; licences; various legal presumptions; and cooling-off periods.

This brings us also to the limits of contract law—or, rather, it raises questions of the definition of contract law, and of private law more generally. Some argue that regulatory private law is an oxymoron, and instead we should draw a sharp distinction between private law and regulation, usually in order to keep private law pure from any instrumentalism.[36] Others understand private law as just one type of regulation, and contract law simply as the law that regulates contractual relationships.[37] Still others insist on distinguishing between regulatory and non-regulatory ('classical') private law, reserving a natural place only for the latter in the civil code.[38] There are both academic-disciplinary and political stakes in this debate, and they overlap in part. Economists often understand regulation as an intervention in otherwise free markets, which may be justified (only) in the case of market failures, which, however, are believed to be exceptional. Lawyers today still often understand private law as relatively unpolitical, in contrast to public law, which is naturally political and from which it should remain largely autonomous. The market versus regulation, law versus regulation, and law versus politics divides converge when private law is understood as the unpolitical law of free markets, and regulation as the political interventions in those markets. Over the years, these sets of divides have been the main points of attack in the

[35] With Radin, *Contested Commodities* (n. 15) ch. 7, and *passim*, we can understand such a regulatory approach as partial (de)commodification. As we will see later, she recommends partial commodification as the preferred legal response in most cases of contested commodities.

[36] See E. J. Weinrib, *Corrective Justice* (2012), at 307: 'An instrumentalist approach makes three errors. First, it imports outside goals for immanent concepts of private law. Second, it ignores the relationship between a plaintiff and a defendant. Third, it wrongly converts all private law into public law.' See earlier, E. J. Weinrib, *The Idea of Private Law* (1995), at 48–50 and *passim*. C. Leone, 'The Missing Stone in the Cathedral: Of Unfair Terms in Employment Contracts and Coexisting Rationalities in European Contract Law' (2020) (doctoral thesis on file at the University of Amsterdam), at 12–15, proposes a sharp distinction between private law and regulation, understood as different rationalities (but contrary to Weinrib she vindicates a deformalized corrective justice as private law's rationality).

[37] H. Collins, *Regulating Contracts* (1999), at 7 and *passim*.

[38] See Michaels, 'Of Islands and the Ocean: The Two Rationalities of European Private Law', in R. Brownsword *et al.* (eds), *Foundations of European Private Law*, (2011) 139, distinguishing two rationalities of private law, 'juridical' and 'instrumental', the former focusing on relationships between individuals and having its natural place in the code or the common law (the ocean), the latter focusing on the regulation of markets and having the legal form of statutes (the islands); H.-W. Micklitz, 'The Transformation of Private Law through Competition', 22 *ELJ* (2016) 627, at 628: 'traditional private law (the grand codifications and the common law) and regulatory private law have to be kept distinct.'

various waves of critical private law scholarship.[39] In all these debates on the proper place and understanding of private law and regulation, freedom of contract usually serves as a key focal point.

I. The Black Market

When contract law refuses to recognize and enforce certain contracts because they are contrary to public policy, this does not mean in all cases that such transactions will not be concluded or performed. Indeed, for several of the examples given above (e.g. weapons, drugs, banned books, alcohol, human organs, sexual services, gestational services), in the jurisdictions where these contracts are banned (or were at some point), well-established black markets have existed. As we will see, this reality where immoral transactions go underground, which carries its own economic, health, and safety risks for the parties and for society at large, is more relevant from the point of view of some political theories than others.

J. Value Pluralism and the Common Good

A final dimension of our question is: what impact should the fact of value pluralism in pluralist societies have on the justifiability of the refusal by the law to enforce contracts with reference to the 'common good' or 'public values'? As we saw in Chapter 2, very different views exist on what role, if any, public institutions can legitimately have in implementing values, including perfectionist, constrained pluralist, radical pluralist, and neutralist views. There, we also saw that the question is intricately related to meta-ethical questions, including ontological ones concerning the existence and nature of values (especially realism versus anti-realism) and epistemological ones concerning their capability for truth, and our access to it (cognitivism versus non-cognitivism). As we will see in this chapter, with regard to contracts and grounds for their invalidity, these abstract and meta-questions become very concrete.

2. Utilitarian

A. Externalities

From a utilitarian point of view, freedom of contract is important, albeit not intrinsically, as for libertarians and liberal-egalitarians (see later, in Sections 4 and 3, respectively), but instrumentally. As we saw in Chapter 5, the reason why utilitarians support

[39] For European private law, see e.g. Caruso, 'The Missing View of the Cathedral: The Private Law Paradigm of European Legal Integration', 3 *ELJ* (1997) 3; Kennedy, 'The Political Stakes in "Merely Technical" Issues of Contract Law', 10 *ERPL* (2002) 7; Hesselink, 'The Politics of a European Civil Code', 10 *ELJ* (2004) 675; Bartl, 'Internal Market Rationality, Private Law and the Direction of the Union: Resuscitating the Market as the Object of the Political', 21 *ELJ* (2015) 572.

the binding force of contract is that they expect an increase in social welfare from voluntary exchanges. The reason is that a contract provides prima facie good evidence for the preferences of the contracting parties ('revealed preferences'). Therefore, if both parties freely agree to a contract then it can be presumed, in principle, that the transaction enhances the welfare of both of them. Indeed, the contract might be Pareto efficient, since it might make the parties better off without making anyone else worse off. From a welfarist point of view, then, the general justification for freedom of contract is exactly the same as what justifies the binding force of contract, i.e. that contractual choices made freely by the parties provide a good proxy for their preferences, as presumed by the neoclassical rational agent model and to be confirmed, in due course, by behavioural studies. This explains the strong attachment of welfare economists to private exchange, private ordering, and freedom of contract, and their correlated scepticism towards the capacity of collective decision makers.[40]

However, utilitarians do not favour unlimited freedom of contract. They reject the enforcement of contracts in certain cases, even when there is little doubt that the contract will make the contracting parties better off. These are the cases where a contract has what economists call negative externalities.[41] Mutually beneficial contracts should not be enforced when they make the parties better off at the (greater) expense of third parties. Welfare theory, and utilitarianism more generally, being collectivist approaches, also when it comes to contract law, focus on social utility, not mere private utility. Therefore, in the utilitarian calculus of social welfare everyone who is affected counts equally. This includes not only the contracting parties themselves, and their benefits, but also non-consenting third parties, and their costs. So, if a contract also affects the welfare of persons other than just the contracting parties, then these external welfare effects should count in just the same way as the welfare effects on the parties themselves. (In economic terms, in the case of negative externalities there is overproduction of whatever good or services the contract is about, because the market price is too high, set as it is at the level of the private marginal costs rather than the social marginal costs.[42])

The problem, however, is that in reality almost all contracts have externalities.[43] When I buy my groceries at the supermarket I make the owner of the small shop next door worse off, in their own estimation (which is the relevant utilitarian standard) than if I bought my groceries at their shop. In other words, in our world contracts will only very rarely—if ever—be Pareto efficient.[44]

In another world, however, all contracts could be Pareto efficient. In a hypothetical world without transaction costs, the contracting parties would trace and find all potentially affected third parties and start negotiations with them in order to obtain their consent. In such a world, where everyone would negotiate with everyone that might

[40] M. J. Trebilcock, *The Limits of Freedom of Contract* (1993), at 7.

[41] See e.g. S. Shavell, *Foundations of Economic Analysis of Law* (2004), ch. 5.

[42] Hermalin, Katz, and Craswell, 'Contract Law', in A. M. Polinsky and S. Shavell (eds), *Handbook of Law and Economics* (2007) 30, ch. 1.

[43] Trebilcock (n. 40) 58: 'Almost every transaction one can conceive of is likely to impose costs on third parties'; G. Calabresi, *The Future of Law and Economics: Essays in Reform and Recollection* (2016), at 24–25: 'Individual decisions with respect to any number of goods create externalities—positive or negative'.

[44] Calabresi, 'The Pointlessness of Pareto: Carrying Coase Further', 100 *Yale L.J.* (1991) 1211.

be affected by their actions until an equilibrium of agreements is reached, there would be no externalities. All potential externalities would be internalized into contracts. So, from a Coasean point of view, the real problem with regard to externalities is transaction costs.

As we saw in Chapter 2, the Kaldor-Hicks standard for efficiency is more lenient than the Pareto standard, because it allows for trade-offs.[45] It only demands that the winners could compensate the losers and still be better off. However, this still does not solve the problem of externalities. The reason is that transaction costs, which prevent externalities from being internalized through bargaining, thus also prevent all relevant preferences from being revealed. So, how are we to know, in the absence of actual bargaining, which third parties are affected by the contract and how much? And how can contract law provide the parties with proper incentives for internalizing externalities if contract law makers do not know the locus or size of contractual externalities? Put differently, while it is generally acknowledged by economists that externalities constitute a market failure,[46] it is not so clear what, if anything, the legal response—and in our case specifically the contract law response—to the pervasive presence of negative externalities should be.

Two very different conclusions have been drawn when applying this to the real world.[47] On one view we should assume that markets function well enough to allow for bargaining with regard to the most important externalities. Therefore, the presumption should be that the main externalities have already in fact been internalized and that the prices consumers pay already incorporate the cost of production to third parties. On the second view, in contrast, the fact that most contracts have externalities means that decisions about their enforcement will always create winners and losers. Another way of putting this is that the question of freedom of contract—which contracts to enforce and which not—always has distributive implications. Therefore, the question will have to be answered on the basis of principles of distributive justice. Positing Kaldor-Hicks as a neutral answer to the question of the scope of contract simply will not do. As Calabresi, one of the founders of the law and economics movement, made very clear:

[45] Trade-offs presume commensurability. In this case, the measure is money. Commensurability is a key premise for commodification, and a key point of attack in commodification-critique, as we will see later.

[46] R. Cooter and T. Ulen, *Law and Economics* (6th ed., 2012), at 39.

[47] Many economists have concluded that welfare economics is largely indeterminate on contractual externalities. See Trebilcock (n. 40) 59: 'the concept of externalities is one of the least satisfactory concepts in welfare economics'. See, more generally, C. J. Dahlman, 'The Problem of Externality', 22 *Journal of Law and Economics* (1979) 141, at 156:

> The conclusion is rather startling: transaction costs per se have nothing to do with externalities. What is involved is a value judgment: if you believe that markets internalize everything, you will believe that externalities do not exist; on the other hand, if you believe that markets do not internalize side effects, you will believe in the persistence of externalities as deviations from an attainable optimum. This is not science; it is metaphysics: value judgments and political goals will enter into the determination of whether externalities occur in our world. You cannot show analytically that the government, in principle and in all cases, handles externalities better than the market; nor can you prove the opposite: it all depends on what point of reference you choose.... This is not positive economics; it is a political discussion at least until we can better justify the choice of appropriate reference points. It is thus doubtful whether the term 'externality' has any meaningful interpretation, except as an indicator of the political beliefs and value judgments of the person who uses (or avoids using) the term.

> without a real-world look at a particular situation, followed by the application of an explicit distributional theory to that situation, the attempt to make Kaldor-Hicks efficiency into a general normative guide must fail. It can be no more than a disingenuous attempt to convert a distributional theory of uncertain validity into one that has genuine distributional neutrality.[48]

Imposing uncompensated Kaldor-Hicks moves through coercive law, as would be the case with the legal enforcement of all contracts which have externalities, has non-neutral distributional consequences, which may be justifiable but for their justification we need an argument found in some theory of distributive justice.[49]

B. Market Inalienability

Market inalienability is usually attributed by economists to reasons other than welfare maximization.[50] The reason is that in the absence of externalities, market inalienability is always inefficient. If we take the agreement between the parties as revealing their preferences, then presumably the transaction makes both parties better off, in their own estimation, and if there are no externalities then the contract is Pareto efficient. Therefore, if goods or services for which there would be a market are kept off the market (or if market access is made more difficult) by law—for example through criminalization, invalidity of contracts, or regulation—then to that extent there is a welfare loss. In the words, of Cooter and Ulen, 'prohibitions on transfers are inefficient because they prevent people from getting what they want'.[51]

Calabresi, however, provides an economic explanation for the market inalienability of certain goods, referred to as 'merit goods', of which he distinguishes two types.[52] The first type are goods whose value diminishes—often sharply—when priced on a market. These are goods the commodification of which causes disgust and pain in people other than those willing to buy and sell. Put in the terminology of externalities, the social cost of contracts for such goods would be the mental suffering of people other than the contracting parties. Calabresi refers to these costs as 'moral externalities'.[53] As a result, overall social welfare would be reduced by the commodification of these goods. As Calabresi underlines, utilitarians and welfare economists are not free to make value judgements about these disutilities; they must count them as costs.[54]

48 Calabresi (n. 44) 1224.

49 Ibid. 1225.

50 Hermalin, Katz, and Craswell (n. 42) 47, refer to market inalienability as 'a concept not easily incorporated into economic accounts of exchange'. See also Cooter and Ulen (n. 46) 162, explaining that 'inalienability rests on conventional morality and political philosophies that stress values other than Pareto efficiency'.

51 Cooter and Ulen (n. 46) 161.

52 Calabresi (n. 43) ch. 2. Calabresi borrows the term from Richard Musgrave and James Tobin and specifies (and modifies) its meaning, removing the (direct) significance of merit in their allocation.

53 Ibid. 27.

54 Ibid. Contrast Mill, who refuses to count moral externalities as harm in the sense of the harm principle. See J. S. Mill, *On Liberty* ([first published 1859] 1974), at 151 dismissively: 'there are many who consider as an injury to themselves any conduct which they have a distaste for, and resent it as an outrage to their

A second category of merit goods, which is frequently overlooked, are goods in regard of which most people would find exchange for money acceptable if only the distribution of wealth in our society were not so unequal.[55] Here the commodification per se is not the problem but the fact that, in the world we live in, the rich would be the typical buyers in the markets for these goods and the poor the usual sellers. Examples of contracts for such goods and services arguably include the sales of body parts and gestational and sexual services. Thus, the concept of merit goods helps to explain on utilitarian, welfare grounds the existing limitations of freedom of contract, either through outright bans (illegality and immorality doctrines of general contract law) or through market regulation. Again, as Calabresi underlines, welfare economists are not free patronizingly to dismiss these disutilities as 'irrational', or paternalistically or moralistically to ignore them as genuine social costs, since this would undermine the entire basis of their argument, grounded as it is in subjective preferences: 'Taking individuals' utilities as they are means that such prohibitions are *not* Pareto inferior.'[56]

In summary, if welfarists and utilitarians take moral preferences seriously then many cases of market inalienability, or the regulation of market exchanges (what Radin calls incomplete commodification), and the ensuing limitations of freedom of contract, can be seen, on their own terms, simply as legal responses to market failures.

C. Donative Contracts

Economists tend to reject the consideration requirement, characteristic of the common law of contract, on efficiency grounds, simply because, as one leading handbook puts it, 'many non-exchange promises also enhance economic welfare'.[57] Therefore, as another leading textbook puts it quite straightforwardly, 'the law ought to allow contracts to give gifts'.[58] To the extent that the law's suspicion of donation contracts is motivated by concerns about impulsiveness or other types of 'bounded rationality', legal economists argue, this is best addressed by a form requirement,[59] as is indeed the usual approach in civil law jurisdictions, and also the solution adopted by the DCFR.[60]

feelings'. Cf. F. H. Buckley, *Just Exchange: A Theory of Contract* (2005), at 121: 'Mill rejected the idea that the state might rely upon moral externalities to impeach a contract.'

[55] Calabresi (n. 43) ch. 3.
[56] Ibid. 48 (emphasis in original).
[57] Hermalin, Katz, and Craswell (n. 42) 50. See also Arrow, 'Gifts and Exchanges', 1 *Philosophy and Public Affairs* (1972) 343, at 344: 'It is obvious on the most superficial observation that the allocation of goods and services is not accomplished entirely by exchange, as standard economic models would hold.'
[58] Shavell (n. 41) 383.
[59] Ibid. 50.
[60] See earlier, in Section 1.F.

D. Illegitimate Preferences

It follows directly from utilitarianism's fundamental and radical moral subjectivism, where all values are like tastes (fairness like chocolate), that it must count every source of utility, and the satisfaction of any kind of preference, equally.[61] As Kymlicka points out, this means that utilitarians have no direct way of excluding from the calculus preferences that seem illegitimate, for example racist or sadistic preferences.[62] Therefore, a welfarist contract law could turn out to be much more permissive in this respect than most existing legal systems actually are. For example, giving access against payment to a website showing scenes of animal torture would not be forbidden as long as there were more people enjoying seeing those images than others suffering from seeing them (or from being aware of their existence), or if those who enjoy it do so more intensely than those who disapprove.[63] Such perverse outcomes of unfettered utilitarianism are not advocated in the law and economics literature. But also no explanation is given as to why, from a law and economics point of view, freedom of contract should not extend to such seemingly illegitimate preferences.

E. Pernicious Markets

Oman offers a very different, not efficiency oriented, consequentialist view on the relationship between markets and contract law. His core claim is that 'well-functioning markets are morally desirable, and contract law should be organized to support such markets'.[64] In particular, according to Oman, well-functioning markets deliver three types of moral goods: liberal cooperation, wealth, and liberal virtues (especially support for moral pluralism).[65] Oman explicitly rejects the economic model of perfect competition as the ideal for a well-functioning market: 'Morally evil market outcomes are consistent with economic efficiency, and the morally desirable consequences of the market I defend do not depend on markets producing formally efficient allocations'.[66] If, however, the purpose of contract law is to support markets that produce morally desirable outcomes, then it makes no sense to enforce contracts when they are immoral. As he observes, 'if contract law exists to support well-functioning, desirable markets, it is entirely natural that we should withhold enforcement from contracts that will create pathological markets'.[67] Markets can turn pernicious, and produce

[61] Cf. Sandel (n. 27) 14: 'Part of the appeal of markets is that they don't pass judgment on the preferences they satisfy. . . . Markets don't wag fingers. They don't discriminate between admirable preferences and base ones.'

[62] W. Kymlicka, *Contemporary Political Philosophy: An Introduction* (2nd ed., 2002), at 26.

[63] Cf. also Radin, *Contested Commodities* (n. 15) 8, in response to Posner's appalling 'argument' that the reason rape must be forbidden is that it bypasses the market in sexual relations (marital or otherwise): 'Posner does not cite as an objection the idea that the purported pleasure of the rapist should not count at all, because this argument is not cognizable within the framework of market rhetoric. Rape is no different from any preference satisfaction.'

[64] N. Oman, *The Dignity of Commerce: Markets and the Moral Foundations of Contract Law* (2016), at 1.

[65] Ibid. ch. 3.

[66] Ibid. 30–31.

[67] Ibid. 17.

morally undesirable outcomes, Oman, argues, in three different ways:[68] when they can cause harm (the slave trade is the most obvious example); when they introduce a commercial ethos in interpersonal interactions where this is inappropriate (commodification); and when they destroy value (e.g. when arbitral awards are sold). In all these cases contract enforcement would not be supportive of a well-functioning market and, therefore, would not be morally justified.

Having said that, the reasoning seems unduly indirect. Why not say directly that we should refuse to enforce contracts that produce morally undesirable outcomes, rather than suggesting that we should declare void contracts that support markets that carry morally undesirable consequences? The detour via the dignity of the market seems wholly dispensable; we could directly concentrate on the moral dignity of the contracting parties and affected third parties, and on evil or pernicious contracts rather than on markets turning pernicious or evil. So, when Oman claims that 'pernicious markets mark the limits of contract',[69] he seems to be getting things backward. It is contract law that, by marking pernicious contracts as immoral, sets the limits of the market.

3. Liberal-Egalitarian

A. Removing Bad Options

As Kimel points out, 'the association of liberalism with the ideal of freedom of contract is quite natural'.[70] Yet, for liberal perfectionists the notion of freedom of contract has a distinct meaning which differs, in particular, from the way it is defined by libertarians. While libertarians, as we will see in the next section, understand freedom of contract as non-interference by the state in the contractual choices freely made by private parties (negative freedom), for liberal perfectionists freedom of contract means the freedom for people to be the authors of their own lives by making autonomous choices among various valuable options (positive freedom). Three elements are important here.

First, the state's task is not limited to non-interference. Raz argues that the state should undertake positive action to make an autonomous life possible by offering the appropriate social forms.[71] For contract this means, it seems, that the state must make free contracting possible by making available a diverse range of valuable contracting options.[72] Secondly, what matters is that the range of contracting options should be sufficiently wide and diverse, not that any particular option be included in the range.[73] From the liberal perfectionist point of view, negative freedom is at the service of

[68] Ibid. ch. 8.

[69] Ibid. 160.

[70] D. Kimel, *From Promise to Contract: Towards a Liberal Theory of Contract* (2005), at 118.

[71] J. Raz, *The Morality of Freedom* (1986), at 391.

[72] In this sense, Dagan, 'Pluralism and Perfectionism in Private Law', 112 *Colum. L. Rev.* (2012) 1409; Dagan, 'Autonomy, Pluralism, and Contract Law', 76 *Law Contemp. Probl.* (2013) 19. On Dagan's view, which has evolved since and now relies less on Raz, see further later.

[73] Raz (n. 71) 410.

positive freedom.[74] This means that we must judge the acceptability of a limitation to the freedom of contract in terms of the range of options that remains available, not the specific options that are removed or the reasons for their removal.[75] Thirdly, the available options must be valuable. The state has no task in offering options that are not valuable.[76] Indeed, Raz explicitly rejects 'moral privatization', i.e. 'a tendency to separate morality from the state'.[77] Here we see the perfectionist nature of the Razian approach.[78] It is based on an objective understanding of the good: autonomy is valuable because it enables people to have a good life, which, in turn, legitimates the removal of bad options. In the words of Raz, 'some options one is better off not having'.[79] In practice, this means, for our purposes, in particular, that the state should not support immoral contracts: 'Since autonomy is valuable only if it is directed at the good it supplies no reason to provide, nor any reason to protect, worthless let alone bad options.'[80] However, many different (indeed mutually incompatible) ways of life are valuable. Therefore, Raz's perfectionism is closely related to his 'moral pluralism'.[81]

In particular, liberal perfectionism explicitly supports setting moral limits to the market. As Raz observes:[82]

> the struggle for the right to freedom of contract, and more generally for the freedom of all economic activity, was conducted against a background which sets limits to the market which were taken for granted by almost all liberals. Citizenship was not up for sale. One's right to life could not be disposed of for money. Sexual services were not exchangeable against appointments to the civil service.

While, on the one hand, Razian liberal perfectionism thus permits banning certain contract options because they lack value, on the other hand, freedom of contract requires an active role for the state in ensuring that enough of a person's remaining options are valuable ones. As Raz points out, 'autonomy requires a choice of goods. A choice between good and evil is not enough'.[83] Think, in particular, of his imaginative examples of 'the man in the pit', who cannot get out for the rest of his life but has just enough food to survive, and (especially) 'the hounded woman', who finds herself on a desert island constantly hunted by a wild animal.[84] Neither the man in the pit nor the hounded woman enjoys an autonomous life. Similarly, someone who has only

[74] Ibid. 410.

[75] In contrast, as we will see, for certain other political theories it is the reasons for removal that are decisive. For discourse theory, for example, they have to be general and reciprocal.

[76] See Kimel (n. 70) 131, presenting (and endorsing) Raz's view: 'personal autonomy is valuable only when exercised in pursuit of the good'.

[77] J. Raz, *Ethics in the Public Domain: Essays in the Morality of Law and Politics* (1994), at 98.

[78] See explicitly Raz (n. 71) 417: 'the autonomy principle is a perfectionist principle. Autonomous life is valuable only if it is spent in the pursuit of acceptable and valuable projects and relationships. The autonomy principle permits and even requires government to create morally valuable opportunities, and to eliminate repugnant ones'.

[79] Ibid. 410.

[80] Ibid. 411. In the same sense, Kimel (n. 70) 128.

[81] See Raz (n. 71) 399: 'valuing autonomy leads to the endorsement of moral pluralism'.

[82] Ibid. 251.

[83] Ibid. 379.

[84] Ibid. 373–374.

boring or dangerous contract options available does not enjoy true freedom of contract, even if no specific contracts are banned. The key question thus becomes: how to distinguish good options from bad ones.

Raz rejects what he calls 'epistemic abstinence', i.e. the idea that disagreement about values should provide a reason for the government to abstain from including values among the reasons for its decisions.[85] Disagreement also abounds in other parts of our culture. Think of scientific expertise with regard to all sorts of risks. Scientists do not consider disagreement a reason to abstain from giving their expert opinion, nor even as a reason to qualify their opinion. Nor does the government when having to decide on a policy, or the legislator, when considering the merits of a proposal for legislation, regard the existence of divergent opinions among experts as a reason per se to disregard all the evidence deriving from the field of expertise at hand. The same should apply, Raz argues, for reasons relating to good and bad (and evil), right and wrong, the valuable project and worthless lifestyles. When an evil law is proposed law makers should vote against it for that reason, not for some other, more neutral reason. Exactly, the same applies on this view, it would seem, for evil—and otherwise bad—contracts. They should not be supported by contract law.

B. Freedom of Contracts—in the Plural

1. Normatively Attractive Contract Types

Choice theory is naturally supportive of freedom of contract, or, rather, of freedom of contracts (in the plural), as Dagan and Heller would put it.[86] Following Raz, they argue that the state should make a sufficiently wide and diverse range of contracting options available, adding specifically that this should be achieved through the formulation of contract types.[87] They formulate their core idea as follows: 'contractual freedom means the ability to choose from among a sufficient range of off-the-shelf, normatively attractive contract types'.[88] Where Raz holds, in explicitly perfectionist vein, that the options made publicly available must be valuable, Dagan and Heller employ the less 'full-blown' perfectionist—but frankly also more obscure—formula of 'normatively attractive' contract types.[89]

The normatively attractive contract types to be made available by the liberal state, it seems, by definition would not be caught by any doctrine of contractual immorality.

[85] Raz (n. 77) chs 4 and 5.

[86] See H. Dagan and M. Heller, *The Choice Theory of Contracts* (2017), at 2.

[87] See ibid. 2: 'contractual freedom means the ability to choose from among a sufficient range of off-the-shelf, normatively attractive contract types', and at 106–107 ('An adequate range of types').

[88] Ibid. 2.

[89] See e.g. ibid. 137. Footnote 18, at 163 does not clarify much: 'We deliberately use the adjective "normatively attractive" to describe the contract types the state must supply because—although we do not commit ourselves to full-blown Razian autonomy—we believe that it is "a mistake to lose sight of the value of the activity that is being chosen through one's exercise of autonomy."' The question remains whether their conception of value is subjective (as in utilitarian preferences) or objective (as in various forms of perfectionism, which include not only Razian liberal perfectionism but also various communitarian understandings of the common good). Moreover, it is not clear how the attractiveness can be normative. Normative relates to the ought. An attractive ought? Or, contract types that ought to be attractive?

For why would any legal order consider its own contract types immoral? While the aim of their project is to move contract law thinking and practice beyond general contract law, Dagan and Heller envisage a residual freedom to conclude untypical contracts.[90] However, they do not discuss what role, if any, a doctrine of contracts contrary to public policy or good morals should play with regard to such 'freestanding' contracts. In particular they do not clarify whether these innominate contracts must also be 'normatively attractive' in order to be enforceable.

Dagan and Heller agree with Raz that a state ban on certain specific contract options does not constitute in itself a limitation of freedom of contract. Indeed, making certain options unavailable for a given contract type may even be freedom-enhancing: 'limits within particular contract types can expand human freedom by expanding meaningful choice'.[91] This is the case since, given the liberal state's obligation to ensure 'intra-sphere multiplicity',[92] for every contracting sphere there will be multiple types to choose from. However, the case would be quite different, it seems, if the law removed entire spheres of life from the scope of contracting. Therefore, the extent of the freedom of contracts under the choice theory will depend at least as much on the recognition and definition of contract spheres and sub-spheres.[93]

Thus when the question arises whether commercial surrogacy or the sale of kidneys should be offered as an emerging 'utopian' type, serving local minoritarian or utopian values,[94] this raises the question not only of which contract types, but also which (sub-)spheres should be legally recognized. Put differently, which kinds of human transactions should be within the scope of contractual choice? This seems an important concern for liberals. A risk-averse strategy of simply not recognizing any contract (sub-)spheres, or offering any contract types, that could offend conservatives or other moralists seems deeply problematic from the point of view of liberalism.

As seen in Chapter 3, Dagan and Heller generally reject the proceduralist democratic route for answering such questions.[95] This raises the question of what substantive standard(s) they have for determining which spheres of live should be within the scope of contract law and which others should remain outside it. Put differently, the core aim of their theory is contract law that 'expands the range of meaningful choices people can make to shape their own lives',[96] but what does choice theory have to say about how to limit choice? How should the limits to freedom of contracts be determined?

Presumably their view in this regard is not libertarian, since Dagan and Heller are generally quite dismissive of libertarianism. The Razian option, i.e. to offer only valuable options, would be an easy way out, but it would come at the price of a thick, perfectionist conception of the good, while, as we just saw, Dagan and Heller have been distancing themselves gradually from Razian perfectionism. Nor does the choice

[90] See ibid. 83: 'a residual category of freestanding contracting'.
[91] Ibid. 6 and 137.
[92] Ibid. 6 and 82.
[93] The question of who should be responsible for the definition of the contracting spheres was discussed in Chapter 3.
[94] Cf. Dagan and Heller (n. 86) 4 and 109.
[95] Ibid. 90.
[96] Ibid. 60.

theory, as presented, offer a conception of the person or of value, or, for that matter, address the question of commodification and the related subject/object dichotomy.

2. Self-determination-erasing Markets

However, in a subsequent separate paper, Dagan explicitly addresses the relationship between the market and autonomy as self-authorship.[97] He argues—just as for contract—that the market's fundamental *telos* is to enhance autonomy. The key implication is that a market fails *qua* market if it fails to be inclusive (e.g. by discriminatorily failing to ensure access to everyone). Moreover, this may also be the case when a market undermines autonomy. And this is what happens, he argues, in certain cases of commodification. Dagan mainly focuses his discussion on commodification in the labour market. However, the argument also applies to commodification through other markets. As he writes, 'there are certain types of contract—even beyond the obvious example of slavery—which instrumentalize people to such an extent that might efface their humanity by erasing their self-determination'.[98] Indeed, presumably this provides a reason to be suspicious concerning the existence of markets in a certain types of good in the first place, given that he writes, quite generally, that 'the law of the market must avoid the commodification of people and interpersonal relationships'.[99] In each case, it seems, the test should be the same: would the legal recognition and enforceability of the contract type at hand illegitimately undermine one (or both) of the contract parties' self-determination? The typical response of the law of the market should not be a ban—complete decommodification in Radin's terminology that Dagan adopts—but merely partial commodification, via market regulation.[100]

What this means in concrete cases, for concrete markets for concrete types in concrete contract spheres, is difficult to say. However, the standard for legal intervention, even if not limited only to the near-slavery cases found in sweatshops, but including also, say, cases where self-determination is seriously undermined or threatened, still seems to be relatively permissive. Laser tag games, as in *Omega*, and also activities such as dwarf tossing would probably be permitted. And even in the cases where poverty is the reason that makes a person offer sexual or gestational services or sell their organs, it is not clear that self-determination is best served by making the transaction illegal.

What is clear, however, is that Dagan's view is fundamentally different from Raz's in that he does not propose to remove bad options. Nor does he follow Anderson in the direction of a theory of value. Rather, the only value that can justify moral limits to the market is the value that justifies the market itself, i.e. autonomy. Autonomy, understood as self-authorship, is 'the market's ultimate value',[101] not—or at least not merely—a means for realizing other values. And the autonomous person—and the related subject/object divide—is understood as prior to her contextual valuations rather than as a (partial) result of these.[102] Overall, Dagan's concept of the autonomous

97 Dagan, 'Markets for Self-Authorship', 28 *Cornell Journal of Law and Public Policy* (2018) 577.
98 Ibid. 598.
99 Ibid. 578.
100 Radin's view is more communitarian and will therefore be discussed later, in Section 5.F.
101 Dagan (n. 97) 578, 589, and 598.
102 Anderson's view will discussed later, in Section 5.C.

person, with its reference to the humanity and self-determination of the choosing subject, starts to display some Kantian traits.

C. Regarding Others

1. External Preferences and the Rights of Others

As we saw earlier, it is a key characteristic of utilitarianism, and of the normative welfare economics grounded in it, that it remains agnostic with regard to the merits of the preferences that different members of society happen to have. Dworkin has attacked this agnosticism. In particular, Dworkin criticizes utilitarianism's failure to distinguish between personal preferences about the goods and bads a person herself will obtain, and external preferences about the goods and bads that others should have.[103] External preferences clearly are genuine preferences.[104] Their satisfaction can bring a lot of pleasure, while the failure to satisfy them can be very painful. Therefore, they should count normally in the utilitarian aggregation of (expected) preference satisfaction to be derived from a law or policy under consideration. However, Dworkin argues, if utilitarians do in fact include external preferences in the social utility or social welfare calculus, then in a sense they illegitimately double count the preferences of certain members of society, i.e. those who happen to have external preferences concerning the matter at hand. As a result, the strong egalitarian appeal of utilitarianism, i.e. its claim to count every person only once—exemplified by what Mill referred to as 'Bentham's dictum, "everybody to count for one, nobody for more than one"'[105]—would be corrupted.[106]

However, it is not always easy to disentangle external preferences from personal ones, as the latter are frequently parasitical upon the former (e.g. a racist who wants to be a member of an all-white club). Therefore, for example, in a democratic law making process it will be impossible, as a practical matter, only to count personal preferences. It is for this reason, Dworkin argues, that we need individual political rights to protect us against the external preferences of the majority. Thus, external preferences are at the heart of Dworkin's general theory of the normative foundation of rights.[107]

For our purposes, this would mean essentially that the contracting parties should have a right that protects them against the external preferences of others against their contracts. That would amount in practice to a right to freedom of contract, or, as it is more often called nowadays, to the constitutionalization of freedom of contract.[108]

103 R. Dworkin, *Taking Rights Seriously* (1977), at 234 ff and 275 ff.

104 Mill (n. 54) 152–153 refuses to count the dissatisfaction of external preferences held by the 'moral police' as relevant harm that could justify legal interference under the harm principle: 'With the personal tastes and self-regarding concerns of individuals the public has no business to interfere'.

105 Mill, 'Utilitarianism', in J. S. Mill and J. Benham, *Utilitarianism and Other Essays* ([first published 1861] 1987), at 336.

106 Dworkin (n. 103) 235.

107 Ibid. 277.

108 Dworkin himself seems to reject a right to freedom of contract, apparently on the ground that it is inconceivable that limitations to freedom of contract could be grounded in external preferences (ibid. 278). This may be true for the minimum wage laws that were struck down by the US Supreme Courts in *Lochner*, the example Dworkin cites, but it seems much less certain, for example, in the case of moralistic objections

The justification for the right to freedom of contract would be that individuals should be protected against majority decisions aiming to ban or regulate certain contracts, on the basis of the external preferences the majority in society against the contract (its conclusion, its performance), e.g. because it commodifies a good that should not be exchanged for money.[109]

However, as Hart explained, there are serious problems with this reasoning.[110] The most important one is that this purely procedural argument against some sort of double counting completely ignores the *content* of the external preferences. Applied to the case of freedom of contract this would mean discarding not only negative external preferences, against freedom of contract,[111] but also positive external preferences, held by those who do not for their own purposes (their own conception of the good life) wish to rely on any of the available contract options, but are happy that other people have the widest possible choice. Dworkin aims to ground rights in equality: we need rights to protect us against the external preferences of the majority. Rights will safeguard us from being treated as second-rate citizens relative to those whose external preferences happen to belong to the majority. As Hart points out, on this reasoning, the more tolerant a society becomes, the fewer rights we will have.[112] However, more importantly, on this view the reason for us having rights has nothing to with the intrinsic moral value of the activity protected by them. But surely the wrong done to persons whose contracts are declared void on moralist or paternalist grounds is not merely that they are treated as second rate citizens, compared to those whose external preferences are counted double, but also—and perhaps more importantly—that the law treats their conception of the good as inferior. As Hart underlined, there are certain liberties that we should not be deprived of, whatever the decision procedure.[113]

2. Accommodating Immoral Contracts

As we saw in Chapter 6, Shiffrin convincingly argues that the unconscionability doctrine in the US does not need to be paternalistic.[114] The same would apply to European doctrines such as unfair exploitation. The reason, in both cases, is that we may understand the motivation for the doctrine and its application as self-regarding. The aim is

against commodification (as opposed to egalitarian concerns about the typical sellers of the commodified services or goods).

[109] Dagan and Heller seem to rely on a version of this argument when they claim, against Oman, that his objection against grounding contract in autonomy 'is premised on a demand that law respects the "external preferences"' of those who do not believe in autonomy as much as Dagan and Heller and their followers do. See, respectively, Oman, 'Contract Law and the Liberalism of Fear', 20 *Theoretical Inquiries in Law* (2019) 381, who points to the fact of pluralism in liberal societies, with specific reference to 'religious believers who reject core assumptions of autonomy theory', and Dagan and Heller, 'Freedom, Choice, and Contracts' 20 *Theoretical Inquiries in Law* (2019) 595, at 603–604. Interestingly, with regard to surrogacy contracts Dagan and Heller do allow a regulatory role for 'external public concerns'. See Dagan and Heller (n. 86) 120.

[110] Hart, 'Between Utility and Rights', 79 *Colum. L. Rev.* (1979) 828.

[111] Or, in the case of Dagan and Heller, against freedom of contracts (with the 's'), as the choice between different contract types is the core freedom in the choice theory of contract, as we saw.

[112] Hart (n. 110) 840.

[113] Ibid. 841.

[114] S. V. Shiffrin, 'Paternalism, Unconscionability Doctrine, and Accommodation', 29 *Philosophy and Public Affairs* (2000) 205.

not to overrule the judgement of the person protected by the doctrine about her own best interests. Indeed, by invoking the doctrine that party indicates that she is of the opinion that setting the contract aside would serve her interest. The real reason is that a society, as organized in the state, refuses to be implicated, in this case through the state's institution of contract law, in the immoral project pursued by the exploitative contract. However, Shiffrin argues, that is not necessarily the end of the story, at least not in a liberal state. The reason is that liberal-egalitarians ought to be committed to toleration and accommodation. As a result, on the liberal-egalitarians view, we will sometimes have to accommodate practices that we disapprove of, which may even include practices and projects we consider immoral. And accommodation duties may not be limited to non-interference (something that also libertarians should be fine with). Liberals (unlike libertarians) may sometimes also have to lend their active support to practices they disapprove of. Shiffrin outlines a theory of liberal accommodation, proposing several elements relevant for consideration. Her conclusion is that the exploitative contracts and clauses that unconscionability doctrines typically aim to set aside are not of the kind that require liberal accommodation.

Shiffrin focuses her discussion on the unconscionability doctrine. However, her argument clearly has wider implications, including for our question, i.e. the invalidity of contracts contrary to public policy and good morals. Let's consider first the paternalism issue. For most, if not all, of our examples (such as contracts for selling weapons, soft and hard drugs, *Mein Kampf*, pornography, human organs, human milk; providing sexual services, gestational services, laser tag games, dwarf tossing; polygamous PACS, penalty clauses, clauses excluding liability for intentional harm), it can be argued plausibly that the reasons for refusing to enforce them are self-regarding reasons: the legal order wants to keep its hands clean and not be implicated in—what it considers to be—immoral practices. However, here too the absence of paternalism is not the end of the story, at least not for a liberal (as opposed notably to a libertarian). Because here, even much more so than in the case of unconscionability, the question of liberal accommodation arises. Let's have a closer look at the factors that Shiffrin deemed relevant in identifying whether a certain sphere of activity is appropriate for accommodation. As she writes:

> These factors might include: whether the decisions being supported are highly personal and critical to one's sense of self (e.g., religion cases); whether the decisions are highly personal ones involving the body; whether the denial of accommodation will engender significant harm or loss of agency (medical care, abortion) for the agent; whether the denial of accommodation will make the agent's projects infeasible; and whether the decisions being supported are ones that are difficult to make and involve hard cases, difficult judgments, or areas in which agents are highly vulnerable or susceptible to overvaluing the opinions or effects on others. On the other side, looking at the costs to be borne by those who accommodate, we should consider what sort of support or involvement by others is required: whether it involves mere financial support or other sorts of involvement, whether the support is direct or indirect, whether the support suggests agreement or affiliation, and so on—whether the degree of support or involvement by the bystanders seriously implicates their integrity or interferes

with their capacities to pursue their own autonomous aims, and whether a practice of accommodation in this domain would be especially subject to free-riding.[115]

If it is indeed the case, as Shiffrin argues, that 'in social, highly interconnected settings, respect for autonomy may involve lending assistance to behavior we disagree with',[116] and if liberal-egalitarians should be particularly committed to this idea, as she also points out, then this dramatically changes the pictures. For, while for all the examples above it could be plausibly argued that contractual invalidity would not need to be considered paternalistic, at the same time, it seems, liberal accommodation would require contract enforcement in most of these cases.

Having another look at our examples in the light of the factors on the side of the contracting parties to be accommodated, arguably none of these contracts seem critical to the parties' sense of self, nor would their invalidity in most cases seem to lead to a significant loss of agency for the agent (as it would in abortion). In most cases, the denial of accommodation also would not make the agent's projects infeasible as black markets exist for most of these goods. In contrast, several of them are highly personal ones involving the body: selling human organs and human milk, providing sexual services, and providing gestational services. As to the question of whether the decisions being supported are ones that are difficult to make and involve hard cases, difficult judgements, or areas in which agents are highly susceptible to overvaluing the opinions of others: this does indeed seem to be the case at least for contested commodities (human organs, human milk, sexual services, gestational services), but perhaps also more widely (risk of stigma).

And looking at the other side, i.e. the factors for those who accommodate, in our case the society as a whole: the support is not merely financial and is quite direct. Whether support suggests agreement is a more tricky question. This depends on the nature of contractual obligation (either its actual, objective essence or its perceived role in society), on which there exists strong disagreement as we saw in Chapter 5. However, if we understand contractual validity as entailing not merely enforcement but also public recognition of the contract, then to that extent validity would suggest agreement, while invalidity would suggest disapproval (and even denigration and stigma).[117] (But the argument risks becoming circular if we also consider that the society ought to accommodate many contracts that it actually disapproves of or if it is widely known that the society enforces such contracts solely for reasons of accommodation.) Involvement in immoral contracts does not seem to interfere with the capacities of society or of its members to pursue their own autonomous aims, nor does accommodation in this domain seem especially subject to free-riding.

In summary, the accommodation factors seem to provide quite some concrete guidance in the (comprehensive) liberal-egalitarian determination of the proper limits of freedom of contract.

115 Ibid. 248.

116 Ibid. 250.

117 See Tjon Soei Len, 'Consumer Protection, Sexual Services and Vulnerability: Exploring Social Justice in European Contract Law', 11 *ERCL* (2015) 127; Tjon Soei Len, 'Equal Respect, Capabilities and the Moral Limits of Market Exchange: Denigration in the EU Internal Market', 1 *Transnational Legal Theory* (2017) 1, at 3. On Tjon Soei Len's political-liberal view, see further later.

D. Basic Structure, Basic Liberties, and Basic Capabilities

1. Immoral Contracts in a Well-ordered Society

As we saw in Chapters 5 and 6, Rawls believed that political principles of justice, such as the two principles of justices as fairness, should not apply directly to contract law. In a well-ordered society, he thought, there would be an appropriate division of labour between the basic structure of society, responsible for ensuring background justice, on the one hand, and the rules applicable to transactions between individuals, on the other.[118] This view of the proper subject of political justice has direct and radical implications for our present question. For if contract law is not part of the basic structure of a well-ordered society, then from a Rawlsian point of view, whether or not there is any freedom of contract in a country, and whether or not contracts against public policy and public morality are enforced, is irrelevant in determining whether or not the society is well-ordered and just.

Imagine three different societies. In society A, all contracts are legally recognized and enforced, including those that might be considered 'immoral' or 'illegal' by some standard. In this society, if there is breach of, for example, a contract to kill someone, a contract to publish images of animal torture, a usurious contract, or a contract for the sale of a kidney, the promisee is entitled to a remedy, such as damages or even specific performance. In society B, no contract is enforceable. In this society, there may be a system of private law that simply declares all contracts void, or provides only derisory remedies for breach. Or it could even be a society that has no system of private law and leaves it to the citizens themselves to find effective means for the private enforcement of agreements (e.g. through physical threats) and for deciding which agreements will be enforced by those means. In society C, contracts are enforceable in principle but there are exceptions for certain cases where contract law withholds legal recognition and enforceability, notably in the case of immoral or illegal contracts. Are these three contract law systems all compatible with a well-ordered society? And are all three societies equal from the point of view of justice? Is Rawlsian justice as fairness really indifferent between societies A, B, and C? Unless contract law, or at least its basic structure, is considered to be part of the basic structure of society, it seems, not even the basic liberties, protected by the first principle of justice as fairness, would constitute a potential limit to the freedom of contract. Or, seen from the other side, to the extent that the legal recognition and enforcement of a contract to kill, or to publish images of animal torture, or usurious contracts, or contracts for the sale of a kidney, undermines a person's basic liberties or her reasons for self-respect, is it realistic to expect that this could be prevented or redressed by other social or political institutions, i.e. the ones that according to Rawls properly belong to the basic structure? Presumably, in a well-ordered society there would be criminal sanctions against murder as well as against the publication of images of animal torture, but should the person who fails to commit the murder or to publish the pictures or videos of tortured animals nevertheless be held liable for breach of contract? That seems perverse. And more to the point here,

[118] J. Rawls, *Justice as Fairness: A Restatement* (2001), at 53–54.

how could such a society still be a well-ordered one, where citizens recognize each other as free and equal?

Rawls made it very clear that 'freedom of contract as understood by the doctrine of laissez-faire' is not a basic liberty and, therefore, not protected by the first principle of justice.[119] However, as we also saw in Chapter 5, Kordana and Tabachnick argue that a just society in the Rawlsian sense should provide at least certain contract options.[120] A society is not just in the political liberal sense if there is no freedom of contract at all. In other words, for Kordana and Tabachnick society B is not a just society. However, can a similar argument not be made—perhaps even more convincingly—for the opposite case? Can a society like society A, where all agreements are enforceable in a court of law, whatever their content, really be a just and well-ordered society in the Rawlsian sense? And is there not an argument in political-liberal justice to be made for a version of a society like society C? In other words, aren't the doctrines of contracts contrary to public policy and good morals at least potentially the kind of background rules against which individuals make their own choices and pursue their aims based on their own conception of the good life?

A rather doctrinal way out of this conundrum would be to argue that the political constitution undisputedly is part of the basic structure of society and that the question of whether constitutional rights have horizontal effect, as a constitutional question, is therefore subject to the principles of justice. From this it would follow that a well-ordered society has a just constitution and that the just constitution gives certain horizontal effects to certain constitutional rights, that indirect horizontal effects are compatible with a well-ordered society, and that indirect horizontal effects take place through general clauses such as good morals (as is the case, for example, in Germany), and that therefore in a just and well-ordered society in the Rawlsian sense certain contracts, especially those the enforcement of which would undermine basic liberties of third parties or of the contracting parties themselves (e.g. their human dignity) or would be incompatible with the conception of the moral person underlying the Rawlsian understanding of justice (in particular, a capacity for a conception of justice and for a conception of the good), would be void. This reasoning is doctrinal in that it bypasses the need for contract law itself to be just, by arguing that a just constitution requires horizontal effects (direct or indirect) of certain fundamental rights. However, the more fundamental, substantive moral idea is that the enforcement of contracts violating human rights of the parties themselves or of third parties seems incompatible, at least in certain cases, with a well-ordered society in the Rawlsian sense.[121]

2. Impairing Basic Capabilities

Tjon Soei Len, adopting the point of view of Nussbaum's capabilities approach (which endorses political liberalism),[122] argues that—what she calls—'the defining structure of contract', i.e. the rules that define what a society recognizes as a valid and enforceable

[119] J. Rawls, *A Theory of Justice* ([first published 1971] 1999), at 54.

[120] Kordana and Tabachnick, 'Rawls and Contract Law', 73 *Geo. Wash. L. Rev.* (2005) 598.

[121] On the horizontal effect of fundamental rights under Rawlsian justice as fairness, see J. Klijnsma, *Contract Law as Fairness: A Rawlsian Perspective on the Position of SMEs in European Contract Law* (2014), at 68 ff.

[122] M. C. Nussbaum, *Creating Capabilities: the Human Development Approach* (2011), at 89.

contract, should be regarded as part of the basic structure of society, or, in Nussbaum's terminology, society's responsibility bearing structure.[123] Therefore, these rules and doctrines are subject to the demand of minimum justice, which is to secure the central capabilities at least up to a minimum level.[124] And for that reason, she argues, contracts impairing the basic capabilities of the contracting parties, or of others, should not be legally recognized and enforced. In particular, she argues that doctrines of contractual immorality should also consider the interests and entitlements of others, notably everyone's right to respect for their basic capabilities. As a test case, she discusses the consumer sales of clothes produced in a sweatshop. She argues that such contracts, even though mutually beneficial to the parties, should be held contrary to good morals and therefore void because the transaction necessarily implies the impairment of the basic capabilities of others.[125]

Specifically for the internal market, she argues that the EU cannot leave the definition of acceptable market conduct, and the prevention of injustice in the internal market, entirely to the Member States. Instead, it should formulate a European standard of minimum contract justice.[126] Moreover, the EU's current 'hands-off' approach to the moral limits of its own internal market, she argues, 'gives rise to a political liberal concern regarding denigration, that is, a failure to treat European citizens with equal respect'.[127] She illustrates this risk with the example of sexual morality. By failing to demarcate the moral limits of its own internal market, the EU leaves open the possibility that Member States may ban contracts for sexual services, through doctrines like contractual illegality and immorality, on the basis of reasons that refer to controversial comprehensive doctrines.[128] These may include, for example: religious reasons; ideas about the corruption of the true nature or essential value of sex; the selective use of arguments about health risks that could be directed with equal force to other activities such as certain professional sports; or arguments about gender inequality that fail to differentiate between the experiences of different sex workers some of whom regard their work as female empowerment.[129] As Tjon Soei Len observes:

> when the state refuses to recognise a market exchange as a contract for reasons of [this] sort, the state expresses moral disapproval of the market pursuits that parties

[123] L. K. L. Tjon Soei Len, *Minimum Contract Justice: A Capabilities Perspective on Sweatshops and Consumer Contracts* (2017), at 42 ff.

[124] Nussbaum's list of central capabilities was discussed in Chapter 6.

[125] Tjon Soei Len (n. 123) 145, and *passim*.

[126] Ibid. 146.

[127] Tjon Soei Len, 'Equal Respect, Capabilities and the Moral Limits of Market Exchange' (n. 117) 3.

[128] For an earlier critical discussion of such reasons, see Nussbaum, '"Whether from Reason or Prejudice" Taking Money for Bodily Services', in M. C. Nussbaum, *Sex and Social Justice* (1999) 276, where she observes (ibid. 276) that 'all of us, with the exception of the independently wealthy and the unemployed, take money for the use of our body' and specifically compares sex work with academic work (ibid. 283), observing that 'the fact that we do not think that the professor ... alienates her mind, or turns her thoughts into commodities ... should put us on our guard about making similar conclusions in the case of the prostitute'.

[129] See also Tjon Soei Len, 'Consumer Protection, Sexual Services and Vulnerability' (n. 117) 134. On the other hand, as she points out (ibid. 128), where contracts for sexual services are valid under national laws, in the cases (probably the majority) where the sex worker is in a vulnerable position, the applicability of European consumer protection rules, that treat the client as the weaker party, risks exacerbating the sexual services provider's vulnerability.

are engaged in. At the same time, the state expresses its endorsement of the moral views on which that disapproval is based.[130]

Instead, she argues, the EU should ensure that no European citizen is denigrated in the internal market.

3. Concentrated Externalities

As we saw in Chapter 6, Bagchi locates her understanding of contract law in a liberal state broadly within the Rawlsian frame. With regard to the negative impacts of human activities upon others, she proposes a distinction between two types of externalities—diffuse and concentrated—and a corresponding institutional division of labour, between public regulation and private law.[131] The idea is that when a certain activity has externalities for the public at large (e.g. environmental pollution), then *ex ante* public regulation is preferable, while *ex post* private law remedies are better suited where the victims are more concentrated and individualized.

The best-known contract law response to contractual externalities, as we saw, are the doctrines of contracts against public policy or good morals.[132] On Bagchi's view, then, the application of this doctrine should be reserved to cases of concentrated externalities. The idea would be that the *ex post* evaluation of the facts of the case at hand, extrapolating them to typical parties similarly situated, is likely to reach better results than *ex ante* regulation. In addition, Bagchi argues—indeed this her main point—that the same approach should also be extended to the interpretation of contract. Whenever a clause is ambiguous it should be interpreted in such a way that it creates the least externalities for third parties. In other words, in a liberal state, contract interpretation should prevent people from being unduly confronted with the negative consequences of 'other people's contracts'.

Although the distinction between diffuse and concentrated externalities and the corresponding institutional division of labour between public regulation and private law is intuitive, there is also a risk of (partial) confusion of interest and norms. While it is clear that courts *ex post* are better placed than the legislature *ex ante* when it comes to determining which parties external to a contract have a legitimate claim to the protection of their interests against the impacts of other people's contracts, it is less clear that private litigation is a better method than democratic deliberation for determining which types of interests should count in the first place. Take the question of external preferences, discussed previously. Should the welfare losses (whether in terms of disgust or property prices) of people living near places where dwarf tossing (the 'Embassy Club' discotheque in Morsang-sur-Orge),[133] playing at killing each other (the 'Omega Spielhallen' in Bonn),[134] or sexual services (the red light district in Amsterdam) are

[130] Tjon Soei Len, 'Equal Respect, Capabilities and the Moral Limits of Market Exchange' (n. 117) 12.

[131] Bagchi, 'Other People's Contracts', 32 *Yale Journal of Regulation* (2015) 211.

[132] In addition there is invalidity for illegality, i.e. when a contract prohibited by statute is also void, as, for example, in the case of cartel agreements. See Art. 101 TFEU.

[133] *Manuel Wackenheim v. France*, Communication No 854/1999, U.N. Doc. CCPR/C/75/D/854/1999 (2002).

[134] Case C-36/02, *Omega Spielhallen- und Automatenaufstellungs-GmbH v. Oberbürgermeisterin der Bundesstadt Bonn* (EU:C:2004:614).

offered, count as harm? And what about the impact on specific contracts of general claims that certain goods are corrupted when they are exchanged for money:[135] can such moral externalities even be categorized as concentrated or diffuse? It seems that the institutional division of regulatory labour in a liberal state depends at least in part on a prior idea of what kind of externalities a liberal state should take into account in the first place, based, for example, on prior commitments to fundamental rights and freedoms. And given 'the fact of reasonable pluralism', as Rawls called it, it is not so clear that private law litigation, which concentrates first and foremost on the interest of the private parties, is a better means than public deliberation for considering the diffuse public views found in liberal societies with a view to determining relevant liberal principles.

Having said that, once the prior commitments of the liberal state are settled in a general way (e.g. in constitutional rights having indirect horizontal effects, via a general clause, on the invalidity of contracts contrary to good morals) and it comes to interpreting these prior abstract commitments with a view to determining their concrete implications for the rights and obligations between private parties, then what Rawls called 'the burdens of judgement' (i.e. the different life experiences with which we come to matters of justice, in this case the interpretation of the same right for different cases) may become particularly relevant. Especially in the case of concentrated externalities, judicial 'situation-sense' may be a better way of properly considering the relevant interests and points of view of everyone truly affected.[136]

4. Libertarian

Freedom of contract is a central tenet of libertarian neoliberalism. Libertarians regard freedom of contract—in terms of Berlin's famous distinction[137]—as a matter of negative liberty, i.e. as freedom from state interference.[138] And doctrines invalidating contracts for reasons of illegality and immorality are met with great suspicion.

A. Self-ownership

According to Nozick, each individual has an unconditional right to freedom of contract concerning her own property and her own person. For Nozick, this right to freedom of contract derives from the absolute character of the right to ownership, including self-ownership, which includes an absolute right to free exchange.

135 This is Sandel's core claim, which will be discussed later.

136 On situation-sense, see K. N. Llewellyn, *The Common Law Tradition: Deciding Appeals* (1960), at 121 ff.

137 Berlin, 'Two Concepts of Liberty', in H. Hardy (ed.), *Liberty* (2002) 166.

138 Cf. also Dagan and Heller (n. 86) 4: '"freedom of contract" stands for a popular version of Lochner era laissez-faire capitalism. Even within contract theory, the term retains that libertarian flavor. It is most often associated with an understanding of freedom in terms of negative liberty'. Cf. also Kronman, 'Contract Law and Distributive Justice', 89 *Yale L.J.* (1980) 472, at 474: 'The libertarian theory of contract law is premised upon the belief that individuals have a moral right to make whatever voluntary agreements they wish for the exchange of their own property, so long as the rights of third parties are not violated as a result.'

Thus, in Nozickian contract law there is very little room (if any) for legal doctrines such as illegality and—in particular—immorality. For a libertarian, there are few public policy reasons eligible to lead to the invalidity of a contract. Nozick explicitly writes: 'Voluntary consent opens the border to crossings.... My nonpaternalistic position holds that someone may choose (or permit another) to do to himself *anything*, unless he has acquired an obligation to some third party not to do or allow it.'[139] From this point of view there does not seem to be any reason why, for example, commercial surrogacy,[140] sexual services, organ selling, sale of soft and hard drugs, sale of weapons,[141] or dwarf tossing should not become the object of a legally recognized and enforceable contract. The same would apply for voluntary COVID-19 infection, with or without remuneration, as part of a vaccine study.[142] Rather, in all these cases, in the eyes of a Nozickian libertarian the invalidity of the contract for illegality or immorality would probably amount to an illegitimate interference with (self)ownership.

Turning to the example of the *Omega* case, Nozickian libertarians clearly would see no difficulty whatsoever in allowing the laser tag game,[143] as the participation in the game was consensual. Indeed, they would fiercely object against any interference with the freedom of contract in such a case. Nozick underlines that 'the state may not use its coercive apparatus ... in order to prohibit activities to people for their own good or protection'.[144] So, if people want to play at killing each other that is fine, as long as the game is entirely voluntary (and remains limited to playing). According to Nozick, pursuant to the principle of self-ownership one could even become a voluntary slave.[145] What matters is that it is consensual. Not respecting free exchange: now that would mean an affront to human dignity. It would make individuals become means to the ends of others (i.e. to their moralist conceptions of the good).

B. Inalienable Rights

Barnett regards his theory as Nozickian, as we saw in Chapter 5. Nevertheless, he concedes that some rights are inalienable. He writes:

> The subjects of most rights transfer agreements are entitlements that are indisputably alienable. In such cases the rules of contract law are entirely sufficient to explain and justify a judicial decision. However, in rare cases—such as agreements amounting to

[139] R. Nozick, *Anarchy, State, and Utopia* (1974), at 58 (emphasis in original).

[140] I refer especially to the 'rent a womb' aspect here. Cf. Brenhouse, 'India's Rent-A-Womb Industry Faces New Restrictions', *Time*, 5 June 2010. When it comes to giving up one's genetically own child there clearly is (at some point) one more person's liberty involved.

[141] On the ground that there is a difference between owning weapons and using them. Certain uses may well be prohibited in the interest of protecting life and limb of third parties.

[142] See Chini,'Volunteers Offered €4,000 to Be Infected with the Coronavirus', *The Brussels Times*, 9 March 2020; Callaway, 'Hundreds of People Volunteer to Be Infected with Coronavirus. Support Grows for a Controversial "Human Challenge" Vaccine Study—But No Trial Is Yet Planned', *Nature*, 22 April 2020.

[143] The *Omega* case was presented earlier, in Section 1.G.

[144] Nozick (n. 139) ix.

[145] Ibid. 331: 'The ... question about an individual is whether a free system will allow him to sell himself into slavery. I believe that it would. (Other writers disagree.)'

> slavery arrangements or requiring the violation of another's rights—contract law's dependency on rights theory will be of crucial importance in identifying appropriate concerns about the substance of voluntary agreements. For example, agreements to transfer inalienable rights—rights that for some reason cannot be transferred— . . . , would not, without more, be valid and enforceable contracts.[146]

Frankly, that does not bring us much further. Indeed, the claim that inalienable rights cannot be transferred is entirely definitional. The question is which libertarian reasons might exist for considering certain rights inalienable. In other words, what reasons in liberty might there be for disallowing the transfer of an entitlement? Indeed, it seems very difficult, for example, to make a case on strictly libertarian grounds against most types of commodification.

C. Degrading Promises

As we saw in Chapter 5, Fried understands the legally binding force as being based on the moral obligation to keep a promise.[147] This raises the question of what should happen to immoral promises. Are immoral promises conceivable? The answer seems positive (think, say, about a promise to lie). If so, can they be morally binding? That seems more doubtful. If they are not morally binding can they still be legally binding and enforceable? That seems even more doubtful—unless, of course, other reasons than a promise can justify the legal recognition and enforcement of the transaction at hand, but that would bring us outside promise theory. While Fried recognizes duress as a ground to 'dispense from obligation',[148] as well as unconscionability,[149] he does not generally address the question of whether illegality or immorality may also render contracts void. Still, in his discussion of unconscionability we find a glimpse of what his approach might be. And it seems moralistic rather than libertarian. He writes: 'Imagine an agreement between adult, competent persons to engage in some degrading sexual practice. Respect for their autonomy may mean that the law will not interfere with their arrangement, but surely it does not require that judges, jurors, and bailiffs involve themselves in enforcing its implementation.'[150] Presumably, a Nozickian libertarian would disagree strongly—and not only she. For it is not at all clear that the libertarian state—or a liberal-egalitarian one, for that matter—would refuse to recognize and enforce the contract merely because in the state's view the

[146] Barnett, 'A Consent Theory of Contract', 86 *Colum. L. Rev.* (1986) 269, at 293.

[147] C. Fried, *Contract as Promise: A Theory of Contractual Obligation* ([first published 1981] 2nd ed., 2015), at 14.

[148] Ibid. 92. Sceptical, Radin, *Contested Commodities* (n. 15) 52: 'Invalidating "contracts" produced under duress is no more than free-market hygiene.'

[149] In the second edition he explicitly follows Shiffrin's 'magisterial treatment' of the problem, which was discussed in Chapter 6 and also in this chapter. See ibid. 154: 'the law will not prevent the promisor from paying a stale debt or honoring an unwritten obligation. And so it is with unconscionable bargains: the law will not prevent promisors from honoring them, but it will not lend its agency to what it believes is harsh, unfair, or just plain ugly. It says: "This is an awful way to treat another human being. Go ahead and do it if you want, but don't ask me to help."'

[150] Ibid. 155.

practice was 'degrading'. The case might well be different, of course, for the communitarian state, depending on the community's values and traditions with regard to sexual practices.

In another book, *Modern Liberty*, Fried dismisses what he calls 'the complaint that goes under the nonsense tag "commodification"'.[151] However, there too, although he rejects the criminalization of prostitution, he argues that 'the government does not need to underwrite what they do by, for instance, licensing and certifying prostitutes or even enforcing contracts for prostitution'.[152] The argument here seems akin to Shiffrin's clean-hands argument for a society's refusal to enforce unconscionable contracts, except for the notable absence of the entire accommodation part of it (about lending support to practices one does *not* underwrite). In any case, unless Fried's argument is limited to moral reasons in the narrow sense of what we reciprocally owe to each other as human beings (such as the prohibition of exploitation), here too it seems to open the door to pervasive contract law moralism, where disgust or even mere disapproval suffices to refuse contract enforcement. Whatever it is, that cannot be a libertarian position.

D. Contractual Freedom as Discovery Procedure

One would expect to find also in Hayek a strong advocate of freedom of contract, not so much because of an inalienable right to property, including self-ownership, but rather because any attempt to interfere with the free market ('the spontaneous order'), with a view to protecting some public interest or other, inevitably constitutes merely the first step towards total governmental planning. Not only would this bring us inevitably on the 'road to serfdom',[153] but also it would be futile because of the incurable ignorance of those who would be deciding on the public policy reasons for interfering with freedom of contract.[154] In particular, the latter argument of competition as discovery procedure, has also been endorsed for European contract law, for example by Grundmann, who writes that 'competition, and in particular freedom of contract, have indeed proven to be probably the most powerful discovery device. Therefore in principle, legislatures should not have the say, and often they do not even have (superior) knowledge'.[155]

However, in reality Hayek's own view on freedom of contract was surprisingly moderate. It is true that in *Law, Legislation and Liberty*, he repeatedly cites the binding force and the freedom of contract as the foundations of an open and free society. However, in *The Constitution of Liberty* he expresses his view specifically on contractual invalidity and it appears rather nuanced. He writes:

[151] C. Fried, *Modern Liberty and the Limits of Government* (2007), at 74.
[152] Ibid. 138.
[153] F. A. Hayek, *The Road to Serfdom* ([first published 1944] 2005).
[154] Hayek, 'Competition as Discovery Procedure', in Hayek, *New Studies in Philosophy, Economics and the History of Ideas* (1978), ch. 12; F. A. Hayek, *Law, Legislation and Liberty*, Vol. I ([first published 1982] 1993), at 13.
[155] Grundmann, 'European Contract Law(s) of What Colour?', *ERCL* (2005) 184, at 195.

> No modern state has tried to enforce all contracts, nor is it desirable that it should. Contracts for criminal or immoral purposes, gambling contracts, contracts in restraint of trade, contracts permanently binding the services of a person, or even some contracts for specific performances are not enforced. Freedom of contract, like freedom in all other fields, really means that the permissibility of a particular act depends only on general rules and not on its specific approval by authority. It means that the validity and enforceability of contract must depend only on those general, equal, known rules by which all other legal rights are determined, and not on the approval of its particular content by an agency of the government.[156]

This seems to be more an argument for statutory general rules, as opposed to the contextual application of general clauses on good morals such as § 138 *BGB*, than an argument for extensive freedom of contract. And, most surprisingly, it seems to allow, in principle, for the invalidity of contracts in most of the examples presented in the Introduction to this chapter. Sales contracts for weapons, soft and hard drugs, and human organs, and service contracts for sexual services, gestational services, and perhaps also laser tag games and dwarf tossing, could be declared void—or the transactions could be heavily regulated—even merely for the reason that the contract has a 'criminal' or 'immoral' purpose, it seems, as long as this is done via generally applicable rules (typically a statute), that the parties can know in advance. One possible explanation for this surprising view of the constitution of contractual liberty might be that immoral contracts are—or should be—only peripheral to a market economy. Hence, their prohibition would not bring any significant loss. However, such a view would hardly be libertarian. Indeed, it would sound more like a utilitarian argument of the kind made, as we saw, by welfare economists.

E. *Alemo* as a European *Lochner*

Some positions taken by participants in the European contract law debate can be assimilated to libertarian political philosophy. In the first place, this includes all discourses speaking of interference with 'the freedom of contract' as if such a freedom already existed in some pre-positive sense—as if European citizens enjoyed a natural right to freedom of contract that certain EU rules then illegitimately interfered with. Such arguments are quite recurrent, and in German legal scholarship they are almost standard.[157] As we saw, the European Commission's Action Plan was also phrased in similarly libertarian (or neoliberal) language: in the common frame of reference, it stated that 'contractual freedom should be the guiding principle; restrictions should only be foreseen where this could be justified with good reasons'.[158]

Naturally, pleas for the constitutionalization of freedom of contract also tend to be closely connected to libertarian philosophy. On such views, a constitutional right to freedom of contract would simply mean the positivization of a natural right

[156] F. A. Hayek, *The Constitution of Liberty* ([first published 1960] 2006), at 201–202.
[157] As one example, see Basedow, 'Freedom of Contract in the European Union', *ERPL* 16 (2008) 901.
[158] Commission Action Plan (n. 24) 62; see also at 92–94.

that individuals already have. In this regard, the *locus classicus* is, of course, *Lochner v. New York* (1905), where the US Supreme Court overturned a maximum-hours law for bakers and thus, effectively, constitutionalized freedom of contract.[159] The US Supreme Court has long since changed course. However, the CJEU might be moving in the opposite direction. In *Alemo-Herron*, after a reminder of its settled case law that the provisions of EU directives must be interpreted in a manner consistent with the fundamental rights as set out by the Charter of Fundamental Rights of the European Union (CFREU), the CJEU held that the freedom to conduct a business, which is protected by Article 16 CFREU, is a 'fundamental right [which] covers, inter alia, freedom of contract'.[160] In the past it had often been argued, especially by ordoliberals, that such a constitutional right to freedom of contract was already enshrined in the (structure of the) European treaties;[161] however, the Court had always rejected these claims.[162] Today, *Alemo* may be regarded as a European *Lochner*—similarly symbolic, albeit probably with a much narrower scope and impact. Yet, European libertarians (most often referred to as 'neoliberals') may hail it as a first step in the right direction.[163]

5. Communitarian

A. Private Contracts and the Common Good

Communitarians question the importance of self-determination. They only have limited confidence in individual rational choice. That gives them less reason than other political philosophies to be champions of freedom of contract. Communitarians are also, more than any of the other political philosophies under discussion in this book, inclined to question the legal validity of certain contracts when this is considered necessary for the respect of community values and tradition. In other words, communitarian perfectionism naturally leads to a more limited range of contracting options

[159] *Lochner v. New York*, 198 U.S. 45 (1905). In his dissenting opinion Oliver Wendell Holmes observed that 'a constitution is not intended to embody a particular economic theory'. Cf. M. J. Horwitz, *The Transformation of American Law 1870–1960: The Crisis of Legal Orthodoxy* (1992), at 5.

[160] Case C-426/11, *Alemo-Herron and Others v. Parkwood Leisure Ltd* (EU:C:2013:521). For critical discussions, see Weatherill, 'Use and Abuse of the EU's Charter of Fundamental Rights: On the Improper Veneration of "Freedom of Contract"', *ERPL* (2014) 167; Bartl and Leone, 'Minimum Harmonisation after *Alemo-Herron*: The Janus Face of EU Fundamental Rights Review', *European Constitutional Law Review* (2015) 140; Hesselink, 'The Justice Dimensions of the Relationship Between Fundamental Rights and Private Law', in H. Collins (ed.), *European Contract Law and the Charter of Fundamental Rights* (2018) 167.

[161] See e.g. Brandner and Ulmer, 'The Community Directive on Unfair Terms in Consumer Contracts: Some Critical Remarks on the Proposal Submitted by the EC Commission', 28 *CMLR* (1991) 647, at 652; Leible, 'Fundamental Freedoms and European Contract Law', in S. Grundmann (ed.), *Constitutional Values and European Contract Law* (2008) 63, at 65; Herresthal, 'Constitutionalisation of Freedom of Contract in European Union Law', in K. S. Ziegler and P. M. Huber (eds), *Current Problems in the Protection of Human Rights: Perspectives From Germany and the UK* (2013) 89, at 91.

[162] See e.g. Case C-484/08, *Caja de Ahorros y Monte de Piedad de Madrid* (EU:C:2010:309), at 45–49.

[163] Contrast, Weatherill (n. 160) 167: 'I am aware that by writing this note I am contributing to saving this alarming decision from its deserved fate in a cold and watery grave. But, sadly, we are not allowed simply to consign maverick rulings of the Court to oblivion. We have to address them. What I try to do here is to expose the deeply flawed reasoning and assumptions that underpin the ruling in *Alemo-Herron* in the hope that it will not be repeated.'

than libertarians, liberals, and utilitarians would require or recommend. In particular, they have no principled difficulty in allowing conceptions of public morality and decency—what liberal-egalitarians would call 'external preferences'—to play a role in determining the range of contracts that are legally enforceable.

Thus, in most communitarian ideas of contract law the doctrines of immorality and illegality will play a comparatively prominent role. For a communitarian there is no good reason for a society to recognize and enforce contracts that are immoral by the standards of the society's own culture and tradition. Indeed, instead the communitarian state (i.e. the political community through its public institutions) should make sure that contract law also contributes to the common good. In the words of Kymlicka, 'a communitarian state can and should encourage people to adopt conceptions of the good that conform to the community's way of life, while discouraging conceptions of the good that conflict with it'.[164] And there is no reason why a communitarian should refrain from applying this agenda also to contract law—quite the contrary. Just as a communitarian state is a perfectionist state, so too is a communitarian contract law a perfectionist contract law, equally committed to encouraging practices in accordance with the community's ways of life and discouraging practices deviating from it.

As a result, in each of the examples mentioned in the Introduction to this chapter (i.e. commercial surrogacy, laser tag, etc.) contracts could be held invalid for being contrary to public policy or good morals, depending on the standards prevailing in the specific community at hand. Crucially, the latter should be determined, not necessarily through majority decision but, rather, hermeneutically (the generally preferred communitarian method), as a matter of interpretation of the community's own culture, traditions, and values.

Having said that, we should not identify contract law communitarianism, and its approach to the moral limits to freedom of contract, simply with moralism and conservatism. Indeed, much of the—often progressive—critique of commodification and market imperialism is grounded in the communitarian critique of dominant liberal and utilitarian conceptions of the person and of value. As we will see, this critique is sophisticated and nuanced, often much more so than the concepts of value, preference, and choice they target.

B. Blocked Exchanges

Walzer's pluralist theory of distributive justice distinguishes different spheres of justice, each with its own distributive principles appropriate for a specific type of social goods (membership, security and welfare, money and commodities, free time, recognition, and political power, among others).[165] Injustices occur, in particular, according to Walzer, when goods or their distributive principles cross the boundaries between spheres. Therefore, on this view, in particular, preserving the boundaries of the sphere where commodities are exchanged for money is a core concern of distributive

164 Kymlicka (n. 62) 220.
165 M. Walzer, *Spheres of Justice: A Defense of Pluralism and Equality* (1983).

justice.[166] And 'blocked exchanges' are the principal means by which the boundaries are upheld.[167] Thus, Walzer understands illegitimate commodification, i.e. the undue expansion of the sphere of money ('the dominance of money outside its sphere'),[168] as unjustified redistribution. In line with his geographical metaphor Walzer refers to political redistribution, i.e. political boundary revision, as 'moral irredentism'.[169] Similarly, on this view we could regard the contract law doctrines that block exchanges by invalidating contracts contrary to public policy or good morals as moral border control.

C. The Plurality of Value

At first sight, Anderson's pluralist theory of value resembles Walzer's in that it also concentrates on sphere differentiation.[170] However crucially, while Walzer presents a pluralist theory of distributive justice, distinguishing different spheres of justice, Anderson offers a theory of value, differentiating spheres of valuation. Her theory is pragmatist in that it understands comparative value judgements as functionally related to specific contexts.[171] At the same time, however, the theory has several distinctly communitarian traits.[172]

For Anderson, rational choice is strongly grounded in a plurality of ethical contexts.[173] She rejects the individualistic understanding of value. As she puts it, 'the good is grounded in communities of valuing, not just individualistic liking'.[174] Thus she emphasizes the role of social norms in valuation and rational choice: valuing happens by 'embedding' a good in a set of social practices.[175] Moreover, she defines democratic citizenship in terms of fraternity.[176] Finally, her backward-looking emphasis on diachronic narrative unity in self-understanding, where the past confers meaning upon present choices,[177] resonates with the hermeneutical approach to identity, culture, and tradition characteristic of communitarianism. Therefore, and because this book does

[166] Ibid. ch. 4.
[167] Ibid. 100.
[168] Ibid. 120.
[169] Ibid. 120
[170] E. Anderson, *Value in Ethics and Economics* (1993), at 143.
[171] Ibid. 47.
[172] Anderson's theory has in common with Razian liberal perfectionism that it concentrates on the social conditions for autonomy, demanding a wide range of significant options to choose from as a precondition for freedom. However, she differs from Raz (and from Dagan and Heller) in her anti-consequentialist focus on spheres of expressive valuation, rather than on a range of legal forms (e.g. contract types) to choose from, and in the communitarian way she embeds these different valuations.
[173] Rejecting the dichotomies between reason and emotions and between reason and social norms (ibid. 45), she endorses Taylor's understanding of practical reason. 'To be practically rational', she writes, is just 'to make sense of ourselves and our actions on the basis of reasons we can reflectively endorse' (ibid. 65).
[174] Anderson (n. 170) 94, with reference to Walzer (n. 165).
[175] Anderson (n. 170) 24.
[176] Ibid. 158.
[177] Ibid. 24 and 34. She refers to A. MacIntyre, *After Virtue* (3rd ed., 2007), ch. 15 ('The Virtues, the Unity of a Human Life and the Concept of Tradition'), where he proposes, with regard to narrative selfhood, 'to envisage each human life as a whole, as a unity, whose character provides the virtues with an adequate telos' (at 204) and points out that 'the narrative of any one life is part of an interlocking set of narratives' (at 218).

not discuss philosophical pragmatism separately as a leading contemporary political theory, it seems appropriate to discuss Anderson's important theory here.[178]

Anderson's expressive pluralist theory of value has direct implications for the ethical limitations of the market, including the limits to freedom of contract on ethical grounds. In particular, her emphasis on the plurality of goods, each properly valued in accordance with its own set of social norms in its own social sphere, provides the basis for a fundamental critique of commodification and of market imperialism. 'Economic goods', she observes, 'are goods that are properly valued as commodities and properly produced and exchanged in accordance with market norms'.[179] The proper mode of valuation for commodities is 'use', as opposed to other, higher modes of valuation such as 'respect'. The market sphere, characterized by market exchanges of economic goods subject to market norms, must be differentiated from other spheres, for example the sphere of personal relations—a sphere of intimacy and commitment where personal goods are shared and where the norms of gift exchange prevail.[180] Anderson points to prostitution as 'the classic example of how commodification debases a gift value and its giver'.[181] Commodified sex, she argues, is degraded and degrading: 'The commodification of sexual "services" destroys the kind of reciprocity required to realize human sexuality as a shared good. Each party values the other only instrumentally, not intrinsically. But the nature of the good exchanged implies a particular degradation of the prostitute.'[182] Her argument is not meant as a conclusive case for the prohibition of prostitution, but rather as an argument for the legitimacy of state regulation in order to bring ethical limits to the market, thus restoring boundaries between different social spheres, where different goods are valued on the basis of different social norms.

More generally, sphere differentiation does not necessarily mean sphere segregation. Sometimes partial commodification, through institutions combining market with non-market norms, may be appropriate.[183] This suggests practical solutions like regulation as opposed to market bans and contractual invalidity, even though Anderson does not explain how proper valuation would take place in such hybrid situations. What is clear, however, is that Anderson adopts rather thick, perfectionist conceptions both of the person and of the good, in direct and explicit contrast to liberal understandings of practical reason, value, choice, and markets.

[178] Cf. Van Staveren, 'Communitarianism and the Market: A Paradox', 67 *Review of Social Economy* (2009) 25, who discusses Anderson as a 'well-known communitarian' and as one of the 'major communitarian philosophers', together with Etzioni, MacIntyre, and Walzer.

[179] Anderson (n. 170) 143.

[180] Ibid. 150.

[181] Ibid. 154.

[182] Ibid. 154.

[183] Ibid. 147. Critical nevertheless, Van Staveren (n. 178) 33: 'Anderson's dichotomous categories of commodities versus moral goods and economic value versus shared value do not help much in furthering our understanding of how moral and economic behaviour are related—instead it conveniently ignores and hides the ways in which they are interdependent.'

D. Corruption

In *What Money Can't Buy: The Moral Limits of Markets*, Sandel traces how, in the past three decades, market reasoning, i.e. the logic of buying and selling, has pervaded our lives, also reaching many spheres of life 'where it does not belong' and eroding appropriate moral standards.[184] He discusses many striking instances of how market principles crowd out ethical standards—some exceptional, others much more mundane.

Sandel's approach is strongly perfectionist, claiming that there are higher and lower, as well as right and wrong, ways of valuing goods. He formulates two main objections against the transgression of market reasoning into other spheres of life,[185] i.e. (1) the fairness objection and (2) the corruption objection.[186] As to the first objection, when the contracting parties have very unequal bargaining power there is reason to worry about how free, voluntary, and autonomous their agreement to sell the goods or service at hand really was. The corruption objection, instead, is directed against the commodification of goods that should not be sold on the market even in a more egalitarian society. The reason is the corrosive tendency of markets: certain goods are tainted, demeaned, and degraded when turned into commodities.[187] As Sandel explains:

> the argument from corruption cannot be met by establishing fair bargaining conditions. If the sale of human body parts is intrinsically degrading, a violation of the sanctity of the human body, then kidney sales would be wrong for rich and poor alike. The objection would hold even without the coercive effect of crushing poverty.[188]

Sandel's notion of corruption strongly builds upon Anderson's idea of proper valuation.[189]

When the norms of the market crowd out the moral norms governing other spheres of life, then, in the first place, in some instances this may well be inefficient. In other words, the objectives of commodification are not reached because social welfare is not increased but reduced. The most famous example in this regard is the sale of human blood crowding out blood donation in the US, as a result of which the quality of blood went down (more of the supplied blood was contaminated), while the administrative costs and the prices went up.[190] However, the wider and more important effect, Sandel

[184] Sandel (n. 27) 7. For a similarly bleak reconstructive diagnosis, albeit with different accents, see T. Judt, *Ill Fares the Land: A Treatise on Our Present Discontents* (2010), *passim*, e.g. at 1–2: 'Something is profoundly wrong with the way we live today. For thirty years we have made a virtue out of the pursuit of material self-interest: indeed, this very pursuit now constitutes whatever remains of our sense of collective purpose. We know what things cost but have no idea what they are worth.'

[185] Ibid. 110. See earlier Sandel, 'What Money Can't Buy: The Moral Limits of Markets', *The Tanner Lectures on Human Values*, delivered at Brasenose College, Oxford May 11 and 12, 1998, at 98 ff.

[186] The distinction corresponds roughly to the two types of reasons for limiting freedom of contract distinguished in this book and discussed respectively in the previous chapter (Chapter 6) and the present one (Chapter 7).

[187] Sandel (n. 27) 9–10.

[188] Sandel, *Tanner Lectures* (n. 185) 94.

[189] Explicitly, Sandel (n. 27) 208, footnote 18.

[190] R. Titmuss, *The Gift Relationship: From Human Blood to Social Policy* ([first published 1970] 2018). Another famous example was the experiment conducted in private day-care centres in Haifa, Israel. Parents were often late in picking up their children, as a result of which teachers had to wait before they could go home. When fines for delay were introduced the number of late comers went up, rather than down. The

submits, is that moral standards are eroded.[191] This is a moral loss at the interpersonal level. Altruism is like a muscle, he suggests: it needs exercise to grow and remain strong.[192] It is also a loss at the societal and political level. From the point of view of Sandel's thick communitarian republicanism, political communities are based on fraternity and virtue.[193] From this thick communitarian conception of republican citizenship, he criticises the commodification of military service, i.e. the privatization of war, which, just like the privatization of prisons, he argues, corrupts the good of self-government.[194]

As one relatively banal example of how market norms crowd out civic norms, Sandel describes the different ways in which today we can pay to jump the queue,[195] ranging from priority boarding at airports, express lanes ('Lexus lanes') at certain American freeways, to 'concierge doctors' (who are available 24/7), with the result, he observes, that 'the ethics of the queue—"first come, first served"—is being displaced by the ethics of the market—you get what you pay for"'.[196] A society probably should not ban jumping the queue schemes, even if they erode moral standards, but what about some more challenging examples? Think of emission trading schemes. Isn't a market in pollution rights intrinsically immoral? Shouldn't the sale of emission rights be declared null and void? The EU has done the exact opposite: it has set up the world's largest greenhouse gas emissions market.[197] Sure enough, when operating efficiently such markets may make a significant contribution to the reduction of greenhouse gas emissions.[198] However, that does not per se answer the question posed: isn't it immoral to buy the right to pollute?[199] An emissions trading scheme, even if effective in slowing down global warming, also normalizes pollution and therefore seems to send the wrong moral message. As Sandel observes, 'turning pollution into a commodity to be bought and sold removes the moral stigma that is properly associated with it'.[200] Consequently, a market in the right to pollute carries a moral cost, Sandel suggests, in that it 'outsources an obligation', which erodes moral standards.

Sandel does not propose any final answers for any of the examples he discusses. The main reason for this is that people differ in their moral judgements. His point is rather that a political debate should be started on the moral limits of the market. For our present purposes, this would mean a debate on which contracts should be banned for the reason that buying and selling certain goods corrupts and degrades them and crowds out the norms and standards for their proper valuation. Even more specifically, this

explanation seems to be that parents read the penalty as a price for a new service; market norms crowded out social norms. See Gneezy and Rustichini, 'A Fine Is a Price', 29 *J. Legal Stud.* (2000) 1.

191 These effects can also be re-read as welfare effects but, as Sandel asks: why should we?

192 Sandel (n. 27) 130.

193 Sandel, *Tanner Lectures* (n. 185) 108.

194 Ibid. 109 ff.

195 Sandel (n. 27) ch. 1.

196 Ibid. 28.

197 Directive (EU) 2018/410, OJ 2018 L 76, Amending Directive 2003/87/EC, OJ 2003 L 275, to enhance cost-effective emission reductions and low-carbon investments, and Decision (EU) 2015/1814.

198 Cf. Commission, 'EU ETS Handbook' (2015), at 5: 'It allows a set environmental outcome to be achieved at lowest costs.'

199 Sandel, 'It's Immoral to Buy the Right to Pollute', *New York Times*, 15 December 1997.

200 Ibid.

would be a debate on the role EU contract law should have in setting moral limits to the internal market.

E. Societal Disintegration

A classic statement of the idea that societies will disintegrate unless the law enforces morality and suppresses vice, can be found in the response, in a lecture in 1959, by Lord Devlin—who later became a member of the House of Lords—to the Wolfenden report, that had been published in 1957, and that had recommended the decriminalization of homosexual acts in private between consenting adults. In a still often cited passage, where he compared vice to treason, Devlin wrote:

> it is not possible to set theoretical limits to the power of the State to legislate against immorality. It is not possible to settle in advance exceptions to the general rule or to define inflexibly areas of morality into which the law is in no circumstances to be allowed to enter. Society is entitled by means of its laws to protect itself from dangers, whether from within or without. ... The law of treason is directed against aiding the king's enemies and against sedition from within. The justification for this is that established government is necessary for the existence of society and therefore its safety against violent overthrow must be secured. But an established morality is as necessary as good government to the welfare of society. Societies disintegrate from within more frequently than they are broken up by external pressures. There is disintegration when no common morality is observed and history shows that the loosening of moral bonds is often the first stage of disintegration, so that society is justified in taking the same steps to preserve its moral code as it does to preserve its government and other essential institutions. The suppression of vice is as much the law's business as the suppression of subversive activities; it is no more possible to define a sphere of private morality than it is to define one of private subversive activity. It is wrong to talk of private morality or of the law not being concerned with immorality as such or to try to set rigid bounds to the part which the law may play in the suppression of vice.[201]

Hart famously responded to Devlin's lecture, which led to the Hart-Devlin debate, an early precursor to the liberal-communitarian debates that would dominate political philosophy in the 1980s.[202] Hart does accept the very general notion of morality as 'the cement of society', in the sense that without any shared morality there would be nothing more than a group of individuals. However, he firmly rejects, as 'absurd', the identification of a society with current shared morality, since this would be tantamount to refusing to allow for any change in social morality—the ultimate conservative position.[203] Clearly, in a society where the direct suppression of vice (however defined, but most likely on the basis of a dominant religious doctrine), and more generally the legal

[201] P. Devlin, *The Enforcement of Morals* ([first published 1965] 1970), at 12–14.
[202] H. L. A. Hart, *Law, Liberty, and Morality* (1963).
[203] Ibid. 48–52.

enforcement of morals, became a task for contract law,[204] immorality as a ground for contractual invalidity would be a centrally important doctrine indeed.

Devlin's argument is essentially a slippery slope argument. With regard to commodification, similar arguments have been made: once we start allowing, say, the commodification of the human body there is no end to it and our society will fall apart. For example, at the end of his famous study comparing the sale of human blood in the US with the donation system in the UK, Titmuss concluded that 'the commercialisation of blood and donor relationships represses the expression of altruism [and] erodes the sense of community'.[205] As Arrow remarked, Titmuss's slippery slope argument about the expansion of the market is the mirror image of Hayek's claim that limitation of free markets will inevitably bring us onto the road to serfdom.[206] However, as Arrow also observed, 'the thing about the argument of instability is that it is, after all, strictly an empirical one. It simply may not be true'.[207]

Yet, according to Buckley, a softer form of the disintegration thesis commends itself even today. Acknowledging that the claim concerning societal disintegration is ultimately an empirical one, he argues that a more moderate version is likely to be empirically more plausible. With reference to empirical evidence on the spill-over costs of divorce (e.g. the emotional suffering of children in broken families), he claims that 'from today's perspective, it is Hart who looks naive and Devlin who appears the realist'.[208] Because nobody is certain that the moral costs of all voluntary contracts for society are zero, he claims, the thin perfectionism of the doctrine of contractual illegality may well provide a viable middle way between 'moral fascism' and 'civil libertarianism'.[209] As he observes, 'reasonable men may differ on the moderate perfectionism implicit in the doctrine of illegality in common law. In deliberating over whether to enforce a contract, we are not asked to choose between moral tyranny and the destruction of society. The stakes are lower than that, all around'.[210] That may well be true. However, just as it is not clear what is the specifically moral cost of allowing divorce, it is also far from obvious what the specifically moral costs of certain types of contracts are, let alone—most to the point here—whether they would lead or contribute in any way to the disintegration of our society properly understood.

F. Incomplete Commodification

Published in 1996, today Radin's *Contested Commodities* is a modern classic in private law theory.[211] Radin presents her own view explicitly as pragmatic.[212] However,

[204] In Devlin (n. 201), chapter 3 is dedicated to 'Morals and the Law of Contract'. To be fair, Devlin's reading of the English contract law was not a very moralistic one: 'The English law of contract is a hotchpotch of the common law, equity, and state. Taken as a whole it is biased in favour of commerce rather than morality.'

[205] Titmuss (n. 190) 245–246.

[206] Arrow, 'Gifts and Exchanges', 1 *Philosophy and Public Affairs* (1972) 343, at 360–361.

[207] Ibid.

[208] Buckley (n. 54) 130.

[209] Ibid. 134.

[210] Ibid. 135.

[211] Radin, *Contested Commodities* (n. 15). The book builds upon Radin, 'Market-Inalienability' (n. 15), one of the most cited law journal articles.

[212] In Radin, 'Market-Inalienability' (n. 15) 1904–1905, she explicitly leaves open the choice between sceptical (Rorty) and realist (Putnam) strands in pragmatic meta-ethics. What matters to her, is what unites

many of her arguments seem strongly communitarian: not only her endorsement of much of the communitarian critique of liberalism, which was central to the liberal-communitarian debate, but also the importance she attributes to community standards, the common good, and embeddedness.

Radin rejects the use of spatial metaphors of spheres and boundary crossing that aim at compartmentalizing our lives.[213] In particular, she challenges Walzer's idea that the market has its proper sphere, and should be kept in check, and that boundary crossing will lead, via a slippery slope, to market imperialism ('domino theory').[214] Blocking exchanges, she argues, is not the solution. Instead, we should reimagine personhood and human flourishing.[215] In particular, she proposes a thoroughly contextualized understanding of personhood:[216] in other words, a thick conception of the self. As she explains, 'a thick theory of the self correlates with an expansive role for inalienability'.[217] Thus, her approach is avowedly perfectionist, explicitly challenging liberal neutrality.[218] Anderson's theory, which we saw earlier, developed in parallel with Radin's theory and there are some striking similarities between the two. The main difference between them, however, is Radin's emphasis on pragmatic compromise.

Rejecting the extremes of universal commodification and universal non-commodification, Radin argues for the 'middle way' of 'incomplete commodification'.[219] For contract law, this means neither laissez-faire nor pervasive bans, but regulated contracts. In practice, therefore, incomplete commodification must be understood as a series of pragmatic compromises. As one example, Radin proposes to permit only unpaid surrogacy.[220] While various concerns would require a total ban, she argues, the difficulty in enforcing it 'because it infringes on people's choices' suggests the pragmatic compromise of banning only paid surrogacy. However, an infringement upon people's choices is typical of any banned commodification. Therefore, it is not so clear exactly what the reasoning is behind the compromise, other than—very pragmatically—trying to meet in the middle.

G. Legal Consciousnesses

A rather different aspect of the communitarian focus on tradition is that legal communitarians will be quick to observe that the question of whether contracts contrary to public policy should be invalid is hardly an abstract one. They will point to the longstanding tradition, both in the common law (with the doctrine of illegality)[221]

all versions of pragmatism, i.e. its anti-foundationalist focus on non-ideal theory. In addition to these neo-pragmatists, she also draws extensively on Dewey's theory of democracy.

213 Radin, *Contested Commodities* (n. 15) 46.
214 Ibid. 47.
215 Ibid. 54.
216 Ibid. 56.
217 Ibid. 60.
218 Ibid. 73.
219 Ibid. xiii.
220 Ibid. 144.
221 See A. W. B. Simpson, *A History of the Common Law of Contract: The Rise of the Action of Assumpsit* (1975), at 50 ff.

and in the civil law (with contracts *contra bonos mores*)[222] of the invalidity of contracts that are held to be contrary to public policy. In other words, it has been our tradition in Europe, going back to Roman and medieval law, to invalidate immoral and illegal contracts. As in the previous chapters, here too the value of experience is hard to ignore. It would be foolish to disregard it entirely and try to start from scratch. On the other hand, both public opinion and moral theory have developed significantly in recent decades, often more rapidly than the law, in part because sometimes there simply are not enough cases brought to the courts to 'update' some of the outdated groups of cases (*Fallgruppen*) that can still be found in the leading commentaries. Therefore there is also an intrinsic risk of conservatism when the older cases are uncritically treated as experience and tradition.[223]

An emphasis in legal communitarianism on the differences between legal traditions yields yet another picture. The common law of contract, with its consideration requirement, regards contracts as essentially an exchange, thus deliberately and categorically excluding 'gratuitous promises' from the scope of contract. This immediately gives contract law a commercial outlook. By contrast, in the civil law tradition civil codes have long recognized the contract of donation as one contract type among others. This gives contract law a more moralizing outlook. Indeed, some civil codes specifically acknowledge that the donative intent may derive from an existing moral obligation.[224]

Taking this argument one step further, approaches to contractual morality can also be understood in terms of national legal sentiments. Some of Micklitz's recent work seems to have taken such a national-communitarian turn. In his latest book, he analyses private law in terms of national 'legal consciousnesses'. He defines a legal consciousness as 'the mode of thinking that typifies the social psychology of a particular society, predominantly shaped by the understandings of the societies' most influential philosophers'.[225] In line with methodological nationalism, i.e. the assumption that political views and values differ chiefly between nations, he foregrounds national

[222] See Zimmermann (n. 7) 706–715. See also Mayer-Maly, 'Was leisten die guten Sitten?', 194 *Archiv für die civilistische Praxis* (1994) 105.

[223] In addition, there are dramatic historical lessons concerning the risk of general clauses, such as good morals, being abused by totalitarian regimes. See, for example, the infamous decision of the German Supreme Court in 1936, where it ruled that the concept of 'good morals' in § 138 *BGB* had the content as determined by the Nazi worldview. See *Reichsgericht*, 13 March 1936, *RGZ* 150, 1, 4: 'Der Begriff "eines Verstoßes gegen die guten Sitten", wie er in §138 und in §826 *BGB* enthalten ist, erhält seinem Wesen nach den Inhalt durch das seit dem Umbruch herrschende Volksempfinden, die nationalsozialistische Weltanschauung'.

[224] See e.g. § 534 German Civil Code on donations to meet a moral duty. Cf. also Art. IV.H.-1:203 DCFR.

[225] H.-W. Micklitz, *The Politics of Justice in European Private Law: Social Justice, Access Justice, Societal Justice* (2018), at 38. The concept seems akin to the notion of 'legal *mentalité*' that Legrand introduced to indicate the depth of the common law versus civil law divide. See Legrand, 'European Legal Systems Are Not Converging', 45 *ICLQ* (1996) 52, at 63: 'the common law *mentalité* is not only different, but is actually *irreducibly* different, from the civil law *mentalité* as found in Continental Europe. These two legal traditions reflect two modes of experiencing the world.' (emphasis in original) For a definition of the concept, see ibid. 60:

> The essential key for an appreciation of a legal culture lies in an unravelling of the cognitive structure that characterises that culture. The aim must be to try to define the frame of perception and understanding of a legal community so as to explicate how a community thinks about

differences in thinking about private law in Europe. In particular, he contrasts three such 'legal consciousnesses', i.e. the English ('liberal and pragmatic'), the French ('intellectual'), and the German ('paternalistic-legalistic') ones.[226] He claims that 'these ideal types help to explain the deeper foundations in the legal consciousness that are reflected in the way in which the citizens perceive justice, perceive the role of the state and their own responsibilities'.[227] Whatever the merits of such reductionist and essentializing accounts of private law as national legal consciousness, it is clear that *Volksgeist* views of this kind can easily also be applied to contractual immorality and public policy.[228] In particular, the distinction of national legal consciousnesses within the EU vindicates the idea of national pluralism along the lines of *Omega*.[229] On this view, it is perfectly understandable that German law paternalistically banned the laser tag game; that English law would have a more liberal (consenting adults) and pragmatic (allowing playing at killing each other might prevent actual murders) response; and that the French would address the issue from the point of view of universal human rights, as contained in the revolutionary *Déclaration des droits de l'homme et du citoyen* (1789), or, alternatively, would get lost in a debate on pertinent '*grandes idées*' or in deconstructing the notion of contractual morality. However, there is a clear risk, it would seem, not only of stereotypes, but also, and especially, of undue disregard for value pluralism—and for pluralisms of legal consciousnesses—*internal* to each of these nation states: what about the German intellectual, the French pragmatic, and the English paternalist?

6. Civic Republican

A. Freedom of Contract as Domination

As we saw earlier, contemporary civic republicans define freedom as non-domination.[230] There is a significant difference in this respect between republicans, on the one hand, and liberals and (especially) libertarians, on the other. While the latter view legal coercion as bad in itself, the former 'view state coercion, in particular coercion that occurs under a suitable form of law, as something that is not so potentially objectionable, being on a par with obstruction by natural obstacles rather than with

the law and why it thinks about the law in the way it does. The comparatist must, therefore, focus on the cognitive structure of a given legal culture and, more specifically, on the epistemological foundations of that cognitive structure. It is this epistemological substratum which best epitomises what I wish to refer to as the legal *mentalité* (the collective mental programme), or the interiorised legal culture, within a given legal culture. (emphasis in original).

[226] Micklitz (n. 225), Part I. See earlier, H.-W. Micklitz, 'Failure or Ideological Preconceptions? Thoughts on Two Grand Projects: The European Constitution and the European Civil Code', in K. Tuori and S. Sankari (eds), *The Many Constitutions of Europe* (2010) 109.

[227] Micklitz (n. 225) 32.

[228] Chapter 4 discussed (methodological) private nationalism and its implications for the debate on Europeanization.

[229] Case C-36/02, *Omega Spielhallen- und Automatenaufstellungs-GmbH v. Oberbürgermeisterin der Bundesstadt Bonn* (EU:C:2004:614).

[230] P. Pettit, *Republicanism: A Theory of Freedom and Government* (1997).

coercion by arbitrary powers'.[231] And as we also saw, there is no reason to think that Pettit's argument should be limited to public law.

Therefore, from the republican perspective of freedom as non-domination, limitations of freedom of contract are not even prima facie problematic. This means that a civic republican may well conclude that if dwarf tossing, playing at killing each other, or prostitution is typically a consequence of—or risks being conducive to—domination, then forbidding such a contract through a general rule would not mean a limitation of freedom, but rather a protection of it. In such cases, therefore, a republican like Pettit may very well accept state interference with what is usually regarded as contractual freedom. As we saw in Chapter 5, from Pettit's republican point of view 'the free contract cannot serve the role of automatic legitimator—even prima facie legitimator—of what happens under the terms of the contract'.[232] What is crucial, however, is that the interference with the contract should be non-arbitrary in order to be capable of being legitimate.

Just as in the cases discussed in Chapter 6, here too the 'eyeball test' is likely to be a relevant criterion in many cases: can the sex worker, the dwarf who is tossed, or the person selling their kidney look their contracting parties in the eye, 'without reason for the fear or deference'; can they 'walk tall and assume the public status, objective and subjective, of being equal in this regard with the best'?[233] Or, on the contrary, do they depend on the arbitrary power of their counterparties?

B. Skirting around Political Conflict

While Pettit derives a substantive standard of justice from the republican commitment to freedom as non-domination, for Bellamy republicanism remains entirely procedural. For him, freedom as non-domination translates into political constitutionalism, the core of which, as we saw in Chapter 3, is majoritarian legislation.[234] At first sight, the implication for any limitations to freedom of contract for reasons of public policy would seem to be twofold. First, any such limitations should be legislative. Secondly, the required 'public reasoning' about the limitations to freedom of contract should be understood in a purely procedural sense,[235] in that it must be ensured through the ordinary legislative process concluded ultimately by majority voting. Obviously, there should be no counter-majoritarian measures. In particular, the majority view should not be constrained by a constitutionalized catalogue of human rights. In this regard, Bellamy's view is in direct and explicit opposition to the view of Dworkin, which we saw earlier.

According to Bellamy, 'claims to moral expertise rest on dubious foundations'.[236] Therefore, one would assume, judges have no more special expertise than any other

231 Ibid. 84.
232 Ibid. 164.
233 P. Pettit, *On the People's Terms: A Republican Theory and Model of Democracy* (2012), at 84.
234 R. Bellamy, *Political Constitutionalism: A Republican Defence of the Constitutionality of Democracy* (2007).
235 Ibid. ch. 5.
236 Ibid. 40.

citizen in determining which contracts should be held contrary to good morals. Yet, Bellamy's support for analogical, case-by-case reasoning by courts as an appropriate means for overcoming reasonable disagreement within the circumstances of politics, as 'a way of skirting around political conflict', raises some doubt in this regard.[237] If the focus on concrete precedents helps courts, and the parties to a dispute, in avoiding discussions about underlying conflicts of principle—as Bellamy suggests—what does this mean for the moral limits to freedom of contract? Perhaps here too the situation-sense of the common law judge could provide an appropriate solution to thorny questions about commodification?[238] However, as already pointed out in Chapter 3, that would mean that an argument that started out as a valiant case for majoritarian legislation would slide into a defence of judicial law making in politically controversial cases, such as contracts for gestational services, dwarf tossing, etc.

Bellamy underscores his point, referring to Sunstein's argument for analogical, rather than principled, reasoning in politically controversial cases. And as it happens, Sunstein illustrates his point with the example of a case where a US court had to decide whether a surrogacy contract violated a statutory prohibition on selling babies.[239] In that case, the judges reasoned analogically, considering the similarities and differences between surrogacy and baby selling, with the majority finding that the two situations were different. The important point, however, according to Sunstein, was the special form of the argument: 'There was no deep theoretical claim about the limits of the marketplace or about the sale of human beings. The court described the justification behind the ban at a relatively low, commonsensical level of abstraction.'[240]

In summary, it is not entirely clear whether political constitutionalism would favour contractual illegality via democratic legislation or rather through incremental judicial law making on the basis of general doctrines such as contractual immorality. What is crystal clear, however, is that from Bellamy's 'democratic political constitutionalist' understanding of freedom as non-domination—in sharp contrast with Pettit's version of republicanism—we can derive no substantive answer, not even a tentative one or a direction, with regard to any of the examples we have been discussing in this chapter.

C. Voluntary Serfdom

In common law jurisdictions, contracts in restraint of trade are prima facie void for reasons of public policy.[241] One possible rationale for the doctrine of restraint of trade, relatively close to its name, is the public interest in preserving free competition. However, that objective cannot easily explain all the cases. Saprai offers as a fresh rationale: republican freedom as non-domination.[242] 'The restraint of trade doctrine is

237 Ibid. 84.

238 See Llewellyn (n. 136).

239 *Surrogate Parenting Associates v. Kentucky*, 704 S.W.2d 209 (1986).

240 C. R. Sunstein, *Legal Reasoning and Political Conflict* (2018), at 87.

241 See, e.g. *Schroeder Music Publishing Co v. Macaulay* (1974) 3 All ER 616, concerning a contract binding a young unknown songwriter exclusively to a publisher for five years (renewable for another five), without the latter being under any obligation to publish any of the former's work.

242 P. Saprai, *Contract Law Without Foundations: Towards a Republican Theory of Contract Law* (2019), ch. 7 ('Restraint of Trade and Freedom').

not only or even principally motivated by economic concerns', he argues, 'the deeper explanation is one of preventing the domination of one contractual party by the other'.[243] The idea is that courts refuse to enforce contracts where one party is subjugated to the arbitrary will and choice of the other, lest they become complicit in domination.

The paradigm republican case of an unfree person is a slave. And contract law should not lend a hand to self-enslavement. The typical cases of contract clauses in restraint of trade are contractual and post-contractual non-compete clauses in employment contracts (and in the sales of businesses).[244] When such clauses are wholly unreasonable because they are excessive in terms of geographical scope, time, activities concerned, and protected interests, and therefore void for that reason, then arguably they amount, at least to a degree, to contracts of modern serfdom. Even though the focus is on preventing a very unequal contractual relationship between the parties, Saprai argues, the concern is a public one. This is evident not only because the doctrine does not require any coercion or similar at the moment of conclusion of the contract, but because the invalidity does not depend on the exercise of any remedy by the party restrained by the contract: contracts in restraint are automatically null and void. As Saprai puts it, 'the state through its courts has a duty not to assist or be complicit in the abuse of contractual principles like promise and freedom of contract to engineer these forms of servitude'.[245]

D. The Republic and the Market

There are different republican ways of looking at the market. In particular, one view distinguishes the market from the republic, and another one conceives of a republican market.

1. Republican Freedom Versus Market Freedom

MacGilvray offers a historical reconstruction of the invention of market freedom, contrasting it with republican freedom.[246] On this view, as he underlines,[247] the 'republican conception of freedom provides a viable alternative not only to the negative and positive liberty traditions, but to market freedom itself'. The contrast between republican and market freedom, he argues, presents us with a choice 'between *responsibility* and *irresponsibility* as models of human freedom'.[248] On this view, it seems, freedom of contract, at least in its traditional laissez-faire understanding, would side with the model of individual irresponsibility. The republican responsibility-taking, by contrast, would necessarily be collective, since 'republican freedom can only be enjoyed in the company and through the cooperation of other people—it is, in this sense, a

243 Ibid. 137.

244 In several civil law jurisdictions, there are specific rules on non-compete clauses in, for example, labour contracts. See e.g. Art. 7:653 Dutch Civil Code.

245 Saprai (n. 242) 146.

246 E. MacGilvray, *The Invention of Market Freedom* (2011).

247 Ibid. 183.

248 Ibid. 183 (emphasis in original).

"relational" good'.[249] And taking collective responsibility, one would assume, entails setting moral limits to the market through appropriate institutions, which may well include contract law, including doctrines invalidating contracts contrary to public policy and good morals.

Specifically with regard to the EU, Kocharov, argues that 'the internal market tends to be based on liberal legitimation while the AFSJ tends to rely on republican legitimation'.[250] Although the distinction should not be reified—Kocharov herself proposes a continuum view—here too the idea is that different types of freedom govern market and non-market issues.

2. Homo Economicus versus Zoon Politikon

A related distinction, with a slightly different emphasis, is between two different conceptions of the person, i.e. the human person as economic man or woman (homo economicus),[251] a rational maximizer of her own welfare, versus the human person as political animal (zoon politikon).[252] Today, the idea that the *polis* is constitutive of the human person and that political participation is an essential part of human fulfilment is found mostly in perfectionist, communitarian versions of republicanism. From this point of view, the logic of the market may be considered a threat to political culture. As we saw, for example, Sandel is concerned that 'commodification corrupts the good of self-government' in various domains of public life.[253] In other words, through commodification the market crowds out the republic, and the consumer replaces the virtuous citizen. On this view, the task of the republic is to push back the market, while the task of the individual market citizens is to rediscover themselves as political citizens. The direct consequence for contract law would be a reduction of the realm of contract—in other words, a limitation of freedom contract—and probably a tendency towards decommodification, perhaps with the help of doctrines such as immorality and illegality.

3. The Market as *Res Publica*

By contrast, other republicans regard the republic as constitutive of the market. For example, Pettit underlines that the market should not be regarded as a natural entity, but rather as a *res publica*: 'The rules of public order constitute the possibility of private life in the way in which the rules of a game like chess constitute the possibility of playing that game.'[254] Pettit explicitly mentions the rules of contract law as such constitutive

[249] Ibid. 179.

[250] The AFSJ is the 'area of freedom, security and justice', to which Title V of the TFEU (Arts 67–89) is dedicated. Chapter 3 (Art. 81) is dedicated to judicial cooperation in civil matters. The AFSJ goes back to the 'third pillar', which was based on intergovernmental cooperation, and was integrated eventually into the EU by the Lisbon Treaty, making the ordinary legislative procedure become applicable.

[251] Cf. e.g. A. Smith, *The Wealth of Nations* ([first published 1776] 1982), at 19: 'It is not from the benevolence of the butcher, the brewer, or the baker that we expect our dinner, but from their regard to their own interest.' Cf. D. Kahneman, *Thinking, Fast and Slow* (2011), at 411–415, contrasting Econs with Humans.

[252] Aristotle, *The Politics* (1981), at 1253a1: 'man is by nature a political animal'.

[253] Sandel, *Tanner Lectures* (n. 185) 109.

[254] Pettit, 'Taking Back the Economy: The Market as Res Publica', *opendemocracy.net*, 31 January 2013, available at www.opendemocracy.net/ourkingdom/philip-pettit/taking-back-economy-market-as-res-publica (last visited 16 July 2020).

rules.[255] Similarly, Bellamy points out that 'to argue government ought not to interfere with the freedom of the market ignores the fact that this liberty is structured by the establishment, through governmental action, of property rights and contract law'.[256]

The republican market, it seems, is a regulated one.[257] In particular, republican market regulation might include rules of public order in the narrower sense of banning certain contracts from the market, especially those that would allow one person to dominate another. In other words, from the point of view of a republican understanding of markets as *res publicae*, contracts which lead to domination are as troubling as contracts that result from domination (i.e. the ones we saw in Chapter 6). In summary, the view of the market as *res publica* could yield a specifically republican conception of market freedom, as opposed to liberal, libertarian, and utilitarian understandings of free markets, and a related republican conception of freedom of contract.

7. Discourse Theory

A. Citizens Achieving Clarity about the Limits of Contract

From a Habermasian discourse-theoretical point of view, the starting point is, again, that private and public autonomy are co-original, which means that they mutually presuppose each other. In the words of Habermas, 'all rights ultimately stem from the system of rights that free and equal legal subjects would mutually accord to one another'.[258] This applies just as much for contractual rights as for any other right. Therefore, when 'freedom of contract' is 'limited' on the basis of doctrines like public policy and public morality, for example in order to declare the sale of a kidney invalid, then this does not amount to a *limitation* of private autonomy by legitimate law, but rather a *change* in the understanding of private autonomy: private autonomy, as we understand it here and now, does not extend to the legally valid conclusion of contracts, such as a contract for the sale of a human kidney. Or, to put it yet differently, the sphere where legal subjects do not have to give account for their actions, providing publicly acceptable reasons,[259] does not extend to the conclusion and performance of contracts for the buying and selling of a human kidney.

[255] Ibid.

[256] Bellamy (n. 234) 157. See also R. Bellamy, *A Republican Europe of States: Cosmopolitanism, Intergovernmentalism and Democracy in the EU* (2019), at 153:

> Some neo-liberals of an anarchist persuasion have ... claimed that markets emerge through conventions and are capable of operating without any need for a state. Yet, as critics of this position—including many libertarians—note, the operation of markets requires the establishment of property rights and freedom of contract, which are only likely to be secured in an impartial and authoritative way by a state capable of enforcing duties. Not only would a pure free market, without any political assignment of rights and duties, be liable to being unjust, it would be largely unworkable as well.

[257] See Pettit (n. 233) 263–264: 'The business that government is charged with taking up will certainly include ... the regulation of various markets.'

[258] J. Habermas, *Between Facts and Norms: Contributions to a Discourse Theory of Law and Democracy* ([first published 1992] 1996), at 409.

[259] Ibid. 120.

The expectation under discourse theory would be, it seems, that a legitimate contract law, i.e. one that has come about in a process where the interests and reasons of all are heard, would not enforce contracts that do not respect the dignity of individuals. However, whether laser games, dwarf tossing, prostitution, or surrogacy contracts are indeed such contracts cannot be said in advance of deliberation, as a result of the procedural nature of the approach, which does not demand any specific outcome, not even the broad contours of a substantive outcome. This is so because of the epistemic role of the public sphere, the centre-periphery divide, and the performative character of public deliberation, all of which were discussed extensively in Chapter 3.

Moral discourses, understood in the narrow sense of referring to what we all mutually owe each other as human beings and of making claims to universal moral rightness, should be at the core of deliberations about contractual immorality, chiefly in their positive form of human rights (although these positive rights, or their official interpretation, can be contested too, on moral grounds). For the validity of ethical discourses, which refer to a conception of the good, either individual or social (the common good), discourse theory requires the unanimous acceptability by all members of the given ethical community.[260] This places strong restrictions on attempts, coming from communitarians and other perfectionists, to limit freedom of contract in the name of public morality—in a way quite similar to political liberalism. For example, Habermas does not allow religious arguments into public discourse.[261] However, contrary to Rawls, Habermas does not propose any self-standing principles of justice for resolving disagreements among people with different conceptions of the good. Nor does he offer any meta-principles for distinguishing ethical and moralistic reasons from strictly moral reasons; these boundary issues can be resolved only by the people themselves within the democratic debate.[262]

As a procedural theory, with a central role for democratic deliberation, and one that distinguishes (normatively) between discourses of law making (by democratic legislatures) and discourses of law application (by courts), a discourse-theoretical approach is likely to prefer the doctrine of illegality (prohibition by statute, enacted by the democratically legitimated law maker) above the doctrine of immorality (the 'general clause' of 'good morals', as interpreted by unelected judges), especially since the kind of cases under discussion here tend to be highly controversial ones. The main reasons for this preference refers to the epistemic dimension and the (crucially important) performative nature of deliberation. As Habermas underlines, 'under postmetaphysical conditions, the only legitimate law is one that emerges from the discursive opinion-and will-formation of equally enfranchised citizens'.[263] Thus, paraphrasing Habermas's

[260] For the distinction between different types of justificatory discourse—pragmatic, ethical, and moral—see Habermas, 'On the Pragmatic, the Ethical, and the Moral Employment of Practical Reason', and Habermas, 'Remarks on Discourse Ethics', in J. Habermas, *Justification and Application; Remarks on Discourse Ethics* (1995), ch. 1, and ch 2.

[261] On this question, see, for example, his debates with Ratzinger and Taylor. See J. Habermas, *Between Naturalism and Religion* (2008), especially ch. 4 ('Prepolitical Foundations of the Constitutional State?') and ch. 5 ('Religion in the Public Sphere: Cognitive Presuppositions for the "Public Use of Reason" by Religious and Secular Citizens').

[262] Cf. Bohman and Rehg, 'Jürgen Habermas', in E. N. Zalta, *Stanford Encyclopedia of Philosophy*, available at https://plato.stanford.edu/entries/habermas/ (last visited 16 July 2020).

[263] Habermas (n. 258) 408.

'radically democratic hunch',[264] private parties cannot come to enjoy true freedom of contract unless they themselves, in the common exercise of their political autonomy, achieve clarity about the interests and standards that can justify the refusal by contract law to recognize and enforce certain contracts.

B. Ethical Discourses

Forst builds upon Habermas's discourse theory adding certain elements that are particularly relevant for the question that concerns us here.

1. The Threshold of Justification

As we saw earlier,[265] Forst distinguishes five different types of contexts of justification (not to be confused with spheres and similar spatial differentiations), each with its own corresponding appropriate type of discourse, conception of autonomy, and conception of the human person: moral, ethical, legal, political, and social contexts. Most relevant here is the distinction between moral and ethical contexts and their respective appropriate discourses. That distinction is particularly relevant because the right to justification with reciprocal and general reasons prevents us from imposing our ethical values upon others who do not share them (lack of reciprocity of reasons). While ethical values are entirely appropriate reasons for justifying and criticizing conduct among members of the same ethical community or towards oneself, they can be legitimately elevated to legal norms that apply to the entire political community[266] only if they can reach the justificatory threshold of reciprocal and general non-rejectability. As Forst explains, 'ethical arguments, if they want to wrap themselves in the cloak of justice, must be able to pass the threshold of reciprocity and generality. This is precisely how to prevent particular value orientations (those of a majority, for instance) from being imposed on others without sufficient reason or authority.'[267]

The direct implications for contractual illegality and morality are clear. Ethical reasons referring to a particular conception of the good life—of what is valuable in life or what kind of persons we essentially are or ought to be, etc.—cannot on their own justify a limitation of freedom of contract (or the rejection thereof).[268] A doctrine declaring contracts null and void, because they are illegal or immoral, on the basis of ethical reasons that fail to pass the test of reasonable non-rejectability, would unjustifiably try to project some people's values onto others with the help of contract law.

By contrast, all relevant moral reasons, which are, as we saw, reasons concerning what we owe to each other as human beings, can legitimately inform doctrines of invalidity of contracts contrary to public policy or good morals. Such reasons may include, notably, reasons of interpersonal and distributive justice and the violation of human rights (which, however, are not necessarily identical to the 'fundamental' or

264 Ibid. xiii. On this hunch and its implications, see also Chapter 1.
265 In Chapters 2 and 5.
266 And often beyond, in the case of private law, via the rules of private international law.
267 R. Forst, *The Right to Justification: Elements of a Constructivist Theory of Justice* (2013), at 8.
268 As to the latter point, the threshold applies for arguments in either direction, i.e. more or less freedom of contract. There is no libertarian default. See further later, in Section 7.B.3.

constitutional rights recognized in certain jurisdictions—the category may be both wider and narrower).

This does not mean that only moral reasons (about what we owe to each other), and never ethical reasons (about the good life), can count as the 'good morals' to which the familiar contract law doctrines refer; it merely means that the ethical values and arguments referring to the common good will have to meet the threshold of moral acceptability to justify the declaration of certain contracts as null and void. What is at stake here is respect for everyone's (morally grounded) right to second-order ethical autonomy, i.e. the autonomy to live in accordance with one's own conception of the good. As Forst observes, 'the political community cannot choose one of the first-order conceptions as the basis for answering the question concerning the extent to which law and politics should guarantee the exercise of ethical autonomy'.[269] For contract law this means that the political community cannot choose one of the controversial conceptions of the good (individual or common) as a basis for deciding in which cases to enforce a contract and in which ones not.

2. Metaphysical Agnosticism

It is important to realize that Forst's view does not imply that moral norms are objectively knowable while ethical values are nothing more than subjective tastes. On the contrary, Forst explicitly remains agnostic with regard to the reality and cognitive content of ethical values. In full respect of the plurality of the normative world, his claim concerns merely the limits of practical reason. As he points out:

> It is not the case that a position standing in the Kantian tradition can only recognize and ascribe cognitive content to those values which (so to speak) have passed through a moral filter. This would amount to a 'colonization' of ethical evaluations by morality, which violates the plurality of the normative world. ... The difference between ethical values and moral norms is not metaphysical in nature, but is only owing to the distinction between contexts of justification; the theory of morality can remain agnostic in relation to the question of the 'reality' of ethical values.[270]

For our purposes here, this means that the point is not that ethical values could never justify the invalidity of contract because the adherence to a value is nothing more than a mere subjective preference, like a taste for chocolate ice cream. Those who wish to impose their values on others, for example when it comes to contested commodities, do not need to prove that their values are real, true, or objectively knowable. What they must do, however, is convince others that their argument for or against banning contracts concerning certain goods or services passes the threshold of reciprocity and generality. For example, this may well be the case when moral norms are at stake, especially when there is a risk of violation of human rights, in particular the right to human dignity.

[269] Forst (n. 267) 132.
[270] Ibid. 71.

3. No Libertarian Default

Finally, it is important to underline that, just as under Rawlsian political liberalism, under discourse theory there is no place for a libertarian default. It is not the case that legitimate law making takes place against an empty background of generic freedom. Under Rawlsian justice as fairness, in a well-ordered society, as we saw, specific basic liberties must be protected (with lexical priority over the difference principle), not generic 'liberty'.[271] Very similarly, from the point of view of the Forstian right to justification it is not the case that the presence of state coercion is any more in need of justification than its absence.[272] Non-interference can be just as problematic as interference—and frequently even more so. For our question of the 'interference with freedom of contract' (the interference with the interference, as it were)[273] on grounds of public policy or good morals this means that not only arguments for the limitation of freedom of contract but also arguments against contractual invalidity must pass the threshold of justifiability with general and reciprocal reasons. The threshold applies for arguments in either direction, i.e. more or less freedom of contract.

8. Concluding Remarks

The EU is quite jealous of its internal market. Easy market access is ensured only for Member States. And in the Brexit negotiations after the UK's decision to withdraw from the EU, a central question was about continued access to the internal market, as sellers and buyers, for businesses and consumers residing in the UK. In other words, the geographical limits of the internal market are well defined and well protected. A similar political eagerness cannot be found for the task of determining the moral limits to the internal market. In a sense, this is not surprising since the question is politically quite divisive. At stake is nothing less than the much heralded and vilified freedom of contract.

In this chapter, we saw that not only the answers, but even the reading of the normative question about the invalidity of contracts contrary to public policy and good morals differs radically from one political theory to another. Is the state allowed to be judgemental about contracts freely concluded by consenting adults? In particular, is the state free to set contracts aside in the pursuit of paternalistic and moralistic policies? Is a society held to support practices it disapproves of, and to facilitate transactions it considers wrong or bad, by making them legally enforceable as valid contracts? Should our external preferences be counted when it comes to the legal recognition of other people's contracts? Can the invalidity of contracts legitimately be a matter of political will and majority decision, or should a pluralist society accept only certain types

[271] See J. Rawls, *Political Liberalism* ([first published 1993] 2005), at 291: 'No priority is assigned to liberty as such, as if the exercise of something called "liberty" has a preeminent value and is the main if not the sole end of political and social justice.' Rawls clarified this point in his theory in response to criticism from H. L. A. Hart, 'Rawls on Liberty and Its Priority', 40 *U. Chi. L. Rev.* (1973) 534.

[272] Forst, 'The Justification of Basic Rights: A Discourse-Theoretical Approach', 45 *Netherlands Journal of Legal Philosophy* (2016) 7, at 24, explicitly rejects 'a libertarian "presumption of liberty"'.

[273] The interference with the interference, since, as was explained in the Introduction to this chapter (and in Chapter 5), if anything, it is the binding force of contract that interferes with libertarian liberty.

of reasons and not others? As a political community, do we need to prevent the commodification of certain goods that should be valued differently than through money and make them market-inalienable? Do any negative externalities of contracts call for a regulatory response from contract law?

Among the fundamental political questions central to this book, the question of the moral and (other) public policy limits to the freedom of contract has proved to be the most divisive by far. Rather than an overlapping consensus, we have found divergence and dissensus among the political philosophies under discussion.[274] Moreover, on this question the differences run particularly deep. Most notably, the charge of over-commodification raises very fundamental—and ultimately metaphysical—questions, not only about the nature of value, but also about the subject-object divide, which the various political theories answer in radically different ways. Specifically, the question of immoral contracts, and the examples discussed in this chapter, also provided a challenging test case for liberals, regarding their commitment to neutrality, and, conversely, for communitarians, concerning their support for contract law moralism and paternalism. Some readers may have discovered themselves more communitarian—or more liberal—than they thought they were.

And yet, the strong disagreements we found among political theories do not necessarily speak against a specifically European answer to the question of what money can legitimately buy in the internal market. Unless we adopt a (methodologically) nationalist perspective, our discussion here does not suggest that the difficulty in determining proper limits to freedom of contract on moral or public policy grounds should be any greater at the European level than in national contract law systems. Most of the arguments we saw about limiting freedom of contract in certain cases—whether in favour or against—did not have a specifically local but rather a more universal vocation, referring as they did to quite general conceptions of human values, the human person, freedom, and tolerance. In other words, it should not necessarily be much more difficult to determine proper moral limits to the EU's internal market than to any local market.

One possibly fruitful starting point for a European effort could be the CFREU, which could perhaps provide a guide in formulating at least minimum standards for contractual immorality in a morally properly functioning internal market. This would mean that in principle contracts violating human rights of the contracting parties or of third parties, should be declared void (when that sanction is proportionate).

It is possible, however, that moral reasons, even though they have universal vocation, are interpreted differently—legitimately—in different societal contexts. This fact could provide a justification, not so much for foundational moral pluralism, but rather for a margin of appreciation. This also seems the normatively most convincing reading of the CJEU's *Omega* ruling, where the dispute was about the proper limitations to the exercise of market freedoms for reasons of public policy, in the light of the right to human dignity—i.e. the dignity we all share as human beings—which by definition must be a universal right. Therefore, any divergent understandings in the Member States concerning the implications of this right for proper limits to market

[274] It should be recalled that all six theories under discussion here are considered to be reasonable theories and doctrines, i.e. ones that are fundamentally respectful of each other.

freedoms—and by implication for the limits to freedom of contract, when the case is a horizontal one between private parties—is best justified, it seems, by what Rawls called 'the burdens of judgement', i.e. the different life experiences with which we come to the interpretation of the same right. And the relevant experiences are always in part collective, as in the case of the trauma of the atrocities of World War II, which informs the contemporary understanding in Germany of human dignity.

Because of the strong divergence among leading contemporary political theories on the questions of contracts against good morals or public policy, there seems to exist a particularly strong need for a legitimate procedure for finding acceptable answers to these questions. This holds true independently of whether the question arises—or ought to arise—at the European or the national level of law making, or on both. Concretely, it seems that typically statutory illegality should be the preferred option, rather than judge-made law based on a general clause such as § 138 *BGB* and similar. However, this may not always be the case. Sometimes, especially in the case of concentrated externalities, as Bagchi aptly calls them, judicial situation-sense may be a better way to properly consider the interests and points of view of everyone affected. And in many cases a combination of *ex ante* democratic deliberation on a legislative formulation of the relevant moral standards (e.g. inspired by Shiffrin's factors of accommodation) with *ex post* judicial determination of their implications for the validity of concrete contracts, may be the most legitimate way of determining moral and other public policy limits to freedom of contract.

8
Optionality

1. Introduction

A. Optional Contract Law

The applicability of contract law rules is partly at the disposal of the contracting parties, on different levels. First, they can freely choose not to conclude specific types of contract, or contracts with specific parties, or indeed any contracts at all (freedom from contract).[1] Secondly, when concluding a contract, the contracting parties can set aside many—and in commercial contracts most—of the rules that would otherwise be applicable, if different terms than the ones provided by the law suit them better. These are the non-mandatory (or 'suppletive' or 'default') rules of contract law (and, in some countries, of the general law of obligations). Thirdly, in cross-border contracts, between parties from different jurisdictions, the parties may set aside, entirely or in part, the national law that would be applicable under conflict-of-law rules, by making a 'choice of law' for another legal system. Finally, the parties can decide to opt out of the state's judicial system altogether—and frequently de facto also much of the legal system—by choosing to submit their disputes exclusively to arbitration or other types of alternative dispute resolution.[2] As we will see, at each of these levels there are significant limits to choice, both legal and factual.

The reality of contract optionality, and its limits, in both national and EU contract law raises the normative question of what justifies the existence of such optional contract law. Why would public institutions have the task of providing elaborate sets of contract law rules if private parties can set them aside as they please? What kind of considerations should determine the content of legal rules that are merely optional? Should the choice mechanisms be subjected to careful public scrutiny?

[1] To be more precise, by shaping their contract in a certain way, and not another, the parties can, to their choice, either ensure or prevent the applicability of the contract law rules relating to certain specific contract types. However, the legal classification is not in the hands of the parties. An employment contract does not become a contract of commercial agency merely through re-labelling by the parties. Still, it is in the hands of the parties to organize their contractual relationship in such a way (e.g. by ensuring the self-employed agent's independence) that it meets the legal definition, as a result of which the legal category properly applies, and all the rules that come with it.

[2] Cf. Bernstein, 'Opting out of the Legal System: Extralegal Contractual Relations in the Diamond Industry', 21 *J. Legal Stud.* (1992) 115. The large field of self-regulation through contracts, which raises many issues both empirical and normative, will not be further discussed here as, by definition, it does not involve political deliberation and institutions, which are the focus of this book.

Justifying Contract in Europe: Political Philosophies of European Contract Law. First Edition. Martijn W. Hesselink, Oxford University Press. © Martijn W. Hesselink 2021. DOI: 10.1093/oso/9780192843654.003.0008

B. Terminology and its (Geo)Politics

Different adjectives have been used to refer to optional contract law. This is the case especially for the familiar sets of contract law rules that the parties can set aside in their contracts, which have been variously called: dispositive, default, non-mandatory, and supplementary. Each of these terms has distinct connotations (of gap filling, starting point, (non)bindingness, supplementing), also reflecting different political agendas, as we will see.

There has also been a temporal evolution. Dispositive (and its equivalent in various languages) was for a long time the term most often used in Europe. However, in recent years, under the influence of law and economics (including behavioural law and economics), the American term 'default' rules is being used more frequently (and is usually not translated). Previously, the Court of Justice of the European Union (CJEU) mainly used the adjective 'supplementary', but it has also recently started speaking of 'default'.[3]

Throughout this chapter, the terms 'non-mandatory rules' and 'default rules' will be used interchangeably, except where indicated otherwise, when a specific political agenda is discussed.

C. EU Options

Compared to the classical questions of the binding force and freedom of contract, and the somewhat more recent question of weaker party protection (discussed in Chapters 5, 7, and 6, respectively), the political salience of the normative question of whether (and if so, when) certain contract law rules should be merely optional is more specifically related to the EU context, for three reasons. First, because, contrary to the national contract laws of the Member States, the contract law *acquis*, i.e. the existing EU law in the area of contracts, is overwhelmingly mandatory, i.e. non-optional. A second reason is the Rome I Regulation.[4] Obviously private international law was not invented by the EU; however, the Rome I Regulation on the law applicable to contractual obligations is one of the few EU legal instruments that are directly applicable to contractual obligations (in contrast to the directives, which require transposition into national law). The Rome I Regulation is based on the principle of free choice of law,[5] subject to mandatory weaker party protection,[6] and indicates which legal system is applicable when parties to a cross-border contract have failed to make a choice of law.[7] Finally, the legal text that became the main focal point in the political and academic debate on the future of European contract law was a proposal for an optional EU sales law. The idea of an 'optional instrument' had been floated by the European

[3] See e.g. Case C-266/18, *Aqua Med sp. z o.o. v. Irena Skóra* (EU:C:2019:282), at para. 33: 'provisions that apply by default, that is to say, in the absence of other arrangements established by the parties in that regard'.
[4] Regulation (EC) 593/2008, on the Law Applicable to Contractual Obligations (Rome I), OJ 2008 L 177.
[5] See Art. 3 (Freedom of choice).
[6] See especially Art. 6 (consumer contracts) and Art. 8 (individual employment contracts).
[7] Art. 4 (applicable law in the absence of choice).

Commission in 2001,[8] after which the notion of a '28th regime' became a recurrent theme in EU policy documents.[9] However, the most significant and concrete step in this regard was the Commission's proposal for a regulation on a Common European Sales Law (CESL), made in 2011.[10] The CESL was meant to operate as a second national regime for cross-border contracts and would have become applicable only when the contracting parties themselves had opted into it.[11] The CESL proposal was withdrawn by the European Commission in 2014. However, even though the CESL is by now long dead, and similar proposals are unlikely to be made by the Commission any time soon, let alone be adopted by the Council, it is nevertheless worthwhile discussing its justifiability here. This is not only as an exercise in counterfactual thinking[12] or to learn from mistakes, but also because the question of whether the CESL could be justifiable with good reasons, and whether the reasons actually given by the European law maker (and its opponents) were of such a kind, remains important for a better understanding the normative foundations of European contract law and its future.

D. Opting In and Opting Out

Optional contract law can operate through two different mechanisms, i.e. opt-in or opt-out. The non-mandatory rules of contract law constitute an opt-out regime. They are applicable unless the parties set them aside in their contract, either explicitly or by making a substantively contrary contractual arrangement. In other words, they apply by default. Another familiar example of an opt-out model is the United Nations Convention on Contracts for the International Sale of Goods (Vienna, 1980) (the 'Vienna Sales Convention' or 'CISG') which provides for a non-national regime for the international sale of goods between businesses. Many countries, including most EU Member States, have ratified this Convention.[13] The Vienna Sales Convention contains rules of substantive contract law—as opposed to mere conflict-of-law rules—thus providing for a non-national sales law regime. It is based on an opt-out mechanism, in that it is applicable to international business to business (B2B) sales contracts, as the

[8] See Commission Communication, 'On European Contract Law' (COM(2001) 398 final), at 17. See also Commission Communication, 'A More Coherent European Contract Law: An Action Plan' (COM(2003) 68 final), at 23.

[9] See e.g. Commission Communication, 'A Digital Agenda for Europe' (COM(2010) 245 final); 'Project Europe 2030: Challenges and Opportunities', Report to the European Council by the Reflection Group on the Future of the EU 2030, May 2010; 'A New Strategy for the Single Market at the Service of Europe's Economy and Society', Report to the President of the European Commission José Manuel Barroso by Mario Monti, 9 May 2010.

[10] Commission Proposal for a Regulation on a Common European Sales Law (COM(2011) 635 final) (hereinafter 'CESL proposal'). In addition, the European institutions were already considering the introduction of further optional instruments for other contracts, especially in the area of financial services, notably insurance. See e.g. Opinion of the European Economic and Social Committee on 'The European Insurance Contract' (2005/C 157/01), at 8.6; Storme, 'An Optional Instrument for Insurance Contract Law: The Point of View of Legal Practice' (2010), Note requested by the European Parliament's Committee on Legal Affairs, PE 425.610.

[11] See Art. 3 CESL proposal (n. 10).

[12] See Venzke, 'What If? Counterfactual (Hi)Stories of International Law', 8 *Asian Journal of International Law* (2018) 403.

[13] Today, Ireland, Malta, and Portugal are the only EU Member States who have not ratified the CISG.

default regime, unless the parties provide otherwise in their contract.[14] By contrast, the CESL would have been an opt-in regime: it could only become applicable through an explicit positive choice by the parties. Obviously, an opt-in usually also implies an opt-out (and vice versa). For example, a choice of law, in private international law, for the applicability of a certain legal system, implies an opt-out of the otherwise applicable national law indicated by conflict rules.

E. Exemplary Role (*Leitbildfunktion*)

One way of looking at unfair terms law is by seeing it as rules limiting the way in which parties can set aside default rules (and the rights and obligations contained therein): under EU law, in contracts with consumers, in principle this cannot be done through standard terms. Put differently, if sellers and service providers want to set aside their customers' or their own obligations, as provided by default rules, they will have to resort to transparent negotiated terms.

This idea is also reflected in the way the CJEU interprets the unfairness test in the Unfair Terms Directive.[15] In determining whether a term that has not been individually negotiated is unfair in the sense of Article 3 of the Directive, because it 'causes a significant imbalance in the parties' rights and obligations arising under the contract, to the detriment of the consumer', the Court takes as the reference point the default rules set aside by that term. This exemplary role for default rules in determining unfairness is referred to in German as their *Leitbildfunktion*. The Court has summarized its approach as follows:

> the Court has held that in order to ascertain whether a term causes a 'significant imbalance' in the parties' rights and obligations under a contract to the detriment of the consumer, particular account must be taken of which rules of national law would apply in the absence of an agreement by the parties in that regard. Such a comparative analysis will enable the national court to evaluate whether and, as the case may be, to what extent, the contract places the consumer in a legal situation less favourable than that provided for by the national law in force.[16]

Specifically with regard to the deleting of rights through standard terms, the Court clarifies that:

> it is for the referring court to assess whether that contractual term, in so far as it restricts the rights which, under the rules of national law, the consumer enjoys under the contract and imposes on him an additional obligation not envisaged by those

[14] Art. 6, United Nations Convention on Contracts for the International Sale of Goods (1980).

[15] Directive 93/13/EEC on unfair terms in consumer contracts, OJ 1993 L 95.

[16] Case C-226/12, *Constructora Principado SA v. José Ignacio Menéndez Álvarez* (EU:C:2014:10), at para. 21. The CJEU first adopted this approach to the significant-imbalance test in Case C-237/02, *Freiburger Kommunalbauten GmbH Baugesellschaft & Co. KG v. Ludger Hofstetter and Ulrike Hofstetter* (EU:C:2004:209), and further consolidated it in Case C-415/11, *Mohamed Aziz v. Caixa déstalvis de Catalunya, Tarragona i Manresa (Catalunyacaixa)* (EU:C:2013:164).

> rules, constitutes a sufficiently serious impairment of the legal situation which national law confers on that consumer as a party to the contract.[17]

As Leone points out, there is a proportionality element in this test:

> Default rules of national contract law become, in this construction, the point of reference for assessing whether the consumer's legal position has been significantly impaired by the contentious term: the more a term deviates from the otherwise applicable rules, to the consumer's disadvantage, the more likely it is that the term should be considered unfair.[18]

The implication is that, to this extent, the optionality (the non-mandatory nature) of the relevant contract law rules becomes gradual too.

Moreover, the exemplary role is reflected very strongly in a second set of cases, where it provides the *justification* for the exclusion from unfair terms control of any terms reflecting non-mandatory rules. Pursuant to Article 1(2) of the Directive, contract terms 'which reflect mandatory statutory or regulatory provisions' are excluded from the substantive scope of the directive. Although the word 'mandatory' is ambiguous here, the preliminary recitals to the Directive are very clear.[19] Accordingly, the Court of Justice has long confirmed that exclusion also covers non-mandatory rules. And the rationale for the exclusion is precisely the *Leitbildfunktion*: such rules must be presumed to reflect the national law maker's view of a fair balance between the rights and obligations of the parties.[20] Thus, when sellers and service providers write terms that correspond to what the law they were free to set aside already provides for (to that extent, redundant terms), then EU unfair terms law does not require even the determination of their fairness.[21] This is not merely a presumption but an assumption of fairness of national non-mandatory rules. That is indeed a very strong exemplary role (*Leitbildfunktion*).[22]

[17] Case C-226/12, *Constructora Principado SA v. José Ignacio Menéndez Álvarez* (EU:C:2014:10), at para. 28.

[18] C. Leone, 'The Missing Stone in the Cathedral: Of Unfair Terms in Employment Contracts and Coexisting Rationalities in European Contract Law' (2020) (doctoral thesis on file at the University of Amsterdam), at 58–59.

[19] See Recital (13): 'the wording "mandatory statutory or regulatory provisions" in Article 1(2) also covers rules which, according to the law, shall apply between the contracting parties provided that no other arrangements have been established'.

[20] Case C-92/11, *RWE Vertrieb AG v. Verbraucherzentrale Nordrhein-Westfalen eV* (EU:C:2013:180), at para. 28: 'it may legitimately be supposed that the national legislature struck a balance between all the rights and obligations of the parties to certain contracts.'

[21] Remember that the Directive is a minimum harmonization directive; Member States are free to bring terms reflecting default rules within the scope of unfairness control. Of course in doing so they would suggest that some of their own laws—or their applicability to consumer contracts—might be unfair.

[22] Presumably, an important part of the rationale for this scope rule is diplomacy: if terms reflecting national law were within the scope of the Directive then at times the Court would have to determine—in effect—whether certain national contract laws—or their application in consumer contracts—were unfair towards consumers. And this could be just as awkward in the case of non-mandatory rules as regarding mandatory ones. However, this rationale applies directly only for national rules that were considered also specifically in relation to the type of contracts concerned. And that is not always the case. Problems may arise, especially when non-mandatory rules of general contract law or the general law of obligations are also applicable to consumer contracts. For example, the rule of nominalism in money debts, which may be a fair

Finally, there is a third context where the exemplary role is at work. When a term is unfair in the sense of the Directive, the question arises of whether courts are allowed to replace that term with the default rule that was set aside by the term. The Court has accepted this and the rationale for allowing substitution is, again, the *Leitbildfunktion*: substitution is fine since the default rule is presumed to be based on the national legislature's determination of a fair balance between the rights and obligations of the contracting parties, and, therefore, must be fair by definition.[23]

F. The Political Philosophy of Optional Contract Law

Do the leading contemporary political theories have anything to say about optional contract law, e.g. concerning its nature, rationale, justifiability, or content? A negative answer would suggest, for example, that non-mandatory contract law rules—which constitute the bulk of contract law in most European countries—are politically neutral or insignificant. That would in itself be a remarkable finding given that in most Member States they are enacted through the usual democratic legislative process. However, as we will see most political theories do have something to say on non-mandatory rules and regard them as far from insignificant or neutral.

2. Utilitarian

A. Incomplete Contracts and Default Rules

In a world without transaction costs, rational contracting parties would write complete contracts. They would fully provide, by appropriate contract clauses, for all possible states of the world at the moment—or during the time—the contract is meant

default rule in most cases, might turn out to be unfair in the context of foreign currency loans to consumers. In other words, the question arises of what *Leitbild* the law maker had in mind. Therefore, arguably only those national non-mandatory rules whose fairness was specifically considered for the type of contracts and type of parties under consideration should be considered outside the scope of the directive. And whether that is the case should be determined by the national court. In other words, there should be an assumption of fairness of the national non-mandatory rule but only a presumption of the fairness of their scope of application including also consumer contracts, a presumption that can be rebutted by evidence that the national legislator did not specifically consider consumer contracts. This argument was proposed by Advocate General Kokott in her Opinion (EU:C:2020:217) in Case C-81/19, *NG and OH v. SC Banca Transilvania SA* (EU:C:2020:532), at para. 42: 'the national legislature could only strike a balance between the parties inasmuch as it envisaged the specific arrangement between the parties'.

[23] However, this is only assured when the types of contract under consideration were on the horizon of the law maker when deliberating on the default rule. That is not necessarily the case for default rules of general contract law (or the general law of obligations) when it comes to their application to specific contracts, in particular specific consumer contracts. Therefore, in this context the presumption of fairness of national default rules can be rebutted for their application in certain consumer contracts. See Case C-260/18, *Kamil Dziubak and Justyna Dziubak v. Raiffeisen Bank International AG* (EU:C:2019:819), at para. 61. It was this reasoning that was picked-up by Advocate General Kokott, by way of analogy, for the different question under consideration in Case C-81/19, *NG and OH v. SC Banca Transilvania SA* (EU:C:2020:532), discussed in the main text as the second exemplary role.

to be performed. In the real world, in contrast, all contracts are incomplete in at least some respects. And where the costs of drafting and negotiating a contractual provision for a certain contingency are higher than their expected benefit, for example where the parties' interests are diametrically opposed with regard to the provision for a very unlikely event, then it is rational for the parties to leave the matter open. However, if there are enough other contracting parties concluding contracts similar enough to allow for the common use of a clause in several contracts, there could be economies of scale that could make the drafting of such a provision become efficient after all. Having said that, it will not be easy for parties drafting such a clause to market it and still keep its content sufficiently secret to prevent free riders from pre-empting a return of the drafters' investment. This collective action problem could be solved if the state stepped in by providing a set (or several sets) of efficient default rules.

This is the welfarist case for 'default rules'. By enacting efficient contract law rules that apply 'by default' (i.e. rules that will become applicable unless the parties replace them with others, in a way very similar to the default settings of our electronic devices)[24] as automatic gap fillers, the legislator can help the parties in saving transaction costs, because they thus will only have to spend resources on drafting and negotiating contractual provisions relating specifically to their particular transaction. The combination of the clauses in the contract and the default rules that have not been set aside by the contract, are said to reflect, together, the common intention of the parties. And as we saw in Chapter 5 (consent as a proxy for preference), a contract agreed to by both parties is presumed to benefit them both and, therefore, to increase social welfare (i.e. to be Pareto efficient) unless the consent was the result of a market failure (e.g. information asymmetry, monopoly, externalities). Thus, by making available such default rules contract law can fulfil its task of facilitating efficient market transactions.

From this welfarist perspective, therefore, it is the law maker's task to fill gaps in contracts by providing efficient default rules. And for this purpose, it becomes crucial to determine which default rules are efficient. This is crucial because, from a welfarist point of view, inefficient default rules are counter-productive since the parties will have to incur costs in order to contract around them. Unfortunately, however, the task of drafting efficient default rules has not proved to be an easy one for law makers.

The basic idea in the economic theory of default rules is that parties save most transaction costs when the non-mandatory rules correspond most to the contract that would be the outcome of their own negotiations not hindered by transaction costs (the hypothetical bargain).[25] The logical consequence of this is that, ideally, there should be as many sets of non-mandatory rules as contracts. However, it is obvious that although such a legal system would maximally save the contracting parties transaction costs, it would also be very costly for the taxpayer. Almost certainly, such a system would not save any costs at all—quite the contrary—since the legislator would have to incur enormous expenses in finding out which contract clauses the parties would want.

[24] The term 'default' was originally derived from the notion of default settings on computers, e.g. in word processing programmes such as MS Word.

[25] See e.g. R. Cooter and T. Ulen, *Law and Economics* (6th ed., 2012), at 293; Hermalin, Katz, and Craswell, 'Contract Law', in A. M. Polinsky and S. Shavell (eds), *Handbook of Law and Economics* (2007), ch. 1, at 87. The idea that the law should help the parties in saving transaction costs is obviously based on the Coase Theorem (see Coase, 'The Problem of Social Cost', 3 *Journal of Law and Economics* (1960) 1).

The second-best option is based on the idea that most contracts have some things in common, even though they are concluded by different parties, in different places, with different preferences. The law, therefore, should provide rules that the typical parties to typical contracts would opt for. This solution is second-best since parties still have to sustain the transaction costs associated with the fact that they have idiosyncratic preferences (they may be untypical parties and/or wish to conclude an untypical contract). Moreover, it raises the question of which rules typical parties to typical contracts would opt for. It may seem that in this second-best approach law makers would have to collect statistical information. For example, they could collect representative samples of contracts and see what kind of things the parties agree upon and provide for. Of course, in the real world legal systems already do include non-mandatory rules. Therefore, in reality the legislator would collect information regarding the existing non-mandatory rules which do *not* have the preference of the parties, i.e. the rules from which their contracts deviate. The empirical survey of contract samples could point to those rules.

However, there may be an easier way out. As we saw, it could be assumed—and many proponents of normative law and economics make the assumption—that contracting parties are rational maximizers of their own welfare. Surprising as this assumption may seem,[26] the benefit for the economic model of contracts is that it simplifies the analysis and therefore the economist's mission to provide policy advice. Instead of having to focus on the real preferences of real people, on this view, we can limit our task to figuring out what a homo economicus would want: what kind of contract would two 'rational' individuals with matching preferences and with full information but without any economic power over each other conclude? Indeed, this approach even makes it possible to depersonalize the analysis altogether and phrase the results in elegant mathematical functions that can be visualized in neat graphs.

Arguably, the assumption is most plausible with regard to contracts between sophisticated economic actors ('firms').[27] Among them, defaults that maximize joint surplus are likely to be most popular.[28] Thus, if default rules for commercial contracts

[26] Rakoff, 'The Implied Terms of Contracts: of "Default Rules" and "Situation-Sense"', in J. Beatson and D. Friedmann (eds), *Good Faith and Fault in Contract Law* (1995) 191, at 200: 'judges are deciding on the default rules applicable, not to abstract bargaining games, but to real life situations'. For a general anthropological critique, see P. Bourdieu, *The Social Structures of the Economy* (2005), at 209 and *passim*:

> Homo oeconomicus, as conceived (tacitly or explicitly) by economic orthodoxy, is a kind of anthropological monster: this theoretically minded man of practice is the most extreme personification of the scholastic fallacy, an intellectualist or intellectualocentric error very common in the social sciences, by which the scholar puts into the heads of the agents he is studying—housewives or households, firms or entrepreneurs, etc.—the theoretical considerations and constructions he has had to develop in order to account for their practices.

[27] Schwartz and Scott, 'Contract Theory and the Limits of Contract Law', 113 *Yale L.J.* (2003) 541, at 546. In the same sense, H. Dagan and M. Heller, *The Choice Theory of Contracts* (2017), at 53 and 104.

[28] The idea is that firms will try to maximize profit for their shareholders. See Schwartz and Scott (n. 27) 550–551. But see Bourdieu (n. 26) 206–207:

> It is, in fact, clear that for the rational calculations of an enlightened 'decision-maker', we have to substitute the political struggle among agents who tend to identify their specific interests (linked to their position in the firm and their dispositions) with the interests of the firm and whose power can no doubt be measured by their capacity to identify, for better or for worse, the interests of the firm with their interests within the firm.

were drafted with the objective of maximizing joint surplus in mind, rather than, say, considerations of fairness, fewer resources would be wasted by firms in setting unwanted defaults aside.[29]

Nevertheless, even this task may not be a very easy one. First, there is the question of what would be the optimal level of abstraction.[30] The lower the degree of abstraction the more specific the default rule can be, and the more precisely it is likely to fit with the specific transaction, and, consequently, the closer it can come to the parties' actual preferences. However, the higher the level of abstraction, the higher the degree of generality, and, hence, the more transactions that can be covered by the same default rule (economies of scale). A combination is also possible: part of the transaction is dealt with at one level of abstraction and part of it on another. Indeed, several twentieth-century civil codes, especially those of the Germanic type, have such a multi-layered structure, with increasingly specific sets of rules in the law of juristic acts (in the General Part), the general law of obligations, the general law of contracts, and the law of specific 'nominate' contracts, respectively.[31]

A related problem is classification. The diversification of default regimes (in accordance with the type of party, the type of contract, the market sectors, etc.) leads to openings for opportunistic behaviour *ex post*, i.e. once a dispute has arisen. The more distinctions that contract law draws—between different types of parties, different types of contracts, and different market sectors—the more possibilities there will be for a party to challenge the applicability of an unfavourable regime.[32] The parties can avoid this problem to some extent through careful drafting (which would, of course, increase transaction costs). However, it should be noted that there is a limit to the degree of legal certainty they can achieve, especially since in most legal systems classification is ultimately a matter for the court, and not the parties, to decide on.

Once the proper level of abstraction is determined, the question of which non-mandatory rule is most likely to enhance social welfare must be considered. Here, law and economics has not yet produced much firm ground so far. The main problem seems to be that hardly any reliable empirical data exist. The example of efficient breach is significant. The question of which remedy would be the preferred default remedy from an economic point of view—i.e. damages or specific performance—is probably the contract law question that has attracted most attention from economic analysts. Yet, as we saw in Chapter 5, the academic debate has still not led to a generally accepted result, ready to be transposed into legislation.[33] On the contrary, some

[29] Schwartz and Scott (n. 27) 551.

[30] An example: if I buy an e-book on the internet, this transaction can be conceived of as an electronic consumer sale of digital content, as a consumer sale, as a sale, as a synallagmatic contract (in civil law jurisdictions), as a contract, which is a source of obligations (which in civil law jurisdictions triggers the general law of obligations), and as a juristic act (in certain civil law jurisdictions).

[31] E.g. the German *Bürgerliches Gesetzbuch (BGB)* (1900), the Portuguese *Código Civil* (1967), and the Dutch *Burgerlijk Wetboek (BW)* (1992).

[32] This seems to be a decisive argument against De Geest's proposal for 'several hundreds of smaller codes' which should be 'extremely detailed' and which should also contain mandatory rules. See De Geest, 'Information Problems Caused by Regulatory Competition, and their Solution: International Standard Codes', in S. Grundmann and J. Stuyck (eds), *An Academic Green Paper on European Contract Law* (2002) 373.

[33] Or into judge-made contract law, as the case may be.

scholars believe that damages are the most efficient default remedy,[34] while others argue for specific performance.[35] In essence, the state of the debate on efficient breach brings us back to the problem of the degree of abstraction. Is it possible to draft a non-mandatory rule likely to produce efficient results in most cases without this rule being completely idiosyncratic?

Moreover, further nuances seem to be in order here. Legal economists indicate, for example, that a rule based on the hypothetical bargain is not always the most efficient rule. A different kind of rule ('penalty default') is likely to produce more efficient results, for example where information asymmetry (where one party knows more than the other) may lead to an inefficient allocation of risk.[36]

Given that law makers lack the information needed for writing efficient default rules, in practice they often resort to default standards, i.e. open-ended concepts such as 'reasonableness', 'good faith', etc. However, such standards are likely to be inefficient since their indeterminacy gives incentives for opportunistic *ex post* behaviour (moral hazard) while at the same time they do not contribute much towards saving parties transaction costs since standards are relatively easy to write, not only for law makers but also for contracting parties. Indeed, for this reason Schwartz and Scott argue that the presence of a gap in a contract that could be filled by a standard should be taken as evidence that the parties did *not* want that standard.[37]

Scott and Schwartz have argued that the project of default rules has failed: 'firms would reject the "default project" if they could because the project generates many inefficient terms that contracting parties must incur costs to avoid'.[38] Similarly, Eric Posner concludes more generally (as we saw in Chapter 5) that the economic analysis of contract law has failed,[39] because its hypotheses are either so general that they cannot be tested empirically, or they can be tested but their implications are so specific that they

34 Because it avoids the costs of double transactions or negotiations under a bilateral monopoly.

35 Because it makes the parties, not the courts, set prices.

36 See Ayres and Gertner, 'Filling Gaps in Incomplete Contracts: An Economic Theory of Default Rules', 99 *Yale L.J.* (1989) 87. The classical example is a 19th century English case on remoteness of damage, *Hedley v. Baxendale* (1854) 9 Exch 341. In that case, the mill shaft in a flour mill had broken. A common carrier had agreed to transport the broken shaft to a third party who was meant to make a new shaft after its model. The owners had told the carrier that the shaft had to be delivered immediately, but had failed to point out that they had no spare shaft, and that therefore any delay would mean that the mill could not work, which would result in a loss of profits. The court decided that this special damage was too remote and therefore could not be recovered. The economic rationale for this rule is said to be that it provides incentives for efficient communication between the parties, which allows the parties efficiently to allocate the risk to the lowest cost-bearer (typically, via a combination of insurance and a limitation of liability).

37 Schwartz and Scott (n. 27) 604.

38 Ibid. 609. They limit their claims explicitly to commercial contracts.

39 Posner, 'Economic Analysis of Contract Law After Three Decades: Success or Failure?' (2003) 112 *Yale L.J.* 829. Critical, Craswell, 'In That Case, What Is the Question? Economics and the Demands of Contract Theory', 112 *Yale L.J.* (2003) 903, at 913, 924:

> While it may be that the ultimate goal of a normative theory is to be able to recommend a particular rule—and, of course, to justify that recommendation—normative analysis can still be useful even if it falls short of that ultimate goal. . . . If we instead see the normative goal slightly differently—that is, if we see it as the goal of shedding as much light as we can on the morally relevant effects of contract rules, and on the costs and benefits of those effects—then, by this standard, the past thirty years should count as a success.

do not reach the minimum level of generality necessary for manageable legislation.[40] This resonates with the experience that law and economics cannot provide clear answers to most of the practical questions that drafters of non-mandatory contract law rules need to answer. For example, in the light of what we saw, it seems virtually impossible to decide, on economic grounds, which comprehensive set of rules—e.g. the *BGB*, *Code Civil*, Principles of European Contract Law (PECL), Draft Common Frame of Reference (DCFR), or CESL—would contribute most to increasing social welfare.[41]

B. Altering Rules

As a more general matter, other things being equal, the world is a better place in the eyes of a utilitarian to the extent that the law corresponds to the preferences of individuals. One way of achieving this is by giving individuals the choice among different sets of legal rules, allowing them to choose, from among the available sets, the one they expect to make them best off. However, even in such a scenario, from the utilitarian perspective, problems may still arise.

First, the free choice by the contracting parties of their own legal regime will only enhance social utility if it does not lead to externalities. Such externalities do exist, for example, if the availability of choice leads to a race to the bottom which may remove from the market options that certain contracting parties might have strongly preferred.

Secondly, the choice of law will not increase the welfare of the parties if it is ill-informed. This is not merely a theoretical possibility. Much of the discussion on the CESL proposal turned on the question of how the parties could know and compare the different available legal regimes. Consumer protection groups, for example, emphatically rejected the CESL proposal because they feared that the choice of law would be made unilaterally by the trader and only in cases where this would best suit the trader's interests (in which case, and to that extent, it would typically be against the interests of the consumer), and that even where consumers were allowed a real margin of negotiation, typically they would not have the necessary information and legal skills to compare and evaluate the available options.[42]

Ayres has pointed out, in more general terms, the importance for successful optional law of having the right 'altering rules', as he calls them. These are the rules that

[40] A striking example is the analysis by L. Kaplow and S. Shavell, *Fairness Versus Welfare* (2002), at 172 ff: their repeated mantra is that contract rules should make both parties better off; however, their analysis remains completely abstract.

[41] Cf. Posner (n. 39) 865.

[42] The European Commission had tried to reduce this problem by introducing formalities and information requirements for the opt-in (CESL proposal (n. 10) Art. 9). The choice had to be made separately and after the parties had received information (Standard Information Notice (SIN)). However, this solution was criticized for going both too far and not far enough. It went too far because the warning suggested that the CESL was intrinsically dangerous or risky while in the vast majority of cases the choice was supposed to make the consumer better off overall (in terms not merely of consumer rights but also of price and quality). For if it did not, the European legislator should not have made the CESL available as an option in the first place (see Art. 114(3) and Art. 169 TFEU). Secondly, the SIN was not enough because it only informed the consumer about the merits of the CESL but not about the alternatives, as a result of which an informed choice would still not be possible.

determine how parties can opt into or out of a legal regime. He argues that efficiency minded law makers, in setting altering rules, should consider not only the costs of altering (i.e. transaction costs) but also the social costs of various kinds of error, especially errors by the parties (e.g. uninformed consent to an opt-out) and judicial errors (e.g. party language mistakenly understood as opt-out).[43] Moreover, classical reasons for making a term mandatory (externalities and paternalism) may also justify making the opt-out from a default rule more difficult ('sticky-defaults').[44] His focus is mainly on opting out and defaults. However, opting into a legal regime also always constitutes an opt-out, except, that is, if one accepts the controversial notion of a '*contrat sans loi*'.[45]

C. Shopping Abroad for Law

A number of efficiency-minded legal scholars have started referring to 'law as product' and have claimed the existence of a 'law market'.[46] That refers to the idea of a market where private parties shop for law and where states offer their laws as products that private parties can buy into. To be sure, the market for law would be a somewhat unusual one since the buyers do not have to pay, at least not directly. Moreover, the buyers buy their products through contracts, not with the state (the supplier), but with each other (as joint demanders). However, it seems the terminology is meant to be understood more broadly, as offering a new (i.e. economic) perspective on the availability of a choice of law in cross-border cases.

The possibility to choose the applicable law, which is well-established in private international law, would be unthinkable in other legal fields (e.g. imagine the possibility of choice of law in cross-border criminal cases). As a result of the possibility of choice of law, in a sense there exist as many private law systems as there are options. We could even speak of a do-it-yourself legal system.[47] Still, there are not as many options as there are preferences. The private law market is not an unregulated market. Supply and demand takes place within the regulatory framework of ordinary mandatory rules (of contract law, property law, etc.) and internationally mandatory rules (through private international law). In principle, the ideas of the law market and law as product do not change (or require change) in the currently existing choice of law rules. They merely offer a different understanding and explanation of party autonomy in cross-border contracts. Having said that, if the justification lies in an increase in welfare then, of course, this model naturally supports a push towards deregulation wherever limitations to the freedom to choose your own law are not welfare-enhancing.

43 Ayres, 'Regulating Opt Out: An Economic Theory of Altering Rules', 121 *Yale L.J.* (2012) 2032.

44 Ibid.

45 For a comparative overview, see Gannagé, 'Le contrat sans loi en droit international privé', 11 *Electronic Journal of Comparative Law* (2007), available at http://www.ejcl.org/113/article113-10.pdf (last visited 22 July 2020).

46 E. A. O'Hara and L. E. Ribstein, *The Law Market* (2009); Eidenmüller, 'Recht als Produkt', 64 *JuristenZeitung* (2009) 641.

47 On the DIY legal system, see Hesselink, 'How Many Systems of Private Law Are There in Europe? On Plural Legal Sources, Multiple Identities and the Unity of Law', in L. Niglia (ed.), *Pluralism and European Private Law* (2013) 199, at 235–236.

Indeed, the normative welfare economist assumption of market efficiency is adopted by Eidenmüller and by O'Hara and Ribstein, accepting limitations to choice of law only for cases of demonstrated externalities and lack of free choice, thus shifting the burden of proof of the justifiability of market regulation in the familiar manner.

The law market is a market where law is the product on offer. However, as discussed previously, the market itself is shaped by law—a product of law and, in particular, choice-of-law rules. Therefore, Eidenmüller is right in underlining that the law market does not undermine the primacy of politics. On the contrary, an effective law market depends on political decisions, made by the legislator or courts that alone can make it come about.[48] Eidenmüller regards the EU as the level of law making where the law market should be located, because the competition should be between states.[49] He argues that the EU should warrant the possibility for Member States to compete with each other on a law market. The legal framework (i.e. especially rules on choice of law) for this market should be shaped by the EU, as indeed has already largely been done in the area of contract law by the Rome I Regulation, especially Article 3 (freedom of choice) and its limits, including those in Articles 6 (consumer contracts), 8 (employment contracts), and 9 (overriding mandatory provisions). The EU could also enrich the competition by introducing products of its own. Thus, in addition to the horizontal competition between the Member States there would also be what Eidenmüller calls vertical competition between the Member States, on the one hand, and the EU, on the other.[50] The EU has already done this with the introduction of the European company (SE); the CESL would have provided a further example.

Although a choice of law is primarily an expression of private autonomy it has a public dimension as well. The reason is that opting out of a legal system always expresses disapproval (at least for the purposes at hand) of the law proposed by one legislator and approval for the law proposed by another. In the longer run, the aggregate effect of several of these individual choices may be that the legislators decide to reconsider their legislative choices.[51] As O'Hara and Ribstein put it, 'the law market fundamentally alters the political process to the extent that it makes people "consumers" or "buyers" of laws rather than simply voters'.[52] The negative consequence may be a race to the bottom. However, the good side may be that interests that were not strongly represented in the law making process (e.g. because of effective lobbying by special interest groups)[53] may obtain an indirect voice by exercising this more limited type of 'exit': not total exit from the country (emigration) but partial exit (i.e. from certain parts of the country's private law only).[54] In any case, it means that the exercise of

[48] Eidenmüller (n. 46) 648.

[49] Ibid. 651.

[50] Ibid. 652.

[51] See e.g. the official motivation for the 2016 contract law reform in France: 'Cette ordonnance vise également à renforcer l'attractivité du droit français'. (*Projet de loi ratifiant l'ordonnance n°2016-131 du 10 février 2016 portant réforme du droit des contrats, du régime général et de la preuve des obligations*).

[52] O'Hara and Ribstein (n. 46) 14.

[53] On this problem, see Chapter 3.

[54] Another limitation is that the exit is offered only in the case of a cross-border contract: most countries do not allow opting out of their laws in purely domestic contracts. This could have changed had the CESL Regulation been adopted. Under the proposed regulation the Member States were allowed to open the choice for its applicability also for purely internal contracts.

private autonomy may undermine or diminish the effectiveness of what was publicly decided.[55] For example, mandatory rules may ban certain contracts or certain contract clauses, but parties may escape this ban by submitting their contract to a more lenient system.[56] However, it is important to underline that in such cases the rule permitting the choice of law that enables a more lenient system to be chosen still derives from a public decision. And this public decision may—and often does (see Rome I)—pose certain limits on the choice of law. Therefore, the primacy of the political process remains in place. The political process of limiting freedom of contract thus operates on two different levels, via national mandatory rules and internationally mandatory rules, respectively. And the autonomy of the parties to build their own legal systems is shaped and limited at these two levels. The idea of self-legislation by the parties (and its limits) was famously expressed (for the first level) by Article 1134(1) (now Article 1103) of the French Civil Code: 'Les conventions légalement formées tiennent lieu de loi à ceux qui les ont faites.' If indeed parties are their own legislators (within the limits of the law) then to that extent they are also their own system builders (within the same limits)—hence, the 'DIY' legal system.[57]

Smits argues that in a globalizing world democratic legitimacy does not have to come about through territorial entities such as national parliaments but can also be achieved through competition.[58] However, it is clear that an unregulated law market would lead to more than just massive externalization of social costs and the survival of the fittest. Taken to its extreme, the idea of an unfettered private law market would ultimately lead to a result where there were as many legal systems as there were individuals: everyone would have their own system.

D. Defective Products and Innovation

Although efficiency-minded scholars have expressed enthusiasm with regard to the idea of optional law, the CESL proposal specifically met with severe criticism from the law and economics front. Several observers argued the quality of the proposal was so

[55] O'Hara and Ribstein (n. 46) 36 speak of 'the eroding effects of choice of law'.

[56] In Germany, it has been argued that unfair terms control in B2B contracts drives businesses out of German law and makes them opt into Swiss law, where there is no unfairness control in B2B contracts. It is not clear whether this 'flight into foreign law' thesis is empirically accurate. Berger, 'Abschied von der Privatautonomie im unternehmerischen Geschäftsverkehr? Zum Differenzierungsgebot im AGB-Recht', *Zeitschrift für Wirtschaftsrecht (ZIP)* (2006) 2149 and Lischek and Mahnken, 'Vertragsverhandlungen zwischen Unternehmen und AGB—Anmerkungen aus der Sicht der Praxis', *ZIP* (2007) 158, offer only anecdotal evidence; Von Westphalen, '30 Jahre AGB-Recht—Eine Erfolgsbilanz', *ZIP* (2007) 149, is sceptical.

[57] See Hesselink (n. 47) 235–236.

[58] Smits, 'Democracy and (European) Private Law: A Functional Approach', in M. Faure and A. van der Walt (eds), *Globalization and Private Law: The Way Forward* (2010) 15; Smits, 'European Private Law and Democracy: A Misunderstood Relationship', in M. Faure and F. Stephen (eds), *Essays in the Law and Economics of Regulation in Honour of Anthony Ogus* (2008) 49; Smits, 'Plurality of Sources in European Private Law, or: How to Live With Legal Diversity?', in R. Brownsword *et al.*, (eds), *The Foundations of European Private Law* (2011) 323. Contrast Mattei, 'Hard Code Now!', 2 *Global Jurist Frontiers* (2002), who rejects the 'soft ideology' behind 'theories of competition between national legal systems as an efficient pattern of private law integration and notions of facilitating, optional "default law" as an efficient alternative to mandatory binding legal rules', and argues for a hard, mandatory European civil code.

poor that it should not be opted into by rational and informed parties.[59] The proposal was labelled as a 'defective product' and as a 'lemon'.[60]

Brexit has brought a further problem in that regard. Eidenmüller argues that the UK had been the most innovative EU Member State when it came to legal products. Therefore, its departure from the EU is bad news from the point of view of horizontal regulatory competition, since the remaining Member States will now have less of an incentive for legal innovation. As he concludes, 'in essence, Brexit will eliminate a highly innovative competitor on the European market for new legal products in private law, reducing the beneficial effects of such competition'.[61]

3. Liberal-Egalitarian

A. Liberal Neutrality and the Content of Default Rules

Craswell has argued forcefully against autonomy-based contract theories, on the grounds that they cannot provide guidance in determining the proper content of default rules, which constitute the bulk of general contract law, for the reason that, by definition, the parties' promises or consent, as acts of autonomy or individual liberty, are silent about how any gaps in their contract should be filled.[62] Therefore, he argues, such theories need to—and in practice do—resort to other values than autonomy or liberty, such as fairness or efficiency. As Craswell explains:

> The reason that ... autonomy-based theories are unhelpful in the selection of default rules is that ... these ... share the characteristic of being completely content-neutral. They give reasons why an individual who has promised to do Ø thereby incurs some form of obligation to do Ø, regardless of how Ø is filled in. The reason for this neutrality is understandable: To do anything more requires a theory that would tell people what kinds of promises they ought to make. Unfortunately, the theorists' reluctance to advise individuals as to how they ought to exercise their freedom to fill in the content of Ø leaves them equally unable to give legal systems any guidance about how to fill in the content of Ø when contracting parties fail to specify their preferred content. As a result, these ... theories have nothing to contribute to the selection of

[59] See e.g. Eidenmüller *et al.*, 'The Proposal for a Regulation on a Common European Sales Law: Deficits of the Most Recent Textual Layer of European Contract Law', 16 *Edinburgh Law Review* (2012) 301. Specifically with regard to related services, see Illmer, 'Related Services in the Commission Proposal for a Common European Sales Law COM(2011) 635 Final: Much Ado About Nothing?' 21 *ERPL* (2012) 131.

[60] Eidenmüller, 'What Can Be Wrong With an Option? An Optional Common European Sales Law as a Regulatory Tool', 50 *CMLR* (2013) 69; Smits, 'Party Choice and the Common European Sales Law, or: How to Prevent the CESL from Becoming a Lemon on the Law Market' 50 *CMLR* (2013) 51. The lemon metaphor—American slang for a defective second hand car—refers to Akerlof, 'The Market for "Lemons": Quality Uncertainty and the Market Mechanism', 84 *Quarterly Journal of Economics* (1970) 488.

[61] Eidenmüller, 'Collateral Damage: Brexit's Negative Effects on Regulatory Competition and Legal Innovation in Private Law', University of Oxford and ECGI, Law Working Paper No. 403/2018 (May 2018).

[62] Craswell, 'Contract Law, Default Rules, and the Philosophy of Promising', 88 *Michigan Law Review* (1989) 489.

default rules governing such important topics as implied terms and conditions, excuses, and remedies for breach.[63]

In the light of this criticism, liberal-egalitarians (and libertarians), it seems, will have to choose between either strict neutrality or implementing some conception of the good. That choice would seem unattractive for liberals, since liberal neutrality would leave us without any rules to fill the gaps in contracts while a non-neutral liberalism, from their perspective, would be a contradiction in terms. Let us see how liberal perfectionist and political liberals, respectively, have responded to Craswell's challenge.

B. A Rich Menu of Contract Types

1. Autonomy through Choice

Optional contract law is central to 'the choice theory of contracts', as presented by Dagan and Heller.[64] In contrast to the utilitarian views we saw in the previous section, where optional contract law is instrumental to the collectivist aim of increasing overall welfare in a society, for liberal perfectionists optional law is of instrumental value for achieving the intrinsic value of individual autonomy. On this view, the main tool by which contract law supports autonomy is by offering, for each contract context, a rich menu of attractive contract types for the parties to choose from.

With their choice theory of contracts Dagan and Heller propose an entirely novel way of looking at contract law, which is liberal perfectionist, in that it has human flourishing through self-authorship at its core. However, it is not susceptible to Craswell's criticism, at least not directly. They argue that we should abandon our traditional focus on general contract law altogether and concentrate instead—both for theory and for reform—on specific contract types. In particular, they argue that in a liberal society the law maker is under an obligation to make a sufficiently wide range of contract types available. Once the parties have chosen one of these types, a whole set of rules will come with it. As a result, through autonomous choice for contract types typically there will be no—or at least many fewer—significant gaps in contracts ('unfilled content of Ø', Craswell's term).

At first sight, this proposal may strike a civil lawyer as not particularly novel, or even regressive. Not only did the 'nominate' contract types historically precede innominate contracts,[65] also, today there would not seem to be any need for reform. For at first sight, the required multiplicity of contract types already seems to be well entrenched in most civil law systems that, in addition to general contract law, usually offer a rich variety of codified contract types. Indeed, in most civil codes, the number of provisions dedicated to specific, 'nominate' contract types far exceeds the space occupied in the code by the rules of general contract law. The same goes for the DCFR, where Book

[63] Ibid. 515–516.
[64] Dagan and Heller (n. 27).
[65] R. Zimmermann, *The Law of Obligations: Roman Foundations of the Civilian Tradition* (1996), at 561 and *passim*.

IV, on specific contracts, is larger than Books I, II, and III, covering the general law of contracts and of obligations, taken together.[66]

Perhaps even more strikingly, it is a core feature of positive EU contract law (against which the European civil code movement was principally directed) that it has indeed moved beyond general contract law: the *acquis communautaire* consists mainly of rules for specific contract types: sales, credit, air transport, timesharing, supply of digital content, commercial agency, contracts in the agricultural and food supply chain, etc. However, on further examination both the existing civil codes and the *acquis* comply only very partially with the demands of the choice theory of contracts. The reason is that they do not seem to meet the diversity requirement central to Dagan and Heller's theory, which is both specific and demanding.

2. Contract Spheres and Types

A core idea in the choice theory of contracts is that for each different contracting sphere there should be an adequate range of attractive types to choose from. Dagan and Heller propose a taxonomy reflecting, they suggest, 'the typical contexts in which people enter contracts', consisting of four contracting spheres, i.e. family, home, employment, and commerce.[67] Thus, Dagan and Heller understand the 'spheres' as rather large sectors of contracting. Of these, commerce seems the largest by far. This is perhaps why they propose a taxonomy of sub-spheres of commerce, i.e. consumer, lending/insurance, sales/business, finance/risk.[68]

For each sphere or sub-sphere of human interaction, it is the law maker's task to offer a sufficiently rich menu of contract types to choose from. Crucially, there also have to be meaningful options to reject. The reason is that autonomy is exercised, and responsibility is taken, by a person for her own self-authored life, not only affirmatively, by a positive choice for a certain option, but also by a negative choice rejecting the other options. For this reason, the law maker must also make some contract types available for which there does not yet—and perhaps never will—exist any significant demand, such as minoritarian or even utopian contract types.[69] It is here that the crucial difference lies with existing systems of contract law, not only in the common law but also in the civil law tradition.[70] Most nominate contracts in civil codes are best explained either as presumptively majoritarian or as historical relicts.[71] Moreover, and most importantly, they usually offer only one type per contracting context. In the terminology of Dagan and Heller, the multiplicity they ensure is across spheres, not intra-sphere. However, from the perspective of their—in this respect Razian[72]—liberal

[66] In the outline edition: pages 138–221 for Books I–III and pages 222–321 for Book IV.
[67] Dagan and Heller (n. 27) 96.
[68] Ibid. 98.
[69] Ibid. 60.
[70] And also, of course, with the idea of the law market we saw earlier, that expects equilibrium between demand and supply, which will clear the market and prevent overproduction, and certainly has no place for state subsidies supporting types that lack demand (except perhaps as a start-up investment in innovation).
[71] The DCFR broke with the traditional contract categories and introduced a novel taxonomy for specific contracts. For the 'functional' methodology that was adopted for distinguishing different types of services, see Loos, 'Towards a European law of service contracts', 9 *ERPL* (2001) 565.
[72] J. Raz, *The Morality of Freedom* (1986) 205, at 373. As we saw in Chapter 7, Dagan and Heller (and Dagan separately in single-authored papers) otherwise aim to differentiate their view from Raz's by adopting a thinner conception of the good, especially with regard to the reasons for removing options.

perfectionism, that is not sufficient. As Dagan and Heller put it pointedly, 'it doesn't enhance freedom if you can choose, for example, either to get married or enter an agency contract'.[73]

Having said that, there is a serious question as to what should count as different contract types within the same (sub-)sphere. Doesn't each contract type in a sense create its own sphere of human interaction? And isn't it somewhat arbitrary in the end which set of types one groups together as types of the same (sub-)sphere? Various family resemblances between many different contract types will probably exist.[74] The idea of 'intra-sphere multiplicity' is that the different types within one sphere or sub-sphere can operate as 'partial functional substitutes'. However, here the reasoning risks becoming circular, since the rationale for intra-sphere multiplicity is the 'autonomy-enhancing function' of contract law.[75] From the point of view of liberal agnosticism with regard to different conceptions of the good couldn't *all* types, in principle, be functional equivalents in the eyes of an autonomous agent—if that is how she wants to write the story of her life? The implication seems to be that choice theory is susceptible to Craswell's challenge after all: autonomy as self-authorship cannot tell us which types might count as functional equivalents within the same sphere. Therefore, how can we know when the objective of intra-sphere multiplicity is met? For all we know even the status quo (in civil law jurisdictions) might do.

3. Choosing the Menu

As we saw in Chapter 3, Dagan and Heller do not regard the legislature as the political institution that most obviously should be the one determining which contracting options should be offered to the public through generally applicable laws. The reason, as we saw, is that in their view this is more a matter of 'institutional competence' than of legitimacy.[76] Similarly, the taxonomy question of how the world of contracting should be divided up, as a matter of contract-law-making, into spheres, is also one that Dagan and Heller think does not require any democratic deliberation or decision-making. Although they acknowledge that their taxonomy is contingent and contestable,[77] they do not seem too concerned that their happy image of contracting as family, home, employment, and commerce may come across as strikingly out of touch with reality, for example, in the eyes of all those who experience contracting mostly in terms of dependence, exploitation, and alienation, and who lack any meaningful access to some of these happy contracting (sub)spheres. To such a person, a different contract law taxonomy, focusing on problems of injustice and inequality, may seem more to the point than the harmonious image of contract law suggested by Dagan and Heller. To be sure, this is not to suggest that Dagan and Heller disregard inequality. They do in fact emphasize that their theory requires substantive equality,[78] as we saw in Chapter 6. The

[73] Dagan and Heller (n. 27) 69.

[74] Cf. L. Wittgenstein, *Philosophical Investigations*, ([first published 1953] 4th ed., 2009) (translation G. E. M. Anscombe, P. M. S. Hacker, and J. Schulte), at §§ 66–67, discussing games and asking whether there is any characteristic common to everything we refer to as 'games'.

[75] Dagan and Heller (n. 27) 13.

[76] Ibid. 130.

[77] Ibid. 96.

[78] Ibid. 87 and 111.

question is rather whether the demands of justice should be made more central to a choice theory of contract law, in particular who should be choosing the taxonomy of a contract law aiming to enhance choice.[79] Very concretely, how will all those to whom contract law will inevitably apply be secured a meaningful say in what will be on the menu and what will be kept off?

4. The Fairness of Choice through Standard Terms

As a practical matter, it seems entirely possible to make a choice for a contract type through standard terms. Indeed, under current law that happens sometimes explicitly, simply by labelling the contract as 'sales' or 'employment' or some other type (even though, as mentioned previously, classification always remains subject to judicial control), or more indirectly, by formulating the rights and obligations of the parties in such a way that the contract is caught by the legal definition of the contract type. Both direct and indirect choice through standard terms also seem possible under the choice theory of contracts. However, the choice theory of contracts does not explicitly address this possibility and its limits.

If the choice takes place through standard terms then in principle it can be subjected to unfairness control. At least for consumer contracts in the EU, this raises the question of how the choice theory relates to the so-called *Leitbildfunktion* (exemplary function) of non-mandatory rules. If it is the task of law makers to provide a range of 'normatively attractive contract types',[80] are they then expressing their views of fairness? Should all the types on the menu be regarded as—and should they in fact be—(equally and) sufficiently fair? That would mean that a choice through standard terms for any of the types could never be unfair. Or does 'normative attractiveness', the standard Dagan and Heller refer to,[81] not relate to fairness and justice, but only to different conceptions of the good (as opposed to the right)? To the extent that sets of rules merely correspond to different values, it seems, under certain circumstances a choice for one type rather than another may indeed be unfair, for example in the cases of various kinds of imbalances between the parties (such as power, experience, expertise, need) while the different available types within the (sub-)sphere involve different degrees of risk-taking. In summary, the exemplary function of standard terms in determining whether a standard term is unfair indirectly raises the question again (but in a different way than in Chapter 7) of Dagan and Heller's understanding of 'normatively attractive contract types', and, thus, of how perfectionist their liberalism still is: what standards do the contract types on the menu have to meet?

Under the *Leitbild* conception, as we saw, the default rules constitute a standard by which courts can evaluate the fairness of a standard term: the more the term deviates from the non-mandatory rule to the disadvantage of the consumer—or, in Radin's powerful expression, deletes their rights[82]—the more the standard term must

[79] See further Hesselink, 'The Right to Justification of Contract', *Ratio Juris* (2020), on which this paragraph draws.
[80] Dagan and Heller (n. 27) 137.
[81] See ibid. 137: 'the state is obligated to ensure the availability of diverse, normatively attractive contract types in each important sphere of human interaction'.
[82] See M. J. Radin, *Boilerplate: The Fine Print, Vanishing Rights, and the Rule of Law* (2013), ch. 2 and *passim*.

be considered unfair. However, it is not clear under the choice theory of contracts that non-mandatory rules are still meant to fulfil this role. It seems that under the choice theory, general contract law is meant to play only the residual role of applying when parties have not opted for one of the types.[83] This may well turn out to occur more frequently than Dagan and Heller expect. In addition, and more importantly here, it is that set of general contract law rules that would, at least under current EU unfair terms law, become the standard for determining the validity of a term, even when the parties were contracting in a specific sphere but had failed to choose a type. This would only be different if choice theory were implemented with one type per sphere being designated as the default, which, however, would not sit too well with the overall theory.

C. Disposable Law and the Basic Structure

1. Can the Basic Structure of Society Be Partly Optional?

As we saw in Chapters 5 and 6, there is controversy among philosophers as to whether contract law should be regarded as part of the basic structure of a well-ordered society as it was understood by Rawls. With respect to optional law, there seem to be further issues in this regard.

There is wide agreement that even if contract law (or its basic structure) were part of the basic structure of society, then contracts themselves still clearly would not be.[84] It might be argued, however, that optional contract law is situated somewhere between contract law and a contract. That makes optional contract law an even less likely candidate for being part of the basic structure, and hence being relevant to social justice, than, say, the non-optional rules of EU contracts law contained in the *acquis*. This follows most clearly if one understands optional contract law, such as national non-mandatory rules ('default rules'), opt-out codes for cross-border contracts (CISG), and those conflict rules that are applicable only in the absence of a choice of law (Article 4, Rome I), merely as gap-fillers, complementing incomplete contracts. The choice itself—whether active or passive—for the applicability of the optional law would, of course, still be subject to law, which would in fact be mandatory; the contracting parties cannot set aside the rules regulating the modalities of choice. And those mandatory rules of contract law and of private international law—the altering rules, as Ayres calls them, as we saw—could perhaps be considered part of the basic structure of society.

Having said that, there is no reason, of course, why a Rawlsian theory of contract law should be committed to the particular merely facilitative, social-cost-reducing utilitarian understanding of non-mandatory rules of contract law.

2. The Difference Principle: A Maximizing Principle?

This raises the question of whether there exists another understanding of optional contract law that would require the presence of non-mandatory contract law rules, under Rawlsian principles of justice, and, thus understood, would determine minimum

83 On 'freestanding contracting', see Dagan and Heller (n. 27) 84.

84 See explicitly J. Rawls, *Political Liberalism* ([first published 1993] 2005), at 282–283.

requirements concerning their content. The reasoning grounded in private autonomy that we just saw is not available for a political liberal, since Dagan and Heller's perfectionist conception of autonomy, celebrating the individual's ability to write the story of her own life, seems far too thick from a Rawlsian perspective, while Rawls's political conception of the person and her autonomy, if indeed it does require at least minimal contracting options, as suggested in Chapter 5, clearly does not go as far as requiring the diverse menu that is necessary, according Dagan and Heller, to ensure human flourishing.[85]

What about the difference principle? Can a case be made that a society's choice whether or not to have optional contract law rules and, if so, what their content should be (minimally), should depend on whether their presence or absence would work for the benefit of the least well off in that society? Whether indeed the difference principle applies to these questions, however, depends on whether default rules are part of the basic structure, which seems to bring us back to where we started.

But what if the difference principle were a maximizing principle, demanding that all institutional choices, or all those related to the basic structure, should contribute to maximally improving the socio-economic position of the least well-off (maximizing the minimum, 'maximin')? Perhaps an empirical case could be made, partly relying on the welfarist argument we saw earlier but substituting the maximization of overall welfare in society with the maximization of bundles of primary goods for the least well-off group in society, to the effect that having a set of default rules could contribute (even if perhaps only marginally) to maximizing the minimum.

As Kordana and Tabachnick point out, 'as is the case with any maximizing principles, the normative conclusions prescribed are a function of the domain over which the principles are applied; the range of application of the maximand must thus be specified'.[86] And defining the scope of the basic structure of society on the basis of application of a principle whose scope of application is supposed to be defined by that very basic structure, may still seem an impermissible bootstrapping argument. On the other hand, however, the scope of basic structure, i.e. the definition of which social, political, and economic institutions should be held mainly responsible for justice in a society, would seem to be an important issue that principles of justice may want to have a say on. In other words, the principles of justice may have to be reflexive, requiring the application of the principles to the determination of their own scope, in which case the circularity would be virtuous, rather than vicious.[87] Or perhaps, vindicating the non-categorical nature of justice as fairness, this is simply due to the fact that normative principles of justice are meant to be derived in part from the conditions of empirically existing societies.[88]

[85] Cf. J. Rawls, *Justice As Fairness: A Restatement* (2001), at 156: 'The liberalisms of Kant and Mill may lead to requirements designed to foster the values of autonomy and individuality as ideals to govern much if not all of life. But political liberalism has a different aim and requires far less.'

[86] Kordana and Tabachnick, 'Rawls and Contract Law', 73 *Geo. Wash. L. Rev.* (2005) 598, at 602.

[87] On the reflexive and recursive character of practical reason, see O'Neill, 'Reason and Politics in the Kantian Enterprise', in O. O'Neill, *Constructions of Reason: Explorations of Kantian Practical Philosophy* (1989), ch. 1.

[88] Because of this empiricism, O'Neill (O. O'Neill, *Bounds of Justice* (2000), at 2), and Ripstein (A. Ripstein, *Force and Freedom: Kant's Legal and Political Philosophy* (2009), at 3), reject Rawls's claim that his theory is Kantian.

Some of Rawls's writing suggests that he did in fact consider the difference principle to be a maximizing principle (albeit constrained of course by the first principle, protecting basic liberties, and the first part of the second principle, protecting fair equal access to opportunities). For example, he writes: 'the basic structure of society is arranged so that it maximizes the primary goods available to the least advantaged to make use of the equal basic liberties enjoyed by everyone'.[89] However, on other occasions he understands the difference principle as being 'essentially a principle of reciprocity',[90] which seems to imply merely that those who benefit from certain policies of law must make sure that all others also benefit from it.[91] The reciprocity reading of the difference principle seems less demanding as it is not intrinsically a maximizing principle (maximizing reciprocity seems a strange political objective).

Scheffler explicitly rejects what he calls the 'strong distributivist thesis that contract law should be designed solely to serve the purposes of the difference principle, leaving no room for other values than distributive justice to inform contract law'.[92] Instead, he prefers what he calls 'weak distributivism', that requires only that contract law 'avoid worsening the economic position of the least favoured members of society'.[93] However, as he points out himself, weak contract law distributivism may well collapse into strong distributivism, because it is not clear what should count as the baseline relative to which the position of the least well-off should not be worsened.[94] This question is particularly pressing from the *ex ante* perspective of law making, where the status quo has not yet been established. From that point of view, not choosing to maximize the position of the least well-off may well be understood to worsen their position.

Scheffler considers contract law as part of the basic structure of society, which brings contract law in any case within the scope of the question of strong versus weak distributivism. Although he does not specifically address default rules the stakes in that debate for our question are relatively clear. Under strong distributivism, default rules may have to be at the full service of improving the economic conditions of the least well-off in society, for instance by contributing to an increase in the 'size of the pie', if this contributes via redistribution through tax-and-transfers or other trickle-down mechanisms to improving the position of the least privileged, even if only marginally. This would crowd out any other normative considerations in the design of non-mandatory rules of contract, not only those based on other values (such as autonomy or solidarity), but also—and especially—those based on considerations of interpersonal justice that are usually understood to inform the exemplary function (*Leitbildfunktion*) of non-mandatory rules.

[89] Rawls (n. 84) 326.
[90] Rawls (n. 85) 64.
[91] Ibid. 64: 'What the difference principle requires, then, is that however great the general level of wealth—whether high or low—the existing inequalities are to fulfil the condition of benefiting others as well as ourselves.'
[92] Scheffler, 'Distributive Justice, the Basic Structure and the Place of Private Law', 35 *OJLS* (2015) 1, at 10.
[93] Ibid.
[94] Ibid. 13.

3. The Option of Abrogating a Legal Obligation

We can also look at default rules from the other end, and ask whether certain rules of contract law that the parties can freely set aside should in fact be mandatory. In other words, we may sometimes want to challenge the optional character of certain contract law rules. Indeed, today the question of optionality of contract law rules is a regular part of the drafting process and political deliberation on modern private law reforms, where often nobody questions the merits of a rule but its mandatory or optional character is heavily debated.

Most modern civil codes indicate explicitly for each rule whether it is mandatory or optional.[95] The same applies for EU contract law directives and regulations.[96] However, in jurisdictions lacking such a legislative practice, for example because contract law is mostly judge-made, the question may arise differently. For example, it may be argued that a clause setting aside certain contract law rules should be considered contrary to public policy or public morality and therefore void. That reasoning brings us within the scope of the question central to Chapter 7. Still, what is specific here is that the issue of whether the term is immoral or contrary to public policy is in effect about whether the contracting parties have the option to delete a contractual right, obligation, or remedy provided by law. That is why it makes good sense to discuss it here.

As we saw in Chapter 5, Shiffrin objects to what she calls 'the overprivatization of private law', with reference specifically to a trend in the US towards the increased enforcement of remedial clauses.[97] These are clauses where the parties take control over the legal response to breach of contract, for example in liquidated damages clauses in common law jurisdictions and penalty clauses in civil law jurisdictions. But, as another example, we can also think of rescission clauses, which determine which breaches of contract automatically terminate the contract without any judicial intervention. Shiffrin questions the acceptability of such remedial clauses. She writes:

> What seems distinctive (and distinctively troubling) about remedial clauses is that they aim to substitute a private, particularist judgment for what, traditionally and for good reason, has been a public, general, impartial judgment about the significance of a legal wrong. For this reason, a regime of presumptively enforceable remedial clauses represents a further, distinct inroad against public values and the rule of law.[98]

[95] But contrast French law, even after the 2016 reform. Cf. Fauvarque-Cosson, 'The French Contract Law Reform and the Political Process', 13 *ERCL* (2017) 337, at 352–353: 'In France as in the vast majority of countries, contract rules are usually not mandatory, unless otherwise provided by the rule itself. Most of the provisions do not specify whether or not they are mandatory.'

[96] In EU contract law non-mandatory rules are the exception. This is the case, in part, because the bulk of EU contract law aims to protect consumers and other weaker parties (see Chapter 6). Another reason is doubt about legal basis. Can the divergence of national non-mandatory rules, which can be freely set aside by the parties, ever constitute an obstacle to the proper function of the internal market, as required by Art. 114 TFEU? Some observers read the CJEU's ruling in Case C-339/89, *Alsthom Atlantique SA v. Compagnie de construction mécanique Sulzer SA* (EU:C:1991:28), at para. 14, as answering this question negatively. Contra, Hesselink, 'Non-Mandatory Rules in European Contract Law', 1 *ERCL* (2005) 43, with further references. See further later.

[97] Shiffrin, 'Remedial Clauses: The Overprivatization of Private Law', 67 *Hastings L.J.* (2016) 407.

[98] Ibid. 442.

And she concludes, pointedly, that 'the judiciary's special role in crafting and meting out remedies should not be outsourced'.[99]

From the perspective of an already existing system of contract law that determines contractual rights, obligations, and remedies, the decision to make certain rules become optional, i.e. ones that the parties can set aside by substituting them with terms that suit their interests better, looks indeed very much like the privatization of contract law. This brings us back to the Rawlsian question discussed earlier, but with a vengeance. If contract law or a part of it, say the basic structure of its remedial system, is indeed part of the basic structure of society, then is it acceptable that this part of the basic structure is privatized, making—in this case—the set of available remedies become optional, at the choice of the parties?

4. Non-binary Rules: The Case of Sticky Defaults

There is one more reason, deriving not so much from Rawlsian principles as from the nature of default rules (and opt-out regimes in general), why the non-mandatory character of certain contract law rules may not constitute a proper reason for categorically excluding them from the basic structure of society, and consequently from being subject to the principles of justice. Default rules may be sticky.

A certain rule, even though non-mandatory, may be difficult to set aside. And an attempt to overrule it may fail, for example when a court concludes that the contract term was too generic or too vague to set the specific rule aside. Or, conversely, the default rule might be so general (e.g. part of the general law of obligations) that the parties did not realize it might apply to their contract. Or, indeed, the parties might be unaware of its existence. This may be the case even for an entire set of rules, for example when unsophisticated parties to a transnational commercial sales contract—which may consist of nothing more than an email from a buyer ordering certain goods and an acceptance of that order by the seller—are wholly oblivious of the existence of the CISG, from which they would have been free to opt out. A final possibility is that a default rule is so widely accepted as a familiar background provision (normalization effect) that a negotiating party may be reluctant to propose opting out of it, because that could raise suspicion, even as to her general reliability, which might risk upsetting the entire deal.[100]

In all these cases, a rule that may have been non-mandatory in theory in certain cases may become de facto mandatory in practice.[101] It is important to realize in this

[99] Ibid. It is important to realize that Shiffrin understands the replacement of the primary legal obligation to perform the contract with a secondary one to pay damages, as 'the abrogation of a legal duty'. Moreover, in her view, the original duty may at least sometimes be understood also as a moral duty and therefore its breach also as a moral wrong. The result of allowing remedial clauses is, then, on this view, that a moral duty (e.g. to keep one's promise) that had been *publicly* recognized as a legal duty, and whose breach would constitute a wrong, is abrogated by *private* means. See ibid. 429: 'the abrogation of a legal duty through nonpublic means'. Still, contractual obligations are legally recognized obligations, whether they coincide sometimes with a moral obligation or not. Therefore, the option of their private abrogation, e.g. through the operation of a rescission clause, may be more widely troubling on liberal-egalitarian views (and other non-libertarian ones).

[100] Ben-Shahar and Pottow, 'On the Stickiness of Default Rules', 33 *Florida State University Law Review* (2006) 651.

[101] Hesselink (n. 96).

regard that a rule that was non-mandatory, and to that extent not binding on the parties *ex ante*, is just as binding *ex post* between parties who have failed to set it aside, as any mandatory rule. As a factual matter, therefore, the optionality of contract law rules is directly negatively proportionate to their stickiness. And this gradual nature of optionality weakens the argument for a categorical distinction between mandatory and non-mandatory contract law rules when it comes to determining whether they should be considered part of the basic structure of society, and therefore subject to the principles of justice. Indeed, especially in the case of familiar background provisions, a case could be made, it seems, that these are part of the institutions responsible for preserving background justice.[102]

5. Options and Alternatives: Access to Choice

Even though Rawlsian social justice might be indifferent, as we saw, with regard to the presence, absence, and content of non-mandatory rules of contract law, for the reason that these are not matters pertaining to the basic structure of society, the reverse is not necessarily true. For if Rawlsian principles of justice applied to optional contract law this could make a real difference. From the perspective of liberal-egalitarian conceptions of social justice, a key question concerning optional contract law seems to be the fair distribution of access to choice. Therefore, beyond the question of the scope of social justice, in a liberal-egalitarian response to the question of whether (European) contract law could or should be partly optional, the focus would probably be more specifically on the nature of the option. In particular, many liberals would probably emphasize the importance of substantive (as opposed to merely formal) freedom of choice. They would want to know whether the parties opting into or out of certain contract law rules—whether individual rules or a whole set of them—would have a real choice in the sense of also having other attractive options.

In particular, the capabilities approach, as developed by Sen and Nussbaum and applied to European contract law by Tjon Soei Len,[103] has emphasized that freedom of choice requires much more than the absence of force. Someone's capability to choose may also be impaired, for example, by lack of education or by various other types of inequalities entrenched in society. Therefore, it could be argued, opting into or out of optional contract law as a result of 'adaptive preferences' should not count as an expression of freedom of contract in any real sense. For example, the decision to work as a self-employed agent rather than under an employment contract very often is not a positive choice to take advantage of the opportunities of the gig economy but rather a take-it-or-leave-it option offered by the employer. Think also of Micklitz's theory of access justice, discussed in Chapter 6, with its central focus on the access

[102] On the responsibility of the basic structure of society for preserving 'background justice', see Rawls (n. 84) 265 ff.

[103] L. K. L. Tjon Soei Len, *Minimum Contract Justice: A Capabilities Perspective on Sweatshops and Consumer Contracts* (2017); Tjon Soei Len, 'Equal Respect, Capabilities and the Moral Limits of Market Exchange: Denigration in the EU Internal Market', *Transnational Legal Theory* (2017) 1. For capabilities approaches to contract law, see also the contributions to S. Deakin and A. Supiot (eds), *Capacitas: Contract Law, Capabilities and the Legal Foundations of the Market* (2009).

to certain contract types, i.e. the privatized utilities, that must go well beyond mere non-discrimination.[104]

Nor is the political interest in access to choice limited to legal theory. With regard to the CESL proposal, for example, the main political controversy concerned the question of whether the CESL would become genuinely optional for both parties. The Social-democrats and Greens in the European Parliament were worried—and the European Consumer Organisation (BEUC) had forcefully argued—that in practice sellers would decide unilaterally on whether the CESL would become applicable to a consumer contract and that they would impose their choice on consumers on a take-it-or-leave-it basis. Moreover, they argued, sellers would only opt into the CESL where that was in their interests, in particular when the CESL would provide a lower level of consumer protection than the otherwise applicable national law, which, in turn, would undermine the protective purposes of Article 6, Rome I. In reply, the European Commission and certain business organizations argued that there could be a win-win situation whenever sellers gained so much in efficiency from being able to offer their products under one single contract law regime, that they could accept a higher level of consumer protection in the CESL than would be economically sustainable if the law applicable to their (online) retail remained a multitude of divergent national contract laws. To this argument the Commission added that the expected beneficial increase in choice was not limited to a choice between different contract law regimes. The real increase in consumer choice would come from the possibility to buy from foreign sellers, which would lead to a wider range of products and lower prices becoming available as a result of the removal of obstacles to cross-border trade. This debate showed very clearly that an increase in choice may be understood very differently, and that the political disagreements—and the egalitarian justice concerns—have at least as much to do with who gets to choose, and how, as with what is on the menu.

4. Libertarian

A. Gap Filling as Non-Interference

The argument by Craswell discussed earlier in relation to liberal contract theories, i.e. that they cannot account for the large part of contract law that is not mandatory, also applies to—indeed was chiefly directed against—the libertarian theories of Fried and Barnett. When it comes to guidance for the legal system in deciding which non-mandatory 'background rules' to adopt, Craswell writes:

> the principle of individual freedom is equally unhelpful, for it implies only that individuals should be left free to change whatever default rule the law adopts as a starting point. Once again, some other value must be invoked to explain why one starting point ought to be picked by the law in preference to another.[105]

[104] H.-W. Micklitz, *The Politics of Justice in European Private Law: Social Justice, Access Justice, Societal Justice* (2018).

[105] Craswell (n. 62) 490.

Fried had already acknowledged as much and had taken recourse to other principles, especially the 'principle of sharing', which he considered unproblematic since 'the recourse to principles of sharing to fill the gaps does not threaten to overwhelm the promissory principle, for the simple reason that the parties are quite free to control the meaning and extent of their relation by the contract'.[106] This may well be true, but the same would apply for most other values that could inform the content of default rules.

Hayek even went a bit further than Fried, arguing that default rules may be positively beneficial, because they facilitate transactions without interfering with liberty. As he wrote:

> freedom of contract, like freedom in all other fields, really means that the permissibility of a particular act depends only on general rules and not on its specific approval by authority. . . . This does not exclude the possibility . . . of the state's laying down rules for the interpretation of contracts which will supplement the explicitly agreed terms. The existence of such recognized standard forms of contract which, so long as contrary terms are stipulated, will be presumed to be part of the agreement often greatly facilitates private dealings.[107]

Yet, this argument too bypasses Craswell's challenge: libertarianism cannot explain default rules. The liberty principle does not require their presence, nor does it—*qua* liberty principle—require any specific content for them. Their substance must come from elsewhere—in this case, from the utilitarian agenda of facilitating transactions, it seems. All that liberty requires is that none of these rules ever becomes mandatory.

B. The Sound of Silence

By contrast, Barnett disagrees with Craswell. He argues that silence may constitute consent to non-mandatory rules. 'Under certain circumstances', he writes, 'it is meaningful to say that one's silence in the face of default rules that one can change constitutes consent to the application of such rules'.[108] This is the case, in particular, when the default rules reflect 'the commonsense expectations of persons in the relevant community of discourse'.[109] If we accept this proposition, Barnet argues, we also know which optional contract law rules the law maker should adopt: the ones that meet the common-sense expectations of the relevant community. That task is not necessarily an easy one, but Barnett is confident that the common law judge has been shown throughout history to be well equipped for this task. Indeed, he suggests that 'the correspondence between common sense and common law is no coincidence'.[110] However, just as a hypothetical contract, even the most reasonable one, is not a contract at all, as

[106] C. Fried, *Contract as Promise: A Theory of Contractual Obligation* ([first published 1981] 2nd ed., 2015), at 73.
[107] F. A. Hayek, *The Constitution of Liberty* ([first published 1960] 2006), at 202.
[108] Barnett, 'The Sound of Silence: Default Rules and Contractual Consent', 78 *Va. L. Rev.* (1992) 821, at 906.
[109] Ibid. 829.
[110] Ibid. 911.

Dworkin famously pointed out against the Rawlsian construct of the original position, so too does the mere reasonableness of a default rule not turn the parties' silence into consent to its application.[111] Therefore, in analogy to Dworkin, we can point out that silence is not simply a pale form of actual consent; it is no consent at all—or at least not of the kind one would expect libertarian liberty to demand.

Just as we saw for the liberal perfectionist understanding of non-mandatory contract law rules, so too for the libertarian view of Barnett, it is not clear that it is compatible with the *Leitbildfunktion* that non-mandatory rules fulfil under EU unfair terms law. For if these rules are understood to correspond to 'commonsense expectations' it is not self-evident that these expectations should necessarily (i.e. as a matter of common sense) be expectations concerning justice and fairness. In any case, common sense expectations of justice may well be expectations merely of minimal justice (or minimum expectations of justice), which may be inadequate as a standard for the fairness of contract terms. Of course, this is not necessarily a problem from the libertarian point of view since libertarians tend to reject the unfairness of the control of contract terms in the first place (because they regard it as theft), as we saw in Chapter 6.

If indeed default rules should correspond to 'commonsense expectations of persons in the relevant community of discourse', then there are more direct ways of accounting for that demand than via libertarian silence. Communitarianism, philosophical pragmatism, and discourse theory could all offer more straightforward accounts. The fact remains that while common-sense default rules developed through the common law method of law making will not interfere with negative liberty, it is difficult to see that liberty also demands them. That is, it is not clear that liberty demands the presence of default rules, nor that common sense should inform their content, nor indeed that non-mandatory rules should be judge-made.

In the closing paragraph of *Anarchy, State, and Utopia*, Nozick famously wrote:

> The minimal state treats us as inviolate individuals, who may not be used in certain ways by others as means or tools or instruments or resources; it treats us as persons having individual rights with the dignity this constitutes. Treating us with respect by respecting our rights, it allows us, individually or with whom we choose, to choose our life and to realize our ends and our conception of ourselves, insofar as we can, aided by the voluntary cooperation of other individuals possessing the same dignity. How dare any state or group of individuals do more. Or less.[112]

Clearly, a state that failed to offer optional contract law rules would hardly be daring to do less than the minimal state requires. Indeed, it would be doing more. The same point can also be made the other way around. As Dagan points out, Nozick's vision of

[111] Dworkin, 'The Original Position', 40 *U. Chi. L. Rev.* (1973) 500, at 501:

> Rawls does not suppose that any group ever entered into a social contract of the sort he describes. He argues only that if a group of rational men did find themselves in the predicament of the original position, they would contract for the two principles. His contract is hypothetical, and hypothetical contracts do not supply an independent argument for the fairness of enforcing their terms. A hypothetical contract is not simply a pale form of an actual contract; it is no contract at all.

[112] R. Nozick, *Anarchy, State, and Utopia* ([first published 1974] 2013), at 333–334.

utopia as a framework of utopias, 'a place where people are at liberty to join together voluntarily to pursue and attempt to realize their own vision of the good life in the ideal community but where no one can impose his own utopian vision upon others',[113] will not get off the ground unless the state facilitates people's choices by offering legally structured options.[114] However, in order to justify a state offering 'a diverse menu of comprehensive life-style options', as Dagan puts it,[115] libertarian negative and formal liberty will not suffice; liberal-egalitarian positive and substantive freedom will be needed. In other words, rather than the minimal night-watchman state, utopian private law seems to require the liberal state. (Having said that, it is also not clear, as we saw, that Dagan's choice theory can offer much guidance in determining the proper content of the available options.)[116]

C. Formal Choice of Law

As a general matter, most libertarians of course would favour optional over non-optional instruments of European contract law. As previously stated, libertarians emphasize free choice and reject state intervention. Moreover, unlike liberal-egalitarians, they would regard formal freedom as sufficient. In particular, they would not be too worried about the unequal bargaining between a professional seller and a consumer in relation to choice of law, whether for an optional second national regime (such as the CESL as it was proposed) or for choice of law for a foreign system.

Indeed, Article 6 Rome I, pursuant to which a choice of law cannot deprive a consumer of the protection she would enjoy under the mandatory provisions of her own national law, does not make any normative sense from a libertarian perspective, because it prevents parties from fully exploiting their superior bargaining power. For a Nozickian libertarian, this would follow from the principle of self-ownership. If a strong business, on the one hand, and a consumer or a small business, on the other, freely opt into or out of a legal system, then that free choice legitimates the applicability of the optional system even if the consumer or small business had no attractive alternative options. Remember Nozick's view, which we saw in Chapter 5: 'a person's choice among differing degrees of unpalatable alternatives is not rendered nonvoluntary by the fact that others voluntarily chose and acted within their rights in a way that did not provide him with a more palatable alternative'.[117] Self-ownership includes the freedom to outwit other parties or to exploit one's superior bargaining power. This means that a libertarian would have been likely to be very critical of all the formalities surrounding opting into the CESL and would have denounced these as paternalistic and illegitimate for that reason, just as she would reject the EU legislator's decision to limit the principle of 'freedom of choice', as heralded by Article 3 Rome I ('A contract shall be governed by the law chosen by the parties'), with a view to protecting the weaker party

[113] Ibid. 312.
[114] Dagan, 'The Utopian Promise of Private Law', 66 *University of Toronto Law Journal* (2016) 392.
[115] Ibid. 397.
[116] On the difficulty choice theory has in accounting for the *Leitbildfunktion* of optional contract law, see earlier, in Section 3.B.4.
[117] Nozick (n. 112) 263–264.

in consumer, insurance, and employment contracts, respectively, under Articles 6, 7, and 8 Rome I.

Instead, one step further in the direction of unfettered choice of law would be to allow the parties to choose privately drafted alternatives, rather than state law. As Mills points out, 'this would be a double-privatisation under which it is not just the power of choice given to private parties, but the power of creating the object of choice as a substitute for state-provided law'.[118] Clearly, such an option would be more than welcomed by libertarians (as well as anarchists).

D. Private Ordering in an Open Society

According to Basedow, party autonomy in private international law is grounded first and foremost in *a priori* natural freedom, which is normatively prior to the national systems of positive private law. As he puts it, 'party autonomy as seen in international contract law . . . is rooted in the pre-governmental right of individuals to subject themselves to a particular positive legal order through acts of private volition'.[119]

However, in addition to the natural law foundation of party autonomy in an innate right to individual liberty, as developed in the political philosophy of the European Enlightenment (especially by Locke and Kant), Basedow offers another argument, this time coming from twentieth-century philosophers. He combines Popper's defence of the open society,[120] in our case a globalized economy built upon myriad cross-border contracts, with Hayek's considerations about incurable ignorance of central planners,[121] in our case law makers' structural incapacity to grasp the realities of cross-border contracting, into an argument in favour of private ordering in private international law. As he sums up:

> the opening of societies and economies progressively deprives State rule-makers of their ability to have a sufficient awareness of the typical transnational situations and to forge corresponding rules. Similar to what was postulated by von Hayek, knowledge of the factual circumstances which is material for the regulation of international transactions is much more likely to be vested, in open societies, in private individuals than in Governments or courts of law. As a consequence, private rule-making,

[118] A. Mills, *Party Autonomy in Private International Law* (2018), at 529. According to Mills, the normative foundations of party autonomy in private international law should be found in various forms of libertarianism. See ibid. 66 ff.

[119] J. Basedow, *The Law of Open Societies: Private Ordering and Public Regulation in the Conflict of Laws (Collected courses of the Hague Academy of International Law, Vol. 360)* (2013), at 205. In spite of the prepositive roots in a natural right to liberty, however, Basedow, acknowledges, probably more than most libertarians, that private autonomy needs positive law to determine its scope (see ibid. 206).

[120] K. Popper, *The Open Society and its Enemies* ([first published 1945] 2011). Although Popper was a co-founder, together with Hayek, Mises, and Friedman among others of the Mont Pelerin Society, one of the catalysts of neoliberalism, his own political thinking defies categorization solely as a libertarian as it also has certain social-democratic and conservative aspects. Cf. W. Gorton, 'Karl Popper: Political Philosophy', *Internet Encyclopedia of Philosophy*, available at https://www.iep.utm.edu/popp-pol/ (last visited 23 July 2020).

[121] Hayek 'The Use of Knowledge in Society', 35 *American Economic Review* (1945) 519.

> whether in a collective way by associations and other private bodies or by the individual through private choice of law, comes to the fore.[122]

Under these circumstances, Basedow sees four legitimate remaining roles for public rule making, one of which is the provision of default rules for the cases where the parties have not dealt with this through their private ordering, i.e. conflict rules indicating the applicable law when the parties have failed to make a choice of law.[123] However, it is far from clear why the endemic problem of dispersed knowledge would affect the drafting of non-mandatory rules any less than that of mandatory ones.

E. Libertarian Paternalism

As already discussed, most libertarians would favour optional over non-optional instruments. And as a general matter they might intuitively prefer opt-in over opt-out models. Yet, even an opt-out model, such as the Vienna Sales Convention (CISG),[124] could be acceptable to a libertarian, as an instance of what has been labelled 'libertarian paternalism'. This seemingly oxymoronic idea of libertarian paternalism has been advocated by Thaler and Sunstein.[125] Given the fact that real people, as established by behavioural studies, often do not correspond to the model of a homo economicus who always makes the choices that are in her own best interest (by a subjective standard), and that there is no truly neutral way in which to present options, Thaler and Sunstein argue that policy and law makers might as well present available options in such a way that people are 'nudged' towards the option that, in the estimation of the law maker, is in people's own best interest, by making it the default option.[126] Thaler and Sunstein speak of 'choice architecture'.[127] This approach is libertarian, they argue, in that it does not entail any government coercion: everyone remains entirely free in their own choices. And it is paternalistic in the sense that the government determines, albeit in a non-binding way, what is in the best interest of its citizens.

An opt-out contract code, it seems, could equally be defended in these terms. For example, to the extent that the CISG contains a regime that is in the best interest of unsophisticated parties to cross-border commercial sales contracts it might be justified in the eyes of a libertarian paternalist. The same could also have applied for an opt-out CESL (which, to be clear, was never proposed). To the extent that the optional instrument was in the best interest of parties concluding cross-border contracts (which arguably would have been the case if its level of consumer protection was very high, as was the case for the proposed CESL according to its drafters and the European

[122] Basedow (n. 119) 102.

[123] Ibid. 103. The other three (which seem to overlap in part), are market failure, externalities, and public policy.

[124] Art. 6, United Nations Convention on Contracts for the International Sale of Goods (1980).

[125] Thaler and Sunstein, 'Libertarian Paternalism', 93 *American Economic Review* (2003) 175; Sunstein and Thaler, 'Libertarian Paternalism Is Not an Oxymoron', 70 *U. Chi. L. Rev.* (2003) 1159.

[126] R. H. Thaler and C. R. Sunstein, *Nudge: Improving Decisions About Health, Wealth and Happiness* (2009).

[127] Ibid. 3.

commission), then making it the default regime would have been a form of 'choice architecture' that would have 'nudged' consumers and SMEs into what was in their own best interest, without, however, coercing them. They would still have remained free to opt out.

However, it is far from clear that many libertarians would accept libertarian paternalism. In their book, Thaler and Sunstein argue that their approach is neither left nor right and transcends the major political division. Although, many libertarians have a very different notion of free markets from Sunstein (who served in the Obama administration as 'administrator of the White House Office of Information and Regulatory Affairs'),[128] in particular, they hold a view which categorically excludes any form of state paternalism, whether hard, soft, or nudged.

Another question is the normative one of whether nudging is objectionable for other, non-libertarian reasons. Many people regard nudges by the government as a manipulative, even Orwellian, way of playing with our minds. As Sunstein acknowledges, a legitimacy condition for nudge has to be that it must be transparent, i.e. that affected parties know that choice architecture is in place; officials 'must not hide it from the public' (which frankly seems only a rather minimal form transparency).[129] That risk is not likely to occur with regard to optional contract law, since civil codes and common law judgments do not usually contain any hidden sections. However, as Gerald Dworkin observes, beyond the intransparency cases it is not so clear that there exists a coherent manipulation concept that could single out cases where nudging is wrongful.[130]

5. Communitarian

A. Default Rules as Customary Law

The notion of 'customary law', referring to a social practice that is observed by people regarding it as a legal obligation (*opinio iuris*), fits well with the communitarian understanding of law as being rooted in and emanating from community standards. While historically very important in medieval times and early modern times in some European countries (think only of the *Coutume de Paris* and the *Sachsenspiegel*), the role of customary law in private law sharply declined with the great codifications. Civil codes still frequently refer to 'customary practice' or 'usage' as a standard.[131] However, in contract law, the doctrine of good faith with its ever expanding role has largely

[128] Around the same time, the libertarian Barnett was actively involved in the constitutional challenges to the Affordable Care Act. See Barnett, 'We Lost on Health Care. But the Constitution Won.', *Washington Post*, 29 June 2012; Barnett, 'Foreword', in J. Blackman, *Unprecedented: The Constitutional Challenge to Obamacare* (2013). Cf. 'Vindication for Challenger of Health Care Law', *New York Times*, 26 March 2012.

[129] Sunstein, 'The Ethics of Nudging', 32 *Yale Journal on Regulation* (2015) 413, at 428.

[130] Dworkin, 'Paternalism', in E. N. Zalta (ed.), *Stanford Encyclopedia of Philosophy*, at 4.5, available at https://plato.stanford.edu/entries/paternalism/ (last visited 23 July 2020).

[131] Several provisions in the German *BGB* explicitly refer to custom or to 'customary practice' (*Verkehrssitte*), e.g. § 157 (Interpretation of contracts) and § 242. See also the reference to 'usage' in Art. 1194 French Civil Code: 'Contracts create obligations not merely in relation to what they expressly provide, but also to all the consequences which are given to them by equity, usage or legislation.'

crowded out custom in the context of interpretation, for example, or as a basis for ancillary duties.[132]

Beyond custom as a distinct unwritten source of law, it is also possible to understand the written law as in essence customary. As we saw in Chapter 3, such bottom-up and evolutionary understandings of the law (common law and civil law), where it is the task of the law maker, either incrementally on a case-to-case basis or by way of codification, to enforce community standards as law, matches well with communitarian political principles. Such an understanding of the nature of private law may fit best with non-mandatory rules, which are usually less driven than mandatory rules by the political agenda of the day. Therefore, on a communitarian reading, non-mandatory rules can be understood as the law maker's restatement and enforcement of generally accepted and observed community standards.[133] Having said that, given their origin in community values and practices, in the eyes of a communitarian it is not self-evident that these rules should be optional.

B. Against Choice Atomism

More generally, the idea of optional contract law is not particularly attractive from a communitarian point of view. As we saw in earlier chapters, communitarians tend to be rather sceptical about individual self-determination and rational choice by the unencumbered self. Instead they point out that every person, and hence also that person's valuations and choices, is always socially and culturally embedded in a community. In other words, they reject what we could call choice atomism. In this respect, the argument with regard to optional law is structurally quite similar to the one concerning freedom of contract we saw in Chapter 7.

Taylor observes that it is not the case, as a narcissist might think, that our subjective choice bestows value upon the option we choose. On the contrary, meaningful choice is possible only against the background of an already existing horizon of significance. In particular, our various options are significant only in relationship to significant others.[134] As he argues, against Mill:

> unless some options are more significant than others, the very idea of self-choice falls into triviality and hence incoherence. Self-choice as an ideal makes sense only because some *issues* are more significant than others.... Which issues are significant, *I* do not determine. If I did, no issue would be significant.... So the ideal of self-choice supposes that there are *other* issues of significance beyond self-choice.[135]

[132] In the US, the Uniform Commercial Code refers to custom for contract interpretation. Very critical, Bernstein, 'Custom in the Courts', 110 *Northwestern University Law Review* (2015) 63, who argues that this role for custom should be abandoned in favour of a more formalist approach to contract interpretation, at least in contracts between businesses.

[133] As we saw earlier, Barnett's reading of common law default rules as the reflection of common sense expectations prevailing in the relevant community, was surprisingly communitarian for a libertarian.

[134] C. Taylor, *The Ethics of Authenticity* (1991).

[135] Ibid. 39 (emphasis in original).

From this point of view it becomes all-important which options there are on the menu. And to choose from a menu, in our case, say, of contract types, is a matter of trying to determine, dialogically,[136] in relation with our significant others, which of them is most valuable.

C. An Unrooted Code

With specific regard to an optional code of contracts, such as the CISG, or the CESL as it was proposed, communitarians are likely to be puzzled. They would be mystified by the idea of opting into a non-national legal system. They would wonder how one can opt into a legal tradition or a legal culture, because, as we saw, that is how they conceive of a legal system. Therefore, they would regard the instrument, and the contracts governed by it, as unrooted, i.e. as not embedded in any community. In particular, the idea of a '28th regime' legal system could not make any sense to them because it would have been no political community's system and therefore not a legal system in any meaningful sense at all.

Such a position is not dissimilar to the one adopted by those scholars who emphasized, in relation to the European Commission's CESL proposal, that the CESL could not work—at least initially and for a long time afterwards—because of the absence of any thick legal culture expressed in case law and academic commentaries providing meaning to the abstract text, making it come alive and making the application of it become foreseeable. Without an interpretative tradition and an epistemic community, they argued, the text would for a long time—and perhaps forever—remain sterile. Legislative enactment does not suffice for a legal text to obtain legal authority.[137]

Moreover, opting into a European legal system implies opting out of one's own system. Communitarians think that this just cannot be done. All of us are always already situated and embedded in social practices and contexts that we cannot simply opt out of. There is no unencumbered self that could make such a choice: I am (part of) my tradition, including my national legal tradition. There may even be epistemic limits to my proper understanding of another legal system.[138]

The idea of an optional instrument as a second national system (instead of a 28th system) that would have become applicable as national law (and not via Rome I), would have been even more unsettling in the eyes of a communitarian. From her perspective, either this would have suggested some sort of schizophrenic national identity or the project would have been doomed to fail (as it eventually did, even before it got off the ground) because the second national system would actually not have been truly national at all. All the familiar arguments against 'legal transplants' would also be directed against the second regime. It would be argued that the instrument would be

136 Ibid. 33.

137 N. Jansen, *The Making of Legal Authority: Non-Legislative Codifications in Historical and Comparative Perspective* (2010).

138 See Legrand, 'European Legal Systems Are Not Converging', 45 *ICLQ* (1996) 52, at 76, with reference to A. MacIntyre, *Whose Justice? Which Rationality?* (1988). Ever since this seminal article, the epistemic limits to understanding foreign law has been one of Legrand's core themes.

rejected by the local community, as a *Fremdkörper*, or a 'legal irritant' that cannot be domesticated.[139]

D. Contracts without a Homeland

The idea of an optional instrument for cross-border contracts was in clear contrast with the traditional Savignian idea of re-nationalizing international contracts, via conflict rules that refer a legal relationship to its proper 'seat' or even its 'homeland'.[140] However, it should be added that classical conflict rules simply ignore the non-national (because transnational) nature of cross-border contracts. It was exactly because they do not belong to one single nation or legal culture that a truly transnational regime of substantive contract law rules was deemed necessary.[141] For, even from a legal culturalist perspective, is it not artificial—and perhaps even disrespectful of the identity of one side of the contractual relationship—to treat the contractual relationship as belonging to one single national community?[142] The Vienna Sales Convention (CISG)—as well as the European Company (*Societas Europea*) in the field of company law—could be regarded as an acknowledgement of the transnational identity of certain legal relationships. Or, to be more precise, to provide the private parties to those relationships at least with the option of recognition for their transnational legal identity, by choosing contractual statelessness.

E. Law as a Contested Commodity

As Stark points out, in the case of regulatory competition, in particular the idea of a law market, discussed earlier, in Section 2.C, where law is considered a product, we observe the commodification of law itself.[143] However, as she argues with reference to Anderson and Sandel, this may lead to the corruption of the very notion of law. When law is understood as being 'for sale', then we value it in the wrong way. In the process, various normative considerations, in particular the political values of democracy, state autonomy, and (perfectionist) political authority, are 'crowded out by the imperatives of success in a global law market'.[144] Ultimately, Stark's aim is not to adopt a strongly

[139] See Teubner, 'Legal Irritants: Good Faith in British Law or How Unifying Law Ends Up in New Divergences', 61 *MLR* (1998) 11, at 12: '"Legal irritants" cannot be domesticated; they are not transformed from something alien into something familiar, not adapted to a new cultural context, rather they will unleash an evolutionary dynamic in which the external rule's meaning will be reconstructed and the internal context will undergo fundamental change.'

[140] See F. C. von Savigny, *System des heutigen Römischen Rechts*, Vol. 8 (1849), at 360: 'dass bei jedem Rechtsverhältnis dasjenige Rechtsgebiet aufgesucht werde, welchem dieses Rechtsverhältnis seiner eigentümlichen Natur nach angehört oder unterworfen ist, (worin dasselbe seinen Sitz hat)'. See also ibid. 361: 'der Sitz (die Heimat) jedes Rechtsverhältnisses'.

[141] Many members of the Lando Commission were professors of private international law, dissatisfied with the project of conflict rules, in particular the idea of the international or European unification of conflict rules rather than of substantive private law rules.

[142] Cf. Michaels and Jansen, 'Private Law Beyond the State? Europeanization, Globalization, Privatization', 54 *AJCL* (2006) 843, at 880.

[143] J. Stark, *Law for Sale: A Philosophical Critique of Regulatory Competition* (2019).

[144] Ibid. 172.

communitarian stance but rather to offer a framework for better understanding of optional law as an essentially 'contested commodity'.[145]

6. Civic Republican

From the perspective of civic republicanism, the exercise of an option offered by (European) contract law may be regarded in some cases as private domination, but in others as public contestation. As we will see, being a political theory mainly of freedom, civic republicanism also (i.e. just like liberal-egalitarianism and libertarianism, but unlike utilitarianism and communitarianism) has more to say on procedure of choice than about the preferred content for the options.

A. Opting in as Dominated Choice

As Pettit writes:

> we can expand non-domination, not just by reducing existing domination, but by novel extensions of the area over which, and the ease with which, a subject can exercise undominated choice, at whatever level of intensity. We can introduce or facilitate undominated choices in areas where they do not currently exist or are very costly.[146]

This idea could be applied, it seems, also to an optional instrument of contract law, such as the—proposed and withdrawn—CESL. For people living in countries where certain products are currently not on offer or only at a very high price the availability of an optional contract law facilitating cross-border contracting, especially between consumers and SMEs, could mean an increase in undominated choice in this sense.

However, to what extent would a choice for the CESL actually have been an undominated choice? Consumer groups argued forcefully that the choice for the CESL would be dominated entirely by the seller:

> The optional Instrument is not what it pretends to be: the entire concept of an 'optional' tool in business to consumer contracts disregards the inequality of bargaining power and the reality of pre-formulated standard contracts in consumer relations. In fact there is no choice between the parties in b2c contracts as the trader imposes the contract terms and conditions. The 'choice' to use the CESL is merely a technical element of the CESL concept, but for the consumer there is no choice offered to select from two legal regimes the one they prefer. This choice is only available to business.[147]

145 Ibid. ch. 5.

146 P. Pettit, *Republicanism: A Theory of Freedom and Government* (1999), at 75.

147 Pachl, 'The Common European Sales Law—Have the Right Choices Been Made? A Consumer Policy Perspective', 19 *Maastricht Journal of European and Comparative Law* (2012) 180. The author is the Deputy Director general of BEUC (Bureau Européen des Unions de Consommateurs), the European Consumer Organisation.

Had the CESL been introduced as was envisaged, then probably for cross-border consumer-buyers the question of whether the CESL would become applicable to their contracts in most cases would have depended solely on the arbitrary choice of the seller. Therefore, it seems, for the consumer this would indeed have meant a dominated choice in the republican sense. Put differently, when it came to opting into EU sales law consumers would hardly have been in a position, with regard to their professional counterparties, to look them in the eye without reason for fear or deference, as republican freedom demands.[148]

With the withdrawal of the CESL proposal by the European Commission the risk of dominated opt-ins or opt-outs has not disappeared. Dominated choices may exist just as well in regular choices of law in cross-border contracts, for different national legal systems under Rome I, or for—or, rather against (given the opt-out regime)—uniform rules such as the CISG. It is true that Rome I provides categorical protection in consumer, insurance, and employment contracts, but it does not offer any protection more generally against unequal bargaining or other instances of dominated choice. For small businesses in particular, this means that the question of whether a different national system than the one indicated by the conflict rules of Rome I will come to govern their contract, or, in the case of sales, an opt-out of the CISG will be made, may depend entirely on the arbitrary choice made by the stronger party.

The same applies for the non-mandatory rules of national contract law. Whether these legal rules will be set aside by the contract is in the hands of the parties. However, whether that option given by contract law to the parties is justifiable will depend, in the eyes of a civic republican, first and foremost on the risk that the choice to set these contract law rules aside, is going to be dominated by one of the contracting parties, and on what measures contract law has taken to limit that particular risk. Mere consumer protection against unfair terms seems insufficient in this regard. When dominating contracting parties delete the rights that their counterparties would have if a default rule were not set aside by the contract, then it is not clear that these counterparties will be able, as they should, 'to walk tall and look others in the eye'.[149] And, crucially, when it comes to domination by contract, from the republican point of view there does not seem to be any categorical difference in this regard between consumers and professionals.[150]

B. Opting out as Political Contestation

1. Choice of Law as Active Citizenship

A civic republican might also look at the question of whether (European) contract law should be partly optional in a rather different way. She might wonder whether the fact of actively choosing the applicable law could be regarded as an expression of active

[148] P. Pettit, *On the People's Terms: A Republican Theory and Model of Democracy* (2012), at 43.

[149] Ibid. 83.

[150] Instead, there may exist a difference in this regard between natural and legal persons, such as companies.

citizenship.[151] At first sight, the idea may not seem very plausible. How could a choice of the law that should govern one's contractual relationship count as an act of political participation—a contribution to the welfare of the polity? Isn't the setting aside of certain non-mandatory rules, a choice for the applicable law to a cross-border contract, or indeed the opting into (CESL) or out of (CISG) a legal instrument containing substantive contract law rules, an eminently private matter, i.e. a choice made by individuals in their private capacity, rather than in their political role as citizens? However, on closer examination this may be different to the extent that a choice for the optional instrument itself becomes political.

This may be the case, in the first place, where an individual or a company opts into in an instrument of EU law deliberately as an expression of its European identity, or as a contribution to further European integration. The experience with the European company (*Societas Europaea*, SE), for example, shows that some companies have opted into that legal form with a view to their European (or post-national) identity.[152] Similarly, certain businesses and even individuals might have wanted to opt into the CESL, in part, for reasons of identity politics.[153] Moreover, choices of law are likely to have political consequences, whether or not this is the aim of the private parties involved, because each of these individual choices has the political dimension—amplified by aggregation—of an endorsement or rejection of the choices made by national legislatures—of voting with one's feet, as it were. The possibility of choice of law thus has a political dimension of giving voice to contestation through exit. This has been underlined, as a positive trait, as we saw, by advocates of the law market paradigm, who argue, in the best utilitarian tradition, that a choice of law can help to undermine the capture by highly organized but minoritarian special interests of the political process. In this regard, it is important to remember that the republican notion of democracy is essentially contestatory; it is not about majority voting.[154] As Pettit underlines with regard to the republican view of the democratic process:

> the process envisaged is essentially one of contestation, not one that necessarily involves majority decision-making. There is no suggestion that the people in some collective incarnation, or via some collective representation, are voluntaristically supreme. Under the contestatory image, the democratic process is designed to let the requirements of reason materialize and impose themselves; it is not a process that gives any particular place to will.[155]

[151] Cf. R. Bellamy, *Citizenship: A Very Short Introduction* (2008), at 16; A. Kymlicka, *Contemporary Political Philosophy: An Introduction* (2002), at 288–289.

[152] On the desire, for marketing reasons, to confirm a European identity as one important reason for some companies to become an SE, see Lenoir, 'The *Societas Europaea* (SE) in Europe: A Promising Start and an Option with Good Prospects', 4 *Utrecht Law Review* (2008) 13, at 15; N. Lenoir, *La Societas Europaea ou SE—Pour une citoyenneté européenne de l'entreprise, Rapports officiels, Ministère de la justice* (Documentation Française, 2007).

[153] Hesselink, 'The Case for a Common European Sales Law in an Age of Rising Nationalism', 8 *ERCL* (2012) 342.

[154] Indeed, this seems to imply that civic republicans would also be sceptical in seeking the content of default rules in the hypothetical bargains of typical parties (majoritarian defaults) that utilitarians might favour.

[155] P. Pettit, *Republicanism: A Theory of Freedom and Government* (1997), at 201.

2. Free Movement between National Contract Laws as Reactive Contestation

Pettit distinguishes between 'authorial' (electoral) and 'editorial' (contestatory) ways in which the people may exercise power over their government, and proposes as an instance of the latter what he calls 'reactive contestation'. The reactive form of democratic control, he argues, 'materializes so far as the authorities are guided in their decision-making by people's reactions or by the anticipation of how people will react: this, so far as they are inhibited by the fear of provoking a negative reaction, or reinforced by the attraction of provoking a positive'.[156] Could non-mandatory rules not derive republican legitimacy from the fact that they constitute a contestable exercise of legislative power? 'The non-arbitrariness of public decisions', Pettit writes, 'comes of their meeting, not the condition of having originated or emerged according to some consensual process, but the condition of being such that if they conflict with the perceived interests and ideas of the citizens, then the citizens can effectively contest them'.[157] Could it be argued plausibly that this is what non-mandatory contract law rules—and other types of optional contract law, such as international choice of law rules—do, i.e. provide space for editorial contestation through exit? Possibly.

However, it should be recalled that Pettit emphatically rejects the idea of a law that comes about through design. He insists that 'the point is to create a testing environment of selection for the laws, rather than to have laws that are consensually designed'.[158] Indeed, he writes, 'the main contrast between the conception of democracy in which the central notion is contestability and the standard, consent-centred conception is precisely that ours relies on a process of selection whereas those conceptions rely on a process of design'.[159] This raises the question of what a republican should make of a set of non-mandatory contract law legal rules, an optional instrument (opt-out, such as CISG, or op-in, as in the withdrawn CESL proposal), or private international law rules combining choice of law with defaults indicated by conflict rules (as in Rome I). Put differently, if legal design is problematic from a republican point of view, then does this also apply to the deliberate design of mechanisms for non-dominated choice?

It has been argued that the EU free movement rights should be understood, in part, as having the function of providing space for political contestation (and emancipation) through the possibility (and threat) of exit.[160] To the extent that opting out of contract law rules (whether through a choice of law, in cross-border cases, or by setting aside certain non-mandatory contract law rules), can indeed be understood, at least in some cases, as political contestation (voting with your feet), as discussed earlier, in Section B.1, then it becomes a relevant question of whether free movement rights also apply to optional law. In this respect the *Alsthom Atlantique* decision of the CJEU is relevant. In that case, from 1989, the Court held that 'the parties to an international contract of sale are generally free to determine the law applicable to their contractual

[156] Pettit, 'Democracy, National and International', 89 *The Monist* (2006) 301, at 309.
[157] Pettit (n. 155) 185.
[158] Ibid. 278.
[159] Ibid. 201–202.
[160] De Witte, 'Integrating the Subject: Narratives of Emancipation In Regionalism', 30 *European Journal of International Law* (2019) 257.

relations and can thus avoid being subject to French law'.[161] From this *obiter dictum* it seems to follow that only internationally mandatory rules (*lois de police*) can constitute a violation of the free movement of goods, as they are the only ones from which the parties cannot deviate, neither by substantive contract clauses nor by a choice of the applicable law. As a result, non-mandatory rules of substantive law as a category could never constitute an obstacle to free movement. Indeed, this has been the conclusion of several observers.[162] However, the Advocate-General in this case had reached the opposite conclusion, arguing that, in this regard, it is irrelevant whether the contract law rule is mandatory or was chosen by the parties as the law governing their contract.[163] This opinion seems to make more sense as a matter of EU law, given that default rules can be very 'sticky', i.e. very difficult to set aside in practice, as we saw earlier, and therefore 'de facto mandatory'.[164] At the same time, this reading also seems to lend some further support for the civic republican understanding of the exercise of free movement rights as a means of reactive political contestation.

7. Discourse Theory

A. Optional Law through Discourse

It is not clear that optional contract law raises any specific concerns or enthusiasm from the perspective of Habermasian discourse theory. At most—but perhaps a bit far-fetched—one could argue that a contract law that is (or could be) optional is more likely than a mandatory contract law to become the object of debate and, thus, spark an exchange of opinions. The fact that individuals have to choose continuously (as opposed to the ordinary case where it is the legislator who chooses, and does so only once) raises the continuous need for them to develop reasons for or against the optional laws. They may exchange experiences and opinions on this. As a result of this process, they may come to regard the law of contract more as their own. In other words, with the availability of an option they may feel more the 'authors' of the laws that govern their contracts than they otherwise would. However, all this will fail of

[161] Case C-339/89, *Alsthom Atlantique SA v. Compagnie de construction mécanique Sulzer SA* (EU:C:1991:28) (n. 96) para. 14. The case was about a rule of national contract law, but one which was mandatory: the French rule of product liability which places an irrebuttable presumption on producers (towards anybody else than producers in the same sector) to have known of any hidden defect in their products. Therefore, in this case the only way for the producer to avoid liability would have been to make a choice for the law of the buyer's place of residence. However, the scope of the *obiter dictum* is broader, it obviously also concerns non-mandatory rules.

[162] See e.g. S. Grundmann, *Europäisches Schuldvertragsrecht* (1999) at 68; Muir Watt, 'Choice of Law in Integrated and Interconnected Markets: A Matter of Political Economy', *Ius Commune Lectures on European Private Law* (2003) 7.

[163] See Opinion of Advocate-General Van Gerven (EU:C:1990:404), footnote 15. In French: 'Il est à cet égard indifférent que la règle de droit en question doive obligatoirement être appliquée à la relation juridique en question ou que, pour les contrats internationaux, les parties au contrat l'aient choisie comme règle applicable à leurs relations juridiques.' The Dutch (original) and the French language versions are clearer on this point than the English one.

[164] Hesselink (n. 96).

course if the choosing process is power-ridden (*vermächtet*), as it often will be, especially in case of unequal bargaining.

If indeed it is true that the addressees of optional contract laws must also be able to regard themselves as their authors, what does this mean for the question of which options there should be, in which fields, and how many? This is not so clear. The key to a tentative answer might be found in the distinction between different types of discourses.[165] As we saw in Chapter 3, private law making is legitimately informed not only by moral reasons but also by ethical and pragmatic reasons.[166] However, Habermasian discourse theory would require any pertinent moral discourses to prevail over ethical and pragmatic ones for these questions as well.

From the Habermasian point of view, the exemplary role (*Leitbildfunktion*) of non-mandatory rules of contract law can be approached from two different angles. First, if indeed that role is based on the assumption that 'the national legislature struck a balance between all the rights and obligations of the parties to certain contracts',[167] then, from the perspective of discourse theory, it seems that the only way to live up to that assumption is through an inclusive democratic deliberation, fully informed by a lively public sphere, which also includes the points of view of those at the periphery of politics, etc.[168] In other words, from a Habermasian point of view the presumption (or assumption) of fairness on which the *Leitbildfunktion* is based entails a further assumption, i.e. of the robust democratic legitimacy the non-mandatory rules—or 'supplementary provisions', as the CJEU calls them.[169] Secondly, the question can be asked: does Habermasian procedural justice require the *Leitbildfunktion*? The answer seems to be yes. Indeed, the exemplary role may even be regarded as the incarnation of the proceduralist approach of private law, in this case default rules of contract law.[170] Negatively, it seems clear that Habermasian discourse theory cannot support the utilitarian idea of majoritarian defaults, according to which the content of default rules should be found in the hypothetical bargain that the majority of typical parties would favour. The majoritarian approach is wrong, from a discourse-theoretical perspective, since democratic law making should not be decisionistic—an act of will—but deliberative, i.e. trying to convince each other with reasons;[171] counting (hypothetical) preferences is not a legitimate way of making generally applicable laws, even in the case of laws that are applicable only by default, i.e. insofar as the private parties have not replaced them by a different arrangement of their contractual relationship.

[165] See J. Habermas, *Justification and Application: Remarks on Discourse Ethics* (1995), chs 1 and 2.

[166] J. Habermas, *Between Facts and Norms: Contributions to a Discourse Theory of Law and Democracy* (1996), at 154.

[167] See Case C-92/11, *RWE Vertrieb AG v. Verbraucherzentrale Nordrhein-Westfalen eV* (EU:C:2013:180), at para. 28, and more recently Case C-81/19, *NG and OH v. SC Banca Transilvania SA* (EU:C:2020:532), at para. 26.

[168] See Chapter 3.

[169] Case C-26/13, *Arpád Kásler and Hajnalka Káslerné Rábai v. OTP Jelzálogbank Zrt* (EU:C:2014:282), at paras 80–85; Case C-81/19, *NG and OH v. SC Banca Transilvania SA* (EU:C:2020:532), at paras 28 and 35.

[170] On the proceduralist paradigm of private law, see Habermas (n. 166), section 9.1.

[171] Ibid. 179: a majority decision 'only represents a caesura in an ongoing discussion', recording 'the interim result of a discursive opinion-forming process'.

B. A Right to Justification of Non-Mandatory Law?

The issue of optional law raises an interesting question from the perspective of the Forstian right to justification with general and reciprocal reasons. Pursuant to the requirement that justification should respect the reciprocity of reasons,[172] the question arises: can we ever be said to project our values onto others when we are enacting laws that are merely optional? First, a version of Heller and Dagan's argument comes to mind:[173] wouldn't the objection against offering an option (say, a contract type, or an optional instrument) that is attractive only in the eyes of a certain ethical community be an impermissible exercise of external preferences? Secondly, there is the argument that the right to justification applies directly and strictly only to the basic structure of society.[174] And although arguably the basic structure of society includes at the least the basic structure of contract law (contract law's core),[175] it is not clear, as we saw, that non-mandatory rules are part of that core, except perhaps because of their exemplary role in unfair terms control.

On the other hand, there is a certain *ex post* perspective to the right to justification, when everyone has the right, in principle, to question the justifiability of certain rules applying to them. From that perspective, and especially in the cases of sticky defaults (e.g. in the case of strong societal normalization effects)[176] or unequal bargaining (due to a lack of social autonomy),[177] it is not clear that the answer 'you could have opted out' is always going to provide a sufficient reason. Put differently, it is not clear from the point of view of the right to justification that we should too easily accept a reified understanding of the perhaps sometimes too formal distinction between mandatory and non-mandatory rules. If rules that are formally non-mandatory lead de facto to relationships of domination or exploitation, then better reasons than their formal optionality may be required to justify them.

C. Optional Law as Deliberation

As we saw in Chapter 5, Lomfeld understands both contract law and contracts themselves as deliberation.[178] Specifically with regard to the non-mandatory rules of contract law he states explicitly that 'defaults demand justification';[179] however, unfortunately he does not elaborate further. Yet, if indeed 'a contract is a discursive institution that promises further reasons'[180] and 'every contract is a social contract',[181] then its seems fair to assume that on Lomfeld's view optional law requires justification

172 R. Forst, *The Right to Justification: Elements of a Constructivist Theory of Justice* (2013), at 6.
173 This argument was discussed in Chapter 7.
174 Forst (n. 172) 80.
175 Hesselink (n. 79).
176 On the social phenomenon of normalization, see M. Foucault, *Sécurité, territoire population: Cours au collège de France 1977–1978* (2004), at 58–59.
177 Forst (n. 172) 136.
178 Lomfeld, 'Contract as Deliberation', 76 *Law Contemp. Probl.* (2013) 1.
179 Ibid. 13.
180 Ibid. 16.
181 Ibid. 16.

at both levels, i.e. law making (the content of the optional rules and the choice mechanism) and the choice made by the parties, and that in principle all relevant values can play a role at each of these levels. This latter point follows from the foundationally (i.e. radically) pluralist nature of Lomfeld's theory of contract, which is categorically different in this respect from both Habermas's and Forst's understandings of discourse theory, committed as the latter authors are to the priority of moral discourse over both ethical and pragmatic discourses.[182] The result is that, on the one hand, contract law as deliberation constrains choices with regard to optional contract law (as stated, on two levels), but, on the other hand, the deliberation (between the parties and among law makers) is radically open. In any case, as expected, given its procedural character, the theory does not offer any substantive answers concerning the desirability of optional contract law or its preferred or required content.

8. Concluding Remarks

All the political theories we saw are generally favourably disposed towards optional contract law, even if for quite different reasons. There exists an overlapping consensus, we could say. Utilitarians support optional contract law, especially opt-out regimes such as default rules, because they can make people better off by saving them transaction costs. Liberal perfectionists are enthusiastic about the possibility for individuals to achieve self-fulfilment by picking their favourite contract type from among a range of options, while political liberals may remain agnostic unless optional contract law can be shown to belong to the core social-political institutions, in which case their main concern will be to ensure robust substantive freedom of choice. Libertarians are fine with optional contract law, because, being merely optional, it will not interfere with liberty, while, here as elsewhere, for them formal freedom of contract suffices. Communitarians are puzzled about the idea of designing optional law, but could accept default regimes as expressing local customs and common-sense understandings of the community. A civic republican might regard a choice of law as an expression of active citizenship (voting with your feet). And discourse theorists might understand the opting in and out of contract law rules as a discursive practice, making it easier for the addressees of contract law to regard themselves also as its co-authors.

Having said that, from the perspectives of each of these political theories there may also be reasons for concern. Several of these we saw in action with regard to the European Commission's CESL proposal, which had been intended to become applicable to cross-border contracts through an opt-in by the contracting parties. Utilitarians doubted whether the CESL corresponded to the actual preferences of many contracting parties. Liberal-egalitarians were concerned that the free choice might be merely formal, not an expression of substantive freedom with attractive alternatives available. The civic republican worry was that the choice for the CESL would be dominated by sellers. The concern from discourse theory was that the drafting process was not sufficiently inclusive towards citizens at the periphery of Europe. However, the

[182] See explicitly, ibid. 1.

most critical responses came from communitarians: they had difficulty with the idea of designing a new legal system, that individuals could opt into, given the communitarian understanding of a legal system as the expression of the values and traditions of the community, while the CESL (at least initially) would have belonged to no one.

Within the EU, the non-mandatory rules of contract law, which operate as defaults that the parties can set aside through their contracts, are located almost exclusively at the national level. Yet, non-mandatory rules play an important role in EU contract law. The reason is the decision by the CJEU to regard national default rules as the reference point in determining the unfairness of contract terms under the Unfair Terms Directive of 1993. Today, this exemplary role (*Leitbildfunktion*) of 'supplementary provisions' of national contract law, as the CJEU calls them, is well-established. On this view, non-mandatory rules represent the legislature's determination of a fair balance between the rights and obligations of the contracting parties, expressing its conception of substantive interpersonal justice,[183] taking into account the specific type of contractual relationship and (especially) the type of parties. However, as we saw, not all political theories can easily justify the exemplary role of optional contract law.

[183] In this sense, see Canaris, 'Wandlungen des Schuldvertragsrechts—Tendenzen zu seiner "Materialisierung"', 200 *Archiv für die civilistische Praxis* (2000) 273, at 285:

> Dieses [i.e. das vertragsergänzende dispositive Recht] ist nämlich seiner Intention nach grundsätzlich auf die Schaffung einer gerechten Zuordnung von Pflichten und Rechten, Lasten und Vorteilen, Risiken und Chancen der Vertragsparteien angelegt und bildet daher weitgehend den Versuch zu einer Konkretisierung der Gebote der iustitia commutativa, insbesondere des objektiven oder materiellen Äquivalenzprinzips (im weiteren, d.h. nicht auf die Hauptleistungen geschränkten, sondern das gesamte Vertragsgefüge umfassenden Sinne).

9
Concluding Remarks

1. Political Philosophies of European Contract Law

A. Thirty-six Boxes: What Do They Tell Us?

This book discussed six fundamental political theories from the perspectives of six contemporary political theories. The result, which is also visible in the structure of the book, was a grid of 6 × 6 = 36 boxes (see Table 9.1).[1] Each box contains an answer to a political question of European contract law coming from a distinct political theory. The objective was in each case to offer a critical discussion of the theory at hand, read in its best light (principle of charity), rather than as a strawman. The analysis may be understood as applied (micro) political philosophy.

What does the resulting matrix of the political philosophy of European contract law tell us? To be sure, the aim was certainly not scientism. And neither the rows, columns, and boxes, nor the distinctions underlying them, should be reified. Other taxonomies of contemporary political philosophy are certainly possible, as explained in Chapter 1. So, what conclusions can we draw from this project? I would like to offer here two sets of conclusions: first, some conclusions that follow in a more narrow sense from the findings; and, secondly, some wider concluding observations, triggered by the findings but going beyond their scope.

Table 9.1 Matrix of the political philosophy of European contract law

	Democratic basis	European	Binding force	Weaker parties	Public policy	Optionality
Utilitarian	*	*	*	*	*	*
Liberal-egalitarian	*	*	*	*	*	*
Libertarian	*	*	*	*	*	*
Communitarian	*	*	*	*	*	*
Civic republican	*	*	*	*	*	*
Discourse-theory	*	*	*	*	*	*

[1] In reality, within each political theory I distinguished several more specific strands, effectively—but somewhat less visibly—leading to some hundred smaller boxes.

Justifying Contract in Europe: Political Philosophies of European Contract Law. First Edition. Martijn W. Hesselink, Oxford University Press. © Martijn W. Hesselink 2021. DOI: 10.1093/oso/9780192843654.003.0009

B. Six Political Philosophies of Contract

A first basic finding is that the contemporary political theories do indeed yield answers to the fundamental political questions of European contract law submitted to them. In some cases, the answers are more determinate and specific; in others they remain more general or indeterminate. In other words, certain theories with regard to certain questions do not provide answers concrete enough to be of practical use to law makers. However, in other cases the general political theories provide very clear and specific guidance. To the extent that the questions discussed in this book (the horizontal axis of the matrix, if you like) are indeed among the most fundamental political questions of contract law in Europe today, pointing to aspects of contract law where the status quo or its reform would seem to be in particular need of justification, the combined answers to the six questions (each of the horizontal rows in the matrix), constitute, for each of the political theories, something like an account of the basic political structure of European contract law.

It is important to be precise with regard to this conclusion. It was never the premise of this book that all there was to say, normatively speaking, about contracts, contractual relationships, and contract law was within the realm of the political and its theory. The claim, that with regard to contract law we can ask normative questions that, with reason, we can consider political, does not at all imply or suggest that all important contract law questions are properly understood as political or ultimately political, even if we limit ourselves to normative questions. In particular, there is the realm of morality and its theory, which may overlap to a large extent, depending on the theory, with the political and its normative theory in political morality. However, neither of them can be reduced, without loss, to the other. As a related point, the relationship between the political and the interpersonal aspects of private law is complex. On the one hand, contract law is part of the law of the land (of the *polis*), and to that extent political. On the other hand, contract law is the law of the contract, governing the contractual relationship, and to that extent interpersonal. This means also that contract law inevitably has a public and a private aspect, and also dimensions of both social and interpersonal justice. So, while this book claims to have presented six political theories of (European) contract law, it does not claim that the resulting picture (i.e. the matrix) presents all there is to be shown and said about the normative theory of (European) contract law.

To this, we must add that even as a representation of the political theory of European contract law the matrix is far from complete. Not all influential political theories were discussed here. This was in part because of very practical considerations regarding the feasibility of the project and the readability of the book, but also because the political debate is fundamentally open and its potential arguments and theories, therefore, are infinite. Moreover, both from an academic point of view (the rejection of scholastics) and from a political point of view (the rejection of a conservative default) there is reason not to give too much weight to whether a theory is influential today. Not only do all political theories aspire to becoming influential (in the academic and political arenas, respectively, and interconnectedly), it was also an explicit ambition of this book to open up the political debate on European contract law by presenting articulated and principled alternatives to the status quo, i.e. to the *acquis communautaire* and the existing debate on it. Utopian proposals can open people's minds towards new horizons, widening the scope of what seems realistic and feasible, and so changing the understanding of which views are moderate and which extreme, and of where the political centre is located.[2] This applies as much for (European) contract law as for any other branch of the law. And radical proposals, i.e. proposals going to the root of the problem—in this case injustices in European contract law, for example—are exactly the ones one would expect to come out of theories, grounded as they usually are in first principles.

In addition, most critical approaches to law, including contract law and EU law, have a normative aspect too. Immanent critique questions the normative premises of (in our case) (European) contract law, points to contradictions among its normative aspirations, and examines whether the law fully lives up to its own normative promises—all of this with a view to liberating the normative potential of (in our case) the law of contract in Europe. Critical theories have been at the basis of various emancipation movements. And critical perspectives and challenges are clearly fundamental to any meaningful political debate, also in the area of European contract law.[3] They remained mostly outside the scope of the present project, focused as it was on normative questions ('ought'-statements with question marks), to which critical theories (*qua* critical theories) by definition do not offer any direct answers, while we need such answers, nevertheless. Still, they are part of the normative picture.

Finally, it is perhaps good to point out that European contract law is at the crossroads of European law and contract law. Thus, it can be regarded as a substantive field of European law,[4] but also as a specific field (or aspect) of contemporary contract law. The same holds true for its theory. In part, the normative theory of European contract law is informed by—and offers answers to—the questions that concern contract theorists around the world. For another part, however, it draws on—and offers new insights for—the (nascent) normative theory of European law. This represents a further limitation to the scope of findings and claims in this book. This was not an inquiry into the natural law of contract; its scope was contingent and local. The question of whether some of its findings and claims can be extrapolated beyond contract (in EU law theory) or beyond the EU (in contract theory) was not within the strict scope of this project.

C. Legal Arguments and Political Theories

A second general finding is that many of the positions in the debate on European contract law, taken by scholars and law makers over the past two decades, can be

[2] Cf. D. Kennedy, *A Critique of Adjudication: Fin de Siècle* (1997), arguing that the political left and right have no core business. Contrast, N. Bobbio, *Destra e sinistra: ragioni e significati di una distinzione politica* (1999).

[3] For an early attempt, see Hesselink, 'The Politics of European Contract Law: Who Has an Interest in What Kind of Contract Law for Europe?', in S. Grundmann and J. Stuyck, *An Academic Green Paper on European Contract Law* (2002) 181.

[4] This is reflected in the fact that this book is part of a series of monographs on European law, based on the general course in the summer school of the Academy for European Law.

assimilated to positions held by (or following from) the contemporary political theories under discussion here. Put differently, this book found structural similarities, on a significant scale, between justificatory discourses proposed in the political debate, on the one hand, and reasons following from political principles and values, on the other. Sometimes participants in the political debate explicitly referred to a certain political philosophy, but more often they did not. However, whenever European contract law scholars or law makers, in order to justify their position, invoke a principle or value that happens to be the core value or principle of an articulated political theory, we can plausibly conclude that the argument can properly be understood as libertarian, communitarian, etc. This is the case for discourses in support of the existing law, and for criticisms of it, as well as for reform proposals. To be more precise, such structural similarities could be found whenever the legal arguments in the debate were in fact normative (or evaluative).

The tracing of the normative foundations of arguments in the political debate on European contract law among legal scholars can contribute to a better understanding of some of these arguments. Once it is clearer where they come from, normatively speaking, it is also easier to understand where they may lead. In particular, in this way specific arguments, criticisms, and proposals about European contract law can be linked up to wider visions of society, and to broader agendas for reform. This could be referred to, using the metaphor introduced earlier, as placing arguments, where appropriate, into one of the 36 boxes. Two words of caution are needed here. First, the emphasis must be on 'where appropriate'. It should be a box where the argument fits in quite naturally and fully, without any strain or use of force. Secondly, what is being discussed here is the categorization of arguments, not their proponents. The aim is emphatically not to put people into boxes, labelling legal scholars as communitarian, etc. That would be wholly misguided. First, because it would be not only hazardous but also disrespectful to attribute political identities to others.[5] Secondly, such labels would be based on an unwarranted assumption that the scholar at hand is a monist, and, moreover, has a consistent political view over time (which is not necessarily a merit, be it in academia or in politics). Thirdly, it would mean a striking and unwarranted deviation from this book's focus, which is on the justification of contract law in Europe with reasons. It is reason-centric, not author-centric. With regard to stakeholders and politicians, the case can be somewhat different. They come to the political debate, not generically as full persons or as citizens, but explicitly in a specific role. Therefore, it would not be disrespectful to identify them, as stakeholders and politicians, with their positions. Still, given the focus of the project, I have preferred to focus on the positions taken by political players rather than discussing whether the European Commission is neoliberal (libertarian) or BEUC is social-democratic (liberal-egalitarian).

The other side of this second general conclusion, that arguments in the political debate on (European) contract law can be traced back or assimilated to contemporary political theories, is that the positions for European contract law that can be shown to follow from these political theories (which was the first general conclusion) are

[5] The case is different when political philosophers self-identify as 'liberal', 'republican', etc.; this happens only rarely (especially in Europe) in the case of legal scholars.

actually operative ideas in the academic and political debates on European contract law and its future. This is true for all six theories under discussion here, albeit not necessarily to the same degree.[6] This conclusion (in combination with the first one) is significant in the light of the recurrent reductions, in the academic debates, of complex matters to binary choices. For example, in contract theory, especially in the (dominant) North-American contributions, the debate on the normative foundation of contract law is often presented as a choice between ('moral') promise theories and ('economic') joint surplus theories. This book has shown (1) that at least six different contemporary political theories offer concrete arguments for the debates on fundamental questions of European contract law and (2) that, in the European context, we can see these arguments at work. Therefore, the second general conclusion of this book cautions against reductionism in accounts of the normative foundations of contract law.

Another practical implication is that these six in-depth political theories of European contract law, based on leading contemporary political philosophies, may be of use when participants in the debates, academic or political, want to propose new normative arguments or articulate better how the arguments they are putting forward are normatively grounded. Similarly, they can show where a normative argument in the political or academic debate comes from, normatively speaking. In other words, the diverse answers presented and critically discussed in this book can be of assistance to participants in the academic and political debates in articulating their normative intuitions. Similarly, they can also be used to obtain a better sense of what exactly is wrong with a normative argument made by the Commission, a legal scholar, or another participant in the political debate.

Finally, this second finding perhaps suggests how similar results could be obtained with regard to political theories or political questions currently outside the scope of this book. How would other political theories answer the same questions, and how would the same theories answer other important political questions? How could the matrix be extended along either of its two axes, increasing the number of boxes, thus covering better the range of actually or potentially operative political ideas on European contract law? Also in this sense, the analysis contributes to opening up the academic and political debates.

D. The Basic Political Structure of European Contract Law

A third finding was that different theories considered different questions more important. This was also visible, throughout the various chapters, in theories claiming more room for answering one question than for another, and more than claimed by other

[6] The normative focus of reasons entailed that no attempt is made (or suggested) here at any quantitative claims. The materials and methods used here would have been wholly inadequate. At the very least, the project should have started from a convincingly random sample of contributions to the debates. The point here was merely that political theories can be traced in operative political arguments within the debate on European contract law, and that this is true for each of the six political theories discussed in this book, without any claim or suggestion concerning the proportions of their respective contributions (or, for that matter, any suggestions as to how the effectiveness of political ideas, in such a debate or in general, could be measured).

theories when answering the same question. To put it in terms of the matrix again, this could be visualized by giving the 36 boxes in Table 9.1 quite diverse sizes.

This finding also gives reason to qualify the claim, made earlier, that the combined answers to the six questions constitutes, for each of the theories, an account of the basic political structure of European contract law. Strictly speaking this is correct, but it may not in each case be their favourite account, because, from the point of view of the theory at hand, these were not necessarily the six most fundamental political questions of European contract law. From the perspective of some of the theories the list of questions may have been either over- or under-inclusive, or both, in some respects. So, to be more precise, for each theory the analysis has yielded at least a partial account of the basic political structure of European contract law, although for some theories (perhaps many) it is not a complete account; while, from the point of view of the theory at hand, some of the boxes in the row may have seemed redundant and out of place in a discussion of the basic political structure of (European) contract law.

It is important to realize, however, that this is inevitable. For if all the theories considered each of the political questions equally important, then to that extent they would not be different theories at all. Therefore, we should understand this finding as a significant one. It underscores how deep the pluralism of political theories of European contract law runs. These theories differ, not only in their answers to political questions, but also in their view of what the most fundamental political questions of (European) contract law are. (The same holds true for presentation. Some theories will regard the order in which the questions in this book were discussed as intuitive or even natural, while it will strike others as illogical. Again, this is inevitable: a neutral order of presentation does not exist.)[7]

The implication is that the basic structure of contract—just like the basic structure of society—is not a neutral, pre-political concept. Normative theories and their principles of justice are not merely applied to a pre-defined basic structure. Rather, principles of justice define the basic structures of society and of contract law. With regard to social justice, this means that the distribuendum constitutes a pointer indicating which aspects of the structure of society are basic. The same applies, *mutatis mutandis*, for contract law and its basic structure. Which part of the structure of contract law (widely understood but by no means limited *ex ante* to its doctrinal structure) is most basic, in the sense of most in need of securing a solid political justification, depends entirely on (or may stand in a dialectic relation to) the fundamental political principles of contract law. As we saw with regard to weaker party protection, it is these principles, for example, which co-determine how much 'regulation' should be considered part of the basic structure of contract law (and vice versa how 'regulatory' contract law ought to be). Similarly, it is the fundamental political principles of contract law too that co-determine where the basic structure of contract law should be understood to be located: at the national or the European level, or both.

In Rawls's theory of justice, the basic structure of society is an empirical concept, referring to the main institutions responsible for social justice in the society at hand, to which the principles of justice are then applied. Rawls's theory is an ideal theory that

[7] I could have rolled dice. That would have meant strict procedural fairness. Instead, I opted for an order where more obviously political themes came first.

refers to a well-ordered society whose basic structure is just. Yet, while the basic structure of society remains contingent and different for each society, it does not seem that the number of possible basic structures that are fully just in the Rawlsian sense can be very large. And the same may be true for contract law. This brings us to the question of what might be referred to as normative comparative law. To the extent that contract theories, including political contract theories of the kind constructed and discussed here, are ideal theories, the question arises of how much room there remains, normatively speaking, for legal diversity. For if a contract theory offers the outline of an ideal basic structure for contract law, then should not contract law makers in every country try to approximate that ideal model? In other words, idealizing elements in contract theories, including political theories of contract, tend towards natural law thinking. Most contract theories do not address this question explicitly; some contract theories, contrary to most comparative law work,[8] claim or assume empirical similarity with regard to the basic structure of contract law.[9]

E. Controversial Political Questions

These were three horizontal conclusions, as it were, focusing on the rows in the table, representing core elements, respectively, of a utilitarian, liberal-egalitarian, libertarian, communitarian, civic republican, and discourse-theoretical political theory of European contract law. Now we move on to vertical conclusions, which by contrast, zoom in on the columns in the matrix. These are conclusions concerning the answers to the same political question across different political theories. Such conclusions were already drawn at the end of each chapter and will not be repeated here. Can any further, more general observations be made in this regard?

Clearly, the analysis undertaken here could not yield any definitive conclusions in the narrow sense of providing conclusive ('valid') answers to the political questions under discussion. I have already pointed this out in Chapter 1, but it is worth repeating here. A discussion of the implications of six political theories, even if these are among the most influential ones in contemporary normative political philosophy, cannot settle the normative issues under discussion here. (Not even temporarily or provisionally as in the Habermasian understanding of a majority decision as being a mere caesura in an ongoing democratic debate.)[10] In particular, a head count among the theories, even if yielding a majority or even unanimity, would prove nothing. First, because its informational basis in political theory would remain rather narrow. By focusing on selected contemporary political theories, the analysis left undiscussed certain other political theories offering their own answers to the same questions. Secondly, because it would suggest, mistakenly, that political theories, and hence their

[8] The main exception is J. Gordley, *Foundations of Private Law: Property, Tort, Contract, Unjust Enrichment* (2006), whose main thesis is that common principles underlie the Western laws of property, contract, tort, and unjust enrichment.

[9] See e.g. P. Benson, *Justice in Transactions: A Theory of Contract Law* (2019), at 29–30.

[10] J. Habermas, *Between Facts and Norms: Contributions to a Discourse Theory of Law and Democracy* (1996), 179. See further, Chapter 3.

theorists, ought to have a particular say (and status) in the matter of determining what the future of European contract law ought to be.[11]

Still, it remains interesting in its own right to see whether divergence or convergence exists, and perhaps even an overlapping consensus on our questions among our theories, even if this would mean nothing more than just that: overlapping consensus, convergence, or divergence on a fundamental political question of European contract law among some of the leading contemporary political theories. As said, I will not repeat here the concluding remarks to each of the questions discussed in Chapters 3 to 8. However, comparing them we can note that the degree of convergence/divergence among the theories differed quite starkly from one question to another. An overlapping consensus could be found on whether contracts should have legally binding force, at least with regard to the minimal idea of rejecting a principle of *pacta non sunt servanda* (Chapter 5). Similarly, there was wide agreement on the general desirability of optional rules of contract (Chapter 8). On the need for a democratic basis (Chapter 3) we saw convergence but no consensus. By contrast, on the Europeanization of contract law (Chapter 4), weaker party protection (Chapter 6), and limitations to freedom of contract for reasons of public policy and morality (Chapter 7) we encountered a strong divergence of opinion. Thus, we saw that some of the fundamental political questions proved more, and others less, controversial among the theories discussed here.

Another interesting 'vertical' conclusion is that coalitions among theories are not stable over different questions. It is not the case, say, that on each of the questions the utilitarians side with the libertarians, or that the liberals and the communitarians always disagree. In other words, there are varying (overlapping) consensuses among different subsets of the already limited number of theories discussed here, concerning the answers to fundamental political questions of (European) contract law, depending on the question at hand.[12]

Both in the (rare) cases of overlapping consensus among all six theories and in the (much more frequent) cases of consensus among a subset of the theories (perhaps best referred to as coalitions rather than as consensus), invariably the overlapping agreement is on outcomes, not on reasons. Theories reach the same conclusions with regard to the proper answer to fundamental political questions of (European) contract law, albeit for entirely different reasons, and grounded in different principles and values as well. In other words, in those cases there is convergence among a number of theories (and occasionally all of them, especially where the question is abstract enough) on outcomes but not on their motivation for those outcomes. Put differently, in a legislative assembly or on a judicial panel these theories could vote for the same proposal, but they might run into great difficulty if they were expected to agree on official motivations as well. In the Rawlsian idiom, in such cases we should perhaps not speak of overlapping consensus, because an agreement only counts as such if it is reached and maintained for the right reasons, which are by definition shared. However, at least for

[11] This raises the question of the expertise of political theorists, contract theorists, and theorists of EU law. What do normative theorists know? This question will be discussed further later, in Section 2.F.

[12] This is not the same point as the one (discussed later, in Section 2.D) about zigzagging, which refers to the varying adherence to political theories in one person over the different questions.

the case of (European) contract law, on such a demanding understanding, it is not clear that any overlapping consensus (as opposed to a mere *modus vivendi*) could ever be reached on core principles.

2. Justifying Contract in Europe

In addition to these conclusions in a more narrow sense, some further observations can be made, that follow in a somewhat wider sense from the research project and its findings, about the justification of contract law in Europe.

A. Nuance and Depth

Nuance and depth are among the most important contributions academic scholars have to offer to political debates. Bringing nuance and depth is what this study has tried to do for the normative debate on European contract law. In contrast to various types of reductions, this book has tried to show complexity. Reduction may be an effective rhetorical tool, in order to foreground one single dimension deemed more important, but it is not necessarily beneficial to politics, good law making, or better mutual understanding in a pluralist society. Therefore, here six key political dimensions of European contract law were discussed each from six different normative perspectives. The book has sought depth by exploring the fundamental principles and values behind arguments used in the normative debates on European contract law and its future, and to assimilate these to political theories, and vice versa. This role for scholarship seems particularly important in times and places where the political debate is polarized and superficial, which generally provides a fertile ground for populism, intolerance, and fanaticism.[13]

I am, of course, not suggesting here that European contract law is a frontier in the battle against intolerance, or that the politics of European contract law has been particularly plagued by populism. But I do think that a political culture of nuance and depth starts from the discussion of specific questions in mutual respect of each other's convictions (which are often heartfelt), as long as these convictions are themselves respectful of others and their views. And I believe that seeking and finding nuance and depth in the political debate on European private law is not trivial in this regard. This conviction is closely linked, of course, to an understanding of the EU, including European private law, as essentially a peace project and in that way, like democracy, as always still to come. This brings me back to the point made in Chapter 1, that we should not throw out the baby with the bathwater. Even if the idea of a European civil code was misguided (too grandiose and perhaps anachronistic too), the spirit of

[13] Thomas Mann pointed out that European humanist values of freedom, tolerance, and doubt rendered it vulnerable (Mann, 'Achtung Europa' (1935), in T. Mann, *Achtung Europa!: Essays 1933–1938* (1995) 147, at 139). Therefore, he called for a militant humanism that would stand up against fanaticism and its relentless attacks on reason, truth, freedom, and justice. S. Zweig, *Die Welt von Gestern: Erinnerungen eines Europäers* ([first published 1942] 2017) similarly contrasted humanism with fanaticism.

overcoming some of the differences that so far had kept Europeans divided (a spirit that was tangible in the meetings of the Lando Commission, the Study Group on a European Civil Code, and the expert group on European contract law) emphatically was not. (I leave aside for the moment whether this spirit is best placed at the service of proposing uniform law.) Nor was the underlying idea misguided that important differences and similarities of views may be found, in the field of private law also, along quite different lines than national boundaries. This work has demonstrated this transversal character of political philosophies of contract law.

B. Justification

A further implication, easy to overlook, is that a meaningful debate is possible on normative questions about European contract law and its future. Each of the theories discussed here justified its proposals, whether they are for reform or for keeping the status quo, with reasons. This means, in the first place, as was anticipated in Chapter 1, that normative questions about European contract law are meaningful questions to ask. And that normative legal scholarship (normative private law theory, normative EU theory) has something to contribute to our understanding of the law, in particular in this case, private law and EU law. Moreover, such a deep and nuanced understanding of the normative stakes in European contract law seems eminently relevant for the practical question of what to do, collectively as a society, about contract law in Europe. In other words, normative legal scholars can make a meaningful contribution to political decision-making on (European) contract law. Indeed, it could be said that the very existence of several articulate normative accounts of European contract law, and the nuanced and profound arguments exchanged between them, as such, constitutes a rejection of normative scepticism, i.e. of the various versions of the notion that normative questions have a real object to which there exist real answers.

None of this is meant to suggest a form of disciplinary imperialism. The meaningfulness of the project of raising, discussing, and trying to answer with reasons, normative questions about contract law and the EU, does not entail in any way, that other types of questions and answers about (European) contract law are any less meaningful or important. Scholarship is not a zero sum game. The world of academic knowledge and understanding is fundamentally unlimited (even though resources are limited). The same applies for arguments in the political debate. Our understanding of reasons for contract law choices does not diminish any findings or hypotheses about their causes (economic, psychological, etc.). Normative insights do not replace empirical insights, and vice versa. In the academic arena as well as in the political one they are fundamentally complementary.

The same applies for critical work. Any amount of insight, however meaningful and eminently relevant for politics, about how reason and reasons are constructed and based on power relationships, does not make the practical questions about what to do, and in particular the evaluative question of what it would be best to do and the normative question of what we ought to do, go away. We still have to decide what, if anything, we as a society ought to do about—in our case—European contract law. Even when we are acutely aware of the fact that Europe, contracts, and the law are constructs, that political questions are mired with power dimensions, and that foregrounding certain questions is not neutral, then the six political questions central to this book are still calling for an answer. Or, at the very least there is the question of which other, better normative questions we should ask next time, with a view to determining what, if anything, we ought to—or could best—do about (European) contract law (including the radical question of whether (European) contract law ought to be abolished altogether). We still need reasons. In other words, critique cannot dispense with justification.

This conclusion about justification with reasons does not imply any further claim that humans are—or ought to be—always rational beings, defined by any specific standard of rationality (notably, economic means-ends rationality). Nor that emotions should not play any role in the political debate and that passion and agonism should be banned from politics. The point is merely that emotions are not reasons and, therefore, do not provide any justification (as opposed e.g. to an explanation). Therefore, if someone asks why a contract was enforced against her, then the fact that law makers were passionate about the *pacta sunt servanda* principle may provide a (causal) explanation, but it does not—in the absence of any further argument—provide a justification. When someone asks for a reason, and we think she is entitled to receive it (i.e. she has a right to justification), then we need something more than empirical data and critical deconstruction. The claim here is merely that trying to determine this 'something else' constitutes a meaningful project—in particular, that it is worth trying to figure out together which reasons about what to do as a society about contracts are better and which ones are worse, and that this book has shown this for the European context.

The idea of nuance and depth in the political debate, both as political values in their own right and as antidotes against intolerance and populism, celebrated previously, does not imply appeasement in the face of injustice, or an appeal for moderate responses to flagrant injustices and—generally—gravitation towards the political centre. On the contrary, the steep rise in inequalities we are facing today is likely to require a radical response. However, it seems important whether any proposed reforms properly address the injustices they respond to. And for that purpose we need to know where exactly the injustice lies. With regard to inequality, for example, this raises the question of inequality of what: among the various inequalities we can demonstrate empirically, which ought to be reduced, and what role should (European) contract law play? These are normative questions. And we need normative arguments to answer them.

Finally, it is important to underline that when it comes to justifiability there should be no status quo bias. The status quo is always in need of justification just as much as any proposed reform (or revolution). A focus on justification does not shift the burden of proof. With regard to inequality, (European) contract law might be either part of the problem or of the solution. European contract law might be an agent of equality or of inequality. What we need to know is whether a proposed reform would make things better or worse, right or wrong. In other words, we need normative standards for justification and contestation. Chapter 6 was an attempt at addressing these difficult questions with regard specifically to weaker party protection.

C. Pluralism

Nuance and depth are closely related to reasonable pluralism, as both their premise and their consequence. If we start from the understanding that there exist different, meaningful ways of looking at the world, which are mutually incompatible in part, then in a society where, as a fact, different people find different accounts more convincing, it seems worthwhile exploring some of the most influential ones among them, in terms of their starting points and their implications. Even if some among these accounts claim that the entire question is a matter of objective truth, i.e. of validity and invalidity of claims, then still, if others disagree, for example claiming that all that counts in this regard is subjective preferences (which on its own terms may be understood as a preference for counting preferences), it seems worthwhile exploring other views in more depth and in all their nuances. In a homogeneous society where everyone endorses and rejects the same ideas, the case would be different, as it would also be if we considered oppression to be an appropriate response to the diversity of worldviews.

At the same time, the acknowledgement of pluralism does not have to lead to mere perspectivism. That is not how the analysis in this book was meant, nor is the case for perspectivism one of its conclusions. The arguments and proposals coming from the different political theories were not merely juxtaposed, as different views of the cathedral, or as building blocks for different cathedrals. The discussion, in each case (for each box, i.e. for each theory's answers to each of the questions), was critical. And as explained in Chapter 1, the critique did not come 'from nowhere'. It was both immanent (i.e. on the theory's own respective terms) and external (i.e. the main criticisms coming from other theories), and indeed transcendent (i.e. from a democratic *a priori*).

Still, the mere finding of a plurality of articulated and principled answers to the same questions does not prove the value or truth of normative pluralism. It might still be the case that only one of the views is true, valid, right, or best. Therefore, the matrix of 36 boxes does not prove normative monists wrong. Making the case for normative pluralism requires a separate argument, distinct from the mere availability of six principled answers to six fundamental normative political questions of (European) contract law. It is true that the structure and presentation of this study may have the rhetorical effect of making pluralism look more plausible by making alternatives become more visible. Showing that not merely one principled monistic theory is possible—as most contributions to contract theory set out to demonstrate—but as many as six (and probably more if more political theories had been included in this project), may perhaps also undermine faith in the unique truth of one's own monistic theory. This effect would be akin to the subversive effect of comparative law, where legal comparison leads to a loss of faith (for some) in the unique truth embodied in one's own national legal system.[14] Yet, loss of faith is not the same as losing a normative argument. And it remains entirely compatible with the display of various alternatives that only one single political theory, indeed only one version of it, contains the normative truth of

[14] Fletcher, 'Comparative Law as a Subversive Discipline', 46 *AJCL* (1998) 683; Muir Watt, 'La fonction subversive du droit comparé', 52 *Revue internationale de droit comparé* (2000) 503. Specifically with regard to the Europeanization of private law, see M. W. Hesselink, *The New European Legal Culture* (2001), 51 ff.

contract law (e.g. by having found its essence) and that all the other theories are false. In terms of the matrix, this would mean that one horizontal row contains the correct answers, while all the other rows were simply wrong.

D. Zigzagging

A core ambition of this project has been to show the various implications of each of these political ideas for fundamental political questions of European contract law. To the extent that my analysis has been as charitable and rigorous as I would hope, avoiding caricature and serious misinterpretations, it has shown six different but direct routes for European contract law making, with no zigzagging—in the matrix, straight horizontal lines. However, it is an interesting question whether it would be acceptable to zigzag. Can one legitimately be a utilitarian for one question and communitarian for another? Can one consider the liberal answer to one question convincing but prefer the republican answer to another question? Empirically, the answer is certainly 'yes'. In the classes I have taught in the past decade in different European universities students were frequently inclined to support one political theory for one question and another theory for another question, zigzagging across the matrix as it were, changing theory when moving on to a different question. Normatively, this would amount to a form of pluralism. As mentioned earlier, normative pluralism requires a normative argument. However, as we see here, such an argument may well be local, referring to a specific combination of principles in a specific context. So, if your intuition is that for some questions you would like to switch to another theory, then this may give reason to reconsider your principles and seek a new reflective equilibrium, perhaps indeed a pluralist one, rather than to give in (as a theorist) to pure intuitionism, which is avowedly unprincipled. Clearly, for dedicated monists there is only one choice available, i.e. not to break ranks, to remain within the bounds of one single horizontal row, and to bite the bullet, as it were, when encountering a question which tempts them to stray. Something like this is what Rawls had in mind when he spoke of holding a 'comprehensive doctrine'.

E. Interpretative Theories

The present analysis has been normative. However, much of what was said may also apply, with appropriate modifications, to legal interpretation. The degree to which you consider that purely normative considerations can appropriately play a role in legal interpretation depends on your theory of legal interpretation and, ultimately, on your theory of law. Usually, the limit seems to be *contra legem* interpretation. There is an analogy here with the doctrine of harmonious interpretation (or indirect effect) in EU law as developed by the CJEU, pursuant to which Member State courts have a duty to interpret national law as much as possible in conformity with EU law.[15] The equivalent

[15] For a clear statement of the doctrine, see Case C-441/14, *Dansk Industri (DI), acting on behalf of Ajos A/S v Estate of Karsten Eigil Rasmussen* (EU:C:2016:278).

duty, which could be adopted by an interpretative theory (or an interpretative version of a normative theory), could be a duty to interpret positive (European) contract law as much as possible in conformity with the principles of the preferred political theory. That would come close to Dworkin's theory of law, and to a Dworkinian theory of contract law, requiring, in addition to 'fit' with the legal materials (usually referred to in Europe as 'sources' of law), also an interpretation congruent with principles of 'political morality'. Many normative contract and private law theories explicitly present themselves as being interpretative in this sense.

F. What Theorists Know

This inquiry has raised, on several occasions, implicitly and explicitly, the question of the limits of academic expertise with regard to normative political questions of (European) contract law. There are two questions here, that are partly interrelated. Both questions belong to meta-ethics, i.e. the philosophical field concerned with the nature of morality. The first is the question about what exists ('out there'). Does morality exist? Do objective substantive values exist? This is the metaphysical question of moral ontology that keeps moral realists and anti-realists divided. Realists believe that moral norms and values are part of reality, even though not as part of the empirical world. Anti-realists, by contrast, deny the reality of morality, while moral agnostics believe that there is no way for us to answer this ontological question. The second question is an epistemological question about the limits of our knowledge: does it make sense with regard to morality and ethics to make truth- (or truth-like) claims and is it possible to determine their validity? The second question overlaps, in part, with the first in that there is little to know about things that do not exist. On the other hand, however, the existence of moral truths does not guarantee that we have or can find a reliable method for determining the validity of truth(-like) claims in their regard.

The questions of moral ontology and epistemology cannot be fully addressed here, let alone be settled, even though they have a very direct bearing on some of our core questions. Therefore, one further conclusion is that the present inquiry has brought us to some of the limits of what we know—and perhaps can know—about normative political questions concerning (European) contract law. Still, it is important to note that these are matters on which there also exists genuine disagreement in meta-ethics. And there is no obvious reason why the sceptical view should be the default. Indeed, as Dworkin points out, that would amount to a substantive position internal to the debate whose rationality or meaningfulness that position aims to contest (i.e. a position of global internal scepticism).

The two most direct implications of these meta-ethical questions for our inquiry were encountered when discussing the issues of normative pluralism and the role of experts. Starting with the first: if objective values do not exist (as the ethical anti-realist claims) or cannot be known (as the epistemic sceptic of ethics believes) or if there is no way we can answer these questions with confidence (as the ethical agnostic holds), then there is no point in discussing the validity of contract theories based on objective values or objective conceptions of the individual or common good. And it would be positively problematic to make such a conception become the basis of generally binding contract laws. This applies both to theories based on the premise that contract law is based on a harmonious system of several objective values, and to essentialist theories claiming that contract law is based on one ultimate value: contract law's essential *telos*. Put differently, the reality and knowability of contract law's essential value is the premise of essentialist theories. By contrast, a version of ethical anti-realism, scepticism, or agnosticism will invariably underlie the views rejecting contract law essentialism and proposing some form of pluralism instead. In particular, the procedural approaches offering normative principles of justice for dealing with the problem of how people with different value commitments can live together mutually respecting one another, are based on the premise that none of these citizens demonstrably has the truth on their side with regard to the value or values objectively underlying (European) contract law. In other words, doubt about the reality and knowability of contract law's essential value is the premise of pluralist theories. For it would be at least as problematic if we ignored what we know to be contract law's essential value.

The ontological and epistemic questions have direct implications for the role of theorists, in both the academic and the political arenas. If knowledge or understanding with regard to values is impossible, either because values do not exist or because we have no reliable method for determining them, then clearly the insights theorists specializing in these matters have to offer are not any better than the recommendations of alchemists and astrologists. By contrast, if objective values do exist and can be known, to ignore that knowledge would be just as irrational as the stances of no-vaxers and flat-earthers. As these analogies suggest, the implications for politics are immediate: if, for example, the essential value of contract law is self-authorship, why not make that value central to contract law making? And—more to the point here—why not ask experts who specialize in contract as choice to draft a blueprint for a new contract law? As Raz points out, 'moral abstention' makes sense only in the face of indeterminacy, not of mere uncertainty. Disagreement among experts exists in all fields of academic expertise and it is never a reason for scientists and scholars to abstain from giving policy advice on the basis of what they consider to be true to the best of their knowledge.

G. Norms and Facts

There is a limit to the degree to which the theory of (European) contract law can be purely normative. Throughout this book the aim has been to foreground the normative dimension of contract theory by focusing on purely normative questions. As explained in Chapter 1, an important benefit of normative theories is that they *counterfactually* present scenarios—in our case—for contract law in Europe, not only as it could be but also as it ideally should or ought to be. The expectation is that such theories can provide guidance, as 'signposts', on the road towards a better and more just European contract law, i.e. for reforms that go *in the right direction*.

However, it was clear from the beginning that our normative questions make sense (are intelligible) only against the background of our reality, which, however (and luckily), is largely contingent. Indeed, the analysis explicitly started from a (weak) premise, which was in part empirical. Moreover, it situated our normative questions in a context that was even more obviously contingent and concrete. This is a book about justifying contract *in Europe*. Indeed, throughout the book normative answers to our questions coming from the different political theories were constantly related to and confronted with the reality of (European) contract law and of existing positions in the debate (both political and academic). To that extent, as stated in Chapter 1, this book can be read as a critical reconstruction of the making of European contract law in more than two decades of political and academic debates.

We also saw that some of the answers to the normative questions, if transformed into a political programme for the reform of (European) contract law, would amount to a very radical agenda—in some cases little short of revolutionary. This abstract confrontation with the reality of our contemporary society in Europe made some of the theories, or their specific positions, come across not only as utopian or *Weltfremd*, but also in urgent need of a further theory or political agenda for how our current society could and should legitimately be brought closer to the theory's ideal, i.e. a theory and agenda for change—in other words, for the transformation, perhaps radical, of (European) private law. Such a theory or agenda by definition could not remain abstract; it would have to engage very concretely with the facts of our current society and its positive laws if these normative views were to become effective political ideas. Monist theories, in particular, would have to address the question of how to adopt, realistically and legitimately, a European contract law based on one single core value or principle in the light of the fact of a pluralism of worldviews.

Beyond the difference between ideal and non-ideal theory, this study has shown the limits of purely normative theory more generally, and also in the context of (European) contract law. This should not be understood as a pessimistic note to end on, only a realistic one. From the impotence of the mere ought (Hegel) we do not need to conclude that normative theories cannot provide us with powerful ideas. And in a political and academic context where neo-empiricism, naturalism, and anxiety about anything normative still hold sway, I hope to have shown the wealth of ideas for justification and contestation that normative political theory has to offer. Even though normative questions about European contract law remain nothing more than one part of the story—one view of the cathedral of (European) contract law (Calabresi and Melamed), and even if not the missing one (Caruso), certainly one that has been overshadowed in dominant European contract law discourse—it seemed a story worth telling—or, rather, a debate worth opening up further.

H. Democratic Compromise

As already announced in Chapter 1, an inquiry like the one conducted here could not produce as its outcome a blueprint for an ideal European contract law. Nor should that be a reason for disappointment. The objective has been throughout to contribute to re-energizing the academic and political discussions on European contract law and its future, with a critical discussion of some of the most powerful ideas about what European contract law should, and realistically could, become. The objective was to widen and deepen the democratic debate on fundamental political questions of European contract law, thus opening up democratic space.

Could theorists, conversely, also be of assistance in finding some closure, in particular in reaching acceptable political compromises? While there is no reason to suggest any categorical distinction between the kind of critical analysis undertaken in this book and the pondering of arguments by citizens and their politicians with a view to finding an acceptable democratic compromise, there nevertheless seems to exist a greater risk of expert overreach. One reason for caution is that theorists do not seem to have any obvious expertise in balancing values, which seems to go one step further than proposing contract law's ultimate value and indicating its implications. Another, even more important reason is that, as stated, the analysis conducted here was limited only to six contemporary political theories. These theories (or rather, families of those) are certainly among the most influential ones in contemporary political philosophy, but they are not the only ones. Nor is it the case, as also said, that citizens and politicians should be required or expected to ground their political compromises, even principled ones, in political philosophy. For these reasons, it is not clear what any proposed expert compromise—a compound or balance of values and principles and their implications for European contract—would represent.

Another question is whether monistic theories may be intrinsically at odds with democratic compromise. Perhaps in the search for compromise in a pluralist society we should disregard monistic theories. However, on the contrary, there is considerable democratic value in isolating and foregrounding, as monistic theories do, one normative dimension while abstracting from all others. Monist theories help us to see more clearly the difference between arguments (and the values and principles they refer to). We understand better what is at stake in the political debate if we imagine the law maker being guided by the single value or principle that some people strongly believe should be the only one that matters. Thus, we can learn a great deal from monist theories even if (European) contract law, present and future, always will—and should—be the result of a compromise among a plurality of values, principles, and understandings. The democratic debate would be a lot poorer without these distinct contributions focusing on only one such dimension.

Having said that, on their own terms none of the monist theories have any reasons to offer that might be helpful in determining which other values should contribute to shaping contract law and how much: the compromise is something on which these monist theories by definition have nothing to say. From the point view of each of the monist theories, allowing for compromise simply amounts to partial compliance. Their natural inclination would be to maximize the territory of—in our case—European contract law over which their theory holds legislative sway. To that extent, their attitude inevitably must be akin to a Schmittian one; however, with the crucial difference that there is no need for them to understand the other theories engaged in the democratic debate as their enemies.

At the end of the day, we best understand the political theories we saw as proposed elements for a democratic compromise on—in our case—fundamental political questions of European contract law. Should this relatively open-ended conclusion disappoint or worry us? I do not think it should—on the contrary. Each of these political questions of European contract law has various aspects, dimensions, and implications which matter differently to different people. Given that everyone's point of view should count equally, all these various aspects and dimensions—and many others—must be considered in the European contract-law-making process. To try to open up democratic space by widening and deepening the debate on fundamental political questions of European contract law is the best contribution normative political theories could make to justifying contract in Europe.

Table of Cases

For the benefit of digital users, table entries that span two pages (e.g., 52–53) may, on occasion, appear on only one of those pages.

CJEU CASES (IN ALPHABETICAL ORDER)

NATIONAL AND INTERNATIONAL CASES

France

Germany

Netherlands

United Kingdom

United Nations Human Rights Committee

United States

Table of Legislation

For the benefit of digital users, table entries that span two pages (e.g., 52–53) may, on occasion, appear on only one of those pages.

EUROPEAN LEGISLATION

Conventions, Institutional Agreements and Treaties (in alphabetical order)

Directives (in chronological order)

Regulations

Decisions

EU Legislative Proposals and Withdrawals

European Parliament Resolutions

INTERNATIONAL AGREEMENTS, CONVENTIONS AND INSTRUMENTS

Index

For the benefit of digital users, indexed terms that span two pages (e.g., 52–53) may, on occasion, appear on only one of those pages.

Note: The terms civic republicanism, communitarianism, discourse theory, liberal-egalitarianism, libertarianism, and utilitarianism can also be found as sub-headings under chapters 2–8.